Biologically-Inspired Techniques for Knowledge Discovery and Data Mining

Shafiq Alam
University of Auckland, New Zealand

Gillian Dobbie
University of Auckland, New Zealand

Yun Sing Koh
University of Auckland, New Zealand

Saeed ur Rehman
Unitec Institute of Technology, New Zealand

A volume in the Advances in Data Mining and
Database Management (ADMDM) Book Series
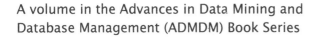

Information Science
REFERENCE
An Imprint of IGI Global

Managing Director:	Lindsay Johnston
Production Editor:	Jennifer Yoder
Development Editor:	Erin O'Dea
Acquisitions Editor:	Kayla Wolfe
Typesetter:	Kaitlyn Kulp
Cover Design:	Jason Mull

Published in the United States of America by
Information Science Reference (an imprint of IGI Global)
701 E. Chocolate Avenue
Hershey PA 17033
Tel: 717-533-8845
Fax: 717-533-8661
E-mail: cust@igi-global.com
Web site: http://www.igi-global.com

Library of Congress Cataloging-in-Publication Data

Biologically-inspired techniques for knowledge discovery and data mining / Shafiq Alam, Gillian Dobbie, Yun Sing Koh, and Saeed ur Rehman, editors.
pages cm
Includes bibliographical references and index.
ISBN 978-1-4666-6078-6 (hardcover) -- ISBN 978-1-4666-6079-3 (ebook) -- ISBN 978-1-4666-6081-6 (print & perpetual access) 1. Data mining. 2. Database searching. 3. Biologically-inspired computing. I. Alam, Shafiq, 1980-
QA76.9.D343B56 2014
006.3'82--dc23
2014007987

This book is published in the IGI Global book series Advances in Data Mining and Database Management (ADMDM) (ISSN: 2327-1981; eISSN: 2327-199X)

British Cataloguing in Publication Data
A Cataloguing in Publication record for this book is available from the British Library.

All work contributed to this book is new, previously-unpublished material. The views expressed in this book are those of the authors, but not necessarily of the publisher.

For electronic access to this publication, please contact: eresources@igi-global.com.

Advances in Data Mining and Database Management (ADMDM) Book Series

David Taniar
Monash University, Australia

ISSN: 2327-1981
EISSN: 2327-199X

MISSION

With the large amounts of information available to organizations in today's digital world, there is a need for continual research surrounding emerging methods and tools for collecting, analyzing, and storing data.

The **Advances in Data Mining & Database Management (ADMDM)** series aims to bring together research in information retrieval, data analysis, data warehousing, and related areas in order to become an ideal resource for those working and studying in these fields. IT professionals, software engineers, academicians and upper-level students will find titles within the ADMDM book series particularly useful for staying up-to-date on emerging research, theories, and applications in the fields of data mining and database management.

COVERAGE

- Cluster Analysis
- Customer Analytics
- Data Mining
- Data Quality
- Data Warehousing
- Database Security
- Database Testing
- Decision Support Systems
- Enterprise Systems
- Text Mining

IGI Global is currently accepting manuscripts for publication within this series. To submit a proposal for a volume in this series, please contact our Acquisition Editors at Acquisitions@igi-global.com or visit: http://www.igi-global.com/publish/.

Titles in this Series

For a list of additional titles in this series, please visit: www.igi-global.com

Biologically-Inspired Techniques for Knowledge Discovery and Data Mining
Shafiq Alam (University of Auckland, New Zealand)
Information Science Reference • copyright 2014 • 311pp • H/C (ISBN: 9781466660786) • US $265.00 (our price)

Data Mining and Analysis in the Engineering Field
Vishal Bhatnagar (Ambedkar Institute of Advanced Communication Technologies and Research, India)
Information Science Reference • copyright 2014 • 335pp • H/C (ISBN: 9781466660861) • US $225.00 (our price)

Handbook of Research on Cloud Infrastructures for Big Data Analytics
Pethuru Raj (IBM India Pvt Ltd, India) and Ganesh Chandra Deka (Ministry of Labour and Employment, India)
Information Science Reference • copyright 2014 • 570pp • H/C (ISBN: 9781466658646) • US $345.00 (our price)

Innovative Techniques and Applications of Entity Resolution
Hongzhi Wang (Harbin Institute of Technology, China)
Information Science Reference • copyright 2014 • 398pp • H/C (ISBN: 9781466651982) • US $205.00 (our price)

Innovative Document Summarization Techniques Revolutionizing Knowledge Understanding
Alessandro Fiori (IRCC, Institute for Cancer Research and Treatment, Italy)
Information Science Reference • copyright 2014 • 363pp • H/C (ISBN: 9781466650190) • US $175.00 (our price)

Emerging Methods in Predictive Analytics Risk Management and Decision-Making
William H. Hsu (Kansas State University, USA)
Information Science Reference • copyright 2014 • 425pp • H/C (ISBN: 9781466650633) • US $225.00 (our price)

Data Science and Simulation in Transportation Research
Davy Janssens (Hasselt University, Belgium) Ansar-Ul-Haque Yasar (Hasselt University, Belgium) and Luk Knapen (Hasselt University, Belgium)
Information Science Reference • copyright 2014 • 350pp • H/C (ISBN: 9781466649200) • US $175.00 (our price)

Big Data Management, Technologies, and Applications
Wen-Chen Hu (University of North Dakota, USA) and Naima Kaabouch (University of North Dakota, USA)
Information Science Reference • copyright 2014 • 342pp • H/C (ISBN: 9781466646995) • US $175.00 (our price)

Innovative Approaches of Data Visualization and Visual Analytics
Mao Lin Huang (University of Technology, Sydney, Australia) and Weidong Huang (CSIRO, Australia)
Information Science Reference • copyright 2014 • 464pp • H/C (ISBN: 9781466643093) • US $200.00 (our price)

www.igi-global.com

701 E. Chocolate Ave., Hershey, PA 17033
Order online at www.igi-global.com or call 717-533-8845 x100
To place a standing order for titles released in this series, contact: cust@igi-global.com
Mon-Fri 8:00 am - 5:00 pm (est) or fax 24 hours a day 717-533-8661

Table of Contents

Detailed Table of Contents

  Shafiq Alam, University of Auckland, New Zealand
  Gillian Dobbie, University of Auckland, New Zealand
  Yun Sing Koh, University of Auckland, New Zealand
  Saeed ur Rehman, Unitec Institute of Technology, New Zealand

Knowledge Discovery and Data (KDD) mining helps uncover hidden knowledge in huge amounts of data. However, recently, different researchers have questioned the capability of traditional KDD techniques to tackle the information extraction problem in an efficient way while achieving accurate results when the amount of data grows. One of the ways to overcome this problem is to treat data mining as an optimization problem. Recently, a huge increase in the use of Swarm Intelligence (SI)-based optimization techniques for KDD has been observed due to the flexibility, simplicity, and extendibility of these techniques to be used for different data mining tasks. In this chapter, the authors overview the use of Particle Swarm Optimization (PSO), one of the most cited SI-based techniques in three different application areas of KDD, data clustering, outlier detection, and recommender systems. The chapter shows that there is a tremendous potential in these techniques to revolutionize the process of extracting knowledge from big data using these techniques.

Chapter 2

The chapter considers the method of probabilistic control of mobile robots navigating in random environments and mimicking the foraging activity of ants, which is widely accepted as optimal with respect to the environmental conditions. The control is based on the Tsetlin automaton, which is a minimal automaton demonstrating an expedient behavior in random environments. The suggested automaton implements probability-based aggregators, which form a complete algebraic system and support an activity of the automaton over non-Boolean variables. The considered mobile agents are based on the Braitenberg vehicles equipped with four types of sensors, which mimic the basic sensing abilities of ants: short- and long-distance sensing of environmental states, sensing of neighboring agents, and sensing the pheromone traces. Numerical simulations demonstrate that the foraging behavior of the suggested mobile agents, running both individually and in groups, is statistically indistinguishable from the foraging behavior of real ants observed in laboratory experiments.

Class imbalance is one of the challenging problems for machine-learning in many real-world applications. Many methods have been proposed to address and attempt to solve the problem, including sampling and cost-sensitive learning. The latter has attracted significant attention in recent years to solve the problem, but it is difficult to determine the precise misclassification costs in practice. There are also other factors that influence the performance of the classification including the input feature subset and the intrinsic parameters of the classifier. This chapter presents an effective wrapper framework incorporating the evaluation measure (AUC and G-mean) into the objective function of cost sensitive learning directly to improve the performance of classification by simultaneously optimizing the best pair of feature subset, intrinsic parameters, and misclassification cost parameter. The optimization is based on Particle Swarm Optimization (PSO). The authors use two different common methods, support vector machine and feed forward neural networks, to evaluate the proposed framework. Experimental results on various standard benchmark datasets with different ratios of imbalance and a real-world problem show that the proposed method is effective in comparison with commonly used sampling techniques.

 Fatai Anifowose, Universiti Malaysia Sarawak, Malaysia
 Jane Labadin, Universiti Malaysia Sarawak, Malaysia
 Abdulazeez Abdulraheem, King Fahd University of Petroleum and Minerals, Saudi Arabia

Artificial Neural Networks (ANN) have been widely applied in petroleum reservoir characterization. Despite their wide use, they are very unstable in terms of performance. Ensemble machine learning is capable of improving the performance of such unstable techniques. One of the challenges of using ANN is choosing the appropriate number of hidden neurons. Previous studies have proposed ANN ensemble models with a maximum of 50 hidden neurons in the search space thereby leaving rooms for further improvement. This chapter presents extended versions of those studies with increased search spaces using a linear search and randomized assignment of the number of hidden neurons. Using standard model evaluation criteria and novel ensemble combination rules, the results of this study suggest that having a large number of "unbiased" randomized guesses of the number of hidden neurons beyond 50 performs better than very few occurrences of those that were optimally determined.

 Juan Luis Olmo, University of Córdoba, Spain
 José Raúl Romero, University of Córdoba, Spain
 Sebastián Ventura, University of Córdoba, Spain

Ant programming is a kind of automatic programming that generates computer programs by using the ant colony metaheuristic as the search technique. It has demonstrated good generalization ability for the extraction of comprehensible classifiers. To date, three ant programming algorithms for classification rule mining have been proposed in the literature: two of them are devoted to regular classification, differing mainly in the optimization approach, single-objective or multi-objective, while the third one is focused on imbalanced domains. This chapter collects these algorithms, presenting different experimental studies that confirm the aptitude of this metaheuristic to address this data-mining task.

 Kesheng Wang, NTNU, Norway
 Zhenyou Zhang, NTNU, Norway
 Yi Wang, University of Manchester, UK

This chapter proposes a Self-Organizing Map (SOM) method for fault diagnosis and prognosis of manufacturing systems, machines, components, and processes. The aim of this work is to optimize the condition monitoring of the health of the system. With this method, manufacturing faults can be classified, and the degradations can be predicted very effectively and clearly. A good maintenance scheduling can then be created, and the number of corrective maintenance actions can be reduced. The results of the experiment show that the SOM method can be used to classify the fault and predict the degradation of machines, components, and processes effectively, clearly, and easily.

Chapter 7

An Enhanced Artificial Bee Colony Optimizer for Predictive Analysis of Heating Oil Prices using
Least Squares Support Vector Machines 149

Zuriani Mustaffa, Universiti Utara Malaysia (UUM), Malaysia
Yuhanis Yusof, Universiti Utara Malaysia (UUM), Malaysia
Siti Sakira Kamaruddin, Universiti Utara Malaysia (UUM), Malaysia

As energy fuels play a significant role in many parts of human life, it is of great importance to have an effective price predictive analysis. In this chapter, the hybridization of Least Squares Support Vector Machines (LSSVM) with an enhanced Artificial Bee Colony (eABC) is proposed to meet the challenge. The eABC, which serves as an optimization tool for LSSVM, is enhanced by two types of mutations, namely the Levy mutation and the conventional mutation. The Levy mutation is introduced to keep the model from falling into local minimum while the conventional mutation prevents the model from over-fitting and/or under-fitting during learning. Later, the predictive analysis is followed by the LSSVM. Realized in predictive analysis of heating oil prices, the empirical findings not only manifest the superiority of eABC-LSSVM in prediction accuracy but also poses an advantage to escape from premature convergence.

Chapter 8

Comparison of Linguistic Summaries and Fuzzy Functional Dependencies Related to Data
Mining 174

Miroslav Hudec, University of Economics in Bratislava, Slovakia
Miljan Vučetić, University of Belgrade, Serbia
Mirko Vujošević, University of Belgrade, Serbia

Data mining methods based on fuzzy logic have been developed recently and have become an increasingly important research area. In this chapter, the authors examine possibilities for discovering potentially useful knowledge from relational database by integrating fuzzy functional dependencies and linguistic summaries. Both methods use fuzzy logic tools for data analysis, acquiring, and representation of expert knowledge. Fuzzy functional dependencies could detect whether dependency between two examined attributes in the whole database exists. If dependency exists only between parts of examined attributes' domains, fuzzy functional dependencies cannot detect its characters. Linguistic summaries are a convenient method for revealing this kind of dependency. Using fuzzy functional dependencies and linguistic summaries in a complementary way could mine valuable information from relational databases. Mining intensities of dependencies between database attributes could support decision making, reduce the number of attributes in databases, and estimate missing values. The proposed approach is evaluated with case studies using real data from the official statistics. Strengths and weaknesses of the described methods are discussed. At the end of the chapter, topics for further research activities are outlined.

This chapter examines the capability of Genetic Programming (GP) and different Artificial Neural Network (ANN) (Backpropagation [BP] and Generalized Regression Neural Network [GRNN]) models for prediction of air entrainment rate (QA) of triangular sharp-crested weir. The basic principal of GP has been taken from the concept of Genetic Algorithm (GA). Discharge (Q), drop height (h), and angle in triangular sharp-crested weir (θ) are considered as inputs of BP, GRNN, and GP. Coefficient of Correlation (R) has been used to assess the performance of developed GP, BP, and GRNN models. For a perfect model, the value of R should be close to one. A sensitivity analysis has been carried out to determine the effect of each input parameter. This chapter presents a comparative study between the developed BP, GRNN, and GP models.

Chapter 10

A relevance measure is a measure over the space of features of a learning problem that quantifies the degree of relatedness of a single feature or a subset of features to a target variable. The measure can be used to both detect relevant features (when the target variable is the response variable) and detect redundant features (when the target variable is another input feature). Measuring relevance and redundancy is a central concept in feature selection. In this chapter, the authors show that there is a lack of generality in the features selected based on heuristic relevance measures. Through some counter-examples, the authors show that regardless of the type of heuristic measure and search strategy, heuristic methods cannot optimise the performance of all learning algorithms. They show how different measures may have different notions of relevance between features and how this could lead to not detecting important features in certain situations. The authors then propose a hyper-heuristic method that through an evolutionary process automatically generates an appropriate relevance measure for a given problem. The new approach can detect relevant features in difficult scenarios.

Chapter 11

Biologically inspired data mining techniques have been intensively used in different data mining applications. Ant Colony Optimization (ACO) has been applied for scheduling real-time distributed systems in the recent time. Real-time processing requires both parallel activities and fast response. It is required to complete the work and deliver services on a timely basis. In the presence of timing, a real-time system's performance does not always improve as processor and speed increases. ACO performs quite well for scheduling real-time distributed systems during overloaded conditions. Earliest Deadline First (EDF) is the optimal scheduling algorithm for single processor real-time systems during under-loaded conditions. This chapter proposes an adaptive algorithm that takes advantage of EDF- and ACO-based algorithms and overcomes their limitations.

Chapter 12

Dimitris Kalles, Hellenic Open University, Greece
Alexis Kaporis, University of the Aegean, Greece
Vassiliki Mperoukli, Hellenic Open University, Greece
Anthony Chatzinouskas, Hellenic Open University, Greece

The authors in this chapter use simple local comparison and swap operators and demonstrate that their repeated application ends up in sorted sequences across a range of variants, most of which are also genetically evolved. They experimentally validate a square run-time behavior for emergent sorting, suggesting that not knowing in advance which direction to sort and allowing such direction to emerge imposes a n/logn penalty over conventional techniques. The authors validate the emergent sorting algorithms via genetically searching for the most favorable parameter configuration using a grid infrastructure.

Chapter 13

Tianxing Cai, Lamar University, USA

Industrial and environmental research will always involve the study of the cause-effect relationship between the emissions and the surrounding environment. Qualitative and mixed methods researchers have employed a variety of Information and Communication Technology (ICT) tools, simulated or virtual environments, information systems, information devices, and data analysis tools in this field. Machine-enhanced analytics has enabled the identification of aspects of interest such as correlations and anomalies from large datasets. Chemical facilities have high risks to originate air emission events. Based on an available air-quality monitoring network, the data integration technologies are applied to identify the scenarios of the possible emission source and the dynamic pollutant monitor result, so as to timely and effectively support diagnostic and prognostic decisions. In this chapter, the application of artificial neural networks for such applications have been developed according to the real application purpose. It includes two stages of modeling and optimization work: 1) the determination of background normal emission rates from multiple emission sources and 2) single-objective or multi-objective optimization for impact scenario identification and quantification. They have the capability to identify the potential emission profile and spatial-temporal characterization of pollutant dispersion for a specific region, including reverse estimation of the air quality issues. The methodology provides valuable information for accidental investigations and root cause analysis for an emission event; meanwhile, it helps evaluate the regional air quality impact caused by such an emission event as well. Case studies are employed to demonstrate the efficacy of the developed methodology.

Chapter 14

Diabetes mellitus is one of the most common chronic diseases. The number of cases of diabetes in the world is likely to increase more than two fold in the next 30 years: from 115 million in 2000 to 284 million in 2030. This chapter is concerned with helping diabetic patients to manage themselves by developing a computer system that predicts their Blood Glucose Level (BGL) after 30 minutes on the basis of their current levels, so that they can administer insulin. This will enable the diabetic patient to continue living a normal daily life, as much as is possible. The prediction of BGLs based on the current levels BGLs become feasible through the advent of Continuous Glucose Monitoring (CGM) systems, which are able to sample patients' BGLs, typically 5 minutes, and computer systems that can process and analyse these samples. The approach taken in this chapter uses machine-learning techniques, specifically Genetic Algorithms (GA), to learn BGL patterns over an hour and the resulting value 30 minutes later, without questioning the patients about their food intake and activities. The GAs were invested using the raw BGLs as input and metadata derived from a Diabetic Dynamic Model of BGLs supplemented by the changes in patients' BGLs over the previous hour. The results obtained in a preliminary study including 4 virtual patients taken from the AIDA diabetes simulation software and 3 volunteers using the DexCom SEVEN system, show that the metadata approach gives more accurate predictions. Online learning, whereby new BGL patterns were incorporated into the prediction system as they were encountered, improved the results further.

Radio Frequency (RF) fingerprinting is a security mechanism inspired by biological fingerprint identification systems. RF fingerprinting is proposed as a means of providing an additional layer of security for wireless devices. RF fingerprinting classification is performed by selecting an "unknown" signal from the pool, generating its RF fingerprint, and using a classifier to correlate the received RF fingerprint with each profile RF fingerprint stored in the database. Unlike a human biological fingerprint, RF fingerprint of a wireless device changes with the received Signal to Noise Ratio (SNR) and varies due to mobility of the transmitter/receiver and environment. The variations in the features of RF fingerprints affect the classification results of the RF fingerprinting. This chapter evaluates the performance of the KNN and neural network classification for varying SNR. Performance analysis is performed for three scenarios that correspond to the situation, when either transmitter or receiver is mobile, and SNR changes from low to high or vice versa.

Foreword

Biologically inspired data mining techniques have been widely accepted as a way to improve the existing Knowledge Discovery and Data Mining (KDD) techniques. There has been an enormous growth in the number of biologically inspired techniques that exhibit natural processes, simplicity, extendibility, adaptability, flexibility, and interpretability. The research community has taken the research one step further than basic optimization problems to knowledge discovery and data mining, exploiting the efficiency and accuracy of these techniques.

Artificial Neural Networks (ANN), Genetic Algorithms (GA), and Swarm Intelligence (SI) are leading bio-inspired techniques that have not only contributed to solving traditional optimization problems but also to making their impact on solving other diverse real-world problems including KDD.

The book contains original works on biologically inspired techniques, including ANN, Ant Colony Optimization (ACO) and Ant Programming, Particle Swarm Optimization (PSO), Self Organizing Maps (SOM), Artificial Bee Colony (ABC), GA, and Genetic Programming (GP). The application areas discussed in this book include research on mobile robot dynamics, data classification, machine fault diagnosis, predicting trends in oil prices, civil engineering, real time distributed systems, sequence sorting, air quality monitoring, security of wireless devices.

Overall, the research work presented in this book contributes to the further development of biologically inspired KDD techniques and their applications. We expect in the future more methods from the areas of Bioinformatics and Neuroinformatics to be adopted in the KDD area for solving complex problems, including data mining and knowledge discovery from large streams of data. A promising approach in this respect is neuromorphic computation, both as brain-inspired algorithms and as hardware implementations for high performance and low energy information processing at a large scale. I hope the book will serve the purpose and bring diverse research communities together, validating and evaluating work from two different perspectives. I am pleased in recommending this book to be used as a reference book by both communities of bio-inspired algorithms and KDD.

Nikola Kasabov
Auckland University of Technology, New Zealand

Nikola Kasabov *is the Foundation Director of the Knowledge Engineering and Discovery Research Institute (KEDRI, www.kedri. aut.ac.nz) and Chair of Knowledge Engineering at the School of Computer and Information Sciences at Auckland University of Technology. He is a Fellow of IEEE, Fellow of the Royal Society of New Zealand, Fellow of the Institute of IT Professionals in NZ, Distinguished Visiting Fellow at the Royal Academy of Engineering, UK, and EU Marie Curie Fellow. He holds a MSc and PhD from the Technical University of Sofia. His main research interests are in the areas of intelligent information systems, soft computing, neuro-computing, bioinformatics, brain study, speech and image processing, data mining, and knowledge discovery. He has been actively working in the area of bio-inspired KDD with more than 550 publications published. He is the co-editor-in-chief of the Springer journal Evolving Systems, Editor of the Springer series of Bio-/Neuroinformatics and the Springer Handbook of Bio-/Neuronformatics (2014).*

Preface

Knowledge Discovery and Data Mining (KDD) has become one of the major research areas in data science and data analytics. The more the complexity of the data grows the more grows the need of sophisticated KDD techniques to reveal the knowledge in the data. On the one hand, traditional data analysis tools and techniques have been struggling to tackle this problem, while on the other hand, as a solution biological inspired data mining techniques have been introduced to perform better on different data mining tasks. Data clustering, classification rules mining, association rule mining, sequential pattern mining, outlier detection, feature selection, and recommender systems are some of the area, where biologically inspired techniques have been used. The applications of these techniques include but are not limited to healthcare data, environmental data, sensor data, Web data, semi-structured data, microarray data, and streaming data. Some of the commonly used bio-inspired techniques include Neural Networks, Fuzzy Systems, Genetic Algorithms, Ant Colony Optimization, Particle Swarm Optimization, Artificial Immune Systems, Culture Algorithms, Social Evolution, and Artificial Bee Colony Optimization.

This book is motivated by the desire of bridging the gap between two contemporary fields of Knowledge Discovery and Data Mining (KDD) and biologically inspired optimization techniques. The aim of this book is to highlight the contemporary research in the area of biologically inspired techniques in different data mining domains and the implementation of these techniques in real life data mining problems. The book includes state-of-the-art work in this area and shares the good practices that have enabled this area to grow and flourish. The book provides quality work from established researchers that can be used by the new researchers in the area. Below are highlights of the book.

Chapter 1 introduces some of the main biologically inspired techniques with discussion on advantages and limitations of some of the commonly used techniques. Brief literature overviews of the KDD techniques from Particle Swarm Optimization (PSO) and a Swarm Intelligence (SI)-based optimization are presented. Some of the most cited work significantly impacting work in the area has been overviewed.

Chapter 2 titled, "Probabilistic Control and Swarm Dynamics in Mobile Robots and Ants," discusses probabilistic control of mobile robots navigating in random environments and mimicking the foraging activity of the ants, a widely accepted optimal method with respect to the environmental conditions. The system was tested using mobile agents based on the Braitenberg vehicles equipped with four types of sensors, mimicking sensing abilities of including short- and long-distance sensing of environmental states, sensing of neighboring agents, and sensing the pheromone traces. The outcomes show the similarity of suggested mobile agents, running both individually and in groups, is statistically indistinguishable from the foraging behavior of real ants observed in laboratory experiments.

Chapter 3, "A Measure Optimized Cost-Sensitive Learning Framework for Imbalanced Data Classification," implements Particle Swarm Optimization (PSO), a well-known Swarm Intelligence (SI)-based technique, to solve the class imbalanced data classification problem, which is one of the contemporary challenging problems. The authors present effective wrapper framework incorporating the evaluation measure into the objective function for improving the performance of classification by simultaneously optimizing the best pair of feature subset, intrinsic parameters, and misclassification cost parameter. For evaluation purposes, support vector machine neural networks have been used. Using the standard benchmark classification datasets, the proposed method is compared to commonly used sampling techniques.

Chapter 4 of the book, "Towards an Improved Ensemble Learning Model of Artificial Neural Networks: Lessons Learned on Using Randomized Numbers of Hidden Neurons," describes an application area of Artificial Neural Networks (ANN) using ensemble learning model. The authors argue that ensemble machine learning is capable of improving performance of instability of ANN. The study presents using a linear search and randomized assignment of the number of hidden neurons as an extension to the already presented approaches in the area. Using standard model evaluation criteria and novel ensemble combination rules, the results of this study suggest that having a large number of "unbiased" randomized guesses of the number of hidden neurons beyond 50 performs better than very few occurrences of those that were optimally determined.

Chapter 5, "Ant Programming Algorithms for Classification," presents a detailed literature overview of ant programming approaches to extract comprehensible classifiers. There exist three such algorithms for classification rule mining: two of them for regular classification and one for imbalanced classification. These algorithms mainly differ in the optimization approach, single-objective or multi-objective, and the purpose of the classification task. The chapter collects these algorithms, presenting different experimental studies that confirm the aptitude of this metaheuristic to address the classification task.

Chapter 6, "Machine Fault Diagnosis and Prognosis using Self-Organizing Map," proposes a Self-Organizing Map (SOM) method for fault diagnosis and prognosis of manufacturing systems, machines, components, and processes. The study concentrates on optimizing the discovery process of machine health. The proposed method provides a way to predict manufacturing faults, which can be used to develop a good maintenance strategy for the optimum number of corrective maintenance. Self-organizing maps have been shown useful to classify the fault and predict the degrading of machines, components, and processes effectively, clearly, and easily.

Chapter 7, "An Enhanced Artificial Bee Colony Optimizer for Predictive Analysis of Heating Oil Prices using Least Squares Support Vector Machines," uses one of the emerging technique from Swarm Intelligence, called Artificial Bee Colony (ABC) optimization, for prediction analysis. The proposed approach is based on the hybridization of Least Squares Support Vector Machines (LSSVM) with an enhanced Artificial Bee Colony (eABC) technique. An interesting application area of the research "oil prices prediction" has been proposed in this study. The technique works in two phases. Initially a Levy mutation is introduced to keep the model from falling into local minimum; later, the predictive analysis is succeeded by the LSSVM. Realized in predictive analysis of heating oil prices, the empirical findings manifest the superiority of eABC-LSSVM in prediction accuracy.

Chapter 8, "Comparison of Linguistic Summaries and Fuzzy Functional Dependencies Related to Data Mining," overviews the task of performing data mining based on fuzzy logic. The chapter explores the ways to discover potentially useful knowledge from relational database by integrating fuzzy functional dependencies and linguistic summaries. The finding of this work says that using fuzzy functional dependencies and linguistic summaries in a complementing way could mine a variety of valuable information from relational databases, which can result in decision-making, reducing the number of attributes in databases, and estimating missing values.

Chapter 9 explores the research work in the area of genetic programming for civil engineering. The chapter, "Application of Artificial Neural Network and Genetic Programming in Civil Engineering," investigates Genetic Programming (GP) and Artificial Neural Network (ANN) models for prediction of air entrainment rate (QA) of triangular sharp-crested weir. The authors present a comparative study between the developed Back Propagation (BP), Generalized Regression Neural Network (GRNN), and GP models.

Chapter 10, "A Promising Direction towards Automatic Construction of Relevance Measures," quantifies a given feature for its relevancy to a target variable. Measuring relevance and redundancy is a central concept in feature selection and features reduction. The authors identify the lack of generality as a core problem and show that regardless of the type of heuristic measure and search strategy, heuristic methods cannot optimize the performance of all learning algorithms. They propose a hyper-heuristic method that through an evolutionary process automatically generates an appropriate relevance measure for a given problem. The new approach can detect relevant features in difficult scenarios.

In chapter 11, Earliest Deadline First (EDF) and Ant Colony Optimization (ACO) have been used for adaptive scheduling of the distributed systems. The chapter titled, "Adaptive Scheduling for Real-Time Distributed Systems," proposes the use of Artificial Intelligence methods towards more realistic domains requiring real-time responses. The finding of the research reports that Ant Colony Optimization (ACO) performs quite well for scheduling real-time distributed systems during overloaded conditions.

Chapter 12, "Discovery of Emergent Sorting Behavior using Swarm Intelligence and Grid-Enabled Genetic Algorithms," uses simple local comparison and swap operators for sorting sequences. The authors present the basic concepts and an experimental validation of Emerge-Sort, a sorting algorithm that does not depend on being told which way a sequence should be sorted and yet manages to sort that sequence based on randomly applied simple local operators. The authors experimentally validate square run-time behavior for emergent sorting and suggest that not knowing in advance which direction to sort and allowing such direction to emerge imposes a penalty over conventional techniques.

Chapter 13, "Application of Biologically Inspired Techniques for Industrial and Environmental Research via Air Quality Monitoring Network," proposes a systematic methodology for simultaneous identification of an emission source and emission rate. The authors assess the application of artificial neural networks for this purpose.

Chapter 14, "Online Prediction of Blood Glucose Levels using Genetic Algorithm," presents an interesting application area of the genetic algorithms. The authors propose a computer-based system that predicts Blood Glucose Level (BGL) in diabetic patients so that they can manage their blood glucose level.

The last chapter of the book, "Security of Wireless Devices using Biological-Inspired RF Finger-printing Technique," proposes the use of ANN for a growing area of communication security. Radio Frequency (RF) fingerprinting, a means of providing an additional layer of security for wireless devices, is a security mechanism inspired from biological fingerprint identification systems. RF fingerprinting classification is performed by selecting an "unknown" signal from the pool, generating its RF fingerprint, and using a classifier to correlate the received RF fingerprint with each profile RF fingerprint stored in the database. The authors evaluate the performance of the KNN and neural network classification in three different scenarios. The experimental study compares the outcome for these different scenarios.

Shafiq Alam
University of Auckland, New Zealand

Gillian Dobbie
University of Auckland, New Zealand

Yun Sing Koh
University of Auckland, New Zealand

Saeed ur Rehman
Unitec Institute of Technology, New Zealand

Chapter 1
Biologically Inspired Techniques for Data Mining:
A Brief Overview of Particle Swarm Optimization for KDD

Shafiq Alam
University of Auckland, New Zealand

Yun Sing Koh
University of Auckland, New Zealand

Gillian Dobbie
University of Auckland, New Zealand

Saeed ur Rehman
Unitec Institute of Technology, New Zealand

ABSTRACT

Knowledge Discovery and Data (KDD) mining helps uncover hidden knowledge in huge amounts of data. However, recently, different researchers have questioned the capability of traditional KDD techniques to tackle the information extraction problem in an efficient way while achieving accurate results when the amount of data grows. One of the ways to overcome this problem is to treat data mining as an optimization problem. Recently, a huge increase in the use of Swarm Intelligence (SI)-based optimization techniques for KDD has been observed due to the flexibility, simplicity, and extendibility of these techniques to be used for different data mining tasks. In this chapter, the authors overview the use of Particle Swarm Optimization (PSO), one of the most cited SI-based techniques in three different application areas of KDD, data clustering, outlier detection, and recommender systems. The chapter shows that there is a tremendous potential in these techniques to revolutionize the process of extracting knowledge from big data using these techniques.

INTRODUCTION

Knowledge Discovery and Data mining (KDD) helps us understand some characteristics of data in large repositories by passing the data through different operations such as data selection, pre-processing, transformation, data mining and post processing. Data mining, which is the core of KDD, extracts informative patterns such as clusters of relevant data, classification and association rules, sequential patterns and prediction models for different types of data such as textual, audio-visual, and microarray data.

DOI: 10.4018/978-1-4666-6078-6.ch001

Recently a huge increase in the use of Swarm Intelligence (SI) based optimization techniques for KDD has been observed. Particle Swarm Optimization (PSO) is one of the most highly cited SI techniques for KDD because it has the simplicity, and extendibility to be used for different data mining tasks. For instance in data clustering, optimization based techniques have been proposed to address different issues that affect the performance of clustering techniques. These issues include selection of the initial parameters, optimizing the centroids, convergence to a solution, and trapping in unfeasible solutions. When involving optimization in the process, it either uses an optimization technique as a data-clustering algorithm or adds optimization to the existing data clustering approaches. Optimization based clustering techniques treat data clustering as an optimization problem and try to optimize an objective function either to a minima or maxima. In the context of data clustering, a minimization objective function can be the intra-cluster distance and maximization can correspond to the inter-cluster distance.

While adding optimization to the data mining process, the results achieved so far are promising. Optimization has significantly improved accuracy and efficiency while solving some other problems such as global optimization, multi-objective optimization and avoiding being trapped in local optima (Kuo et al., 2011) (Alam et al., 2008) (Das et al., 2009) (Van der Merwe, & Engelbrecht, 2003). The involvement of intelligent optimization techniques has been found effective in enhancing the performance of complex, real time, and costly data mining processing. A number of optimization techniques have been proposed to add to the performance of the clustering process. Swarm Intelligence is one such optimization area where techniques based on SI have been used extensively to either perform clustering independently or add to the existing clustering techniques.

This chapter introduces the use of PSO in three KDD areas; data clustering, outlier detection, and recommender systems. The next section explains the concept of swarm intelligence.

SWARM INTELLIGENCE

Swarm Intelligence, inspired by the biological behavior of animals, birds, and fish, is an innovative intelligent optimization technique (Abraham et al., 2006) (Engelbrecht, 2006). SI techniques are based on the collective behavior of swarms of bees, fish schools, and colonies of insects while searching for food, communicating with each other and socializing in their colonies. The SI models are based on self-organization, decentralization, communication, and cooperation between the individuals within the team. The individual interaction is very simple but emerges as a complex global behavior, which is the core of swarm intelligence (Bonabeau & Meyer, 2001). Although swarm intelligence based techniques have primarily been used and found very efficient in traditional optimization problems, a huge growth in these techniques has been observed in other areas of research. These application areas vary from optimizing the solution for planning, scheduling, resource management, and network optimization problems. Data mining is one of the contemporary areas of application, where these techniques have been found to be efficient for clustering, classification, feature selection and outlier detection. The use of swarm intelligence has been extended from conventional optimization problems to optimization-based data mining.

A number of SI based techniques with many variants have been proposed in the last decade and the number of new techniques is growing. Among different SI techniques, Ant Colony Optimization (ACO) and Particle Swarm Optimization (PSO) are the two main techniques, which are widely used for solving discrete and continuous optimization problems. In the next sections we will discuss the foundation PSO followed by its use in KDD.

PARTICLE SWARM OPTIMIZATION

Particle Swarm Optimization (PSO) is Swarm Intelligence based metaheuristic algorithm proposed by Kennedy and Eberhart (Kennedy& Eberhart, 1995), which takes its inspiration, from the cooperation and communication of a swarm of animals. This swarming behavior can be observed in flocks of flying birds, schools of fish swimming, and the communication mechanism in honey bees. The intelligence, which emerges from such behavior, causes the swarm to mimic complex global patterns. Below we describe general concepts of PSO while the next section will explain PSO with special reference to PSO for data clustering.

In PSO, each individual in the swarm, called a particle, behaves like an agent of a highly decentralized and intelligent environment. Each particle of the swarm contributes to the environment by following very simple rules, thus cooperates and communicates with other particles of the swarm. A complex global collective behavior emerges in the swarm. This complex global behavior, which is a result of following collective effort and following simple rules, is exploited to solve a complex optimization problem. High decentralization, cooperation amongst the particles and simple implementation makes PSO efficiently applicable to optimization problems (Eberhart et al., 2001). PSO has three main components, particles, learning components of the particles, and the velocity of the particles. In a problem space where there may be more than one possible solution and the optimal solution of the problem is required, a particle represents an individual solution to the problem. The learning of the particles comes from two sources, one is from a particle's own experi-

ence called cognitive learning and the other source of learning is the combined learning of the entire swarm called social learning. Cognitive learning is represented by personal best (pBest) and social learning is represented by the global best (gBest) value. The pBest solution is the best solution the particle has ever achieved in its history. The gBest value is the best position the swarm has ever achieved. The swarm guides the particle using parameter gBest. Together cognitive and social learning are used to calculate the velocity of each particle to their next position. The following is the velocity equation for the particle:

$$V_i\left(t+1\right) = \omega \times V_i\left(t\right) + q1r1\left(pBest_i\left(t\right) - X_i\left(t\right)\right)$$
$$+ q2r2(gBest_i\left(t\right) - Xi(t))$$

where Vi(t) is the current velocity of the particle, Vi(t+1) is the new velocity. The value Xi(t) is the current position of the data vector, q1, and q2 are constants which weight the social, and cognitive components pBest and gBest respectively, and r1, r2 are random numbers ranging from 0 to 1. The velocity of the particle directs the particle to its new better position using the following equation:

Xi(t + 1) = Xi(t) + Vi(t + 1)

where Xi(t + 1) is the new position, Xi(t) is the current position of the particle and $V_i\left(t+1\right)$ is the new velocity of the particle.

When applied to optimization problems, a typical PSO algorithm starts with the initialization of a number of parameters. One of the important initializations is selecting the initial swarm. The number of particles in the swarm depends upon the complexity of the problem. An initial choice of solutions is normally made randomly. However an initial guess that spreads the particles uniformly in the solution space can speed up the emergence towards an optimal solution. A typical initial number of particles for PSO in a swarm ranges from 20 to 40 but varies from application to application and problem to problem.

PARTICLE SWARM OPTIMIZATION FOR DATA CLUSTERING

Particle Swarm Optimization (PSO) has been widely used for clustering different types of data. It has been used as an independent clustering approach as well as hybridized with other data clustering techniques. The literature reports a

significant amount of usage of PSO as a part of other clustering techniques where PSO is used for selection of optimal values for certain clustering parameters. It has also been used for tuning of different parameters of an existing clustering algorithm to improve the efficiency of the technique and enhance the quality of the output. As an independent technique, the social and cognitive learning component of PSO has been used to guide the centroid of the clusters without involving another clustering method.

Most of the PSO based clustering techniques cited in Table 1 have addressed some of the com-

Table 1. Descriptions of PSO-based techniques

PSO Based Technique	Description
(Merwe & Engelbrecht, 2003)	In this work PSO has been used with k-means clustering. There is a fixed number of particles, each representing the centroids of all clusters, while the swarm starts with multiple solutions. In subsequent iterations, a new set of solution is generated to improve on the previous solutions. The results were evaluated against K-mean, and PSO-hybridized k-means clustering based on classification accuracy and error rate.
(Xiao et al., 2004)	The authors in this work have used Self Organizing Maps (SOM) for data clustering while PSO has been used to optimize the weights of the SOM. Gene expression data was used for the evaluation of this technique.
(Chen & Ye, 2004)	This work is quite similar to the work presented in Van der (Merwe & Engelbrecht, 2003) but instead of using k-means, the authors have only used PSO to perform data clustering. For experiments, fuzzy C-means has been used for comparison of intra-cluster distance as a fitness function.
(Omran & Engelbrecht, 2005)	In this work a Dynamic Clustering algorithm based on binary PSO (DCPSO) was proposed to cluster and segment images. This approach also use k-means with PSO, but the version of PSO that the authors have selected is the discrete PSO instead of standard PSO.
Cohen & de Castro, 2006)	Cohen et al. presented a novel approach using a complete swarm presenting one clustering solution at a time. The particle of the swarm represents one centroid instead of a set of centroids.
(Chen & Zhang, 2007)	This approach uses a similar approach of adding k-mean to PSO as used in the previous approaches. However, the authors have added random trajectories to the velocity of the particles to enhance the coverage of the particle.
(Zahara, & Kao, 2009)	Kao et al. added Nelder-Mead (NM) simplex method to k-means for the first time and PSO for performing data clustering. This approach has reduced the computation cost; one of the major bottlenecks of PSO based techniques.
(Yang, et al. 2009)	In this work, instead of using k-means with PSO, the authors have hybridized k-harmonic means with PSO and to avoid initial sensitivity to centroids.
(Alam et al., 2008)	Evolutionary PSO (EPSO-clustering) is another way to perform clustering without hybridizing it with the traditional clustering approach, instead moving the centroid using the pBest and gBest measure. The best set of solutions comes after a round of evolutionary iterations of the swarm through intermediate generations.
(Alam et al., 2010)	Another similar work to EPSO-clustering is Hierarchical PSO (HPSO-clustering), which extends EPSO to perform hierarchical agglomerative clustering. This is the first ever PSO based hierarchical clustering algorithm.

mon aspects of data clustering, such as enhancing the efficiency and improving the accuracy of the techniques, and ended up either having as good results as the existing techniques or some improvements in one or other aspect of solving the data clustering problem. From the trends that we have observed during a literature review, it is evident that the future of the PSO based clustering is promising as more and more application areas are benefiting from the qualities of these approaches.

PSO BASED OUTLIER DETECTION

Outlier detection is one of the recent KDD areas, where instead of finding common patterns in the data such as clusters of data, classification rules, association rules, which are applicable to a considerable portion of the data, anomalies in data are detected (Breunig et al., 2000). Outliers, anomalies, deviations, exceptions, rare instances and irregularities are terms used in the data mining community to represent such observations that do not comply with the patterns that exist in datasets. Hawkins (Hawkins, 1980) defines the outlier as "*an observation that deviates so much from other observations as to arouse suspicions that it was generated by a different mechanism*". Outliers, if they remain undetected distract different distance measures and can cause incorrect interpretations of the data. Outliers affect statistical measures such as means, standard deviation, asymmetry and tail behavior as well as data mining operations such as clustering, classification, and association rule mining. The inclusion or exclusion of outliers in analysis depends upon the purpose of mining. Sometimes removing or replacing outliers can improve the quality of extracted patterns. Any noise added to the data, which has sufficient deviation from the rest of the data of the repository, can skew the analysis process substantially. An example of such observations is the sessions from web-bots in web data logs, which sufficiently deviate from normal web user sessions. Because web-bots are outliers, they can be excluded from further analysis, as they do not represent genuine web user behavior. Such outliers may lead to wrong analysis and hence to a wrong prediction which can result in incorrect decisions. However, sometimes the study of outliers can be helpful in modeling the decision making process. Fraudulent bank transactions are one such example where one wants to retain the outliers in the data and analyze it to help in modeling the security alert systems.

Outlier detection methods vary from unsupervised, semi supervised and unsupervised techniques (see Table 2). Some methods only consider univariate data while others can handle multivariate data. The process of outlier detection can be performed in a supervised or unsupervised manner. Some of the widely used outlier detection methods include distance based outlier detection, density based outlier detection and clustering based outlier detection and traditional statistical outlier detection methods. A very popular distance-based outlier detection method (Knox & Ng, 1998) is the most commonly used unsupervised technique, which defines an outlier as a data point that has an exceptionally large distance to the other data points or its nearest neighbors. Distance-based detection has been used to detect individual as well as clusters of outliers (Angiulli & Pizzuti, 2005) (Bay & Schwabacher, 2003). Density-based techniques define outliers in terms of the density of their neighborhood. A local outlier is filtered out from the population if it does not have many data points around it. Different statistical techniques have also been used to detect univariate outliers in the data, which includes Box plot and histogram analysis. A popular statistical outlier method is the z-Score method where the mean and the standard deviation of the data are used to identify outlier observations. Distribution-based methods, Control Chart Technique (CCT), and Linear Regression Technique (LRT), are also used for outlier detection. Rosner's test, Dixon's test and Grubbs' test are some other statistical tests that detect potential outliers in data.

Table 2. Descriptions of PSO based outlier detection techniques

(Alam, 2012) EPSO based outlier detection	In this work the basic idea of detection of outliers in the data has been presented. A data point located far away from the centroid of the cluster based on some threshold distance during the evolutionary PSO based clustering is considered an outlier.
(Alam et al., 2010) HPSO based outlier detection	The EPSO based outlier detection was extended to HPSO-based outlier detection where more a robust algorithm has been designed and tested on data from UCI and NASA web usage data. The proposed approach isolates sets of outliers during hierarchical agglomerative clustering. We used HPSO-clustering to identify different suspected observations that are at a significant distance from the centroids of the clusters during a clustering hierarchy.
(Alam et al., 2014) HPSO based Web bot detection	Following the approach of HPSO-clustering based outlier detection; the authors have extended their work to detect web bots in web usage data. Web bots or crawlers are the software agents that crawl through web pages to extract contents of the pages or look for specific material for search engine optimization and other marking purposes. The approach was tested on a real life data set where there were real web bot requests in the data as well as where outliers were manually injected to the data. The results show that almost all the manually injected outliers were detected using the proposed approach.
(Mohemmed et al., 2010)	Another similar work on outlier detection is proposed by Mohemmed et al., where PSO is used to optimize the distance measures instead automatically based on a trial and error approach. The approach integrates a feature selection ability and distance optimization to automatically detect the outliers from a dataset. The proposed approach outperformed the traditional local outlier factor approach.

PSO BASED RECOMMENDER SYSTEMS

Web based recommender systems are tools that suggest web users a resource based on the patterns generated from web users' activities (Mobasher & Srivastava, 2000) (Mobasher et al., 2000) (Cho, 2002). In the context of web usage, all genuine web users exhibit some specific patterns in their browsing behavior. Similarly, the same patterns can also be observed in the usage of web resources. For example, a user is more likely to visit a particular web resource if similar web users are interested in the particular web resource. The historical information of a web user and web resource, which are stored in a web log, provide a way to predict future usage of a web resource by a web user. Recommender systems exploit this information, which predicts the potential interests of web users, based on the history of the web users, the history of similar users, the history of usage of a resource, and the history of usage of other similar resources. Recommender systems generate the set of most suitable choices among these resources

(Resnick et al., 2002). Because of the amount of data and the complexity of the data that needs to be analyzed for data for recommender systems, recently optimization based techniques have been proposed to tackle this problem.

PSO has been proposed as one of the ways to generate web based recommendations in an efficient manner. We proposed the use of PSO to cluster similar web users into groups where recommendation can be generated based on the similarity of different groups. HPSO-clustering is used to develop usage mining based recommender systems, which divide the data into different interest groups, and as a result improve the efficiency of the approach because they do not look at the entire dataset. This is the first ever work to the best of our knowledge that has used PSO for recommender systems. We tested the approach on benchmark data for clustering, and web bot detection, before implementing it for recommender systems. Overall the approach is good on traditional precision and recall measures and generates meaningful recommendations with improved performance.

FUTURE WORK

Data clustering, outlier detection, and recommender systems are well-researched areas, but usage of Swarm Intelligence and particularly PSO has not previously been investigated thoroughly. We cited the different relevant work, looked at different models, and outlined some of the pros and cons of different techniques. Evolutionary techniques and recommender systems are vibrant and rapidly changing areas and have not been researched, and as a result it is difficult to generalize the approaches. As future work different approaches that generalize these techniques to heterogeneous data and different application areas can be carried out and would make a valuable contribution to the field. We outline some of the potential future areas in PSO based clustering and outlier detection, PSO based web usage clustering, and recommender systems.

Web Usage Clustering: One of the major problems in clustering web usage data is the heterogeneous nature of the data. We would like to combine the time dimensions of data, the data download, and browsing sequence of the web user to cluster similar web users. We would also like to see how the semantic dimensions i.e. contents similarity can add to the accuracy of web usage clustering and can produce more accurate and compact clusters.

HPSO Clustering and Outlier Detection: In optimization based clustering, automation of parameters and generalization of the techniques are two major future research directions. Scalability of the HPSO-clustering to be used in a multi-agent environment, in a distributed environment, and for simultaneous clustering are some other open areas. Scaling the outlier detection to high dimensional data is another future direction.

Recommender System: Although in our research we have shown that our PSO based clustering approaches could be used for recommender systems, the system needs more refinement in the following areas:

1. Develop better modeling techniques for web usage based recommender systems.
2. Further experimentation for the validity of recommendations.
3. Add more similarity measures to the clustering process to best suit the recommender system.
4. Generalization of the approach for heterogeneous data and different applications.
5. Propose an incremental updating of the knowledge base.
6. Implementation in a distributed environment.

CONCLUSION

In the last few years, a huge increase has been observed in the usage of optimization-based techniques to tackle data mining problems. The use of Swarm Intelligence based optimization techniques has increased many times. A survey conducted in (Alam et al, 2014) shows that alone PSO has an average increase of about 150% in the number of articles published over the last 10 years. The simplicity, scalability, and efficiency of PSO have attracted a huge interest in this technique to be used for data mining problems. In this chapter, we have outlined some of the work in data clustering, web usage clustering, outlier detection and recommender systems. It is evidence that there is a huge potential for such techniques to be used for data mining in general, and the above application areas in particular.

Overall these biologically inspired techniques have tremendous potential to contribute in solving KDD problems in an efficient and accurate manner.

REFERENCES

Abraham, A., Guo, H., & Liu, H. (2006). Swarm intelligence: foundations, perspectives and applications. In *Swarm Intelligent Systems* (pp. 3–25). Springer. doi:10.1007/978-3-540-33869-7_1

Alam, S. (2012). *Clustering, swarms and recommender systems.* (Doctoral dissertation). Research-Space@ Auckland.

Alam, S., Dobbie, G., Koh, Y. S., & Riddle, P. (2014). Web Bots Detection Using Particle Swarm Optimization Based Clustering. In *Proceedings of IEEE Congress on Evolutionary Computation* (CEC). Beijing, China. IEEE.

Alam, S., Dobbie, G., & Riddle, P. (2008). An evolutionary particle swarm optimization algorithm for data clustering. In *Proceedings of IEEE Swarm Intelligence Symposium*, (pp. 1-6). IEEE.

Alam, S., Dobbie, G., Riddle, P., & Naeem, M. A. (2010). Particle swarm optimization based hierarchical agglomerative clustering. In *Proceedings of IEEE/WIC/ACM International Conference on Web Intelligence and Intelligent Agent Technology* (WI-IAT), (Vol. 2, pp. 64-68). Toronto, Canada: IEEE.

Alam, S., Dobbie, G., Riddle, P., & Naeem, M. A. (2010). A swarm intelligence based clustering approach for outlier detection. In *Proceedings of IEEE Congress on Evolutionary Computation* (CEC), (pp. 1-7). IEEE.

Alam, S., Dobbie, G., Sing Koh, Y., Riddle, P., & Ur Rehman, S. (2014). Research on Particle Swarm Optimization Based Clustering: A systematic review of literature and techniques. In *Swarm and Evolutionary Computation*. Elsevier. doi:10.1016/j.swevo.2014.02.001

Angiulli, F., & Pizzuti, C. (2005). Outlier mining in large high-dimensional data sets. *IEEE Transactions on Knowledge and Data Engineering, 17*(2), 203–215. doi:10.1109/TKDE.2005.31

Bay, S. D., & Schwabacher, M. (2003). Mining distance-based outliers in near linear time with randomization and a simple pruning rule. In *Proceedings of the ninth ACM SIGKDD international conference on Knowledge discovery and data mining* (pp. 29-38). Washington, DC: ACM.

Bonabeau, E., & Meyer, C. (2001). Swarm intelligence: A whole new way to think about business. *Harvard Business Review, 79*(5), 106–114. PMID:11345907

Breunig, M. M., Kriegel, H. P., Ng, R. T., & Sander, J. (2000). LOF: Identifying density-based local outliers. *SIGMOD Record, 29*(2), 93–104. doi:10.1145/335191.335388

Chen, C. Y., & Ye, F. (2004). Particle swarm optimization algorithm and its application to clustering analysis. In *Proceedings of IEEE International Conference on Networking, Sensing and Control, 2004* (Vol. 2, pp. 789-794). Taipei, Taiwan: IEEE.

Chen, J., & Zhang, H. (2007). Research on application of clustering algorithm based on PSO for the web usage pattern. In *Proceedings of International Conference on Wireless Communications, Networking and Mobile Computing WiCom 2007* (pp. 3705-3708). Shanghai, China: IEEE.

Cho, Y. H., Kim, J. K., & Kim, S. H. (2002). A personalized recommender system based on web usage mining and decision tree induction. *Expert Systems with Applications, 23*(3), 329–342. doi:10.1016/S0957-4174(02)00052-0

Cohen, S. C., & de Castro, L. N. (2006). Data clustering with particle swarms. In *Proceedings of IEEE Congress on Evolutionary Computation*, (pp. 1792-1798). Vancouver, Canada: IEEE.

Das, S., Chowdhury, A., & Abraham, A. (2009). A bacterial evolutionary algorithm for automatic data clustering. In *Proceedings of IEEE Congress on Evolutionary Computation*, (pp. 2403-2410). Trondheim, Norway. IEEE.

Eberhart, R. C., Shi, Y., & Kennedy, J. (2001). *Swarm intelligence*. Elsevier.

Engelbrecht, A. P. (2006). *Fundamentals of computational swarm intelligence*. John Wiley & Sons.

Hawkins, D. M. (1980). *Identification of outliers* (Vol. 11). London: Chapman and Hall. doi:10.1007/978-94-015-3994-4

Kennedy, J., & Eberhart, R. (1995). Particle swarm optimization. In *Proceedings of IEEE International Conference on Neural Networks* (Vol. 4, No. 2, pp. 1942-1948). Perth, Australia. IEEE.

Knox, E. M., & Ng, R. T. (1998). Algorithms for mining distancebased outliers in large datasets. In *Proceedings of the International Conference on Very Large Data Bases* (pp. 392-403). Berlin: Morgan Kaufmann Publishers.

Kuo, R. J., Wang, M. J., & Huang, T. W. (2011). An application of particle swarm optimization algorithm to clustering analysis. *Soft Computing*, *15*(3), 533–542. doi:10.1007/s00500-009-0539-5

Mobasher, B., Cooley, R., & Srivastava, J. (2000). Automatic personalization based on Web usage mining. *Communications of the ACM*, *43*(8), 142–151. doi:10.1145/345124.345169

Mobasher, B., Dai, H., Luo, T., Sun, Y., & Zhu, J. (2000). Integrating web usage and content mining for more effective personalization. In *Electronic commerce and web technologies* (pp. 165–176). Springer. doi:10.1007/3-540-44463-7_15

Mohemmed, A. W., Zhang, M., & Browne, W. N. (2010). Particle swarm optimisation for outlier detection. In *Proceedings of the 12th annual conference on Genetic and evolutionary computation* (pp. 83-84). Portland, OR: ACM.

Omran, M., Salman, A., & Engelbrecht, A. P. (2005). Dynamic clustering using particle swarm optimization with application in unsupervised image classification. In *Proceedings of Fifth World Enformatika Conference* (ICCI 2005) (pp. 199-204). Springer.

Resnick, P., & Varian, H. R. (1997). Recommender systems. *Communications of the ACM*, *40*(3), 56–58. doi:10.1145/245108.245121

Van der Merwe, D. W., & Engelbrecht, A. P. (2003). Data clustering using particle swarm optimization. In *Proceedings of IEEE Congress on Evolutionary Computation*, (Vol. 1, pp. 215-220). Canberra, Australia. IEEE.

Xiao, X., Dow, E. R., Eberhart, R., Ben Miled, Z., & Oppelt, R. J. (2004). A hybrid self-organizing maps and particle swarm optimization approach. *Concurrency and Computation*, *16*(9), 895–915. doi:10.1002/cpe.812

Yang, F., Sun, T., & Zhang, C. (2009). An efficient hybrid data clustering method based on K-harmonic means and Particle Swarm Optimization. *Expert Systems with Applications*, *36*(6), 9847–9852. doi:10.1016/j.eswa.2009.02.003

Zahara, E., & Kao, Y. T. (2009). Hybrid Nelder–Mead simplex search and particle swarm optimization for constrained engineering design problems. *Expert Systems with Applications*, *36*(2), 3880–3886. doi:10.1016/j.eswa.2008.02.039

ADDITIONAL READING

Alam, S., Dobbie, G., Koh, Y. S., & Riddle, P. (2013, April). Clustering heterogeneous web usage data using Hierarchical Particle Swarm Optimization. In 2013 IEEE Symposium on Swarm Intelligence (SIS), Singapore (pp. 147-154). IEEE.

Alam, S., Dobbie, G., & Riddle, P. (2009). Exploiting swarm behaviour of simple agents for clustering web users' session data. In Data Mining and Multi-agent Integration (pp. 61-75). Springer US.

Alam, S., Dobbie, G., & Riddle, P. (2012). Towards recommender system using particle swarm optimization based web usage clustering. In *New Frontiers in Applied Data Mining* (pp. 316–326). Springer Berlin Heidelberg. doi:10.1007/978-3-642-28320-8_27

Alam, S., Dobbie, G., Riddle, P., & Koh, Y. S. (2013). Analysis of Web Usage Data for Clustering Based Recommender System. In *Trends in Practical Applications of Agents and Multiagent Systems* (pp. 171–179). Springer International Publishing. doi:10.1007/978-3-319-00563-8_21

KEY TERMS AND DEFINITIONS

Data Clustering: Data clustering is a data mining technique to group the data into identical groups based on the characteristics of the data.

Outlier Detection: Outlier detection is the process of identifiying anomalies and abnormal behaviour in huge data sets.

Particle Swarm Optimizaiton: Particle swarm optimization is a meta heuristic to solve optimization problems based on the method from bird flocking, fish schooling and other similar behaviours in animals.

Swarm Intelligence: Swarm intelligence is the collective behavior of decentralized, self-organized systems, inspired by the group behaviour of animals.

Web Bot Detection: It's the implementation of outlier detection methods to detect web crawlers in the web usage data.

Web Usage Mining: It is the study of extracting useful data from the activities of web users.

Chapter 2
Probabilistic Control and Swarm Dynamics in Mobile Robots and Ants

Eugene Kagan
The Weizmann Institute of Science, Israel

Alon Sela
Tel-Aviv University, Israel

Alexander Rybalov
Jerusalem College of Technology, Israel

Hava Siegelmann
University of Massachusetts at Amherst, USA

Jennie Steshenko
University of Massachusetts at Amherst, USA

ABSTRACT

The chapter considers the method of probabilistic control of mobile robots navigating in random environments and mimicking the foraging activity of ants, which is widely accepted as optimal with respect to the environmental conditions. The control is based on the Tsetlin automaton, which is a minimal automaton demonstrating an expedient behavior in random environments. The suggested automaton implements probability-based aggregators, which form a complete algebraic system and support an activity of the automaton over non-Boolean variables. The considered mobile agents are based on the Braitenberg vehicles equipped with four types of sensors, which mimic the basic sensing abilities of ants: short- and long-distance sensing of environmental states, sensing of neighboring agents, and sensing the pheromone traces. Numerical simulations demonstrate that the foraging behavior of the suggested mobile agents, running both individually and in groups, is statistically indistinguishable from the foraging behavior of real ants observed in laboratory experiments.

INTRODUCTION

Starting with pioneering works in cybernetics, the progress in computational machinery and robotic research is strongly inspired by the studies of intellectual behavior of living organisms.

A basic role in such studies plays the activity of individual ants and dynamics of their colonies, providing the main source of insights for developing multi-agent robotic and intellectual systems (McFarland & Bösser, 1993; Weiss, 1999). On the other hand, the progress in optimization methods

DOI: 10.4018/978-1-4666-6078-6.ch002

and mathematical modeling of collective behavior of automata leads to better understanding of animal and insect activity (Cole & Cheshire, 1996; Couzin, *et al.*, 2005; Gordon, 2010; Sumpter, 2010; Viswanathan, et al., 2011).

Similarly to living organisms, the teleological activity of autonomous mobile robots in a random environment implies certain decision-making processes which allow fulfilling the mission in spite of environmental uncertainty and the changes in the environment as a result of the robot's actions. To specify such behavior, usually the robots' controllers are considered as probabilistic automata with certain learning abilities and are studied following two general approaches. According to the classical approach, the consideration begins with a definite mission of the mobile robot, for which an optimal or near-optimal control and navigation are specified. The second approach, in contrast, starts with certain observed activity of a living organism, mainly – its motion in the environment, and based on that a mobile robot is developed, equipped with the appropriate sensors and controllers, such that it mimics the living organism activity. Below, we follow the second approach and consider biologically-inspired navigation of mobile robots controlled by probabilistic automata.

The studies in modeling of living organisms activity using probabilistic automata can be traced back to the rise of cybernetics in the end of 1940s, and in 1960s the basic automata models of the simplest forms of biological behavior were developed (Fu, 1967; Fu & Li, 1969; Tsetlin, 1963). Additionally, during that time the studies of interacting automata have been started (Chandrasekaran & Chen 1969; Tsetlin, 1973) that led to the considerations of the dynamics of automata colonies (Verbeeck & Nowé 2002) following the same approach that is used in the studies of the colonies of ants. In the last few decades, the studies aimed to develop the artificial agents that mimic the intellectual abilities of living organisms, such as insects and even mammals, are combined

in the unified framework known as ANIMAT (ANImal-autoMAT). Starting from 1991, the results obtained in this direction are presented in the proceedings of the annual conference "From Animals to Animats" (1991-2012).

The presented work is motivated at most by the problem of search and foraging by mobile robots and their societies (Chernikhovsky, *et al.*, 2012; Israel, *et. al.*, 2012; Kagan, *et al.*, 2010, 2012). This task requires the definition a method of the most effective way of searching for the hidden object if only its location probabilities are known. In the framework of the studies of mobile agents, such problem requires a definition of the agents' behavior, who perform the search task. Starting from its original formulation in 1942, this problem was considered using different optimization techniques. A detailed review of the methods and results obtained in optimal control of mobile robots in the tasks of search and evasion is presented in the paper by Chung, Hollinger & Isler (2011); additional information on probabilistic search and optimization techniques can be found in the book by Kagan & Ben-Gal (2013b). However, because of the high complexity of the search problem and wide variety of conditions, which have to be taken into account, in most cases an optimal search planning is far from a successful solution, and the Stone remark that "planning of search is not solely an analytical exercise. Since subjective judgments are crucial to good search planning, search will always, to some degree, be an art" (Stone, 1983, p. 231), is still relevant.

To overcome these difficulties, we considered the methods of navigation and control of mobile robots in order to obtain a resulting motion of the robots such that it is as much as possible the same as the foraging activity of the ants. Such a consideration follows general assumption that animals, and particularly insects, forage optimally, that is "the evolution and adaptation of foraging behavior should approximately reach completion with individuals foraging in ways close to (i.e.

statistically indistinguishable from) those that maximize their expected fitness, subject to any functional constraints" (Pyke, 1984, p. 524).

In this chapter, we present the recent findings in probabilistic control and apply them to the navigation of mobile robots and their societies. The main goal is to develop methods of probabilistic control of mobile robots acting as societies such that the resulting behavior of the robots will be as close as possible to the observed behavior of foraging ants and their colonies. Following the assumption that the ants' foraging behavior is optimal, the resulting agents' behavior will be as optimal as is that of the ants. In particular, the chapter considers the interactions between the agents and their usage of common memory, and presents the methods of sensor fusion and probabilistic motion control.

The suggested methods and techniques are applied for specifications of swarm dynamics in the robots' societies. The obtained results are verified by a comparative analysis of the simulated dynamics of robots and the observed and simulated behavior of foraging ants and their colonies.

Certainly, the chapter presents only one possible approach of control, locomotion and sensing abilities of the mobile agents and does not pretend to cover a wide variety of methods used in swarm robotics and in probabilistic control of swarms. In addition, to make the chapter available to the non-robotic community, we intentionally avoided any specific terminology used in swarm robotics. For an essential review of probabilistic control of swarms see the paper by Lerman, *et al.* (2005). A detailed contemporary review of the methods used in the models of swarms and underlying ideas is presented in the excellent books by Passino (2004) and by Trianni (2008). Specific issues regarding optimization using swarms are given by Gazi & Passino (2011), and very friutfull ideas on general definition of swarm behavior using Langevin and Fokker-Plank equations are suggested by Hamann (2010), who also gives a short and concise review of the methods of swarn robotics.

The research is partially supported by the grant #00014-09-1-0069 of the Office of Naval Research, USA.

COMMON DYNAMIC MEMORY AND COMMUNICATION IN A SWARM

In the section, we present a general vision of mobile agents acting in a dynamic environment considered as their common dynamic memory depending on the agents' activity. During path planning and selection of actions, the agents consider the states of the memory and the behavior of the neighbors.

Activity of Mobile Agent in an Environment

Traditionally, a mobile robot is considered as a computation device or as a controller equipped with sensors and motors that can freely change its location in an environment, with respect to a certain mission (Siegwart & Nourbakhsh, 2004). The environment, it its turn, is considered as an arena or terrain with changeable states, in which the mobile agents act and which states change.

At each time moment, the robot receives the current state of the environment, interprets it and translates it to the local map that provides the positioning of the robot in a global map of the environment. Knowing its global position and the state of the environment, the robot chooses and executes the action required by the mission. Finally, the robot plans its further path in the environment, determines the next local movement and executes it. The scheme of these actions is shown in Figure 1.

In the simplest case, the robot does not conduct any action and its mission is to react to the states of the environment, while in more complicated scenarios, the mission of the robot is specified by certain criteria to the resulting trajectory. In

Figure 1. Actions of a mobile robot in an environment. The robot receives the state of the environment, determines its local and global position and makes the decision regarding the action and the next movement.

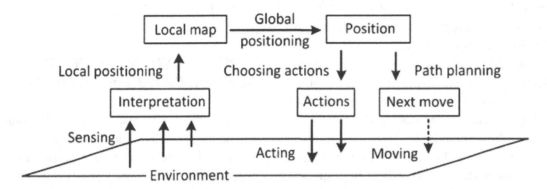

addition, notice that often the next move of the robot is considered as a kind of action and the choice of the actions and the path planning are considered as the same decision-making process. Then, following Wooldridge, the agent is defined as "a computer system that is *situated* in some *environment*, and that is capable of *autonomous action* in this environment in order to meet its design objectives" (Weiss, 1999, p. 29; italics by Wooldridge).

Basic Signal/Reaction Activity of a Braitenberg Vehicle

To clarify the activity of a mobile robot according to the states of the environment, let us consider the movement of a simple two-wheeled robot known as the Braitenberg vehicle (Braitenberg, 1986). In its basic configuration, the vehicle is equipped with sensors and wheels with individual motors. The sensors receive the signals and the controller transmits them to the motors such that the wheel's speed is proportional to the value of the sensed signal. The vehicle is shown in Figure 2.

In this configuration, there are two possible types of connectivity between the sensors and the motors, which define different types of the robot's movement. In the first type, the left sensor is connected with the left motor and the right

sensor is connected with the right motor; thus, a stronger signal received at the left sensor results in a right turn and a stronger signal received at the right sensor results in a left turn of the robot. In the second type, in opposite, the left sensor is connected with the right motor, and the right sensor is connected with the left motor; thus, a stronger signal at the left sensor results in a left turn and a stronger signal at the right sensor results in a right turn of robot. The movement of the robots with the different types of connectivity is illustrated by Figure 3.

The figure shows that for the first type of connectivity (left-to-left/right-to-right connections), since the right sensor is closer to the light source, the right wheel rotates faster than the left wheel, and the vehicle orients away from the light. In contrast, for the second type of connectivity (left-to-right/right-to-left connections), the stronger signal from the right sensor proceeds to the left motor, and the vehicle orients towards the light source. More varitype behavior of the Braitenberg vehicle is obtained by the use of additional sensors and/or by additional control of the signals, which are passed from the sensors to the motors (Braitenberg, 1986). The other types of mobile robots, which follow the similar signal/reaction scheme, are reviewed in the books by Clark (1997) and by Siegwart & Nourbakhsh (2004).

Figure 2. A Braitenberg vehicle with two wheels, two motors and two sensors. The controller regulates the connectivity between the sensors and the motors and specifies the speed of each wheel proportionally to the sensed signals.

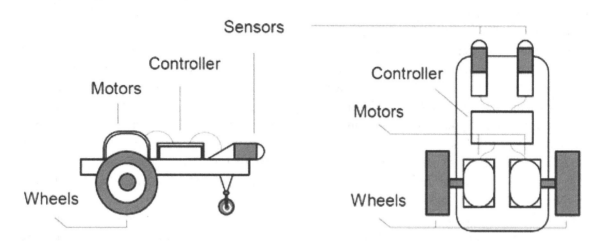

Figure 3. Movements of a Braitenberg vehicle with different connections between its sensors and motors. For the left-to-left/right-to-right connections the vehicle turns away from the light source, while for the left-to-right/right-to-left connections the vehicle turns toward the light source.

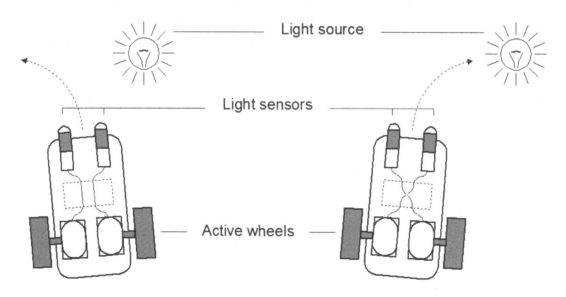

Dynamic Environment

The considered Braitenberg vehicle reacts to the environment's states, and its actions include only the movements of the vehicle. Now assume that, in addition to the movements, the robot's actions result in changes to the environment, that are in turn perceived by the robot's sensors. Such changes can include signing the visited locations or a reconstruction of the environment in the local neighborhood of the robot, and since their result are distinguished as environment states, the robot considers them in further actions and path planning. Using the analogy with ants, such changes are the same as deploying pheromone at certain locations and as gathering materials and food from the environment. Finally, assume that the environment is represented by a natural-like terrain rather than by an artificial static scene that is the terrain allows certain changes that do not depend on the mobile robot activity. For example, in the search tasks such changes are resulted by the target's motion or by random fluctuations of the environment states. In such a case, the robot in its activity should consider this random dynamics of the environment both while choosing the current actions and in further activity and path planning.

Such interactions between the agent and its environment form the most basic feedback model that is in the scope of cybernetics starting from its origins. However, in the framework of mobile agents these dynamics resulted in novel approach usually called embodied cognition (Shapiro, 2011) and strongly applied in ANIMAT researches. In these researches, it is explicitly specified that

1.   The agent is able to change the environment both by definite actions and by signing a certain location;
2.   The environment is dynamic and can change its states according to its internal rules;

3.   The agent is able to sense and to use the states as they resulted both by the agent's action and by the environmental dynamics in further activity and path planning.

Then, the environment is considered "as an active resource whose intrinsic dynamics can play important problem-solving roles" and the agent's sensing and acting system is included into the computational loop (Clark, 1997, p. 83-84). In other words, the environment is considered as an external memory, which is used by the agent in its computations, but which has certain independent dynamics.

Notice that at the same time, the vision of the environment as a part of computational process appeared in the field of quantum robots (Benioff, 1998), where, because of quantum effects, the robots are not completely distinguished from the environment and act in close interaction with the environmental states according to quantum mechanical laws. Later, this approach was modeled using simple Braitenberg-type mobile robots with different control schemes (Raghuvanshi, *et al.*, 2007; Rybalov, *et al.*, 2010); for the main ideas underlying quantum robots and the methods of their navigation see recent work by Kagan & Ben-Gal (2011).

Communication between Agents in a Swarm

The discussed above interactions between a mobile agent and its dynamic environment allow specifying the communication between the agents via environmental changes. Following the already used analogy between mobile agents and ants, we will distinguish two types of such communication: the first is based on the changes of the environment resulted by its reconstruction, like gathering material or food, and the second – on the signing of certain locations, like deploying pheromone by ants. Then, from the agent's point of view, the changes of the environment of the first type resulted by the actions of the other agents are indistinguishable from random changes resulted by the internal dynamics of the environment, while the changes of the second type are considered as meaningful information, which should be considered with respect to swarm behavior (Garnier, *et al.*, 2013; Payton, *et al.*, 2001). To distinguish these types of communication, we assume that the states of the environment and the signs left by the agents are perceived by different sensors.

The other type of communication deals with the direct exchange of information between the agents. Such communication can be conducted in different ways and can support a transfer of different kinds of information. In particular, for capable enough mobile robots it can follow certain communication protocols (Steshenko, *et al.*, 2011), while for less capable agents it is restricted by visual contact or even by touch. Certainly, in living organisms such information exchange is extremely rich and cannot be reduced to artificial communication between the robots. However, for our tasks, we restrict ourselves with only one type of direct communication between neighboring agents; namely, we assume that the agent obtains information about the relative quantity of its neighbors at its left and right side. Such a vision of direct communication follows the general approach of collective behavior of insects and animals (Gordon, 2010; Sumpter, 2010), and, in particular, their movement in groups (Couzin, *et al.*, 2005). Below, we assume that the agents are equipped with specific sensors, which are able to perceive the indicated information about the neighbors.

Considered Mobile Robot and Basic Assumptions

As indicated above, the considered mobile agent acts in a dynamic environment and is equipped with appropriate sensors and actors that allow chang-

ing and perceiving the states of the environment, signing visited locations and obtaining information regarding the quantity of the neighbors and their velocities. We assume that the sensors that check the states of the agent's neighborhood and the sensors that recognize signed locations act in short distances comparable with the geometric size of the agent; below these distances and the dependence of the sensed value on the distance will be defined in details.

In contrast, the sensors that perceive the states of the environment are divided in two groups; the first group acts in the same manner as previously indicated sensors, while the second group acts in long distances and allows obtaining general information regarding the remote environmental states. In a certain sense, such sensors act similarly to smell sensors in living organisms. We assume that this group of sensors is activated only in the situations, when decision-making based on the information obtained by all other sensors is impossible. Such activity of the sensors follows the approach, which is used in different search tasks, where the mobility of the agents is governed by Lévy flights (Benichou, *et al.*, 2005; Benichou, *et al.*, 2011; Condamin, *et al.*, 2007) or by a maximum probability search with diffusion of information (Chernikhovsky, *et al.*, 2012; Israel, *et al.*, 2012; Kagan, *et al.*, 2010, 2012).

Regarding the locomotion devices, we assume that the mobile robot has the same configuration as a basic Braitenberg vehicle shown in Figure 2, it is equipped with two motored wheels governed by a controller according to the sensed signals. The configuration of the considered robot is shown in Figure 4.

The values obtained by different sensors at each side of the agent are fused, and then the controller of the considered mobile robot acts similarly to the controller of a basic Braitenberg vehicle; if at a certain moment only one pair of the sensors receives the signals, then the robot will move similarly to the vehicle shown in Figure 3. However, if all sensors are active and receive

Figure 4. Considered Braitenberg vehicle with two wheels, two motors and four pairs of sensors. Two long distance sensors perceive information regarding remote environmental states. One pair of short distance sensors obtains information regarding the close environment and the other pair deals with the signatures left by the agents. The pair of sensors of neighborhood checks the relative quantity of the neighboring agents.

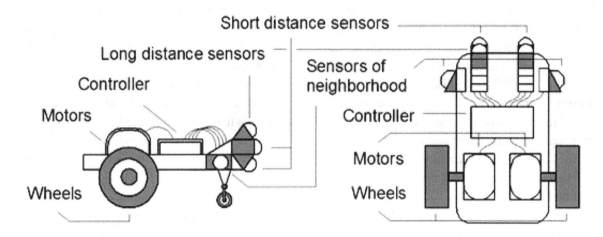

the appropriate information, then according to the corresponding control the mobile agent can demonstrate behavior that is more complicated and can mimic the behavior of living organisms executing various tasks.

In the chapter, we present methods for probabilistic control of mobile agents acting in societies. The developed methods are motivated by search tasks and are aimed to mimic the foraging activity of ants. Our method follows optimization techniques based on the Tsetlin automata (Tsetlin, 1963, 1973). Following the general approach of analog computation (Siegelmann, 1998) and corresponding logical elements (Rybalov, *et al.*, 2012), we start with constructing the multivalued Tsetlin automaton with probabilistic generator functions. Then we define a method for sensor inputs fusion and consider the motion of a single agent acting in a random environment in comparison with the motion of harvester ants. Finally, on the basis of collective behavior of living organisms (Couzin,

et al.,2005; Gordon, 2010; Sumpter, 2010), we define the model of communication between the agents and consider their swarm dynamics.

CONTROL OF MOBILE AGENTS AND THE LOCOMOTION MODEL

In the section, we consider general methods of control based on the Tsetlin automaton and present novel results on a multivalued Tsetlin automaton based on probabilistic generator functions. Using these automata we build the controller of the basic Braitenberg vehicle and the corresponding locomotion model.

Multivalued Tsetlin Automata

Let us start with a Tsetlin automaton that is a minimal automaton, which demonstrates expedient behavior in a random environment and is commonly used for modeling the simplest behavior of biological systems (Tsetlin, 1973). It is assumed that the states of the environment are random variables with the values drawn from the unit interval [0,1]. In the case of mobile agent's activity, the states are associated with the points of the arena or terrain, in which the agents act.

As an input, at each time moment, the automaton is capable to receive a finite number of signals from the environment (environmental states) and to produce a finite number of outputs depending on the internal states. The states of the environment, in their turn, are specified as responses the automaton outputs; so the expedient behavior in the given environment "consists of increasing the number of favorable responses and diminishing the unfavorable ones" (Tsetlin, 1973, p. 3). In the other words, the automaton should demonstrate a certain king of learning and to act with respect to its "knowledge" regarding the favorable responses.

In the simplest case, the Tsetlin automaton is a Boolean automaton, which is defined over the inputs set $X=\{0,1\}$ and the states set $S=\{0,1\}$. The input value $x=0$ is considered as a payoff and the value $x=1$ specifies a reward. The activity of the automaton is defined as follows. Assume that at time t, $t=0,1,2,\ldots$, the automaton is in the state $s(t) \in S$. Then, if at the next time $t+1$ the automaton receives the input $x(t+1)=0$, it changes the

state to the opposite state that is $s(t+1) = \bar{s}(t)$, and if it receives the input $x(t+1)=1$, then it stays in its current state that is $s(t+1)=s(t)$. The output value $y(t+1)$ of the Tsetlin automaton at time $t+1$ is defined by any appropriate Boolean function with respect to the state $s(t+1)$, and to the previous states, if it is needed. The state transitions of the Tsetlin automaton are illustrated in Figure 5.

According to the automaton's strategy, the obtained zero payoff $x(t)=0$ indicates that the automaton is in an unfavorable state that has to be changed, while the obtained reward $x(t)=1$ indicates that the state is favorable, and the automaton stays in this state. It is clear that such activity is equivalent to the negated *xor* operator that is

$$s(t+1) = \overline{xor\left(x(t+1), s(t)\right)}.$$

As it was shown by Tsetlin (Tsetlin, 1963, 1973), such an automaton is the simplest Boolean system, which demonstrates the expedient behavior. This behavior is analogous to the activity of the agent that perceives the environmental state, and it this state is "good", it continues moving in the same direction, while if the state is "bad", the agent changes its direction to opposite.

Let us consider a generalization of the Tsetlin automaton such that for every $t=0,1,2,\ldots$ its

Figure 5. Activity of the Tsetlin automaton with Boolean states and inputs. If input value is x(t)=0, the automaton changes its state to the opposite one, and if the input value is x(t)=1, then the automaton remains it its current state.

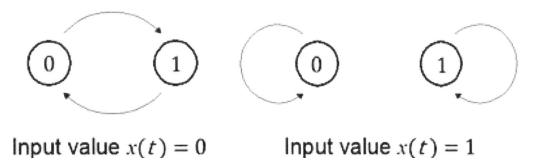

Input value $x(t) = 0$ Input value $x(t) = 1$

inputs, states and outputs are real numbers $x(t)$, $s(t)$, $y(t) \in [0,1]$ and for the Boolean values it behaves equivalently to the automaton governed by the negated *xor*. Certainly, we expect that the resulting multivalued Tsetlin automaton will demonstrate the similar expedient behavior as the Tsetlin automaton with Boolean values.

The actions of this automaton are specified by the use of two parameterized aggregator functions, the uninorm $\oplus_\theta$ and the absorbing norm $\otimes_\vartheta$, which are defined as follows.

Let $u: (0,1) \rightarrow (-\infty,\infty)$ be an invertible continuous strictly monotonously increasing function such that $\lim_{x\to 0} u(x) = -\infty$ and $\lim_{x\to 1} u(x) = +\infty$, and denote by $\theta \in [0,1]$ a parameter such that $u(\theta)=0$. Then the uninorm is the function

$$\oplus_\theta : [0,1] \times [0,1] \rightarrow [0,1]$$

such that for any two variables $x, y \in [0,1]$ its value

$$\oplus_\theta (x, y) = x \oplus_\theta y$$

is defined as (Yager & Rybalov, 1996; Fodor, et al., 1997):

1. $x \oplus_\theta y = u^{-1}\left(u(x) + u(y) \right)$ for any $\theta \in (0,1)$ and $x, y \in (0,1)$;

2. $x \oplus_1 y = x \curlywedge y$ and $x \oplus_0 y = x \curlyvee y$ for any $x, y \in (0,1)$;

3. $x \oplus_1 y = x \wedge y$ and $x \oplus_0 y = x \vee y$ for Boolean $x, y \in \{0,1\}$;

4. $0 \oplus_\theta 0 = 0$, $1 \oplus_\theta 1 = 1$ and $0 \oplus_\theta 1 = 1 \oplus_\theta 0 = \theta$ for any $\theta \in [0,1]$;

5. $x \oplus_\theta \theta = \theta \oplus_\theta x = x$ for any $\theta \in [0,1]$ and $x, y \in [0,1]$; parameter θ is called the neutral element.

In line 2, $\curlywedge$ and $\curlyvee$ stand for the *t*-norm and the *t*-conorm, respectively, that are (Dombi, 1982)

$$x \curlywedge y = f\left(f^{-1}(x) + f^{-1}(y) \right)$$

and

$$x \curlyvee y = g\left(g^{-1}(x) + g^{-1}(y) \right), x,y \in (0,1),$$

where $f: [0,\infty) \rightarrow (0,1]$ is a continuous strictly monotonously decreasing function such that

$$\lim_{\xi \to \infty} f(\xi) = 0 , f(0) = 1$$

and $\lim_{x\to 0} f^{-1}(x) = \infty$, and $g: [0,\infty) \rightarrow [0,1)$ is a continuous strictly monotonously increasing function such that $\lim_{\xi \to \infty} g(\xi) = 1$, $g(0) = 0$ and $\lim_{x\to 1} g^{-1}(x) = \infty$.

Similarly, let $v: (0,1) \rightarrow (-\infty,\infty)$ be a function with the same properties as the function u; that is, v is an invertible continuous strictly monotonously increasing and such that $\lim_{x\to 0} v(x) = -\infty$ and $\lim_{x\to 1} v(x) = +\infty$.

Denote by $\vartheta \in [0,1]$ a parameter such that $v(\vartheta)=0$. Then, the absorbing norm is a function

$$\otimes_\vartheta : [0,1] \times [0,1] \rightarrow [0,1],$$

such that for any two variables $x, y \in [0,1]$ its value $\otimes_\vartheta (x, y) = x \otimes_\vartheta y$ is defined as (Batyrshin, et. al., 2002; Fodor, et. al., 2004):

1. $x \otimes_\vartheta y = v^{-1}\left(v(x) \times v(y) \right)$ for any $\vartheta \in [0,1]$ and $x, y \in (0,1)$;

2. $x \otimes_{\vartheta} y = \overline{xor\left(x, y\right)}$ for any $\vartheta \in [0,1]$ and Boolean $x, y \in \{0,1\}$;

3. $x \otimes_{\vartheta} \vartheta = \vartheta \otimes_{\vartheta} x = \vartheta$ for any $\vartheta \in [0,1]$ and $x, y \in [0,1]$; parameter ϑ is called absorbing element.

It is clear that the absorbing norm $\otimes_{\vartheta}$ extends the negated *xor* operator to the values from the interval [0,1]. In addition, notice that the uninorm $\oplus_{\theta}$ and the absorbing norm $\otimes_{\vartheta}$ considered as logical operators can be related one to another using known logical equalities (Rybalov, *et al.*, 2012).

The functions u and v are called generator functions for the uninorm $\oplus_{\theta}$ and for the absorbing norm $\otimes_{\vartheta}$ correspondingly. These functions can be defined in various ways; for example, the most popular generator function that is used both for the uninorm and for the absorbing norm is

$$u\left(x\right) = v\left(x\right) = \ln \frac{x^{\alpha}}{1 - x^{\alpha}},$$

$x \in (0,1)$, $\alpha > 0$ (Fodor, et. al., 2004). The other generating function, which has several properties that are useful for logic design, is

$$u\left(x\right) = v\left(x\right) = \tan\left(\pi\left(x^{\alpha} - \frac{1}{2}\right)\right),$$

$x \in (0,1)$, $\alpha > 0$ (Rybalov, *et al.*, 2012); in both functions $\theta = \vartheta = \sqrt[\alpha]{1/2}$. In particular, for the last function, if $\alpha=1$ and so $\theta=\vartheta=1/2$, then

$$u\left(x\right) = v\left(x\right) = \tan\left[\pi\left(x - \frac{1}{2}\right)\right],$$

$$u^{-1}\left(\xi\right) = v^{-1}\left(\xi\right) = \frac{1}{2} + \frac{1}{\pi}\arctan\left(\xi\right),$$

$\xi \in \left(-\infty, \infty\right)$, and the corresponding uninorm and absorbing norm are defined as follows:

$$x \oplus_{\frac{1}{2}} y = \frac{1}{2} + \frac{1}{\pi}\arctan\left(\tan\left[\pi\left(x - \frac{1}{2}\right)\right] + \tan\left[\pi\left(y - \frac{1}{2}\right)\right]\right)$$

$$x \otimes_{\frac{1}{2}} y = \frac{1}{2} + \frac{1}{\pi}\arctan\left(\tan\left[\pi\left(x - \frac{1}{2}\right)\right] \times \tan\left[\pi\left(y - \frac{1}{2}\right)\right]\right).$$

The graphs of these uninorm and absorbing norm with $\theta=\vartheta=1/2$ are shown in Figure 6. Below, we apply these functions for the agents' control; certainly similar considerations can be done for other generator functions and the values of θ and ϑ, which determine the slope and curvature of the graphs.

Another way to define the generator functions u and v follows a recent observation that their reverse functions u^{-1} and v^{-1} are equal to certain probability distributions; thus the generator functions u and v are the quantile functions (Kagan, *et al.*, 2013). In particular, the example presented above of the tangent-based generator functions correspond to the Cauchy distribution

$$\mathcal{F}_{m,\alpha}\left(\xi\right) = \frac{1}{2} + \frac{1}{\pi}\arctan\left(\frac{\xi - m}{\alpha}\right)$$

with the median $m=0$ and the parameter $\alpha=1$. Following such an observation, the results $x \oplus_{\theta} y$ and $x \otimes_{\vartheta} y$ of aggregation using uninorm and absorbing norm can be generated randomly according to predefined distributions. Then the aggregation results are interpreted as follows. The

Figure 6. The graphs of the uninorm (left) and the absorbing norm (right) with equivalent tangent based generator functions and $\theta=\vartheta=1/2$

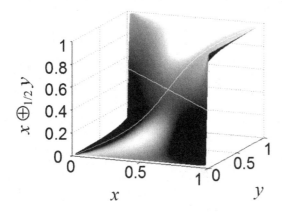 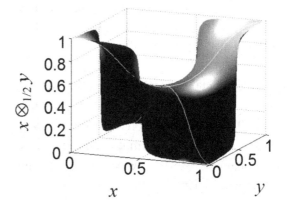

input values x and y are considered either as deterministic values or as probabilities of obtaining favorable responses from the environment. By the generator function u (correspondingly – by the function v), these inputs are mapped to the random variables $\xi_x = u(x)$ and $\xi_y = u(y)$ (correspondingly – to $\zeta_x = v(x)$ and $\zeta_y = v(y)$), which finally are mapped to the output values

$$x \oplus_\theta y = u^{-1}\left(\xi_x + \xi_y\right)$$

(correspondingly – to

$$x \otimes_\vartheta y = v^{-1}\left(\zeta_x \times \zeta_y\right))$$

that are the probabilities that the sum of the variables ξ_x and ξ_y (correspondingly – the product of the variables ζ_x and ζ_y) obtains the value given by the deterministic generator functions. Such an interpretation provides the variability of the aggregation results and allows considering both unavoidable errors in the robots' control and unknown internal processes in living organisms. The outputs of the aggregators can be generated

in two ways. The first one is based on a direct consideration of the random variables ξ_x and ξ_y (and the variables ζ_x and ζ_y), and the second assumes that the generating functions u and v are deterministic and equivalent to certain probability distribution functions, but the neutral element θ and absorbing element ϑ are random variables, obtaining their values in some small interval according to uniform distribution. Below we will follow that second approach.

Now, we are ready to define Tsetlin automata acting over real valued inputs, states and outputs $x(t)$, $s(t)$, $y(t) \in [0,1]$ $t=0,1,2,\ldots$ Since a Tsetlin automaton is defined by the negated *xor* operator, and the absorbing norm $\otimes_\vartheta$ extends this operator to the real values from the interval $[0,1]$, we define the transition function of the multivalued Tsetlin automaton as:

$$s(t+1) = x(t+1) \otimes_\vartheta s(t).$$

According to the definition of the absorbing norm, for Boolean inputs and states this function acts equivalently to the transition function of the original Tsetlin automaton.

As indicated above, the outputs of the Tsetlin automaton can be defined by any appropriate function, which maps the state of the automaton into the output value $y(t+1)$. In the considered automaton, we use the same as in the states' transitions absorbing norm and apply it for aggregation of the current and previous states $s(t+1)$ and $s(t)$ that is:

$$y\left(t+1\right) = s\left(t+1\right) \otimes_{\vartheta} s\left(t\right).$$

For the Boolean inputs, states and outputs, the outputs are equal to the inputs for any state of the automaton, while for the inputs, states and outputs from the interval [0,1] the outputs depend on the internal states. The actions of these two functions for Boolean inputs, states and outputs are shown in the Table 1.

The obtained multivalued Tsetlin automaton governed by the absorbing norm $\otimes_{\vartheta}$ is called $\otimes_{\vartheta}$-automaton. As the original Tsetlin automaton acting with Boolean inputs, states and outputs, the $\otimes_{\vartheta}$-automaton demonstrates a similarly expedient behavior: as greater real valued input of the automaton, as it stronger tends to preserve its state and corresponding output and can be used for definition of a mobile agent which is expected to demonstrate smart-like activity.

Table 1. A characteristic table of the automaton with Boolean inputs, states and outputs, where for any state the output values are equal to the input values

$x(t+1)$	$s(t)$	$s(t+1)$	$y(t+1)$
0	0	1	0
0	1	0	0
1	0	0	1
1	1	1	1

Construction of the Vehicle Controller and Locomotion

The described above multivalued Tsetlin automaton ($\otimes_{\vartheta}$-automaton) defines a controller of the vehicle with one sensor and one motor that changes its velocity with respect to the perceived value. Then, combining two such vehicles and specifying the connections between the sensors and the motors by left-to-right/right-to-left (see Figures 2 and 3), we obtain a simple Braitenberg vehicle that due to the properties of a Tsetlin automaton, is a minimal vehicle, which demonstrates expedient behavior in random environment.

The vehicle includes four $\otimes_{\vartheta}$-automatons, which control the rotations of the wheels according to the sensed signals. The equations, which specify the states' transitions and outputs are the following:

State transitions:

$$s_{left}\left(t+1\right) = x_{left}\left(t+1\right) \otimes_{\vartheta} s_{left}\left(t\right)$$

and

$$s_{right}\left(t+1\right) = x_{right}\left(t+1\right) \otimes_{\vartheta} s_{right}\left(t\right),$$

Outputs:

$$y_{left}\left(t+1\right) = s_{right}\left(t+1\right) \otimes_{\vartheta} s_{right}\left(t\right)$$

and

$$y_{right}\left(t+1\right) = s_{left}\left(t+1\right) \otimes_{\vartheta} s_{left}\left(t\right),$$

where $x_{left}(t+1)$ and $x_{right}(t+1)$ stand for the input values obtained by the left and right side sensors at the time $t+1$, $t=0,1,2,\ldots$, respectively; similarly, $y_{left}(t+1)$ and $y_{right}(t+1)$ denote the output values of the left and right side automatons and $s_{left}(t+1)$ and $s_{right}(t+1)$ denote their internal states. The vehicle is shown in Figure 7.

Basing on the defined controller, the locomotion model of the mobile robot follows the structure of a basic Braitenberg vehicle as shown in Figure 3. We assume that the output signals $y_{left}(t+1)$ and $y_{right}(t+1)$ are passed to the motors in such a manner that the speed of the wheels' rotation is proportional to the signals' values. As a result, as it is expected from a smart agent demonstrating expedient behavior, the robot turns to a favorable environmental state as quickly as is the intensity of the corresponding output of the controller.

Sensor Fusion

Finally, let us specify the fusion of the values obtained from the different sensors. Recall that the considered mobile agent is equipped with four kinds of sensors (see Figure 4). We assume that the values obtained from these sensors on each side of the robot are combined and then the resulting values are passed to the controller as inputs $x_{left}(t+1)$ and $x_{right}(t+1)$ at corresponding times $t=0,1,2,,\ldots$

The obtained values are aggregated by the use of the uninorm $\oplus_\theta$ with the appropriate neutral element. In the most cases, we specify $\theta=1/2$ which corresponds to equal influence of the sensors. Formally, let $z_{left(i)}(t)$ and $z_{right(i)}(t)$, $i=1,\ldots,4$, be the value obtained at the time t by the i-th sensor at the left and the right side of the robot, correspondingly. Following Figure 4 we specify that $i=1$ stands for long-distance sensors, $i=2$ stands for short-distance sensors that perceive the states of the environment, $i=3$ stands for the sensors dealing with the signs left by the agents, and $i=4$ stands for the sensors of the neighborhood. Then, the inputs $x_{left}(t+1)$ and $x_{right}(t+1)$ of the controller are given by the uninorm aggregation of the values $z_{left(i)}(t)$ and $z_{right(i)}(t)$ that are:

Figure 7. Two vehicles with one sensor and one motor controlled by the absorbing norm (left) and the resulting Braitenberg vehicle with left-to-right/right-to-left connections between the sensors and the motors (right). Because of the properties of a Tsetlin automaton, the obtained Braitenberg vehicle is a minimal vehicle, which demonstrates expedient behavior in a random environment.

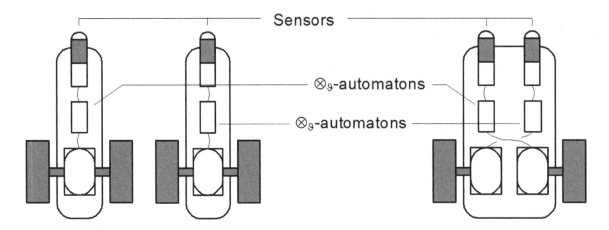

$$x_{left}\left(t+1\right) = z_{left(1)}\left(t+1\right) \oplus_\theta z_{left(2)}\left(t+1\right)$$
$$\oplus_\theta z_{left(3)}\left(t+1\right) \oplus_\theta z_{left(4)}\left(t+1\right)$$

$$x_{right}\left(t+1\right) = z_{right(1)}\left(t+1\right) \oplus_\theta z_{right(2)}\left(t+1\right)$$
$$\oplus_\theta z_{right(3)}\left(t+1\right) \oplus_\theta z_{right(4)}\left(t+1\right)$$

where, as it follows from the definition of the uninorm, the values $z_{left(i)}(t)=\theta$ and $z_{right(i)}(t)=\theta$ mean that the corresponding sensor receives zero value.

Notice that the aggregation using the uninorm is not necessary and any other method, which maps the values of the sensors to the interval [0,1], can be applied. However, being considered as operations over the interval [0,1], the uninorm and the absorbing norm form a definite algebraic system, where $\oplus_\theta$ is a sum and $\otimes_\theta$ is a product (Fodor, *et al.*, 2004; Kagan, *et al.*, 2013), and for both operators there exist complementary operators. Below, we will use the complementary to the uninorm $\oplus_\theta$ that for any $\theta \in (0,1)$ and $x,y \in (0,1)$ is

$$x \ominus_\theta y = u^{-1}\left(u\left(x\right) - u\left(y\right)\right).$$

Such an observation forms a basis for the choice of the uninorm as an aggregator for the sensed valued and supports the notation used for these operators. For briefness, the aggregation using a uninorm is called $\oplus_\theta$-aggregation.

MOTION OF A SINGLE MOBILE AGENT AND THE USE OF COMMON MEMORY

In this section, we implement the suggested control and locomotion models for navigation of a single mobile agent. We consider a hypothetical model of an ant and compare its movement in a random environment with the movement of real ants as they observed in the laboratory experiments.

The Ant's Model and its Kinematics

The suggested model considers the basic locomotion abilities of the ant. In contrast to the widely used approaches dealing with the movement of the ant and formalizing it as a dimensionless point, here we consider the ant as a body of a certain size with distinguished left and right sides. The movements of the ant are specified as results of the left and right side steps.

We assume that the ant has constant spatial size and that its sensors are located at the same constant width as the tips of the legs. In the model, we do not consider the movements of the sensors and assume that they have a constant position relatively to the center of the ant. The real ant and corresponding model are shown in Figure 8.

The modeled movements of the ant follow widely accepted scheme (Wittlinger, *et al.*, 2006; Wittlinger, *et al.*, 2007), where it is considered as a sequence of alternate steps of the left and the right side legs. For our goals, we adopt this model as follows. Given the width W of the ant, we define the lengths of the middle legs by $L=W/2$, which are considered as constants with respect to the considered ant. Now assume that at some time t, the controller obtained the inputs with the values $x_{left}(t)$ and $x_{right}(t)$ such that that according to the outputs $y_{left}(t)$ and $y_{right}(t)$ the left side of the ant shall move by S_{left} units and the right side shall move by S_{right} units, $S_{left} \leq L$ and $S_{right} \leq L$. Then the movement of the ant is conducted by the following steps. At first, the left and right legs are turned over the center of the ant to the angles, which correspond to the halves of the required movements that are $S_{left}/2$ and $S_{right}/2$ respectively. In degrees, these angles are

Figure 8. The Messor ebeninus ant (photo by S. Khodorov) and the model of the ant. The model has constant spatial size and constant positions of the sensors.

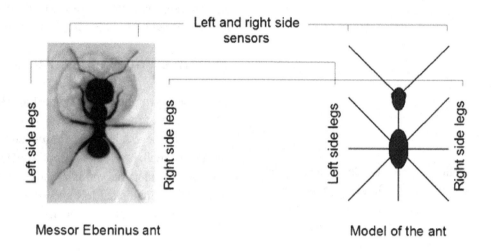

$$\varphi_{left} = S_{left} \frac{360°}{4\pi L}$$

and

$$\varphi_{right} = S_{right} \frac{360°}{4\pi L}.$$

Then, following the rhomb properties, the ant's new center is specified. Finally, the legs are turned over the new center to the angles φ_{left} and φ_{right}.

Such definition of the ant's movement provides proportional movements of the ant's sides according to the values S_{left} and S_{right}; it preserves the ant's model size and allows a simple definition of the ant's direction, which is orthogonal to the ant's legs. The scheme of the ant's movements, which corresponds to the movements of a Braitenberg vehicle, is shown in Figure 9.

The application of the suggested model of the ant instead of the direct usage of the Braitenberg vehicle is motivated by its correspondence with a real ant that allows simple comparison of its trajectories with the trajectories of real ants. Following the indicated in the Introduction a widely accepted assumption that animals and, in particu-

lar, ants demonstrate optimal behavior in a given environment and motion conditions (Pyke, 1984), such comparisons verify the suggested methods of mobile robots' control and form a basis for their further improvements.

Movements in Random Environment without Memory Usage

Numerical simulations address the movements of a mobile agent that follows the scheme of a modeled ant as shown in Figures 8 and 9, and its movements are compared with the observed movements of real ants. In the simulations, it was specified that the ant moves over a square gridded domain of 500×500 cells, and an environmental state $v(i,j) \in [0,1]$, $i,j=1,2,\ldots,500$ at each cell was specified randomly. Following the model, at each time t the ant obtains two input values

$$x_{left}(t) = v\left(i_{left}, j_{left}\right)$$

and

$$x_{right}(t) = v\left(i_{right}, j_{right}\right)$$

Figure 9. The scheme of the ant's movement. The ant turns the left side legs by the angle φ_{left}, then it turns the right side legs by the angle φ_{right}, then again the left side legs by the angle φ_{left} and finally the right side legs by the angle φ_{right}. The resulting position corresponds to the position of the Braitenberg vehicle while it uses left and right side motors and wheels.

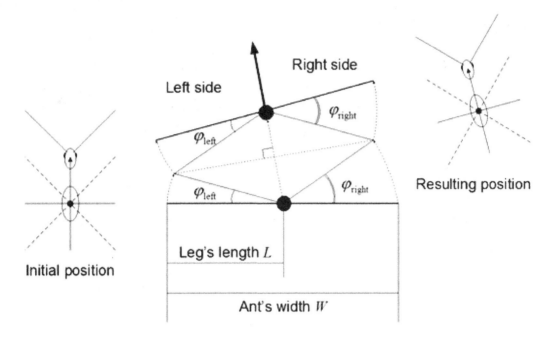

from the domain, where the coordinates (i_{left}, j_{left}) and (i_{right}, j_{right}) are defined according to the ant's location and correspond to the positions of the ant's sensors (see Figure 8). In the $\otimes_\vartheta$-automata used in the controller, we applied the indicated above assumption that the absorbing element ϑ is a random variable. In the simulations, we specified that at each time $\vartheta = 1/2 + \varepsilon$, where ε is a random value drawn from the interval $[-0.1, 0.1]$ according to the uniform distribution. The simulated trial included 1000 time moments $t = 1, \ldots, 1000$. The initial position and the direction of the ant at $t = 0$ were chosen randomly.

Laboratory experiments were conducted with *Messor ebeninus* ants and *Linepithema humile* (Argentinian) ants. The positions of the ants moving over a platform of $200 \times 200 mm$ gridded up to 500×500 cells were recorded by a camera twice per second up to 1000 frames, and the obtained trajectories were used for further statistical comparison with the trajectories obtained in the numerical simulations.

Examples of the trajectory of a *Linepithema humile* worker ant and of the simulated trajectory of the mobile agent are shown in Figure 10.

It is seen that the recorded trajectory of the ant and the simulated trajectory of the mobile agent have the same form; thus, it is meaningful to conduct more accurate statistical comparison of the trajectories. Statistical comparisons of the trajectories were processes as follows (the method was developed in collaboration with A. Novoselsky).

At first, each trajectory τ_i, where i is a number of the trajectory, is smoothed with respect to a scaling factor, which is defined using the steps' length and curvature statistics. In our simulations, we used locally weighted regression smoothing (Cleveland, 1979) with the span of 5% and 10% of the number of time moments.

Figure 10. Trajectory of the Linepithema humile worker ant observed in laboratory experiments and the simulated trajectory of the mobile agent. The ant moved over a square platform 200×200mm gridded up to 500×500 cells (left), and the simulated mobile agent moved over a gridded square domain of 500×500 cells with assigned random values from the interval [0,1] (right). In the right figure, gray color corresponds to the value 1/2, regions in white color denote the cells with the values 1 and the regions in black color denote the cells with the values 0.

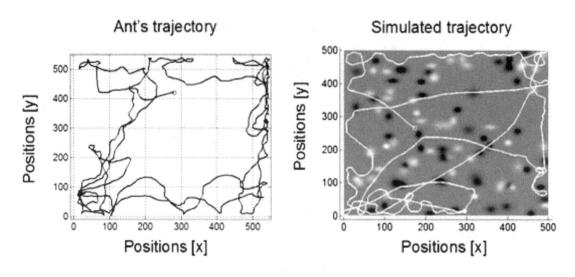

Then, for each trajectory a difference between the given trajectory τ_i and smoothed trajectory ω_i is calculated. It results in the trajectory γ_i, which represents the yawing.

Following usual techniques (Bovet & Benhamou, 1988; Calenge, *et al.*, 2009; Viswanathan, *et al.*, 1999), each smoothed trajectory ω_i and yawing γ_i represented by the sequences $\phi(\omega_i)$ and $\phi(\gamma_i)$ of the turn angles.

Finally, the hypotheses regarding statistical equivalence of the sequences $\phi(\omega_i)$ and $\phi(\omega_j)$ and of the sequences $\phi(\gamma_i)$ and $\phi(\gamma_j)$ are tested with respect to a certain significance value.

The statistical equivalence was checked as follows. The differences

$$\delta_n(\omega) = \phi_n(\omega_1) - \phi_n(\omega_2)$$

and

$$\delta_n(\gamma) = \phi_n(\gamma_1) - \phi_n(\gamma_2),$$

$n=1,2,\ldots,N$, between the angles along the smoothed and yawing trajectories are calculated. These differences $\delta_n(\omega)$ and $\delta_n(\gamma)$, $n=1,2,\ldots,N$, are mutually independent, and for equivalently distributed angles $\phi_n(\omega_1)$ and $\phi_n(\omega_2)$ the differences $\delta_n(\omega)$ are distributed normally with zero mean, and so are the differences $\delta_n(\gamma)$ for equivalently distributed angles $\phi_n(\gamma_1)$ and $\phi_n(\gamma_2)$. Thus, if the *t*-test allows to conclude that $\delta_n(\omega)$ (correspondingly $\delta_n(\gamma)$) are distributed normally with zero mean (and unknown deviation), then we say that the smoothed trajectories ω_1 and ω_2 (correspondingly yawing trajectories γ_1 and γ_2) are statistically equivalent; otherwise, we conclude that the smoothed trajectories ω_1 and ω_2 (correspondingly yawing trajectories γ_1 and γ_2) are statistically different.

The method of comparison of the trajectories is illustrated by Figure 11, which illustrates the trajectory of the *Linepithema humile* worker ant the simulated trajectory of the modeled ant. In the figure, dotted lines correspond to the modeled ant and solid lines correspond to the real ant.

The figure demonstrates the results of the states of the statistical comparisons. Figure 11.a illustrates two original trajectories τ_1 and τ_2 and the histograms step lengths for these two trajectories. Figure 11.b shows the trajectories ω_1 and ω_2, which were obtained by smoothing the original trajectories τ_1 and τ_2, respectively, and the histograms of their turn angles $\phi(\omega_1)$ and $\phi(\omega_2)$. Finally, in the Figure 11.c the yawing trajectories γ_1 and γ_2 and the histograms of their turn angles $\phi(\gamma_1)$ and $\phi(\gamma_2)$ are shown. As indicated above, the *t*-test is applied to the sequences

$$\delta_n\left(\omega\right) = \phi_n\left(\omega_1\right) - \phi_n\left(\omega_2\right)$$

and

$$\delta_n\left(\gamma\right) = \phi_n\left(\gamma_1\right) - \phi_n\left(\gamma_2\right), \; n=1,2,\dots,N.$$

The analysis of the trajectories shown in Figure 11 demonstrates that the trajectories of the modeled and real ant are different (significance value of the *t*-test is $\alpha=0.05$ and the span percent is 5%). The same results were obtained using additional trajectories of the *Linepithema humile* ants (both soldier (20 trajectories) and worker (20 trajectories)), which were compared with different simulated trajectories of the modeled ant.

Notice that in our model, we consider the distributions of the angles and step's lengths at each time $t=0,1,2,\dots$ However, in the other models, which address the other characteristics of the trajectories, the resulting distributions can differ from the obtained ones. In particular, Nouvellet, *et al.* (2009) considered the displacements of the ants and demonstrated that the resulting distributions are normal in coincidence with the behavior of Pharaoh ants (*Monomorium pharaonis*).

From the simulation results and comparisons it follows that both the distributions of the angles in the trajectories of both the considered *Linepithema humile* worker ant and the modeled ant are not normal and that the modeled movement according to short distance sensors differs from the movement of a real ant. In addition, especially in the analysis of *Linepithema humile* soldier ants, it was observed that even a single ant uses an environment as a kind of memory and the trajectories of the ants obtained in sequential simulations are rather different. In particular, the ants acting on a clean platform move both in the central parts of the platform and at its borders however, after several trials, the ants move directly to the borders and move along them without returning to the central parts of the platform. In the next section, we consider the simulations of such behavior.

Movements in Random Environment Using Memory

In the following simulations, we considered the movements of the modeled ant in the environment, which allows signing the visited locations. Such behavior mimics the behavior of the ants' deployed pheromone on certain locations in the environment. Different species of ants use different strategies to deploy pheromone: some of them deploy the pheromone continuously throughout movement, while others sign only the path to food while returning to the nest. In addition, the deployed signatures can differ in their structure; in particular, some of the ants deploy the pheromone in the form of "dotted path" while foraging, and in the form of a "solid path" while returning with the found food. In the simulations, we implement a situation, in which the agent always deploys "pheromone" signatures at visited locations.

Figure 11. (a) Simulated trajectory τ_1 (dotted line) and recorded trajectory of the ant τ_2 (solid line) and distributions of the steps' lengths along the trajectories. (b) Trajectories obtained by smoothing of the trajectories τ_1 and τ_2: ω_1 (dotted line) corresponds to the simulated trajectory τ_1 and ω_2 (solid line) correspond to the ant's trajectory τ_2. The histograms on the right present the distributions of the angles along the smoothed trajectories ω_1 and ω_2. (c) Trajectories that correspond to the yawing along the trajectories: γ_1 (dotted line) corresponds to the simulated trajectory τ_1 and γ_2 (solid line) correspond to the ant's trajectory τ_2. The histograms on the right present the distributions of the yawing angles.

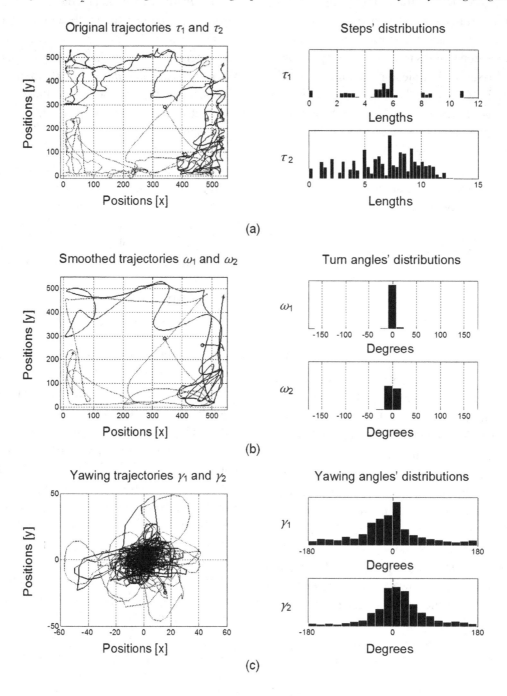

In the first series of simulations, the agent (modeled ant) moved over a domain and deployed the pheromone by itself. An example of the agent's trajectory and corresponding pheromone trace are shown in Figure 12.

Analysis of the obtained trajectories demonstrates that if the agent during its movement deploys "pheromone" and then uses it in the decision-making process regarding its next steps, then the distributions of the angles along the trajectory are not normal, while the distributions of the step's length are normal with mean close to 4 units. In both cases, the hypotheses were tested using the Jarque-Bera test with the significance value $\alpha=0.05$. These results coincide with the above-indicated findings by Nouvellet, *et al.* (2009). Additional comparisons using the method described above (significance value is $\alpha=0.05$) demonstrated an equivalence between the smoothed trajectories of the modeled ants and the trajectories of the *Linepithema humile* worker ants and the difference in their yawing. In other words, the constructed agent differs from the real ant "in small", but following the environment states and pheromone traces it conducts the same mission as a real ant.

In the second series of simulations, the agent moved in the environment with the pheromone deployed both by itself and by the other agents. In these simulations, the first agent moved over the environment without pheromone and deployed it along its trajectory. Then the second agent moved over the environment with the pheromone deployed by the first agent. Then the third acted using the pheromone traces deployed by two previous agents and so on up to the tenth agent. The last eleventh agent moved over the environment with the pheromone traces deployed by ten previous agents.

According to the procedure suggested above, the values obtained from the environment and from the pheromone states were aggregated using the uninorm $\oplus_\theta$ with neutral the element $\theta=1/2$; thus

$$x_{left}\left(t+1\right) = z_{left(2)}\left(t+1\right) \oplus_\theta z_{left(3)}\left(t+1\right),$$

$$x_{right}\left(t+1\right) = z_{right(2)}\left(t+1\right) \oplus_\theta z_{right(3)}\left(t+1\right),$$

Figure 12. Simulated trajectory of the agent (modeled ant) and the remained "pheromone" trace

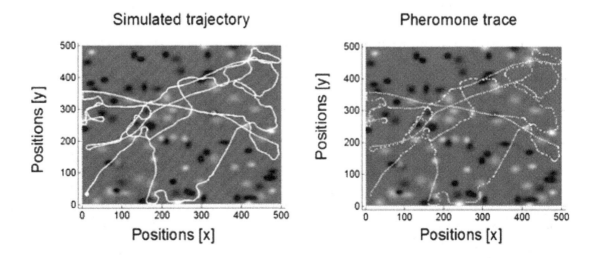

where, as above, $z_{left(2)}(t+1)$ and $z_{right(2)}(t+1)$ stand for the values obtained from the environment by the left and right side sensors, and $z_{left(3)}(t+1)$ and $z_{right(3)}(t+1)$ indicate the pheromone values perceived by the corresponding sensors at the left and right sides of the agent. An example of the trajectories and pheromone traces are shown in Figure 13.

It is seen that the first agent moves over the environment and often crosses the unfavorable regions (indicated by black), while the last agent, which uses the "experience" of the previous ten agents that is represented by the deployed pheromone traces, avoids such regions and mostly follows along the favorable states of the environment (indicated by white). Consequently, for the presented trajectories of the movement over 1000 time units, the total reward that is the sum of the differences between the values in the visited favorable and unfavorable cells for the first agent is 378.37, while for the last agent it is 439.28. If the number of previously moved agents is sufficiently large, the last agent follows the deployed pheromone and visits mostly the favorable regions ignoring the unfavorable ones. Such behavior provides an

optimization of the agent's movement and coincides with the well-known ant-colony optimization techniques (Dorigo & Stutzle, 2004).

Hereby, we obtained a mobile agent, which demonstrates the following:

1. The agent is controlled by the $\otimes_{\vartheta}$-automatons and, consequently, demonstrates expedient individual behavior in a random environment.
2. If the agent is allowed to deploy pheromone traces, and the sensed signals are combined by $\oplus_{\theta}$-aggregation, then the resulting agent's trajectory is statistically equivalent to the observed trajectory of ants, which is assumed to be optimal from a biological point of view.
3. If there are several agents acting in the environment and deploying pheromone, then they tend to visit favorable regions and to ignore unfavorable regions, following the principles of ant colony optimization.

Notice that in the considered models the agents were not allowed to communicate directly with one another. The pheromone traces were perceived

Figure 13. Simulated trajectory of the first agent (left), the "pheromone" traces deployed by ten previously recorded agents and by the considered last agent (center) and the simulated trajectory of the last agent. As in the previous figures, black regions indicate the unfavorable environmental states and white regions indicate favorable environmental states. The pheromone traces are considered as favorable states of the environment and the pheromone values are aggregated with the environmental states using the uninorm $\oplus_{\theta}$ with $\theta=1/2$.

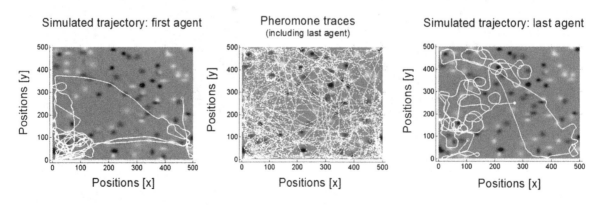

similarly to environmental states, and each agent that moved in the environment independently obtained information from the environment without considering the origin from which this information arrives. Additional improvements of the model are provided by swarm optimization; in the next section, we apply basic principles of swarming and consider their implementations using the suggested mobile agents and their controls.

SWARM DYNAMICS WITH COMMUNICATION AND COMMON MEMORY

In the final section, we implement the suggested above model for consideration of the dynamics of swarm. We assume that the agents communicate using the common memory by signing the visited locations and by sensing the number of the agents acting in a close neighborhood.

Model of the Ants' Communication

In the previous section, we considered the activity of the agent in the environment with the "pheromone" signs remained by the agent itself and by the other agents, which model the communication between the agents by direct use of the common memory (Payton, *et al.*, 2001). In the search problems, such communication represents the changes of the target location probabilities as they resulted by the observations of the search agents (Kagan, *et al.*, 2010). Recently such communication inspired by the ants' behavior was implemented for navigation of mobile robots and allowed emulating and understanding several aspects of self-organization in groups (Garnier, *et al.* 2013). The other type of communication is based on the knowledge about the behavior of the neighboring agents (Couzin, *et al.*, 2005; Gordon,

2010; Steshenko, *et al.*, 2011; Weiss, 1999). Below we address such communication based on a direct observation of the neighboring agents.

As indicated above, we assume that each agent is equipped with a pair of sensors, which perceive relative quantity of the neighboring agents (see Figure 4). The values $z_{left(4)}(t+1)$ and $z_{right(4)}(t+1)$ perceived by the neighborhood sensors depend on two parameters: on the number of neighboring agents and on the distance between the agent and its neighbors. For simplicity, we assume that both are governed by the power function and the results are aggregated by the operator $\ominus_\theta$, which complements the uninorm $\oplus_\theta$, as follows

$$z_{left(4)}\left(t\right) = \left(1 - \theta^{\left(1+n_{left}(t)\right)}\right) \ominus_\theta \left(1 - \theta^{\left(1+d_{left}(t)\right)}\right),$$

$$z_{right(4)}\left(t\right) = \left(1 - \theta^{\left(1+n_{right}(t)\right)}\right) \ominus_\theta \left(1 - \theta^{\left(1+d_{right}(t)\right)}\right),$$

where $n_{left}(t)$ and $n_{right}(t)$ are numbers of neighboring agents at time t at the left and right sides of the agent, and $d_{left}(t)$ and $d_{right}(t)$, $0 \leq d_{left}(t)$, $d_{right}(t) \leq 1$ are normalized average distances between the agent and its neighbors at the left and at the right sides at this time. Such relation represents an assumption that as greater the number of neighbors as stronger they attract the agent, while as far the neighbors are located as less the attraction. In addition, to avoid collisions between the agents, the average distances $d_{left}(t)$ and $d_{right}(t)$ can be shifted so that $z_{left(4)}(t+1)$ and $z_{right(4)}(t+1)$ obtain the values equal to the neutral element θ, while the average distances become less than a certain threshold.

The presented definition of the communication between the agents is, in essence, equivalent to the definition based on the knowledge of the agents' positions, directions and speeds (Couzin, *et al.*, 2005); however, because of distinguishing left and right sides of the agent, our definition is simpler and does not require explicit definition of the direction vector.

Movement of Agents in a Swarm

In the following simulations we considered three types of communications: in the first scenario, the agents communicate using the pheromone traces; in the second, in addition to these traces, the agents consider the number of neighboring agents; and in the third scenario, the agents also use information about the environment's states, which is obtained by long-distance sensors.

In the simulations of the agents' movements following pheromone traces, we considered two cases: in the first one, the agents started in different random points of the environment with different starting directions, and in the second they started at the same point – the center of the domain – and the same starting direction. An example of the final traces of ten agents is shown in Figure 14. Notice that, in contrast to Figure 13, where each agent started only when the previous agent finished its movement, that is at each time there was only one agent in the domain, in the current case, all ten agents moved over a domain simultaneously and the pheromone deployed by one agent was immediately sensed by all other agents.

It is seen that the agents follow the pheromone traces, which at most avoid the unfavorable regions of the environment. Certainly, if the agents start in the same point, then their trajectories are less dispersed over the domain, while if the agents' initial points are arbitrary, they follow the environmental states up to meeting the pheromone trace, and then continue their movement using this trace in addition to the environmental states.

In the simulations of the agents' movement following the environmental states and neighboring agents activity, we considered the dependence of the resulting trajectories on the sensitivity of the neighborhood sensors, which is represented by the neighborhood radius. In general, natural agents like ants are able to sense the other agents at a distance that is comparable with the size of the agent. However, for artificial agents such as mobile robots, the neighborhood radius depends on the type of communication, and can be significantly larger than the agent's size. In the simulation, we implemented a neighborhood of different radii; examples of the resulting traces for a neighborhood with a radius of 15 units, equaling the width of

Figure 14. Final traces of ten agents that start in different random points and different random initial directions (left) and of ten agents that start in the center of the domain with the same top-up initial direction (right). The agents perceive the environmental states and pheromone traces remained by the other agents.

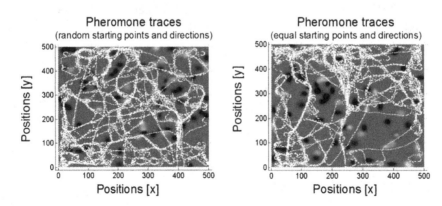

the agent, and for a neighborhood with a radius of 150 units are shown in Figure 15. In both cases, the neighborhood was specified by a semi-circle around the "head" of the agent (see Figure 8), and the numbers of the neighboring agents on the left and right sides were processed independently and then aggregated according to the techniques presented above.

It is seen that if the radius of the considered neighborhood is relatively small, the agents at most follow the environmental states with certain concentrations in the arbitrary regions, where the number of agents becomes large. During the movement in such regions, the influence of the environmental states leads the agents to leave the regions of their concentration and to move to the other regions. If, in contrast, the neighborhood radius is large, the agents eventually change the direction of their movements and at most concentrate in the small regions (in our case – near the bounds of the domain) or follow the same or close trajectories. In addition, notice that because of the strong influence of the neighbors, especially for the large neighborhood radius, the agents less follow the environmental states, and often pass through the unfavorable regions of the environment.

In the next simulation, we combined both previously mentioned types of communication. In addition to the perception of the environmental states, the agents were allowed to perceive pheromone traces and the number of neighbors on the left and right sides. The examples of the resulting traces for ten agents starting in random points with random initial direction and for ten agents starting in the center of the domain with top-up initial direction are shown in Figure 16.

As it was expected, the resulting traces combine the properties of the traces obtained in two previous cases and are similar to the traces obtained in the case of sequential movements of the agents shown in Figure 13. The agents avoid the unfavorable regions and follow the pheromone traces deployed in the environment. In addition, notice that the starting points and the initial directions of the agents do not essentially influence the resulting trajectories.

In the last series of simulations, we considered the movements of the agents, which in addition to the indicated short-distance, pheromone and neighborhood sensors, are equipped with the long-distance sensors (see Figure 4). These sensors are used in cases of uncertainly, when, according

Figure 15. Final traces of ten agents that perceive the environmental states and the number of neighboring agents: on the left, the neighborhood radius is 15 units that is equal to the width of the agent, and on the right the neighborhood radius is 150 units

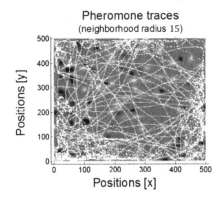
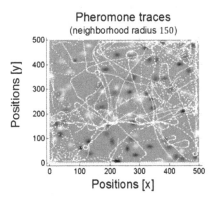

Figure 16. *Final traces of ten agents that perceive the environmental states, the pheromone traces and the number of neighboring agents: on the left, the agents start in different random points and different random initial directions and on the right, the agents start in the center of the domain with the same top-up initial direction. In both cases, the neighborhood radius is 15 that is equal to the width of the agent.*

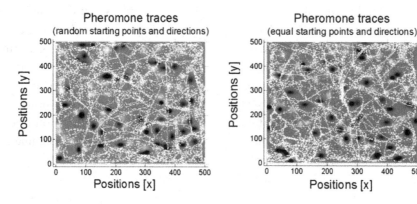

to the signals perceived by the other sensors, the agent terminates its movement. Such behavior is observed in ants, which stop their motion in a completely homogeneous environment. The sensors act as follows.

Assume that the agent is in such a position that its short-distance, pheromone and neighborhood sensors perceive either zero signals or signals, which avoid each other. Then, following the locomotion scheme presented above, the agents terminate the movement and will stay in their location until some change occurs in the environment or in the positions of the other agents. In a static environment, this phenomenon can lead to a situation, in which all the agents stay in their location infinitely long that is, certainly, undesirable. In this situation, the long-distance sensors are activated and perceive certain signals $z_{left(1)}(t)$ and $z_{right(1)}(t)$ from the states of the environment, which are distant from the agent's location. The values $z_{left(1)}(t)$ and $z_{right(1)}(t)$ are defined as follows:

$$z_{left(1)}\left(t\right) = \oplus_{\theta\,j=1}^{N_{left}}\left[v_{left(j)}\left(t\right)\ominus_{\theta}\left(1-\theta^{\left(1+d_{left(j)}(t)\right)}\right)\right],$$

$$z_{right(1)}\left(t\right) = \oplus_{\theta\,j=1}^{N_{right}}\left[v_{right(j)}\left(t\right)\ominus_{\theta}\left(1-\theta^{\left(1+d_{right(j)}(t)\right)}\right)\right],$$

where $v_{left(j)}(t)$ and $v_{right(j)}(t)$ are the environmental states on the left and right sides of the agent at time t such that $0\leq v_{left(j)}(t), v_{right(j)}(t)\leq 1$; $d_{left(j)}(t)$ and $d_{right(j)}(t)$ are the relative distances to the corresponding states from the agent's location, $0\leq d_{left(j)}(t), d_{right(j)}(t)\leq 1$; and N_{left} and N_{right} are the number of the environmental states on the left and right sides of the agent up to which the uninorm $\oplus_{\theta}$ is applied.

To illustrate the activity of the long-distance sensors, let us consider the movements of the agents in the domain, which include one favorable and one unfavorable region and where all other points are neutral. In addition, for illustration purposes, assume that the long-distance sensors are always active. Examples of complete traces of ten agents are shown in Figure 17.

In the simulations, the agents started in random points and had random initial directions. In Figure 17, it is seen that the use of long-distance sensors

Figure 17. Final traces of ten agents moving in the domain with one favorable and one unfavorable regions and using different sensors. (a) Traces of the agents following only the short-distance sensors of the environmental states (left) and traces of the agents following long-distance sensors with observation radius r=150 (right). (b) Traces of the agents, which use both short-distance and long-distance sensors of the environmental states with the perception radius r=15 (left) and r=150 (center and right). The figure in the center illustrates the avoidance of the unfavorable region and the figure in the right illustrates the concentration of the agents in the favorable region. (c) Trace of the agents, which use short- and long-distance sensors of the environmental states and pheromone sensors (left), and the traces of the agent, which, in addition, use the sensors of neighborhood (right).

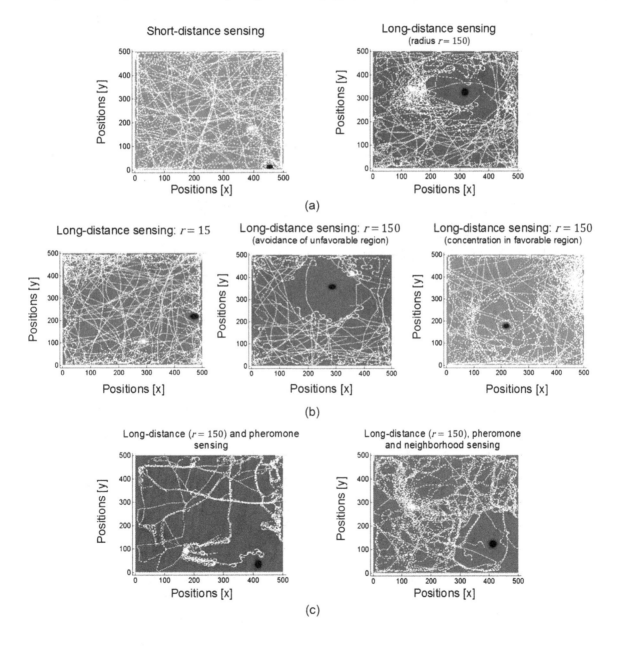

with a small radius of perception does not influence the agents' behavior, while long-distance sensors with a large enough radius of perception allow better avoidance of the unfavorable regions as well as better attraction to the favorable states. Additional application of the pheromone sensors leads to movement along very close trajectories and the application of neighborhood sensors governs the agents to periodical movements between pheromone traces.

Finally, let us consider the influence of the long-distance sensors on the activity of agents moving in a domain with several favorable and unfavorable regions. As in all previous simulations, the domain is of the size 500×500 cells with 100 randomly located favorable and unfavorable regions. Examples of complete traces of ten agents are shown in Figure 18.

The simulation's results demonstrate that if the perception radius of the long-distance sensors

Figure 18. Final traces of ten agents moving in a domain with 100 randomly distributed favorable (white) and unfavorable (black) regions. The agents apply the same short-distance, pheromone and neighborhood sensors and long-distance sensors with different perception radii.

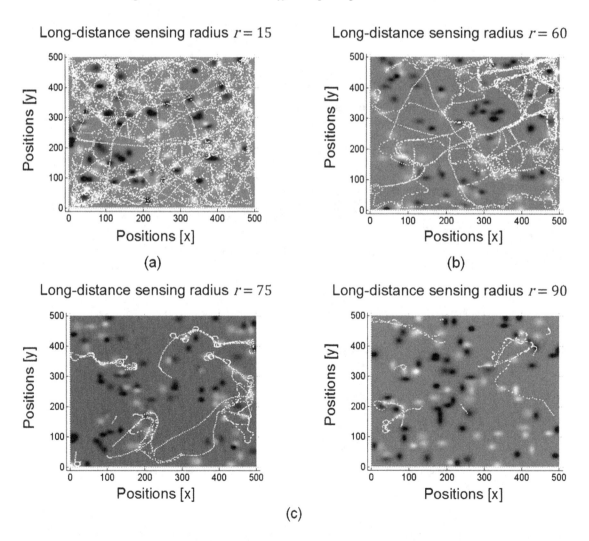

is small (in the shown case it is $r=15$) then they do not influence on the agent's motion and the resulting trajectories of the agents are the same as the trajectories obtained without the long-distance sensors (cf. the trajectories in Figure 18 (a) and the trajectories shown in Figure 16). An increase of the perception radius up to a certain value leads to movements which follow the favorable and avoid the unfavorable regions, and that the passes through the neutral regions (shown in gray) are significantly shorter than similar passes without using the long-distance sensors. In Figure 18 (b), trajectories for long-distance sensors with $r=60$ (cf. Figure 16) are shown. However, additional increase of the perception radius results in shorter trajectories of the agents (see Figure 18 (c)) as it follows the intuition that the redundant information increases the uncertainty and makes the decision-making harder. Notice again that here we assumed that the long-distance sensors are always active, while in certain tasks they are activated only in those cases where the agents cannot make a decision using the other sensors.

DISCUSSION AND FURTHER RESEARCH DIRECTIONS

In the implemented approach, we follow several assumptions regarding the behavior of the mobile agents. A general philosophy, which underlies the model of the agents' interaction with the environment, is the philosophy of embodied intelligence. Certainly, this is not an only kind of general view to the activity of intellectual robots; another point of view is provided by analytical philosophy, which also requires "designing and building a robot that will be a 'rational animal'" (Searle, 2001, p. 142). To obtain an optimal behavior by the agents, they were developed in such a way that they mimic the behavior of ants, which are assumed to be evolutionary optimal foragers in their habitat.

However, since the evolutionary processes are, certainly, ongoing processes, specification of a certain natural behavior as optimal, even in the current state of Nature, is rather discussable.

The suggested method of navigation and control of mobile agents was simulated numerically and the obtained results were compared with the results of laboratory experiments with the ants. The experiments were organized in the manner that was suggested by Hayashi *et al.* (Hayashi, *et al.*, 2008), but instead of closed circle arena we used a square opened platform. For recording the trajectories of the ants, we used a square platform of the size $200 \times 200 mm$ surrounded by water, so the ants were prohibited to leave the platform. The movements of the ants were recorded by usual digital camera in such a manner that the (x, y)-locations of the ant were stored at each frame and the total number of locations was 1000. The environmental states were simulated by slight warming the platform in random points that provided the difference between favorable and unfavorable regions. It is clear, that such experiments with the ants represent rather artificial conditions, and certainly cannot support general statements regarding the ants' behavior in Nature, but provided enough information for our goal of mimicking the ants' behavior by mobile agents acting in given conditions. However, the question of returning to the nest and corresponding odometry techniques it is still open.

Another debatable issue is an implemented communication ability of the agents. In the suggested model, the agents communicate using pheromone traces and by perceiving the number of agents in a nearby neighborhood. However, it is known that ants are able to communicate directly by their physical interactions (Razin, *et al.*, 2013). Moreover, as it was demonstrated in experiments with humans (Woolley, *et al.*, 2010), group intelligence mostly depends on the quality of communication in the group rather than on the

IQ of the group members. Hence, to obtain effective behavior even of simple agents, additional communication channels have to be specified; however, exact requirements for such communication are far from being understood. There other uncertainty is a modeling of the division of labor while conducting a certain task. Recently, such behavior of ants' colonies was considered using general models (Richardson, *et al.*, 2011), but implementation of such models in robot swarms is still unclear; a contemporary review of this topic was recently published by Campbell and Wu (2011).

Following the suggested method of control of mobile agents, the signals received by additional sensors either can be aggregated using the uninorm $\oplus_\theta$ as it was done with the implemented four kinds of sensors or can be considered as controls of the values of the neutral θ and absorbing ϑ elements used in the $\oplus_\theta$-aggregators and $\otimes_\vartheta$-automata. In the last case, the introduced sensors will specify the slope and curvature of the functions defined by the aggregators (see Figure 6) and, consequently, will adjust the obtained decisions. Additional possibilities of both decision-making and aggregation of the sensed signals are provided by application of different distributions as generating functions. Throughout the examples presented in the chapter, we used the Cauchy distribution; however any other probability distribution is applicable and by choosing the distribution, the behavior of the mobile agent can be fine-tuned with respect to the considered task.

The further research, which is planned by our group, addresses some of the indicated open issues. In particular, starting from the methods and procedures, which were designed in the framework of group-testing techniques (Ben-Gal, 2004; Ben-Gal & Caramanis, 2002; Ben-Gal, Herer & Raz, 2003; Kagan & Ben-Gal, 2013b; Kagan & Ben-Gal, 2014), and statistical process control algorithms (Ben-Gal, Morag & Smilovichi, 2003; Ben-Gal & Singer, 2004; Ge & Song, 2013; Oakland, 2003) allow optimization of the agents'

motion and consideration of sensor selection and fusion especially for erroneous detections. Such procedures should provide efficient mapping of the environment basing on the local information obtained by each agent and planning of the observations conducted by individual agents and their groups. The expected results in this direction will form a basis for development of feasible algorithms of optimal swarming and swarm dynamics.

Following the other direction, we plan to address biologically inspired methods of signaling and corresponding grouping and division of labor between the members of the group. The considered communication protocols are inspired by recently investigated models of biological signaling (Bergstrom & Lachmann, 1997, 1998; Hutteger & Zollman, 2010) that allow only occasional per-to-per communication without central unit and provide evolutionary optimal and economic information transfer between the agents. Such signaling is also used as a basis for grouping of the agents for fulfilling the complex tasks, which outtake the abilities of individual agents. The methods grouping are based on the recently developed models of collective animal behavior (Sumpter, 2010) and swarm optimization (Gazi & Passino, 2011), and dynamics of the agents' groups is specified using the models of population dynamics (Turchin, 2003), active Brownian motion (Schweitzer, 2003) and the indicated above models of swarm robotic systems (Hamann, 2010; Triani, 2008).

Evidently, the indicated issues do not exhaust the list of open questions regarding the behavior of mobile agents, which mimic living organisms and their swarms, as well as their sensing, communication and decision-making abilities. Another direction of the further research in the field can address the methods of swarm intelligent and neural networks computation (Siegelmann, 1998). On the other hand, probabilistic analysis of swarms motion (Metzler & Klafter, 2000) in parallel with the analysis of population dynamics (Sumpter, 2010; Turchin, 2003) can help in better understanding of animals behavior.

CONCLUSION

In the chapter, we suggested an approach, which provides simple and flexible techniques of control of mobile agents acting in a random environment such that the resulting behavior of the agents is as optimal as the behavior of natural foragers, like ants.

The method implements generalized Tsetlin automaton based on the probability-based aggregators – uninorm and absorbing norm – that form a complete algebraic system and can be used for constructing modular controllers of mobile agents.

The considered mobile agents are based on the Braitenberg vehicles, which act with respect to short- and long-distance states of the environment. The communication between the agents follows the scheme of pheromone robotics with additional sensing of the density of neighboring agents.

Numerical simulations demonstrate that the suggested control and communication techniques result in the mobile agents' activity, individual and in groups, such that it mimics the behavior of the ants, and so it is as optimal as is that of the ants.

ACKNOWLEDGMENT

HS is thankful to the ONR Program of Computational Neuroscience for their generous support.

REFERENCES

Batyrshin, I., Kaynak, O., & Rudas, I. (2002). Fuzzy modeling based on generalized conjunction operations. *IEEE Transactions on Fuzzy Systems*, *10*(5), 678–683. doi:10.1109/TFUZZ.2002.803500

Ben-Gal, I. (2004). An upper bound for the weight-balanced testing procedure with multiple searchers. *IIE Transactions*, *36*(5), 481–493. doi:10.1080/07408170490426206

Ben-Gal, I., & Caramanis, M. (2002). Sequential DOE via dynamic programming. *IIE Transactions*, *34*(12), 1087–1100. doi:10.1080/07408170208928937

Ben-Gal, I., Herer, Y., & Raz, T. (2002). Self-correcting inspection procedure under inspection errors. *IIE Transactions*, *34*(6), 529–540. doi:10.1080/07408170208928889

Ben-Gal, I., Morag, G., & Smilovichi, A. (2003). A monitoring procedure for state dependent processes. *Technometrics*, *45*(4), 293–311. doi:10.1198/004017003000000122

Ben-Gal, I., & Singer, G. (2004). Statistical process control via context modeling of finite states processes. *IIE Transactions*, *36*(5), 401–415. doi:10.1080/07408170490426125

Benichou, O., Coppey, M., Moreau, M., Suet, P.-H., & Voituriez, R. (2005). Optimal search strategies for hidden targets. *Physical Review Letters*, *94*, 1–4. doi:10.1103/PhysRevLett.94.198101 PMID:16090215

Benichou, O., Loverdo, C., Moreau, M., & Voituriez, R. (2011). *Intermittent search strategies*. Retrieved February 13, 2013, from arXiv.org:1104.0639

Benioff, P. (1998). Quantum robots and environments. *Physical Review A.*, *58*, 893–904. doi:10.1103/PhysRevA.58.893

Bergstrom, C. T., & Lachmann, M. (1997). Signaling among relatives: Is signaling too costly? *Philosophical Transactions of London Royal Society B*, *352*, 609–617. doi:10.1098/rstb.1997.0041

Bergstrom, C. T., & Lachmann, M. (1998a). Signaling among relatives: Beyond the tower of Babel. *Theoretical Population Biology*, *54*, 146–160. doi:10.1006/tpbi.1997.1372 PMID:9733656

Bergstrom, C. T., & Lachmann, M. (1998b). Signaling among relatives: Talk is cheap. *Proceedings of the National Academy of Sciences of the United States of America*, *95*, 5100–5105. doi:10.1073/pnas.95.9.5100 PMID:9560235

Bovet, P., & Benhamou, S. (1988). Spatial analysis of animals' movements using a correlated random walk model. *Journal of Theoretical Biology*, *131*, 419–433. doi:10.1016/S0022-5193(88)80038-9

Braitenberg, V. (1986). *Vehicles: Experiments in synthetic psychology*. Cambridge, MA: MIT Press.

Calenge, C., Dray, S., & Royer-Carenzi, M. (2009). The concept of animal's trajectories from a data analysis perspective. *Ecological Informatics*, *4*, 34–41. doi:10.1016/j.ecoinf.2008.10.002

Campbell, A., & Wu, A. S. (2011). Multi-agent role allocation: Issues, approaches, and multiple perspectives. *Autonomous Agents and Multi-Agent Systems*, *22*(2), 317–355. doi:10.1007/s10458-010-9127-4

Chandrasekaran, B., & Chen, D. W. (1969). Stochastic automata games. *IEEE Transaction on Systems Science and Cybernetics*, *5*(2), 145–149. doi:10.1109/TSSC.1969.300206

Chernikhovsky, G., Kagan, E., Goren, G., & Ben-Gal, I. (2012). Path planning for sea vessel search using wideband sonar. In *Proceedings of 27th IEEE Convention of Electrical and Electronics Engineers in Israel*. IEEE. doi:10.1109/EEEI.2012.6377122

Chung, T. H., Hollinger, G. A., & Isler, V. (2011). Search and pursuit-evasion in mobile robotics: A survey. *Autonomous Robots*, *31*(4), 299–316. doi:10.1007/s10514-011-9241-4

Clark, A. (1997). *Being there: Putting brain, body and world together again*. Cambridge, MA: MIT Press.

Cleveland, W. S. (1979). Robust locally weighted regression and smoothing scatterplots. *Journal of the American Statistical Association*, *74*, 829–836. doi:10.1080/01621459.1979.10481038

Cole, B. J., & Cheshire, D. (1996). Mobile cellular automat models of ant behavior: Movement activity of leptothorax allardycei. *American Naturalist*, *148*(1), 1–15. doi:10.1086/285908

Condamin, S., Benichou, O., Tejedor, V., Voituriez, R., & Klafter, J. (2007). First-passage times in complex scale-invariant media. *Nature*, *450*, 77–80. doi:10.1038/nature06201 PMID:17972880

Couzin, I. D., Krause, J., Franks, N. R., & Levin, S. A. (2005). Effective leadership and decision making in animal groups on move. *Nature*, *433*, 513–516. doi:10.1038/nature03236 PMID:15690039

Dombi, J. (1982). A general class of fuzzy operators, the DeMorgan class of fuzzy operators and fuzziness measures induced by fuzzy operators. *Fuzzy Sets and Systems*, *8*(2), 149–163. doi:10.1016/0165-0114(82)90005-7

Dorigo, M., & Stutzle, T. (Eds.). (2004). *Ant colony optimization*. Cambridge, MA: MIT Press/Bradford Book. doi:10.1007/b99492

Fodor, J., Rudas, I. J., & Bede, B. (2004). Uninorms and absorbing norms with applications to image processing. In *Proceedings of the 4th Serbian-Hungarian Joint Symposium on Intelligent Systems* (pp. 59-72). Academic Press.

Fodor, J., Yager, R., & Rybalov, A. (1997). Structure of uninorms. *International Journal on Uncertainty. Fuzziness and Knowledge-Based Systems*, *5*, 411–427. doi:10.1142/S0218488597000312

From Animals to Animats. (2012). *Proceedings of international conference on simulation and adaptive behavior*. Bradford books/MIT Press/Springer.

Fu, K. S. (1967). Stochastic automata as models of learning systems. In J. T. Lou (Ed.), *Computer and information sciences II* (pp. 177–191). New York: Academic Press.

Fu, K. S., & Li, T. J. (1969). Formulation of learning automata and automata games. *Information Sciences*, *1*(3), 237–256. doi:10.1016/S0020-0255(69)80010-1

Garnier, S., Combe, M., Jost, C., & Theraulaz, G. (2013). Do ants need to estimate the geometrical properties of trail bifurcations to find an efficient route? A swarm robotics test bed. *PLoS Computational Biology*, *9*(3), e1002903. doi:10.1371/journal.pcbi.1002903 PMID:23555202

Gazi, V., & Passino, K. M. (2011). *Swarm stability and optimization*. Berlin: Springer. doi:10.1007/978-3-642-18041-5

Ge, Z., & Song, Z. (2013). *Multivariate statistical process control: Process monitoring methods and applications*. London, UK: Springer. doi:10.1007/978-1-4471-4513-4

Gordon, D. M. (2010). *Ant encounters: Interaction networks and colony behavior*. Princeton, NJ: Princeton University Press.

Hamann, H. (2010). *Space-time continuous models of swarm robotic systems: Supporting global-to-local programming*. Berlin: Springer. doi:10.1007/978-3-642-13377-0

Hayashi, Y., Yuki, M., Sugawara, K., Kikuchi, T., & Tsuji, K. (2008). Analysis and modeling of ant's behavior from single to multi-body. *Artificial Life and Robotics*, *13*, 120–123. doi:10.1007/s10015-008-0571-z

Hutteger, S. M., & Zollman, K. J. S. (2010). Dynamics stability and basins of attraction in the Sir Philip Sidney game. *Proceedings. Biological Sciences*. doi:10.1098/rspb.2009.2105

Israel, M., Khmelnitsky, E., & Kagan, E. (2012). Search for a mobile target by ground vehicle on a topographic terrain. In *Proceedings of 27th IEEE Convention of Electrical and Electronics Engineers in Israel*. IEEE. doi:10.1109/EEEI.2012.6377123

Kagan, E., & Ben-Gal, I. (2011). Navigation of quantum-controlled mobile robots. In A. V. Topalov (Ed.), *Recent advances in mobile robotics* (pp. 311–326). Rijeka, Croatia: InTech. doi:10.5772/25944

Kagan, E., & Ben-Gal, I. (2013a). *Probabilistic search for tracking targets: Theory and modern applications*. Chichester, UK: John Wiley & Sons. doi:10.1002/9781118596593

Kagan, E., & Ben-Gal, I. (2013b). Moving target search algorithm with informational distance measures. *Open Applied Informatics Journal*, *6*, 1–10. doi:10.2174/1874136320130604001

Kagan, E., & Ben-Gal, I. (2014). A group-testing algorithm with online informational learning. *IIE Transactions*, *46*(2), 164–184. doi:10.1080/0740817X.2013.803639

Kagan, E., Goren, G., & Ben-Gal, I. (2010). Probabilistic double-distance algorithm of search after static or moving target by autonomous mobile agent. In *Proceedings of 26th IEEE Convention of Electrical and Electronics Engineers in Israel* (pp. 160-164). IEEE.

Kagan, E., Goren, G., & Ben-Gal, I. (2012). Algorithm of search for static or moving target by autonomous mobile agent with erroneous sensor. In *Proceedings of 27th IEEE Convention of Electrical and Electronics Engineers in Israel*. IEEE. doi:10.1109/EEEI.2012.6377124

Kagan, E., Rybalov, A., Siegelmann, H., & Yager, R. (2013). Probability-generated aggregators. *International Journal of Intelligent Systems*, *28*(7), 709–727. doi:10.1002/int.21598

Lerman, K., Martinoli, A., & Galstyan, A. (2005). A review of probabilistic macroscopic models for swarm robotic systems. In E. Sahin, & W. M. Spears (Eds.), *Swarm robotics (LNCS)* (Vol. 3342, pp. 143–152). Heidelberg, Germany: Springer. doi:10.1007/978-3-540-30552-1_12

McFarland, D., & Bösser, T. (1993). *Intelligent behavior in animals and robots*. Cambridge, MA: MIT Press/Bradford books.

Metzler, R., & Klafter, J. (2000). The random walk's guide to anomalous diffusion: A fractional dynamics approach. *Physics Reports*, *339*, 1–77. doi:10.1016/S0370-1573(00)00070-3

Nouvellet, P., Bacon, J. P., & Waxman, D. (2009). Fundamental insights into the random movement of animals from a single distance-related statistic. *American Naturalist*, *174*(4), 506–514. doi:10.1086/605404 PMID:19737110

Oakland, J. S. (2003). *Statistical process control* (5th ed.). Oxford, UK: Butteworth/Heinemann.

Passino, K. M. (2004). *Biomimicry for optimization, control, and automation*. London: Springer.

Payton, D., Daily, M., Estowski, R., Howard, M., & Lee, C. (2001). Pheromone robotics. *Autonomous Robots*, *11*, 319–324. doi:10.1023/A:1012411712038

Pyke, G. H. (1984). Optimal foraging theory: A critical review. *Annual Review of Ecology and Systematics*, *15*, 523–575. doi:10.1146/annurev.es.15.110184.002515

Raghuvanshi, A., Fan, Y., Woyke, M., & Perkowski, M. (2007). Quantum robots for teenagers. In *Proceedings of 37-th International Symposium on Multi-Valued Logic*. Oslo, Norway: Academic Press.

Razin, N., Eckmann, J. P., & Feinerman, O. (2013). Desert ants achieve reliable recruitment across noisy interactions. *Journal of the Royal Society, Interface*, *10*(82), 20130079. doi:10.1098/rsif.2013.0079 PMID:23486172

Richardson, T. O., Christensen, K., Franks, N. R., Jensen, H. J., & Sendova-Franks, A. B. (2011). Ants in a labyrinth: A statistical mechanics approach to the division labor. *PLoS ONE*, *6*(4), e18416. doi:10.1371/journal.pone.0018416 PMID:21541019

Rybalov, A., Kagan, E., Manor, Y., & Ben-Gal, I. (2010). Fuzzy model of control for quantum-controlled mobile robots. In *Proceedings of 26th IEEE Convention of Electrical and Electronics Engineers in Israel* (pp. 19-23). IEEE.

Rybalov, A., Kagan, E., & Yager, R. (2012). Parameterized uninorm and absorbing norm and their application for logic design. In *Proceedings of 27th IEEE Convention of Electrical and Electronics Engineers in Israel*. IEEE. doi:10.1109/EEEI.2012.6377125

Schweitzer, F. (2003). *Brownian agents and active particles. Collective dynamics in the natural and social sciences*. Berlin: Springer.

Searle, J. R. (2001). *Rationality in action*. Cambridge, MA: MIT Press/Bradford books.

Shapiro, L. (2011). *Embodied cognition*. London: Routledge/Taylor & Francis.

Siegelmann, H. (1998). *Neural networks and analog computation: beyond the Turing limit*. Boston: Birkhüuser.

Siegwart, R., & Nourbakhsh, I. R. (2004). *Introduction to autonomous mobile robots*. Cambridge, MA: MIT Press/Bradford books.

Steshenko, J., Kagan, E., & Ben-Gal, I. (2011). A simple protocol for a society of NXT robots communicating via Bluetooth. In *Proceedings of IEEE Conference ELMAR'11* (pp. 381-384). IEEE.

Stone, L. D. (1983). The process of search planning: current approaches and continuing problems. *Operations Research*, *31*(2), 207–233. doi:10.1287/opre.31.2.207

Sumpter, D. J. T. (2010). *Collective animal behavior*. Princeton, NJ: Princeton University Press.

Trianni, V. (2008). *Evolutionary swarm robotics: Evolving self-organising behaviors in groups of autonomous robots*. Berlin: Springer. doi:10.1007/978-3-540-77612-3

Tsetlin, M. L. (1963). Finite automata and models of simple forms of behavior. *Russian Mathematical Surveys*, *18*(1), 1–27. doi:10.1070/RM1963v-018n04ABEH001139

Tsetlin, M. L. (1973). *Automaton theory and modeling of biological systems*. New York: Academic Press.

Turchin, P. (2003). *Complex population dynamics: A theoretical/empirical synthesis*. Princeton, NJ: Princeton University Press.

Verbeeck, K., & Nowé, A. (2002). Colonies of learning automata. *IEEE Transactions on Systems, Man, and Cybernetics B*, *32*(6), 772–780. doi:10.1109/TSMCB.2002.1049611 PMID:18244883

Viswanathan, G. M., Buldyrev, S. V., Havlin, S., Da Luz, M. G. E., Raposo, E. P., & Stanley, H. E. (1999). Optimizing the success of random searchers. *Nature*, *401*, 911–914. doi:10.1038/44831 PMID:10553906

Viswanathan, G. M., Da Luz, M. G. E., Raposo, E. P., & Stanley, H. E. (2011). *The physics of foraging: an introduction to random searchers and biological encounters*. New York: Cambridge University Press. doi:10.1017/CBO9780511902680

Weiss, G. (Ed.). (1999). *Multiagent systems: a modern approach to distributed artificial intelligence*. Cambridge, MA: MIT Press.

Wittlinger, M., Wehner, R., & Wolf, H. (2006). The ant odometer: Stepping on stilts and stumps. *Science*, *312*, 1965–1967. doi:10.1126/science.1126912 PMID:16809544

Wittlinger, M., Wehner, R., & Wolf, H. (2007). The desert ant odometer: A stride integrator that accounts for stride length and walking speed. *The Journal of Experimental Biology*, *210*, 198–207. doi:10.1242/jeb.02657 PMID:17210957

Woolley, A. W., Chabris, C. F., Pentland, A., Hashmi, N., & Malone, T. W. (2010). Evidence for a collective intelligence factor in the performance of human groups. *Science*, *330*, 686–688. doi:10.1126/science.1193147 PMID:20929725

Yager, R., & Rybalov, A. (1996). Uninorm aggregation operators. *Fuzzy Sets and Systems*, *80*, 111–120. doi:10.1016/0165-0114(95)00133-6

ADDITIONAL READING

Alpern, S., & Gal, S. (2003). *The Theory of Search Games and Rendezvous*. New York: Kluwer.

Bai, F., & Helmy, A. (2006). A survey of mobility modeling and analysis in wireless ad hoc networks. In *Wireless ad hoc and sensor networks* (pp. 1–30). New York: Kluwer.

Baldassarre, G., Nolfi, S., & Parisi, D. (2003). Evolving mobile robots able to display collective behaviors. *Artificial Life*, *9*, 255–267. doi:10.1162/106454603322392460 PMID:14556687

Bartumeus, F. (2009). Behavioral intermittence, Levy patterns, and randomness in animal movement. *Oikos*, *118*, 488–494. doi:10.1111/j.1600-0706.2009.17313.x

Bartumeus, F., & Catalan, J. (2009). Optimal search behavior and classic foraging theory. *J. Phys. A: Math. Theor.*, *42*, 434002. doi:10.1088/1751-8113/42/43/434002

Bartumeus, F., Da Luz, M. G., Viswanathan, G. M., & Catalan, J. (2005). Animal search strategies: a quantitative random-walk analysis. *Ecology*, *86*(11), 3078–3087. doi:10.1890/04-1806

Benichou, O., Chevalier, C., Klafter, J., Meyer, B., & Voituriez, R. (2010). Geometry-controlled kinetics. *Nature Chemistry*, *2*, 472–477. doi:10.1038/nchem.622 PMID:20489716

Brillinger, D. R. (2010). Modeling Spatial Trajectories. In A. E. Gelfand, P. J. Diggle, M. Fuentes, & P. Guttorp (Eds.), *Handbook of Spatial Statistics* (pp. 463–475). CRC Press. doi:10.1201/9781420072884-c26

Buchanan, M. (2008). The mathematical mirror to animal nature. *Nature*, *453*, 714–716. doi:10.1038/453714a PMID:18528368

Choset, H., Lynch, K., Hutchinson, S., Kantor, G., Burgard, W., Kavraki, L., & Thrun, S. (2005). *Principles of robot motion: theory, algorithms, and implementation*. Cambridge, MA, London, England: Bradford Book/MIT Press.

Clark, A. (2003). *Natural-Born Cyborgs – Minds, Technologies, and the Future of Human Intelligence*. Oxford: Oxford University Press.

Erdmann, U., Ebeling, W., Schimansky-Geier, L., & Schweitzer, F. (2000). Brownian particles far from equilibrium. *The European Physical Journal B*, *15*, 105–113. doi:10.1007/s100510051104

Feinerman, O., Korman, A., Lotker, Z., & Sereni, J.-S. (2012). Collaborative search on the plane without communication. In *Proceedings of ACM Conference PODC* (pp. 77-86).

Ferreira, A., Raposo, E., Viswanathan, G., & da Luz, M. (2012). The influence of the environment on Lévy random search efficiency: fractality and memory effects. *Physica A*, *391*, 3234–3246. doi:10.1016/j.physa.2012.01.028

Fewell, J. H. (2003). Social insect networks. *Science*, *301*, 1867–1870. doi:10.1126/science.1088945 PMID:14512616

Gal, S. (1980). *Search Games*. New York: Academic Press.

Hoos, H. H., & Thomas, S. (2004). *Stochastic local search: Foundations and applications*. Amsterdam: Morgan Kaufmann.

Humphries, N. E., Queiroz, N., Dyer, J. R., Pade, N. G., Musyl, M. K., & Schaefer, K. M. et al. (2010). Environmental context explains Levy and Brownian movement patterns of marine predators. *Nature*, *465*, 1066–1069. doi:10.1038/nature09116 PMID:20531470

James, A., Plank, M. J., & Edwards, A. M. (2011). Assessing Levy walks as models of animal foraging. *Journal of the Royal Society, Interface*, *8*, 1233–1247. doi:10.1098/rsif.2011.0200 PMID:21632609

Johnson, K., & Rossi, L. F. (2006). A mathematical and experimental study of ant foraging trail dynamics. *Journal of Theoretical Biology*, *241*, 360–369. doi:10.1016/j.jtbi.2005.12.003 PMID:16442564

Mangel, M., & Clark, C. W. (1986). Towards a unified foraging theory. *Ecology*, *67*(5), 1127–1138. doi:10.2307/1938669

Pavlic, T. P., & Passino, K. M. (2009). Foraging theory for autonomous vehicle speed choice. *Engineering Applications of Artificial Intelligence*, *22*, 482–489. doi:10.1016/j.engappai.2008.10.017

Perna, A., Granovskiy, B., Garnier, S., Nicolis, S. C., Labedan, M., & Theraulaz, G. et al. (2012). Individual rules for trail pattern formation in argentine ants (*Linepithema humile*). *PLoS Computational Biology*, 8(7), e1002592. doi:10.1371/journal.pcbi.1002592 PMID:22829756

Pirolli, P. (2007). *Information foraging theory: Adaptive interaction with information*. New York: Oxford University Press. doi:10.1093/acprof:oso/9780195173321.001.0001

Romanczuk, P., Bar, M., Ebeling, W., Lindner, B., & Schimansky-Geier, L. (2012). Active Brownian particles. *European Physical Journal*, 202, 1–162.

Schonhage, A. (1980). Storage modification machines. *SIAM Journal on Computing*, 9(3), 490–508. doi:10.1137/0209036

Stephens, D. W., & Krebs, J. R. (1986). *Foraging Theory*. Princeton: Princeton University Press.

Stone, L. (2004). *Theory of optimal search* (2nd ed.). Catonsville, MD, USA: INFORMS.

Turchin, P. (1998). *Quantitative analysis of movement: Measuring and modeling population redistribution in animals and plants*. Sunderland, Massachusetts: Sinauer Associates.

Washburn, A. R. (2002). *Search and detection* (4th ed.). Catonsville, MD, USA: INFORMS.

Wilson, S. W. (1991). The animat path to AI. In J. A. Meyer, & S. W. Wilson (Eds.), *From Animals to Animats: Proceedings of the First International Conference on the Simulation of Adaptive Behavior* (pp. 15-21). Cambridge, Massachusetts: The MIT Press/Bradford Books.

Zheng, Y., & Zhou, X. (Eds.). (2011). *Computing with spatial trajectories*. New York: Springer. doi:10.1007/978-1-4614-1629-6

KEY TERMS AND DEFINITIONS

Braitenberg Vehicle: A minimal configuration of the wheeled mobile robot.

Common Memory: An environment including the changeable states, which are interpreted by the agents as meaningful signs and are used for communication between the agents.

Environment: An arena or terrain with changeable states, in which the mobile agents act and which states change.

Expedient Behavior: A behavior of the mobile agent in the environment, which provides greater reward or smaller payoff by avoiding unfavorable states and following the favorable ones.

Mobile Agent: A natural or artificial system, which is capable to autonomous decision-making and movement in the environment. An artificial mobile agent is called mobile robot.

Swarm: A group of mobile agents, which communicate one with another and change their activity with respect to the results of communication.

Tsetlin Automaton: A minimal automaton, which provides an expedient behavior in random environment.

Chapter 3
A Measure Optimized Cost–Sensitive Learning Framework for Imbalanced Data Classification

Peng Cao
Northeastern University, China & University of Alberta, Canada

Osmar Zaiane
University of Alberta, Canada

Dazhe Zhao
Northeastern University, China

ABSTRACT

Class imbalance is one of the challenging problems for machine-learning in many real-world applications. Many methods have been proposed to address and attempt to solve the problem, including sampling and cost-sensitive learning. The latter has attracted significant attention in recent years to solve the problem, but it is difficult to determine the precise misclassification costs in practice. There are also other factors that influence the performance of the classification including the input feature subset and the intrinsic parameters of the classifier. This chapter presents an effective wrapper framework incorporating the evaluation measure (AUC and G-mean) into the objective function of cost sensitive learning directly to improve the performance of classification by simultaneously optimizing the best pair of feature subset, intrinsic parameters, and misclassification cost parameter. The optimization is based on Particle Swarm Optimization (PSO). The authors use two different common methods, support vector machine and feed forward neural networks, to evaluate the proposed framework. Experimental results on various standard benchmark datasets with different ratios of imbalance and a real-world problem show that the proposed method is effective in comparison with commonly used sampling techniques.

DOI: 10.4018/978-1-4666-6078-6.ch003

INTRODUCTION

Recently, the class imbalance problem has been recognized as a crucial problem in machine learning and data mining (Chawla, Japkowicz & Kolcz, 2004; Kotsiantis, Kanellopoulos & Pintelas, 2006; He & Garcia, 2009; He & Ma, 2013). This issue of imbalanced data occurs when the training data is not evenly distributed among classes. This problem is also especially critical in many real applications, such as credit card fraud detection when fraudulent cases are rare or medical diagnoses where normal cases are the majority, and it is growing in importance and has been identified as one of the 10 main challenges of data mining (Yang, 2006). In these cases, standard classifiers generally perform poorly. classifiers usually tend to be overwhelmed by the majority class and ignore the minority class examples. Most classifiers assume an even distribution of examples among classes and assume an equal misclassification cost. Moreover, classifiers are typically designed to maximize accuracy, which is not a good metric to evaluate effectiveness in the case of imbalanced training data. Therefore, we need to improve traditional algorithms so as to handle imbalanced data and choose other metrics to measure performance instead of accuracy. We focus our study on imbalanced datasets with binary classes.

Much work has been done in addressing the class imbalance problem. These methods can be grouped in two categories: the data perspective and the algorithm perspective (He & Garcia 2009). The methods with the data perspective re-balance the class distribution by re-sampling the data space either randomly or deterministically (Chawla, Bowyer, Hall & Kegelmeyer, 2002; Chawla, Lazarevic, Hall & Bowyer, 2003; Chawla, Cieslak, Hall & Joshi, 2008; Barua, Monirul Islam, Yao & Murase, 2013; Galar, Fernández, Barrenechea & Herrera, 2013). The main disadvantage of re-sampling techniques are that they may cause loss of important information or the model overfitting,

since that they change the original data distribution. In addition, the performance of sampling can vary significantly depending upon the data available.

Cost-sensitive learning is one of the most important topics in machine learning and data mining, and attracted high attention in recent years (Akbani, Kwek & Japkowicz, 2004; Ling & Sheng, 2008; Zhou & Liu, 2006). Cost-sensitive learning methods consider the costs associated with misclassifying examples, and try to learn more characteristics of samples with the minority class by setting a high cost to the misclassification of a minority class sample. It has been shown that the problem of learning from imbalanced datasets and the problem of learning when costs are unequal and unknown can be handled in the same manner even though these problems are not exactly the same (Maloof, 2003). Cost-sensitive learning does not modify the data distribution, and is generally more consistent in terms of performance than the sampling techniques (Chris, Taghi, Jason & Amri, 2008; Weiss, McCarthy & Zabar, 2007).

There are two challenges with respect to the training of cost sensitive classifier. The misclassification costs play a crucial role in the construction of a cost sensitive learning model for achieving expected classification results. However, in many contexts of imbalanced dataset, the misclassification costs cannot be determined. Beside the cost, the feature set and intrinsic parameters of some sophisticated classifiers also influence the classification performance. The imbalanced data distribution is often accompanied by high dimensionality in real-world data sets such as text classification and bioinformatics (Blagus, 2013; Van Hulse, Khoshgoftaar, Napolitano & Wald, 2009; Zheng, Wu & Srihari, 2004). Therefore, high-dimensionality poses additional challenges when dealing with class-imbalanced prediction. Optimal feature selection can concurrently achieve good accuracy and dimensionality reduction. The proper intrinsic parameter setting of classifiers, such as regularization cost parameter and the kernel function parameter for SVM, and the structure parameters (i.e. number of hidden layers and their nodes) for neural network, can improve the classification performance. Moreover, these factors including the feature subset choice influence each other, obtaining the optimal factors of imbalanced data learning methods must occur simultaneously. This is the first challenge.

The other is the gap between the measure of evaluation and the objective of training on the imbalanced data (Li, Tsang, Zhou, 2013; Yuan & Liu, 2011). Indeed, for evaluating the performance of a cost-sensitive classifier on a skewed data set, the overall accuracy is irrelevant. It is common to employ other evaluation measures to monitor the balanced classification ability, such as G-mean and AUC. However, these cost-sensitive classifiers measured by imbalanced evaluation are not trained and updated with the objective of the imbalanced evaluation. To achieve good prediction performance, learning algorithms should train classifiers by optimizing the concerned performance measures.

In order to solve the challenges above, we design a novel framework for training a cost-sensitive neural network driven by the imbalanced evaluation criteria. The training scheme can bridge the gap between the training and the evaluation of cost-sensitive learning, and it can learn the optimal factors associated with the cost-sensitive classifier automatically under the guidance of the performance metrics. The search space is expanded exponentially as the class number increases. Moreover the factors to be searched are mixture including continuous and discrete variables. The significance of the scheme has two questions to fix: how to optimize these factors simultaneously; and using what evaluation criteria for guiding their optimization. These two issues are our key steps

for improving the cost sensitive learning in the context of the class imbalance problem without cost information. Our main contributions in this paper are centered around the questions above.

The contributions of this work can be listed as follows:

1. Optimizing the factors (ratio misclassification cost, feature set and intrinsic parameters of classifier) simultaneously for improving the performance of cost-sensitive learning.
2. Imbalanced data classification is commonly evaluated by measures such as G-mean and AUC instead of accuracy. However, for many classifiers, the learning process is still largely driven by error based objective functions. We use the measure directly to train the classifier and discover the optimal parameter, ratio cost and feature subset based on different evaluation functions like the G-mean or AUC. Different metrics can reflect different aspect performance of classifiers.
3. Showing versatility of our proposed framework, we present two different cost-sensitive learning schemes: one based on SVM as a direct method and one based on neural networks as meta learning method.

This chapter will be organized as follows. The basic concepts that are necessary to understand the issues addressed in this paper are described in Section 1, including imbalanced data learning, cost sensitive learning methods and particle swarm optimization. Then our proposed measure optimized framework is presented in Section 2. Section 3 details the experimental results comparing our approaches to other methods proposed in the literature for imbalanced data. Section 4 concludes with general remarks.

BACKGROUND

Imbalanced Data

A common problem faced in data mining is dealing with class imbalance. A dataset is said to be imbalanced if one class (called the majority, or negative class) vastly out-numbers the other (called the minority, or positive class). The class imbalance problem is only said to exist when the positive class is the class of interest. This is due to the fact that if the positive, minority, class is not of interest (i.e., it has no effect on the choice made), then it can be safely ignored. In most practical applications (e.g., loan recommendation, fraud prevention, spam detection, intrusion detection, species modeling, long term epidemiological studies, climate data analysis, etc.), however, the minority class is the class of interest, and therefore the class imbalance problem must be addressed.

Cost Sensitive Learning

The significant shortcomings with the re-sampling approach are the optimal class distribution is always unknown and the criterion in selecting instances is uncertain; furthermore under-sampling may reduce information loss and over-sampling may lead to overfitting or overgeneralization for model constructed. The cost-sensitive learning technique takes misclassification costs into account during the model construction, and does not modify the imbalanced data distribution directly.

Assigning distinct costs to the training examples seems to be the most effective approach of class imbalanced data problem.

The problem of imbalanced data is often associated with asymmetric costs of misclassifying instances of different classes. Medical diagnosis is a prominent example: misclassifying a cancer patient (false negative) may lead to death, while misclassifying a healthy patient (false positive) would lead to expenses associated with unnecessary biopsy and psychological problems. Datasets with different class distributions lead to the effect that conventional machine learning methods are typically biased towards the larger class in the training data.

The cost matrix contains the misclassification information: $C(+,+)$ and $C(-,-)$ are zeros, while $C(-,+)$ and $C(+,-)$ are important cost information to be determined. Moreover, $C(-,+)$ (i.e. when a minority instance is put in a majority class) should be bigger than $C(+,-)$, see Table 1. Table 1 illustrates the confusion matrix and cost matrix. The confusion matrix contains information about actual and predicted classifications done by a classification system.

This study focuses on binary classification, we denote the positive class (+) as the minority and the negative class (-) as the majority. Let $C(i, j)$ be the cost of predicting an instance belonging to class i when in fact it belongs to class j.

Cost-sensitive learning can be classified into two categories: direct methods and wrappers (Ling & Sheng, 2008). Direct methods are cost-sensitive

Table 1. The data sets used for experimentation Confusion and Cost Matrix

Predicted Class		Actual Class	
		Positive class	Negative class
	Positive class	True positive (TP) $C(+,+)$	False positive (FP) $C(+,-)$
	Negative class	False negative (FN) $C(-,+)$	True negative (TN) $C(-,-)$

classifiers in themselves, such as cost sensitive SVM; while wrappers convert any existing cost-insensitive (or cost-blind or cost-agnostic) classifiers into cost-sensitive ones. Wrappers are also called cost-sensitive meta-learning methods.

To show versatility of our method, we present two different cost-sensitive learning schemes: one based on SVM as a direct method and one based on neural networks as meta learning method.

CS-SVM

Support Vector Machines (SVM), which has strong mathematical foundations based on statistical learning theory, has been successfully adopted in various classification applications. SVM maximizes a margin in a hyperplane separating classes, and can be formulated as the following quadratic program:

$$Min \quad \frac{1}{.2}\left\|\mathbf{w}\right\|^2 + C\sum_{i=1}^{n}\xi_i$$
$$s.t. \quad y_i[(\mathbf{w}^T \bullet \mathbf{x}_i) + b] \geq 1 - \xi_i \quad i = 1, \cdots, n$$
$$\xi_i \geq 0$$

$$(1)$$

where C ≥ 0 is a regularization parameter that controls the trade-off between minimizing the errors and maximizing the margin. However, it is overwhelmed by the majority class instances in the case of imbalanced datasets because the objective of regular SVM is to maximize the accuracy, and not purposely to minimize the misclassification cost. The above formulation in Equation 3 implicitly penalizes errors in both classes equally. There may be different costs associated with the two different kinds of errors, making errors on positive examples costlier than errors on negative examples.

SVM have been extensively studied and have shown remarkable success in many applications. However, the success of standard SVM is very limited when applied to the problem of learning from imbalanced datasets. The cost-sensitive version of SVM (CS-SVM or 2C-SVM) (Veropoulos, Campbell & Cristianini, 1999) by assigning different misclassification costs is a good solution to address the above problem. Various proposals of cost-sensitive SVM were made using different error costs for the positive (C+) and negative (C-) classes. CS-SVM is formulated as follows:

$$Min \quad \frac{1}{2}\left\|\mathbf{w}\right\|^2 + C_+\sum_{i:y_i=+1}\xi_i + C_-\sum_{j:y_j=-1}\xi_j$$
$$s.t. \quad y_i[(\mathbf{w}^T \bullet \mathbf{x}_i) + b] \geq 1 - \xi_i \quad i = 1, \cdots, n$$
$$\xi_i \geq 0$$

$$(2)$$

where the C_+, or the $C(-,+)$, is the higher misclassification cost of the positive class, which is the primary interest, while C_-, or the $C(+,-)$, is the lower misclassification cost of the negative class. Using the different error cost for the positive and negative classes, the hyperplane could be pushed away from the positive instances. In this article, we fix $C_- = C$ and $C_+ = C \times C_{rf}$, where C_{rf} is the ratio misclassification cost factor.

In general, the Radial Basis Function (RBF kernel) is a reasonable first choice for the classification of the nonlinear datasets, as it has fewer parameters (γ). For the cost information, Veropoulos el at (Veropoulos, Campbell & Cristianini, 1999) have not suggested any guidelines for deciding what the relative ratios of the positive to negative cost factors should be.

CS-NN

The standard neural network is cost insensitive. In standard neural network classifiers, the class returned is C^* by comparing the probability of each class directly for each instance x according to Equation(3).

$$C^* = \underset{C \in \{1,...,M\}}{argmax}(p_1(C_1 \mid x),...,p_M(C_M \mid x))$$

(3)

where P_i denotes the probability value of each class from the neural network, $\sum_{i=1}^{M} P_i = 1$ and $0 \leq P_i \leq 1$. M is the number of the class.

Many approaches have been developed in the past few years in making the traditional cost-insensitive neural network classification algorithm into cost-sensitive (Kukar & Kononenko, 1998; Zhou & Liu, 2006). The probabilities generated by a standard neural network are biased in the imbalanced data distribution, adjusting the decision threshold moves the output threshold toward inexpensive class such that instances with high costs become harder to be misclassified (Ling & Sheng, 2008). The idea is based on the classifier producing probability predictions rather than classification labels. Results suggest that threshold-moving, replacing the probability a sample belongs to a certain class with the altered probability, which takes into account the costs of misclassification, is found to be a relatively good choice in training CS-NN (Zhou & Liu, 2006). This method uses the training set to train a neural network, and the cost sensitivity strategy is introduced in the test phase. Given a certain cost matrix, the CS-NN with threshold-moving return

the class C^*, which is computed by injecting the cost according to Equation(4) as shown in Box 1.

When M is 2 (binary class), the classifier will classify an instance x into minority class if and only if:

$$p(+ \mid x)C(-,+) > p(- \mid x)C(+,-)$$

(5)

which is equivalent to

$$\frac{p(+ \mid x)}{p(- \mid x)} > \frac{C(+,-)}{C(-,+)} = C_{rf}$$

(6)

It predicts the class by setting a probability threshold dependent on the ratio misclassification cost. Therefore, the final decisions are decide by the misclassification cost specified and probability estimate learned. In the normal classification without considering the cost, the C_{rf} is 1, the decision threshold is 0.5, that means both of the two classes have the same weight. In the cost sensitive context, we need to improve the recognition ability of minority class. Unlike the SVM the ratio cost C_{rf} is used in the training phrase; it is introduced in the validation phase after obtaining a common neural network in the training phrase. When validating, we observe a probability estimate p belonging to positive class on a testing instance, the instance is labeled as the positive class or negative class according to C_{rf} through (6).

Box 1.

$$C^* = \underset{C}{argmax} \frac{1}{\sum_{i=1}^{M} p_i^*(C_i \mid x)} \left\{ p_1^*(C_1 \mid x),...,p_M^*(C_M \mid x) \right\}$$

$$= \underset{C}{argmax} \frac{1}{\sum_{i=1}^{M} cost(C_i)p(C_i \mid x)} \left\{ cost(C_1)p(C_1 \mid x),...,cost(C_M) \times p(C_M \mid x) \right\}$$

(4)

where $Cost(C_i)$ denotes the cost of misclassifying instance of class i. P_i^* denotes the class probabilities from the neural network combined with misclassification cost.

Particle Swarm Optimization

Swarm Intelligence (SI), an artificial intelligence technique for machine learning, is a research branch that models the population of interacting agents or swarms that are able to self-organize. SI has recently emerged as a practical research topic and has successfully been applied to a number of real world problems (Martens, Baesens & Fawcett, 2011). The popularity of swarm intelligence has also instigated the development of numerous data mining algorithms.

Particle swarm optimization (PSO) is a population-based global stochastic search method attributed to Kennedy and Eberhart to simulate social behavior (Kennedy & Eberhart, 1995). Compared to Genetic Algorithms (GA), the advantages of PSO are that it is easy to implement and has fewer control parameters to adjust. Many studies have shown than PSO has the same effectiveness but is more efficient. PSO optimizes an objective function by a population-based search. The population consists of potential solutions, named particles. These particles are randomly initialized and move across the multi-dimensional search space to find the best position according to an optimization function. During optimization, each particle adjusts its trajectory through the problem space based on the information about its previous best performance (personal best, *pbest*) and the best previous performance of its neighbors (global best, *gbest*). Eventually, all particles will gather around the point with the highest objective value.

The position of individual particles is updated as follows:

$$x_i^{t+1} = x_i^t + v_i^{t+1} \tag{7}$$

with *v*, the velocity calculated as follows:

$$v_{id}^{t+1} = w \times v_{id}^t + c_1 \times r_1 \times (pbest_{id}^t - x_{id}^t)$$
$$+c_2 \times r_2 \times (gbest^t - x_{id}^t) \tag{8}$$

where v_i^t indicates velocity of particle *i* at iteration *t*, *w* indicates the inertia factor, C_1 and C_2 indicate the cognition and social learning rates, which determine the relative influence of the social and cognition components. r_1 and r_2 are uniformly distributed random numbers between 0 and 1, x_i^t is current position of particle *i* at iteration *t*, $pbest_i^t$ indicates best of particle *i* at iteration *t*, $gbest^t$ indicates the best of the group. The algorithm is depicted in Algorithm 1.

The output of the algorithm is the best global position (solution) found during all iterations. Even though PSO convergence to a global optimum has not been proven for the general case, the algorithm has been shown efficient for many optimization problem. Moreover, PSO has already been applied in classification problem to obtain optimal relevant parameters of traditional classification model, so as to improve the performance of standard classifier methods. Most of it concerns rule-based classifiers, for instance, PSO is used to extract induction rules to classify data (Sousa, T., Silva, A., & Neves, A., 2004). The standard particle swarm optimizer (PSO) and adaptive Michigan PSO (AMPSO) are applied to the prototype selection problem, and the experimental results show they imrpove the results of the Nearest Neighbor classifiers (Cervantes, A., Galván,. O.M., & Isasi, P., 2009). PSO can also be employed to compute the weights for combining multiple neural network classifiers (Nabavi-Kerizi, S.H., Abadi, M., & Kabir, E., 2010). Additionally, some study demonstrates the feasibility of applying an existing Particle Swarm Optimization approach to feature

Algorithm 1. PSO

```
Input: termination condition; particle update parameters; fitness function f
Initialize particles with random position & velocity
 repeat
     foreach particle i
         if    f(pbest_i) <= f(x_i)
            pbest_i = x_i
        end if
     end foreach
     set gbest as best pbest
     foreach particle i
         update velocity_i and position_i
     end foreach
   until termination condition
   output gbest
```

selection for filtering the irrelevant attributes of the dataset, resulting in a fine Bayesian network built with the K2 algorithm (Chávez, M.C., Casas, G., Falcón, R., Moreira, J.E., & Grau, R., 2007).

MEASURE OPTIMIED COST SENSITIVE LEARNING

Measure Optimized Cost Sensitive Learning Framework

In this section, we present a new measure optimized framework for optimizing the cost sensitive learning (MOCSL), which uses a Particle Swarm Intelligence to carry out the meta-learning, then we introduce the algorithm procedure of MOCS-SVM and MOCS-NN.

Since the evaluation measures describe the overall performance of classifier, it is more appropriate to evaluate and train the classifier as a whole. As we know, SVM and neural network are both driven by error based objective functions. SVM tries to minimize the regularized hinge loss; neural network tries to minimize the square error. We have known the overall accuracy

is not appropriate evaluation measure for imbalanced data classification. As a result, there is an inevitable gap between the evaluation measure by which the classifier is to be evaluated and the objective function according to the classifier is trained. The classifier for imbalanced data learning is needed to be driven by the more appropriate measures. We inject the appropriate measures into the objective function of the classifier in the training with PSO. The common evaluation for imbalanced data classification is G-mean and ROC (Receiver Operating Characteristic) curves. However, for many classifiers, the learning process is still driven by error based objective functions. This paper explicitly treat the measure itself as the objective function when training the cost sensitive learning for improve the performance of classifiers and discovering the best parameter and feature subset. We designed a measure optimized training framework for dealing with imbalanced data classification issue. Chalwa (Chawla, Cieslak, Hall & Joshi, 2008) proposed a wrapper paradigm that discovers the amount of re-sampling for a data set based on optimizing evaluation functions like the F-measure, AUC. To date, there is no research about training the cost sensitive classifier with measure based objective functions. This is one important issue of hindering the performance of cost-sensitive learning.

Another important issue of applying the cost-sensitive learning algorithm to the imbalanced data is that the cost matrix is often unavailable for a problem domain. The misclassification cost plays a crucial role in the construction of cost sensitive approach, and the knowledge of misclassification costs is urgently required for achieving expected classification result. For binary class classification, the cost parameter (ratio misclassification cost) is only one parameter which means the relative cost information, and the cost information to be optimized is only for regulating the accuracy of two classes. However, the values of costs are commonly given by domain experts, it often keep unknown in many domain where it is in fact difficult to specify the precise cost ratio information. It is not exact to set the cost ratio to the inverse of the imbalance ratio (the number of majority instances divided by the number of minority instances); especially it is not accurate for some classifier such as SVM.

Apart from the ratio misclassification cost information, feature subset selection and the intrinsic parameters of the classifier have a significant bearing on the performance. The both of two factors are not only important for imbalanced data classification, but also for any classification. Feature selection is the technique of selecting a subset of discriminative features for building robust learning models by removing most irrelevant and redundant features from the data. Optimal feature selection can concurrently achieve good accuracy and dimensionality reduction. Unfortunately, the imbalanced data distribution are often accompanied by the high dimensional in real-world data sets such as text classification and bioinformatics. It is important to select features that can capture the high skew in the class distribution (Blagus, 2013; Van Hulse, Khoshgoftaar, Napolitano & Wald, 2009; Zheng, Wu & Srihari, 2004). Moreover, proper intrinsic parameter setting of classifiers,

such as regularization cost parameter and the kernel function parameter for SVM, as well as the structure parameters (i.e. number of hidden layers and their nodes) for neural network, can improve the classification performance. For example, for SVM, it is common to use the grid search to optimize the regulation parameter and the kernel parameter. Moreover, these three factors influence each other. Therefore, obtaining the optimal ratio misclassification cost, feature subset and intrinsic parameters must occur simultaneously.

Based on the reason above, our specific goal is to devise a strategy to automatically determine the optimal factors during training of the cost sensitive classifier oriented by the imbalanced evaluation criteria (G-mean and AUC). It is a wrapper framework for empirically discovering the potential misclassification cost ratio, feature subset, and intrinsic parameters for cost sensitive learning (CSL).

In this paper, for the multivariable optimization, especially the hybrid multivariable, the best methods are swarm intelligence technique. We choose the particle swarm optimization (PSO) as our optimization method due to its fast and effective solution space exploration. In addition, many experiments claim that PSO has equal effectiveness but superior efficiency over the GA (Hassan, Cohanim & De Weck, 2005).

Because feature is discrete and parameters are continuous, and the variable needed to be optimized are enormous and mixed. The PSO is a good solution for hybrid multi-variables to be utilized.

The PSO was originally developed for continuous valued spaces; however, many problems have in addition features defined for discrete valued spaces where the domain of the variables is finite. We need to combine the discrete and continuous values in the solution representation since the costs and parameters we intend to optimize are continuous while the feature selection is discrete. Each feature is represented by a 1 or 0 for whether it is selected or not. The major difference between the discrete PSO (Khanesar, Teshnehlab & Shoorehdeli, 2007) and the original version is that the velocities of the particles are rather defined in terms of probabilities that a bit will change to one. Using this definition a velocity must be restricted within the range [0, 1], to which all continuous values of velocity are mapped by a sigmoid function:

$$v'^t_i = sig(v^t_i) = \frac{1}{1 + e^{-v^t_i}} \quad (9)$$

Equation 9 is used to update the velocity vector of the particle while the new position of the particle is obtained using Equation 10.

$$x^{t+1}_i = \begin{cases} 1 & if \quad r_i < v'^t_i \\ 0 & otherwise \end{cases} \quad (10)$$

where r_i is a uniform random number in the range [0,1].

Many methods are proposed to deal with the issue of the imbalanced data classification by means of swarm intelligence. Chawla et al implement a genetic algorithm based framework to weight the contribution of each classifier by an appropriate fitness function, such that the classifiers that complement each other on the unbalanced dataset are preferred, resulting in significantly improved performances (Chawla & Sylvester, 2007). Yuan et al proposed to train the standard AdaBoost on training sets oversampled by SMOTE and, in an offline mode, retrain the weights of base classifiers assigned by the standard AdaBoost using Genetic Algorithms (GAs) with G-mean as the fitness function to boost the performance of AdaBoost on imbalanced datasets (Yuan & Ma, 2013). Both of the above methods also belong to wrapper methods of optimizing some parameters. In addition, Yu et al proposed ACOSampling that is a novel undersampling method based on the idea of ant colony optimization (ACO) to address

this problem (Yu, Ni & Zhao, 2013). Gao et al a powerful technique for two-class imbalanced classification problems by combining the synthetic minority over-sampling technique (SMOTE) and the particle swarm optimisation (PSO) aided radial basis function (RBF) classifier (Gao, Hong, Chen & Harris, 2011).

Evaluation Metrics

Evaluation measures play a crucial role in both assessing the classification performance and guiding the classifier modeling. The purpose of cost-sensitive learning is usually to build a model with total minimum misclassification costs. However, it should be based on the known cost matrix condition. In this article, the purpose of our cost sensitive learning is to get a best AUC or G-mean evaluation metric. And we train the cost sensitive learning using performance measures as the objective functions directly. Through training the cost sensitive classifier with measure based objective functions, we can discover the best factors in terms of the different evaluation. For imbalanced datasets, the evaluation metric should take into account the imbalance. The average accuracy is not an appropriate evaluation metric. We used the G-mean and AUC to evaluate the cost sensitive classifiers. The evaluation metrics value is taken as the fitness function to adjust the position of a particle. These two different evaluations reflect different aspect of the classifier. The AUC concerns the ranking ability more and the G-mean concerns the two accuracies of both classes at the same time.

The G-mean is the geometric mean of specificity and sensitivity, which is commonly utilized when performance of both classes is concerned and expected to be high simultaneously (Kubat & Matwin, 1997). It is a good indicator on overall performance, and has been used by several researchers for evaluating classifiers on imbalanced datasets (Akbani, Kwek & Japkowicz, 2004; Barua, Monirul Islam, Yao & Murase, 2013).

According to the confusion matrix mentioned in the section 1, we define the sensitivity, specificity and G-mean as follows:

$$Sensitivity = \frac{TP}{TP + FN}$$

$$Specificity = \frac{TN}{TN + FP} \qquad (11)$$

$$G - mean = \sqrt{Sensitivity * Specificity}$$
$$(12)$$

ROC analysis (abbr. of Receiver Operating Characteristic) has been recently introduced to evaluate machine learning algorithm. ROC curves measure the separating ability of a classier between two classes. It depicts all possible trade-off between TP rate and FP rate. Closely related to ROC, AUC represents a ROC curve as a single scalar value by estimating the area under the curve, varying between 0 and 1. The AUC measures the performance of ranking a randomly chosen positive example higher than a randomly chosen negative example. In this case, it represents the performance of ranking an instance from the minority class higher than instances in the majority class. The value 1of AUC represents all positives being ranked higher than all negatives. The authors in (Ling, Huang, & Zhang, 2003) have empirically and formally prove that AUC is a statistically consistent and more discriminating measure than accuracy. It is also as the measure criteria for evaluating performance of classification on the imbalanced dataset (Chawla, Cieslak, Hall & Joshi, 2008; Klement, Wilk, Michaowski

& Matwin, 2009). Since AUC is believed to be a better performance measure than accuracy for imbalanced classification problems, and independent of class prevalence. Many existing learning algorithms been modified to deal with the new objective (Tang, Wang & Chen, 2011).

MOCS-SVM

The solution (i.e. particle) of MOCS-SVM includes three parts: the ratio misclassification cost C_{rf}, the intrinsic parameters (C and γ) of classifier, and the feature subsets. Figure 1 illustrates the mixed solution representation in the PSO. If n features are required to decide which features are chosen, then $n+3$ decision variables must be adopted. The value of n variables of feature ranges between 0 and 1. If the value of a variable is less than or equal to 0.5, then its corresponding feature is not chosen. Conversely, if the value of a variable is greater than 0.5, then its corresponding feature is chosen. In addition to feature selection, three decision variables, C, C_f and γ, are required.

Figure 2 shows the flowchart for MOCS-SVM. First, the population of particles is initialized, each particle having a random position within the D-dimensional space and a random velocity for each dimension. Second, each particle's fitness for the CS-SVM is evaluated. G-mean or AUC is a criteria used to design a fitness function. Thus, for the particle with high G-mean or AUC produce a high fitness value. The fitness has been taken as the G-mean or AUC. If the fitness is better than the particle's best fitness, then the position vector is saved for the particle. If the particle's fitness is better than the global best fitness, then the position vector is saved for the global best. Finally the

Figure 1. Solution representation of MOCS-SVM

Ratio cost	Intrinsic parameters		Feature subset				
C_{rf}	C	γ	f_1	f_2	...	f_{n-1}	f_n

Figure 2. The flowchart of the proposed MOCS-SVM

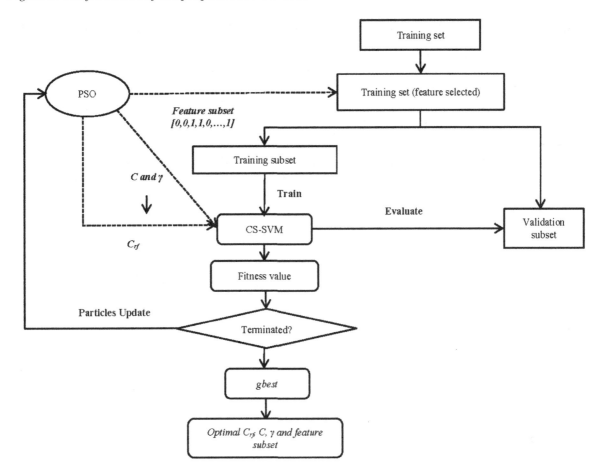

particle's velocity and position are updated until the termination condition is satisfied. Associated with the characteristics of exploitation and exploration search, PSO can deal with large search spaces efficiently, and hence has less chance to get local optimal solution than other algorithms.

The detailed algorithm MOCS-SVM to optimize cost sensitive SVM by imbalanced data measure is shown in Algorithm 2. It is a wrapper framework for empirically discovering the potential misclassification cost ratio, feature subset, and intrinsic parameters (C and γ) for CS-SVM oriented by the imbalanced evaluation criteria (G-mean and AUC).

The choice of the fitness function is important because it is on this basis that the PSO evaluates

the goodness of each candidate solution for designing our classification system. We employ a 5-fold cross-validation to represent an unbiased estimation of the generalization performance of classifier for each candidate solution. We first split the training data set into five partitions. Each partition is used once as a testing fold, with the remaining 80% as the training fold.

MOCS-NN

In the training of the feed-forward neural network, it is often trained by adjusting connection weights with gradient descent. Another alternative is to use swarm intelligence to find the optimal set of weights (Yuan & Liu, 2011). Since the gradient

Algorithm 2. MOCS-SVM

```
Input: Training set D; termination condition T; population size SN; metric E;
NumFolds =5
Randomly initialize particle population positions and velocities (including
cost matrix,
intrinsic parameters, and feature subset)
repeat
 foreach particle i
        Construct the Dᵢ with the feature selected by the particle i
        Separate Dᵢ randomly into NumFolds folds
        for k=1 to NumFolds
    Train CS-SVM with cost matrix and intrinsic parameters optimized by the
particle i
        on the k-th training fold Trtᵏᵢ
        Evaluate the cost sensitive classifier on the Trvᵏᵢ, and obtain the value
Mᵏᵢ based on E
 end for
 Mᵢ=average(Mᵏᵢ);Assign the fitness of particle i  with Mᵢ
        if   fitness (pbestᵢ) <= fitness (xᵢ)
then pbestᵢ = xᵢ
 end if
end foreach
set gbest as best pbest
  foreach particle i
        update velocityᵢ and positionᵢ  with Equations 2 and 3.
end foreach
until termination condition
output optimal parameters, cost ratio and feature subset of gbest
```

descent is a local search method vulnerable to be trapped in local minima, we opted to substitute the gradient descent with PSO in our use of PSOCS-NN in order to alleviate the curse of local optima. We use a hybrid PSO algorithm similar to the PSO-PSO method presented in (Carvalho & Ludermir, 2007). In the PSO-PSO Methodology, a PSO algorithm is used to search for architectures and a PSO with weight decay (PSO: WD) is used to search for weights. We also used two nested PSOs, where the outer PSO is used to search for architectures (including the feature subset which determines the input node amount as well as the number of the hidden nodes) and misclassification costs; the inner PSO is used to search for weights of the neural network defined by the outer PSO. The procedure of inner PSO is the same as the method proposed in (Mazurowski, M.A., Habas, P.A., Zurada, J.M., Lo, J.Y., Baker, J.A. & Tourassi, G.D. 2008), and the major motivation of using evolutionary techniques over gradient based learning algorithms for training neural networks is to alleviate the curse of local optima. We assume there is only one hidden layer. The solution of the outer PSO includes three parts: the cost, the number of the hidden nodes and the feature subset, and the solution of the inner PSO contains the vector of the connection weights. The amount of the variables to be optimized in the inner PSO is determined by the number of the hidden nodes in the outer PSO. Figure 3 illustrates the mixed solution representation of the two PSOs. Figure 4 shows the flowchart for MOCS-NN. The detailed algorithm for MOCS-NN is shown in Algorithm 3.

EXPERIMENTAL STUDY

Dataset Description

To evaluate the classification performance of our proposed methods in different classification tasks, and to compare with other methods specifically devised for imbalanced data, we tried several da-

Figure 3. Solution representation of MOCS-NN

	Ratio cost	number of the hidden nodes		Feature subset			
Outer PSO	C_{rf}	N		f_1	f_2	...	f_{n-1}	f_n
Inner PSO	*Weight vector*						
	w_1	w_2	...			w_{N-1}	w_N

Figure 4. The flowchart of the proposed MOCS-NN

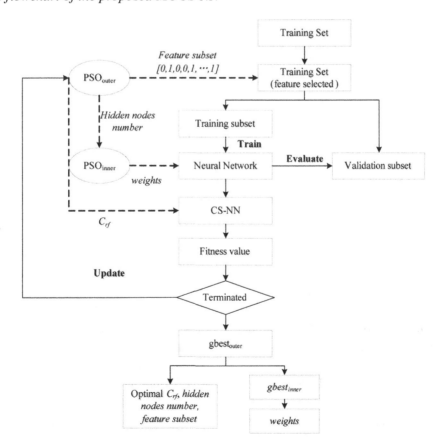

Algorithm 3. MOCS-NN

Input: Training set D; Termination condition of two PSO T_{outer} and T_{inner};
    Population size of two PSOs SN_{outer} and SN_{inner}
Randomly initialize outer-PSO population (including costs, number of the hidden nodes, and feature subset)
repeat   % *outer PSO*
foreach particle^i
Construct D^i with the feature selected by the particle^i
Separate D^i randomly into Trt^i (80%) for training *and* Trv^i (20%) for validation
Randomly initialize inner-PSO population (connection weights) in each particle^i
    repeat   % *inner PSO*
 foreach particle$^i j$
Obtain the number of the hidden nodes from the particle^i
Construct a neural network with the weights optimized by the particle$^i j$
Validate the neural network on the Trt^i and assign the fitness of particle$^i j$ with the G-mean
        end foreach
  Inner-PSO particle population updates
    until T_{inner}
    Obtain the optimal connection weight vector in the $gbest^i_{inner}$ of the inner PSO
    Evaluate the neural network classifier with cost optimized by the particle^i as well as
        the connection weights optimized on the Trv^i, and obtain the value M^i based on G-mean
    Assign the fitness of particle^i with M^i
end foreach
 Outer-PSO particle population updates
until T_{outer}
Output: the number of the hidden nodes, costs, feature subset and the connection weights of the $gbest_{inner}$

tasets from the UCI database. There is no standard dataset for imbalanced classification, and most of these selected UCI datasets have multi-class labels. We used all available datasets from the combined sets used in (Akbani, Kwek & Japkowicz, 2004). This also ensures that we did not choose only the datasets on which our method performs better. We also keep the same minority class as the paper (Akbani, Kwek & Japkowicz, 2004) using

one class as the positive class (minority), while the union of all others as the negative class. The minority class label (+) is indicated in Table 2. The datasets chosen have diversity in the number of attributes and imbalance ratio. Moreover, the datasets used have both continuous and categorical attributes.

We first split the data set into ten partitions. Each partition is used once as a testing fold, with

Table 2. The data sets used for experimentation. The dataset name is appended with the label of the minority class (+).

Dataset (+)	Instances	Features	Class balance
Hepatitis (1)	155	19	1:4
Glass (7)	214	9	1:6
Segment (1)	2310	19	1:6
Anneal (5)	898	38	1:12
Soybean (12)	683	35	1:15
Sick (2)	3772	29	1:15
Car (3)	1728	6	1:24
Letter (26)	20000	16	1:26
Hypothyroid(3)	3772	29	1:39
Abalone (19)	4177	8	1:130

the remaining 90% as the training fold. This results in ten pairs of training and testing folds (10-fold cross-validation), and to prevent overtraining, the training set is separated into training subset (80%) for constructing the classification model and test subset (20%) for evaluating and calculating the fitness value in each fold. The training and validation sets were characterized by the same ratio of both class. I made vertical comparison and horizontal comparison. The vertical comparison means the comparison between our method proposed and the intermediate method or basic method, such as basic classifier, cost sensitive learning and grid search optimization for CS-SVM. The horizontal comparison is the comparison between our method MOCSL and the state-of the-art methods for class imbalance learning.

Experiment 1 (Vertical Comparison): How the MOCSL Improves

In the vertical comparison, we made the comparison between basic classifier with and without the feature selection, cost sensitive learning (CSL), our method proposed using measure oriented training for CSL by PSO (MOCSL) with and without the feature selection. For SVM, we also apply the

common grid search optimization method for comparison. For the basic classifier with feature selection, it is a common wrapper feature selection method with evaluating by classification performance. As for the CSL, the misclassification cost ratio is search iteratively for maximize the measure score within a range of cost value. As for the optimizing the CS-SVM using grid search, we also need to treat this misclassification cost ratio as a hyperparameter, and locally optimize this parameter. However, it is not feasible to use a triple circulation for optimizing the best parameters, so we optimize the best parameter pair(C and γ), then locally optimize the cost ratio parameter based on the best parameter pair(C and γ) before. All SVMs model in this experiment use the same kernel, RBF, and for basic SVM and CS-SVM, the intrinsic parameters are chosen with default values ($C=1$ and $\gamma=1$). In the basic neural network and CS-NN, the number of neurons in the hidden layer was the average number between the input and output neurons.

For the PSO setting of our method, MOCSL, the initial parameter values of it in our proposed method were set according to the conclusion drawn in (Carlisle, 2001). The parameters were used: $C_1=2.8, C_2=1.3, w=0.5$. For empirically providing good performance while at the same time keeping the time complexity feasible, particle number was set dynamically according to the amount of the variables optimized (=1.5×|variables need to be optimized|), and the termination condition could be a certain number of iterations (500 cycles) or other convergence condition (no changes any more within 2×|variables need to be optimized| cycles).

Along with these parameters in PSO, the other parameters are the upper and lower of limit parameter of model to be optimized. For SVM, the ranges for C and γ are based on a grid search for SVM parameters as recommended in (Hsu, Chang & Lin, 2003). The range of C is $(2^{-5}, 2^{15})$, and the range of C is $(2^{-15}, 2^3)$. For the neural network, the upper and lower limits of the connection weights were set to 100 and -100 respectively in the inner PSO; the upper and lower limits of the hidden node amount were empirically set to 5 and 20 respectively in the outer PSO. The range of ratio misclassification cost factor C_r was empirically chosen between 1 and 100×*ImbaRatio* (the ratio between the instance amounts of two classes).

In this experiment, we assess the overall quality of classifiers with only the AUC evaluation metric. The average AUC scores are shown in the Table 3. From the result in Table 3, we found that simultaneously optimizing the feature subset, parameter and cost ratio generally help the base classifiers learned on the different data sets, regardless of feature selecting or not.

For the classifier with the default model intrinsic parameters, the neural network is better than SVM, it is because that SVM is much more sensitive to the choice of model intrinsic parameter than neural network. The default model parameters of SVM cannot get the best performance.

Meanwhile, for SVM, under the condition where the feature selection is not carried out, we found the optimization for all the factors simultaneously using PSO outperform the optimization using extent grid search, which optimize the intrinsic parameter firstly, then search the optimal misclassification cost parameter based on the best intrinsic parameters. It lacks sufficient search in the parameter space, many potential parameters pairs not to be abtained in the parameter space. Hence, it shows that the parameters need to be search at the same time. We believe that a wrapper method can allow one to empirically discover the

Table 3. Experimental results (AUC) of the MOCSL method with and without feature selection, as well as basic method and grid search for SVM

Dataset	SVM						Neural Network				
	Basic		CSL	Grid-CSL	MOCSL		Basic		CSL	MOCSL	
	without FS	FS	without FS	without FS	without FS	FS	without FS	FS	without FS	without FS	FS
Hepatitis	0.632	0.714	0.707	0.801	**0.861**	0.855	0.851	0.847	0.855	0.859	**0.877**
Glass	0.952	0.957	0.953	0.955	0.994	**1**	0.932	0.945	0.956	0.987	**0.994**
Segment	1	1	1	1	1	1	0.999	1	**1**	1	1
Anneal	0.876	0.925	0.957	**1**	**1**	**1**	0.886	0.898	0.888	0.909	**0.932**
Soybean	1	1	1	1	1	1	**1**	1	**1**	1	1
Sick	0.728	0.761	0.788	0.848	0.908	**0.975**	0.817	0.823	0.862	0.924	0.941
Car	0.990	0.987	0.990	0.999	**1**	**1**	0.996	0.996	0.998	**1**	1
Letter	0.898	0.895	0.909	0.983	0.980	**0.999**	0.955	0.962	0.972	0.979	**1**
Hypothyrid	0.830	0.855	0.887	0.945	0.973	**0.988**	0.951	0.963	0.963	0.968	**0.972**
Abalone	0.638	0.712	0.722	0.839	0.867	0.893	0.851	0.853	0.884	**0.891**	0.875

relevant parameters, as it is certainly intrinsically tied in with the data properties. Many results are particularly suggestive because they show that the degree of imbalance is not the only factor that hinders learning. Consider the Anneal data set, which is certainly not the most unbalanced data set. Both SVM and neural network have a very poor performanc. However, there is a significant improvement offered by the wrapper methods.

We also found the feature selection step for these classifiers when working on the imbalanced data classification for both the basic classifier and the MOCSL. In the MOCSL, the use of feature selection was found to improve the AUC on the most datasets.

We have demonstrated the ability to optimize the parameters and input of classifier model for an evaluation function, resulting in effective generalization performance.Therefore, we can draw the conclusion that the simultaneously optimizing

the intrinsic, misclassification cost parameter and feature selection with the imbalanced evaluation measure guiding improve the classification performance of the cost sensitive learning on the different datasets. Moreover, the average AUC score of MOCS-SVM is better than MOCS-NN, which demonstrate that our wrapper approach improve the SVM much more than neural network.

Genetic algorithms also have the potential to generate both the optimal feature subset and parameters at the same time. Figure 5 shows a graphical evolution in terms of the average of AUC of execution of PSO based wrapper and GA based wrapper on four datasets. Both the methods performs feature selection and parameters setting in an evolutionary way. Compared with GA method, PSO based approach generally achieve higher AUC. Moreover, we can also see that for a given AUC value, PSO based wrapper methods tends to take fewer iterations to converge.

Figure 5. The comparison between GA and PSO in terms of AUC and number of iterations. (a) Sick. (b) Anneal. (c) Hepatitis. (d) Hypothyid.

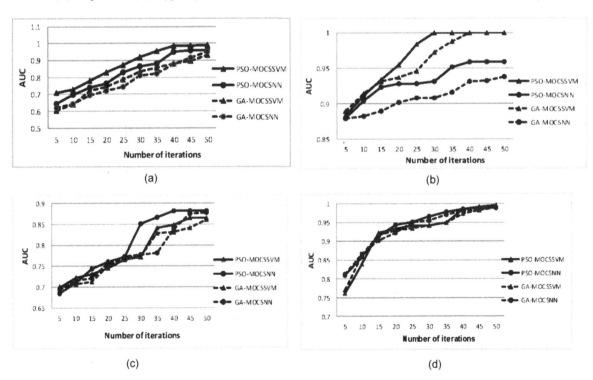

(a)

(b)

(c)

(d)

Compared with GAs, PSO does not need complex operators such as crossover and mutation, it requires only primitive and simple mathematical operators, hence it is computationally inexpensive in terms of both memory and runtime

Experiment 2 (Horizontal Comparison): MOCSL vs. the State-of the-Art Methods

The horizontal comparison means the comparison that our method and the other state-of-the-art imbalanced data classifiers, such as the random under-sampling (RUS), SMOTE over-sampling (Chawla, Bowyer, Hall & Kegelmeyer, 2002), SMOTEBoost (Chawla, Lazarevic, Hall & Bowyer, 2003) and SMOTE combined with asymmetric cost classifier (Akbani, Kwek & Japkowicz, 2004). For the under-sampling algorithm, the SMOTE and SMOTEboost, the re-sampling rate is unknown. The common method for RUS is that majority class of the training data is randomly under-sampled until the sizes of both classes are the same. The common method for SMOTE is that the minority class was oversampled at the different rates from 100% to 500% and choose the average of these different results of different ratio oversampling as the final result. In our experiments, in order to compare equally, no matter under-sampling or over-sampling method, we also use the evaluation measure as the optimization objective of the re-sampling method to search the optimal re-sampling level. The increment step and the decrement step are both set as the 10%. This is a greedy search, which process repeats, greedily, until no performance gains are observed. The optimal re-sampling rate is decided in a greedy iterative fashion according to the evaluation metrics. Thus, in each fold, the training set is separated into training subset and validating subset for searching the appropriate rate parameters. The evaluation metrics are also used with the G-mean and AUC. For the SMOTE with asymmetric cost

classifier, for each re-sampling rate searched, the optimal misclassification cost ratio is determined by grid search under the evaluation measure guiding under the current over-sampling level of SMOTE. Any algorithm that tries to improve on it inevitably sacrifices some specificity in order to improve the sensitivity. G-mean metric is the best of the three measures because it combines both the sensitivity and the specificity and takes their geometric mean.

The experiment results are shown in the Table 4 and Table 5. As shown in bold in Table 4 and 5, our MOCSL outperforms all the other approaches on the great majority of datasets. Irrespective of the wrapper evaluation function, the wrapper approaches always result in an improved G-mean and AUC over the base classifier. For MOCSL based on the SVM (MOCS-SVM), it did not get the best result only on the Glass dataset; For MOCSL based on the neural network (MOCS-NN), there are only two dataset (Soybean and Hypothyroid) not to be winner. From the results, we can see that the random under-sampling is with worst performance. This is because that it is possible to remove certain significant examples. Especially for SVM, undersampling the majority class causes larger angles between the ideal and learned hyperplane.

Both the SMOTE and SMOTEBoost generally help the base classifiers learned on the different data sets. Using the SMOTE based technique of oversampling the minority instances, we can make the distribution of positive instances denser. SMOTE or SMB synthetically generates new instances between two existing positive instances which helps in making their distribution more well-defined. However, SMOTE itself makes some assumptions about the training set. For instance, it assumes that the space between two positive instances is assumed to be positive and the neighborhood of a positive instance is also assumed to be positive, which may not always be true. Since our algorithm uses SMOTE, it also

Table 4. Experimental comparison between MOCSL method and other imbalanced data classification methods based on the SVM

Dataset	Metric	RUS		SMOTE		SMB		SMOTE-CSL		MOCSL	
		AUC	GM	AUC	GM	AUC	GM	AUC	GM	AUC	GM
		Optimization Metric		Optimization Metric		Optimization Metric		Optimization Metric		Optimization Metric	
Hepatitis	AUC	0.663	0.528	0.754	0.721	0.788	0.759	0.813	0.783	**0.855**	0.823
	GM	0.598	0.487	0.672	0.667	0.558	0.592	0.628	0.729	**0.805**	0.801
	Fea	19								7	8
Glass	AUC	0.955	0.948	0.988	0.986	0.981	0.978	0.992	0.975	1	0.995
	GM	0.817	0.803	0.844	0.858	0.874	0.862	0.965	**0.988**	0.986	0.971
	Fea	9								5	4
Segment	AUC	1	1	1	1	1	1	1	1	1	1
	GM	0.993	1	1	1	1	1	1	1	0.998	1
	Fea	19								10	11
Anneal	AUC	0.882	0.866	0.912	0.876	0.891	0.889	0.957	0.934	1	1
	GM	0.616	0.535	0.758	0.821	0.761	0.784	0.819	0.835	0.999	1
	Fea	38								14	12
Soybean	AUC	1	0.992	1	1	1	1	1	1	1	1
	GM	0.876	0.953	0.947	0.965	0.992	0.997	1	0.997	1	1
	Feature	35								12	12
Sick	AUC	0.784	0.742	0.822	0.799	0.841	0.824	0.931	0.874	**0.975**	0.954
	GM	0.206	0.141	0.452	0.528	0.508	0.512	0.811	0.825	0.893	**0.915**
	Feature	29								9	7
Car	AUC	1	1	1	1	1	1	1	1	1	1
	GM	0.964	0.964	0.962	0.958	0.979	0.981	0.995	**0.998**	0.996	**0.998**
	Feature	6								4	4
Letter	AUC	0.907	0.896	0.966	0.956	0.987	0.965	0.988	0.980	**0.999**	0.995
	GM	0.925	0.933	0.947	0.954	0.934	0.922	0.965	0.961	0.983	**0.985**
	Fea	16								12	10
Hypothyroid	AUC	0.876	0.843	0.971	0.915	0.967	0.955	0.973	0.971	0.988	**0.989**
	GM	0.482	0.612	0.853	0.894	0.876	0.903	0.876	0.901	0.964	**0.968**
	Fea	29								9	14
Abalone	AUC	0.781	0.613	0.822	0.754	0.799	0.780	0.846	0.812	**0.893**	0.855
	GM	0.618	0.687	0.712	0.814	0.645	0.744	0.698	0.817	**0.853**	0.785
	Fea	8								4	5

makes a similar assumption. In some complex datasets where this assumption may not hold, such as Hepatitis and Sick, our algorithm will perform slightly worse than the other algorithms.

The over-sampling algorithm that tries to improve on it inevitably sacrifices some specificity in order to improve the sensitivity; but the degree of sensitivity improved is larger than the one of speci-

Table 5. Experimental comparison between MOCSL method and other imbalanced data classification methods based on the neural network

Dataset	Metric	RUS		SMOTE		SMB		SMOTE-CSL		MOCSL	
		AUC	GM	AUC	GM	AUC	GM	AUC	GM	AUC	GM
		Optimization Metric		Optimization Metric		Optimization Metric		Optimization Metric		Optimization Metric	
Hepatitis	AUC	0.751	0.611	0.795	0.74	0.823	0.815	0.841	0.827	**0.893**	0.877
	GM	0.756	0.793	0.829	0.835	0.812	0.807	0.822	**0.851**	0.832	0.848
	Fea	19								10	9
Glass	AUC	0.932	0.919	0.985	0.964	0.987	0.988	0.975	0.953	0.987	**0.994**
	GM	0.845	0.847	0.841	0.851	0.843	0.885	0.931	0.965	0.963	**0.970**
	Fea	9								5	5
Segment	AUC	1	0.999	1	1	1	1	1	1	1	1
	GM	0.996	0.993	0.998	0.999	0.995	0.998	0.999	1	0.998	1
	Fea	19								14	14
Anneal	AUC	0.919	0.902	0.884	0.856	0.878	0.839	0.911	0.847	**0.932**	**0.932**
	GM	0.676	0.702	0.766	0.799	0.797	0.848	0.861	0.914	0.907	**0.934**
	Fea	38								18	16
Soybean	AUC	1	1	1	1	1	1	1	1	1	1
	GM	0.862	0.948	0.988	1	1	1	0.997	1	0.999	1
	Fea	35								14	15
Sick	AUC	0.768	0.721	0.843	0.817	0.853	0.856	**0.965**	0.885	0.962	0.941
	GM	0.325	0.354	0.682	0.699	0.726	0.748	0.822	0.816	0.899	**0.907**
	Fea	29								13	11
Car	AUC	0.812	0.806	0.999	0.986	0.998	0.990	1	1	1	1
	GM	0.725	0.786	0.923	0.944	0.945	0.939	0.951	**0.988**	0.975	0.969
	Fea	6								4	5
Letter	AUC	0.916	0.925	0.958	0.929	1	0.943	1	0.998	1	1
	GM	0.943	0.957	0.953	0.959	0.938	0.966	0.972	0.963	**0.978**	0.971
	Fea	16								11	10
Hypothyroid	AUC	0.889	0.861	0.944	0.923	**0.979**	0.952	0.944	0.935	0.977	0.972
	GM	0.651	0.673	0.823	0.841	0.842	0.853	0.897	0.917	0.955	**0.958**
	Fea	29								12	13
Abalone	AUC	0.797	0.751	0.811	0.793	0.804	0.771	0.837	0.828	**0.888**	0.875
	GM	0.644	0.726	0.733	0.748	0.741	0.756	0.828	0.857	0.823	**0.856**
	Fea	8								5	6

ficity improved. However, they have a potential disadvantage of distorting the class distribution. SMOTE combined with different cost classifier is better than single only SMOTE over-sampling, and it is the method that share most of the second best results. For some dataset, such as Segment, Soybean and Car, the AUC can be achieved 1, which indicates perfect ranking performance, and the two classes can be differenated easily.

There is not a distinct positive correlation between the objective functions in the wrapper-mode and corresponding improvements in the final evaluation. In majority the cases, the G-mean value from the G-mean wrapper is higher than the one of the AUC wrapper, but in some cases, the G-mean value from the AUC wrapper is higher, such as Hepatitis and Abalone datasets for MOCS-SVM and Glass and letter datasets for MOCS-NN. Even for MOCS-SVM, the average G-mean from AUC optimization is better than the one from G-mean optimization. From this, we believe these results in more generalized performances when using AUC as the wrapper evaluation function, which is the similar conclusion as the paper (Chawla, Cieslak, Hall & Joshi, 2008), where the F-measure on some data sets when using AUC as the wrapper evaluation metric rather than the F-measure. We believe that employing the AUC evaluation measure as optimization objective could lead to more generalized performances. Similarly, the two evaluation metrics wrapper optimization for the same classifier result in different misclassification cost, feature subset and intrinsic parameters, since that they optimize different properties of the classifier.

The feature selection is as important as the re-sampling in the imbalanced data classification, especially on the high dimensional datasets. However, the feature selection is always ignored. Our method conduct the feature selection in the wrapper paradigm, hence improve the classification performance on the data sets which have higher dimensionality, such as Anneal, Sick and Hypothyroid. As expected using different classifiers also results in different feature subset. Because different algorithms have different biases and a feature that may help one algorithm may hurt another, so the feature subsets are different according to different wrapper classifiers. The feature number and feature are both different.

Although all methods are optimized under the evaluation measure optimized, we can see clearly that MOCSL is almost always equal to, or better

than other methods. What is most important is that our method does not change the data distribution. The re-sampling based on the SMOTE may make the model overfitting, resulting in the generalization is not as good as the training.

Many papers conclude that there is no consistent clear winner between the sampling approaches and the cost-sensitive technique. However, the conclusions were based on the default condition without the sufficient search in the parameters space. In this paper, we have empirically show that the under the evaluation measure guiding, the performances of cost sensitive learning with cost, feature subset and intrinsic parameter optimized are better than the re-sampling methods with sampling level optimized.

Due to the nature of PSO, searching of cost setups might be time-consuming with some applications. This approach is still respectable considering that this searching is usually an off-line procedure such that the learning speed is not a crucial issue.

Experiment 3: Lung Computer-Aided Detection

Many lung nodule computer-aided detection (CAD) methods have been proposed to help expert radiologists in their decision making. A CAD scheme for nodule detection in CT can be broadly divided into two major steps, an initial nodule identification step and a false-positive reduction step (Li, 2007). The purpose of false-positive reduction is to remove these false positives (FPs) as much as possible while retaining a relatively high sensitivity. It is a typical class imbalance issue since that the two classes are skewed and have unequal misclassification costs. The imbalanced data issue usually occurs in computer-aided detection systems since that the healthy class is far better represented than the diseased class in the collected data (Rao, Fung & Krishnapuram, et al, 2009; Yang, Zheng, Siddique, & Beddoe, 2008), including other CAD, such as breast, colony.

Constructing an accurate classification method requires a training data set that represents different aspects of nodule features. As we know, feature extraction plays an important role in computer aided detection. However, there is not a single outstanding feature that can discriminate the nodule from non-nodule completely. This is due to the fact that the nodules vary enormously in volume, shape, and appearance, and the sources of false positives are different. The majority of false positives are mainly caused by blood vessels and other normal anatomic structures. Some of the false positives can be easily distinguished from true nodule, however, a large portion of them are difficult to distinguish. Therefore, for getting a high classification accuracy in candidate nodule classification, we should extract more features from many aspects, such as intensity, shape and gradient. Our feature extraction process generated 43 image features. Using these features, we construct the input space for our classifiers. This section gives a brief introduction to the features we have collected for analysis and selection. Table 6 describes the features extracted from the candidate nodule Volume-Of-Interest (VOI) for classification.

Our database consists of 98 thin section CT scans with 106 solid nodules, obtained from Guangzhou hospital in China. These databases included nodules of different sizes (3-30mm). We obtained the appropriate candidate nodule samples objectively using a candidate nodule detection algorithm, which identifies 85 true nodules as positive class and 462 non-nodules as negative class from the total CT scans; the class imbalance ratio is 5.4. The imbalance level is not extremely high, but the misclassification costs of each class are extremely different. The imbalance level is dependent on reliability and accuracy of the initial detection processing. The Generation of the nodule candidates is displayed in Figure 6.

Experiments show that the framework proposed improves the evaluation metric, AUC in Table 7. For high dimensional candidate nodule dataset, our methods outperform the other common approach. It means that our method can be applied on the nodule or other lesion detection medical images. The measure optimization is only used the AUC metric.

CONCLUSION

Learning with class imbalance is a challenging task. Cost sensitive learning is an important approach without changing the distribution because

Table 6. Feature set for candidate nodule classification

#	Feature Type	Feature	Description
1-7	Intensity	Intensity statistical feature	The gray value within the objects was characterized by use of seven statistics (mean, variance, max, min, skew, kurt, entropy).
8-12		sub-volume distribution feature	The average intensity within each sub-volume along the radial directions
13-19	Shape	SI statistical feature	The volumetric shape index (SI) representing the local shape feature at each voxel was characterized by use of seven statistics.
20-26		CV statistical feature	The volumetric curvedness (CV), which quantifies how highly curved a surface is, was characterized by use of seven statistics.
27-29		volume, surface area and compactness	
30-36	Gradient	Concentration statistical feature	The concentration characterizing the degree of convergence of the gradient vectors at each voxel, was characterized by use of seven statistics
37-43		Gradient strength statistical feature	The gradient strength of the gradient vectors at each voxel, was characterized by use of seven statistics

Figure 6. Initial detection result of candidate nodules. TPs indicated by arrow, other spots are FPs

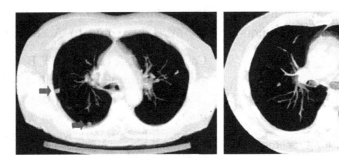

Table 7. Experiment result of candidate nodule classification

Method	Metric	Base	CSL	RUS	SMOTE	SMOTEBoost	SMOTE-CSL	MOCSL
SVM	AUC	0.681	0.785	0.603	0.948	0.948	0.956	**0.969**
	GM	0.208	0.662	0.590	0.826	0.818	0.867	**0.937**
NN	AUC	0.872	0.899	0.873	0.926	0.925	0.938	**0.946**
	GM	0.513	0.650	0.439	0.858	0.864	0.909	**0.921**

it takes into account different misclassification costs for false negatives and false positives. Since the cost matrix, the intrinsic algorithm parameters and the feature subset are important factors for the cost sensitive learning, and they influence each other, it is best to attempt to simultaneously optimize them using an object optimized wrapper approach. We propose a wrapper paradigm optimized by the evaluation measure of imbalanced dataset as objective function with respect to misclassification cost, feature subset and intrinsic parameter of classifier. The optimization processing is through an effective swarm intelligence technique, the Particle Swarm Optimization (PSO). Our measure optimized framework could wrap around an existing cost-sensitive classifier. We demonstrated its applicability with SVM and neural networks, two completely different classifiers. The proposed method has been validated on some benchmark dataset as well as a real world dataset (Lung medical image), which is typically an imbalanced data set with different misclassification cost. The experimental results presented in this study have demonstrated that the proposed

framework provided a very competitive solution to other existing state-of-the-arts methods, in optimization of G-mean and AUC for combating imbalanced classification problems. These results confirm the advantages of our approach, showing the promising perspective and new understanding of cost sensitive learning.

FUTURE RESEARCH

Several interesting problems related to this research are still open for future investigation. The following is a list of some possible directions.

1. More investigations on other base classifier.

In this study, we only demonstrated its applicability with SVM as well as neural network which are commonly used in the imbalanced data learning. Other standard classification systems, such as bayesian network classifier, decision tree, and K-NN, are all reported to be affected by the class imbalance problem. Our measure optimized framework can be applied on other classifiers. In future research, we will extend and investigate how the cost sensitive learning wrapper algorithms effect different base classification systems.

2. More investigations for multiple classes classification.

Most existing imbalance learning techniques are only designed for and tested in two-class scenarios. They have been shown to be less effective or even cause a negative effect in dealing with multi-class tasks. In the future research, we will extend the framework to the multiclass imbalanced data classification.

3. More investigations for other objective function.

The setup of optimized parameters is specific not only to the given data, but also to the learning objective and the base classifier. The kind of objective function can be chosen based on the training objective of the given problem; the alternative performance measures such as F-measure can also be incorporated.

REFERENCES

Akbani, R., Kwek, S., & Japkowicz, N. (2004). Applying support vector machines to imbalanced datasets. In *Proceedings of the 2004 European conference on machine* learning (pp. 39-50). Pisa, Italy: Academic Press.

Barua, S., Monirul Islam, M., Yao, X., & Murase, K. (2013). MWMOTE: Majority weighted minority oversampling technique for imbalanced data set learning. *IEEE Transactions on Knowledge and Data Engineering.*

Blagus, R. (2013). Improved shrunken centroid classifiers for high-dimensional class-imbalanced data. *BMC Bioinformatics, 14*(1), 64–76. doi:10.1186/1471-2105-14-64 PMID:23433084

Carlisle, A., & Dozier, G. (2001). an off-the-shelf PSO. In *Proceedings of Particle Swarm Optimization Workshop* (pp. 1-6). Academic Press.

Carvalho, M., & Ludermir, T. B. (2007). Particle swarm optimization of neural network architectures and weights. In *Proceedings of the 7th international conference on hybrid intelligent systems* (pp. 336-339). Kaiserlautern, Australia: Academic Press.

Cervantes, A., Galván, O. M., & Isasi, P. (2009). AMPSO: A new particle swarm method for nearest neighborhood classification. *IEEE Transactions on Systems, Man, and Cybernetics. Part B, Cybernetics, 39*(5), 1082–1091. doi:10.1109/TSMCB.2008.2011816 PMID:19336325

Chávez, M. C., Casas, G., Falcón, R., Moreira, J. E., & Grau, R. (2007). Building fine bayesian networks aided by PSO-based feature selection. In *Proceedings of Advances in Artificial Intelligence* (pp. 441–451). Academic Press. doi:10.1007/978-3-540-76631-5_42

Chawla, N. V., Bowyer, K. W., Hall, L. O., & Kegelmeyer, W. P. (2002). SMOTE: Synthetic minority over-sampling technique. *Journal of Artificial Intelligence Research, 16*, 321–357.

Chawla, N. V., Cieslak, D. A., Hall, L. O., & Joshi, A. (2008). Automatically countering imbalance and its empirical relationship to cost. *Data Mining and Knowledge Discovery, 17*(2), 225–252. doi:10.1007/s10618-008-0087-0

Chawla, N. V., Japkowicz, N., & Kolcz, A. (2004). Editorial: special issue on learning from imbalanced data sets. *SIGKDD Explorations, 6*(1), 1–6. doi:10.1145/1007730.1007733

Chawla, N. V., Lazarevic, A., Hall, L. O., & Bowyer, K. W. (2003). SMOTEBoost: Improving prediction of the minority class in boosting. In *Proceedings of the Seventh European conference Principles and Practice of Knowledge Discovery in Databases* (pp. 107-119). Cavtat-Dubrovnik, Croatia: Academic Press.

Chawla, N. V., & Sylvester, J. (2007). Exploiting diversity in ensembles: Improving the performance on unbalanced datasets. In *Proceedings of the 7th International Workshop on Multiple Classifier Systems* (pp. 397-406). Prague, Czech Republic: Academic Press.

Chris, S., Taghi, M. K., Jason, V. H., & Amri, N. (2008). A comparative study of data sampling and cost sensitive learning. In *Proceedings of IEEE International Conference on Data Mining Workshops*. Pisa, Italy: IEEE.

Galar, M., Fernández, A., Barrenechea, E., & Herrera, F. (2013). Eusboost: Enhancing Ensembles for Highly Imbalanced Data-sets by Evolutionary Undersampling. *Pattern Recognition*. doi:10.1016/j.patcog.2013.05.006

Gao, M., Hong, X., Chen, S., & Harris, C. J. (2011). A combined SMOTE and PSO based RBF classifier for two-class imbalanced problems. *Neurocomputing, 74*, 3456–3466. doi:10.1016/j.neucom.2011.06.010

Hassan, R., Cohanim, R., & De Weck, O. (2005). A comparison of particle swarm optimization and the genetic algorithm. In *Proceedings of the 46th AIAA/ASME/ASCE/AHS/ASC Structures, Structural Dynamics and Materials Conference*. Austin, TX: AIAA.

He, H., & Garcia, E. A. (2009). Learning from imbalanced data. *IEEE Transactions on Knowledge and Data Engineering, 21*(9), 1263–1284. doi:10.1109/TKDE.2008.239

He, H., & Ma, Y. (2013). *Imbalanced Learning: Foundations, Algorithms, and Applications*. Wiley-IEEE.

Hsu, C.W., Chang, C.C., & Lin, C.J. (2003). *A Practical Guide to Support vector Classification*. National Taiwan University Technical Report.

Kennedy, J., & Eberhart, R. C. (1995). Particle swarm optimization. In *Proceedings of IEEE International Conference on Neural Networks* (pp.1942–1948). Nedlands, Australia: IEEE.

Khanesar, M. A., Teshnehlab, M., & Shoorehdeli, M. A. (2007). A novel binary particle swarm optimization. In *Proceedings of Mediterranean Conference on Control & Automation* (pp. 1–6). Athens, Greece: Academic Press.

Klement, W., Wilk, S., Michaowski, W., & Matwin, S. (2009). Dealing with Severely Imbalanced Data. In *Proceedings of Workshop on Data Mining When Classes are Imbalanced and Errors Have Costs, PAKDD*. Bangkok, Thailand: PAKDD.

Kotsiantis, S., Kanellopoulos, D., & Pintelas, P. (2006). Handling imbalanced datasets: A review. *GESTS International Transactions on Computer Science and Engineering, 30*(1), 25–36.

Kubat, M., & Matwin, S. (1997). Addressing the Curse of Imbalanced Training Sets: One-Sided Selection. In *Proceedings of the 14th International Conference on Machine Learning* (vol. 97, pp. 179-186). Academic Press.

Kukar, M., & Kononenko, I. (1998). Cost-sensitive learning with neural networks. In *Proceedings of European Conference on Artificial Intelligence* (pp.445–449). Brighton, UK: Academic Press.

Li, N., Tsang, I., & Zhou, Z. (2013). Efficient Optimization of Performance Measures by Classifier Adaptation. *IEEE Transactions on Pattern Analysis and Machine Intelligence, 35*(6), 1370–1382. doi:10.1109/TPAMI.2012.172 PMID:22868653

Li, Q. (2007). Recent progress in computer-aided diagnosis of lung nodules on thin-section CT. *Computerized Medical Imaging and Graphics, 31*, 248–257. doi:10.1016/j.compmedimag.2007.02.005 PMID:17369020

Ling, C. X., Huang, J., & Zhang, H. (2003). AUC: A Statistical Consistent and More Discriminating Measure than Accuracy. In *Proceedings of the 18th International Conference on Artificial Intelligence* (pp. 329-341). Acapulco, Mexico: Academic Press.

Ling, C. X., & Sheng, V. S. (2008). Cost-sensitive learning and the class imbalance problem. In *Encyclopedia of Machine Learning* (pp. 231–235). Academic Press.

Maloof, M. A. (2003). Learning when data sets are imbalanced and when costs are unequal and unknown. In *Proceedings of International Conference on Machine Learning Workshop on Learning from Imbalanced Data Sets*. Melbourne, FL: Academic Press.

Martens, D., Baesens, B., & Fawcett, T. (2011). Editorial Survey: Swarm Intelligence for Data Mining. *Machine Learning*, *82*(1), 1–42. doi:10.1007/s10994-010-5216-5

Mazurowski, M. A., Habas, P. A., Zurada, J. M., Lo, J. Y., Baker, J. A., & Tourassi, G. D. (2008). Training neural network classifiers for medical decision making: The effects of imbalanced datasets on classification performance. *Neural Networks*, *21*, 427–436. doi:10.1016/j.neunet.2007.12.031 PMID:18272329

Nabavi-Kerizi, S. H., Abadi, M., & Kabir, E. (2010). A PSO-based weighting method for linear combination of neural networks. *Computers & Electrical Engineering*, *36*(5), 886–894. doi:10.1016/j.compeleceng.2008.04.006

Rao, R. B., Fung, G., Krishnapuram, B., Bi, J., Dundar, M., & Raykar, V. ... Stoeckel, J. (2009). Mining medical images. In *Proceedings of the Third Workshop on Data Mining Case Studies and Practice Prize, Fifteenth Annual SIGKDD International Conference on Knowledge Discovery and Data Mining (KDD 2009)*. Paris, France: ACM.

Sousa, T., Silva, A., & Neves, A. (2004). Particle swarm based data mining algorithms for classification tasks. *Parallel Computing*, *30*(5-6), 767–783. doi:10.1016/j.parco.2003.12.015

Tang, K., Wang, R., & Chen, T. (2011). Towards maximizing the area under the ROC Curve for multi-class classification problems. In *Proceedings of the 25th AAAI Conference on Artificial Intelligence* (pp. 483-488). San Francisco, CA: AAAI.

Van Hulse, J., Khoshgoftaar, T. M., Napolitano, A., & Wald, R. (2009). Feature selection with high dimensional imbalanced data. In *Proceedings of the 9th IEEE International Conference on Data Mining Workshops* (pp. 507–514). Miami, FL: IEEE.

Veropoulos, K., Campbell, C., & Cristianini, N. (1999). Controlling the sensitivity of support vector machines. In *Proceedings of the international joint conference on artificial intelligence* (pp. 55–60). Stockholm, Sweden: Academic Press.

Weiss, G., McCarthy, K., & Zabar, B. (2007). Cost-sensitive learning vs. sampling: Which is best for handling unbalanced classes with unequal error costs? In *Proceedings of the 2007 International Conference on Data Mining* (pp. 35-41). CSREA Press.

Yang, Q., & Wu, X. (2006). 10 challenging problems in data mining research. *International Journal of Information Technology & Decision Making*, *5*(4), 597–604. doi:10.1142/S0219622006002258

Yang, X., Zheng, Y., Siddique, M., & Beddoe, G. (2008). Learning from imbalanced data: a comparative study for colon CAD. In *Proceedings of the Medical Imaging* (Vol. 6915). Academic Press.

Yu, H., Ni, J., & Zhao, J. (2013). ACOSampling: An ant colony optimization-based undersampling method for classifying imbalanced DNA microarray data. *Neurocomputing*, *101*, 309–318. doi:10.1016/j.neucom.2012.08.018

Yuan, B., & Liu, W. H. (2011). A Measure Oriented Training Scheme for Imbalanced Classification Problems. In *Proceedings of the Pacific-Asia Conference on Knowledge Discovery and Data Mining Workshop on Biologically Inspired Techniques for Data Mining* (pp. 293–303). Shenzhen, China: Academic Press.

Yuan, B., & Ma, X. (2012). Sampling + Reweighting: Boosting the Performance of AdaBoost on Imbalanced Datasets. In *Proceedings of the 2012 International Joint Conference on Neural Networks* (pp. 2680–2685). Brisbane, Australia: Academic Press.

Zheng, Z., Wu, X., & Srihari, R. (2004). Feature selection for text categorization on imbalanced data. *ACM SIGKDD Explorations*, *6*(1), 80–89. doi:10.1145/1007730.1007741

Zhou, Z. H., & Liu, X. Y. (2006). Training Cost-Sensitive Neural Networks with Methods Addressing the Class Imbalance Problem. *IEEE Transactions on Knowledge and Data Engineering*, *18*(1), 63–77. doi:10.1109/TKDE.2006.17

KEY TERMS AND DEFINITIONS

Artificial Neural Network: Artificial neural networks are computational models inspired by animal central nervous systems (in particular the brain) that are capable of machine learning and pattern recognition.

CAD: Computer-aided detection (CAD) technology works like a second pair of eyes in helping to detect and mark potential areas of concern on the mammogram and CT.

Classification: A task of predicting a certain outcome based on a given input.

Cost Sensitive Learning: Cost-Sensitive Learning is a type of learning in data mining that takes the misclassification costs into consideration.

Feature Selection: Feature selection is the process of selecting a subset of the features occurring in the training set and using only this subset as features in future classification.

Genetic Algorithm: A search heuristic that mimics the process of natural selection.

Imbalanced Data: The data set contains an unequal distribution of data samples among different classes.

Misclassification Cost: Misclassification costs are basically weights applied to specific outcomes. These weights are factored into the model and may actually change the prediction.

Particle Swarm Intelligence: Particle Swarm Optimization (PSO) is a biologically inspired computational search and optimization method.

SVM: In machine learning, support vector machines (SVM) are supervised learning models with associated learning algorithms that analyze data and recognize patterns, used for classification and regression analysis.

Swarm Intelligence: Swarm intelligence (SI) is the collective behavior of decentralized, self-organized systems, natural or artificial. The concept is employed in work on artificial intelligence.

VOI: Volume of interest.

Chapter 4
Towards an Improved Ensemble Learning Model of Artificial Neural Networks:
Lessons Learned on Using Randomized Numbers of Hidden Neurons

Fatai Anifowose
Universiti Malaysia Sarawak, Malaysia

Jane Labadin
Universiti Malaysia Sarawak, Malaysia

Abdulazeez Abdulraheem
King Fahd University of Petroleum and Minerals, Saudi Arabia

ABSTRACT

Artificial Neural Networks (ANN) have been widely applied in petroleum reservoir characterization. Despite their wide use, they are very unstable in terms of performance. Ensemble machine learning is capable of improving the performance of such unstable techniques. One of the challenges of using ANN is choosing the appropriate number of hidden neurons. Previous studies have proposed ANN ensemble models with a maximum of 50 hidden neurons in the search space thereby leaving rooms for further improvement. This chapter presents extended versions of those studies with increased search spaces using a linear search and randomized assignment of the number of hidden neurons. Using standard model evaluation criteria and novel ensemble combination rules, the results of this study suggest that having a large number of "unbiased" randomized guesses of the number of hidden neurons beyond 50 performs better than very few occurrences of those that were optimally determined.

DOI: 10.4018/978-1-4666-6078-6.ch004

INTRODUCTION

Artificial Neural Networks (ANN) has become a "household" technique in the Computational Intelligence (CI) and data mining application community. It is the most popular and commonly used technique for most predictive modeling tasks. Since it is readily available as a toolbox in the MATLAB software (Demuth et al., 2009), it is easily applied on non-linear and most challenging academic and industrial problems. The journey of the application of CI techniques in petroleum engineering has been interesting. It started with the derivation of empirical equations for the estimation of most petroleum reservoir properties such as porosity and permeability. These equations were used to establish linear relationships between certain observed parameters and the target reservoir property. Later, these equations were found to be inferior to linear and multivariate regression tools in terms of predictive performance. When the capabilities of CI techniques, especially ANN, was discovered by petroleum engineers, focus was shifted from the linear and multivariate regression tools as they could not compete with the latter (Eskandari et al. 2004). Consequently, CI became well embraced in the petroleum reservoir characterization research and has been reported to perform excellently well (Zahedi et al. 2009; El-Sebakhy, 2009). Due to the nice graphical user interface and its ease of use, ANN became popular and commonly used among petroleum engineers.

However, despite the common use of this technique, it poses a number of challenges one of which is the determination of the appropriate network design architecture. One of the important parameters in the ANN design architecture is the number of hidden neurons. The process of determining the optimal number of neurons in the hidden layer has remained an open challenge in the ANN application literature (Bodgan, 2009). So far, two methods have been employed to handle this situation: continuation of the age-long trial-and-

error method (Petrus et al., 1995) and optimization techniques using evolutionary algorithms (Hassan et al., 2005; Maertens et al., 2006).

Each of these methods has its limitations and disadvantages. The trial-and-error method, on one hand, requires so much time and effort. Upon these, it still ends up getting caught in the local optima rather than the global. Since this method involves trying different numbers of hidden neurons consecutively and sometimes haphazardly, it is very easy to miss the global optima between two chosen points and settle down to a sub-optimal value. This method is usually and often affected by the "human factor" of getting tired after a few trials and settling down to the best of the set. However, this best of the set may not be the global best but simply the best among the tried possibilities.

The use of evolutionary algorithms to automatically optimize the number of hidden neurons, on the other hand, leads to high computational complexity, consumption of enormous computing memory resources and increased execution time. Since the evolutionary algorithms are based on exhaustive search heuristic algorithms, some of them have been reported to also end up in the local optima (Anifowose et al., 2013a; Bies et al., 2006; Gao, 2012). There is the need to look elsewhere for a solution. CI hybrid techniques have also been studied in the literature. However, like the ANN technique, hybrid models are only able to handle one hypothesis at a time, hence would not be an appropriate solution to this problem. In view of the limitations of these two conventional methods, we are proposing in this chapter a novel ensemble methodology that utilizes the power of unbiased random guesses in the assignment of the number of hidden neurons.

In our previous studies, we have proposed two ensemble solutions: one with the optimal number of hidden neurons determined by using a linear and sequential search within a range of 1 to 50 neurons (Anifowose et al., 2013b); and the other with the number of hidden neurons merely guessed using an unbiased randomized algorithm (Anifowose et al., 2013c). The two ensemble models comprised 10 instances of the base learners with different statistical distribution of the datasets leading to 10 hypotheses for each dataset. A set of newly proposed combination rules were used to determine and evolve the best hypothesis from the set of 10 hypotheses that represent the results of the base learners. The two respective ensemble models performed better than those of the conventional bagging method and the RandomForest technique. Though, the results were satisfactory but there were still rooms for improvement as some of the results showed that there could be possibilities for better performance by going beyond the maximum limit of 50 neurons in the search range.

In this chapter, we propose extensions of these two ensemble algorithms. The petroleum engineering case of reservoir characterization is used to test and evaluate the performance of the proposed ensemble models. There is no need to compare the proposed extensions with their bagging implementations and the RandomForest technique since the previous versions of the former have already outperformed the latter. The reservoir characterization process includes the prediction of various petroleum reservoir properties such as porosity and permeability for consequent population of full-field reservoir simulation models. The major motivation for proposing extensions of these algorithms is the continued quest for better predictive models in petroleum reservoir characterization. A marginal improvement in the prediction accuracies of reservoir properties has a huge potential impact on exploration, production and exploitation tasks leading to more efficient production of energy. Specifically, the major objectives of this study are:

- To increase the search space for the number of hidden neurons of the two proposed ensemble algorithms to 100. With this increased degree of freedom in the possible choice of the number of hidden neurons,

we hope that the models would identify more optimal values for the better performance of the ensemble models.

- To analyze the comparative performance of the proposed extension with their previous implementations.
- To recommend best practices in the implementation of ensemble models of ANN with randomized numbers of hidden neurons.

In order to achieve the above stated objectives, we give a rich and relevant background on petroleum reservoir characterization for the basic understanding of the average non-petroleum reader. We also present the basic concept of and the mathematical and statistical justifications for the ensemble machine learning. We give the generic algorithms of the ensemble methods and the progress made on its most recent applications in the petroleum industry with emphasis on reservoir characterization. We present a detailed research methodology featuring a description of the datasets used, the evaluation criteria, the ensemble combination rules, diversity checks and the implementation strategy. We analyze the results, give recommendations and draw relevant conclusion based on the results of the study.

Contribution to Knowledge and Consequences of Study

The main contributions of this chapter are:

- The novel introduction randomized algorithm in the determination of optimal number of hidden neurons of ANN.
- The innovative integration of the randomized algorithm with the ensemble learning modeling methodology.
- The successful application of the proposed ensemble methods in the prediction of the most important petroleum reservoir properties.

We hope this chapter will spur more interest in the readers for further studies in the integration of randomized algorithms in other identified parameters of ANN as well as in other CI techniques. We also hope that more studies on the application of ensemble learning in petroleum engineering with reveal better understanding of the applicability of the randomized algorithm as well as the application of other ensemble learning paradigms in this field. Further research successes in this regard will lead to more improvements in the prediction accuracy of reservoir properties produced by the models. Even a marginal improvement in predictive accuracies will have a multiplier effect on the performance of full-field reservoir simulation models for more effective exploration and production of energy.

BACKGROUND

Petroleum Reservoir Characterization

Petroleum reservoir characterization is the process of building a reservoir model that incorporates all the pertinent characteristics of the reservoir with respect to its ability to store and produce hydrocarbons. Reservoir characterization models are used to simulate the behavior of the reservoir fluids under different sets of subsurface conditions and to find the optimal techniques that will maximize their exploration and production (Schlumberger, 2013). It plays a crucial role in modern reservoir management as it maximizes the integration of static and dynamic data from different sources such as wireline, core, seismic and production logs in making sound reservoir decisions. It also maximizes the multidisciplinary synergistic collaboration among technical disciplines such as petroleum engineering, geology, geophysics, oil and gas production engineering, petrophysics, economics, and data management to improve the reliability of reservoir predictions. The ultimate goal of any reservoir characterization process is

"a reservoir model with realistic tolerance for imprecision and uncertainty" (Helmy et al., 2010, pp. 5353-5354).

The major objectives of petroleum reservoir characterization are to focus on modeling independent reservoir units, predicting well behavior, understanding past reservoir performance, and forecasting future reservoir conditions. The petroleum reservoir characterization process helps in the location of and quantification of the amount of hydrocarbons; and estimation of water salinity. Some of the properties of reservoirs that are of interest to petroleum engineers include the lithology, water saturation, wellbore stability, bed thickness, porosity, permeability, etc. Out of these, porosity and permeability are the most important as they are key indicators of reservoir quality and quantity.

Conventionally, the reservoir characterization process involves the acquisition of log data from the reservoirs of interest using various logging tools. Nowadays, a number of sophisticated tools, usually automated by sensors, have emerged and integrated into drilling and production processes. Some of the tools include Logging While Drilling (LWD), Sensing While Drilling (SWD) and Measurement While Drilling (MWD) (Schlumberger, 2013). Porosity is a measure of the percentage of pores in a rock sample. The higher this percentage is, the more its ability to hold hydrocarbons, water and gas. Permeability, on the other hand, is a measure of the interconnectivity of the individual pores in a rock sample. In most rock types, the porosity is directly related to permeability. However, in carbonate geological formations, such relationship is not always true (Jong-Se, 2005).

Porosity measurements are directly obtained in the laboratory from core samples brought from the field. It is expressed mathematically as (Amyx et al., 1960):

$$\varnothing = \frac{V_p}{V_B} \tag{1}$$

where ϕ = porosity, V_P = pore volume and V_B = bulk volume.

When calculated from density logs, porosity has been estimated using the following relations (Coates et al., 1997):

$$\varnothing_d = \frac{\rho_{ma} - \rho_b}{\rho_{ma} - \rho_f} \qquad (2)$$

where ϕ_d = density-derived porosity; ρ_{ma} = matrix density; ρ_b = bulk density; and ρ_f = fluid density.

From sonic log, porosity has been expressed as (Wyllie et al., 1956):

$$\varnothing_s = \frac{\Delta t - \Delta t_{ma}}{\Delta t_f - \Delta t_{ma}} \qquad (3)$$

where ϕ_s = sonic-derived porosity; Δt = transit time; Δt_f = fluid transit time; and Δt_{ma} = transit time for the rock matrix.

On the other hand, a number of equations have been derived for the estimation of permeability from laboratory-measured properties. Among the popular ones is the Darcy's equation (Shang et al., 2003):

$$k = \frac{q * \mu * L}{A - \Delta P} \qquad (4)$$

where k = permeability (Darcy); q = flow rate (cc/sec); μ = viscosity (cp); L = length (cm); A = cross-sectional area (cm^2); and ΔP = pressure difference (Atm).

Another popular equation derived for the calculation of permeability from other properties is the Kozeny-Carman equation (Kozeny, 1927; Carman, 1937) expressed as:

$$k = \frac{\varnothing^3}{F_s \tau^2 A_g^2 (1 - \varnothing)^2} \qquad (5)$$

where k = permeability (μm^2), ϕ = porosity (a fraction); F_s = shape factor; τ = tortuosity; and A_g = surface area per unit grain volume (μm^{-1}). The term, $F_s \tau^2$, is called the Kozeny constant.

From Equation (5), several extensions were derived. These include Wyllie and Rose (1950), Timur (1968), Coates and Denoo (1981) and Amaefule et al. (1993). We posit that all these equations can be expressed in linear terms. Lately, linear and multivariate regression tools were applied and found to outperform the derived equations. With the embrace of CI application in petroleum engineering, it has been argued that such natural phenomena as porosity and permeability cannot be adequately estimated by linear relations. However, with relevant data representing the dynamics of the subsurface, CI techniques have reportedly outperformed the statistical regression tools. Most recently, ensemble machine learning paradigm has been reported (Chen at al., 2004; Anifowose et al., 2013a, 2013b; Helmy et al., 2013) to have better generalization than individual CI techniques.

Due to the above premise, this chapter focuses on the prediction of porosity and permeability of heterogeneous petroleum reservoirs using the proposed ensemble algorithms.

Ensemble Machine Learning in Petroleum Reservoir Characterization

The capabilities of standard CI techniques are limited in that they are able to propose only one hypothesis to a problem at a time. However, ensemble machine learning techniques have the capability to combine the results of different base learners to solve a problem. The ensemble learning technique has been called different names such as mixture of experts (Masoudnia & Ebrahimpour, 2012; Xu & Amari, 2009; Yuksel et al., 2012), committee of machines (Bhatt, 2002; Chen & Lin, 2006; Sadeghi et al., 2011), committee of experts (Baruque & Corchado, 2010; Bastos, 2013), etc. This new learning paradigm is deeply rooted in human sociology where a mixture of various expert opinions is combined to evolve a final decision. Such a decision is often called an "ensemble" decision. It is said that the judgment of a committee is superior to those of individuals, provided the individuals have reasonable competence (Re & Valentini, 2010).

The ensemble learning paradigm is used to improve the performance of a model by selecting the best instance of individual expert decisions while reducing the risk of an unfortunate selection of a poor one (Polikar, 2006; Rokach, 2010). A generic regression algorithm for the ensemble methodology can be given as in Algorithm 1.

According to the algorithm, ensemble modeling starts with the creation of a desired number of base learners. No literature has recommended any specific number, hence, the choice is open. However, the rule-of-thumb is that the base learn-ers should be as much as need to ensure enough diversity. Each base learner is then given a different bootstrap sample of the data. Any other ensemble variable that can ensure diversity can be used. This may include using different learning algorithms, number of hidden neurons, activation functions, and other relevant model parameters. The results of each base learner were collected, combined with recommended combination algorithms and the ensemble solution is evolved.

The most popular conventional ensemble methods are the Bootstrap Aggregating (often abbreviated as Bagging) (Breiman, 1996) and Boosting (Ferreira & Figueiredo, 2012; Marzio & Taylor, 2012) for classification and regression tasks. The bagging method was implemented in RandomForest (Breiman, 2001; Lin & Jeon, 2002; Cutler et al., 2012), an ensemble model of many instances of Decision Tree technique, while the boosting was implemented in AdaBoost (Schapire, 2003), a shortened form of Adaptive Boosting. Bagging is a meta-algorithm that works by having each model in the ensemble contribute in the overall result with equal weight. To improve model variance, it trains each model in the ensemble using a randomly drawn subset of the

Algorithm 1. A Generic Regression Algorithm for Ensemble Learning Methodology

```
1.      Create a number of base learners, n, (with optimal learning param
        eters and diverse characteristics)
2.      For each base learner, B_i
3.            Takes a sampling of data for training or a training algo
              rithm or an activation function,                    etc.
4.            Use the testing set to generalize on previously unseen
              validation data.
5.            Generate decision, D_i
6.      Next i
7.      Combine all individual decisions:
```

$$\sum_{i=1}^{n} D_i$$

```
8.      Use appropriate algebraic algorithm to select the learner with the
        best performance.
```

training set (Lippert, 2013). On the other hand, boosting works by incrementally building an ensemble while training each new model instance to empower the previous misclassified models of the training instances.

A pertinent question to ask at this point is: how does ensemble modeling improve model variance? A succinct answer was given by Lippert (2013) who saw the ensemble learning paradigm as a tradeoff between bias and variance. Consider a regression problem with target values Y as the sum of some unknown deterministic function $f(X)$ mapping inputs X to the target values and some random noise (R) which corrupts the target values. It could be safely assumed that the noise is zero-mean since any bias would be incorporated into the deterministic function $f(X)$. This results in the mathematical expression:

$$Y = f\left(X\right) + R \qquad (6)$$

The variable R could be thought of as being randomness induced from not having perfect features or it could be a truly random source of corruption. A good approach is to estimate $f(X)$ by another function $g(X)$ using the training data. Consequently, this will cause the Mean Square Error (MSE) of the function $g(X)$ in predicting the original target Y to result in three terms: the irreducible error due to the variance in R (known as the Bayes Limit), the squared bias, and the variance as expressed in the following equation:

$$MSE = E\left[\left(Y - g\left(x\right)\right)^2\right] =$$
$$E\left[(f\left(X\right) + R - g * X))^2\right] = \qquad (7)$$
$$\sigma^2 + Bias(g(X))^2 + Var(g\left(X\right))$$

The bias is the average error of $g(X)$ in estimating $f(X)$ over all possible inputs. Since some of the errors will be positive and negative, the

MSE will balance out over the long run provided the model is unbiased. The variance indicates the statistical spread the errors have in estimating $f(X)$ with $g(X)$. This way, a larger variance would mean that the magnitudes of the errors are very large despite that they might average out to zero. It should be noted that bias and variance are measured with respect to the estimation of $f(X)$ and not Y since R is random and therefore truly unpredictable. Trading off between bias and variance is very similar to balancing between overfitting and underfitting (Hastie et al., 2009). Overfitting typically leads to a low bias, but a very high variance, while underfitting gives the opposite. When a model is optimized by tuning its parameters, we seek a balanced point between bias and variance that minimizes the prediction error in the overall estimation.

In an ensemble model, there are a relatively large number of models each with zero or near-zero bias. From the above discussion, the variance of the ensemble solution can be reduced by averaging the individual solutions provided the individual solutions have enough diversity. Intuitively, since each separate model gives a prediction that is somewhere near the right answer, then averaging the results should be a lot closer to the right answer than most of the individual models. This leads to a very important requirement in the ensemble scheme viz. diversity. This implies that each model in the ensemble has to give a different prediction. If each model gives the same prediction, then averaging the predictions would be of no benefit as it would reduce to the same prediction as a single model. The issue of diversity with respect to our work in this chapter will be further discussed in the Research Methodology section.

Since our work is on a regression problem, we focus on the bagging and RandomForest methods in this chapter. The algorithms for the bagging (Breiman, 1996) and RandomForest (Breiman, 2001) methods are shown in Algorithm 2 and 3 respectively.

Algorithm 2. The Bagging Method

1. Start model with all parameters set as optimal as possible.
2. Set N to the number of desired instances.
3. Set T to the desired percentage of data for bootstrapped training data.
4. Do for $n = 1$ to N
5.   Randomly extract T % of the data for training
6.   Use the training data to train the model, S_n
7.   Use the test data to predict the target variables
8.   Keep the result of the above as Hypothesis, H_n
9. Continue
10. Compute the average of all Hypotheses,
$$Hfinal\ (x)\ =\ \arg_n^{max}\ \mu_j\left(x\right)$$

     using the Mean() rule:

$$\mu_j\left(x\right) = \frac{1}{n}\sum\sum_1^n H_n(x)$$

Algorithm 3. RandomForest Technique

1. Starting with a tree:
   a. Set N = number of training cases.
   b. Set M = number of features.
   c. Select a subset m of input variables such that m << M.
   d. Do for n = 1 to N
          i. Train this tree with a bootstrap sample of the training data.
          ii. Use the rest of the cases to estimate the prediction error of
              the tree.
          iii. Replace the bootstrap sample.
       Continue
   e. Calculate the best split based on these m variables in the training set.
2. The above procedure is iterated over all trees in the ensemble.
3. Calculate the mean of the performance of all trees. This represents the
   performance of the Random Forest technique.

Both algorithms start in the same way as discussed with Algorithm 1. However, the bagging method (Algorithm 2) uses the bootstrap sampling of the data as its main algorithmic focus. It also uses the averaging of the results of the base learners as another distinguishing factor in its procedure. Both the bootstrap sampling and the averaging combination methods are the main procedures that differentiate it from other methods. Algorithm 3, on the other hand, applies only to Decision Trees. It combines the bootstrap sampling with a random selection of input variables to differentiate itself from other methods and techniques. Similar to the bagging method, it uses the averaging method to combine the results of the base learners and evolve the ensemble solution.

The performance of the ensemble learning is statistically justified as the uncorrelated errors of individual classifiers can be eliminated by averaging (Dietterich, 2000). Since the probability of getting *r* incorrect votes is a binomial distribution, the risk of taking a wrong ensemble decision is very low. More details of the ensemble learning paradigm can be found in Polikar (2006, 2009) and Zhou (2009). In addition to the aforementioned, very detailed tutorials of various ensemble methods can be found in Baruque & Corchado (2010); Masoudnia & Ebrahimpour (2012) and Yuksel et al. (2012).

The ensemble learning methodology has found a good number of applications in diverse fields. It has mostly been applied in the bio-informatics (Peng, 2006; Chen & Zhao, 2008; Helmy et al., 2012) and in most classification and regression tasks such as predictions of recovery rates (Bastos, 2013), describing robot arm kinematics (Bishop & Svens´en, 2003) and medicine (Johansson et al., 2009). These applications featured ensemble models of techniques like regression tree, Bayesian network, and neural networks respectively. Applications of the ensemble learning concept in the petroleum field are very few. Among the available ones are Bhatt (2002); Chen & Lin (2006); Sadeghi et al. (2011); and Helmy et al. (2013) featuring individual techniques comprising neural networks, empirical formulae, Support Vector Machines, neural networks and Adaptive Neuro-Fuzzy Inference System, and neuro-fuzzy technique respectively.

What differentiates our work from those of the few existing studies? Bhatt (2002) and Helmy et al. (2013) used the bagging approach with their ensemble models trained using different bootstrap samples of the available data. Chen & Lin (2006) is an ensemble model of three empirical formulas that are popularly used in the petroleum engineering field. The three formulas were fed on the same dataset. The three used the same averaging combination strategy to evolve their ensemble solutions. Sadeghi et al. (2011) integrated empirical formulas, multiple regression and neuro-fuzzy in a committee machine such that the base learners were fed on the same dataset while using a genetic algorithm to combine the results. Our work comprises ensemble models of ANN with different numbers of hidden neurons that are obtained from a search space of 1 to 100 using linear search and randomized selection strategies. Hence, our work stands out clearly from those of others.

RESEARCH METHODOLOGY

Description of Datasets and Criteria for Model Evaluation

Since this study is an extension of existing ones and for the purpose of fair comparison among results, the same datasets used in Anifowose et al. (2013b; 2013c) were continued in this study. The design, testing and validation of our proposed ensemble models were based on three porosity and three permeability datasets. The porosity datasets were obtained from a petroleum reservoir in the Northern Marion Platform of North America (Site 1) while the permeability datasets were obtained from a reservoir in the Middle East (Site 2). The datasets from Site 1 have six predictor variables for porosity, while the datasets from Site 2 have eight predictor variables for permeability. These are shown in Table 1 and 2. The datasets were chosen to be of various sizes. This is another way to test the capability of the proposed model to handle datasets of varying sizes as part of our model validation and to increase the confidence in the result of our study.

Following the standard machine learning approach to modeling, each of the datasets was divided into training and testing subsets in the 70:30 ratio using a stratified sampling method as used

Table 1. Predictor variable for porosity

Predictors for Porosity
1. Core
2. Top Interval
3. Grain Density
4. Grain Volume
5. Length
6. Diameter

Table 2. Predictor variable for permeability

Predictors for Permeability	
1.	Gamma Ray Log
2.	Porosity Log
3.	Density Log
4.	Water Saturation
5.	Deep Resistivity
6.	Micro-spherically Focused Log
7.	Neutron Porosity Log
8.	Caliper Log
9.	Magnetic Resonance Log
10.	Induction Log
11.	Electrical Log
12.	Conductivity

in our previous studies. This method randomly selects a certain percentage of the entire data for training while ensuring that each data sample has equal chance of being selected. The remaining percentage was then used for testing. This way, the selection of the training and testing subsets was unbiased. A snapshot of this stratification result is shown in Table 3.

Criteria for Model Evaluation and Ensemble Combination Rules

Similar to the datasets and for the purpose of fair comparison among results, the same criteria used in the previous studies were used to evaluate the performance of our proposed ensemble models viz. correlation coefficient (R-Square), root mean-squared error (RMSE) and mean absolute error (MAE). The R-Square measures the statistical correlation between the predicted and actual values. It is expressed as:

$$R - \text{Square} = \frac{n\sum xy - \left(\sum x\right)\left(\sum y\right)}{\sqrt{n\left(\sum x^2\right) - \left(\sum x\right)^2}\sqrt{n\left(\sum y^2\right) - \left(\sum y\right)^2}}$$

(8)

The RMSE is a measure of the spread of the actual x values around the average of the predicted y values. It computes the average of the squared differences between each predicted value and its corresponding actual value. It is expressed as:

Table 3. Division of datasets into training and testing

	Site 1 (Porosity)			Site 2 (Permeability)		
Wells	1	2	3	1	2	3
Data Size	415	285	23	355	477	387
Training (70%)	291	200	16	249	334	271
Testing (30%)	124	85	7	106	143	116

$$RMSE = \sqrt{\frac{\sum_{i=1}^{n}(x_i - y_i)^2}{n}} \qquad (9)$$

The MAE is a statistical measure of dispersion. It is computed by taking the average of the absolute errors of the predicted y values relative to the actual x values. It is given by:

$$MAE = \frac{1}{n}\sum_{i=1}^{n}|x_i - y_i| \qquad (10)$$

After applying the above criteria on the individual base learners, we then used the Max(R-Square), Min(RMSE) and Min(MAE) rules to obtain the overall performance of our proposed ensemble model. We further introduced two policies to guide the judgments of these rules in cases of non-consensus: majority and preference. The majority policy is applied when the R-Square and one of the error criteria agree on a single representative learner while the preference policy is applied when there is no consensus in the choice of the representative learner among the three criteria. In the latter case, we gave more weight to the R-Square due to its ease of interpretation, common use in literature and for effective comparison across the three ensemble models implemented in this study. The following section discusses the justification for preferring the Max/Min rule to the conventional averaging in the bagging method.

Justification for the Max/ Min Combination

As mentioned earlier, some ensemble based techniques use the simple averaging and sometimes a weighted averaging combination rules (Hoeting et al., 1999) while the RandomForest technique for classification uses the mode or majority vote rule and its variants (Polikar, 2009). What about simply selecting the best among individual so-

lutions (SelectBest) as the ensemble solution? A similar question: "Is Combining Classifiers Better than Selecting the Best One?" was posed by Džeroski and Zenko (2004). They evaluated several state-of-the-art methods for constructing ensembles of heterogeneous classifiers with stacking. They however concluded that they (ensemble models combined by stacking) perform (at best) comparably to selecting the best classifier from the ensemble by cross validation. This is definitely a positive point in favor of the Max/Min combination method rather than being negative. In addition to this, it has been shown that the averaging method, though theoretically correct, "has an expected error that is bounded to be at most twice the expected error" of the SelectBest classifiers (Haussler et al., 1994). Domingos (2000) also posited that the averaging method has a tendency to promote overfitting, and does not perform as well empirically as other ensemble techniques. Averaging may have an excellent smoothening effect in the signal processing field, statistically, the average is not better than the maximum value.

In view of this, we posit that since the SelectBest combination method looks for the best among the available individual solutions to evolve the ensemble solution, it is perfectly in line with the persistent quest in the petroleum engineering and reservoir characterization fields for the best results for more efficient exploration, production and exploitation of the world energy resources.

Model Implementation and Diversity Checks

Model diversity is a major requirement for a successful ensemble solution. It has been empirically shown that ensembles tend to yield better results when there is a significant diversity among the models (Kuncheva & Whitaker, 2003; Minku et al., 2010; Tsymbal et al., 2005). Among the various ways of creating diversity in an ensemble model (Brown et al., 2005; Wang & Yao, 2013) is to take bootstrap samples of the training dataset. This we did in our proposed algorithms (Algorithms 4 and 5) as we ensured that each base learner in our ensemble models has a different bootstrap sample of the data for training. In order to demonstrate the existence of the required diversity in our work, we have used two of the measures of ensemble diversity proposed by Dutta (2009) viz. Diversity Correlation Coefficient (DCC) and Mutual Information Entropy (MIE). The mathematical details of these diversity measures are available in our previous studies (Anifowose et al., 2013a; 2013b). Basically, we require that the DCC be very low (< 0.50 preferred) while the MIE should be as close to zero as possible.

The existence of diversity in our proposed models was checked in two stages viz. pre- *in situ* (or intra-implementation) and post-implementation. The pre-implementation relates to the diversity associated with the assignment of the number hidden neurons before implementation while the post-implementation relates to the diversity associated with the predicted target values after implementation. The results of all these are presented in the next section.

While the proposed models were implemented according to Algorithms 4 and 5 respectively, the other optimized parameters used in the ensemble models apart from the number of hidden neurons are as follows:

- Number of input neurons for porosity = 6
- Number of input neurons for permeability = 8
- Number of layers = 2
- Number of training epochs = 100
- Training algorithm = *trainlm* (Levenberg–Marquardt)
- Activation function at the summation layer = sigmoid
- Activation function at the output layer = linear

For referencing convenience, we adopt the following acronyms for all the four ensemble models that are analyzed and compared in this study:

- Previous1 - The ensemble model of ANN with optimal number of hidden neurons extracted from searches between 1 and 50.
- Previous2 - The ensemble model of ANN with numbers of hidden neurons randomly selected between 1 and 50.
- Proposed1 - An extension Previous1.
- Proposed2 - An extension Previous2.

Algorithm 4 was implemented on six datasets. Each ensemble model has 10 base learners. It used the stratified sampling approach to divide each dataset into training and testing subsets. A linear search was conducted for the number of hidden neurons from 1 to 100. For each round, the training subset was used to train the base learner and the testing set was used to predict the output. The results of both were used to evaluate the performance of each base learner in order to determine the learner than performed best. That would correspond to the number of hidden neurons used to produce such output. This is repeated for each dataset. The optimal sets of model from each dataset is evaluated to evolve the ensemble solution.

Algorithm 5 was similarly implemented on six datasets with 10 base learners in each ensemble model. The only difference here is using a randomized algorithm to guess the number of hidden neuron for each base learner. For each dataset, the optimal sets of learners is evaluated to evolve the ensemble solution.

Results, Discussion and Recommendations

Starting with the diversity checks, we introduced three levels: pre-implementation, *in situ* and post-implementation. The pre-implementation diversity check was carried out before the implementation of the ensemble models. This happened during the pre-processing step of selecting and assigning the number of hidden neurons. We called the diversity check that was carried out during the implementation of the models *in situ*-implementation checks.

Algorithm 4. Linear and sequential search for optimal hidden neurons

```
1.  Start with the other relevant optimized parameters
2.  Do for k = 1 to 6 //there are 6 datasets
3.          Do for n = 1 to 10 //there are 10 instances of ANN
4.                  Randomly divide data into training and testing
5.                  Do for m = 1 to 100 //try different number of neurons
6.                          Use the training data to train the base
                            learner, Sₙ
7.                          Use the testing data to predict the target
8.                          Update result of each run, m
9.                  Continue// try next m
10.             Select the best of the m values
11.         Continue // pick next base learner
12.         Keep the result of the above as Hypothesis, Hₙ
```

13.   Compute the best performance of all hypotheses, $H_{final}(x) = arg_n^{max} \mu_j(x)$

14.   By using the decision rules as follows:

$$\text{a. Mean rule: } \mu_j\left(x\right) = \frac{1}{n}\sum\sum_1^n H_n(x)$$

$$\text{b. Maximum rule: } \mu_j\left(x\right) = \max_{i=1,\ldots,n} H_n(x)$$

$$\text{c. Minimum rule: } \mu_j\left(x\right) = \min_{i=1,\ldots,n} H_n(x)$$

```
15. Continue  // Repeat for the next dataset
```

Algorithm 5. Randomized assignment of hidden neurons

```
1.      Start with the other relevant optimized parameters
2.      For k = 1 to 6 //there are 6 datasets
3.          For n = 1 to 10 //10 base learners
4.              Divide data into training and testing
5.              Number of hidden neurons = Rand(1:100)
6.              Train the model Sₙ with training data
7.              Test the model Sₙ with testing data
8.              Keep result as Hypothesis, Hₙ
9.          Next n
10.     Compute the best of all hypotheses:
```

$$H_{final}(x) = \arg_n^{max} \mu_j(x)$$

```
11. Next k //Repeat for the next dataset
```

The diversity that occurred in the results of the implemented models was called post-implementation checks. The results of the pre-, *in situ-* and post-implementation diversity checks for the two proposed models are shown in Figure 1 to 6. The comparative results of the proposed models with respect to the previous ones are shown in Figure 7 to 9 respectively in terms of correlation coefficient

Figure 1. Pre-implementation diversity check results for Proposed1 model

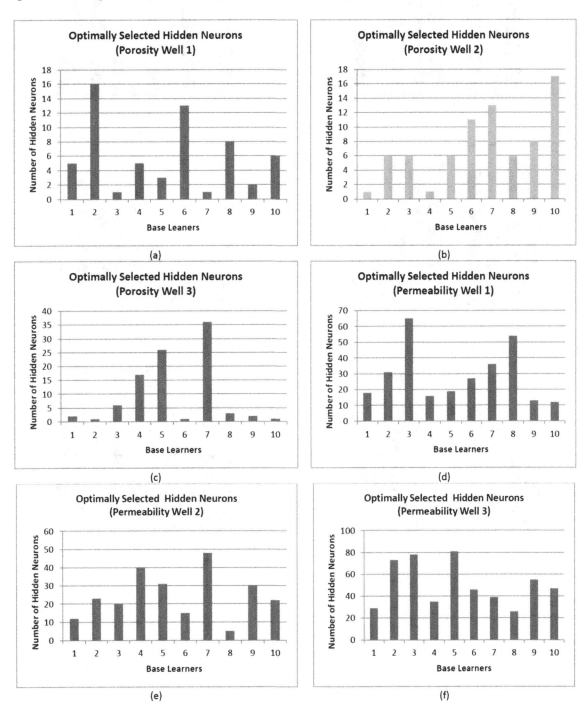

Figure 2. Pre-implementation diversity check results for Proposed2 model

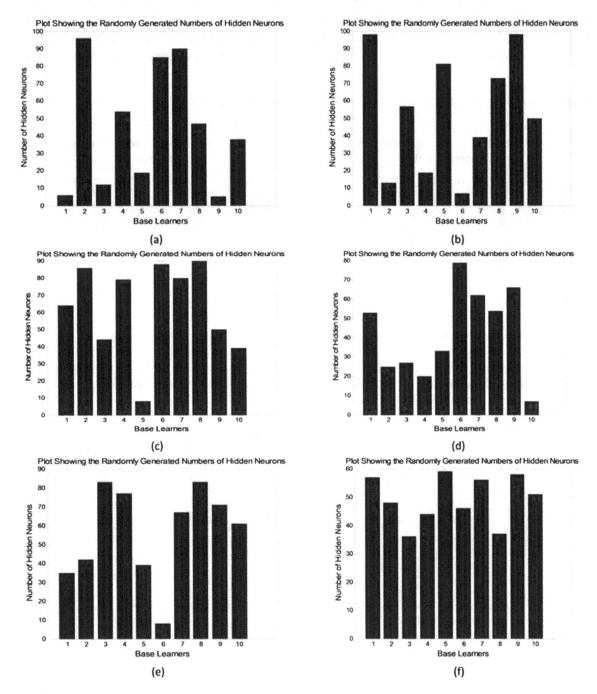

Figure 3. In situ-implementation diversity check results for Proposed1 model

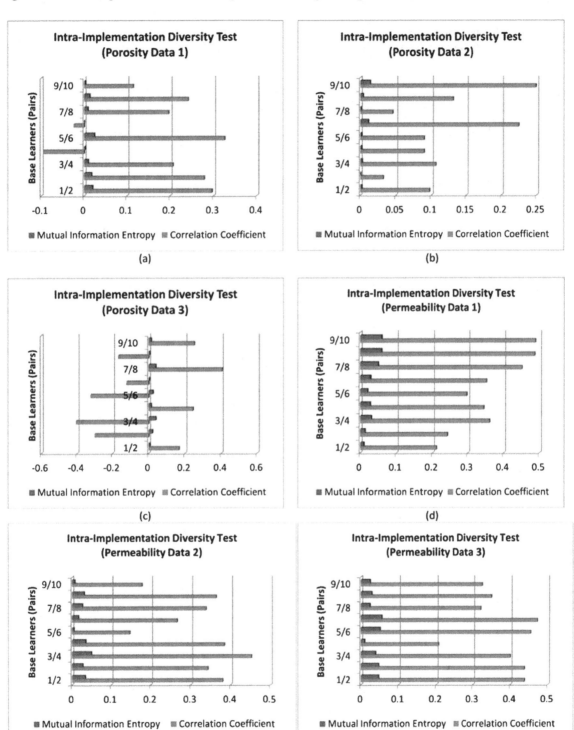

Figure 4. In situ -implementation diversity check results for Proposed2 model

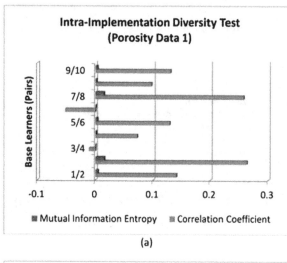

(a)

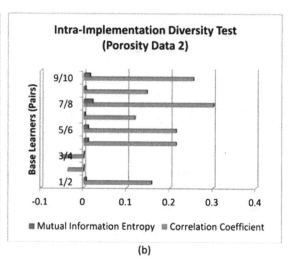

(b)

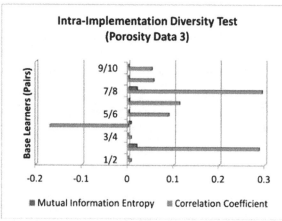

(c)

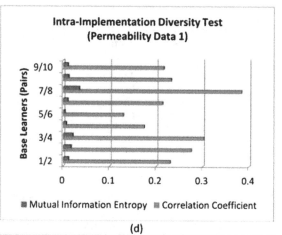

(d)

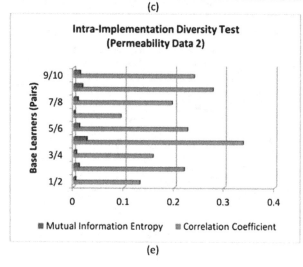

(e)

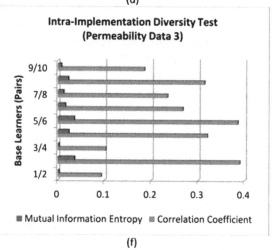

(f)

Figure 5. Post-implementation diversity check results for Proposed1 model

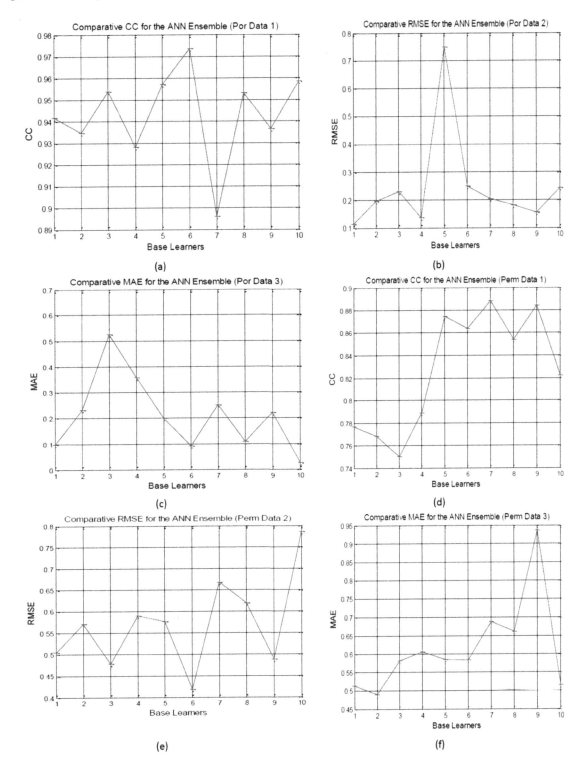

Figure 6. Post-implementation diversity check results for Proposed2 model

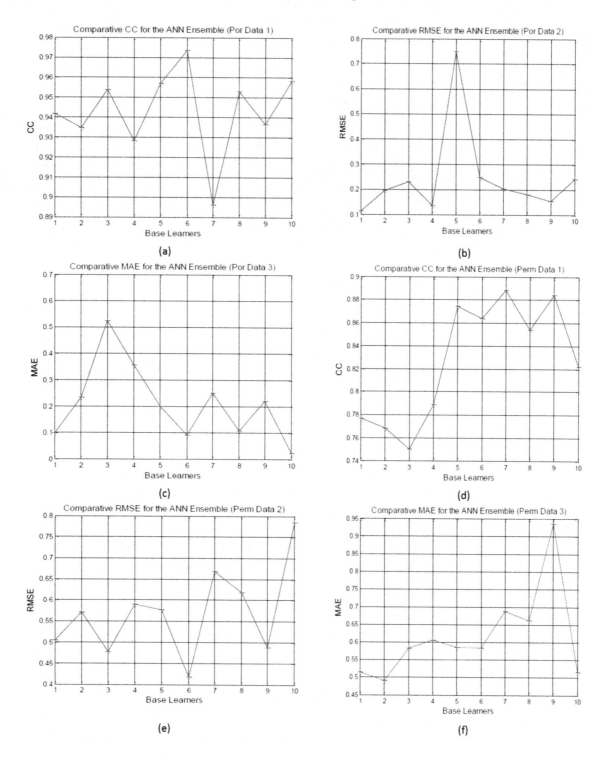

(CC), root mean square error (RMSE) and mean absolute error (MAE). Some of the comparative performances of the exhaustively searched and randomly guessed numbers of hidden neurons are shown in Figure 10.

Figure 1 and 2 showed the results of the pre-implementation diversity check of the respective proposed models indicating that there is a lot of diversity in the optimally selected number of hidden neurons for the Proposed1 model (Figure 1) and the randomly assigned numbers for the Proposed2 model (Figure 2). In both cases, the number of hidden neurons assigned to each base learner is rather scattered and irregular than being serial and regular. Figure 3 and 4 showed the results of the *in situ*-implementation diversity checks indicating that the required values of DCC and MIE are satisfactorily met for the Proposed1 model (Figure 3) and the Proposed2 model (Figure 4). In both cases, the values of DCC are mostly less than 0.5 while those of MIE are mostly below 0.1. Following the same trend, the results of the

post-implementation diversity checks concerning the diversity of the results obtained from the implemented models are shown in Figure 5 and 6. Similarly, the performances of the base learners were diverse in terms of CC, RMSE and MAE on all porosity and permeability datasets for both the Proposed1 (Figure 5) and Proposed2 (Figure 6) models. The haphazard and irregular patterns obtained from these evaluation criteria are indications of the high diversity in the performances of the base learners. We described the diversity check results in Figure 1, 2, 5 and 6 as purely graphical checks while those presented in Figure 3 and 4 are the graphical representations of the numerical checks previously discussed in the DCC and MIE criteria.

Comparing the two proposed models with their previous versions, Figure 7 shows a very competitive performance among all models and for all the datasets. The respective models outperformed each other on different datasets. However, the error measures offer a clearer picture on the

Figure 7. Correlation coefficient comparison for all models

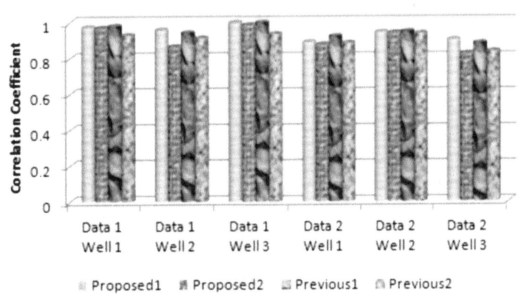

Figure 8. Root mean square error comparison for all models

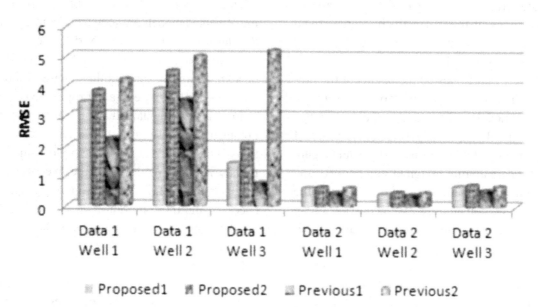

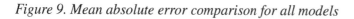

Figure 9. Mean absolute error comparison for all models

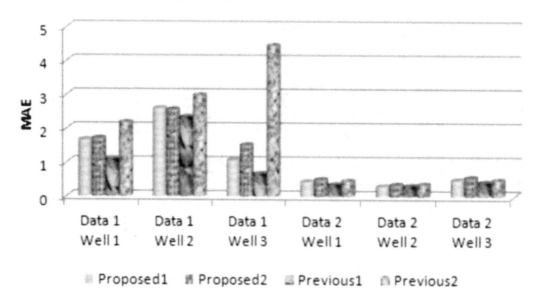

Figure 10. Examples of hidden neuron search (a) with no improvement and (b) with improvement; beyond 50

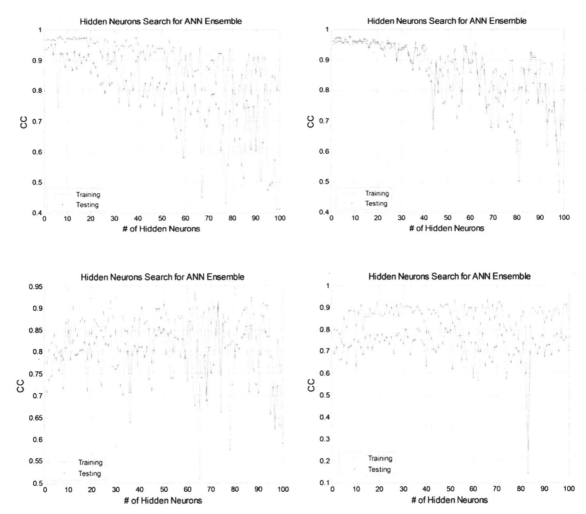

competitive edges displayed by some of the models over the others. Considering the RMSE criterion, Figure 6 showed that for most of the porosity and permeability datasets, Previous1 had less RMSE than Proposed1 while Proposed2 has less error than Previous2. However, the differences are more apparent for the porosity datasets than those of permeability. Figure 8 also agrees with the RMSE comparative results as it showed that the mean absolute errors of Previous1 are less than those of Proposed1 while Proposed2 has lower error

values than those of Previous2 for all porosity and permeability datasets.

Despite that extending the search space for the selection of optimal numbers of hidden neurons to 100 yielded some optimal points well above the previously fixed 50 as shown in Figure 1(d) (base learners 3 and 8 with 65 and 54 neurons respectively) and Figure 1(f) (base learners 2, 3, 5 and 9 with 73, 78, 81 and 55 neurons respectively), that did not improve the overall performance of the Proposed1 over Previous1. This may seem to appear that there is perfect agreement with the recommendation of Demuth et al. (2009) that most non-linear problems can be solved with no more than 50 hidden neurons, hence extending the search space beyond 50 adds no value to the overall performance of the Proposed1 model. However, there is a marked improvement in the performance of Proposed2 over Previous2 as a result of the extension of the randomized search space from 50 to 100.

What is the explanation for this seeming anomaly? We argue that, in reality, going beyond 50 in the search for the optimal numbers of hidden neurons should add more value to the overall accuracy of the prediction systems as shown in the improved results of Proposed2 (Figure 8 and 9). However, the occurrences of optimality beyond 50 are very few (only six out of the entire 60 chances) in the case of the Proposed1 model compared to 34 occurrences (five in Figure 2(a), six in Figure 2(b), seven in Figure 2(c), five in Figure 2(d), six in Figure 2(e) and five in Figure 2(f)) of random choices of the numbers of hidden neurons beyond 50 in the case of Proposed2. Therefore, the more occurrences of hidden neuron assignments beyond 50 in Proposed2 added more value to the overall prediction system. During the implementation of Proposed1 model, while we found that there were no better choices of optimal hidden neurons beyond 50 with some datasets (Figure 10a), it was interesting that we found with yet other datasets points where there were really better choices (Figure 10b).

Another factor that worked in favor of the Proposed2 model is the role of the randomized algorithm in the increased search space. Randomized algorithms have been reported to offer excellent performance due to their fairness in many applications (Arora & Barak, 2009; Bovet & Crescenzi, 2006; Cormen et al, 2001). This algorithm further worked for Propsoed2 as the ensemble paradigm has been reported to work best for unstable systems (Cunningham & Zenobi, 2001). ANN has been noted as one of the computational intelligence techniques that are very unstable (Kostrykin & Oleynik, 2013; Petrus et al., 1995; Stergiou, 2013). Hence, the optimal numbers of hidden neurons discovered in Proposed1 may not have performed optimally when used in the model in a new run of the program. We hereby posit and recommend that contrary to the recommendation of Demuth et al. (2009), using a fair and unbiased randomized algorithm to "guess" and assign the number of hidden neurons beyond 50 in an ANN ensemble model leads to improved overall prediction performance. This position is perfectly in agreement with Huang & Babri (1998) who postulated that ANN with at most N neurons is enough to train N samples.

FUTURE RESEARCH DIRECTIONS

Despite the discovery in this study that the randomized method of assigning the number of hidden neurons is capable of addressing and solving the challenge of determining the number of hidden neurons in ANN, we are further motivated to confirm the consistency of this discovery with other reservoir properties and more diversified datasets. In view of this, more studies will be conducted with the prediction of water saturation, oil viscosity, formation volume factor, bubble point pressure, solution gas-oil ratio, oil gravity and gas specific gravity. All these are important properties of oil and gas reservoirs after porosity and permeability. The consistency and agreement of the results with this study will further establish the randomized method of parameter assignment in machine learning applications especially in petroleum engineering.

Beyond the assignment of the number of hidden neurons, the randomized method can be extended to the selection of learning algorithms and number of layers, and initialization of weights and biases of ANN. Due to the reported instability of ANN and the excellent handling of this phenomenon by our proposed randomized algorithm with increased search space, we are determined to extend our research beyond ANN by considering other techniques with similar behavior as ANN. The following are few of the possibilities that can be considered:

- Selection of the radius of influence in Generalized Regression Neural Networks.
- Selection of the number of hidden neurons in Extreme Learning Machines.
- Selection of the regularization parameter of Support Vector Machines.
- Selection of the minimum tree splits in Decision Trees.

Our immediate focus will be on Decision Trees which has been reported to be similarly unstable and hence prone to the problem of overfitting (Cunningham & Zenobi, 2001; Mitchell, 1997). The same randomized algorithm will be applied to other even stable techniques such as Support vector Machines that require numeric parameters to be set for optimality.

CONCLUSION

We have presented a study comparing two ensemble models of ANN with their previously published versions. The new versions investigated the effect of increasing the search space for the determination of the optimal number of hidden neurons using linear search for optimality and using a randomized algorithm for the selection. The proposed models were implemented using six porosity and permeability datasets from heterogeneous petroleum reservoirs. The required diversity was checked at three stages of the implementation namely pre-implementation, *in situ*- and post-implementation. All the checks showed that the selection and assignment of the number of hidden neurons, the correlation and mutual entropy

of the base learners and the performance of the base learners after the implementation all met the diversity requirement.

The results of the implemented models were then evaluated using standard evaluation criteria. The comparative results showed that there was no improvement when very few assignments of the number of hidden neurons beyond 50 were made. However, a marked performance improvement was recorded with many occurrences of randomly "guessed" numbers of hidden neurons beyond 50. This puts a question on the recommendation of Demuth et al. (2009) and confirms the postulation of Huang & Babri (1998) with respect to the limit on the number of hidden neurons for the excellent performance of ANN. The conclusions reached in this study can be presented as follows:

- In as much as the recommendation of Demuth et al. (2009) may hold in some cases, we found that it may not hold in all cases. Hence, it should be followed with caution.
- Given the instability of ANN, searching exhaustively for the optimal number of hidden neurons may not solve the optimality problem.
- Rather than searching exhaustively, using unbiased random guess in an ensemble model is a better approach to solve the ANN's optimality problem.
- Proper care should be taken to get as much of the random guesses as possible beyond 50 in order to get the optimal performance required of ANN.

This study has recommended that using a fair randomized algorithm to "guess" and assign the number of hidden neurons beyond 50 in an ANN ensemble model leads to improved overall prediction performance.

ACKNOWLEDGMENT

One of the authors would like to acknowledge the support provided by King Abdulaziz City for Science and Technology through the Science & Technology Unit at King Fahd University of Petroleum & Minerals for funding this work under Project No. 11-OIL2144-04 as part of the National Science, Technology and Innovation Plan.

REFERENCES

Amaefule, J. O., Altunbay, M., Tiab, D., Kersey, D. G., & Keelan, D. K. (1993). Enhanced reservoir description: using core and log data to identify hydraulic (flow) units and predict permeability in uncored intervals/wells. In *Proceedings of the SPE 68th Annual Technical Conference and Exhibition.* Houston, TX: SPE/Onepetro Database.

Amyx, J. W., Bass, D. M. Jr, & Whiting, R. L. (1960). *Petroleum Reservoir Engineering, Physical Properties.* New York: McGraw-Hill.

Anifowose, F., Labadin, J., & Abdulraheem, A. (2013a). A least square-driven functional networks type-2 fuzzy logic hybrid model for efficient petroleum reservoir properties prediction. *Neural Computing & Applications.* doi:10.1007/s00521-012-1298-2

Anifowose, F., Labadin, J., & Abdulraheem, A. (2013b). Ensemble learning model for petroleum reservoir characterization: A case of feed-forward back-propagation neural networks. In J. Li, et al. (Eds.), *International Workshop on Data Mining Applications in Industry and Government under the 17th Pacific-Asia Conference on Knowledge Discovery and Data Mining, Gold Trends and Applications in Knowledge Discovery and Data Mining* (LNCS), (vol. 7867, pp. 71-82). Berlin: Springer.

Anifowose, F., Labadin, J., & Abdulraheem, A. (2013c). Ensemble Model of artificial neural networks with randomized number of hidden neurons. In *Proceedings of the 8th International Conference on Information Technology in Asia* (pp. 1-5). Kuching, Malaysia: IEEEXplore.

Arora, S., & Barak, B. (2009). *Computational complexity: a modern approach.* New York: Cambridge University Press. doi:10.1017/CBO9780511804090

Baruque, B., & Corchado, E. (2010). The committee of experts approach: ensemble learning. In *Fusion Method for Unsupervised Learning Ensembles* (pp. 31–47). Springer-Verlag. doi:10.1007/978-3-642-16205-3_3

Bastos, J. A. (2013). Ensemble predictions of recovery rates. *Journal of Financial Services Research*, 1–17.

Bhatt, A. (2002). *Reservoir properties from well logs using neural networks.* (Unpublished doctoral dissertation). Norwegian University of Science and Technology.

Bies, R. R., Muldoon, M. F., Pollock, B. G., Manuck, S., Smith, G., & Sale, M. E. (2006). A genetic algorithm-based, hybrid machine learning approach to model selection. *Journal of Pharmacokinetics and Pharmacodynamics*, *33*(2), 195–221. doi:10.1007/s10928-006-9004-6 PMID:16565924

Bishop, C. H., & Svens'en, M. (2003). Bayesian hierarchical mixtures of experts. In *Uncertainty in Artificial Intelligence: Proceedings of the Nineteenth Conference* (pp. 57-64). Morgan Kaufmann.

Bogdan, M. W. (2009). Neural network architecture and learning algorithms: how not to be frustrated with neural networks. *IEEE Industrial Electronics Magazine*, *3*(4), 56–63. doi:10.1109/MIE.2009.934790

Bovet, D. P., & Crescenzi, P. (2006). *Introduction to the theory of complexity*. San Francisco, CA: Prentice Hall.

Breiman, L. (1996). Bagging predictors. *Machine Learning, 24*(2), 123–140. doi:10.1007/BF00058655

Breiman, L. (2001). Random forests. *Machine Learning, 45*(1), 5–32. doi:10.1023/A:1010933404324

Brown, G., Wyatt, J., Harris, R., & Yao, X. (2005). Diversity creation methods: a survey and categorization. *Information Fusion, 6*(1), 5–20. doi:10.1016/j.inffus.2004.04.004

Carman, P. C. (1937). Fluid flow through a granular bed. *Transactions of the Institution of Chemical Engineers, 15*, 150–156.

Chen, C. H., & Lin, Z. S. (2006). A committee machine with empirical formulas for permeability prediction. *Computers & Geosciences, 32*(4), 485–496. doi:10.1016/j.cageo.2005.08.003

Chen, D., Quirein, J., Hamid, S., Smith, H., & Grable, J. (2004). Neural network ensemble selection using multiobjective genetic algorithm in processing pulsed neutron data. In *Proceedings of the 45th Annual Logging Symposium*. Noordwijk, The Netherlands: SPE/Onepetro database.

Chen, Y., & Zhao, Y. (2008). A novel ensemble of classifiers for microarray data classification. *Applied Soft Computing, 8*, 1664–1669. doi:10.1016/j.asoc.2008.01.006

Coates, G., & Denoo, S. (1981). The producibility answer product. *Technology Review, 29*(2), 55–63.

Coates, G. R., Menger, S., Prammer, M., & Miller, D. (1997). Applying NMR Total and Effective Porosity to Formation Evaluation. In *Proceedings of the 1997 SPE Annual Technical Conference and Exhibition*. San Antonio, TX: SPE/Onepetro database.

Cormen, T. H., Leiserson, C. E., Rivest, R. L., & Stein, C. S. (2001). *Introduction to algorithms*. Cambridge, MA: The MIT Press.

Cunningham, P., & Zenobi, G. (2001). Case representation issues for case-based reasoning from ensemble research. In Case-Based Reasoning Research and Development (LNCS), (vol. 2080, pp. 146-157). Springer.

Cutler, A., Cutler, D. R., & Stevens, J. R. (2012). Random forests. In C. Zhang, & Y. Ma (Eds.), *Ensemble Machine Learning* (pp. 157–175). Springer. doi:10.1007/978-1-4419-9326-7_5

Demuth, H., Beale, M., & Hagan, M. (2009). *Neural Network Toolbox™ 6 User's Guide*. New York: The MathWorks Inc.

Dietterich, T. G. (2000). Ensemble methods in machine learning. In *International Workshop on Multiple Classifier Systems* (LNCS), (vol. 1857, pp. 1-15). Springer-Verlag. DOI: 10.1007/s10693-013-0165-3

Domingos, P. (2000). Bayesian averaging of classifiers and the overfitting problem. In *Proceedings of the 17th International Conference on Machine Learning (ICML)* (pp. 223—230). San Francisco, CA: Morgan Kaufmann.

Dutta, H. (2009). Measuring diversity in regression ensembles. In B. Prasad, P. Lingras, & A. Ram (Eds.), *Proceedings of the 4th Indian International Conference on Artificial Intelligence* (pp. 2220-2236). New York: IICAI.

Džeroski, S., & Zenko, Z. (2004). Is Combining classifiers better than selecting the best one? *Machine Learning, 54*(3), 255–273. doi:10.1023/B:MACH.0000015881.36452.6e

El-Sebakhy, E. A., Asparouhov, O., Abdulraheem, A., Al-Majed, A., Wu, D., Latinski, K., & Raharja, I. (2012). Functional networks as a new data mining predictive paradigm to predict permeability in a carbonate reservoir. *Expert Systems with Applications, 39*(12), 10359–10375. doi:10.1016/j.eswa.2012.01.157

Eskandari, H., Rezaee, M.R., & Mohammadnia, M. (2004). Application of multiple regression and artificial neural network techniques to predict shear wave velocity from wireline log data for a carbonate reservoir, South-West Iran. *CSEG Recorder, 42 - 48.*

Ferreira, A. J., & Figueiredo, M. A. T. (2012). Boosting algorithms: a review of methods, theory, and applications. In C. Zhang, & Y. Ma (Eds.), Ensemble Machine Learning (pp. 35-85). Springer Science+Business Media.

Gao, W. (2012). Study on new improved hybrid genetic algorithm. In D. Zeng (Ed.), *Advances in Information Technology and Industry Applications (LNEE)* (Vol. 136, pp. 505–512). SpringerLink. doi:10.1007/978-3-642-26001-8_66

Hassan, R., Cohanim, B., De Weck, O., & Venter, G. (2005). A comparison of particle swarm optimization and the genetic algorithm. In *Proceedings of 46th AIAA/ASME/ASCE/AHS/ASC Structures, Structural Dynamics, and Materials Conference* (pp. 1-13). Austin, TX: AIAA.

Hastie, T., Tibshirani, R., & Friedman, J. (2009). *The elements of statistical learning: data mining, inference, and prediction* (2nd ed.). Springer-Verlag. doi:10.1007/978-0-387-84858-7

Haussler, D., Kearns, M., & Schapire, R. E. (1994). Bounds on the sample complexity of Bayesian learning using information theory and the VC dimension. *Machine Learning, 14,* 83–113. doi:10.1007/BF00993163

Helmy, T., Al-Harthi, M. A., & Faheem, M. T. (2012). Adaptive ensemble and hybrid models for classification of bioinformatics datasets. *Transaction on Fuzzy. Neural Network and Bioinformatics: Global Journal of Technology and Optimization, 3*(1), 20–29.

Helmy, T., Anifowose, F., & Faisal, K. (2010). Hybrid computational models for the characterization of oil and gas reservoirs. *International Journal of Expert Systems with Application, 37,* 5353–5363. doi:10.1016/j.eswa.2010.01.021

Helmy, T., Rahman, S. M., Hossain, M. I., & Abdulraheem, A. (2013). Non-linear heterogeneous ensemble model for permeability prediction of oil reservoirs. *Arab Journal of Science and Engineering, 38,* 1379–1395. doi:10.1007/s13369-013-0588-z

Hoeting, J. A., Madigan, D., Raftery, A. E., & Volinsky, C. T. (1999). Bayesian model averaging: a tutorial. *Statistical Science, 14*(4), 382–401.

Huang, G. B., & Babri, H. A. (1998). Upper bounds on the number of hidden neurons in feedforward networks with arbitrary bounded nonlinear activation functions. *IEEE Transactions on Neural Networks, 9*(1), 224–229. doi:10.1109/72.655045 PMID:18252445

Johansson, U., Löfström, T., & Norinder, U. (2009). Evaluating ensembles on QSAR classification. In *Proceeding of Skövde Workshop on Information Fusion Topics* (pp. 49-54). Skövde, Sweden: Univeristy of Skövde.

Jong-Se, L. (2005). Reservoir properties determination using fuzzy logic and neural networks from well data in offshore Korea. *Petroleum Science and Engineering, 49,* 182–192. doi:10.1016/j.petrol.2005.05.005

Kostrykin, V., & Oleynik, A. (2013). On the existence of unstable bumps in neural networks. *Integral Equations and Operator Theory, 75*(4), 445–458. doi:10.1007/s00020-013-2045-5

Kozeny, J. (1927). Uber Kapillare Leitung des Wassers im Boden: Sitzungsber. *Akad. Wiss. Wien, 136*, 271–306.

Kuncheva, L., & Whitaker, C. (2003). Measures of diversity in classifier ensembles. *Machine Learning, 51*, 181–207. doi:10.1023/A:1022859003006

Lin, Y., & Jeon, Y. (2002). *Random forests and adaptive nearest neighbors* (Technical Report No. 1055). University of Wisconsin.

Lippert, R. (2013). *The wisdom of crowds: using ensembles for machine learning*. Retrieved from http://blog.factual.com/the-wisdom-of-crowds

Maertens, K., Baerdemaeker, J. D., & Babuska, R. (2006). Genetic polynomial regression as input selection algorithm for non-linear identification. *Journal of Soft Computing, 10*, 785–795. doi:10.1007/s00500-005-0008-8

Marzio, M. D., & Taylor, C. C. (2012). Boosting kernel estimators. In C. Zhang, & Y. Ma (Eds.), *Ensemble Machine Learning* (pp. 87–115). New York, NY: Springer. doi:10.1007/978-1-4419-9326-7_3

Masoudnia, S., & Ebrahimpour, R. (2012). Mixture of experts: a literature survey. *Artificial Intelligence Review*. doi:10.1007/s10462-012-9338-y

Minku, L. L., White, A. P., & Yao, X. (2010). The impact of diversity on online ensemble learning in the presence of concept drift. *IEEE Transactions on Knowledge and Data Engineering, 22*(5), 730–742. doi:10.1109/TKDE.2009.156

Mitchell, T. (1997). *Machine learning*. Boston, MA: WCB/McGraw-Hill.

Peng, Y. (2006). A novel ensemble machine learning for robust microarray data classification. *Computers in Biology and Medicine, 36*, 553–573. doi:10.1016/j.compbiomed.2005.04.001 PMID:15978569

Petrus, J. B., Thuijsman, F., & Weijters, A. J. (1995). *Artificial Neural Networks: An Introduction to ANN Theory and Practice*. Springer.

Polikar, R. (2006). Ensemble based systems in decision making. *IEEE Circuits and Systems Magazine*, 21-45.

Polikar, R. (2009). Ensemble learning. *Scholarpedia, 4*(1), 2776. doi:10.4249/scholarpedia.2776

Re, M., & Valentini, G. (2010). Simple ensemble methods are competitive with state-of-the-art data integration methods for gene function prediction. [). DLBP.]. *Proceedings of the Machine Learning in System Biology, 8*, 98–111.

Rokach, L. (2010). Ensemble-based classifiers. *Artificial Intelligence Review, 33*(1-2), 1–39. doi:10.1007/s10462-009-9124-7

Sadeghi, R., Kadkhodaie, A., Rafiei, B., Yosefpour, M., & Khodabakhsh, S. (2011). A committee machine approach for predicting permeability from well log data: A case study from a heterogeneous carbonate reservoir, Balal oil Field, Persian Gulf. *Journal of Geopercia, 1*(2), 1–10.

Schapire, R. E. (2003). The boosting approach to machine learning: an overview. In *Nonlinear Estimation and Classification* (pp. 143–171). New York, NY: Springer. doi:10.1007/978-0-387-21579-2_9

Schlumberger Oilfield Glossary, Reservoir Characterization. (n.d.). Retrieved August 19, 2013, from http://www.glossary.oilfield.slb.com/en/

Shang, B. Z., Hamman, J. G., Chen, H., & Caldwell, D. H. (2003). A model to correlate permeability with efficient porosity and irreducible water saturation. In *Proceedings of the SPE Annual Technical Conference and Exhibition.* SPE/Onepetro database.

Stergiou, C. (2013). *What is a neural network?* Retrieved August 25, 2013, from http://www.doc.ic.ac.uk/~nd/surprise_96/journal/vol1/cs11/article1.html

Timur, A. (1968, July-August). An investigation of permeability, porosity, and residual water saturation relationship for sandstone reservoirs. *The Log Analyst.*

Tsymbal, A., Pechenizkiy, M., & Cunningham, P. (2005). Diversity in search strategies for ensemble feature selection. *Inference, 6*(1), 83–98.

Wang, S., & Yao, X. (2013). Relationships between diversity of classification ensembles and single-class performance measures. *IEEE Transactions on Knowledge and Data Engineering, 25*(1), 206–219. doi:10.1109/TKDE.2011.207

Wyllie, M. R. J., Gregory, A. R., & Gardner, G. H. F. (1956). Elastic wave velocity in heterogeneous and porous media. *Geophysics,* 41–70. doi:10.1190/1.1438217

Wyllie, M.R.J., & Rose, W.D. (1950). Some theoretical considerations related to the quantitative evaluation of the physical characteristics of reservoir rock from electrical log data. *Transactions of the American Institute of Mechanical Engineers,* 105–118.

Xu, L., & Amari, S. (2009). Combining Classifiers and Learning Mixture-of-Experts. In J. Rabuñal Dopico, J. Dorado, & A. Pazos (Eds.), *Encyclopedia of Artificial Intelligence* (pp. 318–326). Hershey, PA: Information Science Reference.

Yuksel, S. E., Wilson, J. N., & Gader, P. D. (2012). Twenty years of mixture of experts. *IEEE Transactions on Neural Networks and Learning Systems, 23*(8), 1177–1193. doi:10.1109/TNNLS.2012.2200299 PMID:24807516

Zhou, Z.-H. (2009). Ensemble learning. In S. Z. Li (Ed.), *Encyclopedia of Biometrics* (pp. 270–273). Berlin: Springer.

ADDITIONAL READING

Alpaydin, E. (2010). *Introduction to machine learning* (2nd ed.). Houston, Texas: The MIT Press.

Baker, L., & Ellison, D. (2008). Optimisation of pedotransfer functions using an artificial neural network ensemble method. *Geoderma, 144,* 212–224. doi:10.1016/j.geoderma.2007.11.016

Bock, K. W. D., & Poel, D. V. (2010). Ensembles of probability estimation trees for customer churn prediction. In N. Garcıa-Pedrajas et al. (Eds.), *Trends in Applied Intelligent Systems, 23rd International Conference on Industrial Engineering and Other Applications of Applied Intelligent Systems, IEA/AIE 2010, Cordoba, Spain, June 1-4, 2010, Proceedings, Part II* (pp. 57–66). Germany: Springer-Verlag.

Bramer, M. (2002). Using J-prunning to reduce overfitting in classification trees. *Knowledge-Based Systems, 15,* 301–308. doi:10.1016/S0950-7051(01)00163-0

Bray, Z., & Kristensson, P. O. (2010). Using ensembles of decision trees to automate repetitive tasks in web applications. In *Proceeding EICS '10 Proceedings of the 2nd ACM SIGCHI symposium on Engineering interactive computing systems* (pp. 35-40). New York, NY: ACM.

Chandra, A., & Yao, X. (2006). Evolving hybrid ensembles of learning machines for better generalization. *Neurocomputing, 69*, 686–700. doi:10.1016/j.neucom.2005.12.014

Chen, D., Quirein, J., Hamid, H., Smith, H., & Grable, J. (2004). Neural network ensemble selection using multiobjective genetic algorithm in processing pulsed neutron data. In *SPWLA 45th Annual Logging Symposium* (pp. 1-13). Houston, Texas: SPE/OnePetro Database.

De Felice, M. D., & Yao, X. (2011). Short-term load forecasting with neural network ensembles: a comparative study. *IEEE Computational Intelligence Magazine, 6*(3), 47–56. doi:10.1109/MCI.2011.941590

Fei, H., Qing-Hua, L., & De-Shuang, H. (2008). Modified constrained learning algorithms incorporating additional functional constraints into neural networks. *Information Science, 178*(3), 907–919.

Heaton, J.T. (2008). *Introduction to neural networks with Java.* Chesterfield: Heaton Research, Inc.

Ho, T. K. (1995). Random decision forest. In *Proceedings of the 3rd International Conference on Document Analysis and Recognition* (pp. 278–282).

Ho, T. K. (1998). The random subspace method for constructing decision forests. *IEEE Transactions on Pattern Analysis and Machine Intelligence, 20*(8), 832–844. doi:10.1109/34.709601

Jong-Se, L. (2005). Reservoir properties determination using fuzzy logic and neural networks from well data in offshore Korea. *Journal of Petroleum Science Engineering, 49*, 182–192. doi:10.1016/j.petrol.2005.05.005

Jreou, N. S. G. (2012). Application of neural network to optimize oil field production. *Asian Transaction on Engineering, 2*(3), 10–23.

Karsoliya, S. (2012). Approximating number of hidden layer neurons in multiple hidden layer BPNN architecture. *International Journal of Engineering Trends and Technology, 3*(6), 714–717.

Landassuri-Moreno, V., & Bullinaria, J. A. (2009). Neural network ensembles for time series forecasting. In *Genetic and Evolutionary Computation Conference (GECCO)* (pp. 1234-1242). New York: ACM.

Liaw, A., & Wiener, M. (2002). Classification and regression by random forest. *R News, 2*(3), 18–22.

Liu, Y., Starzyk, J. A., & Zhu, Z. (2007). Optimizing number of hidden neurons in neural networks. In *Proceedings of the 25th IASTED International Multi-Conference on artificial intelligence and applications* (pp. 121-126). Innsbruck, Austria: Acta Press.

Minku, L. L., & Yao, X. (2012). DDD: a new ensemble approach for dealing with concept drift. *IEEE Transactions on Knowledge and Data Engineering, 24*(4), 619–633. doi:10.1109/TKDE.2011.58

Mohaghegh, S. (2000). Virtual intelligence and its applications in petroleum engineering: artificial neural networks. *Journal of Petroleum Technology, Distinguished Lecture Series*, June, 2000.

Monedero, I., Biscarri, F., León, C., Guerrero, J. I., González, R., & Pérez-Lombard, L. (2012). Decision system based on neural networks to optimize the energy efficiency of a petrochemical plant. *Expert Systems with Applications, 39*(10), 9860–9867. doi:10.1016/j.eswa.2012.02.165

Panchal, G., Ganatra, A., Kosta, Y. P., & Panchal, D. (2011). Behaviour analysis of multilayer perceptrons with multiple hidden neurons and hidden layers. *International Journal of Computer Theory and Engineering*, *3*(2), 332–337. doi:10.7763/IJCTE.2011.V3.328

Pardoe, D., Ryoo, M., & Miikkulainen, R. (2005). Evolving neural network ensembles for control problems. In *Proceedings of the 2005 conference on Genetic and evolutionary computation* (pp. 25–29), New York, NY: ACM.

Rivals, I., & Personnaz, L. (2000). A statistical procedure for determining the optimal number of hidden neurons of a neural model. In *Second International Symposium on Neural Computation (NCi2000)*. Berlin, German: NAISO Academic Press.

Shibata, K., & Ikeda, Y. (2009). Effect of number of hidden neurons on learning in large-scale layered neural networks. In *ICCAS-SICE 2009* (pp. 5008–5013). Fukuoka, Japan: ICCAS-SICE.

Sun, J., & Li, H. (2012). Financial Distress prediction using support vector machines: ensemble vs. individual. *Applied Soft Computing*, *12*(8), 2254–2265. doi:10.1016/j.asoc.2012.03.028

Tang, E. K., Suganthan, P. N., & Yao, X. (2006). An analysis of diversity measures. *Machine Learning*, *65*, 247–271. doi:10.1007/s10994-006-9449-2

Tang, E. K., Suganthan, P. N., & Yao, X. (2006). An analysis of diversity measures. *Machine Learning*, *65*, 247–271. doi:10.1007/s10994-006-9449-2

Wu, J., & Rehg, J. M. (2012). Object detection. In C. Zhang, & Y. Ma (Eds.), Ensemble Machine Learning: Methods and Applications. Vol. 8, Springer Science+Business Media.

Yu, L., Wang, S., & Lai, K. K. (2008). Forecasting crude oil price with an EMD-based neural network ensemble learning paradigm. *Energy Economics*, *30*, 2623–2635. doi:10.1016/j.eneco.2008.05.003

Zaier, I., Shu, C., Ouarda, T. B. M. J., Seidou, O., & Chebana, F. (2010). Estimation of ice thickness on lakes using artificial neural network ensembles. *Journal of Hydrology (Amsterdam)*, *383*, 330–340. doi:10.1016/j.jhydrol.2010.01.006

KEY TERMS AND DEFINITIONS

Artificial Neural Networks: A machine learning technique that emulates the biological nervous system.

Ensemble Learning: The machine learning paradigm that combines the individual results of standard techniques to evolve a single improved solution to a problem.

Hidden Neurons: The processing units in the hidden layer of an Artificial Neural Network model that processes variable inputs to produce target outputs.

Linear Search: A sequential search for an optimal value in a bounded space.

Permeability: A petroleum reservoir property that measures the interconnectivity of the pores identified in a reservoir rock sample.

Petroleum Reservoir Characterization: A discipline in petroleum engineering that is concerned with the estimation of various reservoir properties.

Porosity: A petroleum reservoir property that measures the amount of pores in a reservoir rock sample.

Randomized Algorithm: An algorithm that generates a number from a normal distribution within a bounded space such that each number has equal chance of being selected.

Chapter 5
Ant Programming Algorithms for Classification

Juan Luis Olmo
University of Córdoba, Spain

José Raúl Romero
University of Córdoba, Spain

Sebastián Ventura
University of Córdoba, Spain

ABSTRACT

Ant programming is a kind of automatic programming that generates computer programs by using the ant colony metaheuristic as the search technique. It has demonstrated good generalization ability for the extraction of comprehensible classifiers. To date, three ant programming algorithms for classification rule mining have been proposed in the literature: two of them are devoted to regular classification, differing mainly in the optimization approach, single-objective or multi-objective, while the third one is focused on imbalanced domains. This chapter collects these algorithms, presenting different experimental studies that confirm the aptitude of this metaheuristic to address this data-mining task.

INTRODUCTION

Data mining (DM) tasks and some parts of the knowledge discovery process can be addressed as optimization and search problems, in account of their difficulty to be modeled and the high size of the space of solutions. To this end, biologically-inspired techniques appear as a good technique,

since they are techniques tolerant to certain imprecision and uncertainty that are able to model in an approximate way natural phenomena.

The DM classification task focuses on predicting the value of the class given the values of certain other attributes (referred to as the predicting attributes). A model or classifier is inferred in a training stage by analyzing the values of the

DOI: 10.4018/978-1-4666-6078-6.ch005

predicting attributes that describe each instance, as well as the class to which each instance belongs. Thus, classification is considered to be supervised learning, in contrast to unsupervised learning, where instances are unlabeled. Once the classifier is built, it can be used later to classify other new and uncategorized instances into one of the existing classes.

Genetic programming (GP) (Koza, 1992) was the first biologically-inspired automatic programming technique used for addressing the classification task of DM. A survey focused on the application of GP to classification can be found in (Espejo, Ventura, & Herrera, 2010). Another automatic programming technique, less widespread but more recent than GP, is ant programming (AP) (Roux & Fonlupt, 2000) which uses ant colony optimization as the search technique to look for computer programs. Actually, individuals in AP are known as artificial ants and they encode a solution that is represented by a path over a graph or a tree. Recent research has put the spotlight on the application of AP to DM, specifically to classification (Olmo, Romero, & Ventura, 2011) and association rule mining (Olmo, Luna, Romero, & Ventura, 2013), demonstrating the suitability of this metaheuristic to find good and comprehensible solutions to these tasks.

In this chapter we present the AP algorithms for inducing rule-based classifiers that have been presented in literature. Two of them are devoted to regular classification, and they mainly differ in the optimization approach, while the third proposal is specific for imbalanced classification (Olmo et al., 2012). All the algorithms can cope both with binary and multiclass data sets.

The first section of this chapter presents the original single-objective AP algorithm for classification, called GBAP (Grammar-Based Ant Programming). The second section describes the multi-objective AP proposal, called MOG-BAP (Multi-Objective GBAP). The third section explains the main workings of the imbalanced APIC (Ant Programming for Imbalanced Clas-

sification) algorithm. The fourth section presents the experimental studies carried out to show the performance of these algorithms. Finally, the last section gives some concluding remarks and ideas for future work.

THE GBAP ALGORITHM: GRAMMAR-BASED ANT PROGRAMMING

This section introduces the first AP algorithm for classification, called GBAP, which is based on the use of a context-free grammar (CFG) for ensuring the generation of individuals syntactically valid, as well as the other AP algorithms presented in this work. The algorithm evolves a population of rules from the training set that are combined at the end of the last generation into a decision-list like classifier. Then, the model induced is test over the test set and the results obtained are reported. The flowchart of GBAP is shown in Figure 1, and its characteristics are described in the following subsections.

Environment and Rule Encoding

The AP models presented here are founded on the use of a context-free grammar (CFG) that defines all the possible states that individuals can visit. Actually, the environment that permits ants to communicate indirectly with each other is the derivation tree that can be generated from the grammar, as shown in Figure 1. This grammar is expressed in Backus-Naur form, and its definition is given by $G = (\Sigma_N, \Sigma_T, P, S)$:

$$G = (\Sigma_N, \Sigma_T, P, S)$$

$$\Sigma_N = \{<\text{Rule}>, <\text{Antecedent}>, <\text{Consequent}>, <\text{Condition}>\}$$

$$\Sigma_T = \{-->, \text{AND}, =, !=, attr_1, attr_2, ..., attr_n, value_{1,1}, value_{1,2}, ..., value_{1,m}, value_{2,1}, value_{2,2}, ..., value_{2,m}, ..., value_{n,1}, value_{n,2}, ..., value_{n,m}\}$$

Figure 1. Flowchart of GBAP

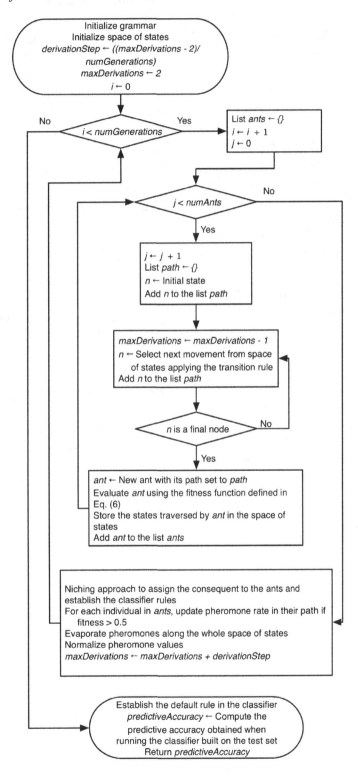

S = <Rule>

P = {<Rule>:= --> <Antecedent> <Consequent>, <Antecedent>:= <Condition> | AND <Antecedent> <Condition>, <Consequent>:= <Condition>, <Condition>:= all possible valid combinations of the ternary operator attr value}

Here, Σ_N is the set of non-terminal symbols, Σ_T is the set of terminal symbols, P is the set of production rules, and S stands for the start symbol. Notice that the grammar could be adapted to other specific problems, for instance by adding other logical operators such as not equal or the disjunctive operator. Any production rule is composed of two parts. The first one is the left hand side, which always refers to a non-terminal symbol. This non-terminal symbol might be replaced by the second part, the right hand side of the rule, which consists of a combination of terminal and non-terminal symbols. Production rules are internally implemented in prefix notation and should always be derived from the left. This implies that each transition from a state i to another state j is triggered after applying a production rule to the first non-terminal symbol of state i. This design decision was taken because of performance reasons, in order to save on computational costs when assessing rules' quality.

The environment comprises all possible expressions or programs that can be derived from the grammar in a given maximum number of derivations. The initial state corresponds to the start symbol of the grammar. A path over the environment corresponds to the states visited by any ant until reaching a feasible solution. The last state of a path corresponds to a final state or solution, comprised only of terminal symbols. Thus, concerning individuals' encoding, the AP algorithms presented here follow the ant=rule approach (a.k.a. Michigan approach). However, it is worth noting that when a given ant reaches a final state, it just encodes the antecedent of the rule. Each AP algorithm employs a different approach for assigning a consequent to each rule. In this case, GBAP uses a niching approach that will be described later in the fitness evaluation section.

Heuristic Measures

Another important characteristic of the algorithms proposed is that they consider two complementary heuristic measures, in contrast to typical ACO algorithms, which use only one. The metric to be

Figure 2. Space of states at a depth of four derivations. Double-lined states stand for final states.

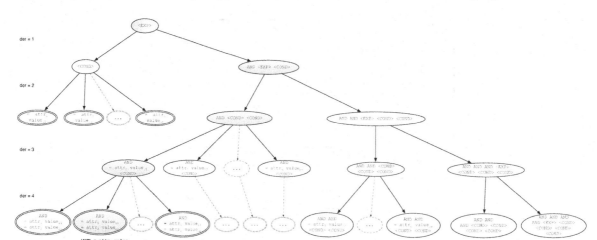

applied depends on the kind of transition involved, since they cannot be applied at once. Two cases are considered: final transitions, if the transition involves the application of a production rule that selects an attribute of the problem domain, and intermediate transitions, otherwise.

In the case of intermediate transitions, a measure associated with the cardinality of the production rules is considered. It is referred to as *Pcard*, and it increases the likelihood of selecting transitions that may lead a given ant to a greater number of candidate solutions. It is based on the cardinality measure proposed in (Geyer-Schulz, 1995). Thus, given a state i having k subsequent states, j being a specific successor among those k states, and where d derivations remain available, this heuristic measure is computed as the ratio between the number of candidate solutions that can be successfully reached from the state j in d-1 derivations, and the sum of all possible candidate solutions that can be reached from the source state i in d derivations, as shown in the following Equation:

$$Pcard_{ij}^{k} = \frac{cardinality(state_j, d-1)}{\sum_{k \in allowed}(cardinality(state_k, d-1))}$$

In contrast, the component considered for final transitions differs depending on the AP algorithm. Both GBAP and MOGBAP use the well-known information gain measure, which computes the worth of each attribute in separating the training examples with respect to their target classification. This measure is widely used. Actually, regarding ACO algorithms for classification, Ant-Miner (Parpinelli, Freitas, & Lopes, 2002), which was the first ACO algorithm proposed for this task, uses it as the only heuristic measure. Most of its extensions and variants do the same.

Fitness Evaluation

The fitness function that GBAP uses in the training stage for measuring the quality of individuals generated in a given generation is the Laplace accuracy. This measure was selected because it suits well to multiclass classification problems due to the fact that it takes into account the number of classes in the data set. It is defined as:

$$fitness = \frac{1 + TP}{k + TP + FP}$$

where TP and FP stands for true positives and false positives, respectively, and k refers to the number of classes in the data set.

Concerning the assignment of the consequent, GBAP follows a niching approach analogous to that employed in (Berlanga, Rivera, Del Jesus, & Herrera, 2010), whose purpose is to evolve different multiple rules for predicting each class in the data set while preserving the diversity. Depending on the distribution of instances per class of a particular data set, it is often not possible for a rule to cover all instances of the class it predicts. Therefore, it is necessary to discover additional rules predicting this class. The niching approach is in charge of this issue, so that it will not overlap the instances of another class. In addition, it is appropriate to remove redundant rules. Moreover, it lacks the drawbacks that sequential covering algorithms present with respect to instances discard.

In the niching algorithm developed, every instance in a data set is called a token, and all ants compete to capture them. At the beginning, an array of dimension k is created per individual, one for each class, and k fitness values are computed for each one, assuming that the respective class is assigned as consequent to the individual. Then, the following steps are repeated for each class:

1. Ants are sorted by the fitness associated to this class in descending order.
2. Each ant tries to capture as many tokens as it covers in case of tokes whose class corresponds to the computing class and also if the token has not been seized by any other ant with higher priority previously.
3. Ants' adjusted fitness for this class are computed as:

$$adjusted Fitness = fitness \cdot \frac{captured Tokens}{class Tokens}$$

Once the k adjusted fitness values have been computed, one for each class in the training set, the consequent assigned to each ant corresponds to the class for which the best-adjusted fitness has been reported. To conclude, individuals having and adjusted fitness greater than zero and, therefore, cover at least one instance of the training set, are added to the classifier.

Transition Probability

The ACO metaheuristic follows a constructive method where every solution is created according to a sequence of steps or transitions guided by some information. The information that biases each step is considered in the transition rule, which defines the probability that a given ant moves from a state i to another state j:

$$P_{ij}^k = \frac{(\eta_{ij})^\alpha \cdot (\tau_{ij})^\beta}{\Sigma_{k \in allowed}(\eta_{ik})^\alpha \cdot (\tau_{ik})^\beta}$$

where k is the number of valid subsequent states, α is the heuristic exponent, β is the pheromone exponent, η is the value of the heuristic function, and τ indicates the strength of the pheromone trail. Note that the heuristic function has two excluding components: they are not applicable in the same

situations, which results in the fact that always one of the two components will be equal to zero.

When computing the transition rule, the algorithm enforces that the movement to the state j allows reaching final states in the number of derivations that remain available at that point. If not, a probability of zero will be assigned to this state and, therefore, it will never be chosen.

Pheromone Updating

As it was aforementioned, higher pheromone levels in a given transition lead ants to choose this transition with a higher likelihood. Ants communicate with each other by means of the pheromone that they deposit in the environment, in such a way that those ants encoding good solutions will deposit more pheromone in the transitions they have followed than ants encoding bad solutions. On the other hand, evaporation is required since it avoids the convergence to a locally optimal solution.

In GBP, reinforcement and evaporation are the operations involved regarding pheromone maintenance. All ants of the current generation are able to reinforce the pheromone amount in their path's transitions only if the quality of the solution encoded exceeds an experimentally fixed threshold of 0.5. This threshold avoids a negative influence on the environment of those solutions considered not good enough. The quantity of pheromones spread by a given ant is proportional to its fitness:

$$\tau_{ij}(t+1) = \tau_{ij}(t) + \tau_{ij}(t) \cdot fitness$$

where $\tau_{ij}(t)$ indicates the existing quantity of pheromone in the transition from state i to state j, $\tau_{ij}(t+1)$ is the new amount of pheromones that will be in the same transition after the pheromone deposition, and *fitness* represents the quality of the individual.

All transitions in the path of a given individual are reinforced equally. The evaporation takes place over the whole space of states. For a given transition, the amount of pheromone after performing the evaporation is:

$$\tau_{ij}(t+1) = \tau_{ij}(t) \cdot (1 - \rho)$$

where ρ represents the evaporation rate.

THE MOGBAP ALGORITHM: MULTI-OBJECTIVE GRAMMAR-BASED ANT PROGRAMMING

This section explains the main workings of MOG-BAP, which is the multi-objective version of the algorithm presented before. The flowchart of this algorithm is shown in Figure 3, and the particular characteristics of this algorithm are described next, focusing on the differences that it presents with respect to GBAP.

Environment and Rule Encoding

The CFG used in MOGBAP is the same as in GBAP. Therefore, the environment also adopts the shape of a derivation tree. Individuals are encoded also following the individual=rule approach, and the final state of a path over a derivation tree encodes the antecedent of the rule. However, MOGBAP does not delegate the niching approach to assign a consequent to the rules. Instead, for a given rule, it directly assigns the consequent corresponding to the most frequent class covered by this antecedent among the training instances.

Multi-Objective Fitness Evaluation

The quality of individuals in MOGBAP is assessed on the basis of three conflicting objectives: sensitivity, specificity and comprehensibility.

Sensitivity and specificity are two measures widely employed in classification problems, even as a scalar function of them. Sensitivity indicates how well a rule identifies positive cases. On the contrary, specificity reports the effectiveness of a rule's identifying negative cases or those cases that do not belong to the class studied. If the sensitivity value of a rule is increased, it will predict a greater number of positive examples, but sometimes at the expense of classifying as positives some cases that actually belong to the negative class. Both objectives are to be maximized.

$$sensitivity = \frac{TP}{TP + FN}$$
$$specificity = \frac{TN}{TN + FP}$$

Since MOGBAP is a rule-based classification algorithm, it is intended to mine accurate but also comprehensible rules. So, somehow, it should also optimize the complexity of the rules mined. Although comprehensibility is a sort of subjective concept, there are several ways to measure the comprehensibility of the rules and the classifier, usually by counting the number of conditions per rule and the number of rules appearing in the final classifier. The latter can not be considered here as an objective, since MOGBAP follows the ant=rule approach, as aforementioned. On the other hand, if the number of conditions per rule is directly used as the comprehensibility metric, it should be minimized. Nevertheless, assuming that a rule can have up to a fixed number of conditions, comprehensibility can be measured as:

$$comprehensibility = 1 - \frac{numConditions}{maxConditions}$$

where *numConditions* refers to the number of conditions appearing in the rule encoded by the

Figure 3. Flowchart of MOGBAP

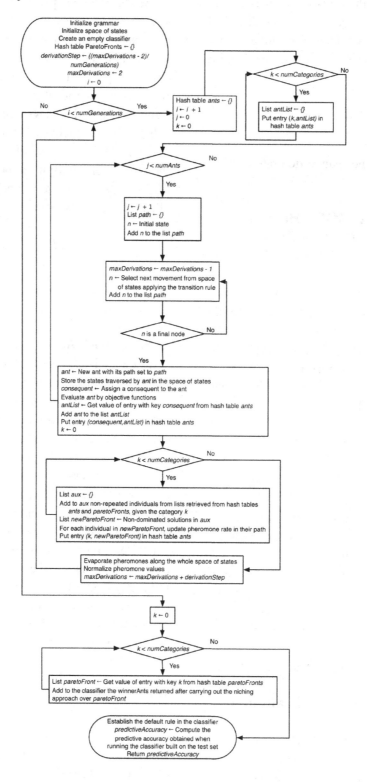

individual, whereas *maxConditions* is the maximum number of conditions that a rule can have (Dehuri, Patnaik, Ghosh, & Mall, 2008).

In MOGBAP, it is easy to compute the maximum number of conditions that an individual can have, because the grammar is known beforehand and the maximum number of derivations allowed is also known. The advantage of using this comprehensibility metric lies in the fact that its values will be contained in the interval [0,1], and the closer its value to 1, the more comprehensible the rule will be. Hence, just as with the objectives of sensitivity and specificity, this objective, too, should be maximized.

Pareto dominance asserts that a given rule ant_1 dominates another rule ant_2, denoted as $ant_1 \succ ant_2$, if ant_1 is not worse than ant_2 in any objective, but is better in at least one of them. The non-dominated set of solutions of a population makes up the Pareto front.

Multi-Objective Strategy

MOGBAP follows a multi-objective strategy that has been specially designed for the classification task. The idea behind this scheme is to distinguish solutions in terms of the class they predict, because certain classes are more difficult to predict than others. Actually, if individuals from different classes are ranked according to Pareto dominance, overlapping may occur, as illustrated in Figure 4, which shows the Pareto fronts found after running MOGBAP for the binary hepatitis data set, considering only the objectives of sensitivity and specificity for simplicity reasons. As can be observed, if a classic Pareto approach were employed, a single front of non-dominated solutions would be found, as shown in the left part of the figure. Hence, among the individuals represented here, such a Pareto front would consist of all the individuals that predict the class 'LIVE' and just one individual of the class 'DIE' (the individual which has a specificity of 1.0). In order for the remaining individuals of the class 'DIE' to be considered, it would be necessary to find additional fronts, and they would have less likelihood of becoming part of the classifier's decision list. On the other hand, the multi-objective approach of MOGBAP shown in the right part of the figure guarantees that all non-dominated solutions for each available class will be found, so it ensures the inclusion of rules predicting each class in the final classifier.

Figure 4. Comparison between a classic Pareto approach and the proposed strategy for the two-class data set hepatitis

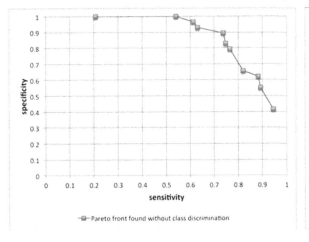 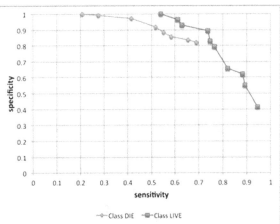

Roughly speaking, the multi-objective approach devised for MOGBAP consists in discovering a separate set of non-dominated solutions for each class in the data set. To this end, once individuals of the current generation have been created and evaluated for each objective considered, they are divided into *k* groups, *k* being the number of classes in the training set, according to their consequent. Then, each group of individuals is combined with the solutions kept in the corresponding Pareto front found in the previous iteration of the algorithm, to rank them all according to dominance, finding a new Pareto front for each class. Hence, there will be *k* Pareto fronts, and only the non-dominated solutions contained will participate in the pheromone reinforcement.

The final classifier is built from the non-dominated individuals that exist in all the Pareto fronts once the last generation has finished. A niching procedure executed over each one of the *k* fronts is in charge of making up the decision list from these rules: the individuals of the front are sorted by the Laplace accuracy and then they try to capture as many instances of the training set as they can. Each ant can capture an instance just in case it covers it and if the instance has not been seized previously by another ant. Finally, only those ants whose number of captured instances exceeds the percentage of coverage established by the user are added to the list of returned ants, having an adjusted Laplace accuracy computed as follows:

$$LaplaceAccuracy_{adjusted} = LaplaceAccuracy \cdot \frac{capturedTokens}{idealTokens}$$

where *idealTokens* is equal to the number of instances covered by the ant.

The resulting ants of carrying out the niching procedure over each Pareto front are added to the classifier, sorted by their adjusted Laplace accuracy. A default rule predicting the majority

class in the training set is added at the bottom of the decision list and the classifier is run over the test set to compute its predictive accuracy.

Pheromone Updating

Only those ants that belong to the Pareto fronts are able to retrace their path and deposit pheromone. For a given ant, all transitions in its path are reinforced equally, and the value of this reinforcement is based upon the quality of the solution encoded, represented by the Laplace accuracy, and also the length of this solution:

$$\tau_{ij}(t+1) = \tau_{ij}(t) \cdot Q \cdot LaplaceAccuracy$$

where *Q* is a measure that favors comprehensible solutions, computed as the ratio between the maximum number of derivations in the current generation and the length of the path followed by the ant (thus shorter solutions will receive more pheromone).

THE APIC ALGORITHM: ANT PROGRAMMING FOR IMBALANCED CLASSIFICATION

Classification algorithms not specifically devised for imbalanced problems generally infer a model that misclassifies test samples of the minority class, which is usually the class of interest, more often that those of the other classes. This typically involves a higher cost in the application domains embraced. Several solutions have been proposed to tackle the class imbalance problem, although there are some open issues (Fernández, García, & Herrera, 2011). In particular, the employment of a separate colony for generating rules predicting a specific class, as well as the employment of a multi-objective evaluation strategy and an appropriate heuristic function allows AP to obtain good results for imbalanced problems. The AP algorithm, called APIC (Ant Programming for Imbalanced Classification), is an algorithm-level approach that can be applied both to binary and multi-class data sets. Concerning binary problems, it does not require to carry out resampling, using the imbalanced data sets without any preprocessing steps in the evolutionary process. On the other hand, concerning multi-class problems, it does not require to reduce the problem using either a one-vs-one (OVO) or a one-vs-all (OVA) decomposition scheme (Galar, Fernández, Barrenechea, Bustince, & Herrera, 2011), where a classifier is built for each possible combination. Instead, it addresses the problem directly, simplifying thus the complexity of the model.

The APIC algorithm induces a classifier from a learning process over a training set. The classifier induced acts as a decision list, and it consists in classification rules in the form IF antecedent THEN consequent. This algorithm adopts some base characteristics from the AP algorithms for standard classification explained previously. However, there are many differences between these models, since APIC has been specifically devised for imbalanced classification. Among others, the most important can be summed up as follows: APIC is a multi-colony algorithm, whereas the others have a single colony; it follows a multi-objective approach, as well as MOGBAP, although in this case different objectives are to be optimized; information gain, which is one of the heuristic function components of the other AP algorithms, is replaced by the class confidence, which is more suitable for class imbalanced problems; and other differences related to pheromone reinforcement and the classifier building.

Introduction to Performance Metrics in Imbalanced Domains

To measure the performance of a classifier in imbalanced domains, accuracy should not be used since it is biased towards the majority class. This bias is even more noticeable as the skew increases.

Instead, the area under the receiver operating characteristic (ROC) curve (AUC) (Fawcett, 2006) is a commonly used evaluation measure for imbalanced classification. ROC curve presents the tradeoff between the true positive rate and the false positive rate. The classifier generally misclassifies more negative examples as positive examples as it captures more true positive examples. AUC is computed by means of the confusion matrix values:

$$AUC = \frac{1 + \dfrac{TP}{TP + FN} - \dfrac{FP}{FP + TN}}{2}$$

This measure considers a tradeoff between the true positives ratio and the false positives ratio.

However, it is necessary to extend its definition for multi-class problems to consider pairwise relations. This extension is known as probabilistic AUC, where a single value for each pair of classes is computed, taking one class as positive and the other as negative. Finally, the average value is obtained as follows:

$$PAUC = \frac{1}{C(C-1)} \cdot \sum_{i=1}^{C} \sum_{j \neq 1}^{C} AUC(i, j)$$

where AUC_{ij} is the AUC having i as positive class, j as negative class, and C stands for the number of classes.

Environment and Rule Encoding

The environment where ants interact with each other also adopts the shape of a derivation tree, since the CFG that controls the creation of new individuals is the same used in GBAP and MOG-BAP. The path encoded by a given individual in APIC also represents the antecedent of a rule, but in this algorithm the consequent is known since there will be as many colonies as classes in the data set, each colony devoted just to generate individuals predicting the corresponding class.

Each colony is evolved in parallel, since individuals generated by one colony do not interfere with those of the other colonies. Moreover, since there are k different colonies, one for each class, it simulates the existence of k different kinds of pheromone, so that specific ants for a given class do not interfere with those of the others.

Heuristic Measures

In APIC, information gain is not used as the final transitions' heuristic. Instead, it uses the class confidence (Liu, Chawla, Cieslak, & Chawla, 2010), since the former biases the search towards the majority class. The class confidence (CC) is defined as follows:

$$CC(x \rightarrow y) = \frac{Support(x \cup y)}{Support(y)}$$

where x stands for the antecedent and y stands for the consequent. This measure allows focusing just on the most interesting antecedents for each class, since we use the support of the consequent in the denominator, which basically counts the number of instances belonging to the class specified as consequent. In turn, the numerator computes the support of the antecedent and the consequent, which is the number of instances covered by the antecedent that also belong to the class specified as consequent.

Transition Probability

The equation of the transition rule differs slightly from that of the previous AP algorithms, due to the existence of several space of states. It is defined as follows, distinguishing the colony to which the individual belongs with the *suffix* class:

$$Pclass_{ij}^{k} = \frac{(\eta_{ij})^{\alpha} \cdot (\tau class_{ij})^{\beta}}{\sum_{k \in allowed}(\eta_{ik})^{\alpha} \cdot (\tau class_{ik})^{\beta}}$$

Pheromone Updating

The evaporation process takes place in a similar manner as in GBAP and MOGBAP, where the pheromone amount in all transitions is decremented proportionally to the evaporation rate. However, in this case there are k different space of states, one for each colony.

Concerning reinforcement, only those ants belonging to the Pareto front are able to retrace their path to update the amount of pheromone in the transitions followed. For a given individual, all transitions in its path are reinforced equally, and the value of this reinforcement is based upon the length (shorter solutions will receive more pheromone) and the quality of the solution encoded (represented by the computed AUC for this individual in the training set):

$$\tau_{ij}(t+1) =$$
$$\tau_{ij}(t) + \tau_{ij}(t) \cdot \frac{maxDerivations}{pathLength} \cdot AUC$$

When the pheromone updating operations have finished, a normalization process takes place in each space of states. In addition, for the first generation of a given colony, all transitions in its space of states are initialized with the maximum pheromone amount allowed.

Multi-Objective Fitness Evaluation

The quality of individuals generated in APIC is assessed on the basis of two objectives, precision and recall. These two measures have been widely

Ant Programming Algorithms for Classification

employed in imbalanced domains, since when used together, remain sensitive to the performance on each class (Landgrebe, Paclik, Duin, & Bradley, 2006). Thus, they are appropriate to be used as objective functions, trying to maximize them simultaneously.

Precision and recall are used to evolve a Pareto front of individuals per each class considered in the training set, because owing to the fact that each colony is in charge of generating individuals predicting a particlar class, there will be *k* Pareto fronts in total. This number matches the number of fronts evolved in MOGBAP, although in this latter the multi-objective strategy devised evolves these fronts at once in the only colony that exists. Notice that AUC is also computed for each individual, since the reinforcement is based on this measure and it is used also to sort the rules in the final classifier.

Once the evolutionary process finishes in all the colonies, to select appropriately the rules that make up the final classifier, a niching procedure is run over the final Pareto front obtained in each colony. This procedure is in charge of selecting non-overlapping rules, adding them to the classifier. As the classifier acts as a decision list, rules are sorted in descending order by their AUC.

EXPERIMENTAL STUDIES

Standard Classification

An empirical study has been conducted to determine whether single-objective or multi-objective are competitive techniques for extracting comprehensible and accurate classifiers. Their results were compared with those obtained by other well-known algorithms belonging to several paradigms. To this end, the experimental study was directed as follows:

- Fifteen real data sets from the UCI machine learning repository were employed in the experimentation, presenting varied characteristics regarding dimensionality, type of attributes and number of classes.

- In order to perform a fair comparison, two preprocessing steps were carried out. First, missing values were replaced with the mode or the arithmetic mean, assuming categorical and numeric attributes, respectively. Second, since the AP algorithms and Ant-Miner cannot cope directly with numerical variables, a discretization procedure was applied to turn all continuous attributes into categorical ones. The Fayyad&Irani discretization algorithm (Fayyad & Irani, 1993) was used for such purpose. Both steps were performed by using WEKA[1].

- A stratified 10-fold cross validation procedure was followed to evaluate the performance of the algorithms. In case of non-deterministic algorithms we used 10 different seeds for each partition, so that for each data set we considered the average values obtained over 100 runs.

- For comparison purposes, we considered several rule-based algorithms belonging to different paradigms. Two AP algorithms, GBAP and MOGBAP. Three ant-based algorithms, Ant-Miner (Parpinelli, Freitas, & Lopes, 2002), Ant-Miner+ (Martens, De Backer, Vanthienen, Snoeck, & Baesens, 2007) and the hybrid PSO/ACO2 algorithm (Holden & Freitas, 2008). Three GP algorithms, a constrained syntax algorithm called Bojarczuk-GP (Bojarczuk, Lopes, Freitas, & Michalkiewicz, 2004); Tan-GP (Tan, Tay, Lee, & Heng, 2002), which implements a niching mechanism that bears some resemblance with the niching procedure used by both AP algorithms; and the recently proposed ICRM algorithm (Cano, Zafra, & Ventura, 2011), which generates very interpretable classifiers. And finally, two classic rule-based algorithms, the reduced error pruning JRIP (Cohen, 1995) and PART (Frank & Witten, 1998), which extracts rules from a decision tree.

- Regarding parameter set-up, GBAP and MOGBAP use the same configuration for the common attributes: a population of 20 ants, 100 iterations, 15 derivations allowed for the grammar, an initial and maximum pheromone amount of 1.0, a minimum pheromone amount of 0.1, an evaporation rate of 0.05, a value of 0.4 for alpha, and 1.0 for beta. The GBAP's attribute that indicates the minimum number of instances covered per rule was set to 3 instances, while MOGBAP's specific attribute of minimum coverage of instances per class was set to 5%. The other algorithms were executed using the parameters suggested by their authors. The following implementations were used: for GBAP and MOGBAP, we used our own implementations in Java. For Ant-Miner and PSO/ACO2, the open source code provided in the framework Myra[2] was employed. In case of Ant-Miner+, the code provided by the authors was used. The three GP algorithms were used using the implementations available in the framework JCLEC[3]. Finally, PART and JRIP were run by using the implementations available in WEKA.

A first experimental study focused on determining whether GBAP and MOGBAP obtained an accuracy performance competitive or better than the obtained by the rest of algorithms. Each row in the top half of Table 1 shows the average accuracy results in test obtained by each algorithm for a given data set, with the standard deviation.

Bold type indicates the algorithm that attains the best result for a particular data set. We can observe at a glance that MOGBAP reaches the best results in a 40% of the data sets considered, while GBAP obtained the best results in a 30%.

To analyze statistically these results, the Iman&Davenport test was applied (Demsar, 2006). This test computes the average rankings obtained by k algorithms over N data sets regarding one measure, distributed according to the F-distribution with (k-1) degrees of freedom, stating the null-hypothesis of equivalence among all the algorithms. The critical interval obtained was C0 = [0, 16.9189], at a significance level of alpha=0.05. The value obtained for the statistic was 47.3491, which exceeds the critical interval and, therefore, the null-hypothesis was rejected, indicating the existence of significant differences between algorithms.

Because of the rejection of the null-hypothesis by the Iman&Davenport test, we proceeded with a posthoc test to reveal the performance differences. We applied at the same significance level of alpha=0.5 the Holm test, which is a step-down posthoc procedure that tests the hypotheses ordered by significance. The results obtained revealed that MOGBAP behaved significantly better than PSO/ACO2, Ant-Miner+, Ant-Miner, ICRM, Tan-GP and Bojarczuk-GP, in this order. In the same manner, GBAP behaved significantly better than those algorithms except PSO/ACO2, with which it does not present significant differences. GBAP and MOGBAP, therefore, behave equally well regarding accuracy.

Then, a comprehensibility analysis using the same tests was carried out to study the complexity of the rule set and the rules mined by each algorithm, which can be observed in the bottom half of Table 1. Column R indicates the average number of rules obtained by an algorithm over each data set, and C/R stands for the average number of conditions per rule. The last but one row of this table represents the average ranking of each

Table 1. Standard classification comparative results: predictive accuracy (%), rule set length and rule complexity

Data set	MOGBAP Acc	σ_{Acc}	GBAP Acc	σ_{Acc}	AntMiner Acc	σ_{Acc}	AntMiner+ Acc	σ_{Acc}	PSOACO2 Acc	σ_{Acc}	Bojarczuk Acc	σ_{Acc}	Tan Acc	σ_{Acc}	ICRM Acc	σ_{Acc}	JRIP Acc	σ_{Acc}	PART Acc	σ_{Acc}
Hepat.	**85.15**	1.52	82.17	12.04	83.27	10.32	81.79	10.30	84.59	9.33	71.05	14.45	81.64	12.34	74.25	12.36	81.54	12.05	84.64	7.66
Sonar	79.49	9.26	**81.98**	7.44	76.95	6.89	76.05	7.22	78.49	8.05	79.82	9.24	73.45	7.70	69.16	8.66	80.33	6.61	77.84	8.10
Breast-c	72.02	9.62	71.40	7.86	**73.42**	7.29	73.05	6.86	68.63	6.87	68.63	10.94	60.59	10.56	63.61	8.28	72.00	6.41	68.48	7.90
Heart-c	**83.13**	4.24	82.84	5.24	78.01	6.69	82.41	5.10	82.25	5.36	70.02	7.08	77.14	6.20	73.86	4.69	82.20	5.12	80.13	6.39
Ionos.	90.55	5.67	**93.02**	4.07	84.39	6.73	92.89	4.02	89.97	4.99	76.48	8.19	87.17	6.13	88.96	7.43	91.70	5.14	88.93	4.02
Horse-c	**83.78**	4.67	82.97	6.34	82.71	4.73	81.79	6.03	82.06	4.93	82.52	6.06	82.15	6.77	82.89	7.21	83.72	6.35	81.5	3.72
Vote	94.89	2.92	94.37	3.57	94.29	3.27	94.66	3.72	94.80	3.81	**95.67**	2.78	95.60	3.65	**95.67**	3.61	95.44	3.52	94.51	3.08
Austr.	**87.38**	4.27	85.47	4.49	85.30	4.12	83.48	3.38	85.19	4.69	85.52	4.50	86.21	4.31	86.84	4.20	86.70	5.15	84.66	4.48
Breast-w	95.41	2.31	**96.50**	1.68	94.69	2.04	94.28	2.86	95.86	1.91	87.39	2.75	94.11	2.76	88.69	2.66	95.71	1.81	95.71	1.82
Credit-g	70.82	3.33	70.79	4.27	70.55	3.72	70.80	3.87	70.36	3.55	63.02	7.03	66.77	6.11	68.90	4.68	70.70	3.26	**72.70**	3.26
Iris	95.33	6.00	**96.00**	4.10	95.20	5.47	94.00	3.59	95.33	6.70	91.73	10.46	95.00	2.80	94.00	5.57	**96.00**	5.33	95.33	6.70
Wine	**98.24**	2.75	97.01	4.37	91.86	6.08	93.86	4.61	90.20	2.86	83.69	9.44	93.44	6.10	90.43	6.12	95.61	5.37	95.03	3.89
Lymph.	80.55	9.74	**81.00**	10.35	75.51	9.59	77.23	10.91	76.59	12.20	77.78	12.77	78.35	9.95	79.29	9.60	78.84	11.49	78.43	14.30
Glass	71.03	8.45	69.13	8.66	65.52	9.26	62.03	9.80	71.16	10.54	39.23	11.34	65.06	10.29	67.50	6.00	69.00	8.70	**73.91**	8.43
Primary	**42.18**	7.19	37.91	6.55	37.75	5.27	37.26	5.43	37.19	5.88	16.41	4.96	26.20	6.13	22.29	5.30	38.11	3.75	38.36	5.09
RANK.	**2.5333**		3.3		6.4667		6.2333		5.7		7.9333		7.2		6.8		3.7333		5.1	

Data set	MOGBAP R	C/R	GBAP R	C/R	AntMiner R	C/R	AntMiner+ R	C/R	PSOACO2 R	C/R	Bojarczuk R	C/R	Tan R	C/R	ICRM R	C/R	JRIP R	C/R	PART R	C/R
Hepat.	9.1	1.99	8.1	1.89	4.8	1.99	3.9	3.25	7.4	2.28	3.1	**1.22**	6.5	4.3	**2.0**	2.00	3.8	2.15	8.4	2.30
Sonar	11.1	2.04	12.3	1.81	5.2	2.07	4.0	3.48	6.1	2.92	3.0	**1.00**	7.6	4.27	**2.0**	2.00	4.6	2.21	17.1	2.12
Breast-c	11.8	1.69	13.2	1.91	6.0	1.28	5.4	2.82	11.8	1.75	3.5	**1.01**	9.0	4.36	**2.0**	2.00	3.3	1.70	17.1	2.12
Heart-c	9.9	2.25	14.5	1.67	5.9	1.20	4.4	2.82	11.9	3.81	**3.0**	3.02	6.5	4.38	5.0	**1.15**	5.3	2.32	17.3	2.35
Ionos.	6.8	1.49	11.1	1.18	8.8	1.41	4.5	4.03			3.1	**1.14**	5.3	4.32	**2.0**	2.00	7.7	1.48	8.2	1.83
Horse-c	9.6	2.03	9.0	1.46	6.3	1.49	4.7	3.41	20.1	3.39	3.0	**1.00**	6.9	4.25	**2.0**	1.90	3.5	1.74	13.2	2.38
Vote	6.6	2.12	17.2	2.19	5.6	1.36	5.2	2.34	6.1	1.33	3.0	**1.00**	3.1	3.21	**2.0**	**1.00**	3.1	1.38	7.7	1.84
Austr.	9.1	2.00	10.1	1.08	6.5	1.53	3.3	2.08	25.8	6.96	3.0	**1.00**	4.9	4.1	**2.0**	**1.00**	5.2	1.80	19.4	2.01
Breast-w	6.1	1.77	6.6	1.65	7.2	1.04	6.4	1.92	10.5	1.10	3.0	**1.00**	3.8	3.82	**2.0**	2.00	6.5	1.74	10.9	1.63
Credit-g	11.6	1.82	22.9	1.82	9.1	1.51	3.3	3.31	52.8	4.20	3.3	**1.17**	9.5	4.25	**2.0**	2.00	7.1	2.54	57.8	2.70
Iris	5.8	1.15	3.7	1.06	4.3	1.03	3.9	1.80	4.0	1.20	4.3	1.29	4.1	2.69	**3.0**	**1.00**	3.0	2.00	4.6	**1.00**
Wine	6.1	1.47	7.2	1.50	5.1	1.33	**2.5**	2.19	4.0	1.73	4.1	**1.27**	5.6	3.88	3.0	2.00	4.2	1.56	6.3	1.77
Lymph.	11.9	1.55	10.2	1.60	4.7	1.69	4.6	2.83	15.6	2.11	5.1	**1.02**	9.1	3.79	**4.0**	1.25	6.9	1.53	10.2	2.30
Glass	17.5	2.22	21.6	1.79	8.4	1.76	12.4	4.10	24.5	3.13	8.2	**1.48**	11.9	4.07	7.0	1.67	8.0	2.03	13.7	2.32
Primary	34.9	2.53	45.9	2.60	12.1	3.35	9.3	8.50	86.5	6.01	23.7	**1.37**	46.6	4.16	22.0	1.88	**8.3**	3.13	48.7	3.23
R	7.5666		8.1666		5.2333		3.8333		7.4333		2.9333		5.5666		**1.4666**		3.7666		9.0333	
C/R	5.1333		3.7		3.7333		8.3333		7.1333		**2.1333**		9.4666		4.4		4.2666		6.7	

algorithm with regards to the rule set length, and the last row indicates the average rankings regarding the number of conditions per rule.

Regarding the number of rules in the classifier, the best result would be to extract one rule predicting each class in the data set. Nevertheless, this may be detrimental for the accuracy of the algorithm, as happens for Bojarczuk-GP and ICRM. At a significance level of alpha=0.05, ICRM obtained significant differences with respect to Ant-Miner, Tan-GP, PSO/ACO2, MOGBAP, GBAP and PART, in this order. Bojarczuk-GP, JRIP and Ant-Miner+ also behaved significantly better than MOGBAP and GBAP regarding this metric.

Concerning the average number of conditions per rule, Bojarczuk-GP obtained significant differences with MOGBAP, PART, PSO/ACO2, Ant-Miner+ and Tan-GP algorithms. Bojarczuk is the unique algorithm capable of behaving statistically better than MOGBAP regarding the complexity of the rules mined. In this sense, there is no algorithm behaving significantly better than GBAP, which also outperforms statistically PSO/ACO2, Ant-Miner+ and Tan-GP.

Imbalanced Classification

It is important to introduce at this point another problem that can affect all kinds of classification problems, but that arises with special relevance when tackling imbalanced data: the problem of data set shift, i.e. the case where the distribution that follows the training data used to build a classifier is different from that of the test data (Moreno-Torres, Raeder, Alaiz-Rodríguez, Chawla, & Herrera, 2012). As depicted in Figure 5, owing to

Figure 5. Shift effect in imbalanced classification

the low presence of instances that belong to the minority class in a given training set, the model learned may misclassify instances of this class when used over the corresponding test set and, in addition, the minority class is very sensitive to misclassifications. Actually, a single error may provoke a significant drop in performance in extreme cases (Fernández, García, & Herrera, 2011).

In this work, to minimize the effects of data set shift, we do not limit to carry out a single cross-validation procedure. Instead, the experimental design has been conducted from ten separate groups of partitions with different seeds. Within a given group, partitions are mutually exclusive, and they preserve as far as possible the same proportion of instances per class as in the original data set, i.e., they are stratified for the sake of introducing minimal shift, trying to avoid sample selection bias, which occurs when the partitions are selected non-uniformly at random from the data set (Moreno-Torres, Raeder, Alaiz-Rodríguez, Chawla, & Herrera, 2012). Then, a 5-fold cross validation procedure is performed per each group of partitions, where each algorithm is executed five times, with a different partition left out as the test set each time, the other four being used for training. The global AUC obtained by a classifier in a given data set is estimated by considering the average AUC over the fifty experiments (five experiments per group of partitions):

$$AUCtest = \sum_{i=1}^{10} \frac{\sum_{j=1}^{5} \frac{AUCP_{ij}}{5}}{10}$$

where P_{ij} stands for the partition j of the group of partitions i, and $AUCP_{ij}$ represents the AUC obtained by the classifier when the partition P_{ij} is left out as the test set.

Moreover, notice that when evaluating the performance of nondeterministic algorithms (all the algorithms, except NN CS and C-SVM CS), ten different seeds are considered, carrying out the stratified 5-fold cross-validation nine additional times, in order to avoid any chance of obtaining biased results. Thus, for a given data set, these algorithms are executed five hundred times in total, whereas in the case of deterministic algorithms, fifty runs are performed.

The experimentation has been split into binary and multi-class sides. APIC is compared against the following baseline algorithms or approaches for binary imbalanced classification: ADAC2 (Sun, Kamel, Wong, & Wang, 2007), a boosting algorithm that produces an ensemble of decision trees; NNCS (Zhou & Liu, 2006), a cost-sensitive neural network; CSVM-CS (Tang, Zhang, Chawla, & Krasser, 2009), a cost-sensitive support vector machine; C4.5-CS (Ting, 2002), a cost-sensitive C4.5 decision tree; RUS+C4.5 (Wilson & Martinez, 2000), random undersampling of over-represented instances, and then application of C4.5 algorithm; SBC+C4.5 (Yen & Lee, 2006), undersampling based on clustering, and then application of C4.5 algorithm; SMOTE+C4.5 (Chawla, Bowyer, Hall, & Kegelmeyer, 2002), which uses SMOTE to generate underrepresented class instances and then applies the C4.5 algorithm; and SMOTE-TL+C4.5 (Tomek, 1976), which first uses SMOTE to generate underrepresented class instances, then removes instances near the boundaries using TL, and finally applies the C4.5 algorithm.

In the case of multi-class imbalance classification, we compared APIC against OVO and OVA decomposition schemes, both using C4.5-CS as base classifier.

Notice that owing to the fact that APIC can cope only with nominal attributes, for the sake of carrying out a fair comparison, training partitions were discretized using the Fayyad&Irani discretization algorithm in order to contain only nominal attributes. Then, the cut points found were used to discretize also the corresponding test partitions. The experiments carried out for the binary experimental study were performed using the implementations available in the KEEL[4] software tool. On the other hand, we use our own implementations for the decomposition schemes used in the multi-class experimental study. The parameter setup used for APIC was the following: population size of 20 ants, 100 generations, a maximum number of 10 derivations, an initial amount of pheromone and a maximum amount of pheromone of 1.0, a minimum amount of pheromone equal to 0.1, an evaporation rate of 0.05, a value of 0.4 for the alpha exponent and a value of 1.0 for the beta exponent. For the other algorithms, parameters advised by the authors in their respective publications were used.

Binary Experimental Study

Each row in Table 2 shows the average AUC results obtained per algorithm in a given binary data set, after performing the experiments as described previously. Data sets are ordered by their imbalance ratio (IR), which can be seen in the second column of the table. APIC obtains the best results in 8 data sets, obtaining also the best result in other 3 data sets, but tied with other approaches. The last row of the table shows the average ranks obtained by each algorithm.

To analyze statistically these results, we performed the Iman&Davenport test. The value obtained for the statistic was 26.9765. Since the critical interval for a probability level of alpha=0.01 is [0, 8.232], the computed statistic value is not comprised in the critical interval, and the null-hypothesis was rejected, which means that there are significant differences among the algorithms regarding the AUC results.

To reveal the performance differences it is necessary to proceed by carrying out a posthoc test. Since all classifiers are compared to a control one, it is possible to perform the Bonferroni-Dunn test (Demsar, 2006). The critical difference value obtained by this test is equal to 2.2818. It is easy to compute those algorithms that behave significantly better than APIC, just adding the critical difference value to the ranking of APIC, which is the control algorithm, and looking at those algorithms whose ranking exceeds the value obtained. These algorithms are those whose ranking value is over 5.015: AdaC2, C45-CS, NN-CS, CSVM-CS, SBC-C4.5, in this order. In addition, our proposal obtains competitive or even better AUC results than SMOTE-TL+C4.5, SMOTE+C4.5 and RUS+C4.5.

Multiclass Experimental Study

Table 3 shows the average AUC results obtained by each algorithm per multi-class data set. Here the IR value shown in the second column represents the highest imbalance ratio between any pair of classes, and data sets are also ordered in terms of their IR. Our proposal, APIC, obtains the best AUC results in 10 of the 15 data sets.

Table 2. Binary imbalanced classification comparative results: AUC

Dataset	IR	APIC	AdaC2	NN CS	C-SVM CS	C4.5 CS	RUS C4.5	SBC C4.5	SMOTE C4.5	SMOTE TL+C4.5
Ecoli0vs1	1.86	0.9811	0.9742	0.9808	0.9811	0.9811	0.9811	0.5000	0.9792	0.9792
Iris0	2.00	1.0000	0.9850	1.0000	1.0000	1.0000	1.0000	0.5000	0.9855	0.9852
Haberman	2.78	0.6410	0.5720	0.5052	0.5000	0.4992	0.6311	0.5528	0.6350	0.6343
Glass0123vs456	3.20	0.9200	0.9193	0.9161	0.7923	0.9131	0.9066	0.6823	0.9181	0.9245
Ecoli1	3.36	0.8917	0.8834	0.7735	0.5003	0.8965	0.8941	0.5378	0.8861	0.8857
Ecoli2	5.46	0.8493	0.8952	0.6892	0.7248	0.8469	0.8423	0.5000	0.8834	0.8772
Glass6	6.38	0.9012	0.8898	0.7800	0.8365	0.9115	0.8994	0.5789	0.9090	0.9093
Yeast2vs4	9.08	0.8598	0.8950	0.7404	0.6573	0.8963	0.9242	0.5016	0.8861	0.8974
Ecoli067vs5	9.09	0.8495	0.7645	0.8207	0.8072	0.5385	0.8741	0.5114	0.8488	0.8434
Yeast0256vs3789	9.14	0.7760	0.5843	0.5575	0.5007	0.4981	0.8011	0.6068	0.7673	0.7850
Ecoli01vs235	9.17	0.8507	0.5597	0.7459	0.7104	0.8612	0.8454	0.5504	0.8423	0.8534
Glass04vs5	9.22	0.9719	0.9927	0.9916	0.9689	0.9927	0.9276	0.5000	0.9709	0.9681
Yeast05679vs4	9.35	0.7830	0.7596	0.5000	0.5000	0.5000	0.7787	0.5099	0.7753	0.7785
Ecoli067vs35	10.00	0.8352	0.5803	0.792	0.7403	0.5842	0.8383	0.5236	0.8461	0.8440
Led7digit02456789vs1	10.97	0.8883	0.7076	0.5595	0.5000	0.8379	0.8667	0.5000	0.8850	0.8703
Cleveland0vs4	12.62	0.7121	0.5874	0.5711	0.5379	0.6487	0.6942	0.5001	0.7489	0.8745
Shuttle0vs4	13.87	1.0000	0.9897	0.9999	1.0000	1.0000	1.0000	0.5000	0.9992	0.9994
Glass4	15.47	0.7885	0.8306	0.5923	0.5082	0.7848	0.8079	0.5660	0.8971	0.8952
Ecoli4	15.80	0.8789	0.8801	0.7345	0.7314	0.7403	0.8068	0.5000	0.8698	0.8764
Abalone9vs18	16.40	0.7095	0.6434	0.5159	0.4999	0.4801	0.6906	0.6624	0.6768	0.6909
Glass016vs5	19.44	0.9131	0.9375	0.5279	0.4980	0.9273	0.8721	0.5009	0.9565	0.9431
Shuttle2vs4	20.50	0.9950	0.9650	0.9959	0.9850	0.9150	0.9150	0.5000	0.9950	0.9985
Glass5	22.78	0.9185	0.9367	0.5246	0.4988	0.9230	0.8812	0.5000	0.9392	0.9338
Yeast2vs8	23.10	0.7739	0.6462	0.7339	0.5614	0.5000	0.7739	0.5045	0.7960	0.8001
Yeast4	28.10	0.8048	0.7279	0.5000	0.5000	0.6033	0.8029	0.5007	0.7643	0.7770
Yeast1289vs7	30.57	0.6285	0.6037	0.5574	0.5031	0.5000	0.5832	0.5000	0.6266	0.6406
Yeast5	32.73	0.9521	0.8567	0.5828	0.5000	0.9481	0.9429	0.5000	0.9418	0.9494
Ecoli0137vs26	39.14	0.7997	0.7774	0.6410	0.5285	0.6836	0.7775	0.5000	0.7977	0.8184
Yeast6	41.40	0.8533	0.7822	0.5860	0.5000	0.5275	0.8504	0.5000	0.8272	0.8243
Abalone19	129.44	0.7100	0.5185	0.5027	0.5000	0.5281	0.6958	0.5808	0.5670	0.5721
Ranking		2.7333	5.1833	6.2500	7.2333	5.3166	3.8000	8.0333	3.5000	2.9500

Table 3. Multiclass imbalanced classification comparative results: AUC

Data set	IR	APIC	OVO C4.5-CS	OVA C4.5-CS
Penbased	1.09	0.9639	0.9561	0.9285
Hayes-roth	1.70	0.7279	0.8333	0.7902
Contraceptive	1.88	0.6765	0.6626	0.6045
Wine	2.71	0.9688	0.9389	0.9257
New-thyroid	5.00	0.9621	0.9621	0.9404
Dermatology	5.55	0.9608	0.9746	0.9599
Balance	5.87	0.7381	0.7125	0.7399
Glass	8.44	0.9486	0.8423	0.8591
Autos	16.00	0.8406	0.8493	0.8820
Thyroid	39.17	0.9686	0.9847	0.9725
Lymphography	40.50	0.9397	0.7247	0.8070
Ecoli	71.50	0.9465	0.8100	0.8516
Pageblocks	164.00	0.9370	0.8984	0.8787
Yeast	295.80	0.8988	0.8166	0.7219
Shuttle	853.00	0.9850	0.9281	0.9695

To realize if there were significant differences, we performed the Wilcoxon rank-sum test (Demsar, 2006) at the significant level of alpha=0.05. We can use this test since there are only three algorithms involved in the study, performing multiple pairwise comparisons among the algorithms. The Wilcoxon rank-sum test statistic is the sum of the ranks for observations from one of the samples. The *p*-value for this test regarding the performance of APIC against OVO using C4.5-CS as base classifier was 0.04792, while in the comparison against the OVA scheme using the same base classifier, the *p*-value obtained was 0.03016. Both values are below 0.05 and, therefore, the null-hypothesis was rejected for both comparisons. As can be observed, OVO behaves slightly better than OVA, but our proposal outperforms them with a confidence level higher than 95%.

CONCLUSION

This chapter presents three AP algorithms for classification rule mining. They are guided by a CFG and use two complementary heuristic measures that conduct the search process of new valid individuals.

In addition to their novelty, concerning GBAP and MOGBAP, their results demonstrate that AP can be successfully employed to tackle standard classification problems, just as GP has demonstrated previously in other research. Specifically, results prove that multi-objective evaluation in AP is more suitable for the classification task than single-objective. They also proved statistically that both AP algorithms outperform most of the other algorithms regarding predictive accuracy, also obtaining a good trade-off between accuracy and comprehensibility.

On the other hand, the third AP algorithm presented, APIC, deals with the classification of imbalance data sets. Its main advantage is that it addresses conveniently both the classification of binary and multiclass imbalanced data sets, whereas traditional imbalanced algorithms are specifically devised to address just one of them. In addition, APIC deals with the classification problem directly, without needing to carry out a preprocessing step to balance data distributions. Results demonstrate that APIC performs exceptionally well both in binary and multiclass imbalanced domains.

As open issues we can mention that it would be interesting to try other kind of encoding schemes for representing individuals. It might be also possible to improve the results of these algorithms by hybridizing them with other techniques. Finally, self-adaptive versions of these algorithms might involve an important benefit for data miners non-expert in the basics of AP and ACO.

REFERENCES

Berlanga, F., Rivera, A., Del Jesus, M., & Herrera, F. (2010). GP-COACH: Genetic Programming-based learning of COmpact and ACcurate fuzzy rule-based classification systems for High-dimensional problems. *Information Sciences*, *180*, 1183–1200. doi:10.1016/j.ins.2009.12.020

Bojarczuk, C., Lopes, H., Freitas, A., & Michalkiewicz, E. (2004). A constrained-syntax genetic programming system for discovering classification rules: Application to medical data sets. *Artificial Intelligence in Medicine*, *30*, 27–48. doi:10.1016/j.artmed.2003.06.001 PMID:14684263

Cano, A., Zafra, A., & Ventura, S. (2011). An EP algorithm for learning highly interpretable classifiers. In *Proceedings of Intelligent Systems Design and Applications (ISDA)* (pp. 325–330). Cordoba, Spain: IEEE. doi:10.1109/ISDA.2011.6121676

Chawla, N., Bowyer, K., Hall, L., & Kegelmeyer, W. (2002). SMOTE: Synthetic minority over-sampling techniques. *Journal of Artificial Intelligence Research*, *16*, 321–357.

Cohen, W. (1995). Fast effective rule induction. In *Proceedings of International Conference on Machine Learning (ICML)*, (pp. 115-123). Tahoe City, CA: ICML.

Dehuri, S., Patnaik, S., Ghosh, A., & Mall, R. (2008). Application of elitist multi-objective genetic algorithm for classification rule generation. *Applied Soft Computing, 8*, 477–487. doi:10.1016/j.asoc.2007.02.009

Demsar, J. (2006). Statistical comparisons of classifiers over multiple data sets. *Journal of Machine Learning Research, 7*, 1–30.

Espejo, P., Ventura, S., & Herrera, F. (2010). Article. *IEEE Transactions on Systems, Man and Cybernetics. Part C, Applications and Reviews, 40*(2), 121–144. doi:10.1109/TSMCC.2009.2033566

Fawcett, T. (2006). An introduction to ROC analysis. *Pattern Recognition Letters, 27*, 861–874. doi:10.1016/j.patrec.2005.10.010

Fayyad, U., & Irani, K. (1993). Multi-interval discretization of continuous-valued attributes for classification learning. In *Proceedings of International Joint Conference on Uncertainly in Artificial Intelligence (IJCAI)*, (pp. 1022-1029). Chambéry, France: IJCAI.

Fernández, A., García, S., & Herrera, F. (2011). *International Conference on Hybrid Artificial Intelligence Systems (HAIS)*, (LNAI), (vol. 6678, pp. 1-10). Berlin: Springer.

Fernández, A., García, S., & Herrera, F. (2011). Addressing the classification with imbalanced data: Open problems and new challenges on class distribution. In *Proceedings of International Conference on Hybrid Artificial Intelligent Systems (HAIS)* (pp. 1-10). Wroclaw, Poland: Springer.

Frank, E., & Witten, I. (1998). Generating accurate rule sets without global optimization. In *Proceedings of International Conference on Machine Learning*, (pp. 144-151). Madison, WI: Academic Press.

Galar, M., Fernández, A., Barrenechea, E., Bustince, H., & Herrera, F. (2011). An overview of ensemble methods for binary classifiers in multi-class problems: Experimental study on one-vs-one and one-vs-all schemes. *Pattern Recognition, 44*(8), 1761–1776. doi:10.1016/j.patcog.2011.01.017

Geyer-Schulz, A. (1995). *Fuzzy rule-based expert systems and genetic machine learning*. Physica-Verlag.

Holden, N., & Freitas, A. (2008). A hybrid PSO/ACO algorithm for discovering classification rules in data mining. *Journal of Artificial Evolution and Applications, 2*, 1–11. doi:10.1155/2008/316145

Koza, J. (1992). *Genetic programming: on the programming of computers by means of natural selection*. Cambridge, MA: The MIT Press.

Landgrebe, T., Paclik, P., Duin, R., & Bradley, A. (2006). Precision-recall operating characteristic (P-ROC) curves in imprecise environments. In *Proceedings of International Conference on Pattern Recognition (ICPR)*, (pp. 123-127). Hong Kong, China: ICPR.

Liu, W., Chawla, S., Cieslak, D., & Chawla, N. (2010). A robust decision tree algorithm for imbalanced data sets. In *Proceedings of SIAM International Conference on Data Mining (SDM)*, (pp. 766-777). Columbus, OH: SIAM.

Martens, D., De Backer, M., Vanthienen, J., Snoeck, M., & Baesens, B. (2007). Classification with ant colony optimization. *IEEE Transactions on Evolutionary Computation*, *11*, 651–665. doi:10.1109/TEVC.2006.890229

Moreno-Torres, J. G., Raeder, T., Alaiz-Rodríguez, R., Chawla, N. V., & Herrera, F. (2012). A unifying view on dataset shift in classification. *Pattern Recognition*, *45*(1), 521–530. doi:10.1016/j. patcog.2011.06.019

Olmo, J., Luna, J., Romero, J., & Ventura, S. (2013). Mining association rules with single and multi-objective grammar guided ant programming. *Integrated Computer-Aided Engineering*, *20*(3), 217–234.

Olmo, J., Romero, J., & Ventura, S. (2011). Article. *IEEE Transactions on Systems, Man, and Cybernetics. Part B, Cybernetics*, *41*(6), 1585–1599. doi:10.1109/TSMCB.2011.2157681

Olmo, J. L., Cano, A., Romero, J. R., & Ventura, S. (2012). Binary and multiclass imbalanced classification using multi-objective ant programming. In *Proceedings of International Conference on Intelligent Systems Design and Applications (ISDA)*, 70-76. doi:10.1109/ISDA.2012.6416515

Parpinelli, R., Freitas, A., & Lopes, H. (2002). Data mining with an ant colony optimization algorithm. *IEEE Transactions on Evolutionary Computation*, *6*, 321–332. doi:10.1109/TEVC.2002.802452

Roux, O., & Fonlupt, C. (2000). Ant programming: or how to use ants for automatic programming. In *Proceedings of International Conference on Swarm Intelligence (ANTS)*, (pp. 121-129). Brussels, Belgium: ANTS.

Sun, Y., Kamel, M. S., Wong, A. K., & Wang, Y. (2007). Cost-sensitive boosting for classification of imbalanced data. *Pattern Recognition*, *40*, 3358–3378. doi:10.1016/j.patcog.2007.04.009

Tan, K., Tay, A., Lee, T., & Heng, C. (2002). Mining multiple comprehensible classification rules using genetic programming. In *Proceedings of IEEE Congress on Evolutionary Computation (IEEE CEC)* (pp. 1302-1307). Honolulu, HI: IEEE.

Tang, Y., Zhang, Y., Chawla, N., & Krasser, S. (2009). SVMs modeling for highly imbalanced classification. *IEEE Transactions on Systems, Man, and Cybernetics. Part B, Cybernetics*, *39*(1), 281–288. doi:10.1109/TSMCB.2008.2002909 PMID:19068445

Ting, K. M. (2002). An instance-weighting method to induce cost-sensitive trees. *IEEE Transactions on Knowledge and Data Engineering*, *14*, 659–665. doi:10.1109/TKDE.2002.1000348

Tomek, I. (1976). Two modifications of CNN. *IEEE Transactions on Systems, Man, and Cybernetics*, *6*, 769–772. doi:10.1109/ TSMC.1976.4309452

Wilson, D., & Martinez, T. (2000). Reduction techniques for instance-based learning algorithms. *Machine Learning*, *38*, 257–286. doi:10.1023/A:1007626913721

Yen, S., & Lee, Y. (2006). Cluster-Based Sampling Approaches to Imbalanced Data Distributions. In *Data Warehousing and Knowledge Discovery* (pp. 427–436). Springer. doi:10.1007/11823728_41

Zhou, Z. H., & Liu, X. Y. (2006). Training cost-sensitive neural networks with methods addressing the class imbalance problem. *IEEE Transactions on Knowledge and Data Engineering*, *18*(1), 63–77. doi:10.1109/TKDE.2006.17

KEY TERMS AND DEFINITIONS

Ant Colony Optimization: A swarm intelligence method that allows to heuristically generating good solutions based on the real observed behaviour of ant colonies, that is, in their search for the shortest path between food sources and their nest by iteratively creating, following and improving trail pheromones deposited by other individuals.

Ant Programming: An automatic programming technique that uses the principles of ant colony optimization in the search for optimal computer programs.

Association Rule: A descriptive rule in the form of *IF antecendent THEN consequent*, where both the antecedent and the consequent are sets of conditions fulfilling the requirement of not having any attribute in common.

Automatic Programming: A technique that aims at finding automatically computer programs from a high-level statement of what needs to be done, without being necessary to know the structure of the solution beforehand.

Context-Free Grammar: A formal grammar consisting of a set of terminal symbols; a set of nonterminal symbols; a set of production rules of the form A → B, where A is a single nonterminal symbol and B is a string of either terminal or nonterminal symbols; and a start symbol from which the initial string is generated. A grammar is said to be context free when its production rules can be applied regardless of the context of a nonterminal.

Genetic Programming: An evolutionary computing technique based on genetic algorithms in which small computer programs in form of lists or tress of variable size are optimized, being specially concerned with maintaining closure during the population initialization and operators application.

k-Fold Cross Validation: A technique to divide data into k sets (k-1 sets for training and 1 for test), which guarantees that results from statistical tests using these data are independent of the sets constructed.

Niching Method: Procedure used in evolutionary computation that allows to maintain the diversity of the population by locating and promoting multiple, optimal subsolutions on the way to a final solution.

Pareto Dominance: In multi-objective problems, the best solutions are sometimes obtained as the trade-off of various objectives, since no optimal solution for every objective could be found. Having two solutions, A and B, B is said to be Pareto dominated by A if A is at least as good as B in all objectives, and better than B in at least one of them.

Rule-Based Classifier: A classifier made of single rules expressed as *IF antecedent THEN class*, which acts as a decision list, having rules ordered by a given criterion. The final rule added to the classifier serves as default rule.

ENDNOTES

[1]   WEKA is available at http://www.cs.waikato.ac.nz/ml/index.html

[2]   Myra is available at http://myra.sourceforge.net/

[3]   JCLEC framework is available at http://jclec.sourceforge.net

[4]   KEEL is available at http://www.keel.es/

Chapter 6
Machine Fault Diagnosis and Prognosis using Self-Organizing Map

Kesheng Wang
NTNU, Norway

Zhenyou Zhang
NTNU, Norway

Yi Wang
University of Manchester, UK

ABSTRACT

This chapter proposes a Self-Organizing Map (SOM) method for fault diagnosis and prognosis of manufacturing systems, machines, components, and processes. The aim of this work is to optimize the condition monitoring of the health of the system. With this method, manufacturing faults can be classified, and the degradations can be predicted very effectively and clearly. A good maintenance scheduling can then be created, and the number of corrective maintenance actions can be reduced. The results of the experiment show that the SOM method can be used to classify the fault and predict the degradation of machines, components, and processes effectively, clearly, and easily.

1. INTRODUCTION

Traditional preventive maintenance schemes as age-replacement are time-based without considering the current health state of the product, and thus are inefficient and less valuable for a customer whose individual asset is of the utmost concern. The major role of degradation analysis is to investigate the evolution of the physical characteristics, or performance measures, of a product leading up to its failure (Lee, Ni, Djurdjanovic, Qiu, & Liao, 2006). A maintenance scheme, referred to as Condition-based Maintenance (CBM), is developed by considering current degradation and its evolution. CBM methods and practices have continued to improve over recent decades. The main idea of CBM is to utilize the product degradation information extracted and identified

DOI: 10.4018/978-1-4666-6078-6.ch006

from on-line sensing techniques to minimize the system downtime by balancing the risk of failure and achievable profits (Vachtsevanos, Lewis, Roemer, Hess, & Wu, 2006). The decision making in CBM focuses on predictive maintenance according to the states of monitored products. It performs maintenance action just when it is needed before the failure happens. To do so, many diagnostic and prognostics tools, methods and algorithms have to be developed to detect and predict the fault as early as possible.

The function of fault diagnosis is to find out root cause of the observed process or machinery degradation. The tasks of fault diagnosis are detecting, isolating, and identifying an impending or incipient failure condition—the affected component (subsystem, system) is still operational even though at a degraded mode. Fault detection means detecting and reporting an abnormal operating condition. Fault isolation means determining which component/system/subsystem is failing or has failed. Fault identification means estimating the nature and extent of the fault. Therefore, through fault diagnosis, the condition of manufacturing machines can be determined accurately impending or incipient failure conditions without false alarms.

Fault prognosis, on the other hand, is predicting the Remaining Useful Life (RUL) according to the current state of product. It predicts when the observed process or equipment is going to fail or degrade to the point that its performance becomes unacceptable. It aims at extrapolating the behavior of process signatures over time and predicts their behavior in the future.

Fault diagnosis and prognosis are the basis for the strategy of CBM which can reduce the maintenance cost and production loss, and improve the reliability and prolong the life of the machines. This chapter mainly discusses how to apply Self-organizing Map (SOM) in fault diagnosis and prognosis for manufacturing systems. The features in time domain of vibration signals are extracted, and then conditions of machine are predicted and

the faults are classified. The following of this chapter is organized as follows. Section 2 reviews the related work in fault diagnosis and prognosis. In Section 3, the concept and principle of Self-organizing map (SOM) are introduced. Section 4 presents the experimental setup for validation of the proposed method. The features extracted from time domain are described in Section 5. Section 6 shows the procedure of experiment and its results. The conclusions are given in Section 7.

2. RELATED WORK

Over the last several decades, there has been a wide range of approaches and implementation strategies for performing manual, semi-automated, or fully automated fault diagnosis and prognosis on critical systems in commercial and defense markets (Vachtsevanos, et al., 2006). In recent years, the fault diagnosis and prognosis has gained much attention in development of Intelligent Systems (Berenji et al., 2006). As mentioned in Section 1, fault diagnosis aims at detecting fault of a machine after their occurrences, while fault prognosis aims at predicting faults before their occurrences. Fault diagnosis is a type of classification problem, and artificial intelligence techniques based classifiers could be used to classify normal and faulty machine conditions effectively and efficiently (Kankar, et al., 2011). Fault prognosis is a type of classification problem as well, and the difference with diagnosis is that the prognosis should classify the whole condition into continuous or several discrete extents of degradation from perfect condition to absolutely failure. Therefore, the artificial intelligence techniques based classifiers could be used in fault prognosis as well because it is also a classification problem. A machine fault diagnosis and prognosis solution consists of two main steps: the one is feature extraction from raw vibration signals or other raw signals to extract some useful features that demonstrate the information of fault, and the other is to use these extracted features for fault diagnosis using various artificial intelligence techniques such as artificial neural networks, support vector machines, etc. (Berenji & Wang, 2006; Kankar, et al., 2011; Laouti, et al., 2011).

For rotating machine, vibration signals are very popular used in fault diagnosis and prognosis. However, the complex and non-stationary vibration signals with a large amount of noise make the challenging in fault diagnosis and prognosis of machines, especially at the early stage. Therefore, development of effective and novel diagnosis and prognosis procedures are needed using different signal analyzing procedures for features extraction and soft computing techniques in order to avoid the system shutdowns, and even catastrophes involving human fatalities and material damage. To analyze vibrations signals and extract features, many different techniques are extensively used. These techniques can be classified into three types: time domain (Chen, et al., 2008; Wang, et al., 2010), frequency domain such as fast Fourier transformation (Corinthios, 1971; Liu, et al., 2010; Rai & Mohanty, 2007) and time-frequency domain such as the short time Fourier transformation (Portnoff, 1980), Hilbert-Huang transform (Yu, Yang, & Cheng, 2007), Wigner-ville distribution (Andria, et al., 1994; Staszewski et al., 1997; Wang, et al., 2008) and wavelet transformation (Chen, et al., 2005; Lin & Qu, 2000; Prabhakar, et al., 2002; Seker & Ayaz, 2003; Tse, et al., 2004; Wu & Chen, 2006; Wu & Liu, 2009; Zheng, et al., 2002). All these time-frequency techniques were developed successfully.

After signal processing and feature extraction, there are many techniques could be used to diagnose the fault and predict remaining useful life of machines. Support vector machine (SVM) learning is used in many applications of machine learning because of its high accuracy and good generalization capabilities (Saravanan, et al., 2008). Li, et al. (2005) proposed a hidden Markov model (HMM)-based fault diagnosis in speed-up and speed-down process for rotary machinery. In

the implementation of the system, one PC was used for data sampling and another PC was used for data storage and analysis. A network communication was also set up between the two computers for data transmission. Wu and Chow (Wu & Chow, 2004) presented a self-organizing map (SOM) based radial-basis-function (RBF) neural network method for induction machine fault detection. The system was implemented by utilizing a PC and additional data acquisition equipment. Due to the strength of artificial neural networks (ANN), such as the ability to easily deal with complex problems without sophisticated and specialized knowledge, the ability to carry out classifications, the ability to deal with non-linear systems and low operational response times after the learning phase, many methods based on ANN have been developed for online surveillance with knowledge discovery, novelty detection and learning abilities (Kasabov, 2001; Markou & Singh, 2003; Marzi, 2004). Artificial Neural Network, Fuzzy Logic System, Genetic Algorithms and Hybrid CI (Computational Intelligence) Systems were applied in fault diagnosis and a case of centrifugal pump was utilized to show how the method works (Sun, et al., 2012; Wang, 2002; Ye, et al., 2010). Lee, et al. (Lee, et al., 2006) developed an intelligent prognostics and e-maintenance system named "Watchdog Agent" with the method of Statistical matching and performance signature and Support Vector Machine (SVM) based diagnostic tool.

3. SELF-ORGANIZING MAP (SOM)

3.1. Artificial Neural Network (ANN)

The pattern classification theory has become a key factor in fault diagnosis and prognosis. Some classification methods for equipment performance monitoring use the relationship between the type of fault and a set of patterns which is extracted from the collected signals without establishing explicit models. Currently, ANN is one of the most popular methods in this domain. ANN is a model that emulates a biological neural network (Wang, 2005). The origin of ANN can be traced back to a seminar paper by McCulloch and Pitts (McCulloch & Pitts, 1943) that demonstrated a collection of connected processors, loosely modeled on the organization of brain, could theoretically perform any logical or arithmetic operation. Then, the development of ANN techniques is very fast which is extensive to many categories containing Back-propagation (BP), Self-organization Mapping (SOM) and Radial Basis Function (RBF), etc. The application of artificial neural network models lies in the fact that they can be used to infer a function from observations. This is particularly useful in applications where the complexity of the data or task makes the design of such a function by hand impractical. This attribution is very nontrivial in diagnostic problems (Wang, 2005).

Robert Hecht Nielsen in 1990 defined ANN as: "An Artificial Neural Network is a parallel, distributed information-processing element (which can possess a local memory and can carry out localized information processing operations) interconnected together with unidirectional signal channels called connections. Each processing element has a single output connection which branches ("fans out") into as many collateral connections as desired (each carrying the same signal - the processing element output signal). The processing element output signal can be of any mathematical type desired. All of the processing that goes on within each processing element must be completely local; i.e., it must depend only upon the current values of the input signal arriving at the processing element via impinging connections and upon values stored in the processing element's local memory (Nielsen, 1990)." It can deal with complex non-linear problem without sophisticated and specialized knowledge of the real systems. It is an effective classification techniques and low operational response times needed after training. The relationship between the condition of component and the features is not linear but

non-linear which the ANN techniques can solve very sufficiently. SOM permits to cluster data where there is no prior knowledge of the results or of the clustering. Therefore, it is very suitable to be applied in condition clustering when the condition is not well defined in the training data. This section mainly introduces the concept and principle of SOM.

3.2. Self-Organizing Map

Machine learning is an approach of using data to synthesize programs. In the particular case when the data are input/output pairs, it is called supervised learning. In a case, where there are no output values and the learning task is to gain some understanding of the process that generated the data, this type of learning is said to be unsupervised (Kankar, et al., 2011). The concept of SOM was introduced by Teuvi Kohonen in 1982 (Kohonen, 1982), and numerous versions, generalizations, accelerated learning scheme, and application of SOM have been developed since then. It is a type of artificial neural network that is trained using unsupervised learning to produce a low-dimensional, discretized representation of the input space of the training samples, called a map. The SOM is the closest of all Artificial Neural Networks architectures and learning schemes to the biological neuron network. Its network is composed by only one layer of neurons arranged in tow dimensional plane with a well-defined topology.

The most important unsupervised ANNs learning algorithm is the Kohonen competitive learning algorithm, and Figure 1 shows a typically example of Kohonen map. The neurons on the output layer (also called competitive layer) can find the organization of relationship among input patterns. The output of each neuron isn't connected to all of the other neurons in the plane, but only to a small number that are topologically close to it. The network map shows the natural relationship between the patterns, that is, each input neuron is connected to every neuron on

Figure 1. Kohonen Model of SOM

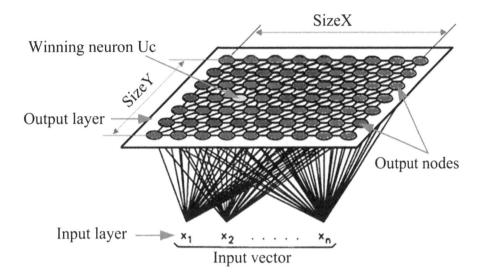

the competitive layer which is organized as two-dimensional grids. The network is presented by a set of training input patterns without target output patterns. At the beginning one of the patterns is chosen randomly, and then each neuron in the input layer of the SOM takes on the value of the corresponding entry in the input pattern. In the competitive learning, only one neuron in the output layer is selected after input occurs, regardless of how close the other neurons are from the best one. This is so-called "Winner takes it all" method.

In generally, the learning process of SOM network can be classified in following steps.

1. Initializing the weight vector randomly ω_{ij}, the learning rate $\eta(t)$ and other relative training parameters.
2. For each input vector, the responses of all neurons in the output layer are calculated and the winning node U_c is selected. The winning node means its weight ω_{ij} best matches the input vector that is the Euclidean Distance is the smallest among all nodes.
3. After the winning node is selected, identifying the neighborhood around U_c, that is the set of competitive units close to the winning

node. Figure 2 shows the two example of a neighborhood around wining node: the one is rectangular lattice and the other is the hexagonal lattice. The size of the neighborhood begins with a large enough size and then decreases with the number of iterations of the network.

4. Updating the weight vectors of node U_c and all nodes in the neighborhood around it by the following function:

$$\omega_j(t+1) =$$
$$\begin{cases} \omega_j(t) + \eta(t) \cdot f(d_c - d_i) \cdot (x - \omega_j(t)) & j \in H(t) \\ \omega_j(t) & \text{otherwise} \end{cases}$$

(1)

$$H(t) = H_0(1 - \frac{t}{T}) \qquad (2)$$

$$\eta(t) = (\eta_{\max} - \eta_{\min})\frac{T-t}{T-1} + \eta_{\min} \qquad (3)$$

where t is the current learning epoch; x is input vector; T is the total number of learning epoch; H_0 is the initial neighborhood size; d_c-d_i is the topological distance between the central neuron c and the current neuron I; f

Figure 2. Different forms of the neighborhood in SOM network around Uc

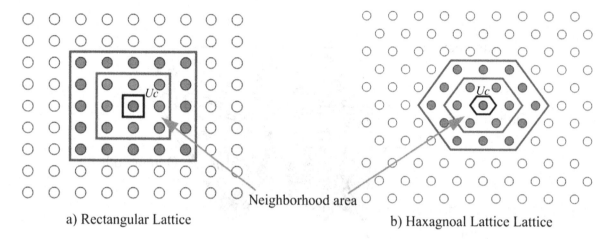

a) Rectangular Lattice   b) Haxagnoal Lattice Lattice

is topology dependent function; $H(t)$ is the actual neighborhood size in tth epoch; $\omega_j(t)$ is the weigh vectors of Uc and its neighborhood in tth epoch; and $\eta(t)$ is the learning rate in tth epoch.

5. Updating the learning rate $\eta(t)$ using Equation (3).
6. Reduce the neighborhood function $H(t)$ using Equation (2).
7. Loop from 2) to 6) until no noticeable changes of the feature map.

The squared distance between an observed data x^j and its corresponding (nearest) node is the quantization error. Summing this quantization error over all data leads to the quantization error of the SOM which indicate the quality of SOM mapping to the original input data. It can be expressed as (Bodt, Cottrell, & Verleysen, 2002):

$$quantization\_error = \sum_{i=1}^{U} \sum_{x_j \in V_i} d^2(x_j, G_i)$$
$$= \sum_{x_j} \min_{1 \le i \le U} d^2(x_j, G_i)$$

(4)

where U is the number of nodes in the SOM, G_i is the ith node, d is the classical Euclidean distance,

V_i is the Voronoi region associated to G_i, i.e. the region of the space nearer to G_i than to any other centroid, and the sums on x_j cover all observed data. According to Equation (1), the process of SOM training is to find the minimum value of quantization error.

Topographic error (TE), in other word, defined as the proportion of data points which the closest and second-closest weight neurons are not adjacent on the neuron lattice (Box 1) (Neme & Miramontes, 2005).

Lattices in which SOMs are formed are almost always regular (Figure 2). By regular, we mean that neurons are connected only to neighbors and that every neuron has approximately the same number of connecting edges (same degree). Topographic errors together with quantization error are two parameters to indicate the quality of SOM mapping.

SOM network has some advantages and some disadvantages. SOM permits to cluster data where there is no prior knowledge of the results or of the clustering. It is able to convert multi-dimensional data clusters into the form of a two-dimensional grid preserving the topological relationship of the data. It may be used where there is ample supply of "good normal" data containing some but little bad or usual data. That is engine monitoring or alarm monitoring. The SOM has very serious

Box 1. Topographic error calculation

$$\varepsilon = \frac{1}{N} \sum_{i=1}^{N} \eta(x_i, \omega_2, \omega_{2,} ..., \omega_U) \quad (5)$$

$$\eta(x_i, \omega_2, \omega_2, ..., \omega_U) = \begin{cases} 1, \text{ if } \forall l \exists j, \ k : l \ \in \{1, ..., \ j-1, j \ +1, \ ..., \ k-1, k \ +1, \ ...U\} \\ \quad \|m_j - x_i\| \le \|m_k - x_i\| < \|m_l - x_i\|, \ |j-k| > 1 \\ 0, \quad \text{otherwise} \end{cases} \quad (6)$$

where:
- N: The number of input data;
- ε : Topographic error;
- U: The number of nodes (lattices).

computational disadvantages, which affects the performance of large scale application running on parallel computers. In order to find which neuron is to be stimulated, the program has to check all of the neurons. This is a big restriction when large SOM network are to be trained. Sometimes grid size may need to be adjusting in response to number of clusters expected.

4. EXPERIMENTAL SETUP

To research how to apply SOM to fault diagnosis and prognosis in rotating machine, a simple experimental setup is established in Knowledge Discovery Laboratory (KDL) at NTNU.

4.1. Experimental Setup

We can only find a medium pressure blower in KDL as the research object. The plan is to run the blower in several simulated conditions and simultaneously collect vibration signals by mounting some accelerometers. The processed vibration signals can be used to train and test SOM. Therefore, the hardware of the setup is: the blower, two accelerometers, a power supply and coupler for

accelerometers, and instrument equipment such as DAQ card, BNC connector etc. Figure 3 shows the hardware of the experimental setup which contains a blower, two vibration sensors, power supply for sensors, connector, DAQ card and a computer. In this setup, the blower is selected as monitoring object and a kind of vibration sensors (Kistler: Type 8702B100) are chosen to collect the signals from the blower. Two sensors are setup on the blower in horizontal and vertical directions which collect the vibration signals in these directions (Figure 4). The signals are collected from the sensors and processed using some signal processing method such as filter, de-noising and compression. Then the features are extracted in time domain, frequency domain or/and wavelet domain which can be used to train and query artificial neural network. After training, the system can determine the state of machine or component using real time signals.

4.2. Experimental Procedure

In the present study, four different degradations of unbalance are simulated using three different parts (Figure 5) which are mounted in the axis end of the blower. The unbalance degradation (condi-

Figure 3. Hardware of experimental setup

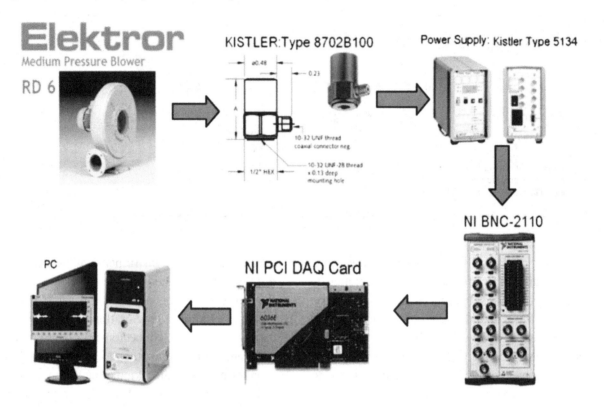

Figure 4. Sensors setup on blower

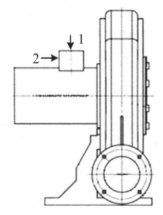

Figure 5. Parts for simulation degradation

tion) contains Low (L), Medium (M), Medium-High (M-H) and High (H) which represent the performance states from perfect to absolutely failure (unbalance). In the first case, power on the blower, collect and store signals from the sensors without amounting any simulation part. Next, power off the blower and mount first part in the axis end and then, power on the blower, collect and store the signals from sensors. Repeat this process until collect all the degrading signals simulated by simulation parts. Figure 6 shows the signals of the second sensor from perfect state to absolutely failure.

5. FEATURE EXTRACTION

Feature selection has a significant impact on the success of pattern recognition for fault diagnosis and prognosis. Root mean square (RMS) value, crest factor, kurtosis, skewness, standard deviation, etc. are the most commonly used statistical measures used for fault diagnosis of rotary machines. Statistical moments like kurtosis, skewness and standard deviation are descriptors of the shape of the amplitude distribution of vibration data, and have some advantages over traditional time and frequency analysis, such as its lower sensitivity to the variations of load and speed, the analysis of the condition monitoring results is easy and convenient, and no precious history of the component life is required for assessing the component condition. In this Chapter, statistical parameters like kurtosis, skewness, etc. are used as features to effectively detect periodic failures:

1. **Peak Value:** The value between the maximum value and minimum value of the vibration signal.

$$Pv = \frac{1}{2}[\max(x_i) - \min(x_i)] \qquad (7)$$

where x_i is the amplitude at sampling point i and N is the number of sampling points.

2. **RMS Value:** RMS is short for root mean square which is a statistical measure of the magnitude of a varying quantity.

Figure 6. Raw signals with different degradations

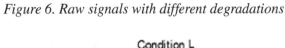

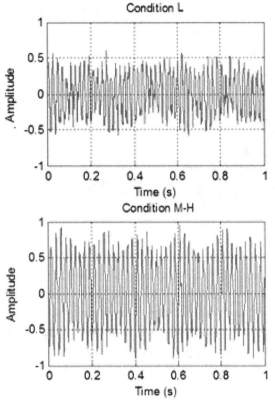

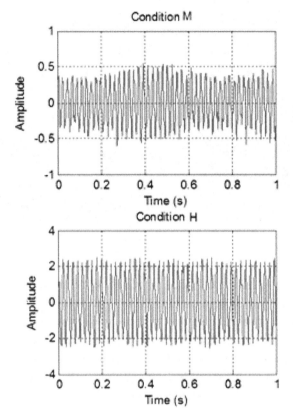

$$RMS = \sqrt{\frac{1}{N}\sum_{i=1}^{N}(x_i)^2} \qquad (8)$$

3. **Standard Deviation:** Standard deviation is measure of energy content in the vibration signal.

$$SD = \sqrt{\frac{1}{N}\sum_{i=1}^{N}(x_i - \bar{x})^2} \qquad (9)$$

4. **Kurtosis Value:** Kurtosis is a statistical measure used to describe the distribution of observed data around the mean. It is defined as the degree to which a statistical frequency curve is peaked.

$$Kv = \frac{\frac{1}{N}\sum_{i=1}^{N}(x_i - \bar{x})^4}{(RMS)^2} \qquad (10)$$

5. **Crest Factor:** The crest factor is also called peak-to-average ratio or peak-to-average power ratio which is a measurement of a waveform, calculated from the peak amplitude of the waveform divided by the RMS value of the waveform.

$$Crf = \frac{Peak \quad Value}{RMS \quad Value} \qquad (11)$$

6. **Clearance Factor:**

$$Clf = \frac{Peak \quad Value}{\left(\frac{1}{N} \sum_{i=1}^{N} \sqrt{|x_i|} \right)^2} \qquad (12)$$

8. **Shape Factor:** Shape factor is dimension-less quantities used in signal analysis that numerically describe the shape of a signal, independent of its size.

7. **Impulse Factor:**

$$Imf = \frac{Peak \quad Value}{\frac{1}{N} \sum_{i=1}^{N} |x_i|} \qquad (13)$$

$$Shf = \frac{RMS \quad Value}{\frac{1}{N} \sum_{i=1}^{N} |x_i|} \qquad (14)$$

Figure 7. Experimental procedure

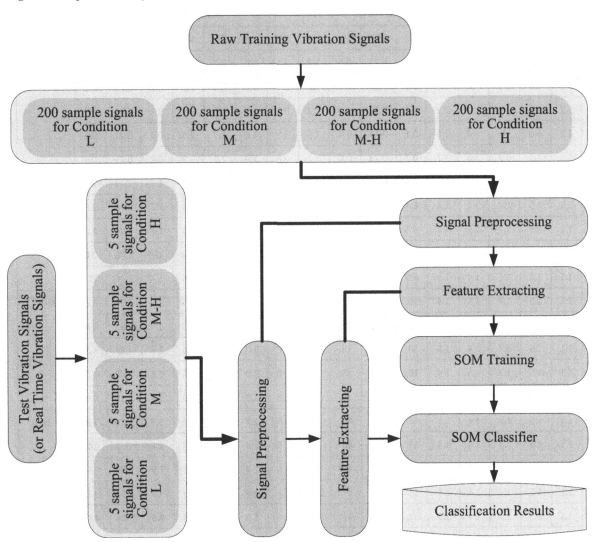

These features are fed as input to the artificial intelligence techniques for fault classification and prediction. In this chapter, SOM neural network are selected as a classification tool for fault diagnosis and prognosis.

6. EXPERIMENT AND ITS RESULTS

In order to verify the effectiveness and correctness of the proposed method, an experiment is designed in the KDL lab at NTNU. The hardware system is shown in Figure 3 which include the monitoring object a blower, two vibration sensors, and other necessary instruments. The sensors mounting direction is shown in Figure 4. Two sensors collect the signals in vertical and horizontal directions. Figure 7 shows the procedure of the experiment. Firstly, for each condition (L, M, M-H and H), 200 samples of vibration signals are collected as raw training data for SOM using two sensors mounting on blower. And then the collected signals are

Table 1. Part of SOM training data

Sensor 1								Sensor 2								Condition
Shf	*Imf*	*Clf*	*Crf*	*Kv*	*SD*	*RMS*	*Pv*	*Shf*	*Imf*	*Clf*	*Crf*	*Kv*	*SD*	*RMS*	*Pv*	
1.3	3.5	4.6	2.7	2.9	0.1	0.21	0.5	1.2	3.5	4.6	2.7	2.7	0.2	0.22	0.6	L
1.2	3.1	4.1	2.4	2.2	0.1	0.20	0.4	1.2	3.1	3.9	2.4	2.7	0.2	0.22	0.5	
1.2	2.8	3.6	2.2	2.1	0.1	0.18	0.4	1.2	3.2	3.9	2.6	2.7	0.2	0.21	0.5	
1.2	3.0	4	2.4	2.5	0.1	0.19	0.4	1.3	3.5	4.8	2.7	2.8	0.2	0.21	0.5	
1.2	3.3	4.3	2.6	2.7	0.2	0.23	0.6	1.1	2.8	3.4	2.3	2.1	0.2	0.25	0.6	
1.1	1.5	1.7	1.4	1.4	6.4	6.44	9.1	1.1	1.8	2.1	1.6	1.7	1.7	1.73	2.8	M
1.1	1.5	1.7	1.4	1.4	6.4	6.48	9.3	1.1	1.8	2.0	1.6	1.6	1.7	1.78	2.8	
1.1	1.5	1.7	1.4	1.4	6.5	6.53	9.3	1.1	1.8	2.0	1.6	1.6	1.7	1.76	2.8	
1.1	1.5	1.7	1.4	1.5	6.4	6.45	9.2	1.1	1.8	2.0	1.5	1.6	1.7	1.76	2.8	
1.1	1.5	1.7	1.4	1.5	6.5	6.51	9.3	1.1	1.7	1.9	1.5	1.6	1.7	1.76	2.7	
1.1	1.5	1.7	1.4	1.4	10.	10.7	15.	1.1	1.7	2	1.5	1.6	2.9	2.92	4.6	M-H
1.1	1.6	1.7	1.4	1.5	10.	10.6	15.	1.1	1.7	1.9	1.5	1.5	2.9	2.91	4.4	
1.1	1.6	1.7	1.4	1.5	10.	10.6	15.	1.1	1.8	2.0	1.6	1.6	2.8	2.82	4.5	
1.1	1.5	1.7	1.4	1.4	10.	10.8	15.	1.1	1.8	2.0	1.5	1.6	2.8	2.88	4.5	
1.1	1.5	1.7	1.4	1.4	10.	10.9	15.	1.1	1.8	2.0	1.5	1.6	2.9	2.96	4.6	
1.1	1.5	1.7	1.4	1.5	32.	32.5	46.	1.1	1.6	1.7	1.4	1.5	9.8	10.2	14.	H
1.1	1.5	1.7	1.4	1.4	33.	33.1	46.	1.1	1.6	1.8	1.4	1.5	10.	10.2	14.	
1.1	1.5	1.7	1.4	1.5	33.	33.2	47.	1.1	1.6	1.8	1.4	1.5	9.9	9.95	14.	
1.1	1.5	1.7	1.4	1.5	33.	33.2	47.	1.1	1.6	1.8	1.5	1.5	9.9	9.94	14.	
1.1	1.5	1.7	1.4	1.5	33.	33.2	47.	1.1	1.6	1.8	1.4	1.5	9.9	9.96	14.	

preprocessed such as de-noising, amplification and filtering, and afterward, the features which were described in section 5 are extracted. The features are used to train SOM neural network. For each condition, 5 samples of the same kind of vibration signals are collected as SOM test data. These signals are processed and the features are collected the same as training data which can be used to test the SOM classifier. And finally the

classification results are presented graphically. As for this experiment, a 12×12 map of SOM is used as classifier which could be trained firstly and then could be used to classify the different conditions of the blower. The total number of training number (epochs) is 500. Table 1 shows parts of training data while Table 2 shows the test data.

Figure 8 shows the training process of the experiment. Figure 8(a) shows quantization er-

Table 2. SOM test data

Sensor 1								Sensor 2								Condition
Shf	*Imf*	*Clf*	*Crf*	*Kv*	*SD*	*RMS*	*Pv*	*Shf*	*Imf*	*Clf*	*Crf*	*Kv*	*SD*	*RMS*	*Pv*	
1.24	2.91	3.75	2.36	2.21	0.179	0.181	0.427	1.18	2.73	3.25	2.3	2.16	0.246	0.252	0.58	L
1.27	3.03	3.93	2.38	2.41	0.187	0.192	0.458	1.28	3.2	4.19	2.51	2.68	0.264	0.267	0.671	
1.21	2.77	3.37	2.3	2.11	0.191	0.199	0.458	1.31	3.44	4.45	2.63	2.9	0.262	0.266	0.702	
1.29	3.25	4.19	2.53	2.95	0.18	0.193	0.488	1.23	3.05	3.83	2.47	2.42	0.257	0.259	0.641	
1.23	2.94	3.7	2.4	2.24	0.193	0.204	0.488	1.24	2.96	3.71	2.4	2.36	0.229	0.229	0.549	
1.11	1.58	1.73	1.43	1.49	6.498	6.499	9.277	1.13	1.88	2.09	1.66	1.63	1.907	1.908	3.174	M
1.11	1.59	1.74	1.43	1.5	6.568	6.571	9.399	1.14	1.79	2	1.58	1.63	1.951	1.954	3.083	
1.11	1.58	1.73	1.43	1.48	6.673	6.671	9.521	1.13	1.77	1.96	1.57	1.59	2.001	2.001	3.144	
1.11	1.58	1.73	1.43	1.48	6.534	6.533	9.308	1.12	1.77	1.95	1.58	1.55	1.93	1.93	3.052	
1.11	1.58	1.73	1.43	1.48	6.528	6.526	9.308	1.13	1.83	2.04	1.62	1.62	1.94	1.94	3.144	
1.12	1.62	1.78	1.45	1.54	11.22	11.23	16.27	1.12	1.74	1.92	1.55	1.62	3.338	3.341	5.188	M-H
1.12	1.62	1.78	1.45	1.54	11.39	11.4	16.54	1.12	1.72	1.89	1.53	1.59	3.401	3.403	5.219	
1.12	1.62	1.78	1.45	1.54	11.26	11.28	16.33	1.12	1.71	1.89	1.53	1.62	3.33	3.332	5.097	
1.12	1.61	1.77	1.45	1.53	11.27	11.28	16.3	1.12	1.7	1.87	1.52	1.59	3.358	3.358	5.097	
1.12	1.62	1.78	1.45	1.53	11.21	11.22	16.3	1.12	1.76	1.94	1.57	1.62	3.277	3.279	5.158	
1.11	1.56	1.7	1.41	1.48	33.66	33.65	47.33	1.1	1.51	1.65	1.37	1.44	10.62	10.61	14.56	H
1.11	1.57	1.72	1.42	1.49	33.45	33.45	47.39	1.11	1.55	1.69	1.4	1.46	10.46	10.46	14.68	
1.11	1.58	1.72	1.42	1.5	33.3	33.31	47.3	1.11	1.57	1.71	1.41	1.48	10.37	10.38	14.68	
1.12	1.61	1.77	1.44	1.53	32.68	32.72	47.15	1.12	1.59	1.75	1.43	1.51	10.25	10.26	14.62	
1.12	1.62	1.78	1.45	1.54	32.65	32.71	47.33	1.11	1.59	1.75	1.43	1.51	10.27	10.28	14.71	

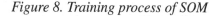

Figure 8. Training process of SOM

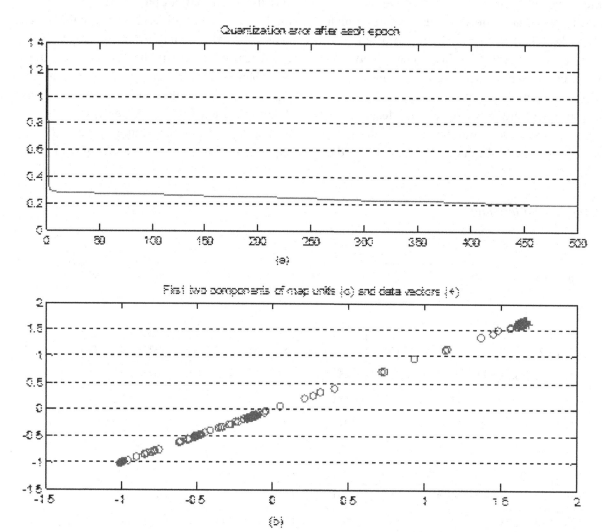

ror after each epoch, and the final quantization error is 0.195 and the final topographic error is 0.068. Figure 8(b) shows the similar and difference between the first two components of map node and data vectors. From the figure, the first two parameters of training data are obvious four groups. From the beginning, the two components of map nodes are distributed randomly, after training, however, most map nodes are distributed four groups around the same groups of training data vectors, and the others are boundary of the map nodes but not distributed in the groups.

Figure 9 shows the results of the experiment. Figure 9(a) shows the U-matrix which is short for unified distance matrix which means the Euclidean distance between the SOM node vectors of the neighboring neurons is depicted in a gray scale image. From this figure, it is easy to see that the maps are classified as four different groups clearly. Figure 9(b) and (c) display the distributions variable Pv and variable RMS. From these two figures, the map is classified as four groups and group boundaries for each variable are very clear. Figure 9(d) shows the label (represent conditions

Figure 9. Classification result of SOM

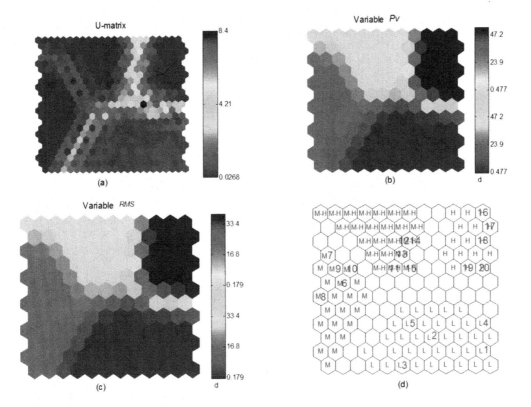

of L, M, M-H and H) predefined for each node if this node represents a kind of condition. From these four figures, the groups could be classified and the boundaries are very clearly. The numbers in Figure 9(d) represent the sequence of the test data which are from 1-5 represent low condition (L), from 11-15 represent middle condition (M), from 16-20 represent middle high condition (M-H) and from 21- 25 represent high condition (H). From this figure, all test data are located their own nodes, and the results are very clear and easy to understand.

After training and test, SOM can be applied for online condition classification of components or machines. Figure 10 shows a current condition of the monitored component, i.e. blower unbalance in this case. It shows that SOM, after training, can be easily applied online for component condition monitoring and the result is very easy to understand even for unskilled staff.

7. CONCLUSION

In this Chapter, the authors described a Self-organizing Map (SOM) classifier applying in fault prediction for a machine (i.e. a blower in this paper) which could be seen as pattern classification as well. The self-organizing map describes a mapping from a higher dimensional input space to a lower dimensional map space. In the experiment in this Chapter, SOM map sixteen dimensional variables into two dimensional maps (12×12). The result of SOM method is very effective, clear and easy to understand. The results of the experiment shows SOM is very suitable for solving this kind of problem like fault prediction, fault classification and other kind of pattern recognitions.

Through this Chapter, the way to continuously monitor the condition of machines, components, systems and processes have been found. The first stage is determining the number of neurons of a

Figure 10. Classification Result of SOM

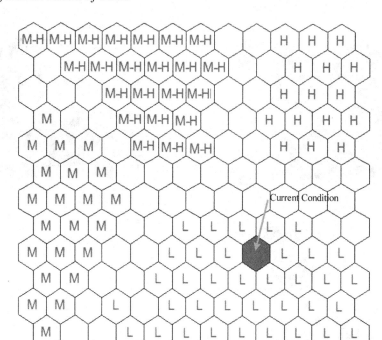

two-dimensional SOM lattice and the number of clusters of the conditions and fault type according to the real machines or systems. The second stage is training SOM map which is mapping the many of variables to the predefined SOM neurons, that is finding the groups of lattice which each of them represent a kind of condition or fault. The third stage is finding the location of the test data or real time data inside the lattice. Finally, the conditions or faults of machines, components, systems or processes could be determined according to the trained lattice and the location of the test data or real time data.

Although the results of this Chapter are really expected, there are still something can be done in the future. In this Chapter, only one type of fault with five conditions is researched. However, this is not enough and not fitting the real situation. In the future, more types of faults and degradations should be considered.

This Chapter only uses offline data to test trained SOM neurons, but in the future, the real time data should be used for real time monitoring, control and maintenance.

Finally, in the future, SOM could be applied in these kinds of problems such as pattern recognition combining with other machine learning method such as Support Vector machine (SVM) and Supervised Back-propagation (SBP).

REFERENCES

Andria, G., Savino, M., & Trotta, A. (1994). Application of Wigner-Ville Distribution to Measurements on Transient Signals. *IEEE Transactions on Instrumentation and Measurement*, *43*(2), 187–193. doi:10.1109/19.293418

Berenji, H. R., & Wang, Y. (2006). *Wavelet Neural Networks for Fault Diagnosis and Prognosis*. Academic Press. doi:10.1109/FUZZY.2006.1681883

Berenji, H. R., Wang, Y., & Saxena, A. (2006). Dynamic Case Based Reasoning in Fault Diagnosis and Prognosis. In *Proceedings of the 14th IEEE International Conference on Fuzzy Systems,* (pp. 845–850). IEEE. doi:10.1109/FUZZY.2005.1452504

Chen, C., Changcheng, S., Yu, Z., & Nan, W. (2005). Fault diagnosis for large-scale wind turbine rolling bearing using stress wave and wavelet analysis. In *Proceedings of 2005 International Conference on Electrical Machines and Systems* (pp. 2239–2244). IEEE. doi:10.1109/ICEMS.2005.202966

Chen, G., Liu, Y., Zhou, W., & Song, J. (2008). Research on intelligent fault diagnosis based on time series analysis algorithm. *Journal of China Universities of Posts and Telecommunications, 15*(1), 68–74. doi:10.1016/S1005-8885(08)60064-3

Corinthios, M. J. (1971). A fast Fourier transformation for high-speed signal processing. *IEEE Transactions on Computers, 20*(8), 843–846. http://doi.ieeecomputersociety.org/ 10.1109/T-C.1971.223359 doi:10.1109/T-C.1971.223359

de Bodt, E., Cottrell, M., & Verleysen, M. (2002). Statistical tools to assess the reliability of self-organizing maps. *Neural Networks, 15*(8-9), 967–978. doi:http://dx.doi.org/10.1016/S0893-6080(02)00071-0

Kankar, P. K., Sharma, S. C., & Harsha, S. P. (2011). Rolling element bearing fault diagnosis using wavelet transform. *Neurocomputing, 74*(10), 1638–1645. doi:10.1016/j.neucom.2011.01.021

Kasabov, N. (2001). Evolving fuzzy neural networks for supervised/unsupervised online knowledge-based learning. *IEEE Transactions on Systems, Man, and Cybernetics. Part B, Cybernetics: A Publication of the IEEE Systems. Man, and Cybernetics Society, 31*(6), 902–918. doi:10.1109/3477.969494

Kohonen, T. (1982). Self-organized formation of topologically correct feature maps. *Biological Cybernetics, 43,* 59–66. doi:10.1007/BF00337288

Lee, J., Ni, J., Djurdjanovic, D., Qiu, H., & Liao, H. (2006). Intelligent prognostics tools and e-maintenance. *Computers in Industry, 57*(6), 476–489. doi:10.1016/j.compind.2006.02.014

Li, Z., Wu, Z., He, Y., & Fulei, C. (2005). Hidden Markov model-based fault diagnostics method in speed-up and speed-down process for rotating machinery. *Mechanical Systems and Signal Processing, 19*(2), 329–339. doi:10.1016/j.ymssp.2004.01.001

Lin, J., & Qu, L. (2000). Feature extraction based on Morlet wavelet and its application for mechanical diagnosis. *Journal of Sound and Vibration, 234*(1), 135–148. doi:10.1006/jsvi.2000.2864

Liu, Y., Guo, L., Wang, Q., An, G., Guo, M., & Lian, H. (2010). Application to induction motor faults diagnosis of the amplitude recovery method combined with FFT. *Mechanical Systems and Signal Processing, 24*(8), 2961–2971. doi:10.1016/j.ymssp.2010.03.008

Markou, M., & Singh, S. (2003). Novelty detection: a review–part 2: Neural network based approaches. *Signal Processing, 83*(12), 2499–2521. doi:10.1016/j.sigpro.2003.07.019

Marzi, H. (2004). Real-time fault detection and isolation in industrial machines using learning vector quantization. *Proceedings of the Institution of Mechanical Engineers. Part B, Journal of Engineering Manufacture, 218*(8), 949–959. doi:10.1243/0954405041486109

McCulloch, W. S., & Pitts, W. (1943). A logical calculus of the ideas immanent in nervous activity. *The Bulletin of Mathematical Biophysics, 5*(4), 115–133. doi:10.1007/BF02478259

Nassim, L. (2011). Support Vector Machines for Fault Detection in Wind Turbines. In B. Sergio (Ed.), *Proceedings of the 18th IFAC World Congress, 2011* (pp. 7067–7072). Milano, Italy: IFAC. doi:10.3182/20110828-6-IT-1002.02560

Neme, A., & Miramontes, P. (2005). Statistical Properties of Lattices Affect Topographic Error in Self-organizing Maps. In W. Duch, J. Kacprzyk, E. Oja, & S. Zadrożny (Eds.), *Artificial Neural Networks: Biological Inspirations* (pp. 427–432). Springer. doi:10.1007/11550822_67

Nielsen, R. H. (1990). *Neurocomputing*. Addison-Wesley.

Portnoff, M. R. (1980). Time-Frequency Representation of. Digital Signals. *IEEE Transactions on Acoustics. Speech and Signal Processing ASSP, 28*(1), 55–69. doi:10.1109/TASSP.1980.1163359

Prabhakar, S., Mohanty, A. R., & Sekhar, A. (2002). Application of discrete wavelet transform for detection of ball bearing race faults. *Tribology International, 35*(12), 793–800. doi:10.1016/S0301-679X(02)00063-4

Rai, V. K., & Mohanty, A. R. (2007). Bearing fault diagnosis using FFT of intrinsic mode functions in Hilbert–Huang transform. *Mechanical Systems and Signal Processing, 21*(6), 2607–2615. doi:10.1016/j.ymssp.2006.12.004

Saravanan, N., Kumar Siddabattuni, V. N. S., & Ramachandran, K. I. (2008). A comparative study on classification of features by SVM and PSVM extracted using Morlet wavelet for fault diagnosis of spur bevel gear box. *Expert Systems with Applications, 35*(3), 1351–1366. doi:10.1016/j.eswa.2007.08.026

Seker, S., & Ayaz, E. (2003). Feature extraction related to bearing damage in electric motors by wavelet analysis. *Journal of the Franklin Institute, 340*(2), 125–134. doi:10.1016/S0016-0032(03)00015-2

Staszewski, W. J., Worden, K., & Tomlinson, G. R. (1997). Time-frequency Analysis Gearbox Fault Detection Using the Wigner Ville Distribution and Pattern Recognition. *Mechanical Systems and Signal Processing, 11*(5), 673–692. doi:10.1006/mssp.1997.0102

Sun, H.-C., Huang, Y.-C., & Huang, C.-M. (2012). Fault Diagnosis of Power Transformers Using Computational Intelligence: A Review. *Energy Procedia, 14*, 1226–1231. doi:10.1016/j.egypro.2011.12.1080

Tse, P. W., Yang, W., & Tam, H. Y. (2004). Machine fault diagnosis through an effective exact wavelet analysis. *Journal of Sound and Vibration, 277*(4-5), 1005–1024. doi:10.1016/j.jsv.2003.09.031

Vachtsevanos, G., Lewis, F., Roemer, M., Hess, A., & Wu, B. (2006). *Intelligent Fault Diagnosis and Prognosis for Engineering System*. John Wiley & Sons, Inc. doi:10.1002/9780470117842

Wang, C., Kang, Y., Shen, P., Chang, Y., & Chung, Y. (2010). Applications of fault diagnosis in rotating machinery by using time series analysis with neural network. *Expert Systems with Applications, 37*(2), 1696–1702. doi:10.1016/j.eswa.2009.06.089

Wang, C., Zhang, Y., & Zhong, Z. (2008). Fault Diagnosis for Diesel Valve Trains based on Time–frequency Images. *Mechanical Systems and Signal Processing*, *22*(8), 1981–1993. doi:10.1016/j.ymssp.2008.01.016

Wang, K. (2002). *Intelligent Condition Monitoring and Diagnosis Systems*. Amsterdam: IOS Press.

Wang, K. (2005). *Applied Computational Intelligence in Intelligent Manufacturing Systems*. Advanced Knowledge International Pty Ltd.

Wu, J., & Chen, J.-C. (2006). Continuous wavelet transform technique for fault signal diagnosis of internal combustion engines. *NDT & E International*, *39*(4), 304–311. doi:10.1016/j.ndteint.2005.09.002

Wu, J., & Liu, C.-H. (2009). An expert system for fault diagnosis in internal combustion engines using wavelet packet transform and neural network. *Expert Systems with Applications*, *36*(3), 4278–4286. doi:10.1016/j.eswa.2008.03.008

Wu, S., & Chow, T. W. S. (2004). Induction Machine Fault Detection Using SOM-Based RBF Neural Networks. *IEEE Transactions on Industrial Electronics*, *51*(1), 183–194. doi:10.1109/TIE.2003.821897

Ye, X., Yan, Y., & Osadciw, L. A. (2010). *Learning Decision Rules by Particle Swarm Optimization (PSO) for Wind Turbine Fault Diagnosis*. Academic Press.

Yu, D., Yang, Y., & Cheng, J. (2007). Application of Time–frequency Entropy Method based on Hilbert–Huang Transform to Gear Fault Diagnosis. *Measurement*, *40*(9-10), 823–830. doi:10.1016/j.measurement.2007.03.004

Zheng, H., Li, Z., & Chen, X. (2002). Gear Fault Diagnosis Based on Continuous Wavelet Transform. *Mechanical Systems and Signal Processing*, *16*(2-3), 447–457. doi:10.1006/mssp.2002.1482

KEY TERMS AND DEFINITIONS

Artificial Neural Networks (ANN): ANNs are computational models inspired by animals' central nervous systems that are capable of machine learning and pattern recognition.

Clustering: Clustering is the task of grouping a set of objects in such a way that objects in the same group (called a cluster) are more similar (in some sense or another) to each other than to those in other groups (clusters).

Condition-Based Maintenance (CBM): CBM is also known as predictive maintenance which means a set of activities that detect changes in the physical condition of equipment (signs of failure) in order to carry out the appropriate maintenance work for maximizing the service life of equipment without increasing the risk of failure.

Fault Diagnosis: Detecting, isolating, and identifying an impending or incipient failure condition—the affected component (subsystem, system) is still operational even though at a degraded mode.

Fault Prognosis: Fault Prognosis is the ability to predict accurately and precisely the Remaining Useful Life (RUL) of a failing component or subsystem. The task of the prognostic module is to monitor and track the time evolution (growth) of the fault.

Feature Extraction: When the input data to an algorithm is too large to be processed and it is suspected to be notoriously redundant then the input data will be transformed into a reduced representation set of features (also named features vector). Transforming the input data into the set of features is called feature extraction.

Machine Learning: Machine learning is a branch of artificial intelligence, concerns the construction and study of systems that can learn from data.

Self-Organizing Map (SOM): SOM is a type of artificial neural network (ANN) that is trained using unsupervised learning to produce a low-dimensional (typically two-dimensional), discretized representation of the input space of the training samples, called a map.

Chapter 7
An Enhanced Artificial Bee Colony Optimizer for Predictive Analysis of Heating Oil Prices using Least Squares Support Vector Machines

Zuriani Mustaffa
Universiti Utara Malaysia (UUM), Malaysia

Yuhanis Yusof
Universiti Utara Malaysia (UUM), Malaysia

Siti Sakira Kamaruddin
Universiti Utara Malaysia (UUM), Malaysia

ABSTRACT

As energy fuels play a significant role in many parts of human life, it is of great importance to have an effective price predictive analysis. In this chapter, the hybridization of Least Squares Support Vector Machines (LSSVM) with an enhanced Artificial Bee Colony (eABC) is proposed to meet the challenge. The eABC, which serves as an optimization tool for LSSVM, is enhanced by two types of mutations, namely the Levy mutation and the conventional mutation. The Levy mutation is introduced to keep the model from falling into local minimum while the conventional mutation prevents the model from over-fitting and/or under-fitting during learning. Later, the predictive analysis is followed by the LSSVM. Realized in predictive analysis of heating oil prices, the empirical findings not only manifest the superiority of eABC-LSSVM in prediction accuracy but also poses an advantage to escape from premature convergence.

DOI: 10.4018/978-1-4666-6078-6.ch007

INTRODUCTION

Over the last decades, there has been a growing interest in energy fuel price predictive analysis and this issue attracts the attention not only from practitioners but also the scientific community. Due to its significant non linearity characteristic, this issue is regarded as challenging task and received an impressive interest from time to time (Tehrani & Khodayar, 2011). In literature, considerable amount of studies on predictive analysis have been published, spanning from conventional statistical techniques to Computational Intelligence (CI) approach. Nonetheless, the obvious non linearity of energy fuel prices makes the conventional statistical techniques such as Autoregressive Integrated Moving Average (ARIMA) (Yusof, Rashid, & Mohamed, 2010) inapplicable. Such situation has led the academia to heed an attention on CI approach, which includes Artificial Neural Network (ANN) (Kulkarni & Haidar, 2009), Support Vector Machines (SVM) (Khashman & Nwulu, 2011) and also Least Squares Support Vector Machines (LSSVM) (Bao, Zhang, Yu, Lai, & Wang, 2011). As a derived version of conventional SVM (Vapnik, 1995), the LSSVM (Suykens, Van Gestel, De Brabanter, De Moor, & Vandewalle, 2002) provides an efficient learning algorithm which offers promising generalization (i.e. the ability of hypothesis to correctly predict on unseen data set) capability. With the adaptation of Structural Risk Minimization (SRM) principle, LSSVM seems to be a good candidate in addressing the over fitting problem which is found in ANN (Xiang & Jiang, 2009). Unlike Empirical Risk Minimization (ERM) which is adopted in ANN, the SRM principle tends to minimize an upper bound of generalization error rather than training error as applied in ERM (Afshin, Sadeghian, & Raahemifar, 2007). This characteristic equips the LSSVM with a great ability for generalization. With such an interesting feature, the application of LSSVM has been broadly utilized in various fields such as classification (Luts, Molenberghs, Verbeke, Van Huffel, & Suykens, 2012), prediction (Zhai & Huang, 2013) and many others. The remarkable performance of LSSVM has also attracted communities from different area includes engineering (Wu & Niu, 2009), finance (Shen, Zhang, & Ma, 2009), meteorological (Mellit, Massi Pavan, & Benghanem, 2013) so on so forth.

Even though LSSVM comes with such an interesting property, the performance of LSSVM greatly relies on the value of hyper-parameters, namely regularization parameter, γ and kernel parameter, σ^2. Both hyper parameters values will directly affect the regression accuracy and generalization of LSSVM. As to resolve this problem, in literature, it is observed that there are two common approaches in optimizing the LSSVM hyper-parameters; experimental technique and theoretical technique (Afshin, et al., 2007). In experimental technique, the Cross Validation (CV) (Afshin, et al, 2007; Mellit, et al., 2013) is commonly utilized. However, since CV requires an exhaustive search over the parameter space, in term of time, it is inefficient (Zhang, Niu, Li, & Li, 2013). In addition, the obtained error rates tend to be unsatisfactory (Yu, Chen, Wang, & Lai, 2009). On the other hand, the latter approach involved the hybridization of LSSVM with various theoretical Evolutionary Computation (EC) algorithm, such as Genetic Algorithm (GA) (Haupt & Haupt, 2004) which is developed based on natural selection (Liao & Balzen, 2013) and Particle Swarm Optimization (PSO) (Kennedy & Eberhart, 1995) which based on analogy of bird flocking and fish schooling. However, this field is still widely open for improvement as currently there exists a few others EC algorithm. Hence, the aim of this study is to utilize Artificial Bee Colony which was introduced in 2005 to optimize the algorithmic parameters of LSSVM. The ABC algorithm is inspired from the foraging behavior of honey bees swarm (Karaboga, 2005). The unique of ABC can be seen in the number of algorithmic parameters which is smaller compared to GA and PSO. Apart of two fundamental control parameters namely population size and maximum number of iteration, ABC only has one control parameter, viz. limit which can be determined based on number of parameters of interest and population size (Karaboga, 2005; Karaboga & Akay, 2009). In addition, the ABC algorithm is easy in implementation as it includes basic mathematical operators (Bolaji, Khader, Al-Betar, & Awadallah, 2013). As analysed in Bolaji, et al., (2013), these two properties are vital for diversity in application and has been proven by enormous published studies on ABC. As to enhance the predictive power of the (basic) ABC algorithm, two significant problems in learning, namely local minimum and data fitting issues are addressed using Levy mutation and conventional mutation respectively. This newly algorithm which is termed as enhanced Artificial Bee Colony (*e*ABC) will later be used to optimize the LSSVM hyper parameters. The details on the justification of enhancement are presented in the Literature Review section. The results obtained from the twofold modifications are later discussed and analysed not only in terms of error rate but also covers the premature convergence issue and the exploration behaviour of the bees during pre and post modifications.

In this study, the *e*ABC-LSSVM contributes in avoiding local minimum and prevents the model from over fitting and/or underfitting. The local minimum problem is addressed using Levy mutation, which is based on Levy Probability Distribution (LPD). As LPD provides an interesting distribution, it helps to enrich the bees searching behaviour which later contributes to achieving global minimum. For this matter, different searching strategy is introduced and this is discussed in The Proposed *e*ABC-LSSVM section. The proposed *e*ABC-LSSVM also provides means (i.e conventional mutation) to overcome the over fitting and/or underfitting problem. Such utilization produces a better generalization performance. The detail on this is also presented in The Proposed *e*ABC-LSSVM section.

In terms of application, this study realizes its proposed algorithm in the predictive analysis of heating oil price. As a refine purification product of crude oil, heating oil plays vital role in the community. Typically used as a substitute for natural gas in power generation (Dunsby, Eckstein, Gaspar, & Mulholland, 2008), the price of heating oil tend to rise due to winter demand and the increment in crude oil prices ("Heating Oil Explained," 2012). Hence, such an application would provide useful insight for investors and economic planners.

LITERATURE REVIEW

This section reviews existing work on variants of ABC, followed by the reviews on price prediction for energy fuel. Meanwhile the last subsection presents discussion on hybridization of LSSVM with Evolutionary Computation (EC) techniques which includes Evolutionary Algorithm (EA) and SI techniques.

Variants of Artificial Bee Colony Algorithm

The accessibility of ABC algorithm has made this algorithm favorable in solving various optimization issues. In literature, it is observed that many improvements have been suggested to enhance the capability of ABC. In Babayigit and Ozdemir (2012), the standard ABC is enhanced to solve numerical function optimization problem. The modification includes on how to calculate the probability and searching mechanism which later proves to be beneficial as compared to the standard ABC.

Some interesting modification to the standard ABC algorithm also includes the induction of mutation and integration with other technique, such as PSO. In Rajasekhar, Abraham, and Pant (2011), the Levy mutation is introduced in order to guide the bees in searching for global optimum. However, the predetermined value of α which belongs to LPD limits the shape of distribution, which consequently affect the searching behavior of the bees. In addition, even though the study introduced a new formulate in producing new solutions, however, the concept of depending on a single equation is still retained, which has been one of the critical concerns in literature (Bilal & Ozdemir, 2012; Sharma, et al., 2011; Subotic, 2011). Meanwhile, in Sharma, Pant, and Bhardwaj (2011), the ABC algorithm is hybridized with PSO for solving continuous optimization problems. The incorporation of PSO with ABC is to overcome the limitation of ABC which highly depends on single equation in producing new solution. The hybridization of ABC with PSO also has been presented in Shi, et al., (2010), termed as IABAP, which has been experimented on four benchmark functions. From the conducted experiment, the IABAP performed better as compared to standard ABC and PSO. Furthermore, an ABC algorithm with diversity strategy, termed as DABC has been presented by Wei and Wan (2011). The motivation of the improvement is to balance the performance of exploitation and exploration process in ABC. Tested on similar test function as in Shi, et al., (2010), the empirical results showed that the overall, the performance of DABC is better than the standard ABC.

Predictive Analysis on Energy Fuel Price

The price of energy fuel, specifically the crude oil is of paramount importance for the individual and the government. Therefore, an efficient predictive analysis of the crude oil price is utmost important. In literature, different techniques have been introduced, but this field is still wide open for improvement as there are still no definite conclusion drawn. In 2012, the crude oil price prediction based on ANN has been presented by Jammazi and Aloui (2012). In the study, the ANN

is integrated with wavelet decomposition and the model is tested on monthly prices of West Texas Intermediate (WTI). The comparison against conventional Back Propagation Neural Network (BPNN) indicated that the presented technique is superior in the context of the study.

In Kulkarni and Haidar (2009), the hybridization of Multilayer Feed Forward Neural Network (MLFNN) and back propagation algorithm is demonstrated for daily WTI crude oil prices. However, the comparison with other techniques was not presented. Upon completing the empirical procedure, the results obtained which were evaluated based on Root Mean Square Error (RMSE) and hit ratio achieved satisfying results. Meanwhile, in Tehrani and Khodayar (2011), the crude oil prices prediction is presented using GA and Feed Forward Neural Network (FFNN) with back propagation algorithm. The GA was utilized to facilitate the learning algorithm and assist in parameter tuning of ANN. Compared against standard ANN, the GA-FFNN performed better in terms of produced lower error rate.

Besides ANN, the application of other technique such as LSSVM for crude oil prices prediction has also been presented and an example can be seen in Bao, et al., (2011). As to enhance the capability of LSSVM, the technique was integrated with wavelet decomposition, termed as W-LSSVM. Realized in two types of crude oil prices, viz. WTI and Brent, the empirical results suggested that the W-LSSVM outperformed the other compared techniques.

Hybridization of LSSVM with Evolutionary Computation Algorithm

As to enhance the generalization performance of LSSVM, many hybrid approaches have been proposed, and this includes GA-LSSVM (Mustafa, Sulaiman, Shareef, & Khalid, 2012) and also PSO-LSSVM (Jiang & Zhao, 2013; (Liao, Zheng, Grzybowski, & Yang, 2011); Xiang & Jiang, 2009) In the study by Mustafa, et al. (2012), the

GA-LSSVM is employed to predict the reactive power and the comparison was performed against the results produced by ANN. The results obtained suggested that GA-LSSVM owns an advantage in terms of computational time. Besides in Mustafa, et al., (2012), the application of GA-LSSVM also has been presented in Yu, et al., (2009) in dealing with predictive analysis of stock market. In the study, the performance of GA-LSSVM model was compared against conventional Back Propagation Neural Network (BPNN), ARIMA, SVM and various LSSVM models. Similarly, the findings of the study are in favour to GA-LSSVM. Meanwhile, the study in Sun and Zhang (2008) and Xie, et al. (2009) proposed the GA-LSSVM for predictive analysis of power spot and dissolved gas concentration respectively. Both studies proved the efficiency of GA-LSSVM for the problem under study. Nonetheless, the shortcomings of GA such as slow in convergence, risk in facing with premature convergence and also difficulty in parameters selection may affect the prediction performance and hence requires careful attention (Chen, Wang, Sun, & Liang, 2008).

The hybridization of bird flocking approach with LSSVM, namely PSO-LSSVM (Jiang & Zhao, 2013) has been proposed to solve the prediction of critical heat flux. Evaluated based on coefficient of determination (R^2), Mean Relative Error (MRE) and Root Mean Square Error (RMSE), the PSO-LSSVM outperformed other comparison algorithms. Besides in Jiang and Zhao (2013), the hybridization of PSO-LSSVM has been previously demonstrated in predictive analysis of water quality (Xiang & Jiang, 2009). The study makes use of the water figures data in China which limits the study for the stated region. Meanwhile, similar study as in Xie, et al., (2009) has also been conducted by using PSO-LSSVM (Liao, et al., 2011). Upon completing the simulation task, it was concluded that the PSO-LSSVM is superior in performance than the identified techniques relative to MAPE and R^2. However, as experienced by GA, PSO also faced with similar

drawbacks; tend to fall into local minimum (Park, Jeong, Shin, & Lee, 2010) and is difficult in parameter selection due to the several algorithmic parameters embedded in the algorithm (Chen, et al., 2008).

Besides GA and PSO, the application of Differential Evolution (DE) is also presented and was realized in prediction of thermal process (Dos Santos, Luvizotto, Mariani, & Dos Santos Coelho, 2012). Empirical experimentation suggested that the proposed model, which is a modified version of DE, demonstrates better predictive power than the standard DE-LSSVM model. Nevertheless, differ to GA and PSO, in terms of diversity in application, the application of DE with LSSVM is not as widespread as experienced by both the GA and PSO. These techniques have not only been applied extensively in optimizing LSSVM hyper-parameters, buy they also shown superiority in the task. Nonetheless, as highlighted previously, the demerits of GA and PSO deserve a careful attention since it would positively affect the generalization capability of LSSVM.

Besides, GA, PSO and DE, another EC approach, viz. Artificial Bee Colony (ABC) algorithm has also been demonstrated to tackle the optimization of LSSVM hyper-parameters (Mustaffa & Yusof, 2011). The study which make used of the financial time series data suggested the superiority of ABC-LSSVM over the experimented technique. However, even though the findings of the study indicated promising results, it is worth noting that the ABC endure with imbalance performance between exploitation and exploration process (Gao & Liu, 2012). Hence, exposing the model into local minimum (Gao & Liu, 2012). This demerit reflects the progressive research trend in studying the search equation of ABC algorithm (Alam, Ul-Kabir, & Islam, 2010; Gao & Liu, 2013; Gao, Liu, & Huang, 2013). On the other hand, the tendency of the algorithm to fall into boundary values (Karaboga & Akay, 2009) also requires for modification as this would make the LSSVM vulnerable with over fitting and under fitting. As to treat such limitations, this study proposed a new hybrid technique which integrates the enhanced Artificial Bee Colony (eABC) algorithm with LSSVM (eABC-LSSVM). This study is experimented on daily energy fuel price to predict short term heating oil prices. In the study, the eABC is employed as an optimization tool to find the optimal values of the LSSVM hyper-parameters.

ESTIMATION MODEL BASED ON LSSVM

LSSVM (Suykens, et al., 2002) is a class of kernel machines which introduces square errors instead of nonnegative errors in the cost function and applies equality constraint rather than inequality constraint of SVM in the problem formulation. This reformulation results in one solves a linear set of equations (i.e. linear programming) instead of Quadratic Programming (QP) solver which in practice is harder to use. The simplification also contributes to easier and faster training task. Thus, a simpler optimization problem can be obtained. As the hyper-parameters optimization of LSSVM involved the proper selection of γ and σ^2, the optimized values of both hyper-parameters are crucial in order to achieve high generalization performance. Too large value of γ will cause LSSVM to over fit the training data while too small value of γ will make the LSSVM model exposed to under fitting problem. On the other hand, for σ^2, too large value will lead the LSSVM to expose with under fitting problem while over fitting is likely to occur when too small value is set for it (Fu, Liu, & Sun, 2010; Wu, Feng, & He, 2007).

Formally, given a training set of N points $\{x_i, y_i\}^N$ with the input values x_i and the output values y_i, for nonlinear regression, the data are generated

by the nonlinear function $y(x) = f(x_i) + e_i$, the aim is to estimate a model of the following form (Suykens, et al., 2002):

$$y(x) = w^T \varphi(x_i) + b = e_i \tag{1}$$

where w indicates the weight vector, $\varphi(.):R^n$ is the function map the input space into a higher dimensional feature space, b represents the bias and e_i denotes the error between the target value and the predicted value at the ith sample point. The input, x_i and output, $y(x)$ are described in Methodology section. The coefficient vector w and bias term b can be obtained through the optimization problem which is formulated as follows (Suykens, et al., 2002):

$$\min_{w,b,e} J(w,e) = \frac{1}{2} w^T w + \gamma \frac{1}{2} \sum_{i=1}^{N} e_i^2 \tag{2}$$

Subject to the equality constraints

$$y_i = w^T \varphi(x_i) + b + e_i, i = 1, 2, \ldots, N$$

The first part of (2) is used to regulate the weight sizes and penalize large weights. On the other hand, the second part of (2) indicates the error in training data. Applying the Lagrangian multiplier to (2) yields:

$$L(w,b,e;\alpha)$$
$$= J(w,e) - \sum_{i=1}^{N} \alpha_i \{w^T \phi(x_i) + b + e_i - y_i\} \tag{3}$$

where α_i are Lagrange multipliers called support values that can be positive or negative in LSSVM formulation due to the equality constraints, γ is the regularization parameter which balances the complexity of the LSSVM model, i.e. $y(x)$, and the training error. The solution in (3) can be obtained by partially differentiating with respect to w, b, e_i and α_i, as express in the following:

$$
\begin{aligned}
\frac{\partial L}{\partial w} &= 0 \to w = \sum_{i=1}^{N} \alpha_i \phi(x_i) \\
\frac{\partial L}{\partial b} &= 0 \to \sum_{i=1}^{N} \alpha_i = 0 \\
\frac{\partial L}{\partial e_i} &= 0 \to \alpha_i = \gamma e_i \\
\frac{\partial L}{\partial \alpha_i} &= 0 \to w^T \phi(x_i) + b + e_i - y_i = 0
\end{aligned}
\qquad i=1,2,\dots
$$

N (4)

By elimination of w and e_i, the optimization problem can be transformed into the following linear equations:

$$
\begin{bmatrix} 0 & y^T \\ y & \Omega + I/\gamma \end{bmatrix} \begin{bmatrix} b \\ \alpha \end{bmatrix} = \begin{bmatrix} 0 \\ 1_v \end{bmatrix}
\qquad (5)
$$

With $y = [y_1; \dots; y_N]$, $\alpha = [\alpha_1, \dots, \alpha_N]$, I is the identity matrix and $1_v = [1;\dots;1]$. The kernel trick is applied as follows:

$$\Omega il = \phi(x_i)T\phi(x_l) = K(x_i,x_l)i, l = 1, \dots, N \qquad (6)$$

The resulting of LSSVM model for regression in (1) becomes:

$$y(x) = \sum_{i=1}^{N} \alpha_i K(x, x_i) + b \qquad (7)$$

where α and b are the solutions of (5). In (7), among possible kernels functions $K(x, x_i)$, such as Gaussian kernel or Radial Basis Function (RBF) kernel, Polynomial kernel or Linear kernel function, RBF kernel is the most used in the practice due to its suitability in dealing with nonlinear cases (Wu, et al., 2007) and give good performance in many prediction cases (Liao, et al., 2011). It is defined by:

$$K(x, x_i) = e^{\frac{\|x-x_i\|^2}{2\sigma^2}} \qquad (8)$$

where σ^2 is a tuning parameter which associated with RBF kernel. By using kernel function, it allows the data which are not linearly separable in input space to become linearly separable in high dimensional feature space. Another tuning parameter, which is regularization parameter, γ can be seen in (2).

OPTIMIZATION BASED ON ABC ALGORITHM

The optimization of ABC algorithm is described in both theoretical and procedure of the algorithm.

ABC: Theory

Categorized as one of the branches in SI technique, ABC algorithm was first invented by Karaboga (Karaboga, 2005) to tackle the numerical optimization problem. The algorithm was developed in response to the observed success and efficiency of collective behaviors of real honey bee swarm in problem solving. Theoretically, the colony of artificial bee is populated by three groups of honeybees, namely Employed Bee (EB), Onlooker Bee (OB) and Scout Bee (SB). The division of the colony is equally distributed where half of it is comprised of the EB and the rest is filled with the OB. Meanwhile, the SB is basically a demoted EB which has to switch its role based on certain condition. This situation is described SB Phase.

ABC: Procedure

The procedure of ABC algorithm is described as follows:

Initialization Phase

In initialization phase, suppose the solution space of the problem is D-dimensional, where D is the number of parameters to be optimized, viz. γ, σ^2 (corresponds to LSSVM) and α (corresponds to LPD). Initial food sources are produced randomly within the range of the boundaries of the parameters of interest (Karaboga, 2005). It defined as follows:

$$x_{ij} = x_j^{\min} + rand(0,1)(x_j^{\max} - x_j^{\min})$$ (9)

where $x_j^{\max}$ and $x_j^{\min}$ are the upper and lower bound of parameters of interest respectively. After the population is initialized, the fitness of food source is calculated using (10) (Karaboga, 2005):

$$fit_i = \frac{1}{(1 + obj.Fun_i)}$$ (10)

where *obj. Fun* is the objective function. In this study, the objective function is served by Mean Absolute Percentage Error (MAPE).

EB Phase

Besides to search for food source, the responsibilities of EBs are also to gather required information. In term of population's size, the size of EB and OB are both equal to number of food sources, which is denoted by *SN*. For each

food source's position, one EB is assigned to it. A new food source is produced according to (11) (Karaboga, 2005):

$$v_{ij} = x_{ij} + \phi i_j(x_{ij} - x_{kj})$$ (11)

where $i = 1, 2, ..., SN, j = 1, 2, ..., D$, ϕ is a random generalized real number within the range [-1, 1],and k is a randomly selected index number in the colony which has to be different from i. In (11), if the values of the produced parameters exceed their boundary, they are automatically switched onto the boundary values (Karaboga & Akay, 2009). In each iteration, only one dimension of each position is changed. After producing the new solution v_{ij}, its fitness is calculated and compared to the previous solution x_{ij} based on greedy selection scheme, where, if the new solution has equal or better quality than the old source, the old source is replaced; otherwise the previous solution is retained.

OB Phase

The OB selects a food source to be exploited with the probability value related to the fitness values of the solution. This probability is defined as follows (Karaboga, 2005):

$$p_i = \frac{fit_i}{\sum_{j=1}^{SN} fit_j}$$ (12)

where fit_i is the fitness of the solution v. *SN* is the number of food sources positions. Later, the OB searches a new solution in the selected food source site using (11), the similar way as EBs exploit. The food source with richer quality would have a larger opportunity to be selected by the OB. Here,

Roulette Wheel mechanism is applied. The food source selection by OB represents the positive feedback in ABC algorithm. It should be noted that even though both EB and OB phases use similar way for food source exploitation, however, in EB phase, every solution will be updated while in OB phase, only the selected one will go through that process.

SB Phase

In SB phase, if the fitness of a found food source by respective EB failed to be improved for a given number of attempts (indicated by limit), it is eliminated. This indicates that the limit parameter determines how fast the solutions are casted away. This action represents the negative feedback in ABC algorithm and the EB of that food source will be demoted as SB and discovers new food source in the vicinity of the hive using random search as defined in (13).

$$x_{id} = x_d^{min} + r(x_d^{max} - x_{dx}^{min})$$ (13)

where *r is* a random real number within the range $[0, 1]$, x_d^{min} and x_d^{max} is the lower and upper borders in the *d*th dimension of the problems space respectively. The random movement by SB represents the fluctuations characteristic in SI. In a certain time, only one SB can be in the population. Basic steps of ABC algorithm are as follows:

1. Initialize the food source positions (population)

2. Each EB is assigned on their food sources.
3. Each OB select a source base on the quality of her solution, produces a new food source in selected food source site and exploits the better source.
4. Decide the source to be cast aside and appoint its EB as SB for discovering new food sources.
5. Memorize the best food source (solution) found so far.
6. If requirement are met, output the best solution, otherwise repeat steps 2-5 until the stopping criterion is met or maximum iteration is achieved.

The correspondence variables in the ABC algorithm (as in optimizing the parameters of interest) is as tabulated in Table 1.

THE PROPOSED eABC-LSSVM

In order to find the optimal value of parameters, the LSSVM is embedded in the ABC algorithm. The optimized value of parameters of interest can be obtained after a termination criterion is achieved. In this study, maximum number of iteration is set as a termination criterion. This is indicated by the value of MAPE produced in the validation set which is performed upon completing the training process. The lower the MAPE, the higher the prediction accuracy is. As to enrich the searching behavior of the bees in the basic ABC algorithm, mutation based on Levy Probability Distribution (LPD) is introduced (Levy, 1937). This is done

Table 1. Correspondence of the variables in the ABC algorithm in optimization of parameters

Data Representation	Variable
D	Number of parameters to be optimized, which is 3, namely γ, σ^2 and α
New food source position, v_{ij}	Feasible solution of the optimization problem (i.e. to obtain optimized value of γ, σ^2 and α)
Quality of nectar	Fitness function, which is the inverse of objective function
Objective Function	MAPE

by formulating a new formula in the exploitation process. On the other hand, as to avoid over fitting and under fitting, conventional mutation approach was employed which is introduced in the decision making process. The illustration of the proposed method is shown in Figure 1.

Hybrid ABC-LSSVM

In this study, there are three parameters of interest: regularization parameter, γ, kernel RBF parameter, σ^2 and α. The γ and σ^2 are associated to LSSVM hyper parameters where γ is responsible in determining the tradeoff between Empirical Risk Minimization (ERM) and Structural Risk Minimization (SRM) while σ^2 controls the value of function regression error (Wu, et al., 2007). On the other hand, α which belongs to LPD, is responsible to control the shape of distribution. All of these parameters are subject to predetermined constraint where [1, 1000] for γ and σ^2, while for α, it is subject to $0 < \alpha < 2$. The goal is to find the ideal values of all parameters that will generate minimum (lowest) value of objective function, where in this study is the MAPE.

Levy Mutation for Improving Exploitation Process of Bees in Search Space (*lv*ABC)

As to deal with the poor exploitation process of standard ABC, Lévy Mutation in ABC (*lv*ABC) is induced in generating solutions, which involves EB and OB phases. The *lv*ABC is introduced based on Lévy Probability Distribution (LPD) which was first coined by P. Levy in 1930 (Levy, 1937). The advantage of LPD relies on its tuning parameter, namely α where different value of α will yield different shapes of probability distribution. The smaller the α, the longer the tail of the distribution. This unique feature developed an efficient searching behavior since it will provide wider search space and reduce the likelihood of revisiting a similar location (Lee & Yao, 2004).

$$L_{\alpha,\theta}(y) = \frac{1}{\pi} \int_0^\infty e^{-\theta q^\alpha} \cos(qy) dq \; y \in R \qquad (14)$$

From (14), the distribution is symmetric with respect to $y = 0$ and has 2 parameters, α and θ. α controls the shape of the distribution, requiring 0

Figure 1. Flowchart of eABC-LSSVM

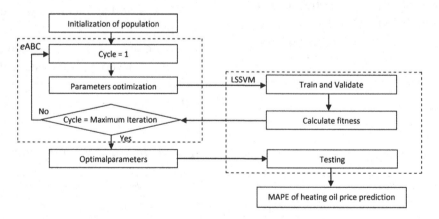

$< \alpha < 2$ while θ is the scaling factor satisfying $\theta > 0$. Since the analytic form of (14) is unknown generally, an algorithm to generate Lévy random number is commonly utilized (Lee & Yao, 2004; McCulloch, 1996).

For θ, it can be set to $\theta = 1$ without loss of generality. To describe this, rescale y to $y' = by$ with some constant b. Then, from (14), the following relation can be obtained:

$$L_{\alpha, \theta}(by) = \frac{1}{b} L_{\alpha, \theta'}(y) \qquad (15)$$

where $\theta' = \theta b^{-\alpha}$. In particular, by setting $\theta' = 1$, (15) becomes:

$$L_{\alpha, \theta}(y') = \theta^{-\frac{1}{\alpha}} L_{\alpha, 1}(y) \qquad (16)$$

Implying that θ is nothing but an overall scaling factor. Thus, with the distribution of $\theta = 1$, the distribution of any other θ can be obtained (Lee & Yao, 2004).

In the EB phase, instead of applying (10), the following equation is introduced:

$$v_{ij} = x_{ij} + (x_{ij} - x_{kj}) \times L \qquad (17)$$

On the other hand, in OB phase, the following equation is used as to replace (10):

$$v_{ij} = x_{ij} + L \qquad (18)$$

Equations (17) and (18) are designed through experimental approach. Here, L is represented by a random number generated by LPD. The main objective is to enrich the searching process by applying different strategies in both phases. In (18), the impact of neighborhood is omitted. The justification is to design the OB to move straightly to the strong solution indicated by the EB. The addition of Levy mutation will induce more advantage in exploration as described above. In this study, all parameters involved are automatically tuned by *e*ABC-LSSVM.

Conventional Mutation for Avoiding Local Minima (*cm*ABC)

The adaptation of conventional mutation is introduced in decision making process, which acts as a precaution step in preventing the model from suffering with over fitting and under fitting problem. In LSSVM, too small value of γ and too big value for σ^2 will make the prediction model does not fit to training data and also will lead to inaccurate prediction model respectively. On the other hand, over fitting problem is likely to be aroused if the value of γ is set too large while too small value is set for σ^2 (Lendasse, Ji, Reyhani, & Verleysen, 2005; Wu, et al., 2007). In the standard ABC-LSSVM (Mustaffa & Yusof, 2011), if the generated parameter value exceeds the boundaries, it will push back to the boundaries (Karaboga & Akay, 2009). However, in the proposed *cm*ABC, instead of forcing the parameter value to the boundary, a mutation strategy is applied. This operation is executed by multiplying the generated random number with the range of boundary that has been determined. In this study, the boundaries are set to the range of [1, 1000]. The equation is expressed as follows (Haupt & Haupt, 2004):

$$new\_param = (ub - lb) * rand\_num \qquad (19)$$

where *new_param* = new parameter; *rand_num* = random number within the range [0, 1]; *ub* = upper bound; and *lb* = lower bound.

The pseudo code of the *e*ABC-LSSVM is given in Figure 2.

Figure 2. eABC-LSSVM algorithm

```
Initialize the food source (possible solutions) positionsxᵢ, i = 1,…, SN
Initialize parameters
Evaluate the nectar amount (fitness value, fitᵢ) of possible solutions based on  training
and  validation sets using LSSVM
Cycle = 1
While Cycle <= MCN
EMPLOYED BEE (EB) PHASE
for each EB
        Produce new solutionsV using Eq.(17)(lvABC)
        ifsolution is out of boundary, apply Eq.(19)
Evaluate new solution V and calculate the fitness value fitᵢvalue based on training
and validation sets using LSSVM
if fitness value fitVᵢⱼ is better than  fitness value fitxᵢⱼ
            Applygreedy selection
end for
Calculate the probability values pᵢ for the best solution
ONLOOKER BEE (OB) PHASE
for each OB
        Select a solution depending on pᵢ
        Produce new solutionsV using Eq.(18)(lvABC)
        if solution is out of boundary, apply Eq.(19) (cmABC)
        Evaluate new solution V and calculate the fitness value fitᵢ value based on training
and validation sets using LSSVM
if  fitness value fitVᵢⱼ is better than  fitness value fitxᵢⱼ
            Applygreedy selection
    If Limit reached
            SCOUT BEE (SB) PHASE
            Abandon its food source
            Search for new ones to replace the abandoned food source
            Evaluate new solution, V and calculate the fitness value fit  based on
            training and validation using LSSVM
        else
            Memorized the best solution
        end if
end for
Cycle = Cycle + 1
End while
Print optimal solution
```

DATA DESCRIPTION AND TRAINING PROCEDURE

Empirical Data

This proposed *e*ABC-LSSVM is realized in predictive analysis of heating oil price. The utilized input for the analysis includes high frequency (daily) of four energy fuels prices time series data, viz. crude oil (CL), heating oil (HO), gasoline (HU)

and propane (PN). The CL is priced by the barrel, while the HO, HU and PN are denominated in gallons. The empirical data considered in this work covers from December 1997 to November 2002, consist of 1248 days (trading days). The datasets utilized are available at *Barchart* website (Barchart, 2012). From the dataset, 70% serves as training data, while the balance of 30% is reserved for validation and testing equally. The samples of dataset are as tabulated in Table 2 while Table 3

Table 2. Samples of original input

Date	CL	HO	HU	PN
1-12-1997	18.63	0.5144	0.5338	0.3200
2-12-1997	18.70	0.5190	0.5316	0.3188
3-12-1997	18.60	0.5220	0.5328	0.3213
4-12-1997	18.59	0.5218	0.5272	0.3198
5-12-1997	18.70	0.5276	0.5262	0.3200

Table 3. Input and output variables

Input	Variable	Output
Daily closing price of crude oil, heating oil, gasoline and propane	CL, HO, HU, PN	HO21owd
Percent change (*%Chg*) in daily closing spot prices from the previous day of CL, HO, HU and PN	CL%Chg, HO%Chg, HU%Chg, PN%Chg	
Standard deviation (*sd*) over the previous 5 days trading days of CL, HO, HU and PN	CLsd5, HOsd5, HUsd5, PNsd5	
Standard deviation (*sd*) over the previous 21 days trading days of CL, HO, HU and PN	CLsd21, HOsd21, HUsd21, PNsd21	

*HO21owd = Heating oil price from day 21 onwards

indicates the variables assigned to the features involved. The input arrangement is as suggested in Malliaris and Malliaris (2008).

From the table, it is shown that besides the daily closing prices of the selected energy fuels, another three derivatives input are also fed to the prediction model. The daily spot price will help the model to fix to current price location while the purpose of including the derivative input is to help the model to learn the underlying relationship that is constant over time (Malliaris & Malliaris, 2008). The standard deviation for 5 and 21 days represent the volatility of the price/rate in a week (sd5) and a month (sd21) during business days.

Test for Correlation

In this study, the correlation among input variables was tested using Pearson Product Moment Correlation Coefficient (Lomax, 2007). The value for correlation is defined as $r = 0.8 - 1.0$ which indicates a high correlation (Ahmed Farid & Salahudin, 2010). Table 4 shows the correlation between selected energy fuels prices.

Test for Non Linearity (Raw Data)

The test to examine the non-linearity behavior was conducted using the Brock, Dechert,

Table 4. Correlation between energy fuel prices from December 1997 to November 2002

	CL	HO	HU	PN
CL	1	-	-	-
HO	0.9597	1	-	-
HU	0.9649	0.9262	1	-
PN	0.8422	0.8812	0.8473	1

Table 5. Results for BDS test

Dimension	CL		HO		HU		PN	
	z-Statistic	Prob.	z-Statistic	Prob.	z-Statistic	Prob.	z-Statistic	Prob.
2	157.0196	0.0000	141.1323	0.0000	159.1354	0.0000	112.7183	0.0000
3	169.1750	0.0000	151.8276	0.0000	171.0004	0.0000	120.7303	0.0000
4	183.9557	0.0000	164.8749	0.0000	185.2621	0.0000	130.4755	0.0000
5	204.9558	0.0000	183.3142	0.0000	205.4883	0.0000	144.4204	0.0000
6	233.4320	0.0000	208.2991	0.0000	232.9067	0.0000	163.3450	0.0000

and Scheickman (BDS, hereafter) test (Brock, Scheinkman, Dechert, & LeBaron, 1996). The justification is to support the employment of non-linear predictive analysis method (i.e. LSSVM). The BDS tests is a 2 - tailed test, where the null hypothesis of independence and identical distribution will be rejected if z > 2 at a significance level of 5% (Vlad, 2010). The results obtained uon completing the BDS test are summarized in Table 5. From the tables, it indicates that the z-Statistic are greater than the critical values significantly. Thus, the null hypothesis is rejected. This implies that time series of interest exhibit a significant non linear behavior which proof the suitability of employing a non linear model for further task.

Data Normalization

In order to eliminate dimension different, data normalization is performed prior to training procedure which is based on the Min Max Normalization (Al-Shalabi, Shaaban, & Kasasbeh, 2006). This procedure is important in increasing the prediction accuracy and facilitates the learning process. The definition of Min Max Normalization is defined as:

$$v' = \left(\left(v - \min_a \right) / \left(\max_a - \min_a \right) \right) * \left(new \max_a - new \min_a \right) + new \min_a$$

(20)

where, v' = New value for variable v; v = Current value; $\min_a$ = Minimum value in data set; $\max_a$ = Maximum value in data set; $new\max_a$ = New maximum value in data set; and $new\min_a$ = New minimum value in data set.

Using (20), all input and output data were standardized and normalized into the range of [0, 1]. The normalized input for the sample in Table 2 is as tabulated in Table 6.

Training, Validation, and Testing

The data set is split into 3 independent subsets, namely training set (for model fitting), validation

Table 6. Samples of normalized input

Date	CL	HO	HU	PN
1-12-1997	0.2989	0.2804	0.2970	0.1803
2-12-1997	0.3015	0.2860	0.2943	0.1698
3-12-1997	0.2977	0.2896	0.2957	0.1734
4-12-1997	0.2973	0.2894	0.2889	0.1712
5-12-1997	0.3015	0.2965	0.2877	0.1715

Table 7. Data proportion for training, validation and testing

Training	Validation	Testing	Description of Data Arrangement
70%	15%	15%	Training = (2,3,4,5,6), (8,9,10,11,12), …, N Validation = $(1+ (n - 1) \times d$, where $d = 6$, $n = 1,2,3, …, N$ Testing (1062 - 1248)

set (for model assessment and to prevent over fitting) and testing set (for real assessment of how well the model generalize) (Marsland, 2009). The proportion for each subset is as tabulated in Table 7. The data arrangement is based on Arithmetic Progression formula (Tan, 2010).

Prediction Error Criteria

To assess the prediction performance of the predictive analysis techniques, three statistical metrics are utilized viz. MAPE (Hyndman & Koehler, 2006), Prediction Accuracy (PA) and Theil's U (Armstrong, 2001). They are defined as follow:

$$MAPE = \frac{1}{N}\left[\sum_{n=1}^{N}\left|\frac{y_n - y(x_n)}{y_n}\right|\right] \qquad (21)$$

$$PA = 100\% - (MAPE \times 100) \qquad (22)$$

$$Theil'sU = \frac{\sqrt{\frac{1}{N}\Sigma_{n=1}^{N}(y_n - y(x_n))^2}}{\sqrt{\frac{1}{N}\Sigma_{n=1}^{N}(y_n)^2} + \sqrt{\frac{1}{N}\Sigma_{n=1}^{N}(y(x_n))^2}} \qquad (23)$$

where $n = 1, 2, …, x$; y_n = Observed values; $y(x_n)$ = Predicted values/approximate values by predictor models; and N = Number of observations.

RESULTS AND DISCUSSION

In this study all experiments were executed on Matlab software and LSSVMlab Toolbox (Pelk-

mans, et al., 2002) was applied to derive all the hybrid LSSVM prediction models. The properties of the proposed technique are set as followed: $SN = 10$, *limit* = $SN*D$ and maximum iteration = 100. For comparison purposes, 3 approaches (ABC-LSSVM, GA-LSSVM, and BPNN) are chosen and a brief review of those techniques is given in the following:

1. **ABC-LSSVM (Mustaffa & Yusof, 2011):** The proposed technique was developed based on this approach.

2. **GA-LSSVM (Mustafa, et al., 2012):** GA-LSSVM is one of the recent state of the art algorithms. GA is pioneered by John Holland, and later popularized by David Goldberg (Haupt & Haupt, 2004). This technique is build based on three fundamental operators, namely selection, crossover and mutation. The properties of GA are set as followed: Population size = 20, maximum iteration = 100, crossover probability = 0.9 and mutation probability = 0.1.

3. **BPNN (Malliaris & Malliaris, 2008):** Inspired from the observation of how human brain works, ANN is tailored to imitate the function of human brain in learning where it adapts example based learning approach (Zhang, Patuwo, & Hu, 1998). As a prominent machine learning technique, BPNN is usually considered as a comparable benchmark to LSSVM (Chen, Wu, & Chen, 2008; Tan, Yan, Gao, & Yang, 2012). The architecture of BPNN is built based on three layers, viz. an input layer, a hidden

layer and an output layer. In determining the property of BPNN such as Learning rate and momentum constant, manual selection approach was utilized within the range $0-1$ (Zhang, et al., 1998).

The empirical results produced by each identified prediction techniques are tabulated in Table 8. From the table, empirical findings indicate that *e*ABC-LSSVM produced promising MAPE, which is 6.3310% when the value of γ and σ^2 is set to 80.2488 and 944.0822 respectively. With that, the prediction accuracy obtained is 93.6690%. This is followed by ABC-LSSVM with 7.1769% of MAPE. The GA-LSSVM which recorded 7.6421% of MAPE is ranked third. Meanwhile, BPNN came in last when the MAPE produced are more than 10%, which is 15.6724%; it is ranked fourth. This makes the prediction accuracy achieved by BPNN is less than 90%, which is not considered to be a highly accurate prediction (Yorucu, 2003). Besides MAPE and prediction accuracy, the result in terms of Theils' U is also analyzed in the experiment. From the table, it is shown that the *e*ABC-LSSVM produced the lowest Theils'U, which is 0.0405 and followed by ABC-LSSVM with 0.0444. The third place goes to GA-LSSVM with 0.0463 and BPNN is still placed last with 0.0978. This supports findings of earlier measurements (i.e accuracy and error rate).

An obvious difference between results obtained from various hybrid LSSVM methods and BPNN is due to different principle governed by those techniques where LSSVM is rooted from SVM, which adopts SRM principle while the ERM principle is practiced in BPNN. By applying SRM, generalization capability of prediction model is enhanced (Bao, et al., 2011) while over fitting is tend to be found in BPNN. This situation is indicated by excellent performance was recorded during training by BPNN, which is 1.2188%. Unfortunately, the good performance during model fitting is incapable to be sustained during testing phase, which results in error more than 10% with 15.6724%. This showed that model fail to generalize well in prediction task. It is also observed that in practice, the BPNN usually require large amount of training data (up to 10 years of historical daily data) to ensure it performs well in prediction (Haidar & Wolff, 2011), and this is not the case for LSSVM (Xiang & Jiang, 2009).

Summarized in Table 9 are the results obtained for the statistical significance level of the difference of the means between two algorithms using paired sample T-test. From the table, it shows that the modifications that have been introduced are significant at 0.05% significance level. That is, the proposed *e*ABC-LSSVM is proved to be superior, not only to ABC-LSSVM, but also superior to the other compared prediction models.

The results produced by *e*ABC-LSSVM and the comparison algorithms are also visualized in Figure 3. From the figure, the actual values are represented in black straight line while *e*ABC-

Table 8. Comparison of eABC-LSSVM with other prediction techniques

	eABC-LSSVM	**ABC-LSSVM**	**GA-LSSVM**	**BPNN**
γ	80.2488	67.8285	106.695	-
σ^2	944.0822	134.4249	37.0208	-
α	1.8135	-	-	-
MAPE Training (%)	8.4098	8.1882	7.8572	1.2188
MAPE Testing (%)	6.3310	7.1769	7.6421	15.6724
PA Testing (%)	93.6690	92.8231	92.3579	84.3276
Theils' U Testing	0.0405	0.0444	0.0463	0.0978

Table 9. Significant test for HO price prediction

Methods	Sig. (2-tailed)
*e*ABC-LSSVM - ABC-LSSVM	.000
*e*ABC-LSSVM - GA-LSSVM	.000
*e*ABC-LSSVM – BPNN	.000

LSSVM and ABC-LSSVM were indicated with red and yellow straight line respectively while the other two methods namely GA-LSSVM and BPNN were represented in green and blue straight line respectively. The training days started from day 1062 to 1248.

To discuss the produced results of *e*ABC-LSSVM and ABC-LSSVM in more details, the graphical results of searching behavior of the bees

between *e*ABC-LSSVM (post modification) and ABC-LSSVM (pre modification) is provided, which can be seen in Figures 4 and 5. In Figure 4, the exploitation process of the agents (i.e. bees) in *e*ABC-LSSVM is progressively performed before optimal γ and σ^2 is found at F [80.2488, 944.0822]. This situation portrayed how the searching space is efficiently utilized and the agents are guided to the desired solution. The optimal results offered in *e*ABC-LSSVM is the benefit gained from LPD based mutation which promotes more intensive searching behaviour. In addition, the adaptation of conventional mutation encourages the model from suffering with over fitting and under fitting situation which increases the chance of getting higher prediction accuracy. As a consequence, the combination of both modifications contributed in achieving the desired solution, viz. global optimal.

Figure 3. Visual results of comparison of eABC-LSSVM with other prediction techniques

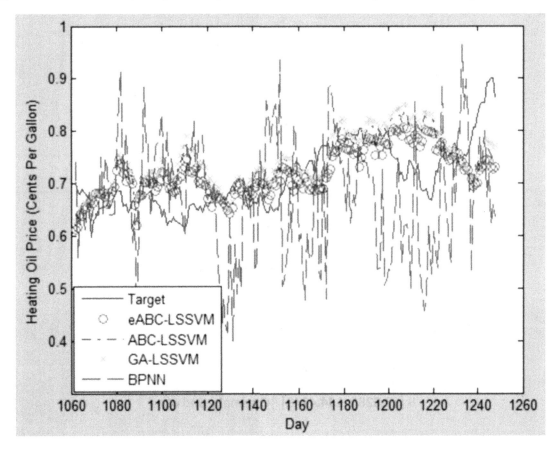

Figure 4. Exploitation of search space by eABC-LSSVM in HO price prediction

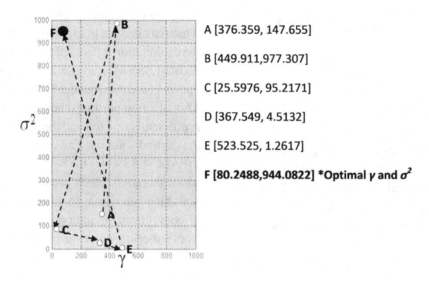

A [376.359, 147.655]

B [449.911, 977.307]

C [25.5976, 95.2171]

D [367.549, 4.5132]

E [523.525, 1.2617]

F [80.2488, 944.0822] *Optimal γ and σ²

Figure 5. Exploitation of search space by ABC-LSSVM in HO price prediction

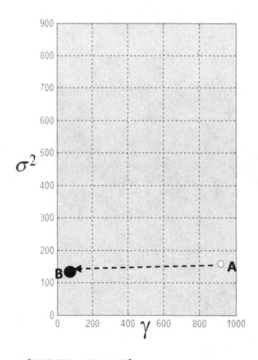

A [932.75, 151.117]

B [67.8285, 134.4249] *Optimal γ and σ²

On the other hand, in ABC-LSSVM, the search space is not fully exploited as the agents easily get stuck into local minimum at coordinate B [67.8285, 134.4249] (see Figure 5). This resulted to higher MAPE obtained by ABC-LSSVM, which is 7.1769%.

Findings of the study also suggest that besides than avoiding local minimum and over fitting/under fitting situation, the *e*ABC-LSSVM also escapes from premature convergence, which is illustrated in Figure 6. The exploitation of the search space is progressively performed by *e*ABC-LSSVM until it converged at iteration 89. From the figure, it is shown that, both GA-LSSVM and ABC-LSSVM experienced premature convergence where it is encountered at the very beginning of the iteration. Nevertheless, contradict situation is shown by *e*ABC-LSSVM. The findings of the

study also indicate that 100 iterations is adequate for the proposed model to converge and produced better results.

FUTURE RESEARCH DIRECTIONS

As ABC embodies algorithmic parameters which are important for the whole optimization performance namely number of population, number of iteration and limit, it would be interesting to proceed the research on the effect of each algorithmic parameters values to the problem under study. Based on literature and own experiments, it is observed that any inappropriate value for the algorithmic parameters may affect the whole optimization process which can lead the model to face with inconvenient issues such as long

Figure 6. Comparison of convergence rate

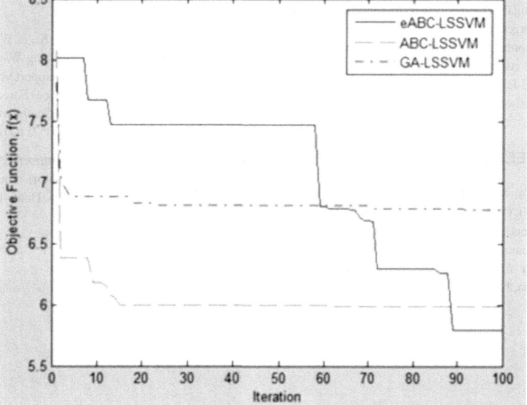

computational time and fail to converge. Besides that, accelerating the convergence speed would be also considered for future research since this is one of the appealing issues in ABC community. Last but not least, in the future work, the proposed *e*ABC-LSSVM is also planned to be applied for predictive analysis of other commodities prices. Thus, such future research is hoped to contribute significant findings in the ABC community.

CONCLUSION

This study proposed a hybrid *e*ABC-LSSVM which is realized in predictive analysis of heating oil price. The modification is devoted to ABC for the purpose of improving the generalization of LSSVM in prediction task. Based on the obtained results, the *e*ABC-LSSVM enjoys superiority over other comparison algorithms by offering lower error rates relative to the criteria utilized. Hence higher prediction accuracy is achieved. Besides proving its superiority in terms of lower error and convergence rate, the modifications introduced also contributes in addressing premature convergence issue. The promising results indicate that *e*ABC-LSSVM is suitable to be applied for the context of the study.

REFERENCES

Afshin, M., Sadeghian, A., & Raahemifar, K. (2007). On Efficient Tuning of LS-SVM Hyper-Parameters in Short-Term Load Forecasting: A Comparative Study. In *Procdings of the IEEE Power Engineering Society General Meeting*. Tampa, FL: IEEE.

Ahmed Farid, J., & Salahudin, F. (2010). *Risk Frameworks and Applications* (2nd ed.). Karachi: Alchemy Technologies Pvt. Ltd.

Al-Shalabi, L., Shaaban, Z., & Kasasbeh, B. (2006). Data Mining: A Preprocessing Engine. *Journal of Computer Science*, 2(9), 735–739. doi:10.3844/jcssp.2006.735.739

Alam, M. S., Ul Kabir, M. W., & Islam, M. M. (2010). Self-adaptation of mutation step size in Artificial Bee Colony algorithm for continuous function optimization. In *Proceedings of the 13th International Conference on Computer and Information Technology* (ICCIT). Dhaka, Bangladesh: ICCIT.

Armstrong, J. S. (2001). *A Handbook for Researchers and Practitioners*. New York: Springer.

Babayigit, B., & Ozdemir, R. (2012). A modified artificial bee colony algorithm for numerical function optimization. In *Proceedings of the IEEE Symposium on Computers and Communications* (ISCC). Cappadocia, Turkey: IEEE.

Bao, Y., Zhang, X., Yu, L., Lai, K. K., & Wang, S. (2011). An Integrated Model Using Wavelet Decomposition and Least Squares Support Vector Machines for Monthly Crude Oil Prices Forecasting. *New Mathematics and Natural Computation*, 7(2), 299–311. doi:10.1142/S1793005711001949

Barchart. (2012). Retrieved November, 2011, from http://www.barchart.com/historicalquote.php?view=quote&sym=CLY00&txtDate=12%2F31%2F09&submit=Get+Data

Bolaji, A. L. A., Khader, A. T., Al-Betar, M. A., & Awadallah, M. A. (2013). Artificial Bee Colony Algorithm, its Variants and Applications: A Survey. *Journal of Theoritical and Applied Information Technology, 47*(2), 434–459.

Brock, W. A., Scheinkman, J. A., Dechert, W. D., & LeBaron, B. (1996). A Test for Independence on the Correlation Dimension. *Econometrics Reviews, 15*(3), 197–235. doi:10.1080/07474939608800353

Chen, Q., Wu, Y., & Chen, X. (2008). Research on Customers Demand Forecasting for E-business Web Site Based on LS-SVM. In *Proceedings of the International Symposium on Electronic Commerce and Security*. Nachang City, China: Academic Press.

Chen, X., Wang, J., Sun, D., & Liang, J. (2008). Time Series Forecasting Based on Novel Support Vector Machine Using Artificial Fish Swarm Algorithm. In *Proceedings of the Fourth International Conference on Natural Computation* (ICNC). Jinan, China: ICNC.

Dos Santos, G. S., Luvizotto, L. G. J., Mariani, V. C., & Dos Santos Coelho, L. (2012). Least Squares Support Vector Machines with tuning based on Differential Evolution Approach Applied to the Identification of a Thermal Process. *Expert Systems with Applications, 39*, 4805–4812. doi:10.1016/j.eswa.2011.09.137

Dunsby, A., Eckstein, J., Gaspar, J., & Mulholland, S. (2008). *Commodity Investing: Maximizing Returns Through Fundamental Analysis*. John Wiley & Sons.

Fu, H., Liu, S., & Sun, F. (2010). Ship Motion Prediction Based on AGA-LSSVM. In *Proceedings of the International Conference on Mechatronics and Automation* (ICMA). Xi'an, China: ICMA.

Gao, W., & Liu, S. (2012). A Modified Artificial Bee Colony. *Computers & Operations Research, 39*, 687–697. doi:10.1016/j.cor.2011.06.007

Haidar, I., & Wolff, R. C. (2011). Forecasting of Crude Oil Price (Revisited). In *Proceedings of the 30th USAEE Conference*. Washington, DC: USAEE.

Haupt, R. L., & Haupt, S. E. (1998). *Practical genetic algorithms*. New York: Wiley Pub.

Heating Oil Explained. (2012). Retrieved October 22, 2013, from http://www.eia.gov/energyexplained/index.cfm?page=heating_oil_home

Hyndman, R. J., & Koehler, A. B. (2006). Another Look at Measures of Forecast Accuracy. *International Journal of Forecasting, 22*, 679–688. doi:10.1016/j.ijforecast.2006.03.001

Jammazi, R., & Aloui, C. (2012). Crude oil price forecasting: Experimental evidence from wavelet decomposition and neural network modeling. *Energy Economics, 34*, 828–841. doi:10.1016/j.eneco.2011.07.018

Jiang, B. T., & Zhao, F. Y. (2013). Particle Swarm Optimization-based Least Squares Support Vector Regression for Critical Heat Flux Prediction. *Annals of Nuclear Energy, 53*, 69–81. doi:10.1016/j.anucene.2012.09.020

Karaboga, D. (2005). *An Idea Based on Honey Bee Swarm for Numerical Optimization (Technical Report)*. Erciyes University.

Karaboga, D., & Akay, B. (2009). A comparative study of Artificial Bee Colony. *Applied Mathematics and Computation, 214*, 108–132. doi:10.1016/j.amc.2009.03.090

Khashman, A., & Nwulu, N. I. (2011). Intelligent Prediction of Crudei Oil Price Using Support Vector Machines. In *Proceedings of the 9th IEEE International Symposium on Applied Machine Intelligenc abd Informatics*. Smolenice, Slovakia: IEEE.

Kulkarni, S., & Haidar, I. (2009). Forecasting Model for Crude Oil Price Using Artificial Neural Networks and Commodity Futures Prices. *International Journal of Computer Science and Information Security*, 2(1).

Lee, C.-Y., & Yao, X. (2004). Evolutionary programming using mutations based on the Levy probability distribution. *IEEE Transactions on Evolutionary Computation*, 8(1), 1–13. doi:10.1109/TEVC.2003.816583

Lendasse, A., Ji, Y., Reyhani, N., & Verleysen, M. (2005). LS-SVM Hyperparameter Selection with a Nonparametric Noise Estimator. In *Proceedings of the 15th International Conference on Artificial Neural Networks: Formal Models and Their Applications* (ICANN). Warsaw, Poland: ICANN.

Levy, P. (1937). *Theorie de l'Addition des Veriables Aleatoires*. Paris, France: Gauthier-Villars.

Liao, R., Zheng, H., Grzybowski, S., & Yang, L. (2011). Particle Swarm Optimization-Least Squares Support Vector Regression based Forecasting model on Dissolved Gases in Oil-Filled Power Transformers. *Electric Power Systems Research*, 81, 2074–2080. doi:10.1016/j.epsr.2011.07.020

Liao, W., & Balzen, Z. (2013). LSSVM Network Flow Prediction Based on the Self-adaptive Genetic Algorithm Optimization. *Journal of Networks*, 8(2), 507–512.

Lomax, R. G. (2007). *An Introduction to Statistical Concepts*. Lawrence Erlbaum Associates, Inc.

Malliaris, M. E., & Malliaris, S. G. (2008). Forecasting Inter-Related Energy Product Prices. *European Journal of Finance*, 14(6), 453–468. doi:10.1080/13518470701705793

Marsland, S. (2009). Machine Learning An Algorithm Perspective. Boca Raton, FL: A Chapman & Hall Book.

McCulloch, J. H. (1996). *J. Huston McCulloch*. Retrieved March 15, 2012, 2012, from http://economics.sbs.ohio-state.edu/jhm/programs/STABRND.M

Mellit, A., Massi Pavan, A., & Benghanem, M. (2013). Least Squares Support Vector Machine for Short-Term Prediction of Meteorological Time Series. *Theoretical and Applied Climatology*, (111): 297–307. doi:10.1007/s00704-012-0661-7

Mustafa, M. W., Sulaiman, M. H., Shareef, H., & Khalid, S. N. A. (2012). Reactive power tracing in pool-based power system utilising the hybrid genetic algorithm and least squares support vector machine. *IET, Generation. Transmission & Distribution*, 6(2), 133–141. doi:10.1049/iet-gtd.2011.0166

Mustaffa, Z., & Yusof, Y. (2011). Optimizing LSSVM using ABC for Non-Volatile Financial Prediction. *Australian Journal of Basic and Applied Sciences*, 5(11), 549–556.

Park, J.-B., Jeong, Y.-W., Shin, J.-R., & Lee, K. Y. (2010). An Improved Particle Swarm Optimization for Nonconvex Economic Dispatch Problems. *IEEE Transactions on Power Systems*, 25(1), 156–165. doi:10.1109/TPWRS.2009.2030293

Pelkmans, K., Suykens, J. A. K., Gestel, T. V., Brabanter, J. D., Lukas, L., Hamer, B., et al. (2002). *LS-SVMlab: A Matlab/C Toolbox for Least Squares Support Vector Machines*. Retrieved from www.esat.kuleuven.be/sista/lssvmlab/

Rajasekhar, A., Abraham, A., & Pant, M. (2011). Levy Mutated Artificial Bee Colony Algorithm for Global Optimization. In *Proceedings of the IEEE International Conference on Systems, Man, and Cybernetics* (SMC). Anchorage, AK: IEEE.

Sharma, T. K., Pant, M., & Bhardwaj, T. (2011). PSO Ingrained Artificial Bee Colony Algorithms for Solving Continuous Optimization Problems. In *Proceedings of the International Conference on Computer Applications and Industrial Electronics* (ICCAIE). Penang, Malaysia: ICCAIE.

Shen, W., Zhang, Y., & Ma, X. (2009). Stock Return Forecast with LS-SVM and Particle Swarm Optimization. In *Proceedings of the International Conference on Business Intelligence and Financial Engineering* (BIFE). Beijing, China: BIFE.

Shi, X., Li, Y., Li, H., Guan, R., Wang, L., & Liang, Y. (2010). An integrated algorithm based on artificial bee colony and particle swarm optimization. In *Proceedings of the Sixth International Conference on Natural Computation* (ICNC). Yantai, China: ICNC.

Subotic, M. (2011). Artificial Bee Colony Algorithm with Multiple Onlookers for Constrained Optimization Problems. In *Procedings of the European Computing Conference* (ECC). Paris: ECC.

Suykens, J. A. K., Van Gestel, T., De Brabanter, J., De Moor, B., & Vandewalle, J. (2002). *Least Squares Support Vector Machines*. Leuven, Belgium: World Scientific Publishing Co. Pte. Ltd.

Tan, G., Yan, J., Gao, C., & Yang, S. (2012). Prediction of water quality time series data based on least squares support vector machines. *Procedia Engineering*, *31*, 1194–1199. doi:10.1016/j.proeng.2012.01.1162

Tan, S. T. (2010). *Applied Mathematics for the Managerial, Life, and Social Sciences* (6th ed.). Richard Stratton.

Tehrani, R., & Khodayar, F. (2011). A hybrid optimized Artificial Intelligent Model to Forecast Crude Oil using Genetic Algorithm. *African Journal of Bussiness Management*, *5*(34), 13130–13135.

Vapnik, V. N. (1995). *The Nature of Statistical Learning Theory* (2nd ed.). New York: Springer-Verlag. doi:10.1007/978-1-4757-2440-0

Vlad, S. (2010). Investigation of Chaotic Behavior in Euro-Leu Exchange Rate. *Journal of Applied Computer Science and Mathematics*, *8*(4), 67–71.

Wu, D., Feng, S., & He, Y. (2007). Infrared Spectroscopy Technique for the Nondestructive measurement of Fat Content in Milk Powder. *Journal of Dairy Science*, *90*, 3613–3619. doi:10.3168/jds.2007-0164 PMID:17638971

Wu, J., & Niu, D. (2009). Short-Term Power Load Forecasting Using Least Squares Support Vector Machines(LS-SVM). In *Proceedings of the Second International Workshop on Computer Science and Engineering* (WCSE). Qingdao, China: WCSE.

Xiang, Y., & Jiang, L. (2009). Water Quality Prediction Using LS-SVM and Particle Swarm Optimization. In *Proceedings of the Second International Workshop on Knowledge Discovery and Data Mining* (WKDD). Moscow, Russia: WKDD.

Xie, H.-L., Li, N., Lu, F.-C., & Xie, Q. (2009). Application of LS-SVM by GA for Dissolved Gas Concentration Forecasting in Power Transformer Oil. In *Proceedings of the Asia-Pacific Power and Energy Engineering Conference* (APPEEC). Wuhan, China: APPEEC.

Yorucu, V. (2003). The Analysis of Forecasting Performance by Using Time Series Data for Two Mediterranean Islands. *Review of Social. Economic & Business Studies*, *2*, 175–196.

Yu, L., Chen, H., Wang, S., & Lai, K. K. (2009). Evolving Least Squares Support Vector Machines for Stock Market Trend Mining. *IEEE Transactions on Evolutionary Computation*, *13*(1), 87–102. doi:10.1109/TEVC.2008.928176

Yusof, N., & Rashid, A. R., & Mohamed, Z. (2010). Malaysia Crude Oil Production Estimation: An Application of ARIMA Model. In *Proceedings of the International Conference on Science and Social Research* (CSSR). Kuala Lumpur, Malaysia: CSSR.

Zhai, J., & Huang, L. (2013). Marketing Prediction Based on Time Series Prediction Algorithm of Least Squares Support Vector Machines. [JCIT]. *Journal of Convergence Information Technology*, *8*(3), 245–250. doi:10.4156/jcit.vol8.issue3.29

Zhang, G., Patuwo, B. E., & Hu, M. Y. (1998). Forecasting with Artificial Neural Network: The State of Art. *International Journal of Forecasting*, *14*, 35–62. doi:10.1016/S0169-2070(97)00044-7

Zhang, W., Niu, P., Li, G., & Li, P. (2013). Forecasting of Turbine Heat Rate with Online Least Squares Support Vector Machine based on Gravitational Search Algorithm. *Knowledge-Based Systems*, *39*, 34–44. doi:10.1016/j.knosys.2012.10.004

ADDITIONAL READING

Blum, C., & Li, X. (2008). Swarm Intelligence in Optimization [Springer Berlin Heidelberg.]. *Optimization*, 43–85.

Bonabeau, E., Corne, D., & Poli, R. (2010). Swarm Intelligence: The State of the Art Special Issue of Natural Computing. *Natural Computing*, *9*, 655–657. doi:10.1007/s11047-009-9172-6

Bonabeau, E., & Meyer, C. (2001). Swarm Intelligence: A Whole New Way To Think About Business. *Harvard Business Review, May*

Chen, N., Lu, W., Yang, J., & Li, G. (2004). *Support Vector Machines in Chemistry*. London: World Scientific Publishing Co. Pte. Ltd.

Civicioglu, P., & Besdok, E. (2013). A Conceptual Comparison of the Cuckoo-Search, Particle Swarm Optimization, Differential Evolution and Artificial Bee Colony Algorithms. *Artificial Intelligence Review*, *39*(4), 315–346. doi:10.1007/s10462-011-9276-0

Cristianini, N., & Shawe-Taylor, J. (2000). *An Introduction to Support Vector Machines and other kernel-based learning methods*. United Kingdom: Cambridge University Press. doi:10.1017/CBO9780511801389

El-Abd, M. (2012). Performance Assessment of Foraging Algorithms vs. Evolutionary Algorithms. *Information Sciences*, *182*, 243–263. doi:10.1016/j.ins.2011.09.005

Frush, S. (2008). *Commodities Demystified*. New York: McGraw-Hill.

Garnier, S., Gautrais, J., & Theraulaz, G. (2007). The Biological Principles of Swarm Intelligence. *Swarm Intelligence*, *1*, 3–31. doi:10.1007/s11721-007-0004-y

Hyndman, R. J., & Athanasopoulos, G. (2012). Forecasting: principles and practice Retrieved from http://otextx.com/fpp/.

Karaboga, D., & Akay, B. (2009). A survey: algorithms simulating bee swarm intelligence. *Artificial Intelligence Review*, (31): 61–85. doi:10.1007/s10462-009-9127-4

Karaboga, D., & Basturk, B. (2007). A Powerful and Efficient Algorithm for Numerical Function Optimization: Artificial Bee Colony (ABC) Algorithm. *Journal of Global Optimization*, *39*, 459–471. doi:10.1007/s10898-007-9149-x

Karaboga, D., Gorkemli, B., Ozturk, C., & Karaboga, N. (2012). A comprehensive survey: artificial bee colony (ABC) algorithm and applications. *Artificial Intelligence Review*, 1–37. doi: doi:10.1007/s10462-012-9328-0

Kotsiantis, S. B., Kanellopoulos, D., & Pintelas, P. E. (2006). Data Preprocessing for Supervised Learning. *International Journal of Computer Science*, *1*(2), 1306–4428.

Labys, W. C. (2006). *Modelling and Forecasting Primary Commodity Prices*. Hampshire: Ashgate Publishing Limited.

Langley, P. (2011). The Changing Science of Machine Learning. *Machine Learning*, (82): 275–279. doi:10.1007/s10994-011-5242-y

Maimon, O., & Rokach, L. (2010). *Data Mining and Knowledge Discovery Handbook* (2nd ed.). New York: Springer. doi:10.1007/978-0-387-09823-4

Martens, D., Baesen, B., & Fawcett, T. (2011). Editorial Survey: Swarm Intelligence. *Machine Learning*, *82*, 1–42. doi:10.1007/s10994-010-5216-5

Martens, D., Baesen, B., & Fawcett, T. (2011). Editorial Survey: Swarm Intelligence. *Machine Learning*, *82*, 1–42. doi:10.1007/s10994-010-5216-5

Mustaffa, Z., & Yusof, Y. (2012). *Levy Mutation in Artificial Bee Colony Algorithm for Gasoline Price Prediction*. Proceedings of the Knowledge Management International Conference (KMICe), Johor Bahru, Johor, Malaysia.

Palit, A. K., & Popovic, D. (2005). *Computational Intelligence in Time Series Forecasting Theory and Engeneering Applications*. London: Springer-Verlag.

Scholkopf, B., & Smola, A. J. (2002). *Learning with Kernels*. London: The MIT Press.

Wahde, M. (2008). *Biologically Inspired Optimization Methods: An Introduction*. Southampton, Boston: WIT Press.

Wang, H., & Hu, D. (2005). *Comparison of SVM and LS-SVM for Regression*. Paper presented at the Proceedings of the International Conference on Neural Networks and Brain (ICNN&B), Beijing.

Weiss, S. M., & Indurkhya, N. (1998). *Predictive Data Mining: A Practical Guide*. San Francisco: Morgan Kaufmann Publishers, Inc.

Yang, X.-S. (2010). *Nature-Inspired Metaheuristic Algorithms* (2nd ed.). United Kingdom: Luniver Press.

KEY TERMS AND DEFINITIONS

Artificial Bee Colony: A SI based optimization technique which is emerged from the observation of honey bees swarm in finding food sources.

Least Squares Support Vector Machines: A variant of of SVM technique which is based on SRM principles.

Levy Probability Distribution: Possess a special feature in term of diversifying results which benefits from its adjustable parameters.

Mutation: Responsible in bringing diversity to the solution.

Optimization: Process of finding minimum or maximum value based on a set of adjustable parameters subject to the constraint.

Predictive Analysis: A form of prediction task which models continuous-valued functions.

Time Series: A set of data which recorded in sequential order.

Chapter 8
Comparison of Linguistic Summaries and Fuzzy Functional Dependencies Related to Data Mining

Miroslav Hudec
University of Economics in Bratislava, Slovakia

Miljan Vučetić
University of Belgrade, Serbia

Mirko Vujošević
University of Belgrade, Serbia

ABSTRACT

Data mining methods based on fuzzy logic have been developed recently and have become an increasingly important research area. In this chapter, the authors examine possibilities for discovering potentially useful knowledge from relational database by integrating fuzzy functional dependencies and linguistic summaries. Both methods use fuzzy logic tools for data analysis, acquiring, and representation of expert knowledge. Fuzzy functional dependencies could detect whether dependency between two examined attributes in the whole database exists. If dependency exists only between parts of examined attributes' domains, fuzzy functional dependencies cannot detect its characters. Linguistic summaries are a convenient method for revealing this kind of dependency. Using fuzzy functional dependencies and linguistic summaries in a complementary way could mine valuable information from relational databases. Mining intensities of dependencies between database attributes could support decision making, reduce the number of attributes in databases, and estimate missing values. The proposed approach is evaluated with case studies using real data from the official statistics. Strengths and weaknesses of the described methods are discussed. At the end of the chapter, topics for further research activities are outlined.

DOI: 10.4018/978-1-4666-6078-6.ch008

INTRODUCTION

The increasing use of information systems by business and governmental agencies has created large amounts of data that contain potentially valuable knowledge (Rasmussen & Yager, 1997). This amount of data should be processed and interpreted to be useful. Modern corporations are becoming more and more dependent on information generated from databases (Vucetic, Hudec, & Vujošević, 2013). Accordingly, decision makers are often not interested in large sheets of figures, but in relational knowledge that is usually overshadowed by large amount of data in relational databases. Hence, data with meaning are more important than pure data. Traditional knowledge discovery in a database provides precise information from the data rather than providing a global review of the whole database. Therefore, it is important to develop methods able to handle imprecision, uncertainty and partial truth, and present revealed information in an understandable way to users.

In this chapter we use fuzzy concept to induce associational rules hidden in the data. Discovering these useful rules from databases is seen as a data mining technique. The fuzzy sets and fuzzy logic are used to find association among attributes of relational database and the character of the discovered dependencies. Approaches presented in this chapter are bio-inspired techniques because of similarity of the fuzzy concept to human reasoning (computing with words instead of crisp numbers and precise measurement). More recently, these techniques are increasingly present as suitable methods for mining knowledge from different kinds of databases.

Dependencies and relations between attributes convey relevant information for users. It is obvious that they may also exist between particular parts of attributes domains which could not have clear boundaries. Feil and Abonyi (2008) pointed out that there is an urgent need for a new generation of computational techniques to assist humans in extracting useful information (knowledge) from

the constantly growing volumes of collected data. Mining this information also requires approaches which enable ambiguity and imprecision in data to be easily handled (Ansari, Biswas, & Aggarwal, 2012).

Initially, Linguistic Summaries (LSs) have been developed to express a relational, concise and easily understandable knowledge about the data (Rasmussen & Yager, 1997). LSs mimic human reasoning in looking for the information by natural language questions and processing data without precise measurements. The concept of LSs has been initially introduced in Yager (1982) and further developed in Hudec (2013b), Kacprzyk and Yager (2001), Kacprzyk and Zadrozny (2009), Rasmussen and Yager (1997), Yager (1989).

Our research uses the LS of the following structure:

Q R entities in database are (have) *S*

where *S* is a summarizer defined as a linguistic term on the domain of the examined attribute, *R* is a linguistic term adding some constraints and *Q* is a fuzzy quantifier as in Zadeh (1983). The truth value of a summary is usually called *validity* and gets value from the [0, 1] interval. For example, the rule: *most of well-paid employees are middle aged,* may have a higher truth value than other rules describing a particular company and its employees.

Data summarization is one of the basic capabilities of any "intelligent" system (Kacprzyk & Zadrozny, 2009). We could say that the same holds for the Fuzzy Functional Dependencies (FFDs). The main aim of FDDs is detecting attributes that have a high value of dependency.

A fuzzy functional dependency, denoted by $X \xrightarrow{\theta} Y$ expresses that a relation exists between the two sets of attributes X and Y. It can be stated as follows: if t and t' have similar values on X, they also have the similar value on Y with linguistic strengths θ (Sözat & Yazici, 2001).

Discovering FFDs in relational databases is the subject of interest in data mining, because FFDs are very informative for making executive decisions, especially in cases when we lack precise and exact information. To illustrate this, let us observe the following empirically obtained statement: "The length of road more or less determines resources required for maintenance" and its linguistic strength is 0.8. In this situation, we could create rules such as:

IF length of road is high THEN resource is high, and IF length of road is small THEN resource is small.

Neural networks, genetic algorithms, swarm-based algorithms and artificial intelligence have played an important role in the field of data mining (Liao, Chu, & Hsiao, 2012). It is suggested that bio-inspired methodologies are found to be major methods in the developing of the data mining techniques nowadays. There are different aspects and trends of the application of the above mentioned methods such as: algorithm architecture (Jimenez, Aroba, Torre, Andujar, & Grande, 2009), system optimization (Fong, 2013), application in different information systems and knowledge-based systems (Hong, Lee, & Wu, 2014), dynamic prediction (Chen & Du, 2009), decision problems (Lessman, Caserta, & Arango, 2011), estimation of missing values for support of flash estimation in economy based on official statistics data (Kľúčik, 2012) etc.

It is worth noting that soft computing or the bio-inspired mode of data mining is not just an assemblage or mixture of all. It should be regarded as a synergy in which each component (fuzzy logic, neural networks, evolutionary algorithms, swarm optimisation, etc.) contributes with methods to address particular parts of complex problems in a complementing rather than competitive way (Feil & Abonyi, 2008). The same holds for methods inside fuzzy logic. Both LSs and FFDs are based on fuzzy logic but they use different methods for extracting relational knowledge from databases. Currently, LSs and FDDs are developing independently even though they could cooperate in mining knowledge and dependencies in databases.

This chapter is focused on constructing FFDs and LSs, reveling dependencies on illustrative examples on data from official statistics, and discussion of obtained results. The chapter also discusses the prospects of improving data mining by integrating LSs and FFDs in a complementing way. Furthermore, it outlines how LSs and FFD can be improved by neural networks and genetic algorithms and suggests future research topics.

RELATIONAL KNOWLEDGE AND DEPENDENCIES IN DATA

Classical approaches for dependencies evaluation based on two-valued logic can result in one of the two extreme situations: attributes are fully dependent and attributes are fully independent. Therefore, the situation when attributes are more or less dependent cannot be detected. In addition, high dependency could be detected on the whole domains of considered attributes, or only in particulars parts of their respective domains. Moreover, these parts of domains usually do not have clear boundaries. This consideration is shown in Figure 1 where tuples t are sorted from the smallest value (t_1) to the highest value (t_n). Fuzzy logic is an option that could provide a solution for these problems.

Mined dependencies and relational knowledge in the data could support decision making and improve the quality of data (e.g. estimation of missing values). The following paragraphs briefly discuss areas where LSs and FFDs are applicable.

Data collection is a demanding task for respondents (e.g. in official statistics). Respondents become more and more reluctant to cooperate in surveys (Giesen, 2011) or pay less attention to the questionnaires which as a consequence has the poor quality of the data (Bavdaž, 2010). During

Figure 1. Dependencies between attributes

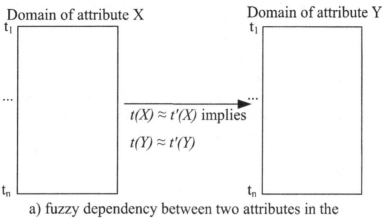

a) fuzzy dependency between two attributes in the whole database

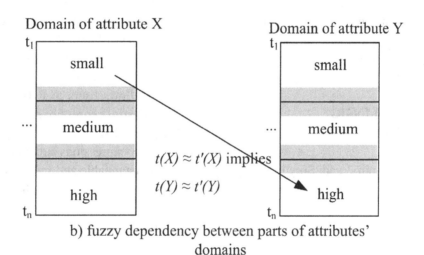

b) fuzzy dependency between parts of attributes' domains

the design of a database, designers and experts cannot detect all redundancies and dependencies between attributes. But during the regular use of databases they become aware that values of some attributes more or less depend on values of other attributes. If we detect a high dependency between some attributes, then we could discard the dependent attribute from the further data collection. The reduced requirements for data will lead to the reduction of the pressure to respondents and could therefore improve the quality of the collected data. Even with maximum effort, some values will remain unavailable. Therefore, efforts focused on estimation of missing values should be continuously improved (de Leeuw, Hox, & Huisman, 2003; Kľúčik, 2011). Handling dependencies could also improve imputation of missing values. If we detect a high dependency between some attributes, we could be able to estimate the missing value of a dependent attribute by using the known values of independent attributes.

Mined dependencies and relational knowledge expressed in a concise and easily understandable way are essential for executive decision making. Mined rules expressed as in: *waste production significantly depends on population density,* or the rule: *most small municipalities have high unemployment rate and small migration,* are significant pieces of supporting information for both public policy making decisions and management decisions. As an example, let us take a company that would like to test the assumption that highly situated municipalities mainly use sources for heating other than gas. In this case, the rule is expressed as: *most of municipalities with high altitude above sea level have low gas consumption.* The validity of rule provides the answer to this question.

Issues explained in the previous paragraphs are recognized in many areas, including data processing in official statistics from data collection to data dissemination. That is the main reason why the case studies in this chapter are focused on database of official statistics.

ROLE OF FUZZY LOGIC IN DATA MINING

Fayyad, Piatestku-Shapiro, and Smyth (1996) have offered the following explanation of data mining: "the notion of finding useful patterns in data has been given a variety of names including data mining, knowledge extraction, information discovery, and data pattern processing. The term data mining has been mostly used by statisticians, data analysts, and the management information systems (MIS) communities" (Feil & Abonyi, 2008, p. 56). The term knowledge discovery in databases (KDD) refers to the overall process of discovering knowledge from data (from defining a goal to consolidating results and disseminating knowledge to users), while the data mining part refers to a step of this process: the application of specific algorithms for extracting patterns or knowledge from data. Before the realization of the data mining step, data should be pre-processed.

After the data mining step, the discovered knowledge should be consolidated and interpreted to be useful for users.

Main steps of KDD are depicted in e.g. Abonyi, Feil, & Abraham (2005), Feil and Abonyi (2008). All these steps describe KDD at large to be applied for variety of tasks and on a variety of data (relational databases, XML data sets, etc.). In this paper we are focused on revealing relational knowledge in an easy and understandable way by FFDs and LSs. With this aim, KDD steps are discussed for possible roles of fuzzy logic, LSs and FFDs. The steps are as follows:

1. Developing and understanding the application domain and the relevant prior knowledge, and defining the goal of the whole process of extracting knowledge from the data. In this step, fuzzy logic is an approach that allows users to define their tasks by linguistic expressions, which envelopes imprecision, ambiguities and partial truth. These expressions are transparent, easily understandable and modifiable for domain experts. Knowing the application domain and the nature of data, the required parameters of a model or relevant attributes can be chosen by the domain expert or automatically form a data set.

2. Creating target data sets. In this step the strategy for data collection should be defined (surveys, import data from other sources or using data stored in company databases). Attributes like cost of realisation of surveys and quality of the available data should be taken into account.

3. Data cleaning and pre-processing. This step includes operations such as the removal of noise, examining outliers and handling missing values. Handling missing values is a complex problem that should be continu-

ously improved (de Leeuw, et al., 2003). In this step, fuzzy logic, for example LSs in cooperation with neural networks and genetic algorithms could provide a solution (Hudec & Juriová, 2013; Kľúčik, 2012).

4. Data reduction and projection. This step is devoted to reducing the number of attributes in relational databases or dimensions in data hyper cubes. Neural networks and neuro-fuzzy systems are often used for this purpose (Feil & Abonyi, 2008). Recent research reveals the potential of FFDs in the reduction of more or less dependent attributes from relational databases (Vucetic, et al., 2013).

5. Matching the goal of the KDD with a suitable data mining method. The goal of data mining could be achieved using methods for clustering, summarisation, dependency detection and modelling, regression, classification, deviation detection.

6. Choosing the data mining models and algorithms. The goal of this step is to decide which models and algorithms are suitable. Often, one algorithm is insufficient. Merging several algorithms in a complementing way where each algorithm addresses a particular part of a KDD task or applying several algorithms to compare the obtained results provides the solution. If the goal is summarisation (concise and easily understandable knowledge describing the whole data set of interest) then LSs seem to be a rational option. In case of dependency modelling and detection (direction and intensity of dependencies among attributes), FFDs could provide the solution. Concerning the classification (mapping entity into one of several predefined classes (crisp way) or into several overlapping classes with different membership degree (fuzzy way)), creating a rule base is an important step. Fuzzy if-then rules can be revealed by FFDs and LSs.

7. Realisation phase. Selected algorithms search and evaluate patterns or relational knowledge in the data.

8. Interpretation. Interpreting mined patterns includes presenting obtained knowledge (relations, rules, etc.) in a useful and understandable way, e.g. list of rules ranked downwards from the rule having the highest validity, or presenting obtained information on thematic maps when the goal of KDD is analysing territorial units.

9. Consolidating discovered knowledge. This includes documenting and reporting results to users.

The following sections examine in detail the theory of FFDs and LSs, examples on real data from the official statistics, and discuss strengths and weaknesses with an overview of future research topics and merging with neural networks and genetic algorithms.

FUZZY FUNCTIONAL DEPENDENCIES

A functional dependency (FD), denoted by $X \rightarrow Y$, expresses that a function exists between two sets of attributes X and Y, and it can be stated as follows: if t and t' share a common value on X, they also have the same value on Y, for any pair of tuples t and t'.

Definition 1: Let r be any relation instance on scheme $R(A_1, A_2, ..., A_n)$, U be the universal set of attributes $A_1, A_2, ...A_n$ and both X and Y are subsets of a universal set of attributes $U = \{A_1, A_2, ..., A_n\}$, $X, Y \subseteq U$. We say that relation r satisfies the functional dependency $X \rightarrow Y$ (reads as "X determines Y") if, for every two tuples t and $t' \subseteq r$, $t(X) = t'(X)$ implies $t(Y) = t'(Y)$.

This definition is based on the concept of equality. If FDs are involved in the fuzzy relation database model (Ma, 2006), then the definition cannot be directly applied because there is no clear way to verify whether the two imprecise values are equal. The concept of FDs has to be extended and generalized.

From FDs to FFDs

Extension of FDs to FFDs has been widely investigated. There are many different definitions of FFDs based on different concepts. The first extension of FDs to FFDs was introduced by Bosc, Kraft, and Petry (2005). They replaced strict equality in FD definition with similarity relation in FDD definition. This dependency is shown as $X \xrightarrow{\theta} Y$, where θ is the strength. It means that if $t(X)$ is similar to $t'(X)$ then $t(Y)$ is also similar to $t'(Y)$ with the strength θ.

Let $\approx(t(X), t'(X))$ denote a similarity measure between $t(X)$ and $t'(X)$. In particular X determines Y with strength θ if and only if: $\min I(\approx(t(X), t'(X)), \approx(t(Y), t'(Y)) \geq \theta$ where $t, t' \in R$ and I is one of the acceptable fuzzy implications.

For example, if $\approx(t(X), t'(X)) = 0.95$ and $\approx(t(Y), t'(Y)) = 0.90$ then fuzzy functional dependency meets $X \xrightarrow{0.9} Y$ with strength 0.90.

One of the most fundamental definitions of FFDs is given in the Sözat and Yazici's (2001) model. First, they introduced a new definition for conformance of tuples where conformance is a degree of similarity for two tuples in a given attribute. Then the formal definition of FFDs is based on the concept of conformance between tuples.

The conformance of attribute A_i defined on domain D_i for any two tuples t_i and t_j presented in relation instance r and denoted by $C(A_i[t_i,t_j])$ is given as:

$$C(A_i[t_i,t_j]) = \min (\mu_{t_i}(A_i), \mu_{t_j}(A_i), s(t_i(A_i), t_j(A_i)), \quad (1)$$

where $\mu_{t_i}(A_i)$ is a membership degree of value attribute A_i to fuzzy set appearing in t_i, $\mu_{t_j}(A_i)$ membership degree of value attribute A_i to fuzzy set appearing in t_j and $s(t_i(A_i), t_j(A_i))$ is a proximity relation between fuzzy sets on the domain A_i.

Definition 2: Let r be fuzzy relation on scheme $R(A_1,...,A_n)$ and U universal set of attributes $A_1,...,A_n$ and both X, Y be subsets of U. Fuzzy relation r is said to satisfy the fuzzy functional dependency $X \xrightarrow{\theta} Y$ (reads X determines Y with linguistic strength θ) if for tuples t_i and t_j in r:

$$C (Y[t_i,t_j]) \geq \min (\theta, C(X[t_i,t_j])) \quad (2)$$

where θ is real number within the range $[0,1]$ describing the linguistic strength. When $\theta = 1$, FFD becomes FD, denoted as $X \rightarrow Y$.

To determine the similarity between fuzzy sets appearing as attribute values in the fuzzy relations we use proximity relation.

Definition 3: A proximity relation is a mapping $s: D \times D \rightarrow [0,1]$ such that for $x, y \in D$:
1. $s(x,x)=1$ (reflexivity)
2. $s(x,y)=s(y,x)$ (symmetry)

Table 1 illustrates proximity relation on the domain of the attribute *Population density* and Table 2 illustrates proximity relation on the domain of the attribute *Production of waste in tones*.

Expert skills are used in the process of determining the proximity relation among the elements of observed domains, i.e. we can acquire those skills by interviewing experts. On the other hand,

Table 1. Proximity relation on the domain of the attribute Population density

s_{PD}	Small	Medium	High
Small	1	0.80	0.30
Medium		1	0.65
High			1

Table 2. Proximity relation on the domain of the attribute Production of waste in tones

s_{PWt}	Small	Medium	High
Small	1	0.65	0.25
Medium		1	0.60
High			1

we can use some parameters, such as distance, density etc. to determine proximity between linguistic terms.

In the classical relational databases, FD $X \rightarrow Y$ is expressed by the classical implication operator I_c. Accordingly, in classical logic IF X THEN Y proposition is denoted as $X \rightarrow Y$. It means that equal Y-values correspond to equal X-values.

However, in fuzzy relational database models where attribute values are not only a single domain's elements but also fuzzy subsets or possibility distributions, the degree of FD $X \rightarrow Y$ does not have to be implicitly equal 1 as in the crisp case. Naturally, its value is from the interval [0, 1]. In that case, the definition of FD is generalized and extended in form of FFD (Chen, Kerre, & Vandenbulckle, 1996). Classical implication operator is replaced with fuzzy implication operators and proximity relation is used instead of equality relation. Fuzzy implication is then an extension of classical implication. IF-THEN proposition, in the case of FFD, is defined with fuzzy implication I_f denoted by $X \xrightarrow{\theta} Y$ and specified as follows:

$$\min I_f (t(X) =_c t'(X), t(Y) =_c t'(Y)) \geq \theta, \ t, \ t' \in r,$$

where "$=c$" is proximity measure, $\theta \in [0,1]$, I_f: $[0,1] \times [0,1] \rightarrow [0,1]$ is fuzzy implication and min 'is presented by *AND* operator.

In the theory of fuzzy logic four models for implication operators exist (Trillas, Cubillo, & del Campo, 2000; Ying, 2002): strong or S-implications that are generalized from crisp implication

$(x => y = \neg x V y)$; Residuated or R-implications; Quantum logic implications Q-implications and Mamdani-Larsen ML-implications. Apart these implications, some applications employ for the implication purposes functions, which do not meet all the axioms to be real implications. In practice, it is very usual to describe implication by t-norms (Gupta & Qi, 1991). This especially holds for the minimum t-norm which is often called Mamdani implication.

In addition, fuzzy implications are a suitable tool for computing FFDs (Fodor, 1991; Oh & Bandler, 1987; Cao & Kandel, 1989). Fuzzy implications have a number of attractive characteristics that make them applicable in FFDs analysis. Firstly, we can use them in fuzzy relations because we can express the dependency strength between the observed attributes by the actual real value. Secondly, fuzzy implications provide a natural framework that incorporates IF-THEN rules necessary for the development of new techniques in knowledge discovery. From our point of view, there are fuzzy implications that meet the acceptance criteria in problems of computation and identification of fuzzy dependencies between the data such as Mamdani, Kleene-Diens, Willomt and Early-Zadeh. On the other hand, fuzzy operators like Lukasiewicz and Gödel implication cannot be used in these connotations, because they do not satisfy acceptance criteria for FFDs analysis (Vucetic, et al., 2013). Table 3 presents fuzzy implications that we can use for discovering FFDs in fuzzy relations.

Table 3. Fuzzy implication operators used for FFDs discovering

Fuzzy Implication	Corresponding Formula for $X \xrightarrow{\theta} Y$
Mamdani	$I_{MM} = \min(x,y)$
Kleene-Diense	$I_{KL} = \max(1\text{-}x,y)$
Early-Zadeh	$I_{EA} = \max(1\text{-}x,\min(x,y))$
Willmot	$Iw = \min[\max(1\text{-}x,y),\ \max(x,1\text{-}x),\ \max(y,1\text{-}y)]$

Realization

A new method for calculating FFDs for relational databases has been suggested recently by Vucetic, et al. (2013). Identifying potential dependencies between attributes of the observed fuzzy relation induces the discovery of hidden and useful knowledge. In order to identify FFDs within the corresponding fuzzy model, the following steps are necessary:

1. Preparing data for analysis (pre-processing, fuzzification, data summarization, and determining proximity relation).
2. Finding sub relations (pairs of tuples) on the observed attributes with potentially hidden fuzzy functional dependencies.
3. Associating fuzzy functional dependencies with corresponding fuzzy implications.
4. Interpreting search results for the purpose of getting the final set of FFDs.

The first step is the construction of fuzzy sets on attributes domains included in calculation of FFDs. This step is a critical part which has significant influence on the final solution. In order to decrease subjectivity and have the same starting step as in LSs (discussed in the next Section), fuzzy sets are constructed using the uniform domain covering method (Tudorie, 2008). This step is common for both approaches and it is explained in Section *Construction of membership functions*.

To assess the dependencies, we apply the following definitions:

- $|T_r| = |r \times r|$, where r is given fuzzy relation.
- For every attribute $A_i \in r$, we compute conformance $C(A_i[t_i,t_j])$ for each pair of tuples.
- T_r represents relation whose columns are $C(A_i[t_i,t_j])$ and entitles t_i and t_j that holds:

$\forall t_i, t_j \in r,\ i \neq j$ pair of tuples $(t_i t_j) \in r \times r$, i.e. $t_i t_j \in T_r$, $C(A_i[t_i,t_j]) \in [0,1]$.

- $X \xrightarrow{\theta} Y$, θ represents linguistic strength of dependency computed with fuzzy implications where $\theta_k \in [0,1]$ is the critical linguistic strength for detecting dependencies between pairs of tuples.
- T_{min} t - norm is used for connecting pairs of tuples where FFDs are satisfied.

In the process of computation of dependencies we use the definition of FFD given in (2), and $C(A_i[t_i,t_j])$ we compute in accordance with the Equation (1). $C(A_i[t_i,t_j])$ is calculated on the pair of tuples (sub relation $r(R)$ of the given relational scheme).

The idea to measure the percentage of tuples where FFDs appear to be very interesting. Following this methodology helps us to discover FFDs and compute a measure which enables us to determine the proportion of tuples P in a fuzzy relation where FFDs are satisfied.

Formally, this is how we get the proportion parameter P:

$$P = \frac{C}{C_{tot}} \qquad (3)$$

where C is the number of sub relations (pair of tuples) with the observed FFD $X \xrightarrow{\theta} Y$, while C_{tot} is the total number of pairs of tuples in relation T_r. We calculate C_{tot} by using the following formula:

$$C_{tot} = \frac{n!}{k!(n-2)!} \qquad (4)$$

where n is the number of tuples in a relational database and k is the number or examined attributes. Usually pairs of attributes are examined, i.e. k = 2.

Proportion parameter P tells us about the frequency of FFDs and on that basis we become able to express the dependencies in the form of linguistic rules.

For example, if P=50% in the FFD *Position* $\xrightarrow{\theta}$ *Salary*, we can put it down in a linguistic form *Position considerably affects the employee's salary,* which end-users easily understand. Perception based on information given by rules is discussed in Batyrshin (2004).

Computational complexity in applying the proposed algorithm may cause serious problems in practice. Increasing the number of tuples, as well as the number of attributes of relational scheme exponentially increases the number of computed transactions. It means that the total number of transactions (possible pairs of tuples with associated values) that need to be computed can be unacceptably large. From a theoretical point of view, advanced computer technology cannot effectively solve exponential problems like this (Pavlus, 2012). In order to mitigate this shortcoming, different techniques such as projection, restriction, powerful computer systems, data summarization based on fuzzification

(Cubero, Medina, Pons, & Vila, 1999), cluster formation, granulation, presenting a number of similar tuples with one representing tuple, etc. have been proposed.

LS FOR EXTRACTING RELATIONAL KNOWLEDGE IN DATA

In the previous section we discussed FFDs and their strengths in detecting dependencies between attributes taking into account the whole domains of examined attributes. On the other hand, if dependency exists only between parts of examined attributes' domains, then FFDs are not able to detect it, or the value of dependency is under the critical linguistic strength θ_k. This kind of dependency could be detected by the LS.

Construction of LS

Initially, LSs have been developed to express relational knowledge about the data (Rasmussen & Yager, 1997) which is concise and easily understandable to humans. Since the natural language is the best way for communication and information mining for humans (from other people or databases) LSs would be a desirable way. They are in line with the bio-inspired concept of computing with words introduced in Zadeh (2002). While in the LSs of structure *Q R entities in database are (have) S,* the *R* is optional (Kacprzyk & Zadrozny, 2009), in evaluation of dependencies this part is mandatory.

Linguistically quantified propositions are written in a general form:

$$Qx(Px) \qquad (5)$$

where Q is a linguistic quantifier, $X = \{x\}$ is a universe of disclosure (e.g. the set of all municipalities) and $P(x)$ is a predicate depicting summariser S e.g. *high water consumption per household*. Predicate P is a fuzzy set $P \in F(X)$. $F(X)$ is a family of fuzzy sets defined on the domain of an examined attribute.

The truth value of an elementary rule (Q *entities in database are S*) is computed by the following equation (Zadrożny & Kacprzyk, 2009):

$$T\left(Qx(Px)\right) = \mu_Q \left(\frac{1}{n} \sum_{i=1}^{n} \mu_{\mathrm{P}}(x_i) \right) \qquad (6)$$

where n is the cardinality of a data set (number of entities), $\frac{1}{n} \sum_{i=1}^{n} \mu_{\mathrm{P}}(x_i)$ is the proportion of objects in a data set that satisfy $P(x)$ and μ_Q is the membership function of a quantifier.

A more complex type of summary, relevant for the aim of this chapter, has the form Q R *entities in database are (have) S*. The example is the rule: *most low polluted municipalities have high altitude and small number of inhabitants*. The procedure for calculating truth value has the following form (Rassmusen & Yager, 1997):

$$T\left(Qx(Px)\right) = \mu_Q \left(\frac{\sum_{i=1}^{n} t\left(\mu_{\mathrm{P}}(x_i), \mu_{\mathrm{R}}(x_i)\right)}{\sum_{i=1}^{n} \mu_{\mathrm{R}}(x_i)} \right)$$

$$(7)$$

where

$$\frac{\sum_{i=1}^{n} t\left(\mu_{\mathrm{P}}(x_i), \mu_{\mathrm{R}}(x_i)\right)}{\sum_{i=1}^{n} \mu_{\mathrm{R}}(x_i)}$$

is the proportion of the R objects in a database that satisfy S, t is a t-norm, μ_Q is the membership function of a quantifier.

This kind of summarisation reflects intensity of relation between parts of attributes domains depicted in Figure 1b.

If the summarizer S consists of several attributes, $\mu_{\mathrm{P}}(x_i)$ is calculated in the following way:

$$\mu_{\mathrm{P}}(x_i) = f(\mu_{Pj}(x_i)) \qquad (8)$$

where P_j is the j-th atomic predicate and f is a t-norm. Detailed examination of t-norms can be found in e.g. Klement, Mesiar, and Pap (2000) and Klir and Yuan (1995). If the R part of a LS contains several attributes connected by the logical *AND* operator, then the same discussion as for $\mu_{\mathrm{P}}(x_i)$ (Equation 8) applies for $\mu_{\mathrm{R}}(x_i)$.

LSs could contain other forms depending on data mining needs. Kacprzyk & Zadrozny (2009) suggested different proto forms from simple to general one. Hudec (2013b) explained extending S and R parts with preferences and using LSs for querying and ranking entities on higher hierarchical level using data on lower hierarchical level.

Obviously, to calculate the validity of all types of LSs, fuzzy sets for summarizers and quantifiers should be constructed. The first step, the critical part, is to construct fuzzy sets on attributes domains. This step was marked as essential in FFDs too. In order to obtain consistent results, we constructed fuzzy sets for LSs and FFDs in the same way by using the uniform domain covering method (Tudorie, 2008; 2009) explained in the Section *Construction of membership functions*. The construction of quantifiers is explained in the following subsection.

One motive for treating gradations, as it is done in fuzzy logic, is to reduce the complexity of mathematical analysis of real problems by the classical approaches (Radojević, 2008b). For example, two elements of the analysed universe can be discerned by the black-white approaches (crisp or two-valued logic) only if one has the examined property and the other does not. A rule is either satisfied or not in a crisp way. If we have several satisfied rules, the relevance is the same. If we want to discern them, another attribute should be added to the rule. Contrary, in linguistic summaries, rules are based on validity degree. Rules are also discerned by intensity of meeting the rule condition.

Construction of the Quantifier

The validity of summaries examined in the chapter is computed by the relative quantifier *most*. A quantifier is constructed as a fuzzy set on the [0, 1] interval (Zadrożny & Kacprzyk, 2009).

For a regular non-decreasing quantifier (*most*) its membership function should meet the following property:

$$x \leq y \Rightarrow \mu_Q(x) \leq \mu_Q(y); \; \mu_Q(0)=0; \; \mu_Q(1)=1. \quad (9)$$

Existing approaches to linguistic data summarization have introduced various quality indicators for quantifier selection to solve this problem (Glöckner, 2006). For practical application the quantifier *most* is suggested in (Kacprzyk & Zadrożny, 2009), which meets the property (9), and has the following form:

$$\mu_Q(y) = \begin{cases} 1, & \text{for } y > 0.8 \\ 2y - 0.6, & \text{for } 0.3 \leq y \leq 0.8 \,. \\ 0, & \text{for } y < 0.3 \end{cases} \quad (10)$$

Another way of modelling a linguistic quantifier is by using the Ordered Weighted Averaging (OWA) operator. If a quantifier is a regular non-

decreasing one (9), then the weight vector of an OWA operator is defined as follows (Yager, 1988):

$$w_i = \mu_Q\left(\frac{i}{m}\right) - \mu_Q\left(\frac{i-1}{m}\right), \quad i = 1,...,m \,. \quad (11)$$

Because of its simplicity and fast calculation, the first approach is used in the chapter. In the case of an OWA operator, the number of municipalities that meet the predicate to some extent could be high (value of *m* in Equation 11) and it is a time consuming task to calculate all values of w_i for such a long vector. In this case (10) is a rational option.

On the other hand, if the mining task is to calculate an "aggregated" linguistic quantifier, e.g. *most of the predicates {P$_i$} are satisfied (i=1... n)*, then the quantifier could be represented by the OWA operator using (11). In that case, the number of predicates is significantly smaller than the number of entities in a database.

However, if we replace numbers in (10) with parameters the following way (Hudec, 2013a):

$$\mu_Q(y) = \begin{cases} 1, & \text{for } y > n \\ (y-m)/(n-m), & \text{for } m \leq y \leq n \\ 0, & \text{for } y < m \end{cases} \quad (12)$$

then we are able to adjust strictness of the linguistic quantifier. A quantifier is stronger and closer to the crisp quantifier *all*, if $n \to 1$ and $m \to n$ (Figure 2). This approach is desirable when we have a larger number of rules. The adjustment of *m* and *n* filters rules and selects only the rules that significantly describe relations in a database.

Given a set of data, we can hypothesize any dependency using appropriate linguistic summarisers (Kacprzyk & Zadrożny, 2009). The validity of truth indicates the strength of relational dependency in the examined subset of attributes.

A detailed explanation is given in case studies later on in the chapter.

Realization

The first step in each linguistic summarisation is to calculate the proportion of objects in a database that satisfy $P(x)$ (Hudec, 2013a). This step contains two sub steps: selection of all entities with membership degree greater than zero to the predicate $P(x)$. This sub step could be solved by arbitrary fuzzy query approaches, e.g. SQLf (Bosc & Pivert 2000), FQL (Wang, Lee, & Chen, 2007) and fuzzy generalized logical condition (Hudec, 2009; Hudec, 2011). The last one was applied in our experiments. In the second sub step the proportion of entities that meet the summarizer is calculated. Finally, in the second step validity of summary is calculated according to the employed quantifier.

There are also tools either focused on summarisation like SummarySQL (Rassmusen & Yager 1997) or query language FQUERY (Kacprzyk & Zadrożny, 1995) which is extended to cover linguistic summarisation (Zadrożny & Kacprzyk, 2009).

This way of realization makes LSs an effective approach for detecting dependencies on specified parts of attributes domains. Figure 1 shows that nine summaries should be executed for the estimation of dependency on whole domains by LSs. Nine queries could be a significant burden for large databases and managing all queries and their validities is not an easy task.

Previous paragraphs examined the situations in which the user or decision maker wants to find relational knowledge between particular attributes. However, if we want to reveal all relevant rules, then the procedure is a standard operations research task (Liu, 2011):

Find Q, S, and R subject to:

$$Q \in \bar{Q}$$

$$S \in \bar{S}$$

$$R \in \bar{R}$$
$$v(Q, S, R) \geq v_k$$

where $\bar{S}$ is a set of relevant linguistic expressions {small, medium, high,...}, $\bar{R}$ is a set defining relevant sub populations of interest, $v_k \in (0, 1]$ is the threshold for the validity of summary, and $\bar{Q}$ is a set of relevant quantifiers {few, about half, most,...} which is reduced to the quantifier *most* for estimation dependencies. Each solution produces a linguistic summary $Q* R * are S*$. All solutions create the relational rule base.

Figure 2. Adjustment of the quantifier most

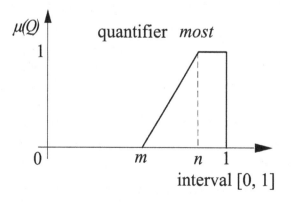

CONSTRUCTION OF MEMBERSHIP FUNCTIONS

In order to reveal FFDs and LSs, the first step is fuzzification of attributes domains. It implies the construction of a family of fuzzy sets *F(X)* on the domain of an examined variable as shown in Figure 3.

Galindo (2008) pointed out that a system will not work properly if it uses ill defined membership functions. Consequently, these functions have to be carefully defined. This also stands for LSs and FFDs where properly constructed fuzzy sets are pivotal for further calculations.

Let D_{min} and D_{max} be the lowest and the highest domain values of attribute *A* i.e. Dom(A) = [D_{min}, D_{max}]. Generally, an attribute's domain is defined in a way that all theoretically possible values could be stored in a database. However, in practice the lowest stored value and the highest stored value are often far from D_{min} and D_{max} respectively. Let *L* and *H* be the lowest and the highest values in the current content of a database respectively (Hudec & Sudzina, 2012). In practice, [*L*, *H*] ⊂ [D_{min}, D_{max}] (either [D_{min}, *L*] or [*H*, D_{max}] are empty or even both of them are empty). A good example is water consumption per household and the number of summer days during the year indicators in the Slovak municipal statistics (Hudec, 2003).

Theoretically possible values are the set of real numbers greater or equal than zero for the first attribute and the interval [0, 365] for the second attribute. However, all collected data are situated only in parts of respective domains. If we want to find whether dependencies and relations between these two attributes exist we should consider only parts of domains that contain data.

The uniform domain covering method (Tudorie, 2008) is an appropriate method for the construction of membership functions for these tasks. At the beginning, values of *L* and *H* are retrieved from the current content of a database. The length of fuzzy set core *β* and the slope *α* (Figure 4) are calculated using the following equations (Tudorie, 2008):

$$\alpha = \frac{1}{8}(H - L) \tag{13}$$

$$\beta = \frac{1}{4}(H - L) . \tag{14}$$

Consequently, required parameters of membership functions *A*, *B* *C* and *D* (Figure 4) are calculated using (13, 14):

$$A=L+\beta; \; B=L+\beta+\alpha; \; C=H\text{-}\beta\text{-}\alpha; \; D=H\text{-}\beta. \tag{15}$$

Figure 3. Linguistic and crisp domains of a database attribute

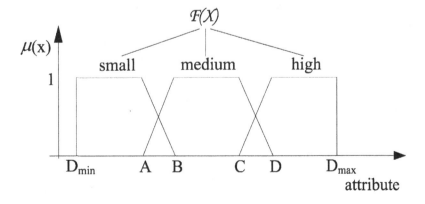

Figure 4. Linguistic and crisp domains of current content of a database attribute

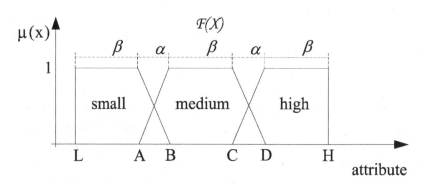

There are other approaches in literature that have been suggested for membership functions construction such as the statistical mean based algorithm (Tudorie, 2008) and logarithmic transformation of domains (Hudec & Sudzina, 2012). They are more suitable for fuzzy data queries to mitigate issues of empty and overabundant answer problems. If the distribution of data inside the respective domains is highly unbalanced and the query is more restrictive (several elementary conditions merged with the *AND* logical operator), then the answer might easily end as empty. If a user wants to obtain some alternative data when initial query ended as empty, then the statistical mean based algorithm and logarithmic transformation of domains are suitable. However, in mining relational knowledge and dependencies from the data, the goal is not data selection but validity of rules depicted in Figure 1. The validity of a rule having value of 0 does not mean that no data meets the query condition, but relation between examined attributes in particular parts of their respective domains is low. For this reason, we should uniformly cover the [L, H] interval.

CASE STUDIES

The focus of this Section is on the evaluation of the suggested methods of FFDs and LSs by means of experiments. The experiments were performed using real data from the Slovak municipal statistics database. We were interested whether a dependency between the attributes *Number of days during year - summer (temperature greater or equal 25 degrees Celsius)* – abbreviated to *Number of warm days* and *Consumption of water – Households per inhabitant* – abbreviated to *Consumption of water* exists in both directions. The second experiment examined dependencies between attributes: *Population density* and *Production of waste in tons*. Experimental results are presented in the two following subsections.

FFDs

In the first step, all attributes were fuzzified into three fuzzy sets: *small*, *medium* and *high* according to the uniform domain covering method (13 – 15).

Experiments were realised in accordance with the definition of the FFD (Definition 2.) and the methodology suggested in this chapter. Concerning the fuzzy implication, the Mamdani implication (Table 3) was employed in the algorithm for detecting FFDs.

Mined dependencies for both experiments are presented in Table 4. The critical linguistic strength θ_k was adjusted to value of 0.70.

Change in the value of θ_k causes changes in the strength of dependency. Designers of information systems, researchers and decision makers involved in mining knowledge from relational databases according to their knowledge, needs and goals of a particular task could adjust value of θ_k. If we change this value to 0.76 the following dependencies are obtained (Table 5.).

The comparison of values in Tables 4 and 5 shows the influence of the modification of the critical linguistic strength on the of dependencies' intensity. For $\theta_k = 0.70$ (Table 4), the consumption of water depends on the number of warm days with a higher degree than in the reverse case. However, when we increase the threshold of critical dependency to value of 0.76 two changes occur: dependencies in both directions are noticeably lower and the reverse case has stronger dependency than the initial one. We could conclude that there is a trend explaining that regardless of climatic conditions the population takes care not to significantly increase consumption, probably due to environmental awareness or low family budgets. The similar conclusion is obtained by LSs.

From the second experiment, the dependency of production of waste on population density is apparent. This trend continues to be obvious after the increase in the threshold of critical dependency to value of 0.76. This result is in accordance with the usual opinion and experiences. One of reasons to use these two attributes is to see how this

method works when our common sense expects strong dependency.

If we replace dependency defined as $C(Y[t_i,t_j]) \geq \min (\theta_k, C(X[t_i,t_j]))$ with $\min I(\approx(t(X), t'(X), \approx(t(Y), t'(Y)) \geq \theta_k (t, t' \in R)$ (Section *From FDs to FFDs*) and apply Mamdani fuzzy implication (Table 3), we can conclude that dependency between the attributes *number of warm days* and *consumption of water* is in 57.51% tuples. Furthermore, by applying LSs we can explore dependencies on particular clusters of domains to reveal the nature of the obtained fuzzy functional dependencies which could be further expressed by IF-THEN rules. These rules could significantly support decision making, reduction of redundancies in databases and estimation of missing values.

The above evaluated dependencies could be translated into linguistic rules or statements. Users could communicate with a database in a human oriented mode. This way of providing results is advisable because natural language envelopes uncertainties and subjectivity which are compatible with the nature of FFDs. Examples of mined statements are as follows:

"Number of warm days has significant influence on consumption of water." and "Population density strongly determines production of waste."

Table 4. Mined dependencies for critical linguistic strength of 0.70

FFD	P
0.70 Number of warm days $\longrightarrow$ Consumption of water	P=37.42%
0.70 Consumption of water $\longrightarrow$ Number of warm days	P=20.09%
0.71 Population density $\longrightarrow$ Production of waste	P= 45.86%
0.70 Production of waste $\longrightarrow$ Population density	P= 24.51%

Table 5. Mined dependencies for critical linguistic strength of 0.76

FFD	P
0.82 Number of warm days $\longrightarrow$ Consumption of water	P=13.70%
0.77 Consumption of water $\longrightarrow$ Number of warm days	P=15.79%
0.78 Population density $\longrightarrow$ Production of waste	P= 43.03%
0.77 Production of waste $\longrightarrow$ Population density	P= 18.80%

The mined rule is readable and understandable for humans. It depicts dependency between the two attributes of interest. The result is based on the evaluation of the whole database. If a user wants to see the influence between these attributes but only in subsets of collected data, then LSs could provide the solution.

LSs

Using the uniform domain covering method (13 – 15) in the same way as for the experiment for FFDs, the attributes were fuzzified into three fuzzy sets: *small*, *medium* and *high*. For the construction of the quantifier *most* the Equation (10) was used.

The first experiment focused on revealing dependencies between *Number of warm days* and *Consumption of water* on their respective sub domains. The obtained dependencies are shown in Table 6 and Table 7 for the reverse case. In all experiments the threshold value is set to 0.2.

The mined information could be interpreted and explained in the following way. As for the first row (Table 6), higher unemployment in many small municipalities (in southern part) and a tendency for saving, causes the water consumption to be not as highly dependent on temperature as expected. As for the last row, there is no need for higher consumption when the number of warm days is small. The mined information could also be used as an initial estimation of the missing values. If for a municipality having low water consumption per inhabitant the value of the number of warm days in an examined year is missing, we could say that this value belongs to fuzzy set *small* with probability of 0.905. However, dependencies in the opposite direction (Table 7) are less strong.

The second experiment was focused on revealing dependencies between *Population density* and *Production of waste in tons*. Mined dependencies are shown in Table 8 and Table 9.

Table 6. Mined dependency: Number of warm days -> Consumption of water

Rule	Validity
Most municipalities having high number of warm days have high consumption of water	Under threshold of quantifier
Most municipalities having medium number of warm days have medium consumption of water	0.695
Most municipalities having small number of warm days have low consumption of water	0.905

Table 7. Mined dependency: Consumption of water -> Number of warm days

Rule	Validity
Most municipalities having high consumption of water have high number of warm days	Under threshold of quantifier
Most municipalities having medium consumption of water have medium number of warm days	Under threshold of quantifier
Most municipalities having low consumption of water have small number of warm days	0.509

The table reveals full dependency between small municipalities and low waste production. The influence of this strong value is that incomes are usually smaller in small municipalities and people try to buy fewer items and use them longer. Dependency exists in the first rule: Municipalities having high population density usually produce high amounts of waste but with lower validity of rule. It is interesting that the validity of the second rule is under the threshold value. If we want to create fuzzy expert system, then the second rule does not describe inhabitant behaviour properly. Generally, it means that dependency does not exist or that there is even a discrepancy in methodology explaining the procedure and metadata in the data collection.

In opposite direction, a strong dependency is again detected between small municipalities and low waste production. We can conclude that these parts of domains are very dependent in both directions.

Comparison of Obtained Results and Discussion

FFDs have revealed a stronger functional dependency (FD) for *Number of warm days ->* *Consumption of water* than vice versa. The same solution was obtained by LSs. FFDs concluded that dependency between temperature and water consumption exists in 57.51% pairs of all database tuples. Furthermore, LSs revealed that dependency is stronger for municipalities having small number of warm days and low water consumption. This experiment has proven that these two approaches could efficiently complement each other providing different types of information but in a consistent and understandable way. The same conclusion holds for the second experiment.

The strength of LSs is in lower time and computational resources demands an examination of dependencies in particular parts of attributes domains. LSs are based on fuzzy queries and do not require modification of relational databases. Their weakness is in subjectivity in construction of quantifiers and therefore, measuring the

Table 8. Mined dependency: Population density -> Production of waste

Rule	Validity
Most municipalities having high population density have high production of waste	0.662
Most municipalities having medium population density have medium production of waste	Under threshold of quantifier
Most municipalities having small population density have low production of waste	1

Table 9. Mined dependency: Production of waste -> Population density

Rule	Validity
Most municipalities having high production of waste have high population density	0.595
Most municipalities having medium production of waste have medium population density	Under threshold of quantifier
Most municipalities having small production of waste have small population density	1

quality of summaries (Castillo-Ortega, Marín, Sánzhes, & Tettamanzi, 2012). LSs also require more interaction with users than FFDs. For skilled data miners this is an advantage but for all other decision makers not skilled in fuzzy logic, this could be a limiting factor. Usually in LSs, a user is left to define all rules of interest and evaluate them. Weakness lies in the fact that the examined database could contain some other rules with a higher degree of validity. Since a fully automatic generation of LSs is not feasible at the moment (Kacprzyk & Zadrożny, 2009), there is room for further research and development. First results in this direction have been presented in van der Heide and Trivinio (2009).

FFDs require significantly more computation resources and time. They evaluate dependency among attributes taking values for each database tuple. When the number of tuples is increasing, the time complexity problem has exponential nature. Because relational databases cannot recognize fuzzy values of attributes, they should be prepared by additional calculations over databases (Vucetic, et al., 2013). For a large database, this is a significant computational burden. On the other hand, complex and deep mining could reveal relevant and reliable results. Another advantage of the proposed method for detecting FFDs is that it evaluates dependencies in both directions, whereas LSs have to execute an additional set of fuzzy queries with replaced positions of attributes in R and S parts of LSs. However, if the dependency is below the threshold value, it could mean either that attributes are independent or that high dependency exists only in a specific part of their domains. Improvements of FFDs are also a field of interest of researchers.

If the goal is to find dependency only between particular parts of domains of two attributes, then LSs are a better option. They can be applied directly without any modifications of the database. If we want to apply FFDs, then the first step should be to create query or view of part of database of interest and continue with all necessary calculations ex-

plained in Section *From FDs to FFDs*. This might be a very demanding task even for the evaluation of only a part of the database. If the goal is to find dependencies between attributes on their whole domains and examine which direction is stronger, FFDs are a better option. If we want to apply LSs, we have to realize series of fuzzy queries and to calculate the average value of dependency, as well as to discover the nature of mined dependencies between attributes of relational databases.

Both approaches share a common advantage and a common disadvantage. The advantage is that a user has control over revealing dependencies and relational knowledge by creating summaries of interest or selecting attributes for estimating dependencies. On the other hand, this could also be a disadvantage because other, even stronger dependencies might exist. There are two main solutions: taking into consideration all possible summaries and reveal summaries with validity greater than threshold value in a way of an operations research task (Liu, 2011) or apply method suggested in der Heide & Trivio (2009). Theoretically, FFDs can work autonomously on the whole database to reveal all relevant dependencies; however, without specifically selected attributes they might end in combinatorial explosion.

The other possibility is applying neural networks or genetic algorithms. Neural networks are able to recognize nonlinear patterns and dependencies between input and output data in the presence of noise and incomplete data sets (Juriová, 2012). Neural networks are usually highly parameterised and require steps such as preparing input data (training sets, validating sets, and data for detecting dependencies) into input format and selecting learning algorithms. These tasks might be complicated for field experts. The same holds for genetic algorithms which are also able to learn from data and uncover new information, e.g. dependencies between attributes.

Theory, illustrative examples, and preliminary experiment results on real data provide some information of use, and both advantages and limitations of FFDs and LSs in the data mining. In a broader sense, taking into account other steps of KDD depicted in Section *Role of fuzzy logic in data mining*, we could apply FFDs and LSs in several steps but further research is required. In the step of developing and understanding the application domain and the relevant prior knowledge, LSs allow users to describe a task using sentences from natural language.

In the step of data cleaning and pre-processing, both approaches are able to tackle the issues of missing values. FFDs are applicable when dependency is detected on the whole domain, whereas LSs could support estimation of missing values on particular parts of domains. However, this holds only in case when a database contains a smaller number of missing values or when relations between attributes are not complex. Otherwise, neural networks and genetic algorithms are more suitable. In that case the purpose of LSs could be to evaluate how these algorithms estimate missing values (Hudec & Juriová, 2013).

FFDs are suitable for the step of data reduction and projection. The nature of FFDs is to reveal dependencies between attributes which are more or less similar. Dependent attributes could be deleted and excluded from further data mining and also excluded in further data collection.

Finally, in steps of interpreting mined relational knowledge and consolidating this knowledge, LSs and FFDs provide a solution by revealed IF-THEN rules, dependencies and relations explained by linguistic terms and degrees of truth. This allows ranking downwards of evaluated rules from rules that best fit the data to rules that less fit relational knowledge in data.

DIRECTIONS FOR FUTURE RESEARCH

Mining dependencies could support decisions in various fields. Some of them are briefly discussed in Section *Relational knowledge and dependencies in data*. Further development of practical solutions should be coordinated between researchers and practitioners.

For research concerning LSs and FFDs the following topics are of interest. Dependencies could have more complex structure when several independent attributes determine one attribute, or when transitive dependency exists. In the case when several independent attributes determine one attribute, LSs could solve the issue. The *R* part of LSs could be extended to envelope more attributes connected to the logical operator, for example: *most of municipalities having low pollution and low unemployment have low migration*. The *AND* operator should be expressed by appropriate aggregation functions. The fuzzy logic is a generalization of the two-valued logic based on truth functionality. As a consequence, its logical operators do not meet all axioms of Boolean logic (Radojević, 2008a). Literature offers many t-norms functions that meet different axioms. For example, min t-norm meets the axiom of idempotency, but not the axiom of non-contradiction. In the case of Lukasiewicz t-norm situation is opposite. A possible field of research would be to examine which t-norms are most suitable for mining dependencies. Research in the real-valued realization of Boolean algebra and its implementation could bring additional knowledge. In case when transitive dependencies exist, FFDs are suitable for finding them. Fuzzy implications are crucial in algorithms for discovering FFDs. There is space for further research in implications and their suitability.

Furthermore, our approach divides fuzzified attributes' domains into three fuzzy sets {small, medium, high} (Figure 1 and Figure 4). Finer granularity of rules can be obtained by constructing five fuzzy sets on attributes domains e.g. {very small, small, medium, high, very high} by uniform domain covering method (Tudorie, 2009). The same holds for the set of quantifiers which could also be extend to more elements. On the other hand, this would induce issues of evaluating more rules. The starting point for solving the problem is summaries expressed as operations research task as explained in (Liu, 2011).

Furthermore, LSs could be used as typical fuzzy queries, but with a touch of the disclosure control (Hudec, 2013c). For example, users want to select and rank districts downwards according to the matching degree of the summary, e.g.: *most small municipalities have high unemployment rate*. The query keeps data that are not free of charge or sensitive (municipalities) hidden. A user obtains only the mined summarised information for each district. Further research is required in this promising direction, e.g. the critical size of data on lower hierarchical level to avoid risk of disclosure. This direction is also suitable when policy makers are not interested in data on the lower hierarchical level, but in mined aggregated information from this level.

Mining dependencies in different fuzzy relational databases is a research aspect which should not be neglected. There are various fuzzy relational database models which will be the subject of future research. Fuzzy databases make way for their practical applicability. Indeed, their wider use is expected in the near future. Also, multi-valued dependencies and their extraction from fuzzy relations are an interesting issue in this connotation. Mining dependencies is an especially promising research field for LSs as research papers are few. The possibility of integrating FFDs by LSs and their comparison may be considered in fuzzy relational databases. It could be a natural extension of the comparison made in this chapter on the relational database.

In the future, we will attempt to modify the proposed algorithm for research in the area of text mining and estimation of missing values in relational databases. These efforts are aimed at extending the presented framework for more complex mining problems. Hybrid techniques, such as LSs and FFDs, provide more opportunities to researchers for resolving this kind of problems. The authors will investigate other bio-inspired techniques in order to improve the model.

Mining and revealing all relevant dependencies, similarities and behaviour among data respondents significantly supports policy and executive decision making and the evaluation of missing values. However, the estimation of missing values is not always a straightforward task. It depends highly on the nature of the collected data. If we focus on municipal statistics and indicators describing climate conditions, we recognise some similarities between municipalities and dependencies between their indicators. If the distance between municipalities is not large and if they have similar altitude above sea level, then climate indicators (number of days with snow coverage, number summer days) are dependable. It means that we can select relevant indicators and examine their dependency on a whole domain by FFD or reveal whether dependency exists on specific parts of domains by LS.

In the case of business and trade statistics (Hudec, et al., 2012; Kľúčik, 2012; Juriová, 2012) the relations among all accessible data (previous trade, administrative data about companies, etc.) are more complicated and it is not easy to exclude some indicators from the evaluation of dependencies. In that case, it is desirable to examine all possible influences by neural networks (Juriová, 2012) or by evolutionary algorithms (Kľúčik, 2012). Neural networks and genetic algorithms are able to search large incomplete data sets in order to reveal relevant information required for the decision making. The main drawback is that the obtained knowledge remains hidden for users.

The suggested cooperation between neural networks and fuzzy logic as a data mining task for estimation of missing values in business and trade statistics is explained in Hudec and Juriová (2013). In the first step, missing values could be estimated by neural networks due to complex relations among attributes, the presence of noise and incomplete data sets. In the next steps, the evaluation of whether imputed values have similar properties as data received from respondents should be carried out.

The evaluation of whether imputed values have similar properties as data received from respondents could reveal how procedures for data imputation work. This way we could create pair of rules, e.g.: *most (about half, few) of responded exports has small (medium, high) number of items (goods)* and run the rules on two parts of a database: collected data and estimated data respectively. If truth values of both rules gravitate to each other, then both parts of a database have similar properties (data distribution), which means that the current algorithm works properly. The opposite result suggests that algorithms should be improved. This example has shown how LSs used together with neural networks can be used for the evaluation of estimated values as well as for revealing useful information from a database.

In the case of examination of territorial units, the mined information may be interpreted and presented on thematic maps using different colours. For example, territorial units which fully meet the summary evaluated on units on the level below (districts-municipalities) can be marked with one colour, territorial units which do not meet the summary can be marked with a second colour and territorial units having the validity of the summary in the [0, 1] interval can be marked with a third colour, having a colour gradient from a faint hue to a deep hue following the value of validity.

CONCLUSION

In this chapter, we have proposed complementary methods based on fuzzy approach to extract rules and useful knowledge from relational databases. An example has been given to illustrate a fuzzy data mining algorithm on real data from the Slovak municipal statistics. Overall, our research has shown how to extract intelligent information from relational databases by FFDs and LSs. These two methods are considered and used as complementing, not competitive. In order to identify possible relations and dependencies between attributes in a database, the first task is to prepare the framework for the analysis. The common part is the construction of a family of membership functions on respective attributes' domains. It can be satisfactorily solved if we calculate parameters of membership functions directly from the current database content using the uniform domain covering method. This way, the subjectivity of a user's opinion about linguistic terms is reduced.

FFD continues with pre-processing based on aggregation, granulation or summarization, creating a table with pairs of tuples, and conformance values on all attributes of relation. The following step finds sub-relations where criteria for the existence of fuzzy dependencies were met. The final step is to associate FFDs with the corresponding fuzzy implications. LSs continue with the creation of a membership function for the relative quantifier, realization of fuzzy queries on a database, calculation of proportion of entities which meet the query, and finally calculation of the validity of a rule by relative quantifiers expressed as fuzzy sets.

Approaches based on fuzzy logic are able to mimic human reasoning in searching for information by natural language questions and processing data without precise measurements. However, this might lead to more subjective results than expected (LSs) or even longer processing of all linguistic terms (FFDs). Quality assessment in LSs and optimisation of FFDs are topics for further research.

It is worth noting that soft computing is not a melange (Feil & Abonyi, 2008). Rather, it is a partnership in which each component (fuzzy logic, neural networks, evolutionary algorithms, swarm optimisation, etc.) contributes with methods to address problems in their respective domains. The same holds for methods inside fuzzy logic. We have demonstrated how FFD and LS complement in revealing intensities of dependencies between data. In order to solve problems which worry practitioners, developing soft computing approaches in a complementing rather than competitive way could provide solutions.

In further research and development we plan to deeply examine the possibilities of both approaches for the estimation of missing values. This is an issue which needs constant improvements in the field of official statistics data collection. The second issue is mitigating combinatorial explosion of FFD by identifying possible candidates for evaluating dependencies. For this purpose, the user or biologically inspired tool could indicate the candidates. Revealing all relevant linguistic summaries could be an operations research task which is another topic for further research. Including other bio-inspired techniques in LSs and FFDs to improve revealing relational knowledge in the data is promising research topic. Finally, adapting LSs to reveal dependencies and relational knowledge in fuzzy relational databases is also an interesting research direction due to their expected wider use in the near future.

REFERENCES

Abonyi, J., Feil, B., & Abraham, A. (2005). Computational Intelligence in Data Mining. *Informatica*, *29*, 3–12.

Ansari, A. Q., Biswas, R., & Aggarwal, S. (2012). Neutrosophic classifier: An extension of fuzzy classifer. *Applied Soft Computing*, *13*, 563–573. doi:10.1016/j.asoc.2012.08.002

Batyrshin, I. (2004). On linguistic representation of quantitative dependencies. *Expert Systems with Applications*, *26*, 95–104. doi:10.1016/S0957-4174(03)00111-8

Bavdaž, M. (2010). Sources of Measurement Errors in Business Surveys. *Journal of Official Statistics*, *26*, 25–42.

Bosc, P., Kraft, D., & Petry, F. (2005). Fuzzy sets in database and information systems, status and opportunities. *Fuzzy Sets and Systems*, *156*, 418–426. doi:10.1016/j.fss.2005.05.039

Bosc, P., & Pivert, O. (2000). SQLf query functionality on top of a regular relational database management system. In M. Pons, M. A. Vila, & J. Kacprzyk (Eds.), *Knowledge Management in Fuzzy Databases* (pp. 171–190). Heidelberg, Germany: Physica-Verlag. doi:10.1007/978-3-7908-1865-9_11

Cao, Z., & Kandel, A. (1989). Applicability of some fuzzy implication operators. *Fuzzy Sets and Systems*, *31*, 151–186. doi:10.1016/0165-0114(89)90002-X

Castillo-Ortega, R., Marín, N., Sánchez, D., & Tettamanzi, A. (2012). Quality Assessment in Linguistic Summaries of Data. In S. Greco, B. Bouchon-Meunier, G. Coletti, M. Fedrizzi, B. Matarazzo, & R. Yager (Eds.), *14th International Conference on Information Processing and Management of Uncertainty in Knowledge-Based Systems IPMU 2012* (pp. 285-294). Berlin: Springer-Verlag.

Chen, G., Kerre, E. E., & Vandenbulcke, J. (1996). Normalization based on fuzzy functional dependency in a fuzzy relational data model. *Information Systems*, *21*, 299–310. doi:10.1016/0306-4379(96)00016-6

Chen, W., & Du, Y. (2009). Using neural networks and data mining techniques for the financial distress prediction model. *Expert Systems with Applications*, *36*, 4075–4086. doi:10.1016/j.eswa.2008.03.020

Cubero, J. C., Medina, J. M., Pons, O., & Vila, M. A. (1999). Data summarization in relational databases through fuzzy dependencies. *Information Sciences*, *121*, 233–270. doi:10.1016/S0020-0255(99)00104-8

de Leeuw, E., Hox, J., & Huisman, M. (2003). Prevention and Treatment of Item Nonresponse. *Journal of Official Statistics*, *19*(2), 153–176.

Fayyad, U. M., Piatestku-Shapiro, G., & Smyth, P. (1996). Knowledge discovery and data mining: Towards a unifying framework. In E. Simoudis, J. Han, & U. M. Fayyad (Eds.), *Advances in Knowledge Discovery and Data Mining* (pp. 82–88). Palo Alto, CA: AAAI/MIT Press.

Feil, B., & Abonyi, J. (2008). Introduction to fuzzy data mining methods. In J. Galindo (Ed.), *Handbook of Research on Fuzzy Information Processing in Databases* (pp. 55–96). London: IGI Global. doi:10.4018/978-1-59904-853-6.ch003

Fodor, J. C. (1991). On fuzzy implication operators. *Fuzzy Sets and Systems*, *42*, 293–300. doi:10.1016/0165-0114(91)90108-3

Fong, H. (2013). Opportunities and Challenges of Integrating Bio-Inspired Optimization and Data Mining Algorithms. In X. S. Yang, Z. Cui, R. Xiao, A. H. Gandomi, & M. Karamanoglu (Eds.), *Swarm Intelligence and Bio-inspired Computation: Theory and Applications* (pp. 385–402). London: Elsevier. doi:10.1016/B978-0-12-405163-8.00018-1

Galindo, J. (2008). Introduction and Trends to Fuzzy Logic and Fuzzy Databases. In J. Galindo (Ed.), *Handbook of Research on Fuzzy Information Processing in Databases* (pp. 1–33). London: IGI Global. doi:10.4018/978-1-59904-853-6.ch001

Giesen, D. (Ed.). (2011). *Response Burden in Official Business Surveys: Measurement and Reduction Practices of National Statistical Institutes*. BLUE-ETS Project Report. Retrieved May 10, 2012, from http://www.blue-ets.istat.it/index.php?id=7

Glöckner, I. (2006). Quantifier Selection for Linguistic Data Summarization. In *Proceedings of IEEE International Conference on Fuzzy Systems* (pp. 720 – 727). Institute of Electrical and Electronics Engineers (IEEE).

Gupta, M. M., & Qi, J. (1991). Theory of t-norms and fuzzy inference methods. *Fuzzy Sets and Systems*, *40*, 431–450. doi:10.1016/0165-0114(91)90171-L

Hong, P. T., Lee, Y. C., & Wu, M. T. (2014). An effective parallel approach for genetic-fuzzy data mining. *Expert Systems with Applications*, *41*, 655–662. doi:10.1016/j.eswa.2013.07.090

Hudec, M. (2003). Urban and Municipal Statistics Project and Information System of the Slovak Republic. *INFO-M*, *5*, 20–22.

Hudec, M. (2009). An Approach to Fuzzy Database Querying, Analysis and Realisation. *Computer Science and Information Systems*, *6*(2), 127–140. doi:10.2298/CSIS0902127H

Hudec, M. (2011). Fuzzy improvement of the SQL. *Yugoslav Journal of Operations Research*, *21*, 239–251. doi:10.2298/YJOR1102239H

Hudec, M. (2013a). Applicability of Linguistic summaries. In N. Mladenović, G. Savić, M. Kuzmanović, D. Makajić-Nikolić, & M. Stanojević (Eds.), *11ᵗʰ Balkan conference on operational research* (pp. 133-140). Belgrade, Serbia: Faculty of Organizational Sciences.

Hudec, M. (2013b). Issues in construction of linguistic summaries. In R. Mesiar, & T. Bacigál (Eds.), *Proceedings of Uncertainty Modelling 2013* (pp. 35–44). Bratislava: STU.

Hudec, M. (2013c). Fuzzy database queries in official statistics: Perspective of using linguistic terms in query conditions. *Statistical journal of the IAOS, 4*, 315-323.

Hudec, M., Balbi, S., Juriová, J., Kľúčik, M., Marino, M., & Scepi, G. … Triunfo, N. (2012). *Report on principles of fuzzy methodology and tools developed for use in data collection (Soft computing and text mining tools for Official Statistics)*. BLUE-ETS Project Report. Retrieved May 15, 2013, from http://www.blue-ets.istat.it/index.php?id=7

Hudec, M., & Juriová, J. (2013). *Evaluation and checking non-response data by soft computing approaches - Case of business and trade statistics*. Paper presented at the New Techniques and Technologies in Statistics, (NTTS 2013). Brussels, Belgium.

Hudec, M., & Sudzina, F. (2012). Construction of fuzzy sets and applying aggregation operators for fuzzy queries. In J. Cordeiro, A. Cuzzocrea, & L. Maciaszek (Eds.), *14th International Conference on Enterprise Information Systems* (ICEIS 2012) (pp. 253-257). Setubal: SciTe Press.

Jiménez, A., Aroba, J., de la Torre, M. L., Andujar, J. M., & Grande, J. A. (2009). Model of behaviour of conductivity versus pH in acid mine drainage water, based on fuzzy logic and data mining techniques. *Journal of Hydroinformatics, 11*(2), 147–153. doi:10.2166/hydro.2009.015

Juriová, J. (2012). *Neural Network Approach Applied for Classification in Business and Trade Statistics*. Paper presented at the 46th Scientific Meeting of the Italian Statistical Society. Rome, Italy.

Kacprzyk, J., & Yager, R. (2001). Linguistic summaries of data using fuzzy logic. *International Journal of General Systems, 30*, 33–154. doi:10.1080/03081070108960702

Kacprzyk, J., & Zadrożny, S. (1995). FQUERY for Access: Fuzzy querying for windows-based DBMS. In P. Bosc, & J. Kacprzyk (Eds.), *Fuzziness in Database Management Systems* (pp. 415–433). Berlin: Physica-Verlag. doi:10.1007/978-3-7908-1897-0_18

Kacprzyk, J., & Zadrożny, S. (2009). Protoforms of Linguistic Database Summaries as a Human Consistent Tool for Using Natural Language in Data Mining. *International Journal of Software Science and Computational Intelligence, 1*, 1–11. doi:10.4018/jssci.2009010107

Klement, E. P., Mesiar, R., & Pap, E. (2000). *Triangular Norms*. Dordrecht, The Netherlands: Kluwer Academic Publishers. doi:10.1007/978-94-015-9540-7

Klir, G., & Yuan, B. (1995). *Fuzzy sets and fuzzy logic, theory and applications*. Prentice Hall.

Kľúčik, M. (2011). *Introducing New Tool for Official Statistics: Genetic Programming*. Paper presented at the New Techniques and Technologies in Statistics (NTTS 2011). Brussels, Belgium.

Kľúčik, M. (2012). *Estimates of Foreign Trade Using Genetic Programming*. Paper presented at the 46th Scientific Meeting of the Italian Statistical Society. Rome, Italy.

Lessman, S., Caserta, M., & Arango, I. M. (2011). Tuning metaheuristics: A data mining based approach for particle swarm optimization. *Expert Systems with Applications, 38*, 12826–12838. doi:10.1016/j.eswa.2011.04.075

Liao, S.-H., Chu, P.-H., & Hsiao, P.-Y. (2012). Data mining techniques and applications – A decade review from 2000 to 2011. *Expert Systems with Applications, 39*, 11303–11311. doi:10.1016/j.eswa.2012.02.063

Liu, B. (2011). Uncertain Logic for Modeling Human Language. *Journal of Uncertain Systems, 5*, 3–20.

Ma, Z. (2006). *Fuzzy database modeling of imprecise and uncertain engineering information.* Berlin: Springer.

Oh, K. W., & Bandler, W. (1987). Properties of fuzzy implication operators. *International Journal of Approximate Reasoning, 3*, 273–285. doi:10.1016/S0888-613X(87)80002-6

Pavlus, J. (2012). Machines of the infinitive – searching for easy answers to hard. *Scientific American, 307*, 52–57.

Radojević, D. (2008a). Interpolative Realization of Boolean Algebra as a Consistent Frame for Gradation and/or Fuzziness. In M. Nikravesh, & L. Zadeh (Eds.), *Forging New Frontiers: Fuzzy Pioneers II Studies in Fuzziness and Soft Computing* (pp. 295–318). Berlin: Springer-Verlag. doi:10.1007/978-3-540-73185-6_13

Radojević, D. (2008b). Real sets as consistent boolean generalisation of classical sets. In L. Zadeh, D. Tufis, F. Filip, & F. G. Diztac (Eds.), *From natural language to soft computing: New paradigms in artificial intelligence* (pp. 150–171). Bucharest: Editing House of Romanian Academy.

Rasmussen, D., & Yager, R. (1997). Summary SQL - A Fuzzy Tool for Data Mining. *Intelligent Data Analysis, 1*, 49–58. doi:10.1016/S1088-467X(98)00009-2

Sözat, M. I., & Yazici, A. (2001). A complete axiomatization for fuzzy functional and multivalued dependencies in fuzzy database relations. *Fuzzy Sets and Systems, 117*, 161–181. doi:10.1016/S0165-0114(98)00152-3

Trillas, E., Cubillo, S., & del Campo, C. (2000). When QM-operators are implication functions and conditional fuzzy relations? *International Journal of Intelligent Systems, 15*, 647–655. doi:10.1002/(SICI)1098-111X(200007)15:7<647::AID-INT5>3.0.CO;2-T

Tudorie, C. (2008). Qualifying objects in classical relational database querying. In J. Galindo (Ed.), *Handbook of Research on Fuzzy Information Processing in Databases* (pp. 218–245). London: IGI Global. doi:10.4018/978-1-59904-853-6.ch009

Tudorie, C. (2009). Intelligent interfaces for database fuzzy querying. *The Annals of Dunarea de Jos University of Galati. Fascicle III, 32*(2), 33–37.

van der Heide, A., & Trivino, G. (2009). Automatically generated linguistic summaries of energy consumption data. In A. Abraham, J. Sánchez, F. Herrera, V. Loia, F. Marcelloni, & S. Senatore (Eds.), *Intelligent Systems Design and Applications* (ISDA 2009) (pp. 553 – 559). Los Alamitos, CA: CPS.

Vucetic, M., Hudec, M., & Vujošević, M. (2013). A new method for computing fuzzy functional dependencies in relational database systems. *Expert Systems with Applications, 40*(7), 2738–2745. doi:10.1016/j.eswa.2012.11.019

Wang, T. C., Lee, H. D., & Chen, C. M. (2007). Intelligent queries based on fuzzy set theory and SQL. In P. Wang (Ed.), *Joint Conference on Information Science* (pp. 1426–1432). Washington, DC: Word Scientific.

Yager, R. (1982). A new approach to the summarization of data. *Information Sciences, 28*, 69–86. doi:10.1016/0020-0255(82)90033-0

Yager, R. (1988). On ordered weighted avaraging operators in multicriteria decision making. *IEEE Transactions on Systems, Man, and Cybernetics, 18*, 183–190. doi:10.1109/21.87068

Yager, R., & Kacprzyk, J. (Eds.). (1997). *The Ordered Weighted Averaging Operators: Theory and Applications*. Boston: Kluwer. doi:10.1007/978-1-4615-6123-1

Yager, R. R. (1989). On linguistic summaries of data. In G. Piatetsky-Shapiro & W. Frawley (Eds.), *IJCAI Workshop on Knowledge Discovery in Databases* (pp. 378–389). Waltham, MA: GTE Laboratories Incorporated.

Ying, M. (2002). Implication operators in fuzzy logic. *IEEE Transactions on Fuzzy Systems, 10*(1), 88–91. doi:10.1109/91.983282

Zadeh, L. A. (1983). A computational approach to fuzzy quantifiers in natural languages. *Computers & Mathematics with Applications (Oxford, England), 9*, 149–184. doi:10.1016/0898-1221(83)90013-5

Zadeh, L. A. (2002). From computing with numbers to computing with words – From manipulation of measurements to manipulation of perceptions. *International Journal of Applied Mathematics and Computer Science, 12*(3), 307–324.

Zadrożny, S., & Kacprzyk, J. (2009). Issues in the practical use of the OWA operators in fuzzy querying. *Journal of Intelligent Information Systems, 33*, 307–325. doi:10.1007/s10844-008-0068-1

ADDITIONAL READING

Abonyi, J., Babuska, R., Verbruggen, H., & Szeifert, F. (2000). Using a priori knowledge in fuzzy model identification. *International Journal of Systems Science, 31*, 657–667. doi:10.1080/002077200290966

Bandemer, H. (2006). *Mathematics of uncertainty: Ideas, methods, application problems*. Halle: Springer.

Beliakov, G., Pradera, A., & Calvo, T. (2007). *Aggregation Functions: A Guide for Practitioners*. Berlin: Springer.

Berzal, F., Blanco, I., Sánchez, D., Serrano, J. M., & Vila, M. A. (2005). A definition for fuzzy approximate dependencies. *Fuzzy Sets and Systems, 149*, 105–129. doi:10.1016/j.fss.2004.07.012

Bojadziev, G., & Bojadziev, M. (2007). *Fuzzy logic for business, finance, and management*. New Jersey: World Scientific Publishing.

Chen, G. (1998). *Fuzzy logic in data modelling, semantics, constraints and database design*. Boston: Kluwer Academic Publisher. doi:10.1007/978-1-4615-4068-7

Chen, S.-M., & Huang, C.-M. (2008). A new approach to generate weighted fuzzy rules using genetic algorithms for estimating null values. *Expert Systems with Applications, 35*, 905–917. doi:10.1016/j.eswa.2007.07.033

De Oliveira, J. V. (1999). Semantic constraints for membership function optimization. *IEEE Transactions on Systems, Man, and Cybernetics, 29*, 128–138. doi:10.1109/3468.736369

Dubois, D., & Prade, H. (1997). The three semantics of fuzzy sets. *Fuzzy Sets and Systems*, *90*, 141–150. doi:10.1016/S0165-0114(97)00080-8

Dubois, D., & Prade, H. (2003). Fuzzy set and possibility theory- based methods in artificial intelligence. *Artificial Intelligence*, *148*, 1–9. doi:10.1016/S0004-3702(03)00118-8

Galindo, J. (Ed.). (2008). *Handbook of Research on Fuzzy Information Processing in Databases*. London: IGI Global. doi:10.4018/978-1-59904-853-6

Galindo, J., Urrutia, A., & Piattini, M. (2006). *Fuzzy databases: Modelling, Design and Implementation*. Hershey: Idea Group Publishing Inc.

Ge, E., & Nayak, R. (2008). An Interactive Predictive Data Mining System for Informed Decision. In J.R. Haritsa, R. Kotagiri, & V. Pudi (Eds.), *13th International Conference, DASFAA 2008* (pp. 694-697). Berlin Heidelberg: Springer.

Glöckner, I. (2003, March). *Fundamentals of Fuzzy Quantification: Plausible Models, Constructive Principles, and Efficient Implementation*. Research Report of the Technical Faculty of University Bielefeld, Germany.

Haris, J. (2006). *Fuzzy logic application in engineering science*. Berlin, Heidelberg: Springer.

Hassani, H., Gheitanchi, S., & Yeganegi, M. (2010). On the Application of Data Mining to Official Data. *Journal of Data Science*, *8*, 75–89.

Hudec, M. (2013, April). *Improvement of data collection and dissemination by fuzzy logic*. Paper presented at the Joint UNECE/Eurostat/OECD Meeting on the Management of Statistical Information Systems, Paris, France.

Kacprzyk, J., & Wilbik, A. (2009). Using fuzzy linguistic summaries for the comparison of time series: an application to the analysis of investment fund quotations. In P. Carvalho, D. Dubois, U. Kaymak, & J. M. C. Sousa (Eds.), *2009 International Fuzzy Systems Association World Congress and 2009 European Society for Fuzzy Logic and Technology Conference (IFSA–EUSFLAT 2009)* (pp. 1321-1326). IFSA and EUSFLAT.

Kacprzyk, J., Wilbik, A., & Zadrony, S. (2006). Linguistic summarization of trends: a fuzzy logic based approach. In *11th International Conference Information Processing and Management of Uncertainty in Knowledge-based Systems* (pp. 2166-2172). Berlin Heidelberg: Springer.

Kacprzyk, J., & Zadrożny, S. (2000). On a fuzzy querying and data mining interface. *Kybernetika*, *36*, 657–670.

Liu, W. Y. (1993). Extending the relational model to deal with fuzzy values. *Fuzzy Sets and Systems*, *60*, 207–212. doi:10.1016/0165-0114(93)90347-K

Liu, W. Y. (1997). Fuzzy data dependencies and implication of fuzzy data dependencies. *Fuzzy Sets and Systems*, *92*, 341–348. doi:10.1016/S0165-0114(96)00173-X

Ma, Z. M., & Yan, L. (2007). Generalization of strategies for fuzzy query translation in classical relational databases. *Information and Software Technology*, *49*(2), 172–180. doi:10.1016/j.infsof.2006.05.002

Ma, Z. M., & Yan, L. (2008). A literature overview of fuzzy database models. *Information Science and Engineering*, *24*, 189–202.

Martino, F., Loia, V., & Sessa, S. (2009). Multi-Dimensional Fuzzy Transforms for Attribute Dependencies. In J. P. Carvalho, D. Dubois, U. Kaymak, & J. M. C. Sousa (Eds.), *Proceedings of the 2009 International Fuzzy Systems Association World Congress and 2009 European Society for Fuzzy Logic and Technology Conference (IFSA–EUSFLAT 2009)* (pp. 53-57). IFSA and EUSFLAT.

Medina, J. M., Vila, M. A., Cubero, J. C., & Pons, O. (1995). Towards the implementation of a generalized fuzzy relational database model. *Fuzzy Sets and Systems, 75*(3), 273–289. doi:10.1016/0165-0114(94)00380-P

Siler, W., & Buckley, J. (2005). *Fuzzy expert systems and fuzzy reasoning.* New Jersey: John Wiley & Sons, Inc.

Taniar, D. (Ed.). (2008). *Data Mining and Knowledge Discovery Technologies.* London: IGI Global. doi:10.4018/978-1-59904-960-1

Tineo, L. (2005). *A Contribution to Database Flexible Querying: Fuzzy Quantified Queries Evaluation.* Unpublished doctoral dissertation, Universidad Simón Bolívar, Venezuela.

Vučetić, M., & Vujošević, M. (2012). A literature overview of functional dependencies in fuzzy relational database models. *Techniques Technologies Education Management, 7*(4), 1593–1604.

Zadeh, L. A. (1971). Similarity relations and fuzzy orderings. *Information Sciences, 3,* 177–200. doi:10.1016/S0020-0255(71)80005-1

Zadeh, L. A. (1978). Fuzzy sets as a basis of theory of possibility. *Fuzzy Sets and Systems, 1,* 3–28. doi:10.1016/0165-0114(78)90029-5

KEY TERMS AND DEFINITIONS

Functional Dependency: Expresses dependency between attributes in terms of equal values on attribute X means equal values on attribute Y. Formally, a functional dependency is an expression denoted as $X \rightarrow Y$ ($X, Y \subseteq R$) and is said to hold in relation r over R if for tuples t_1 and t_2 in r $t_1[X] = t_2[X]$ implies $t_1[Y] = t_2[Y]$.

Fuzzy Functional Dependency: Expresses dependency between attributes in terms of similar values on attribute X means similar values on attribute Y. A definition of functional dependency has been extended using closeness measure for the similarity between fuzzy values and fuzzy implication operator (I) for the if-then propositions. Fuzzy functional dependency is denoted as $X \overset{\theta}{\rightarrow} Y$, where $X, Y \subseteq R$ and θ is the strength.

Fuzzy Implication: Function computing the fulfilment degree of a rule expressed by if X then Y, where the antecedent and the consequent are fuzzy sets. These functions must satisfy certain axioms.

Fuzzy Logic: Dealing with reasoning that is approximate rather than precise allowing us to examine "levels of grey" like the degree of matching of a selection condition, the extent to which a rule is satisfied, the inclusion of objects to several overlapping classes with different matching degrees, and intensity of dependencies.

Fuzzy Quantifiers: Express quantities or proportions in order to provide an approximate idea of the number of elements that meet a certain crisp or fuzzy condition. Relative quantifiers are statement such as "most", "about half", "few" and so on.

Fuzzy Relational Database: Traditional relational databases can operate with only precise (crisp) data. Fuzzy databases intend to envelope imperfect information and represent it in a database. Fuzzy relational databases store data in tables which meet axioms of relational algebra.

Linguistic Summary: A short statement created by human language that expresses relational knowledge in the data. Validity of linguistic summary takes value from the [0, 1] interval describing strength of a relation in the data.

Proximity Relation: Closeness measure between attribute values. The relation is reflexive and symmetric. In addition to introducing fuzziness into relational database models it is necessary to define proximity relations between fuzzy values on the domain's attributes.

Relational Database: Database where precise data (crisp values) are structured and processed in relations that are stored in relational tables. Relational tables meet axioms of relational algebra which initially consists of operators: union, intersection, division, cross product, join projection and selection.

Chapter 9
Application of Artificial Neural Network and Genetic Programming in Civil Engineering

Pijush Samui
VIT University, India

Dhruvan Choubisa
VIT University, India

Akash Sharda
VIT University, India

ABSTRACT

This chapter examines the capability of Genetic Programming (GP) and different Artificial Neural Network (ANN) (Backpropagation [BP] and Generalized Regression Neural Network [GRNN]) models for prediction of air entrainment rate (Q_A) of triangular sharp-crested weir. The basic principal of GP has been taken from the concept of Genetic Algorithm (GA). Discharge (Q), drop height (h), and angle in triangular sharp-crested weir (θ) are considered as inputs of BP, GRNN, and GP. Coefficient of Correlation (R) has been used to assess the performance of developed GP, BP, and GRNN models. For a perfect model, the value of R should be close to one. A sensitivity analysis has been carried out to determine the effect of each input parameter. This chapter presents a comparative study between the developed BP, GRNN, and GP models.

DOI: 10.4018/978-1-4666-6078-6.ch009

INTRODUCTION

A weir is designed to change flow characteristics of river. Different shapes of weir are used such as rectangular weir, triangular or v-notch weir, the broad-crested weir, etc. The amount of dissolved oxygen in a river system is increased by weir. The change in oxygen concentration due to weir is given by the following equation

$$\frac{dm}{dt} = V \frac{dC}{dt} = k_L A \left(C_s - C \right) \qquad (1)$$

where dm/dt is mass transfer rate of gas molecules across an interface, C_s and C are the saturation concentration of oxygen in water at prevailing ambient conditions and the actual concentration of oxygen in the water at time t-difference being proportional to the concentration gradient, k_L is bulk liquid film coefficient, A is the air–water contact area and V is the volume of water associated with this. Ervine, et al. (1980) explained air entrainment mechanisms by weirs. They gave four mechanism of air entrainment.

So, the determination of air entrainment rate (QA) of triangular sharp-crested weir is an imperative task in civil engineering. Researchers determined air entrainment rate and aeration efficiency of different shapes weirs (Baylar & Bagatur, 2000; 2001a; 2001b; 2006; Baylar, et al., 2001a; 2001b; Baylar, 2002, 2003; Baylar & Emiroglu, 2007; Emiroglu & Baylar, 2003a; 2003b; 2005). Baylar, et al. (2008) successfully adopted Adaptive Neuro Fuzzy Inference System(ANFIS) for prediction of QA of triangular sharp-crested weir. ANFIS has been successfully used to model different problems in water (ASCE, 2000; Kisi, 2004a; 2004b; Hanbay, et al., 2006a; 2006b; 2007; Abolpour, et al., 2007; Baylar, et al., 2007). ANFIS can be trained to provide input/output data mappings and one can get the relationship between model inputs and corresponding outputs. It enables the knowledge that has been learnt in the network

training to be translated into a set of fuzzy rules that describe the model input/output relationship in a more transparent fashion. ANFIS makes inference by fuzzy logic and shapes fuzzy membership function using neural network (Altrock, 1995; Brown & Harris, 1995).

However, the developed ANFIS did not give any equation for prediction of air entrainment rate and aeration efficiency of triangular sharp-crested weir.

This chapter adopts two data mining techniques (Artificial Neural Network [ANN] and Genetic Programming [GP]) for determination of Q_A of triangular sharp-crested weir. Figure 1 shows a triangular sharp-crested weir. Two types (Back-propagation [BP] and Generalized Regression Neural Network [GRNN]) of ANN have been developed. ANN was developed originally by McCulloch and Pitts (1943). In ANN, the knowledge lies in the interconnection weights between neuron and architecture of the networks (Jones & Hoskins, 1987). Hebb (1949) described the importance of the synaptic connections in the learning process. Rosenblatt (1958) defined the term 'Perceptron BP network consists an input layer, a sigmoid hidden layer and a linear output layer. It has ability to approximate any function (Demuth & Beale, 1999). Irie and Miyanki (1988) described BP as the most versatile learning algorithm. It is an approximate steepest descent algorithm, in which the performance index is mean square error. It is most useful for non-linear mappings. It works well with noisy data. GRNN consists an input layer, hidden layer and the output layer. It falls into the category of probabilistic neural networks. It is a special case of Radial Basis Networks. In GRNN, the hidden layer contains radial-basis neurons. These radial-basis neurons use the Gaussian transfer function. There are lots of applications of ANN in the literatures (Zhang, et al., 2008; Akdag, et al., 2009; Sharma & Ponselva, 2010; Mardi, et al., 2011; Saraswathi, et al., 2012; Khosravi, et al., 2013). GP is developed based on the concept of genetic algorithm (Koza, 1992). It is an

Figure 1. A triangular sharp-crested weir

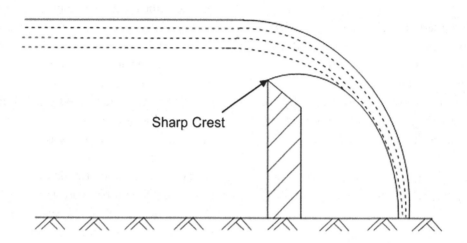

automated invention machine. Researchers have successfully used GP for solving different problems in engineering (Azamathulla, et al., 2008; Guven, et al., 2009; Agarwal, et al., 2010; Yi & Kang, 2011; Azamathulla & Zahiri, 2012; Garg & Jothiprakash, 2013). The above mentioned data mining techniques have been developed by using the database collected from the work of Baylar, et al. (2008). The datasets contain information about discharge (Q), drop height (h), angle in triangular sharp-crested weir (θ) and Q_A. This book chapter has the following aims:

- To examine the capability of BP, GRNN and GP for prediction of a Q_A of triangular sharp-crested weir
- To make a comparison between the developed BP, GRNN and GP models
- To do a sensitivity analysis for obtaining the effect of each input parameter on Q_A

EXPERIMENTAL PROCEDURE

This section will describe the experimental procedure. Figure 2 shows the experimental setup.

Figure 2. Details of experimental setup (Baylar, et al., 2008)

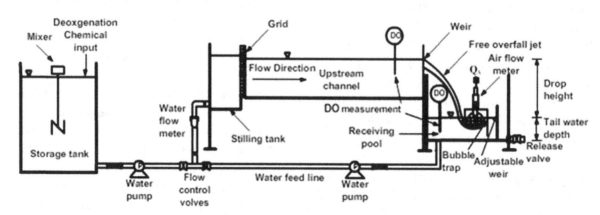

The length of experimental channel was 3.4m. The width and depth of the channel was 0.6m and 0.5m respectively. The maximum flow rate of channel was 4L/s. The water was filed to the stilling tank by pump. An adjustable weir controlled the water depth in the downstream water pool. The area of the downstream water pool was 1.44 m². An air flow meter was kept on the air-hood to measure Q_A. The area of the air-hood was 0.45 m². The following three sizes weirs were used:

- 45^0triangular sharp-crested weir
- 90^0 triangular sharp-crested weir
- 135^0 triangular sharp-crested weir

The value of Q was varied from 1L/s to 4L/s. The value of h was varied from 0.15m to 0.9m. Na_2SO_3 and $CoCl_2$ were added to increase the upstream dissolve oxygen deficit. It has been seen from experimental results that Q and h are important parameters for prediction of Q_A. The value of Q_A increases with increasing h and Q in weirs.

Details of ANN

ANN is a computation model in which mode of data processing replicates the mode of synaptic dynamics in biological network and derives its inspiration from human brain (called as natural neural network). ANN learns from examples (i.e. input and output pairs). The goal of network learning is to generalise the relationship between the input and output. To achieve the goal of generalisation, the network needs to be trained and tested. Thus training and testing are two major tasks in the development of a neural network model. In training (supervised learning), the learning rule is provided with a set of example of proper network behaviour. As the inputs are applied to the network, the network outputs are compared to the targets. The learning rule is then used to adjust the weight and biases of the network in order to move the network output to the target values. BP and GRNN models have been used for determination of Q_A and E_{20} of triangular sharp-crested weir. The details of the above mentioned two ANN models are given below.

Details of BP

This article employs Multi-Layer Perceptrons (MLPs). The training of MLPs is done by Levenberg-Marquardt Backpropagation algorithm (Hagan & Menhaj, 1994). MLPs are perhaps the best-known type of feed forward networks. There are three layers (an input layer, an output layer and a hidden layer) in the BP model. In Backpropagation training process, the network error is back propagated into each neuron in the hidden layer, and then continued into the neuron in the input layer. Figure 3 shows the propagation of error in the BP model. The modification of connection weights and biases is affected by the distribution of error at each neuron. The global network error

Figure 3. Propagation of error in the BP model

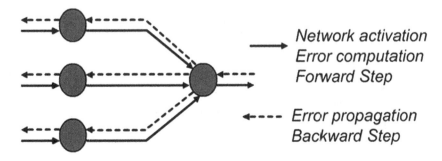

Network activation
Error computation
Forward Step

Error propagation
Backward Step

is reduced by continuous modifications of connection weights and biases. An error goal is set before the network training, and if the network error during the training becomes less than the error goal, the training have to be stopped. The BP algorithm contains the following four steps:

- Feed-forward computation
- Backpropagation to the output layer
- Backpropagation to the hidden layer
- Weight updates

In BP model, it should be guaranteed the continuity and differentiability of the error function. Levenberg-Marquardt Backpropagation algorithm is a variation of Newton's method and is well suited to ANN training. More (1977) gave the details of Levenberg-Marquardt Backpropagation. The details of BP were given by many researchers (Nawi, et al., 2012; Qiao, et al., 2013; Singh & Arya, 2014).

To develop the BP model, the datasets have been divided into the following two groups:

- **Training Dataset:** This is required to develop the BP model. This study uses 101(70% of total datasets) datasets out of 144 as training dataset.
- **Testing Dataset:** This is used to verify the developed BP model. The remaining 43(30% of total datasets) have been used as testing dataset.

The inputs of BP are Q,h, and θ. The output of BP is QA. The statistical parameters of dataset have been shown in Table 1. The datasets are normalized between 0 and 1. The following formula has been used for normalization.

$$d_{normalized} = \frac{\left(d - d_{min}\right)}{\left(d_{max} - d_{min}\right)} \quad (2)$$

where d=any data (input or output), d_{min} = minimum value of the entire dataset, d_{max} = maximum value of the entire dataset, and $d_{normalized}$=normalized value of the data. The program of BP has been developed by using MATLAB.

Details of GRNN

In a GRNN design, hidden layer weights (W_R) are simply the transpose of input vectors from the training set. A Euclidean distance is calculated between an input vector and these weights.

$$dist = \mid X - W_R^j \mid, \quad \text{for } j = 1, \; Q \quad (3)$$

where Q=number of neurons in the hidden layer; X=input vector=[x,y,z], dist=Euclidean distance between X and W_R^J. For prediction of Q_A, X=[Q,h,θ]. The calculated Euclidean distance is then rescaled by the bias, b:

Table 1. Statistical parameters of the dataset

Variables	Mean	Standard Deviation	Skewness	Kurtosis
Q(m³/sec)	0.0025	0.0011	0	1.6400
h(m)	0.5250	0.2571	0	1.7314
θ(degree)	90	36.8706	0	1.5000
Q_A(m³/sec×10⁴)	7.0040	10.2544	1.8896	6.4895

$$b = 0.8326/s \qquad (4)$$

$$n_1 = dist \times b \qquad (5)$$

where n_1 = the adjusted distance, and s = the spread. The radial basis output is then the exponential of the negatively adjusted distance having the form:

$$a_1 = e^{\left[-(n_1)^2\right]} \qquad (6)$$

Therefore, if a neuron weight is equal to the input vector, distance between the two is 0 giving an output of 1. This neuron gives special output. It characterizes the closeness between input vectors and weight vectors. The weight matrix size is defined by the size of the training dataset, while the number of neurons is the number of input vectors. The output layer consists of neurons with a linear transfer function, which is:

$$n_2 = W_L \times a_1 \qquad (7)$$

where W_L is the weight matrix in the output layer.

The details of GRNN is given by Specht (1991). Figure 4 shows a typical architecture of GRNN model. GRNN model uses the same training dataset, testing dataset, normalization technique, inputs and output as used by the BP model. The details of GRNN were given by many researchers (Fan, et al., 2012; Li, et al., 2013; Luu, et al., 2014). The program of GRNN has been developed by using MATLAB.

Details of GP

GP is a model of programming which uses the ideas (and some of the terminology) of biological evolution to handle a complex problem. It is a computing method that generates a structured representation of the data provided. It imitates the biological evolution of living organisms. The technique which was introduced in the early 90s by Koza, though research was started on it in the 1960s itself. Similar to Genetic Algorithms, it initiates a population of computer models composed of functions and terminals, known as chromosomes. It then finds the model that best fits the problem. These functions and terminals are the building blocks of GP models. The functions may be mathematical operators, logic functions or user-defined too. These are then used to develop computer programs out of which the most accurate one is selected based on Darwinian theory. The terminal set contains the arguments for the function. They may be numerical constants, logical constants, variables, etc. These are chosen at ran-

Figure 4. Architecture of GRNN model

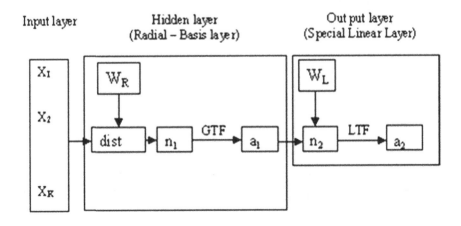

dom and constructed together to form a computer model of a tree-like structure with a root point. The branches extend from each function and end in a terminal.

GP has been developed based on the concept of 'survival of the fittest'. It evolves computer program to perform an underlying process defined by a set of training samples. In 1st step, a random number of equations is created. The fitness of each equation is determined in 2nd step. In 3rd step, parents are selected out of these equations. In 4th step, offsprings are created from parents through the process of reproduction, mutation and crossover. The details of reproduction, mutation and crossover are given by Koza (1992). Crossover replaces a random point in one parent with a random point from the other parent. The main advantage of mutation that it maintains diversity in the population .The best offspring is the solution of the problem. GP uses the same training dataset, testing dataset, normalization technique, input variables and output variable as used by the GRNN model. The program of GP has been constructed by using MATLAB.

RESULTS AND DISCUSSION

Different percentage of training datasets have been tried to get best performance. Figure 5 shows the effect of training dataset (%) on testing performance. It is clear from Figure 5 that all models (BP, GRNN and GP) give best testing performance for 70% training dataset.

In BP model, the optimum BP network that is obtained in the present study is a three-layer feed forward network. Figure 6 shows the final architecture of the BP model with one hidden layer. In this study, the transfer function used in the hidden layer is tansig. Figure 7 shows the distribution of tansig. It squashes elements between -1 and 1. The output layer contains logsig transfer function. It squashes elements between 0 and 1. The distribution of logsig is shown in Figure 8.

The number of neurons in the hidden layer is determined by training several networks with different numbers of hidden neurons and comparing the predicted results with the desired output. Using too few hidden neurons could result in huge training errors and errors during testing, due to

Figure 5. Effect of training dataset (%) on testing performance

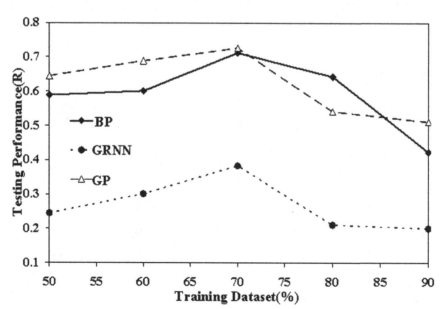

Figure 6. Architecture of the BP model

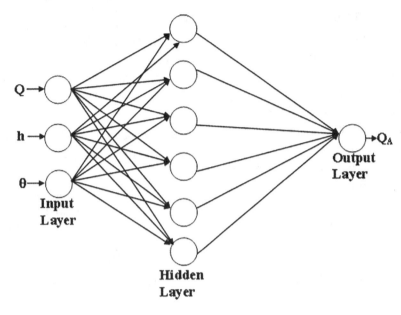

Figure 7. Distribution of tansig

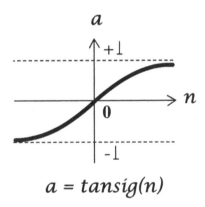

Figure 8. Distribution of logsig

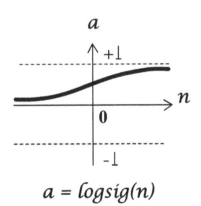

underfitting and high statistical bias. On the other hand, using too many hidden neurons might give low training errors but could still have high testing errors due to overfitting and high variance. Table 2 shows the effect of number of neurons on training performance.

It is clear from Table 2 that 6 neurons give best performance. In this study, the hidden layer with 6 neurons has been used. For BP model, the best results have been obtained at 3000 epochs. An epoch is defined presentation of the complete training dataset during the training of model. Figure 9 shows the performance of the BP for training dataset as well as testing dataset. The performance of BP has been assessed in terms of coefficient of correlation(R). The value of R is determined from the following equation.

$$R = \frac{\sum\limits_{i=1}^{n}\left(Q_{Aai} - \overline{Q}_{Aa}\right)\left(Q_{Api} - \overline{Q}_{Ap}\right)}{\sqrt{\sum\limits_{i=1}^{n}\left(Q_{Aai} - \overline{Q}_{Aa}\right)}\sqrt{\sum\limits_{i=1}^{n}\left(Q_{Api} - \overline{Q}_{Ap}\right)}} \tag{8}$$

Table 2. Effect of no of neurons on training performance

No of Neurons in the Hidden Layer	Training Performance(R)
1	0.540
2	0.623
3	0.621
4	0.645
5	0.694
6	0.745
7	0.701
8	0.696
9	0.634
10	0.521

where Q_{Aai} and Q_{Api} are the actual and predicted Q_A values, respectively, $\overline{Q}_{Aa}$ and $\overline{Q}_{Ap}$ are mean of actual and predicted Q_A values corresponding to n patterns.

The value of R should be close to one for a perfect model. The value of R is also shown in Figure 9. The spread(s), which is the most important parameter in a GRNN, has been determined by using the following procedure.

1. Begin the training of the intended GRNN by assuming a small initial spread value.
2. Evaluate the trained GRNN using the testing data set. This is done simply by comparing the GRNN-predicted Q_A value with the known Q_A value for each case in the testing data set. A root mean squared error (RMSE) of all cases is calculated:

$$\text{RMSE} = \sqrt{\sum\limits_{i=1}^{n}\varepsilon^2 / n} \tag{9}$$

where, e is the difference between the known Q_A value and the predicted Q_A value, and n is the number of cases in the testing data set.

3. Repeat steps (1) and (2) above, a number of times using a gradually increased spread value. With each adopted spread, a GRNN is trained and used to predict Q_A value for each case in the testing data set, and RMSE is then calculated.
4. Plot the RMSE against the corresponding spread value. The spread that yields a minimum RMSE is considered to be the optimum spread.

Using GRNN model, a plot of the calculated RMSE against the assumed spread is obtained as

Figure 9. Performance of the BP model

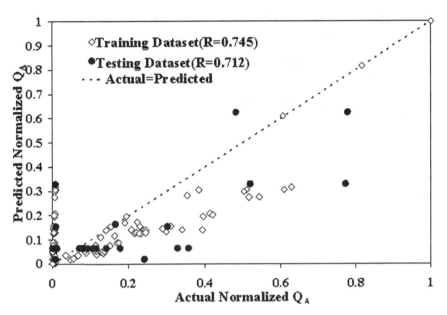

Figure 10. Plot between s vs. RMSE

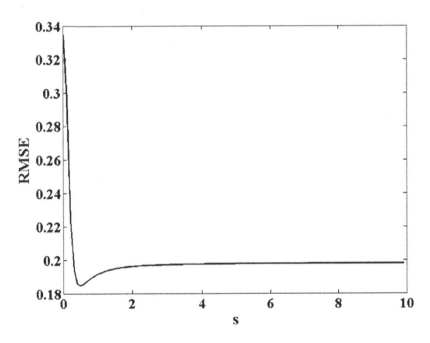

shown in Figure 10. In this case, a spread of 0.47 is obtained, and corresponding RMSE is 0.18. Using this spread, the performance of training and testing datasets has been shown in Figure 11.

For developing GP, size of population is set to 800. A larger population increases chance of evolving a solution. The size of population varies from 500 to 16,000. We have taken the number of

Figure 11. Performance of the GRNN model

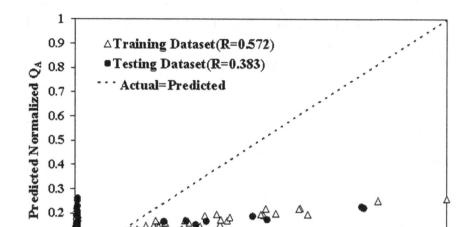

generations has been taken to 200. If we increase the number of generations, then the probability of evolving a solution will be increased. It is also assigned the maximum depth of tree representation allowed during generations=6. The developed GP gives the following equation for determination of Q_A.

$$Q_A = 0.25Q + 0.25h - 0.00025 \exp\left(\exp\left(h + \theta\right)\right)$$
$$+ 0.013 \exp\left(Q + h\right)^2 - 0.258 \cosh^2$$
$$+ 0.012 \exp\left(2h + 2\theta\right) + 0.13 \cos\left(h - Q + \theta\right)$$
$$- 0.298 \exp\left(Q + h - \cos\theta\right) + 0.225$$

(10)

The performance of training and testing dataset has been shown in Figure 12. The performance of BP and GP is better than the GRNN models. The developed ANFIS gave best performance(R=0.999). However, equation was not obtained from the developed ANFIS. BP uses many tuning parameters (number of hidden layers, number of neurons in the hidden layers, transfer function, number of epochs, etc). However, GRNN

uses only one tuning parameter. GP also uses many tuning parameters (number of population, number of generation, etc). The computational time of ANN (BP and GRNN) is very less compare to the GP. The developed GP does not make distinction between search and solution space. There is an iterative training procedure in the backpropagation model. However, GRNN does not require any iterative training procedure. The developed GRNN has excellent approximation ability, fast, and exceptional stability during the prediction stage. The performance of BP is affected by randomly assigned initial weight values. However, the performance developed GRNN is not affected by initial weight values (Cigizoğlu, 2005). BP works poorly on dense data with few input variables.

A sensitivity analysis has been performed to determine the effect of each input (Q,h and θ) on Q_A. The concept of sensitivity analysis has been taken from the work of Liong, et al (2000). According to Liong, et al (2000), the sensitivity(S) of each input parameter has been calculated by the following formula

Figure 12. Performance of the GP model

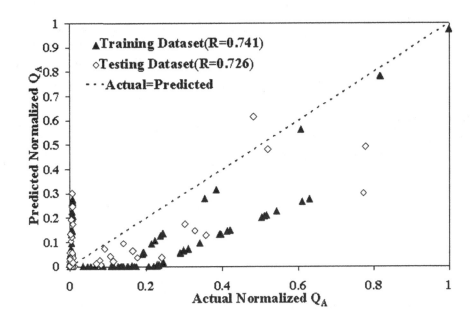

Figure 13. Effect of each input parameter on QA

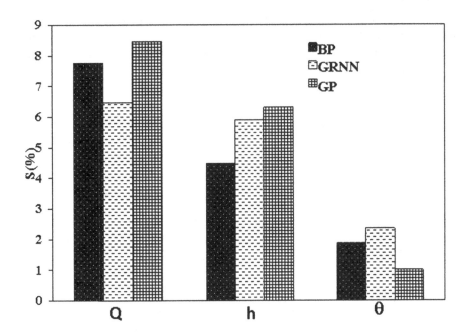

$$S(\%) = \frac{1}{N} \sum_{j=1}^{N} \left(\frac{\% \text{ change in ouput}}{\% \text{ change in input}} \right)_j \times 100$$

(11)

where N is the number of data points. In this study, the value of N is 30. The analysis has been carried out on the trained model by varying each of input parameter, one at a time, at a constant rate of 30%.

The results of sensitivity analysis have been shown in Figure 13. It is clear from Figure 13 that Q has maximum effect of Q_A. θ has least effect on Q_A.

CONCLUSION

This chapter presents BP, GRNN and GP models for prediction of Q_A of triangular sharp-crested weir. For BP model, the procedures to determine data division, data normalizing technique, network architecture selection, transfer function and no of epochs are outlined. In GRNN, the procedure for determination of optimum spread is described. The developed BP and GP give better performance than the GRNN. User can use the developed GP based equation for practical purpose. Sensitivity analysis indicates that Q is more important parameter for prediction of Q_A. It can be concluded that the developed BP, GP and GRNN model can be used for modeling different problems in civil engineering.

ACKNOWLEDGMENT

Authors thank VIT University for funding the above work.

REFERENCES

Abolpour, B., Javan, M., & Karamouz, M. (2007). Water allocation improvement in river basin using adaptive neural fuzzy reinforcement learning approach. *Applied Soft Computing*, 7(1), 265–285. doi:10.1016/j.asoc.2005.02.007

Agarwal, M., Goyal, M., & Deo, M. C. (2010). Locally weighted projection regression for predicting hydraulic parameters. *Civil Engineering and Environmental Systems*, 27(1), 71–80. doi:10.1080/10286600802517491

Akdag, U., Komur, M. A., & Ozguc, A. F. (2009). Estimation of heat transfer in oscillating annular flow using artifical neural networks. *Advances in Engineering Software*, 40(9), 864–870. doi:10.1016/j.advengsoft.2009.01.010

Altrock, C. V. (1995). *Fuzzy logic and neurofuzzy applications explained*. Prentice-Hall.

ASCE Task Committee on Application of Artificial Neural Networks in Hydrology. (2000). Artificial neural networks in hydrology. *Journal of Hydrologic Engineering*, 5(2), 115–137. doi:10.1061/(ASCE)1084-0699(2000)5:2(115)

Azamathulla, H. M., & Zahiri, A. (2012). Flow discharge prediction in compound channels using linear genetic programming. *Journal of Hydrology (Amsterdam)*, 454-455, 203–207. doi:10.1016/j.jhydrol.2012.05.065

Baylar, A. (2002). *Study on the effect of type selection of weir aerators on oxygen transfer.* (Ph.D. thesis). Firat University, Elazig, Turkey.

Baylar, A. (2003). An investigation on the use of venturi weirs as an aerator. *Water Quality Research Journal of Canada*, 38(4), 753–767.

Baylar, A., & Bagatur, T. (2000). Aeration performance of weirs. *Water S.A.*, *26*(4), 521–526.

Baylar, A., & Bagatur, T. (2001a). Aeration performance of weirs. *Water Engineering & Management*, *148*(3), 33–36.

Baylar, A., & Bagatur, T. (2001b). Aeration performance of weirs. *Water Engineering & Management*, *148*(4), 14–16.

Baylar, A., & Bagatur, T. (2006). Experimental studies on air entrainment and oxygen content downstream of sharp-crested weirs. *Water and Environment Journal*, *20*(4), 210–216. doi:10.1111/j.1747-6593.2005.00002.x

Baylar, A., Bagatur, T., & Tuna, A. (2001a). Aeration performance of triangular notch weirs at recirculating system. *Water Quality Research Journal of Canada*, *36*(1), 121–132.

Baylar, A., Bagatur, T., & Tuna, A. (2001b). Aeration performance of triangular-notch weirs. *Journal of the Chartered Institution of Water and Environmental Management*, *15*(3), 203–206. doi:10.1111/j.1747-6593.2001.tb00334.x

Baylar, A., & Emiroglu, M. E. (2007). The role of weir types in entrainment of air bubbles. *International Journal of Science and Technology*, *2*(2), 143–154.

Baylar, A., Hanbay, D., & Ozpolat, E. (2007). Modeling aeration efficiency of stepped cascades by using ANFIS. *Clean – Soil, Air. Water*, *35*(2), 186–192.

Baylar, A., Hanbay, D., & Ozpolat, E. (2008). An expert system for predicting aeration performance of weirs by using ANFIS. *Expert Systems with Applications*, *35*, 1214–1222. doi:10.1016/j.eswa.2007.08.019

Brown, M., & Harris, C. (1994). *Neurofuzzy adaptive modeling and control*. Prentice-Hall.

Cigizoğlu, H. K. (2005). Application of generalized regression neural networks to intermittent flow forecasting and estimation. *J. Hydrol. Engng ASCE*, *10*(4), 336–341. doi:10.1061/(ASCE)1084-0699(2005)10:4(336)

Demuth, H. B., & Beale, M. (1999). *Neural Network Toolbox, users guide*. Natick, MA: The Mathworks, Inc.

Emiroglu, M. E., & Baylar, A. (2003a). Experimental study of the influence of different weir types on the rate of air entrainment. *Water Quality Research Journal of Canada*, *38*(4), 769–783.

Emiroglu, M. E., & Baylar, A. (2003b). The effect of broad-crested weir shape on air entrainment. *Journal of Hydraulic Research*, *41*(6), 649–655. doi:10.1080/00221680309506897

Emiroglu, M. E., & Baylar, A. (2005). The influence of included angle and sill slope on air entrainment of triangular planform labyrinth weirs. *Journal of Hydraulic Engineering*, *131*(3), 184–189. doi:10.1061/(ASCE)0733-9429(2005)131:3(184)

Ervine, D. A. (1998). Air entrainment in hydraulic structures: A review. *Proceedings of the Institution of Civil Engineers Water Maritime and Energy*, *130*(3), 142–153. doi:10.1680/iwtme.1998.30973

Fan, B., Ji, P., & Zhou, K. (2012). The implementation of pipe climbing robot's real-time speech control based on the generalized regression neural network in embedded system. *Applied Mechanics and Materials*, *220-223*, 1986–1989. doi:10.4028/www.scientific.net/AMM.220-223.1986

Garg, V., & Jothiprakash, V. (2013). Evaluation of reservoir sedimentation using data driven techniques. *Applied Soft Computing Journal, 13*(8), 3567–3581. doi:10.1016/j.asoc.2013.04.019

Guven, A., Md. Azamathulla, H., & Zakaria, N. A. (2009). Linear genetic programming for prediction of circular pile scour. *Ocean Engineering, 36*(12-13), 985–991. doi:10.1016/j.oceaneng.2009.05.010

Hagan, M. T., & Menhaj, M. B. (1994). Training Feedforward Networks with the Marquardt Algorithm. *IEEE Transactions on Neural Networks, 5*. PMID:18267874

Hanbay, D., Turkoglu, I., & Demir, Y. (2006a). Complex systems modeling by using ANFIS. In *Proceedings of International Fifteenth Turkish Symposium on Artificial Intelligence and Neural Networks* (pp. 83–90). Academic Press.

Hanbay, D., Turkoglu, I., & Demir, Y. (2006b). A wavelet neural network for intelligent modeling. In *Proceedings of International fifteenth Turkish symposium on artificial intelligence and neural networks* (pp. 175–182). Academic Press.

Hanbay, D., Turkoglu, I., & Demir, Y. (2007). Predicting chemical oxygen demand (COD) based on wavelet decomposition and neural networks. *Clean – Soil, Air. Water, 35*(3), 250–254.

Hebb, D. O. (1949). *The organization of behaviour.* Wiley. McCulloch, W.S., & Pitts, W. (1943). A logical calculus in the ideas immanent in nervous activity. *The Bulletin of Mathematical Biophysics, 5*, 115–133.

Irie, B., & Miyanki, S. (1988). Capabilities of three layer perceptrons. *In Proceedings of IEEE second Int. Conf. on Neural networks* (pp. 641-648). IEEE.

Jones, W. P., & Hoskins, J. (1987, October). Back–propagation a generalized delta learning rule. *BYTE,* 155-162.

Khosravi, A., Nahavandi, S., & Creighton, D. (2013). Quantifying uncertainties of neural network-based electricity price forecasts. *Applied Energy, 112,* 120–129. doi:10.1016/j.apenergy.2013.05.075

Kisi, O. (2004a). River flow modeling using artificial neural networks. *Journal of Hydrologic Engineering, 9*(1), 60–63. doi:10.1061/(ASCE)1084-0699(2004)9:1(60)

Kisi, O. (2004b). Multi-layer perceptions with Levenberg–Marquardt optimization algorithm for suspended sediment concentration prediction and estimation. *Hydrological Sciences Journal, 49*(6), 1025–1040.

Koza, J. R. (1992). *Genetic programming: On the programming of computers by means of natural selection.* Cambridge, MA: MIT Press.

Li, X. H., Fan, Y. S., Cai, Y. X., Zhao, W. D., & Yin, H. Y. (2013). Optimization of biomass vacuum pyrolysis process based on GRNN. *Applied Mechanics and Materials, 411-414,* 3016–3022. doi:10.4028/www.scientific.net/AMM.411-414.3016

Luu, T. P., Low, K. H., Qu, X., Lim, H. B., & Hoon, K. H. (2014). An individual-specific gait pattern prediction model based on generalized regression neural networks. *Gait & Posture, 39*(1), 443–448. doi:10.1016/j.gaitpost.2013.08.028 PMID:24071020

Mardi, M., Nurozi, H., & Edalatkhah, S. (2011). A water saturation prediction using artificial neural networks and an investigation on cementation factors and saturation exponent variations in an Iranian oil well. *Petroleum Science and Technology, 30*(4), 425–434. doi:10.1080/10916460903452033

Md. Azamathulla, H., Wu, F. C., Ghani, A. A., Narulkar, S. M., Zakaria, N. A., & Chang, C. K. (2008). Comparison between genetic algorithm and linear programming approach for real time operation. *Journal of Hydro-environment Research, 2*(3), 172–181. doi:10.1016/j.jher.2008.10.001

More, J. J. (1977). The Levenberg-Marquardt algorithm: Implementation and theory. In G. A. Watson (Ed.), *Numerical Analysis* (pp. 105–116). Springer.

Nawi, N. M., Hamid, N. A., & Zainun, N. Y. (2012). A new modified back-propagation algorithm for forecasting Malaysian housing demand. *Applied Mechanics and Materials, 232*, 908–912. doi:10.4028/www.scientific.net/AMM.232.908

Qiao, C., Sun, S., & Hou, Y. (2013). Design of strong classifier based on adaboost M2 and back propagation network. *Journal of Computational and Theoretical Nanoscience, 10*(12), 2836–2840. doi:10.1166/jctn.2013.3287

Rosenblatt, F. (1958). The perceptron: a probabilistic model for information storage and organization in the brain. *Psychological Review, 68*, 386–408. doi:10.1037/h0042519 PMID:13602029

Saraswathi, R., Saseetharan, M. K., & Suja, S. (2012). ANN-based predictive model for performance evaluation of paper and pulp effluent treatment plant. *International Journal of Computer Applications in Technology, 45*(4), 280–289. doi:10.1504/IJCAT.2012.051128

Sharma, M., & Ponselva, A. (2010). Delayed coker heater analysis using an artifical neural network: The model was used to study the effects of the many variables that affect coke formation. *Hydrocarbon Processing, 89*(2), 75–79.

Singh, B., & Arya, S. R. (2014). Back-propagation control algorithm for power quality improvement using DSTATCOM. *IEEE Transactions on Industrial Electronics, 61*(3), 1204–1212. doi:10.1109/TIE.2013.2258303

Specht, D. F. (1991). A general regression neural network. *IEEE Transactions on Neural Networks, 2*, 568–576. doi:10.1109/72.97934 PMID:18282872

Whigham, P. A., & Crapper, P. F. (2001). Modelling rainfall-runoff using genetic programming. *Mathematical and Computer Modelling, 33*, 707–721. doi:10.1016/S0895-7177(00)00274-0

Yi, L., & Kang, W. (2011). A new genetic programming algorithm for building decision tree. *Procedia Engineering, 15*, 3658–3662. doi:10.1016/j.proeng.2011.08.685

Zhang, G., Jiang, W., & Su, X. (2008). Discussion on the optimization of BP neural network in GPS height conversion. *Journal of Geomatics*, *33*(4), 18–20.

KEY TERMS AND DEFINITIONS

Air Entrainment Rate: The rate at which air bubbles and pockets that are advected within the turbulent flow are called air entrainment rate.

Artificial Neural Network: An artificial neural network is the computational schematic description of the system that has the inclination for machine learning, pattern recognition, etc., It is based on the neural structure of the brain.

Back Propagation: The process of conforming the parameters of a neural network is called Back propagation.

Generalized Regression Neural Network: The general regression neural network (GRNN) is a one-pass learning algorithm with a highly parallel structure. It provides smooth transitions from one observed value to another.

Genetic Programming: Genetic programming is a probabilistic search procedure designed to work on large spaces involving states that can be represented by strings. It gives the best optimized result.

Prediction: Estimating something for a specified thing that will happen in the future or will be a consequence of something.

Triangular Sharp-Crested Weir: A weir is the barrier across the river or open channel which is designed in a manner for modifying the flow character of the water. The weir results an increase in the water level, or head, which is measured upstream of the structure.

Chapter 10
A Promising Direction towards Automatic Construction of Relevance Measures

Lucianne Varn
Independent Researcher, New Zealand

Kourosh Neshatian
University of Canterbury, New Zealand

ABSTRACT

A relevance measure is a measure over the space of features of a learning problem that quantifies the degree of relatedness of a single feature or a subset of features to a target variable. The measure can be used to both detect relevant features (when the target variable is the response variable) and detect redundant features (when the target variable is another input feature). Measuring relevance and redundancy is a central concept in feature selection. In this chapter, the authors show that there is a lack of generality in the features selected based on heuristic relevance measures. Through some counter-examples, the authors show that regardless of the type of heuristic measure and search strategy, heuristic methods cannot optimise the performance of all learning algorithms. They show how different measures may have different notions of relevance between features and how this could lead to not detecting important features in certain situations. The authors then propose a hyper-heuristic method that through an evolutionary process automatically generates an appropriate relevance measure for a given problem. The new approach can detect relevant features in difficult scenarios.

INTRODUCTION

High dimensionality is not usually a desired situation in the context of machine learning and data mining. Often the need for more training examples grows exponentially with respect to the number of dimensions in a problem—an effect known as

the curse of dimensionality. High dimensionality makes the hypothesis space bigger (again often exponentially), which makes finding a good hypothesis computationally more challenging. Feature selection, a practice usually carried out at the preprocessing stage, deals with the high dimensionality issue. While feature selection is

DOI: 10.4018/978-1-4666-6078-6.ch010

not formally defined in the literature, it informally refers to the process of finding a minimal subset of features that is sufficient to solve a learning problem. The sufficiency criterion may refer to improving learning performance (with some definition of performance), maintaining performance at some acceptable level, or even other criteria regarding model complexity, intelligibility, etc.

Feature selection algorithms have, in abstract terms, two main components. The first component is a search mechanism that searches the space of power sets of features which grow exponentially ($O(2^n)$) with respect to the number of features in problems. The second component is an evaluation mechanism which measures the goodness of (candidate) subsets of features. There are two major approaches for evaluation: wrapper and filter (or non-wrapper) (Kohavi & John, 1997). In the wrapper approach, the performance of a learning algorithm (e.g. a decision tree inducer) is used to guide the search. The wrapper approach is computationally intensive; every evaluation involves training and testing a model. In the filter approach, instead of using a learner's performance as a measure of the utility of a candidate subset of features, computationally-cheap heuristics are incorporated. The most common measure of utility in the filter approach is relevance. Relevance quantifies the degree of relatedness between a subset of features and another feature (that does not exist in the subset). Features with a significant degree of relevance to target concepts (such as class labels) are desired, while features with a considerable degree of relevance to each other are considered redundant and thus unwanted. Examples of commonly-used heuristic relevance measures are those based on information theory such as Information Gain (IG) and Information Gain Ratio (IGR) (Last, K, & Maimon, 2001), and those based on statistical methods such as $\chi 2$ (Chi-square) ranking (Liu & Setiono, 1995) and Logistic Regression (Cheng, Varshney, & Arora, 2006).

Filter-based feature selection methods are known to be computationally efficient in comparison with methods taking the wrapper approach. Since filter methods do not use any learning algorithms directly, they are usually described as being "independent of any learning algorithms" (Kohavi & John, 1997). However, it is unclear whether the importance (utility) of features can be determined independently from any learning algorithms. Clearly, filter methods have improved the performance of some learning algorithms over some problems, but a question that remains to be answered is whether "independence from learning algorithms" implies that a highly relevant subset of features found by a filter method is expected to optimise the learning performance of any arbitrary learning algorithm. If the answer is 'no', then what can be done? This chapter investigates these issues and proposes a solution.

PROBLEM STATEMENT

Let $\mathcal{D}$ represent the set of all possible observations in a classification domain; for example $\mathcal{D}$ could be the population of patients receiving a medical diagnosis. A feature (or attribute) is a mapping from $\mathcal{D}$ to a *co-domain*; for example, *height* and *gender* as features can be mappings of the form $height : \mathcal{D} \rightarrow \mathbb{R}^+$ and

$$gender : \mathcal{D} \rightarrow \{male, female\}.$$

If d is a member of the population (a data item), then *height(d)* and *gender(d)* represent the value of the two features for the given data item.

We use $\mathcal{F}$ to represent the set of all features that are available (defined or measurable) for all members of the population. In a supervised learning context $\mathcal{F}$ is partitioned into two sets $\mathcal{X} = \{X_1, X_2, ..., X_{|\mathcal{X}|}\}$ and $\mathcal{Y} = \{Y_1, Y_2, ..., Y_{|\mathcal{Y}|}\}$ such that $\mathcal{X} \cap \mathcal{Y} = \varnothing$, $\mathcal{X} \cup \mathcal{Y} = \mathcal{F}$ and thus

$|\mathcal{X}| + |\mathcal{Y}| = |\mathcal{F}|$. $\mathcal{X}$ is known as the set of input features (*explanatory* variables), and $\mathcal{Y}$ is known as the set of concept or output features (*response* variables). For each data item $d \in \mathcal{D}$, $X_i(d)$ represents the value of the i-th feature. $|\mathcal{X}|$ is the dimensionality of the problem; that is the number of features in the input space.

A subset of features $\mathcal{S} \subseteq \mathcal{X}$ is considered 'good' if it is *relevant* to a response variable and has least *redundancy*. The first formal (mathematical) definition of relevance is almost a century old (Keynes, 1921) and there has been several refinements to the definition since then (Carnap, 1967; Gärdenfors, 1978). Relevance is defined in terms of dependency using the concepts of *joint* and *conditional* probability distributions: a subset of features $\mathcal{S}$ is relevant to a response variable Y (on the basis of a prior evidence that is usually dropped for the sake of simplicity without loss of generality) if and only if

$$P\{Y(d) = y \mid \mathcal{S}(d)\} \neq P\{Y(d) = y\} \quad \forall d \in \mathcal{D}. \tag{1}$$

While this definition gives a good logical foundation for relevance, in practice, it cannot be *directly* used to find relevant features because:

- We often need to measure (quantify) relevance on a scale such that we can compare subsets of features to each other and select ones that are more relevant. A logical definition (that takes values `true' or `false') is not adequate for this purpose.
- In most problems (almost all real-world problems), it is infeasible to estimate the joint distribution of all variables as the training data required to do this is of exponential order. This problem is known as *the curse of dimensionality*.

In the remainder of this chapter we first formalise the two current research directions in measuring relevance and discuss their advantages

and disadvantages. We then use the developed formalism to prove that heuristic relevance measures (including many commonly-used measures) can misjudge the importance of features particularly by seeing relevant features as irrelevant. We then introduce a hyper-heuristic approach to measure relevance and illustrate how it can alleviate the current limitations.

WRAPPING LEARNING ALGORITHMS TO MEASURE RELEVANCE

The goal of learning is to find a model that predicts the value of features in $\mathcal{Y}$ based on the value of features in $\mathcal{X}$. Since in most regression and classification tasks there is only one response variable in $\mathcal{Y}$, without loss of generality we assume that $\mathcal{Y} = \{Y\}$. Using $\mathcal{C} = \{c_1, c_2, \dots c_{|\mathcal{C}|}\}$ as the set of target concepts (e.g. class labels) in the problem; Y represents the actual value of the target concept (e.g class label) for each observation: $Y : \mathcal{D} \to \mathcal{C}$. Let $\mathcal{H}$ be a hypothesis space (e.g. the space of all possible decision trees for a classification problem). Then each hypothesis $h \in \mathcal{H}$ is a mapping from the population into the space of target classes (concepts), i.e. $h : \mathcal{D} \to \mathcal{C}$.

A learning algorithm L (e.g. a decision tree inducer) is a function that takes three arguments and returns a hypothesis:

$$h = L(\mathcal{D}_{train}, \mathcal{S}, Y), \qquad \mathcal{S} \subseteq \mathcal{X}, \mathcal{D}_{train} \subseteq \mathcal{D}. \tag{2}$$

The arguments are a training data set $\mathcal{D}_{train}$ which is a sample from $\mathcal{D}$, a subset of features $\mathcal{S}$ which determines which input features are available to the learner, and the true (actual) output mapping Y. The algorithm induces and returns a hypothesis $h \in \mathcal{H}$ (e.g. a classifier). Deterministic learning algorithms—those that do not have any stochastic components—will always produce the same hypothesis, given the same three input arguments. On the other hand, learning algorithms with stochastic components such as Artificial Neural Networks (with random initial weights) and Genetic Programming (with random initial population and stochastic operators) may generate different hypotheses for even a fixed set of input arguments. Note that these algorithms can become deterministic by introducing a fourth argument (known as a random seed) that specifies the state (or an index to the state) of the random number generator used by the algorithm.

The quality (performance) of a hypothesis h is usually determined based on how closely it mimics Y and is quantified by a cost (error) function. The cost function is typically the approximation error in regression tasks and the misclassification cost in classification tasks. The cost function may also include a term for the length of the model (the model complexity or the number of bits required to encode the model) in order to penalise large and uninterpretable models. We use $e(h, \mathcal{D}', Y)$ to indicate the error (cost) of h on a given data set $\mathcal{D}'$ (a sample from $\mathcal{D}$). The expected error over $\mathcal{D}'$ is

$$E_{\mathcal{D}'}[e(h, \mathcal{D}', Y) \mid h].\qquad(3)$$

where h comes from Equation (2).

From a wrapper point of view, the most relevant subset of features is the one that when passed to L yields the hypothesis with the lowest cost (in feature selection, we are, in addition to low costs, also interested in small subsets). In other words, the most relevant subset can be obtained by optimising the cost over the power set of features, denoted by $2^{\mathcal{X}}$.

Regardless of the search strategy (to navigate in the search space) that is used for optimisation, once a candidate solution has been selected, it must be evaluated. A candidate $\mathcal{S}$ can be directly evaluated by inserting it in Equation (2) and then calculating the error of the resulting hypothesis:

$$Error_{(L, \mathcal{D}', \mathcal{S})} = E_{\mathcal{D}'}[e(L(\mathcal{D}', \mathcal{S}, Y), \mathcal{D}', Y) \mid \mathcal{S}].$$
$$(4)$$

The error can then be used as a measure of the utility of $\mathcal{S}$. This is in fact a wrapper approach as L is directly used to find the worth of a candidate subset. The best subset of features is

$$\mathcal{S}^\star = \arg\min_{\mathcal{S} \subseteq \mathcal{X}}(Error_{(L, \mathcal{D}', \mathcal{S})}).\qquad(5)$$

The biggest issue in finding $\mathcal{S}^\star$ using the above equation is the computational cost associated with it. Using Equation (4) to measure the utility of a candidate subset involves computing L; that is, inducing a new hypothesis and then estimating the cost of the resulting hypothesis. This is computationally expensive and is a motivation to use heuristic measures.

Heuristic relevance measures are relatively simple and cheap-to-compute functions that do not depend on any learning algorithms. They allow for more thorough search strategies and bigger problems. Perhaps the most common heuristic measures are those based on *mutual information* (Bell & Wang, 2000; Peng, Long, & Ding, 2005).

Let $r(\mathcal{S}, Y, \mathcal{D}')$ denote the relevance between a subset of features $\mathcal{S}$ and a response variable Y over a data set $\mathcal{D}'$. Here, finding the most relevant subset reduces to maximising r:

$$\mathcal{S}_r^\star = \arg\max_{\mathcal{S} \subseteq \mathcal{X}}(r(\mathcal{S}, Y, \mathcal{D}')).\qquad(6)$$

In the context of feature selection, r may be combined with some other terms to penalise *redundancy*.

While heuristic measures enjoy computational efficiency, the fact that they quantify relevance independent of any learning algorithm raises a question concerning their generality: Given a relevance measure r, can $\mathcal{S}_r^\star$ maximise the performance of any arbitrarily chosen learning algorithm? The answer to this question can have important practical implications. In many data mining scenarios, selection of relevant features is considered a preprocessing step and is done without any particular learning algorithm in mind. If the answer to the question is 'no', then one needs to choose r based upon anticipated choices of learning algorithms. The next section answers this question.

THE LACK OF GENERALITY IN WRAPPER AND HEURISTIC MEASURES

This section shows, through some counter-examples, that for some classification problems, $\mathcal{S}_r^\star$ cannot optimise the learning performance of all algorithms. It also shows that for two arbitrary learning algorithms L and L', $\mathcal{S}_L^\star$ is not necessarily the same as $\mathcal{S}_{L'}^\star$.

Assume that there are enough computational resources available to find $\mathcal{S}_r^\star$ for a given classification or regression problem; this can be achieved by evaluating r on all subsets of features in $2^{\mathcal{X}}$; that is, performing an *exhaustive* search. Let L_1, L_2, ... be learning algorithms applied to the classification or regression problem in hand. According to Equation (5), the best subsets of features for these algorithms are $\mathcal{S}_{L_1}^\star$, $\mathcal{S}_{L_2}^\star$, and so forth. If $\mathcal{S}_r^\star$ could maximise the performance of all learning algorithms then we must have

$$\mathcal{S}_r^\star = \mathcal{S}_{L_1}^\star = \mathcal{S}_{L_2}^\star = \ldots \qquad (7)$$

To show that for some problems Equation (7) does not hold, we show that for some problems at least one $\mathcal{S}_{L_i}^\star$, $i=1,2,\ldots$, differs from the rest. In other words, we present examples where dif-

ferent learning algorithms have different optimal subsets and thus no unique solution can maximise their performance.

Two benchmark data sets from UCI machine learning repository (Asuncion & Newman, 2007) have been chosen for the examples. The two data sets are:

1. Liver Disorders with 6 input (explanatory) features, 345 instances and 2 classes, and
2. Thyroid Disease with 5 input features, 215 instances and 3 classes.

We have chosen relatively low-dimensional data sets so that we can use a brute-force search to find counter-examples. The following classifiers have been applied to the data sets:

- Multi-Layer Perceptron (MLP)
- Support Vector Machines (SVMs) using LibSVM with Radial Basis kernels
- J48 implementation of C4.5 decision tree with pruning (J48)
- k-Nearest Neighbourhood with Euclidean distance measure (k-NN)
- Naive Bayes (NB)
- Logistic Regression (LR)

All the classifiers are implemented in the Weka framework.

To find $\mathcal{S}^\star$ for each classifier and data set, an exhaustive (brute-force) search is conducted over $2^{\mathcal{X}}$; that is, the error of the classification is evaluated for all subsets of features. A common measure of error for classification is the misclassification ratio:

$$e(h, \mathcal{D}', Y) = \frac{\sum_{d \in \mathcal{D}'} \mathbf{1}_{\{h(d) \neq Y(d)\}}(d)}{|\mathcal{D}'|}. \qquad (8)$$

To estimate the expected value in Equation (4), a sample data set D' is divided into 10 stratified folds D'_1, D'_2, ... D'_{10} and then the average of Equation (8) is calculated via 10-fold cross-validation:

$$\widetilde{Error}_{(L,\mathcal{D}',\mathcal{S})} = \frac{1}{10}\sum_{i=1}^{10} e(L(\bigcup_{j \in \{1,2,\ldots 10\}: j \neq i} D'_j, \mathcal{S}, Y), D'_i, Y).$$

(9)

The search results for the two data sets are presented in Table 1 and Table 2. For each classification algorithm the best subset—that is, $\mathcal{S}^{\star}$, the subset of features that yields the lowest error—is reported. The corresponding estimated error for each subset of features is also reported. The tables show that in both problems, for most cases, "the best" subset of features varies from one classifier to another.

Based on the results in Tables 1 and 2, one can conclude that Equation (7) does not hold for the two benchmark data sets and the presented classifiers. This conclusion is supported by the fact that in many cases the difference between classification errors is quite considerable. The observation serves as counter-examples and imply that no matter what relevance measure r is used, even the optimal solution $\mathcal{S}^{\star}_r$ cannot necessarily maximise the performance of all learning algorithms. This is in a way analogous to the *no free lunch* theorem (Wolpert & Macready, 1997). While the original theorem is on the lack of difference over all permutations of a data scheme, the lack of generality observed in this section is over the set of all learning algorithms.

EVOLVING RELEVANCE MEASURES

The lack of generality in heuristic measures is a two-fold problem:

Table 1. Selected features for the best subset in Liver Disorders data set

Learner	f_1	f_2	f_3	f_4	f_5	f_6	Size	Error
J48	●	●	●		●	●	5	0.307
LR	●		●	●	●	●	5	0.303
MLP	●		●	●	●	●	5	0.275
SVM			●	●	●		3	0.348
k-NN	●		●	●	●	●	5	0.346
NB			●		●	●	3	0.378

Table 2. Selected features for the best subset in Thyroid Disease data set

Learner	f_1	f_2	f_3	f_4	f_5	Size	Error
J48		●	●			2	0.061
LR		●	●		●	3	0.023
MLP		●	●		●	3	0.031
SVM	●	●	●	●	●	5	0.102
k-NN	●	●	●		●	4	0.023
NB	●	●			●	3	0.023

1. A subset of features that is highly relevant according to a relevance measure might not be useful to some classifiers.
2. A subset of features that is relevant to a classifier may not be detected as relevant by some relevance measures.

The first issue is rather related to a poor choice of learning algorithm which can be solved by better design strategies; for example, by trying out a number of learning algorithms and choosing the best one. The second issue, however, is about failure in measuring relevance or more precisely a bad choice of heuristic measure. Similar to the first issue, one might think that a possible solution would be to try different heuristic measures, but the problem is that only a handful heuristic measures are available. This is where hyper-heuristics come into play.

Hyper-heuristics is a new direction in search and optimisation with very promising results (Burke et al., 2003; Ozcan, Bilgin, & Korkmaz, 2008). In heuristic search, the space of solutions (for the problem in hand) is searched and the heuristic is used as a guide to move in the space in order to find better solutions. Heuristic search is subject to the no free lunch theorem; there is no single heuristic that would work for all problems. In hyper-heuristic search, the space of possible heuristics is searched and the algorithm tries to find the right heuristic for the problem in hand. The promising news is that, there could be a free lunch in hyper-heuristics (Poli & Graff, 2009); that is, for a class of problems, a hyper-heuristic algorithm can be devised that can find the right heuristic for each instance of problem from that class.

We propose a hyper-heuristic algorithm that uses genetic programming (GP) to generate new heuristics on the fly. In terms of categorisation of hyper-heuristic algorithms, the proposed work is a heuristic generation algorithm (Burker, et al., 2010).

For a binary classification problem with a (nominal) binary class variable $C \in \{c^+, c^-\}$, we define a new *template relevance measure*, r_φ. We call it a template because its actual behaviour (how it measures the importance of a subset of features) depends on a function φ. The measure is defined as

$$r_\varphi(\mathcal{S}, C) = \left(\frac{\mathrm{Cov}(\varphi(\mathcal{S}), \omega(C))}{\sigma(\varphi(\mathcal{S}))\, \sigma(\omega(C))} \right)^2 \tag{10}$$

where $\mathrm{Cov}(\bullet, \bullet)$ and $\sigma(\bullet)$ denote the covariance and the standard deviation, respectively. The function ω converts the binary class variable C into a numeric variable and is defined as

$$\omega(C) = \begin{cases} +\sqrt{\dfrac{n_N}{n_P}}, & C = c^+ \\[2ex] -\sqrt{\dfrac{n_P}{n_N}}, & C = c^- \end{cases} \tag{11}$$

where n_P and n_N are the numbers of instances belonging to class c^+ and class c^-, respectively, and $n_P + n_N = n$ is the total number of examples in the training set. The two values have been chosen such that the class imbalance is taken into account and as we will see, later equations are simplified. The function φ is of the form $\varphi(X_1, X_2, \ldots, X_{|\mathcal{S}|})$ that takes the value of a subset of features for an object and returns a scalar value in $\mathbb{R}$. By the Cauchy-Schwarz inequality we have

$$|\, \mathrm{Cov}(\varphi(\mathcal{S}), \omega(C)) \,| \leq \sqrt{\sigma^2(\varphi(\mathcal{S}))\, \sigma^2(\omega(C))}$$

Thus the r_φ function is bounded from below and above: $0 \leq r_\varphi(\mathcal{S}, C) \leq 1$. The relationship between $\mathcal{S}$ and $\omega(C)$ can be expressed using r_φ via:

$$E[\omega(C) \mid \varphi(\mathcal{S})] = E[\omega(C)]$$
$$+\sqrt{r_\varphi(\mathcal{S},C)}\sigma(\omega(C))\frac{\varphi(\mathcal{S}) - E[\varphi(\mathcal{S})]}{\sigma(\varphi(\mathcal{S}))}$$

That is, as $r_\varphi(\mathcal{S},C)$ approaches 1, the value of $\omega(C)$ can be approximated by the value of $\varphi(\mathcal{S})$ and since ω is defined as an injective function, C can be predicted correctly which in turn implies that $\mathcal{S}$ is a (highly) relevant subset of features.

Note that the converse does not hold necessarily; that is, C (and so $\omega(C)$) may highly depend on $\mathcal{S}$ while a poor choice of φ can cause the r_φ to be close to zero. This is where hyper-heuristic comes to play in order to find a proper function φ.

The function ω has some properties that makes the calculation of r_φ computationally cheap. The function converts C into a standardised numeric random variable:

$$E(\omega(C)) = p(c^+)\sqrt{\frac{n_N}{n_P}} - p(c^-)\sqrt{\frac{n_P}{n_N}}$$
$$= \frac{1}{n}\left(n_P\sqrt{\frac{n_N}{n_P}} - n_N\sqrt{\frac{n_P}{n_N}}\right) = 0$$

$$(12)$$

where $p(.)$ denotes the probability mass function of the class labels. Consequently:

$$\mathrm{Var}(\omega(C)) = E(\omega^2(C)) - (E(\omega(C)))^2$$
$$= E(\omega^2(C)) = p(c^+)\omega^2(c^+)$$
$$+ p(c^-)\omega^2(c^-) = \frac{n_P}{n}\frac{n_N}{n_P} + \frac{n_N}{n}\frac{n_P}{n_N} = 1$$

$$(13)$$

Using the properties of $\omega(C)$ expressed in Equations (12) and (13), the proposed template can be simplified as the formula in Box 1 which can then, given large enough n examples, be estimated by:

$$\hat{r}_\varphi(\mathcal{S},C) =$$

$$\frac{\left[\frac{1}{n}\sum_{i=1}^{n} y_i\omega(c_i)\right]^2}{\frac{1}{n}\sum_{i=1}^{n} x_i^2 - \left(\frac{1}{n}\sum_{i=1}^{n} y_i\right)^2} = \frac{\left[\sum_{i=1}^{n} y_i\omega(c_i)\right]^2}{n\sum_{i=1}^{n} x_i^2 - \left(\sum_{i=1}^{n} y_i\right)^2}$$

$$(14)$$

where y_i is the i-th observation of the scalar random variable $\varphi(\mathcal{S})$ (which is the result of applying function φ to the value of the subset of features $\mathcal{S}$) and c_i is the corresponding class label. The

Box 1.

$$r_\varphi(\mathcal{S},C) = \left(\frac{\mathrm{Cov}(\varphi(\mathcal{S}),\omega(C))}{\sigma(\varphi(\mathcal{S}))\ \underbrace{\sigma(\omega(C))}_{=1\,\mathrm{by\,equation\,}(13)}}\right)^2$$

$$= \left(\frac{E[(\varphi(\mathcal{S}) - E[\varphi(\mathcal{S})])(\omega(C) - \overbrace{E[\omega(C)]}^{=0\,\mathrm{by\,equation}(12)})]}{\sigma(\varphi(\mathcal{S}))}\right)^2 = \left(\frac{E[\varphi(\mathcal{S})\omega(C) - E[\varphi(\mathcal{S})]\omega(C)]}{\sqrt{E[\varphi(\mathcal{S})^2] - (E[\varphi(\mathcal{S})])^2}}\right)^2$$

$$= \left(\frac{E[\varphi(\mathcal{S})\omega(C)] - \overbrace{E[\varphi(\mathcal{S})]E[\omega(C)]}^{=0\,\mathrm{by\ equation}(12)}}{\sqrt{E[\varphi(\mathcal{S})^2] - (E[\varphi(\mathcal{S})])^2}}\right)^2 = \frac{(E[\varphi(\mathcal{S})\omega(C)])^2}{E[\varphi(\mathcal{S})^2] - (E[\varphi(\mathcal{S})])^2}$$

right hand side of the equations shows that the complexity of computing r_φ is $O(n)$; and in fact it can be estimated in one pass (one loop over all available observations/examples).

Finding a Right Function

In order to find out whether S is relevant to C, one needs to find an appropriate heuristic function φ (of elements of S) that maximises the value of r_φ. By discovering (constructing) a right heuristic any complex relationship between S and C (linear and non-linear) can be discovered. Note that not being able to find such a function does not necessarily mean S is irrelevant to the problem.

We use a Genetic Programming (GP) hyper-heuristic method to search a finite subset of the space of all heuristic functions constructible from a set of *primitive* functions. An evolved GP program defines a function over its variable terminals; the function maps (the value of) a subset of features to a real number. The goal is to find a function that generates the highest relevance (close to 1) when it is used as φ in r_φ. Therefore, in order to calculate the fitness of an individual in the GP search, for each candidate solution (program tree), a new r_φ (heuristic relevance measure) is generated such that φ in Equation (10) is the function defined by the candidate GP program.

Algorithm 1 shows how the fitness of a GP individual is calculated. The class label vector, $\mathbf{c}[i]$, can take only two values in $\{c^+, c^-\}$. The values of n_P and n_N (the number of instances in the two classes) are constants and determined by the training data set. With only one 'for' loop, the algorithm can calculate the fitness of a program in one pass. The value obtained in the last line is an estimate of r_φ calculated based on Equation (14).

TWO EXAMPLE CASE STUDIES

In this section, we demonstrate some preliminary results from the proposed hyper-heuristic measure on two families of classification problems that are deemed difficult to handle by two commonly-used heuristic measures in the literature:

- *Information-theory* family of relevance functions (such as IG (Last et al., 2001)) measure the worth of features by first discretising them (via setting some *split points*) and then measuring the change in the entropy of the class variable.
- *Logistic regression*, as a uni-variate measure, that models the *logit* function for the probability of the positive class (log of odds). The value of $|\beta|$ returned by this measure is the coefficient of the feature in a linear expression. If it has a high magnitude the feature is considered relevant and when it is close to zero the feature is considered irrelevant (Cheng et al., 2006).

For the proposed hyper-heuristic approach, we use the standard tree-based GP in all experiments (Koza, 1992). In this model, each program produces a single floating-point number at its root as the result of its evaluation (output). There is one variable terminal for each feature in the problem. A number of randomly generated constants are also used as terminals. The four standard arithmetic operators were used to form the function set. The division operator, however, is protected; that is, it returns zero for division by zero. All the members of the function set are binary; they take two parameters. The population size is 1024 and the maximum number of generations is set to 50.

Algorithm 1. Given the data set of a binary classification task and a GP program, the relevance between the subset of features used in the program and the target class is calculated

```
Inputs:
```
- $\mathbf{D}$: A dataset of the form $\mathbf{D} = (\mathbf{X}, \mathbf{c})$ where $\mathbf{X} = \{\mathbf{x}_1, \mathbf{x}_2, \ldots, \mathbf{x}_m\}$ is a set of vectors of length n containing samples from the m original features in the problem and $\mathbf{c}$ is a vector of class labels for the corresponding observations in $\mathbf{X}$
- φ: A GP program which acts as a function: $\mathbb{R}^m \to \mathbb{R}$

```
Output: fitness: a real value in [0,1] showing the relevance between the fea-
tures used in φ and the target class.
```

$sum_y, sum_{y^2}, sum_{y\omega} \leftarrow 0$ // initialising the sums

For $i = 1$ **to** n

$\quad y \leftarrow \varphi(\mathbf{x}_1[i], \mathbf{x}_2[i], \ldots, \mathbf{x}_m[i])$ // transformation

$\quad sum_y \leftarrow sum_y + y$

$\quad sum_{y^2} \leftarrow sum_{y^2} + y^2$

$\quad$ **If** $\mathbf{c}[i] = c^+$:

$$sum_{y\omega} \leftarrow sum_{y\omega} + y\sqrt{\frac{n_N}{n_P}}$$

$\quad$ **Else:**

$$sum_{y\omega} \leftarrow sum_{y\omega} - y\sqrt{\frac{n_P}{n_N}}$$

Return $\dfrac{(sum_{y\omega})^2}{n \, sum_{y^2} - (sum_y)^2}$

Multivariate Relationship

Consider a synthetic linear binary classification problem with two input features X_1 and X_2. The class boundary is set to $X_2 = -X_1 + 1$ and $X_1, X_2 \in [0,1)$. According to Equation (1), the two features are both useful for classification because a straight line (passing through the boundary of the two classes) can separate the classes. Indeed, a learning algorithm as simple as a single perceptron can learn the target concept completely.

Now, we look at the two commonly-used heuristic relevance measures to see how they handle multivariate situations like this. We then compare the result to the new hyper-heuristic approach.

We use a sample of 1000 observations from the described problem. The results have been summarised in Table 3.

Information Entropy: The original entropy (without any input features) is 0.7. The best split points along X_1 and X_2 are at 0.5 which reduces the expected value of entropy to 0.55, which is a very small gain considering the high quality of these features; that is, to measures relying on changes in information entropy (such as mutual information), the two features are not very relevant.

Logistic Regression: The standard logistic regression method returns a $|\hat{\beta}|$ of less than 0.2 for each of these features, deeming them unimportant. A multivariate logistic regression, how-

Table 3. Performance of the three methods on the multivariate case

Method	Measure	Value
Information Entropy	Entropy	$H(C) \approx 0.7$
	Conditional entropy	$H(C|X_1) \approx H(C|X_2) \approx 0.55$
	Information Gain	$I(C;X_1) \approx I(C;X_2) \approx 0.15$
Logistic Regression	Coefficient	$\|\hat{\beta}\|_{X_1} \approx \|\hat{\beta}\|_{X_2} \approx 0.2$
Hyper-Heuristic	Relevance	$\mathcal{S} = \{X_1, X_2\}$ and $r_{\varphi(\mathcal{S})} = 0.93$

ever, returns a high estimated coefficient for the two features, seeing them as important.

Hyper-Heuristic: With this method, GP is used to find a φ for which the resulting heuristic relevance can detect the relationship between the explanatory variables (input features) and the response variable (the class label). One of the evolved solutions by GP is the s-expression (sub (add x1 x2) 1) which is actually the equation of the decision boundary. The relevance of $\{X_1, X_2\}$ measured by r_φ at late generations is above 0.9 indicating the two features are relevant.

Multi-Modal Class Distribution

Now we examine a bimodal classification problem; that is, a problem where the probability density function of one of the classes has two peaks and between the two peaks, the density of the other class is higher. We look at a relatively simple case where probability densities are either normal or constructed from a number of normal distributions of the form $N(\mu,\sigma^2)$ where μ is the mean and σ is the standard deviation.

Consider a classification problem with one feature X where some of the positive objects are distributed by $N(2,1)$ and some by $N(8,1)$. The negative class is distributed by $N(5,1)$. The feature X is observably a good feature because by setting up an interval around instances of the negative class (e.g. the interval [3.5,6.5]) the classification problem can be solved. This is equivalent to a simple decision tree with two nodes. Now we study the behaviour of some heuristic relevance measures and then the proposed hyper-heuristic measure on this problem. The results have been summarised in Table 4.

Logistic Regression: Since the class probability does not change linearly with respect to X, the logistic regression method does not consider X to

Table 4. Performance of the three methods on the multi-modal case

Method	Measure	Value
Information Entropy	Entropy	$H(C) \approx 0.61$
	Conditional entropy	$H(C|X) \approx 0.43$
	Information Gain	$I(C;X) \approx 0.18$
Logistic Regression	Coefficient	$\|\hat{\beta}\|_X \approx 0.03$
Hyper-Heuristic	Relevance	$r_{\varphi(X)} = 0.82$

be a good feature, returning a $\hat{\beta}$ coefficient close to zero.

Information Entropy: Since measures based on information entropy need discretisation (in order to estimate probability densities) they try to find the best split point along X (using which, instances from different classes can be separated). However, since not all the instances can be separated around one split point, the feature is not considered relevant. While a more sophisticated discretisation may be able to handle low-dimensional problems like this, for a more complex problem, discretisation would fail.

Hyper-Heuristic: One of the solutions GP evolved for φ is the s-expression (add (mul (sub 5.1 x) (sub 4.8 x)) -3.9) which is a second degree polynomial describing the decision boundary and thus enabling r_φ to detect the relevance of the feature to the target concept.

Comments on the Two Cases

While the scalar values returned by heuristic and hyper-heuristic methods are not directly comparable to each other, they indicate how important a feature is perceived by the measure.

In the multivariate case, although the two features were clearly useful (and sufficient) in separating the two classes, we observed that to some heuristic relevance measures, the features seemed irrelevant. No univariate relevance measure could judge X_1 or X_2 individually important. This is because very little separation can be obtained by using only one of the features. Multivariate measures can detect the importance of the two features. The features seem more useful to those measures that do not use discretisation.

If the distribution of one of the classes in the problem is multi-modal, then the features are likely to be dismissed as irrelevant by measures like logistic regression (due to non-linear relationships) and those depending on information entropy such as mutual information (due to poor discretisation).

DISCUSSION

Each heuristic relevance measure has its own notion of separability of data on the basis of which it assigns a relevance value to a subset of features (or just a single feature). If a group of features provides high separability between instances of different classes but not in a way that is recognisable to the relevance measure, then the features will receive low relevance score and be considered, consequently, irrelevant. Now if that relevance measure was used in a feature selection algorithm (the filter approach), those good features would be eliminated from the problem due to them being seen as irrelevant.

On the other hand, a hyper-heuristic approach like the one proposed, searches for the right heuristic for the problem. In both cases, the proposed method detected the relevance of the features by finding a right heuristic by using GP to evolve a function φ that would lead to a right heuristic.

Hyper-heuristic solutions in general and Genetic Programming in specific are computationally expensive and in loose terms, depending on the problem, it may take hours or even days to complete the task on a single machine. The computational complexity of the problem grows linearly with respect to the number of training examples. This is similar to almost all other machine learning algorithms. Given that training examples are valuable for better learning, there is almost never a concern over large numbers of training examples.

The size of the search space—that is the total number of possible expressions constructible using primitive nodes—grows exponentially with respect to the number of features in a problem. Usually the proportion of desired solutions to all possible candidates does not grow at the same rate as the search space and therefore one needs to do extra computation in order to maintain a reasonable probability of finding a desired solution. This can make the proposed algorithm quite expensive on problems with large numbers of features. On the other hand, since algorithms like this are run only once at the beginning of solving a classification problem, long run times (up to a few days) might be acceptable.

CONCLUSION

Heuristic relevance measures (filter-based feature selection algorithms) can *never guarantee* finding an optimal subset of features; that is, the best subset for any arbitrarily chosen learning algorithm (see the counter-examples). This is an intrinsic limitation of all filter methods. Being "independent from any learning algorithm" must not be interpreted as their results (selected subsets) being compatible with all learning algorithms.

Often feature selection is carried out as a preprocessing task, before it is known what type of learning algorithms will be used on data. It is therefore important to detect all relevant features in a problem regardless of whether a particular learning algorithm is able to use those features. A hyper-heuristic approach to measuring relevance seems to be a promising direction as it would be able to search for a right heuristic for the problem. The proposed hyper-heuristic approach uses GP to find (construct) a function that when inserted into a template, creates the right heuristic for the problem. Our results on two case studies show that the proposed approach can detect the relevance between input features and target concepts in difficult scenarios where commonly-used heuristic relevance measure are not able to detect the relationship between features.

While the chapter focused on classification problems the conclusions can rationally be extended to a wider class of supervised learning algorithms including both classification and regression algorithms.

REFERENCES

Bache, K., & Lichman, M. (2013). *UCI Machine Learning Repository*. Irvine, CA: University of California, School of Information and Computer Science.

Bell, D. A., & Wang, H. (2000). A formalism for relevance and its application in feature subset selection. *Machine Learning*, *41*(2), 175–195. doi:10.1023/A:1007612503587

Burke, E., Kendall, G., Newall, J., Hart, E., Ross, P., & Schulenburg, S. (2003). Hyper-heuristics: An emerging direction in modern search technology. In International series in operations research and management science, (pp. 457-474). Springer.

Burke, E. K., Hyde, M., Kendall, G., Ochoa, G., Özcan, E., & Woodward, J. R. (2010). A classification of hyper-heuristic approaches. In Handbook of Metaheuristics (pp. 449-468). Springer US.

Carnap, R. (1967). *Logical foundations of probability*. University of Chicago Press.

Cheng, Q., Varshney, P. K., & Arora, M. K. (2006). Logistic regression for feature selection and soft classification of remote sensing data. *IEEE Geoscience and Remote Sensing Letters*, *3*(4), 491–494. doi:10.1109/LGRS.2006.877949

Gärdenfors, P. (1978). On the logic of relevance. *Synthese*, *37*(3), 351–367. doi:10.1007/BF00873245

Keynes, J. M. (1909). A treatise on probability. *Diamond (Philadelphia, Pa.)*, *3*(2), 12.

Kohavi, R., & John, G. H. (1997). Wrappers for feature subset selection. *Artificial Intelligence*, *97*(1), 273–324. doi:10.1016/S0004-3702(97)00043-X

Koza, J. R. (1992). *Genetic Programming: On the programming of computers by means of natural selection* (Vol. 1). Cambridge, MA: MIT Press.

Last, M., Kandel, A., & Maimon, O. (2001). Information-theoretic algorithm for feature selection. *Pattern Recognition Letters, 22*(6), 799–811. doi:10.1016/S0167-8655(01)00019-8

Liu, H., & Setiono, R. (1995). Chi2: Feature selection and discretization of numeric attributes. In *Proceedings of the Seventh International Conference on Tools with Artificial Intelligence* (pp. 388-391). IEEE.

O˙˙zcan, E., Bilgin, B., & Korkmaz, E. (2008). A comprehensive analysis of hyper-heuristics. *Intelligent Data Analysis, 12*(1), 3–23.

Peng, H., Long, F., & Ding, C. (2005). Feature selection based on mutual information criteria of max-dependency, max-relevance, and min-redundancy. *IEEE Transactions on Pattern Analysis and Machine Intelligence, 27*(8), 1226–1238. doi:10.1109/TPAMI.2005.159 PMID:16119262

Poli, R., & Graff, M. (2009). There Is a Free Lunch for Hyper-Heuristics, Genetic Programming and Computer Scientists. In *Proceedings of the 12th European Conference on Genetic Programming* (pp. 195-207). Berlin: Springer-Verlag.

Wolpert, D., & Macready, W. (1997). No free lunch theorems for optimization. *IEEE Transactions on Evolutionary Computation, 1*(1), 67–82. doi:10.1109/4235.585893

ADDITIONAL READING

Guyon, I., & Elisseeff, A. (2003). An introduction to variable and feature selection. *Journal of Machine Learning Research, 3*, 1157–1182.

Kohavi, R., & John, G. H. (1997). Wrappers for feature subset selection. *Artificial Intelligence, 97*(1), 273–324. doi:10.1016/S0004-3702(97)00043-X

Koza, J. R., Bennett, F. H. III, & Stiffelman, O. (1999). *Genetic programming as a Darwinian invention machine* (pp. 93–108). Springer Berlin Heidelberg. doi:10.1007/3-540-48885-5_8

Neshatian, K., Zhang, M., & Andreae, P. (2012). A Filter Approach to Multiple Feature Construction for Symbolic Learning Classifiers Using Genetic Programming. *Evolutionary Computation. IEEE Transactions on, 16*(5), 645–661.

Özcan, E., Bilgin, B., & Korkmaz, E. E. (2008). A comprehensive analysis of hyper-heuristics. *Intelligent Data Analysis, 12*(1), 3–23.

Peng, H., Long, F., & Ding, C. (2005). Feature selection based on mutual information criteria of max-dependency, max-relevance, and min-redundancy. *Pattern Analysis and Machine Intelligence. IEEE Transactions on, 27*(8), 1226–1238.

Yang, J., & Honavar, V. (1998). Feature subset selection using a genetic algorithm. In Feature extraction, construction and selection, pp. 117-136, Springer US.

KEY TERMS AND DEFINITIONS

Classifier: A function that given an input vector returns a symbol (class) from a set of predefined symbols (classes). In machine learning, classifiers are automatically made/selected using a set of training data.

Feature: A feature is a mapping (function) from the universal set of objects (Ω), to a set of values (e.g. the set of real numbers). The set of features in a problem domain form a language for describing the objects in the domain. Sometimes features are referred to as *random variables* or *attributes*.

Feature Selection: The process of finding a minimal subset of features (a member of the power set of features) that maximises a performance metric.

Genetic Programming: An evolutionary optimization algorithm in which candidate solutions are computer programs. The search is conducted over the space of programs (functions) that are representable with a pre-specified representation scheme and a pre-defined set of symbols.

Hyper-Heuristics: A hyper-heuristic algorithm produces a heuristic function by searching the space of heuristics or constructing one using some primitive operations.

Redundancy: A feature is redundant with respect to a subset of features if the information it carries is already contained in the given subset and therefore is not needed if the features in the subset are already selected. Redundancy is in fact relevance between input features.

Relevance Measure: A function that measures the degree of relatedness between two (subsets of) features. A high degree of relevance indicates that the information in one of the (subsets of) features is highly reconstructible from the other.

Chapter 11
Adaptive Scheduling for Real-Time Distributed Systems

Apurva Shah
The M. S. University of Baroda, India

ABSTRACT

Biologically inspired data mining techniques have been intensively used in different data mining applications. Ant Colony Optimization (ACO) has been applied for scheduling real-time distributed systems in the recent time. Real-time processing requires both parallel activities and fast response. It is required to complete the work and deliver services on a timely basis. In the presence of timing, a real-time system's performance does not always improve as processor and speed increases. ACO performs quite well for scheduling real-time distributed systems during overloaded conditions. Earliest Deadline First (EDF) is the optimal scheduling algorithm for single processor real-time systems during under-loaded conditions. This chapter proposes an adaptive algorithm that takes advantage of EDF- and ACO-based algorithms and overcomes their limitations.

INTRODUCTION

Scheduling of Real-Time Distributed Systems

Real-time system is required to complete its work and deliver its services on a timely basis. The results of real-time systems are judged based on the time at which the results are produced in addition to the logical results of computations. Therefore, real-time systems have well defined, fixed time constraints i.e. processing must be done within the defined constraints otherwise the system will fail.

Real-time computing systems play a vital role in our society and spectrum of complexity of such systems vary widely from the very simple to extremely complex systems e.g. patient monitoring system in an ICU, flight control system to nuclear power plants. Some other examples of current real-time computing systems are the control of laboratory experiments, the control of engines in automobiles, command and control systems, process control plants, flight control systems, space shuttle and aircraft avionics, robotics, etc.

The distributed system can be defined as a collection of computing nodes interconnected

DOI: 10.4018/978-1-4666-6078-6.ch011

by a high speed local and wide area networks. Utilization of distributed operating system in the provision of distributed parallel environment allows the execution of processes in parallel as well as traditional concurrent execution (Paoli, et al, 1996). There are one or more processors and a certain amount of memory in each node. The nodes don't share memory; message exchange across the network is the only mechanism for communication between them.

There are two strategies for scheduling real-time tasks on multiprocessor and distributed systems: global and partitioning (Oh & Son, 1995). A centralized scheduler will take care of different jobs in case of global scheme but specific jobs are allocated to specific processor in partition scheme. Partitioning schemes are less complex since the overhead of multiprocessor scheduling merely consists in assigning tasks to processors (Thai, 2002). The assignment is performed only once, thereafter well-known uniprocessor scheduling algorithms can be used for each processor.

In client/server distributed systems, the server is often the bottleneck. For example, the growth rate of traffic at the World Wide Web servers has increased exponentially (Yongcheng & Roy, 1995). The same problem is affected to digital library systems also. Improving the server performance is thus crucial for improving the overall performance of distributed information systems.

Priority based scheduling algorithms have been widely applied in real-time systems and scheduling decisions are made immediately upon job releases and completions. These algorithms include Rate-Monotonic (RM), Deadline Monotonic (DM) (Liu & Layland, 1973), Earliest deadline first (EDF), Least Laxity First (LLF) (Mok, 1983), Highest Value First (HVF), Highest Value Density First (HVDF) (Buttazzo, et al, 1995) etc. In these algorithms, priorities of tasks are all calculated based on deadline, laxity time, criticalness, etc. RM and DM algorithms are fixed priority algorithms and priority is decided off-line. In EDF and LLF algorithms, priority changes as time changes and

therefore called dynamic algorithms. EDF and LLF are proved to be optimal scheduling algorithm when the system is preemptive, underloaded and having only one processor (Dertouzos & Ogata, 1974; Mok, 1983). But the same is not true for multiprocessor systems. Moreover, in overload conditions, EDF or LLF algorithm will result in rapidly decreasing of the system performance, even bringing on the domino effect (Buttazzo, et al, 1995; Chengyang, et al,1999).

Application of Swarm Intelligence for Scheduling Problems

Any problem solving is a search for the solution from a vast solution space. Artificial Intelligence (AI) solves the problem efficiently by heuristic search, embedding the domain knowledge which guides the search in an intelligent way. AI has successfully demonstrated its capabilities in almost every field of engineering. It has speed up almost all the applications using its one or many of the following tools:

- Heuristics search
- Fuzzy Logic
- Genetic algorithm
- Swarm Intelligence
- Bayesian Networks
- Artificial Neural Network

Swarm Intelligence (SI) is computational and behavioral metaphor for the problem solving that originally took its inspiration from the nature's examples of collective behaviors- e.g.

- **Social Insects:** Nest building, Foraging, Assembly, Sorting.
- **Vertebrates:** Swarming, Flocking, Herding, Schooling

SI provides a basis, which makes it possible to explore collective (or distributed) problem solving methodology without centralized control or the provision of a global model (Bonabeu, et al, 1999). SI makes system-level behavior appear to transcend the behavioral repertoire of single (minimalist) agent. The swarm lives are distributed in some abstract or real space. For them, local communication allows to get nonlinear global behavior. Structures resulting from individual local interactions develop by a process of self-organization.

Main forms of communication are:

- Point-to-point
- **Broadcast-Like:** Related to schooling & flocking behaviors, that have inspired Practical Swarm Optimization (PSO)
- **Indirect:** It is also called stigmergy. It has led to Ant Algorithms and in particular Ant Colony Optimization (ACO)

ACO is the branch of SI. The ACO algorithms are computational models inspired by the collective foraging behavior of ants (Dorigo & Stutzle, 2004). The ACO algorithms provide inherent parallelism, which is very useful in multiprocessor environment. They provide balance between exploration and exploitation along with robustness and simplicity of individual agent. Each ant is an autonomous agent that constructs a path. There might be one or more ants concurrently active at the same time. Ants do not need synchronization. Forward ant moves to the good-looking neighbor

from the current node, probabilistically. Probabilistic choice is biased by Pheromone trails previously deposited and heuristic function.

Without heuristics information, algorithms tend to converge towards initial random solution. In backward mode, ants lay down the pheromone. In Ant Colony System algorithm, pheromone is added only to arcs belonging to the global-best solution (Dorigo & Gambardella, 1997). Pheromone intensity of all the paths decreases with time, called pheromone evaporation. It helps in unlearning poor quality solution (Dorigo & Stutzle, 2004). After some time, the shortest path has the highest probability.

The pseudo-code of the ACO metaheuristic is shown in Box 1 (Dorigo & Stutzle, 2004).

Advantages of such systems are inherent parallelism and can exhibit high level of robustness, scalability, fault tolerance and effectiveness on unquantified data along with simplicity of individual agent ((Dorigo & Caro, 1999), Ramamritham & Stankovik, 1994). This technique combines global and local heuristics to allow step-by-step decisions by a group of cooperating agents and it seems particularly suitable to efficiently explore the search space of this class of problems that can be formulated as stochastic decisions making processes as well as the traveling salesman problem for which this method has been introduced (Dorigo & Gambardella, 1997, Dorigo, et al, 1996). Several characteristics make ACO a unique approach: it

Box 1. Procedure ACO Metaheuristic()

```
{           while (Stopping Criterion)
            Schedule Activities
            Ant Agents Construct Solutions Using Pheromone()
            Pheromono Updating()
            Daemon Action(); (if required)
               End Schedule Activities
         end while
         return Best Solution Generated
           }
```

is constructive, population-based metaheuristic which exploits an indirect form of memory of previous performance. These combinations of characteristics are not found in any of the other metaheuristic (Dorigo & Stutzle, 2004).

ACO has been applied successfully to solve scheduling problems. It has been compared with some basic heuristics for the Flow Shop Problem (FSP) showing that this approach is very promising for the FSP (Thai, 2002). This technique combines global and local heuristics to allow step-by-step decisions by a group of cooperating agents and it seems particularly suitable to efficiently explore the search space of this class of problems that can be formulated as stochastic decisions making processes as well as the traveling salesman problem for which this method has been introduced (Dorigo & Gambardella, 1997; Dorigo, et al, 1996).

Recently, attempts are being made to solve combinatorial optimization problems using Ant Colony Optimization (ACO) algorithms. Ant Colony Optimization (ACO) is the branch of SI. It is a metaheuristic that allows finding the best solution of hard-to-solve optimization problems (Dorigo & Caro, 1999; Ramos, et al, 2002). The aim of ACO algorithms is to find a path of minimal cost while respecting the constraints (Dorigo & Caro, 1999). ACO has been applied successfully to solve scheduling problems. It has been compared with some basic heuristics for the Flow Shop Problem (FSP) showing that this approach is very promising for the FSP (Stutzle, 1998). This technique combines global and local heuristics to allow step-by-step decisions by a group of cooperating agents and it seems particularly suitable to efficiently explore the search space of this class of problems that can be formulated as stochastic decisions making processes as well as the traveling salesman problem for which this method has been introduced (Dorigo & Gambardella, 1997). It has been also applied for heterogeneous multi-

processor systems (Turneo, et al, 2008; Chang, et al, 2008) and reconfigurable parallel processing systems (Saad, et al, 2006).

ACO has been also applied for scheduling real-time distributed systems (Shah & Kotecha, 2010). During experiments, it has been found that ACO based scheduling algorithm performs well but it takes more time for execution. As time is very critical factor in real-time systems, it is required to overcome this limitation. Therefore an adaptive scheduling algorithm for real-time distributed systems has been proposed and compared with the results of EDF and ACO based algorithms in the same environment.

The chapter has been organized as follows: In the next section the system and task model considered during the experiments is mentioned and then, the proposed algorithm is discussed. Thereafter, simulation method and performance measuring parameters have been explained. Results obtained are discussed after that and the paper ends with a brief conclusion.

THE SYSTEM AND TASK MODEL

The system assumed here is client/server distributed system which is basically loosely coupled homogeneous multiprocessor system. The system is having soft timing constraints and preemption of the tasks is allowed. Each client makes scheduling and resource access control decisions independently. The clients assumed are homogeneous and can be used interchangeably for different kinds of tasks. Each client can execute at most one task at a time.

A task set consists of m independent periodic tasks $\{T_1,...,T_m\}$. In the periodic model of real-time task $Ti = (Ei, Pi)$, a task Ti is characterized by two parameters: an execution requirement Ei, and a period Pi - with the interpretation that the task generates a job at each integer multiple of

Pi and each such job has an execution requirement of *Ei* units and must complete by a deadline equal to the next integer multiple of *Pi* (Baruah & Goossens, 2003; Liu, 2001). A job is the smallest executable unit of the system.

In soft real-time systems, each task has a positive value. The goal of the system is to obtain as much value as possible. If a task succeeds, then the system acquires its value. If a task fails, then the system gains less value from the task (Locke, 1986). In a special case of soft real-time systems, called a firm real-time system, there is no value for a task that has missed its deadline, but there is no catastrophe either (Koren & Shasha, 1995). Here, the proposed algorithm is assuming the system as firm real-time system. The value of the task has been taken same as its computation time required.

THE PROPOSED ALGORITHM

Scheduling real-time tasks on distributed systems consists of two sub-problems: task allocation to processors and scheduling tasks on the individual processors. The task assignment problem is concerned with how to partition a set of tasks and then how to assign these to the processors. The proposed algorithm is based on partitioned scheme that enforces once assigned job to be executed on the same processor. In client/server distributed systems, improving the server performance is crucial in improving the overall performance of distributed information systems. Because of the adopted policy,

- The scheduling at server is without any complex or time consuming logic. It allocates different jobs to different clients one-by-one in sequential order.
- It is the responsibility of the clients to achieve the deadline for different jobs assigned to them. The adaptive algorithm for client has been proposed for the same purpose.

The Adaptive algorithm is combination of two scheduling algorithms: EDF algorithm and ACO based scheduling algorithm. The flowchart of the proposed scheduling algorithm for server and client are shown in Figure 1 and Figure 2.

Figure 1. Scheduling algorithm for server

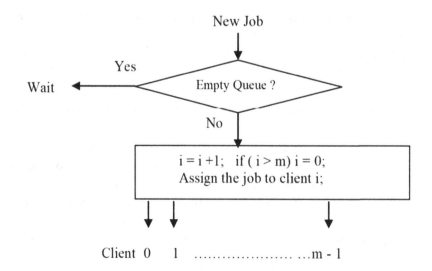

Figure 2. Scheduling algorithm for client

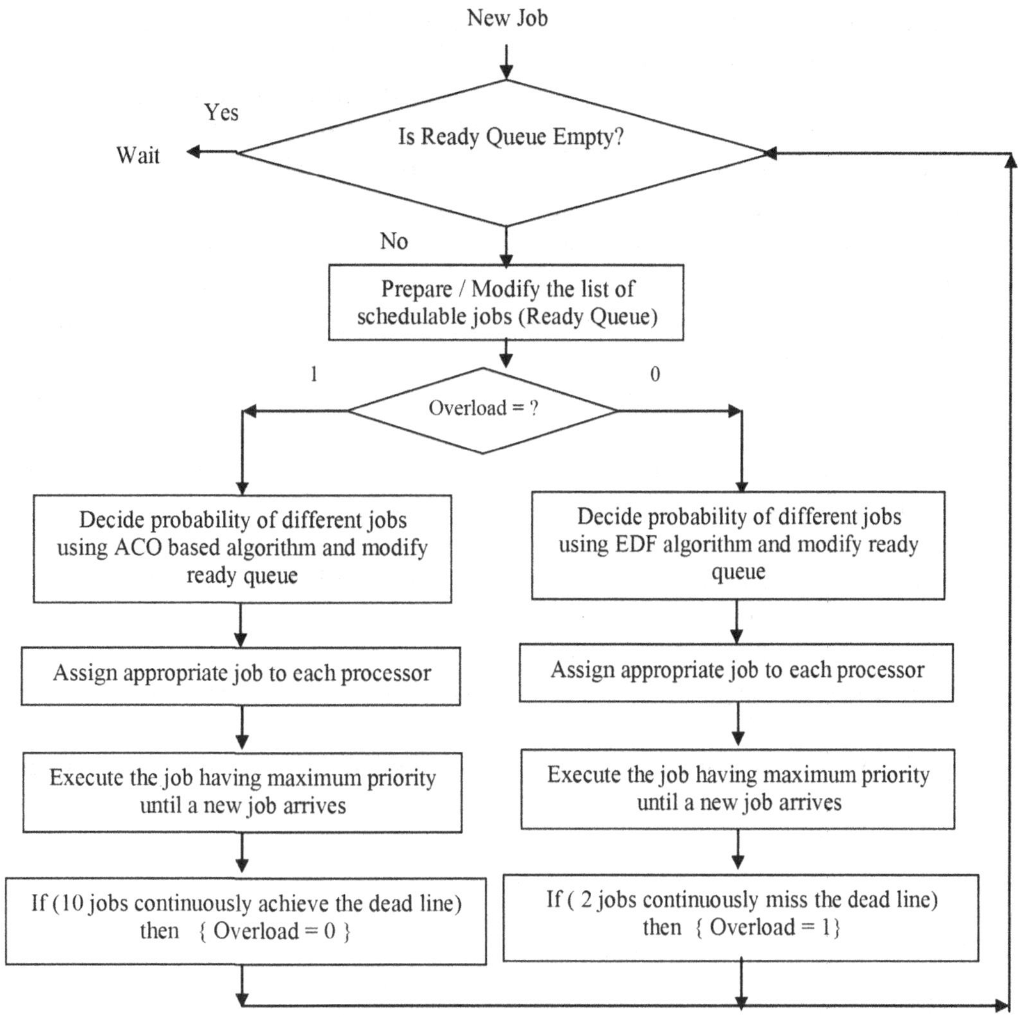

EDF Algorithm

The priority of each task is decided based on the value of its deadline. The task with nearest deadline is given highest priority. This algorithm is considered under restricted-dynamic priority class algorithms. This algorithm is also referred as task-level dynamic-priority and job-level fixed-priority algorithm in the literature. Main property of EDF algorithm is, the priority of a job is determined at run-time and hence, different jobs of a task can

be assigned different priorities. However, once assigned, the priority of a job cannot be changed.

Observations with EDF Algorithm for Distributed Environment

EDF performs very efficiently during underloaded conditions but it has been experimentally proved that its performance is quite poor when the system is even slightly overloaded (Saini, 2005; Locke, 1986).

ACO Based Scheduling Algorithm

Each ant is an autonomous agent that constructs a path. There might be one or more ants concurrently active at the same time. In this algorithm, forward ant moves to the good-looking neighbor from the current node probabilistically. A probabilistic choice is biased by pheromone trails previously deposited and heuristic function. Without heuristics information, the algorithm tends to converge towards initial random solution. Therefore a heuristic function is used which is inversely proportional to the deadline of the task. In backward mode, ants lay down the pheromone. In Ant Colony System (Dorigo & Gambardella, 1997) pheromone is added only to arcs belonging to global best solutions. Pheromone intensity of all the paths decreases with time, called pheromone evaporation. It helps in unlearning poor quality solution (Dorigo & Stutzle, 2004). Accordingly this algorithm also suggests change in pheromone value dynamically.

Main steps for ACO based scheduling algorithm are as per following (Shah, et al, 2010):

1. Construct the tours of different ants and produce the task execution sequences
2. Analyze the generated task execution sequences
3. Update the value of pheromone; and
4. Decide probability of each task and select the task for execution

Each schedulable task is considered, as a node and different ant will start the journey starting from one of the node. Ants will traverse till all nodes are visited. The ants will traverse depending on the value of pheromone and some heuristic function. Pheromone value will be updated on each node depending on the performance of the journey and tasks are sorted as per the probability of the best performance. Finally, most eligible task is selected for execution on each processor.

Observations with ACO Based Algorithm for Distributed Environment

- The ACO based algorithm performs efficiently for distributed, preemptive environment when the system is underloaded.
- During overloaded conditions, performance of the ACO based algorithm is good.
- The limitation of the ACO based algorithm observed is, it takes more time for execution than EDF algorithm. This overhead is a serious problem and proposed to be solved in the proposed adaptive algorithm.

The Adaptive Algorithm

The Adaptive algorithm is combination of both of these algorithms with the goal to overcome limitation of both of the algorithms. It has been proposed as per following:

- During underloaded condition, the algorithm uses EDF algorithm and priority of the job will be decided dynamically depending on its deadline.
- During overloaded condition, it uses ACO based algorithm i.e., priority of the jobs will be decided depending on the pheromone value laid on each schedulable task and the heuristic function which is inversely proportional to its deadline.

Switching Criteria

Initially the proposed algorithm uses EDF algorithm considering that the condition is not overloaded. But when any single job misses the deadline, it will be identified as overloaded condition and the algorithm will switch to ACO based algorithm. After 10 jobs have continuously achieved the deadline, again the algorithm will shift to EDF algorithm considering that overloaded condition has been disappeared.

During underloaded condition, EDF algorithm is used for reducing execution time and during overloaded condition ACO based scheduling algorithm is used for achieving better performance. By this way, adaptive algorithm has taken advantage of both algorithms and overcome their limitations.

SIMULATION METHOD

Simulator

In order to compare the performance of different algorithms, a simulator program has been developed in the C language. The simulator program is having different modules like init pro, add job, delete job, prepare ready q, time clock and timers.

The main functions of different modules are:

- **Init_ pro:** Initializes the task set when a new task arrives
- **Add_ job:** It adds the job to the system at particular time interval for the task
- **Delete_ job:** It deletes the job after it is finished successfully
- **Pprepare_ready_q:** It prepares the ready queue and by this way keep track of ready to run jobs

- **Time_clock:** It arbitrarily generates and maintains the time and by this way it also keep track of timing period required by each job

The simulator program is tasted using standard dynamic and static scheduling algorithms like EDF (Earliest Deadline First), RM (Rate Monotonic), DM (Deadline Monotonic) and LLF (Least Laxity First). It is giving the same results for all the standard algorithms as shown in literature. It has been verified that the simulator program is giving the unbiased and correct results for all the algorithms.

Most of the simulation programs have been executed on PIV Intel machine with 512 MB. SDRAM and Linux Red Hat Operating System. Some of the results are taken on IBM server with dual Xeon 2.8 GHZ processors when more processing power was required.

Simulation of the Proposed Algorithm

The proposed algorithm and EDF algorithm are simulated for client/server distributed system with soft timing constraints. The results are taken using periodic tasks. The relative deadline of the task is considered the same as its period i.e. before the arrival of the next job; present job is expected to be finished. The task set generated for each load value consist of 4 different values of period. For taking results at each load value, we have generated 200 task sets each one containing 3 to 26 tasks.

For periodic tasks, load of the system can be defined as summation of ratio of required computation time and period of each task. The results are taken from under loaded conditions to highly overloaded conditions and tested on more than 36,000 scheduling instances.

The system is said to be overloaded when even a clairvoyant scheduler cannot feasibly schedule the tasks offered to the scheduler. A reasonable way to measure the performance of a scheduling algorithm during an overload is by the amount of work the scheduler can feasibly schedule according to the algorithm. The larger this amount, better the algorithm. Because of this, following two have been considered as main performance measuring criteria:

1. In real-time systems, deadline meeting is the most important and we are interested in finding whether the task is meeting the deadline. Therefore Success Ratio is very important performance metric and defined as (Ramamritham, et al, 1990):

$$SR = \frac{Number\ of\ tasks\ successfully\ scheduled}{Total\ number\ of\ tasks\ arrived}$$

(1)

2. It is important that how efficiently the processors are utilized by the scheduler especially during overloaded conditions. Therefore, the other performance metric is Effective CPU Utilization (ECU) and defined as:

$$ECU = \sum_{i \in R} \frac{V_i}{T}$$

(2)

where,

- V is *value of a task* and,
  - *Value of a task* = Computation time of a task, if the task completes within its deadline.
  - *Value of a task* = 0, if the task fails to meet the deadline.

- R is set of tasks, which are scheduled successfully i.e. completed within their deadline.
- T is total time of scheduling.

3. The execution time required by each scheduling algorithm is very important especially when real-time systems are considered. Therefore, time taken by each scheduling algorithm is also measured.

Finally, all the results are shown in Figure 3 to Figure 5 with different number of processors or clients and discussed in the following section.

EXPERIMENTAL RESULTS

The results obtained with two and five processors are shown in Figures 3 to 5. The results are taken from under loaded condition (load ≤ 0.5) to highly overloaded condition (load≥3). Figures 3 and 4 shows the comparison of SR and ECU of all three algorithms with number of processors is two and five. Figure 5 shows the comparison of execution time taken by each algorithm.

Performance of EDF starts to deteriorate exponentially when load increases just more than 1.00. EDF gives value of ECU and SR 15.37% and 18.15% when the load value is 1.2. The ACO based algorithm performs comparatively better. It gives value of ECU and SR 37.66% and 54.91% respectively when the load value is 1.2. The adaptive algorithm gives the values of ECU and SR 36.19% and 41.97% in the same conditions; i.e. performance of adaptive algorithm is almost same as ACO based algorithm.

During under loaded conditions time taken for execution by the adaptive algorithm is nearer to EDF algorithm. EDF is very fast i.e. its execution time is less but it cannot perform well in

Figure 3. Load vs. % SR and load vs. % ECU with number of processor = 2

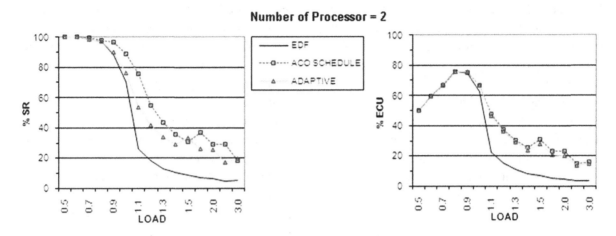

Figure 4. Load vs. % SR and load vs. % ECU with number of processor = 5

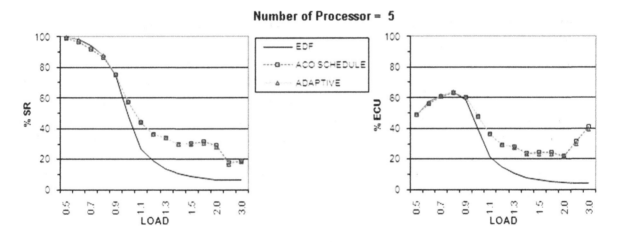

Figure 5. Comparison of required execution time when number of processor is 2 and 5

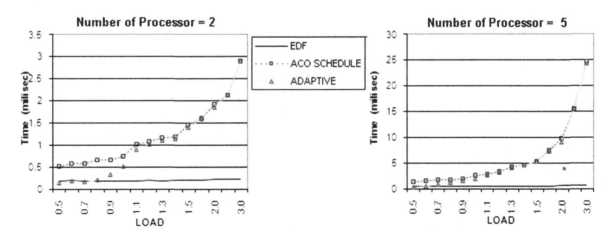

overloaded environment. SR and ECU of EDF are less than 20% when load increases slightly more than one. ACO based algorithm performs well in overloaded conditions also but its execution time is not negligible in any case - either under loaded or overloaded.

The Adaptive algorithm performs well in all type of conditions and gives results which are nearer to ACO. It takes more time only in overloaded condition i.e. in under loaded condition; execution time taken by this algorithm is almost same as EDF algorithm.

The results remain consistent when we increase the number of processors. Figure 3 to Figure 5 demonstrate the same when numbers of processors are 2 and 5.

Observations with Adaptive Algorithm for Distributed Environment

- The server is often the bottleneck in client/ server distributed systems; therefore the proposed algorithm reduces the overhead for server.
- The proposed algorithm performs efficiently for distributed, preemptive environment when the system is underloaded.
- The proposed algorithm performs well in both underloaded and overloaded conditions.
- During underloaded conditions, it takes execution time almost same as EDF algorithms. Moreover, it takes always less time than ACO based algorithm.

CONCLUSION

The proposed algorithm discussed in this paper is for scheduling of client/server system in real-time environment when the tasks are preemptive.

EDF algorithm is not able to sustain in overloaded conditions but its advantage is it is simple and fast in execution. ACO based algorithm is performs well in both underloaded and overloaded conditions but its limitation is that it takes more time during execution. The Adaptive algorithm performs well in both underloaded and overloaded conditions.

Its performance is almost same as ACO based algorithm during overloaded conditions. It takes execution time same as EDF during underloaded conditions. Therefore, it has been proved that the proposed algorithm takes advantage of both algorithms and overcome the limitations of each other. Moreover, the Adaptive algorithm is very useful when future workload of the system is unpredictable.

FUTURE RESEARCH DIRECTIONS

Different Artificial Intelligence techniques can be used for soft real-time multiprocessor and distributed systems. Bio-inspired data mining such as PSO (particle swarm optimization), genetic algorithm and neural networks can be applied for the same environment. For static and dynamic task assignment of distributed environment these algorithms can be applied and results should be compared.

Nowadays, real-time systems do not use virtual memory. These techniques can also be applied for implementing virtual memory when timing constraints are not critical in real-time environment.

REFERENCES

Baruah, S. K., & Goossens, J. (2003). Rate-Monotonic scheduling on uniform multiprocessors. *IEEE Transactions on Computers*, *52*(7), 966–970. doi:10.1109/TC.2003.1214344

Bonabeau, E., Dorigo, M., & Theraulaz, G. (1999). *Swarm Intelligence: From Natural to Artificial Systems*. Oxford University Press.

Buttazzo, G., Spuri, M., & Sensini, F. (1995). Value vs. Deadline scheduling in overload conditions. In *Proceeding of Real-Time System Symposium,* (pp. 90-99). Academic Press.

Chang, P. C., Wu, I. W., Shann, J.-J., & Chung, C. P. (2008). *ETAHM: An energy-aware task allocation algorithm for heterogeneous multiprocessor.* DAC. doi:10.1145/1391469.1391667

Chenyang, L., Stankovic, J. A., Gang, T., & Sang, H. S. (1999). Design and evaluation of a feedback control EDF scheduling algorithm. In *Proceedings of IEEE Real-Time System Symposium,* (pp. 56-67). IEEE.

Dertouzos, M., & Ogata, K. (1974). Control Robotics: The procedural control of physical process. In *Proceeding of IFIP Congress,* (pp. 807-813). IFIP.

Dorigo, M., & Caro, G. D. (1999). The Ant Colony Optimization metaheuristic. In *New Ideas in Optimization.* McGraw-Hill.

Dorigo, M., & Gambardella, L. M. (1997). Ant colony system: A cooperative learning approach to the traveling salesman problem. *IEEE Transactions on Evolutionary Computation, 1*(1), 53–66. doi:10.1109/4235.585892

Dorigo, M., Maniezzo, V., & Colorni, A. (1996). The ant system: Optimization by a colony of cooperating agents. *IEEE Transaction on Systems. Man and Cybernetics- Part B, 26,* 29–41. doi:10.1109/3477.484436

Dorigo, M., & Stutzle, T. (2004). *Ant Colony Optimization.* The MIT Press. doi:10.1007/b99492

Koren, G., & Shasha, D. (1995). D^{Over}: An optimal on-line scheduling algorithm for overloaded real-time systems. *SIAM Journal on Computing, 24*(2), 318–339. doi:10.1137/S0097539792236882

Liu, C. L., & Layland, J. W. (1973). Scheduling algorithms for multiprogramming in a hard real-time environment. *Journal of the ACM, 20*(1), 46–61. doi:10.1145/321738.321743

Liu, J. W. S. (2001). *Real-Time Systems.* Pearson Education.

Locke, C. D. (1986). *Best Effort Decision Making for Real-Time Scheduling.* (Doctoral thesis). Computer Science Department, Carnegie-Mellon University, Pittsburgh, PA.

Mok, A. (1983). *Fundamental design problems of distributed systems for the hard-real time environment.* (Doctoral thesis). MIT, Cambridge, MA.

Oh, Y., & Son, S. H. (1995). Allocating fixed-priority periodic tasks on multiprocessor systems. *J. of Real-Time Systems, 9*(3), 207–239. doi:10.1007/BF01088806

Paoli, D. D., Goscinski, A., Hobbs, M., & Joyce, P. (1996). Performance comparison of process migration with remote process creation mechanism in RHODOS. In *Proc. of 16th ICDCS,* (pp. 554-561). Hong Kong: ICDCS.

Ramamritham, K., & Stankovic, J. A. (1994). Scheduling algorithms and operating support for real-time systems. *Proceedings of the IEEE, 82*(1), 55–67. doi:10.1109/5.259426

Ramamritham, K., Stankovic, J. A., & Shiah, P. F. (1990). Efficient scheduling algorithms for real-time multiprocessor systems. *IEEE Transactions on Parallel and Distributed Systems, 1*(2), 184–194. doi:10.1109/71.80146

Ramos, V., Muge, F., & Pina, P. (2002). Self-organized data and image retrieval as a consequence of inter-dynamic synergistic relationships in artificial ant colonies. In *Proceedings of Second International Conference on Hybrid Intelligent System,* (pp. 500-512). Academic Press.

Saad, E. M., Adawy, M. E., & Habashy, S. M. (2006). Reconfigurable parallel processing system based on a modified ant colony system. In *Proc. of NRSC,* (pp. 1-11). NRSC.

Saini, G. (2005). Application of fuzzy-logic to real-time scheduling. In *Proceedings of 14th IEEE-NPSS Real-Time Conference*, (pp. 60-63). IEEE.

Shah, A., Kotecha, K., & Shah, D. (2010). Dynamic scheduling for real-time distributed systems using ACO. *International Journal of Intelligent Computing and Cybernetics*, *3*(2), 279–292. doi:10.1108/17563781011049205

Stutzle, T. (1998). An ant approach for the flow shop problem. In *Proceeding of EUFIT-98*, (pp. 1560-1564). EUFIT.

Thai, N. D. (2002). Real-time scheduling in distributed systems. In *Proc of PARELEC'02*, (pp. 165-170). PARELEC.

Turneo, A., Pilato, C., Frrandi, F., et al. (2008). Ant colony optimization for mapping and scheduling in heterogeneous multiprocessor systems. In *Proceedings of International Conference on Embedded Computer Systems: Architectures, Modeling and Simulation,* (pp. 142-149). Academic Press.

Yongcheng, L., & Roy, C. (1995). A dynamic priority based scheduling method in distributed systems. In *Proceedings of the International Conference on Parallel and Distributed Processing Techniques and Applications,* (pp. 177-186). Academic Press.

KEY TERMS AND DEFINITIONS

Ant Colony Optimization (ACO): ACO algorithms are computational models inspired b the collective foraging behaviour of ants.

Artificial Intelligence: Artificial intelligence solves the problem efficiently by heuristic search, embedding the domain knowledge which guides the search in an intelligent way.

Distributed System: The distributed system can be defined as a collection of computing nodes interconnected by a high speed local and wide area networks.

Dynamic Scheduling: Dynamic algorithm assigns priority at runtime based on execution parameters of tasks.

Earliest Deadline First (EDF): A greedy strategy turns out to be optimal for scheduling sporadic tasks on a single processor real-time system.

Real-Time System: Real-time system is required to complete its work and deliver its services on the basis of time. The results of real-time systems are judged based on the time at which the results are produced in addition to the logical results of computations.

Scheduling: An essential component of a computer system is the scheduling mechanism that is the strategy by which the system decides which task should be executed at any given time.

Static Scheduling: Static algorithm assigns all priorities at design time and it remains constant for the life time of a task.

Swarm Intelligence: Swarm intelligence is computational and behavioural metaphor for the problem solving that originally took its inspiration from the nature's examples of collective behaviours.

Chapter 12
Discovery of Emergent Sorting Behavior using Swarm Intelligence and Grid-Enabled Genetic Algorithms

Dimitris Kalles
Hellenic Open University, Greece

Vassiliki Mperoukli
Hellenic Open University, Greece

Alexis Kaporis
University of the Aegean, Greece

Anthony Chatzinouskas
Hellenic Open University, Greece

ABSTRACT

The authors in this chapter use simple local comparison and swap operators and demonstrate that their repeated application ends up in sorted sequences across a range of variants, most of which are also genetically evolved. They experimentally validate a square run-time behavior for emergent sorting, suggesting that not knowing in advance which direction to sort and allowing such direction to emerge imposes a n/logn penalty over conventional techniques. The authors validate the emergent sorting algorithms via genetically searching for the most favorable parameter configuration using a grid infrastructure.

INTRODUCTION

Sorting has been one of the first areas of computer science to showcase efficient algorithms to stand the test of time. While algorithms like quick-sort, merge-sort and heap-sort (Cormen, et al., 2009) are good at sorting with relatively few constraining assumptions, research focus gradually shifted to designing algorithms that can harness special cases in the input to accommodate some practical settings. Such special cases refer, for example,

to input that is partially ordered (Manilla, 1985; Estivill-Castro and Wood, 1992), or drawn from a constrained distribution, as is the case in bucket-sort (Cormen, et al., 2009) and spread-sort (Ross, 2002). Moreover, researchers have also studied extremely inefficient sorting algorithms to see whether inefficiencies can be mitigated by very simple changes in these algorithms (Gruber, et al., 2007).

Our motivation to examine sorting is to investigate what is the minimum structure of local

DOI: 10.4018/978-1-4666-6078-6.ch012

operators whose repetitive application ends up in sorted sequences. In our work, we further relax the assumption that we know which way to sort, yet arrive at a sorted sequence by simple local interactions. These are the basic elements of Emerge-Sort (Kalles, et al., 2012), our approach to self-organizing sorting without knowledge of sorting direction, which we experimentally validate across a range of variants, some of which are genetically evolved. We observe an $\Omega(n^2)$ run-time behavior and point out that Emerge-Sort is immune to arbitrary sequence modifications.

A simple example may help to visualize such a context. Consider a database which is distributed across several sites, with each site maintaining a sorting that best suits its local needs (either largest-first or smallest-first). If there is a need to redistribute objects across the sites, according to their order, so as to avoid asking all sites where an object might be located, one can either opt for some sort of centralized control over who-comes-first or, simply, let each object re-arrange itself in the local neighborhood. Additionally, when new objects are inserted dynamically into any of the available sites, one can either explicitly direct each one of them to the correct database partition or, simply, wait until the object finds its way to a partition. Similar problems have been long studied in the distributed computing literature where, up to now, solvability guarantees were accompanied by complex structured multiple passes, sometimes to deal with adversarial behavior in some of these passes (Flocchini, et al., 2004; Prasath, 2010; Israeli & Jalfon, 1993); they have also attracted the attention of the multi-agent systems community (Casadei, et al., 2006; Casadei, et al., 2007) and the consensus reaching community (Bénézit, et al., 2011).

The prominence of locality in the swarm intelligence approach to problem-solving has long been highlighted since many traditional problems (graph partitioning and clustering, among others, as described by Bonabeau, et al. [1998], Bonabeau [1997], Franks and Sendova-Franks [1992] and

Kuntz, et al. [1997]) have been recast in terms of swarm behavior. Swarm intelligence is at the junction of randomized behavior and local operations and has been demonstrated to solve difficult problems such as task scheduling (Bonabeau, et al., 1998). Now, emergent sorting is a behavior that has been documented in insect societies and modeled via swarm intelligence principles (Bonabeau, et al., 1999; Casadei, et al., 2007), albeit in an unconventional way; therein, sorting takes place in 2-D and consists of forming concentric circles where items of similar size are at roughly the same distance from the centre. 2-D sorting has received relatively scant attention since it is usually seen as a (difficult) case of clustering, another classic problem that has been also recently addressed with swarm intelligence (Handl & Meyer, 2008). It is interesting to note that swarm intelligence, beyond emergent sorting, has been also related to autonomic computing research, mainly through the observation of autonomic computing principles in biology inspired systems and the transfer of relevant concepts to problems in distributed computing (Babaoglu, et al., 2006).

Seen from a more conventional computer science perspective, swarm intelligence draws on several aspects of distributed computing (Dijkstra, 1974). It is not surprising that distributed sorting algorithms have been designed and progressively refined to address related problems of increasing relaxation of assumptions. We thus witness Loui (1984) first framing the problem of distributed sorting across n nodes linked in a chain, which, however, he based on an explicit three-stage process; first, elect a leader, then, using a carefully crafted encoding of the numbers to be sorted, insert values in the right place and let all nodes know about that encoding, and, finally, selectively delete values from all nodes, so that each node is left with the proper value of the sorted order. Based on that idea, Gerstel and Zaks (1997) extended the proofs of various properties of distributed sorting algorithms to tree-structures of connected processors. Flochinni, et al. (2004)

tackled various difficult extensions of the basic problem, among which one also observes the un-oriented sorting which is the problem we are examining; however, they assumed knowledge of the length of the sequence to be sorted and they explicitly structured distinct passes over the data. The latter approach was also employed by Fukś (1997), who, also, specified the exact length of each such pass. Hofstee, et al. (1990) did not use passes for their distributed sorting variant but they injected knowledge of the direction of sorting and assumed a minimum number (2) of elements per processor. This latter assumption was relaxed by Sasaki (2002) who, however, still used the orientation assumption and, furthermore, developed an algorithm that implies knowledge of location. Such knowledge has usually been explicitly built in even in the simplest parallel and sequential sorting algorithms, like odd-even sort (Knuth, 1973) and gnome sort (Black, 2010).

It is interesting to see that $\Omega(n^2)$ seems to be the minimum one has to pay for such sorting, though, in the distributed computing context, the cost of messaging is also taken into account and factored into slight variations of the underlying $\Theta(n^2)$ complexity. But, we note that, while these approaches also tackle the problem of election, that very election is central to the eventual sorting activity and costs $\Theta(n\log n)$ if seen in isolation (Dolev et al., 1982). In contrast, we simply apply local operators

which have no knowledge of further steps. From that perspective, we view cellular automata to be also related to our approach (Breukelaar & Bäck, 2005; Gonzaga de Sa & Maes, 1992; Gordillo & Luna, 1994; Mitchell, et al., 1993), also taking into account the genetic discovery of interesting behaviors for such automata (Mitchell, et al., 1993; Andre, et al., 1996) and their influence on distributed co-ordination in consensus reaching problems (Boyd, et al., 2005; Kempe, et al., 2003; Hassin & Peleg, 2001).

The rest of this chapter is structured in three sections. The next one is the core of the paper: we sketch out the basic principles that have lead to Emerge-Sort by showing how simple local operators manage to deliver sorted sequences. Following that, we examine various modifications to the basic operators and, then, design and carry out an extensive genetic search to research which of these are most effective. We conclude the chapter by drawing the key results from our research and by setting forth the key future research viewpoint.

A BRIEF BACKGROUND ON EMERGE-SORT

There are six possible ways to permute a triple (a,b,c) of distinct numbers as shown in Figure 1.

Figure 1. All possible permutations of three numbers

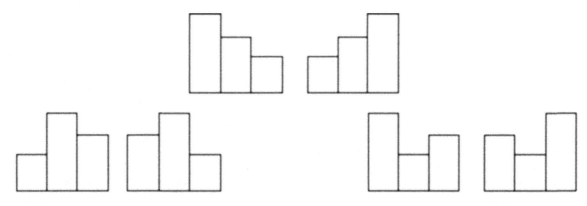

Provided we have no bias as to what direction a triple should be sorted, any top row configuration is good; for the lower row ones, we just swap those two elements that result in a sorted triple (see Figure 2).

It would be difficult to imagine a simpler operator on any three numbers. One could hope that this operator would be able to scale to arbitrarily selected triples of any unordered sequence and that, eventually, would result in an ordered sequence.

It turns out that this is not the case. Consider, for example the sequence 6 3 4 8. A malicious selection of triples could first request that $\boxed{6\ 3\ 4}\ 8$ is transformed into 6 4 3 8 and, then, request that $6\ \boxed{4\ 3\ 8}$ is transformed into 6 3 4 8, *ad nauseam*.

Accordingly, the next best attempt is to minimally extend this operator. Interestingly, the extension is quite simple: instead of actually sorting a triple according to Figure 2, we opt to sort that triple according to its *local* sorting direction bias (which, of course, may conflict with the bias of the neighboring triple). The sorting direction bias is a majority vote among all triple members. Such direction preference (bias) can be initialized at random for each member. In effect, the new local sorting operator (which, we stress, is confined to the triple's limits):

- First, establishes a preference for a sorting direction,

- Then, enforces that direction by locally sorting the triple,

- Finally, modifies the sorting direction bias of the minority vote items.

So, we have substituted the "to make as few moves as possible" approach with a still very simple one, namely "to make as few direction bias changes as possible" (which, of course, means that the arrows shown in Figure 2, about how permutations are turned into sorted triples, are no longer valid). The new approach creates overlapping triples that compete for setting the sorting direction of the sequence. But, this suffices for the sequence to be eventually sorted (Kalles, et al., 2012).

This approach closely follows the concepts of ant based algorithms, as we view sequences of numbers to be societies of individuals which act locally and are unaware of the consequences of their actions on the sequence as a whole (Bonabeau, et al., 1999). No shared knowledge, control or logic exists; individuals are only triggered into action via messaging by objects within their reach. Direction bias flags act as pheromones that are laid on the ground (this is the *stigmergy* concept), inviting others to follow a certain direction (this is the *chemotaxis* concept). Although the society has no hierarchies, large numbers can be viewed as foraging agents who influence others

Figure 2. Required swaps to sort any three numbers

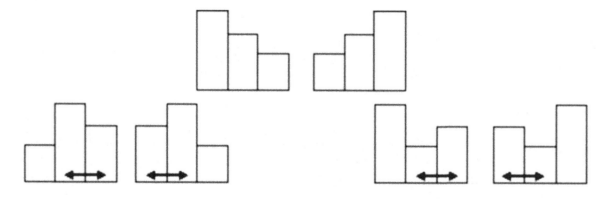

by helping settle direction issues (much like how taller children act when a group of children self-arranges itself in a circle according to height in a schoolyard).

A Proof of Concept

As a convention, let us use *A* to denote an ascending sorting bias (for left-to-right), and *D* to denote a descending sorting bias (again, for left-to-right). Let us also assume that we have a sequence of length *n* to sort. A triple is uniquely identified by the location of its middle element, *i*, with $1 \leq i \leq n$ and we employ a simple wrapping that arranges the sequence in a circle (ring). Additionally, we assume that, at initialization, all numbers in the sequence have equal probability of having a sorting bias direction of *A* or *D*. Note that such a bias only conveys information as to what sorting direction a triple *plans* to employ.

We now show an example of a neck-to-neck competition for establishing the bias; it will then

be easier to develop a general probabilistic argument on why Emerge-sort works.

Let us assume that a sequence has the following bias distribution: *DDDDAAAA*. Some locations (underlined) belong to triples with competing biases: *DDDDAAAA*; let us examine one such contest point at the centre of triple 5: *DDDD* **A** *AAA*. For this point, triples 4, 5 and 6 compete to set its bias. Even if all triples act purely parallel, only one gets the final opportunity to modify that location's bias. For the assumed sequence and contest point, (the left part of) Figure 3 shows what can happen, depending on which triple fires first (we only examine paths of length of at most 3 and omit duplicate triple firings).

We observe that, with a probability of 2/3, a contest point will have its bias belong to a majority class and that, with a probability of 1/3, a bias balance will be sustained.

On the other hand, (the right part of) Figure 3 shows that at non-contest points (for example, at

Figure 3. Bias sequence transformations (for contest and non-contest points)

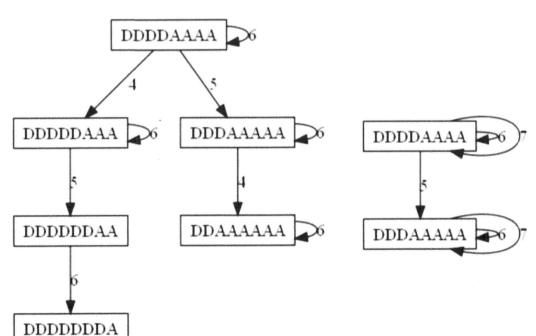

the centre of triple 6: $\underline{D}DD\underline{\mathbf{DA}}\boxed{A}A\underline{\mathbf{A}}$), we observe that with a probability of 2/3, such a point will not undo the balance and that with a probability of 1/3, it will have its bias belong to a majority class.

For the particular configuration set out above, since any of the *A*s and *D*s can be the centre of a triple, it follows that there is a ½ probability that there will again be a balance of four *A*s and four *D*s and there is a ½ probability that either *A*s or *D*s will overwhelm the other.

However, establishing a majority of one sorting direction bias will, quite probably, create more triples of the same bias, increasing the probability that all triples will end up with the same bias. Eventually, this sorts the sequence.

To see why, observe that when all triples have the same sorting direction bias, any triple that is being picked to sort itself will contribute to the overall sorting. A simple measure of unsorted-ness of any sequence is the number of alternating runs, as defined by the times one has to change the upwards or downwards direction when traversing the sequence, end-to-end (usually also referred to as up-runs and down-runs, ending in peaks and valleys correspondingly). For example, the sequence (3, 5, 6, 2) has 2 alternating runs. Any triple has at most 2 alternating runs and it is locally sorted when it has just 1 such run.

Now, assume that, at some point in our sequence, we come across an unsorted triple and that we have achieved a global sorting direction bias of *A* (though each triple is aware of its own bias only). It is easy to enumerate all possible orderings of the triple and its neighbors and show that, after the triple has been sorted, it either decreases the number of alternating runs of its extended neighborhood (and of the whole sequence, as a result) or it leaves that number unchanged (see the Appendix for a full example and the accompanying enumeration); each such alternative has a prob-

ability of ½. The number of alternating runs can be viewed as a potential function, which cannot increase. If we define as a binary random variable the occurrence of an alternating runs reduction at a triple, then the binomial random variable, *X*, that governs the behavior at the sequence level has $E(X)=n/2$ (Doerr, 2011), suggesting that, in one parallel round, $n/2$ triples can be expected to contribute to a reduction of the number of alternating runs. However, since sorted triples are not affected, the next parallel round will deliver a further $n/4$ reduction in the number of alternating runs, so $O(\log n)$ parallel rounds will deliver the final sorted sequence.

To see why all triples converge to the same sorting direction bias, observe that the process governing the conversion of *A*s into *D*s and vice-versa is a Markov chain with two equilibrium distributions, all *A*s or all *D*s, hence the probability of oscillations strictly decreases the longer we examine local triples and eventually one ends up in a sequence with a common flag.

For an example, we show the state transition probability matrix for the quintuple case in Figure 4. When examining an *ADDAA* quintuple, for example, oscillations can occur *ad nauseam* between alternating configurations (for example, if we first examine a triple centered around a *D* item, then the majority of flags features a *D*, which can change again if we examine a triple centered around one of the remaining *A*s) but the probability of this happening strictly decreases with time.

The left part of Figure 4 shows the states; each state is characterized by the number of the minority flags. The $3\rightarrow2$ state suggests that, with a 2/5 probability, one goes to a 2-strong minority of the *opposite* class. Note that the dotted transition to the $3\rightarrow2$ state signifies that this is a diversion from that standard formalism; the $3\rightarrow2$ state is just a 2-strong minority state, for which a standard state has been drawn. However, this does not make a

Figure 4. Quintuple state transition probabilities: Verbose and lean versions

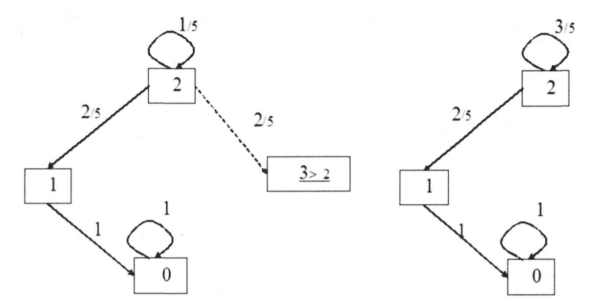

difference in our approach; Emerge-sort does not favor a certain sorting direction, so any majority is good enough.

The right part of Figure 4 shows the simplified and formally correct Markov chain; therein, state numbers indicate the size of *any* minority (therefore, the probability of staying in a 2-strong minority is 1/5+2/5). Note that when a flag in non-existent, then there is no way it can turn up, hence the transition from a 0 to itself; additionally when there is only one instance of a flag, then it will be overturned, hence the transition from 1 to 0.

The quasi-stationary distribution of the underlying Markov process converges to a column of 1's; this is a probabilistic guarantee that all islands will be eventually washed out and it bears nice analogies both to the gambler's ruin problem (Allen, 2010) and to the competing species problem (van Doorn & Pollett, 2009). The eventual outlook of M_n^i (where n refers to the sequence length) is shown as:

$$M_n^i = \begin{bmatrix} 1 & 0 & & \cdots & & 0 \\ 1 & 0 & & \cdots & & 0 \\ 1 & 0 & 0 & \cdots & 0 & 0 \\ \underset{i\to\infty}{} & \underset{i\to\infty}{} & \underset{i\to\infty}{} & & \underset{i\to\infty}{} & \underset{i\to\infty}{} \\ \vdots & 0 & \ddots & \cdots & \ddots & 0 \\ & \underset{i\to\infty}{} & & & & \underset{i\to\infty}{} \\ \vdots & \vdots & & \vdots & & \vdots \\ 1 & 0 & 0 & \cdots & \cdots & 0 \\ \underset{i\to\infty}{} & \underset{i\to\infty}{} & \underset{i\to\infty}{} & & & \underset{i\to\infty}{} \end{bmatrix}$$

Prototype Experimental Validation

To validate Emerge-Sort we describe a series of experiments we have carried out across a range of input sizes and with several initial distributions of A and D biases.

We review in Table 1 the results for $n = 128$. Each line corresponds to 100 experiments (all experiments reported henceforth are based on 100 samples per configuration). The %A column indicates the percentage of elements that have been

Table 1. Results for n = 128 (100 experiments) (Kalles, et al. 2012)

% A	% Sorted Ascending	# Rounds	# Moves
99	100	4614	51
95	100	5163	52
90	99	6099	53
80	97	7778	58
70	96	9346	64
60	68	10697	74
55	63	10985	76
50	54	10949	76

initialized with an *A* sorting direction bias. It is reasonable, of course, that when a large majority of elements has the same sorting direction bias, there is a high probability that the sequence will eventually be sorted according to that bias. The *% sorted Ascending* column confirms just that; i.e. it reports how many of the experiments were eventually sorted in ascending order.

Note that, as earlier argued, it is also reasonable that the faster all sequence elements converge to a common sorting direction bias, the faster it will be able to eventually sort itself. This is confirmed by the *# Rounds* column, which reports the individual number of triples examined. It is also confirmed by the *# Moves* columns, which shows how many numbers are moved per round on average. Since

triples are fired at random, rounds are measured in terms of individual triple inspections.

To substantiate our $\Omega(n^2)$ behavior claim, Table 2 presents the detailed values of the average number of rounds per type of experiment. The *x* column between every two *R* (rounds) columns is the calculated multiplying factor between two *R* numbers that correspond to two experiments that differ by a factor of 2 in the sequence length (and that have the same initial A/D distribution). Numbers in the *x* column are reported to an accuracy of one decimal digit. The pattern is pretty clear.

The results were obtained with an implementation that had a simple but key difference to the naïve protocol; we do not change *any* direction bias within a *sorted* triple.

Table 2. Results for n = 128 up to 2048, in powers of 2 (number of rounds only)

% A	n = 128 #R	x	n = 256 #R	x	n = 512 #R	x	n = 1024 #R	x	n = 2048 #R
99	4614	4.0	18229	4.0	73213	4.0	291097	4.0	1154117
95	5163	3.9	20330	4.1	82648	4.0	331394	4.0	1324288
90	6099	3.9	23877	4.1	96987	3.9	380112	4.0	1518406
80	7778	4.0	31011	3.9	121080	4.0	481221	4.0	1901525
70	9346	3.9	36830	3.9	143110	4.0	574193	4.0	2297483
60	10697	4.0	42739	4.0	171135	4.0	683604	3.9	2675876
55	10985	4.0	44088	4.1	180408	4.0	715828	4.0	2846350
50	10949	4.1	45088	4.1	183031	4.0	735276	4.0	2938168

Indicative $\Omega(n^3\log n)$ results for the naïve protocol are shown in Table 3 and confirm a rapid deterioration for decreasingly unbalanced *A/D* mixtures (50% of *A*s would correspond to a completely balanced mixture).

Since a subtle change in an operator can have such profound consequences (see also Biedl et al. (2004) for a similar context), a systematic investigation of alternatives is warranted to see which are useful.

DISCOVERING VARIANTS OF EMERGE-SORT

As Emerge-Sort is a genre of processes, its most interesting variations relate to how we deal with boundary cases of the basic process. It turns out that subtle points in behavior sometimes create substantial differences. We first use a *n*=256 benchmark for sequence length to discuss these differences (because this value of *n* did allow the interestingly slow variant reported in Table 6 to conclude in a reasonable amount of time) before scaling up for the more promising variants.

Focusing Random Behavior

The basic variant of Emerge-Sort renders triples dormant until one of their elements has participated in a recent (neighboring) triple sorting; then dormant triples are (awakened and) marked as candidates for local sorting. This focuses changes around recently sorted triples and propagates changes in their neighborhood. We now examine some variants in this assumption and we report the results in Table 4 (data in its *basic* columns are drawn from Table 1).

In the *perfect oblivion* variant, triples are randomly selected and sorting slows down. Yet another variant considers triples either to the left or to the right of the triple that was last modified. Essentially this *focuses* most of the *changes* around a point and propagates changes to the left or to the right of it; interestingly, this variant seems to not depend on the mix of *A*s and *D*s in the initial bias distribution. And finally, when one *combines* the concept of awakening dormant triples and focused change (see Figure 5 for a tentative pattern), the number of rounds remains fairly low and constant, while the average number of moves also grows slower.

Table 3. Results for n = 8, 16, 32, 64, 128 – simplest protocol

% A	n = 8		n = 16		n = 32		n = 64		n = 128	
	# R	# M	# R	# M	# R	# M	# R	# M	# R	# M
99	18	3	68	6	261	11	1028	24	9676	54
95	18	3	68	6	538	15	3002	31	21260	69
90	18	3	118	7	1035	21	6735	46	59686	117

Table 4. Results for assessing the impact of randomness variants for n = 256

% A	Basic		Oblivion		Focused-Change		Combined	
	# R	# M	# R	# M	# R	# M	# R	# M
99	18229	101	29357	102	24707	103	19184	101
95	23877	104	36458	105	25124	103	19310	103
90	45088	155	73801	156	24531	113	19724	106

Figure 5. Potential patterns of examining triples in the oblivion (left) and combined (right) variants

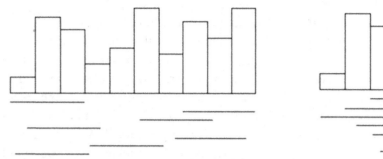 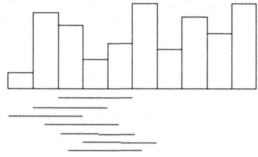

The Nature of Endpoints

Any sequence has endpoints. When a sequence is arranged as a ring, an endpoint is a transparent wall through which any number is allowed to move. If we consider endpoints as being set against a non-transparent wall (see Figure 6), endpoint numbers cannot form a triple and only get an indirect chance to move, via their neighbors' triples.

As shown in Table 5, this does not really affect the results.

Figure 6. Demonstrating how endpoints wrap to form triples

Table 5. Results for assessing the impact of wrap enabling for n = 256

% A	Basic		Endpoint-Excluded	
	# R	# M	# R	# M
99	18229	101	18177	101
95	23877	104	23803	103
90	45088	155	44617	154

The Nature of Neighborhoods

An intuitive extension to the basic process involves assigning the direction bias of a newly sorted triple to its neighboring left and right locations. Surprisingly, this seemingly simple and intuitive outreach delivers an outstandingly inferior performance, as shown in Table 6.

Even here, though, a small further change can have substantial consequences. The above results only refer to what happens when a triple has settled on a direction bias and, incidentally, is also sorted to that bias. If we examine a variant where the neighborhood expansion is only allowed in triples which were actually sorted in just the previous step, then Table 7 paints a totally different picture, highlighting the sensitivity to how neighborhoods are treated. Still, note that it becomes increasingly difficult to home in on a direction bias (see, for example, the spike in terms of expended resources for the 90% case).

Using Genetic Algorithms to Develop Emerge-Sort Variants

In-depth investigation of a series of variants can be a painstaking process. The way we report results above, on a case-by-case basis, offers us, at best, fragmented views since, for any variation, we must *fix* some experimentation parameters. But, deciding the value at which some parameters must be fixed while other parameters are allowed some fluctuation is an exercise in educated intuition.

We can do better by employing a genetic algorithm to come up with tentative parameter combinations, then use these combinations in random sequences and observe whether they manage to self-sort efficiently and, as a result, investigate whether some common patterns of behavior seem to prevail.

Essentially, we are using genetic algorithms (Wilson, 1986; Booker, et al., 1989; Goldberg, 1989) in a genetic programming context (Koza, 1991; Kalles & Papagelis, 2001):

Table 6. Results for assessing the impact of setting neighbors' bias for n = 256

% A	Basic		Triple-Extended	
	# R	# M	# R	# M
99	18229	101	62098	103
95	23877	104	1051290	103
90	45088	155	2195418	113

Table 7. Results for re-assessing the impact of setting neighbors' bias for n = 256

% A	Basic		Triple-Extended	
	# R	# M	# R	# M
99	18229	101	14975	103
95	23877	104	15624	106
90	45088	155	22868	155

- We initialize a set of candidate Emerge-Sort variants by arbitrarily combining aspects of how to treat sequences, as set out previously,
- We evaluate that populations of variants by adopting a fitness function that allows us to estimate whether they can sort effectively a set of sequences,
- We combine (by selection and cross-over) good solutions into offspring thus attempting to cross-fertilize good aspects of how to treat sequences,
- We mutate some offspring to avoid local maxima and, finally,
- We iterate with the new population, until we reach a predefined number of iteration steps.

Note that we do not use the genetic algorithm for sorting but for exploring the space of Emerge-Sort variants. Of course, key to our approach is the selection of how to represent an Emerge-Sort variant. A sorting variant is defined by a combination of the following building blocks:

- Type of random behavior: there are four options for this part (as exemplified in Table 4).
- Type of endpoint treatment: in addition to whether endpoints are allowed to wrap around the sequence or not (as exemplified in Table 5), we have also allowed the possibility for endpoints to be inflected, setting their direction bias explicitly to point to the middle of the sequence. Though this is an injection of knowledge of location, albeit at a small scale, it was deemed an interesting variation to investigate even if it is not part of Emerge-sort.
- Type of neighborhood side-effects: extending the outreach of local operators gives rise to more complex interactions and (as exemplified in Table 6) even intuitively appealing options may turn out to be un-

affordable. This motivated us to design a more elaborate representation for neighborhoods to allow the investigation of combinations of alternatives:

- The first issue concerns what happens when an already sorted triple is examined: the alternatives are to do nothing, to set the neighborhood's bias flags to the triple's bias, or to set these flags to X (don't care).
- A second issue concerns what happens at the boundaries of a just sorted triple. As the experiments reported in Table 6 and in Table 7 highlighted, it makes a difference if we are talking about a triple that was just sorted instead of being found sorted (which is also addressed in the previous issue). The three above alternatives apply.
- A third issue is a dual to the second one; it concerns the boundaries of a not-sorted triple. Again, we use the same three alternatives.

The above coding gives rise to $4 \times 3^3 = 324$ variants. The fitness function we use to assess each evolved variant is simple. We first generate some sequences which are used as test cases for all evolution; note that this means that the A/D mix of each sequence remains the same for all variants tested on that sequence. Each (individual) evolved sorting variant is tested on all such sequences and we calculate the average number of rounds required to sort these sequences (using a *large* number as a penalty whenever the variant fails to sort a sequence). Taking the inverse of that average, we end up with high fitness for those variants that manage to sort most sequences fast.

We used the ECJ package (http://www.cs.gmu.edu/~eclab/projects/ecj/) to implement the genetic algorithm and we integrated the ECJ runtime with Emerge-Sort to allow for a uniform way of creating experimental logs and of specifying global experimental parameters (such as, among others, the size of sequences to be sorted and the maximum allowable number of rounds allowed).

We ran experiments with 100 generations, a population of 100 competing variants, a mutation rate of 0.1 and a cross-over rate of 1. Members were selected via tournament selection and we employed a single-point cross-over. The experiments were carried out in 16-, 32-, 64- and 128-long sequences, therefore our results are based on an analysis of 400 variants, which are the population individuals in the last generation (100 individuals x 4 sequence sizes).

We now present the results in terms of observations on these 400 individuals, starting with the ones where an overwhelming majority of a particular type of behavior was observed and drilling down to discuss peculiarities.

- All 400 variants opted to not touch the current triple when it was observed to be already sorted.
- 389 variants selected the *combined* approach in random behavior whereas only 11 variants selected the *basic* approach (as exemplified in Table 4).
  - Of the 11 variants, only one employed inflection of bias at the endpoints whereas the rest opted to not treat the sequence as a ring (as exemplified in Table 5); additionally, most of them opted to set the neighbors of triples to an *X* bias (as exemplified in Table 7).
  - Of the 389 variants, only one extended the triple's bias to its neighbors (and that was only observed in the 16-long sequences); all the rest either did nothing or opted to set the neighbors to an *X* bias (as exemplified in Table 7), with the latter option being favored to the former by a ratio of about 3:1.
- The treatment of endpoints was quite balanced. Excluding 16-long experiments, which, overwhelmingly rejected endpoint

wrapping or inflection, we observed that 121 (out of the remaining 300) variants favored inflection, 81 favored wrapping and 98 favored the simple approach. We did not observe any pattern to associate the relative frequency of these preferences to the size of the experiments.

Scaling up Genetic Search using a Grid

While genetic search can deliver insight into what works and what does not, it is usually the case that experiments have to be carried out at a substantial scale to allow for the originally developed insight to be confirmed. Though desktop and conventional laboratory infrastructure may indeed be helpful for the insight development stage, production-class experimentation can be best supported by powerful infrastructures. The grid-computing paradigm is, arguably, one where the entry-level requirements for any researcher are relatively low in terms of time invested in return for access to powerful infrastructure, though a certain level of programming expertise is a must. For example, scientific workflows, that are normally required for intensive data processing applications, have usually demanded a substantially steep learning curve, which can challenge the very reason one would like to resort to a grid-based system. Special tools are required for the production of workflows and file transfer tools for transferring files to and from the grid, though recent research also attempts to hide from the user the logistics of computation recovery in less reliable workflow systems (Gu, et al., 2013).

We have, thus, designed and carried out a series of experiments on a grid-computing infrastructure[1] to investigate the behavior of the aforementioned variants at a larger scale; we were particularly interested to see how the apparently best variants would perform in light of increased neighborhood size. This parameter is particular crucial, since it allows us to conjecture that our emergent sorting mechanism describes, essentially, a spectrum of behaviors where co-ordination at a local scale (the neighborhood) allows for emergent behavior to be observed regardless of the neighborhood size.

The high-level implementation decision we made for implementing the genetic search on the grid was to use the MPJ-Express library which implements an MPI-based protocol for Java (www. mpj-express.org). To distribute computations across k sites, we partitioned the population evaluation process for each generation into k-1 slave processes, each of which evaluated POP_SIZE div k-1 atoms, and a master process evaluating POP_SIZE mod k-1 atoms (an atom refers to a sorting variant). To explore a more complex setting, we also adopted a modified scheme of genetic operators and we set the mutation rate at 0.2 and the cross-over rate at 0.8 for all experiments.

As the tools and the software were in place for the larger-scale experiments, we first ran some warming-up experiments which highlighted the importance of the size of the neighborhood relative to the overall sequence. In Table 8, we report on genetic search with 16-long sequences, over 30 generations, with two basic alternatives as regards population size (10, 100) and three alternatives as

regards neighborhood size (3, 5, 7). We used 30 samples for each experiment and report averages.

It is rather not surprising to note that large neighborhoods tend to produce quite early an overwhelming sorting direction that is imposed upon the (relatively speaking, not much larger) sequence and produces fast sorting.

The next experimental round attempted to quantify what results one might get with a hard constraint on the amount of time one can afford to wait for results to be produced. Again, we used 30 samples for each experimental configuration, over 30 generations and set the population size at 30. We then investigated up to which sequence length we would be able to conclude our experiments given a ceiling of 1 hour's worth of waiting. The results are shown in Table 9.

While the 7-long neighborhood configuration did not manage to scale beyond 128-long sequences within the prescribed time limit, it produced results that essentially confirmed the previous findings with respect to its relative superiority to smaller neighborhoods. Also note that the sequence size starts growing, the effects of larger neighborhoods relative to smaller ones are sustained, but the growth of the expended time

Table 8. Time spent to produce results for assessing the impact of neighborhood size for n = 16

POP_SIZE / Neighborhood	3	5	7
10	12.35	8.12	10.25
100	132.15	19.63	15.91

Table 9. Time spent to produce results for assessing the impact of neighborhood size for n up to 128

Sequence Length / Neighborhood	3	5	7
8	10.42	9.12	10.98
16	14.93	12.53	11.12
32	277.35	133.09	65.73
64	1525.88	899.29	513.36
128	3500.65	2411.92	1287.13

starts looking interestingly similar (about ~2.5, effectively suggesting that the $O(n^2)$ complexity of Emerge-Sort can be brought down to sub-square time in a properly distributed environment).

We then focused on 7-long neighborhoods and using the same combination of generations, population size and samples per experiment, we experimented with sequence lengths ranging from 2^3 to 2^{13}, in powers of 2. First of all, we confirmed the *combined* approach of Table 4; we reiterate that this is, indeed, the epitome of swarm intelligence as it shows that, not only localized behavior can bring about global sorting, but that such sorting is more effectively done when local changes *nudge* their neighborhood out of tranquility.

Additionally, we calculated the ratio of time consumed by a 2^x–long sequence experiment over than of the corresponding 2^{x-1}–long experiment. The results (shown in Figure 7, with axis x denoting the exponent of 2^x and axis y denoting the ratio) suggest that, as we increase the size of the sequence to be sorted, the increased neighborhood size starts creating isles of sorted sequences that sustain their sorting direction. This is reflected in the factor-of-2 increase of the expended time, though it initially creates problems for sequences that are not too large compared to the neighborhood size, as we already documented in Table 8.

Note that the eventual factor-of-2 suggests that with the particular computation distribution

we adopted, we manage to end-up with a linear increase in overall time. We note that we report elapsed time for the experiments as we have not yet investigated how to smooth out differences in CPU time reported from different grid computers. This may also explain the apparent outlier behavior of 2^{11}. An argument, however, for suggesting that this particular metric is not too coarse (as elapsed time always is) and can be relied upon, has to do with the observation that grid computers have minimal user-interaction overhead as all job submission and management is done through grid user-interface computers.

DISCUSSION AND RESEARCH DIRECTIONS

We firmly believe that the idea of genetic search in Emerge-sort is not (yet) aimed at developing the best variant; this is a vague goal since we are looking at different number sequences each time. Instead, the goal should be directed at looking into which variants manage to consistently and effectively sort randomly generated sequences and, after some evolution time, examining parameter configurations that prevail in winning variants.

It is an intuitive metaphor to interpret the locality of the bias-setting-and-then-sorting operators in Emerge-sort as a demonstration of

Figure 7. Scaling up the genetic search with 7-long neighborhoods

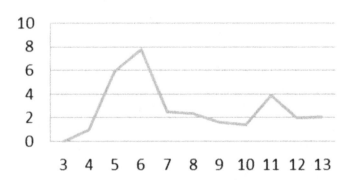

selfishness; where each triple aims to minimize the bias conflict between members. This sets out two further directions to be explored. The first direction has to do with whether one can relate the quantification of what constitutes a good-size neighborhood to research on co-operating groups in social networks (Allen, et al., 2010). The second direction has to do with investigating whether the $n/\log n$ performance degradation from Emerge-Sort to a conventional co-ordinated sorting algorithm of $O(n\log n)$ complexity, is an instantiation of the $\Theta(p/\log p)$ *price of anarchy* tag in congestion games (Roughgarden, 2003) where the edge latency factor is a polynomial of degree at most p.

Of course, as earlier described, it is easier to see that Emerge-sort resembles societies of individuals which act locally and are unaware of the consequences of their actions on the sequence as a whole; even when a triple finds itself ordered it remains idle, being oblivious to a grander common global goal, which might well be the development of a sorting direction opposite to that of the triple at hand. This takes us easily to the $n/\log n$ penalty (over a classical sorting algorithm) that this society pays for not having *a priori* settled the direction issue.

A further issue is whether the the $n/\log n$ delay coefficient is related to the size of the local operators (in our case, we have triples that may affect also affect their neighbors). If we extend the scope of a local operator to a quadruple (or, any n-tuple), it is reasonable to ask whether we inject unnecessarily much local overhead; alternatively, we may ask whether $n/\log n$ is a delay coefficient that characterizes all local operators. In essence, this question raises the issue of trading off computational efficiency for cost of long-range connections (Mitchell, 2006). Such connections also have to do with structural properties of the operators that can be applied to a sequence; Scharnow et al. (2004) discuss how a variety of such operators can lead to interesting similarities in lower bounds for basic evolutionary algorithms,

while He and Yao (2001) and Droste et al. (2002) discuss how slowly-changing objective functions may help one derive relatively tight estimates of convergence times. Hassan and Ingram (2010) examine the related problem of multi-hop one-dimensional networks, essentially suggesting that larger neighborhoods could lead to faster convergence to the quasi-stationary distribution.

Similar problems and behaviors are identified in gossip-based schemes of information diffusion (Kempe, et al., 2003). Note, however, that what differentiates Emerge-sort from consensus-related research is the fact that our operators impose consensus on a locality, whereas classical gossip research makes the fundamental assumption of conservation of global information (Bénézit, et al., 2011; Kempe, et al., 2003), which is crucial to aggregate information schemes, such as averaging (Boyd, et al., 2005), but not to our problem. Also, several consensus schemes admit an approximate solution formulation which factors the accuracy margin (ε) into the asymptotic estimate for convergence (Bénézit et al., 2010).

Majority voting schemes are representative of that family of research, but they aim to ensure that the majority is respected (Bénézit, et al., 2009; Bénézit, et al., 2011), whereas Emerge-sort allows for the possibility that sorting can emerge along a sequence direction despite an initially adversary direction bias distribution among the sequence elements (see, for example, the third, fourth and fifth line in Table 1). Such behavior is also elegantly described in the work of Hassin and Peleg (2001), whose distributed probabilistic polling research suggested that consensus on a ring is bounded by $O(n^2\log n)$, though we stress that this is not a guaranteed consensus on the initial majority, which has been shown to be impossible (Mustafa & Pekeč, 2001). Their results are also quite close to our mechanism, since their validity criterion is similar to the mechanism employed in Emerge-sort, namely that once all items have the same direction bias, no bias changes can occur again. Hassin and Peleg's approach involves pairs (as in classic gossip schemes) and not triples, as we do; however, they also prove a result that working in pairs take $O(n^3 \log n)$ to stabilize, which is probably an indication that the transition from a pair-based to a triple-based neighborhood is a critical performance parameter. The $O(n^2 \log n)$ tag also appears as part of the convergence time of the binary voting via gossip problem, as described by Draief and Vojnović (2012). That work also accommodates the initial majority ratio into the convergence time estimate.

An alternative approach is to accommodate some error in the achieved consensus. In this context, an $O(n^2 \log(1/\varepsilon))$ tag for consensus averaging with an error margin of ε has been obtained by Dimakis, et al. (2008) for rings (where the localized geographic information is minimal). A similar perspective is provided by rumor spreading research (Sauerwald, 2008). Since in Emerge-sort, we not only spread a rumor but also act on it, it may be worth investigating if limitations in the computational power of cellular automata (Mitchell, et al., 1993; Land & Belew, 1995; Capcarrère & Sipper, 2001) can be somehow countered by endowing a neighborhood centre with the capacity to drag into its computational environment a finite number of its neighbors. Likewise, fast results in consensus research come with a price on the accuracy of the final solution (Aysal, et al., 2007) or with the exploitation of geographic information (Dimakis, et al., 2008).

Emerge-sort *should* be formally shown to converge, to enhance its value. Such a research result would have unequivocal consequences and, hence, we consider it of the highest priority. Additionally, the infrastructure we have put in place allows us, now, to investigate fine aspects of complexity; scaling up to large sequences with shorter neighborhoods could allow us to research behavior that might shed some light into differences that may be difficult to observe in smaller-scale experiments (for example, telling apart $\Omega(n^2 \log n)$ and $\Omega(n^3 \log n)$ may be impossible without long inputs; telling apart $\Omega(n^2 \log n)$ and

$\Omega(n^2 \log \log n)$ will likely be impossible without very long inputs). Furthermore, genetic search for more variants can be also extended to study the level of their immunity to perturbation: while they will eventually manage to sort, it is important to find the limit in the rate at which they can absorb changes in the sequences.

CONCLUSION

We have described the basic concepts and an experimental validation of Emerge-sort, a sorting algorithm that does not depend on being told which way a sequence should be sorted and yet manages to sort that sequence, usually alongside a dominant preference among the sequence numbers, based on randomly applied simple local operators.

We have also shown that these local operators need not be absolutely hard-and-fast and slight variations can be accommodated, without compromising the concept of locality. However, we have also shown that, sometimes, these variations end up in considerably delays for sorting; consequently, we have also shown how we investigated the power of some key variants as regards their respective ability to sort, using genetic algorithms. We have thus implemented an approach whereby collections of local operators have been evolved and evaluated with respect to some target sequences to be sorted; the top performing variants have been consistently observed to revolve around some key parameters.

We have also ported our investigation to the grid to analyze the behavior of such variants under more demanding requirements, particularly the ones posed by longer neighborhoods. We have observed, again, indications that performance seems to be subject to the same (coarse) underlying complexity and this is a key indicator of the robustness of the Emerge-sort algorithm.

We have already stated elsewhere that research in Emerge-sort started as an experimental effort into investigating the dynamics of local operators regarding their ability to generate order. While the painstaking analysis of the variants is a formidable theoretical goal, we also now believe that the large-scale experimentation, where these variants are allowed to compete with each other, may also hold some potential as regards uncovering which parameters seem to dominate the performance of these simple local operators. Essentially, we are designing versatile configurations and evolve them with the hope that the fittest will survive; analyzing, then, these "fittest" ones, we hope to be able to uncover behavior that might guide our theoretical analysis. This is a signature approach to genetic search and algorithm design.

ACKNOWLEDGMENT

Emerge-Sort is implemented in Java and is temporarily hosted at http://student-support2.ouc.ac.cy:8080/emergesort/index.html. An earlier version was implemented in Maple. All variants are available on demand for academic purposes.

REFERENCES

Allen, L. (2010). *An introduction to stochastic processes with applications to biology* (2nd ed.). Chapman and Hall/CRC.

Allen, S. M., Colombo, & Whitaker. (2010). Cooperation through self-similar social networks. *ACM Transactions on Autonomous and Adaptive Systems, 5*(1), Article 4.

Andre, D., Bennett, F. H., III, & Koza, J. R. (1996). Discovery by genetic programming of a cellular automata rule that is better than any known rule for the majority classification problem. In *Proceedings of First Annual Conference on Genetic Programming* (pp. 3-11). Stanford, CA: Academic Press.

Aysal, T. C. Coates, & Rabbat. (2007). Distributed average consensus using probabilistic quantization. In *Proceedings of IEEE 14th Workshop on Statistical Signal Processing* (pp. 640-644). Madison, WI: IEEE.

Babaoglu, O., Canright, Deutsch, di Caro, Ducatelle, Gambardella, Ganguly, …. Urnes, T. (2006). Design patterns from biology to distributed computing. *ACM Transactions on Autonomous and Adaptive Systems, 1*(1), 26-66.

Bénézit, F. Thiran, & Vetterli. (2009). Interval Consensus: From Quantized Gossip to Voting. In *Proceedings of IEEE International Conference on Acoustics, Speech, and Signal Processing* (pp. 3661-3664). Taipei, Taiwan: IEEE.

Bénézit, F., Dimakis, Thiran, & Vetterli. (2010). Order-Optimal Consensus Through Randomized Path Averaging. *IEEE Transactions on Information Theory, 56*(10), 5150–5167. doi:10.1109/TIT.2010.2060050

Bénézit, F., Thiran, P., & Vetterli, M. (2011). The Distributed Multiple Voting Problem. *IEEE Journal of Selected Topics in Signal Processing, 5*(4), 791–804. doi:10.1109/JSTSP.2011.2114326

Biedl, T., Chan, T., Demaine, E. D., Fleischer, R., Golin, M., King, J. A., & Munro, J.-I. (2004). Fun-Sort – or the Chaos of Unordered Binary Search. *Discrete Applied Mathematics, 144*, 231–236. doi:10.1016/j.dam.2004.01.003

Black, P. E. (2010). Gnome sort. In *Dictionary of Algorithms and Data Structures*. Retrieved from http://www.nist.gov/dads/HTML/gnomeSort.html

Bonabeau, E. (1997). From classical models of morphogenesis to agent-based models of pattern formation. *Artificial Life*, *3*(3), 191–209. doi:10.1162/artl.1997.3.3.191 PMID:9385734

Bonabeau, E., Theraulaz, & Deneubourg. (1998). Fixed Response Thresholds and the Regulation of Division of Labour in Insect Societies. *Bulletin of Mathematical Biology*, *60*, 753–807. doi:10.1006/bulm.1998.0041

Bonabeau, E. Dorigo, & Theraulaz. (1999). Swarm Intelligence: From Natural to Artificial Systems. Oxford University Press.

Booker, L.B., Goldberg, & Holland. (1989). Classifier Systems and Genetic Algorithms. *Artificial Intelligence*, *40*(2), 235–282. doi:10.1016/0004-3702(89)90050-7

Boyd, S., Ghosh, A., Prabhakar, B., & Shah, D. (2005). Gossip algorithms: Design, analysis and applications. In *Proceedings of 24ᵗʰ Annual Joint Conference of the IEEE and Communication Societies* (Vol. 3, pp. 1653-1664). Miami, FL: IEEE.

Breukelaar, R., & Bäck, T. (2005). Using a Genetic Algorithm to Evolve Behaviour in Multi Dimensional Cellular Automata. In *Proceedings of Conference on Genetic and Evolutionary Computation* (pp. 107-114). Washington, DC: Academic Press.

Capcarrere, M.S., & Sipper. (2001). Necessary conditions for density classification by cellular automata. *Physical Review E: Statistical, Nonlinear, and Soft Matter Physics*, *64*(3), 036113. doi:10.1103/PhysRevE.64.036113 PMID:11580400

Casadei, M., Gardelli, L., & Viroli, M. (2006). Collective Sorting Tuple Spaces. In *Proceedings of 11ᵗʰ International Workshop on Cooperative Information Agents* (pp. 255-269). Delft, The Netherlands: Academic Press.

Casadei, M., Menezes, R., Viroli, M., & Tolksdorf, R. (2007). Using Ant's Brood Sorting to Increase Fault Tolerance in Linda's Tuple Distribution Mechanism. In *Proceedings of 7ᵗʰ Workshop from Objects to Agents* (pp. 173-180). Catania, Italy: Academic Press.

Cormen, T. H., Leicerson, C. E., Rivest, R. L., & Stein, C. (2009). *Introduction to Algorithms* (3rd ed.). MIT Press.

Dijkstra, E. W. (1974). Self-stabilizing systems in spite of distributed control. *Communications of the ACM*, *17*(11), 643–644. doi:10.1145/361179.361202

Dimakis, A.D.G., Sarwate, & Wainright. (2008). Geographic gossip: Efficient averaging for sensor networks. *IEEE Transactions on Signal Processing*, *56*(3), 1205–1216. doi:10.1109/TSP.2007.908946

Doerr, B. (2011). Analyzing randomized search heuristics: Tools from probability theory. In *Theory of Randomized Search Heuristics: Foundations and Recent Developments*. World Scientific. doi:10.1142/9789814282673_0001

Dolev, D., Klawe, & Rodeh. (1982). An *O*(*n*log*n*) unidirectional distributed algorithm for extrema finding in a circle. *Journal of Algorithms*, *3*(3), 245–260. doi:10.1016/0196-6774(82)90023-2

Draief, M., & Vojnović. (2012). Convergence speed of binary interval consensus. *SIAM Journal on Control and Optimization*, *50*(3), 1087–1109. doi:10.1137/110823018

Droste, S., Jansen, & Wegener. (2002). On the analysis of the (1 + 1) evolutionary algorithm. *Theoretical Computer Science*, *276*, 51–81. doi:10.1016/S0304-3975(01)00182-7

Estivill–Castro, V., & Wood. (1992). A Survey of Adaptive Sorting Algorithms. *ACM Computing Surveys*, *24*(4), 441–476. doi:10.1145/146370.146381

Flocchini, P., Kranakis, E., Krizanc, D., Luccio, F. L., & Santoro, N. (2004). Sorting and election in anonymous asynchronous rings. *Journal of Parallel and Distributed Computing*, *64*, 254–265. doi:10.1016/j.jpdc.2003.11.007

Franks, N.R., & Ssendova-Franks. (1992). Brood sorting by ants: distributing the workload over the work-surface. *Behavioral Ecology and Sociobiology*, *30*(2), 109–123. doi:10.1007/BF00173947

Fukś, H. (1997). Solution of the density classification problem with two cellular automata rules. *Physical Review E: Statistical Physics, Plasmas, Fluids, and Related Interdisciplinary Topics*, *55*(3), 2081–2084. doi:10.1103/PhysRevE.55.R2081

Gerstel, O., & Zaks. (1997). The bit complexity of distributed sorting. *Algorithmica*, *18*, 405–416. doi:10.1007/PL00009163

Goldberg, D. (1989). *Genetic Algorithms in Search, Optimization & Machine Learning*. Reading, MA: Addison-Wesley.

Gonzaga de Sa, P., & Maes, C. (1992). The Gacs-Kurdyumov-Levin automaton revisited. *Journal of Statistical Physics*, *67*(3-4), 507–522. doi:10.1007/BF01049718

Gordillo, J. L., & Luna, J. V. (1994). Parallel sort on a linear array of cellular automata. In *Proceedings of International Conference on Systems, Man and Cybernetics* (Vol. 2, pp. 1903-1907). San Antonio, TX: Academic Press.

Gruber, H., Holzer, M., & Ruepp, O. (2007). Sorting the slow way: an analysis of perversely awful randomized sorting algorithms. In *Proceedings of 4th International Conference on Fun with Algorithms* (pp. 183-197). Castiglioncello, Italy: Springer.

Gu, Y., Wu, C. Q., Liu, X., & Yu, D. (2013). Distributed Throughput Optimization for Large-Scale Scientific Workflows Under Fault-Tolerance Constraint. *Journal of Grid Computing*, *11*, 361–379. doi:10.1007/s10723-013-9266-3

Handl, J., & Meyer. (2008). Ant-based and swarm-based clustering. *Swarm Intelligence*, *1*(2), 95–113. doi:10.1007/s11721-007-0008-7

Hassan, S.A., & Ingram. (2010). Modeling of a Cooperative One-Dimensional Multi-Hop Network using Quasi-Stationary Markov Chains. In *Proceedings of IEEE Global Telecommunication Conference* (pp. 1-5). Miami, FL: IEEE.

Hassin, Y., & Peleg. (2001). Distributed Probabilistic Polling and Applications to Proportionate Agreement. *Information and Computation*, *171*, 248–268. doi:10.1006/inco.2001.3088

He, J., & Yao. (2001). Drift analysis and average time complexity of evolutionary algorithms. *Artificial Intelligence*, *127*, 57–85. doi:10.1016/S0004-3702(01)00058-3

Hofstee, H.P., Martin, & van de Snepscheut. (1990). Distributed sorting. *Science of Computer Programming*, *15*(2-3), 119–133. doi:10.1016/0167-6423(90)90081-N

Israeli, A., & Jalfon, M. (1993). Uniform Self-Stabilizing Ring Orientation. *Information and Computation*, *104*(2-3), 175–196. doi:10.1006/inco.1993.1029

Kalles, D., & Papagelis. (2001). Breeding decision trees using evolutionary techniques. In *Proceedings of the International Conference on Machine Learning* (pp. 393-400). Williamstown, MA: Academic Press.

Kalles, D., Mperoukli, V., & Papanderadis, A.-C. (2012). Emerge-Sort: Swarm Intelligence Sorting. In *Proceedings of Panhellenic Conference on Artificial Intelligence* (pp. 98-105). Lamia, Greece: Springer.

Kempe, D., Dobra, A., & Gehrke, J. (2003). Gossip-based computation of aggregate information. In *Proceedings of IEEE Conference on Foundations of Computer Science* (pp. 482-491). Cambridge, MA: IEEE.

Knuth, D. E. (1973). The Art of Computer Programming: Vol. 3. *Sorting and Searching*. Reading, MA: Addison-Wesley.

Koza, J. R. (1991). Concept formation and decision tree induction using the genetic programming paradigm. In *Parallel problem solving from nature*. Springer Verlag. doi:10.1007/BFb0029742

Kuntz, P. Layzell, & Snyers. (1997). A colony of ant-like agents for partitioning in VLSI technology. In *Proceedings of the 4th European Conference on Artificial Life* (pp. 417-424). Brighton, UK: MIT Press.

Land, M., & Belew. (1995). No Perfect Two-State Cellular Automata for Density Classification Exists. *Physical Review Letters*, *74*(25), 5148–5150. doi:10.1103/PhysRevLett.74.5148 PMID:10058695

Loui, M. C. (1984). The complexity of sorting on distributed systems. *Information and Control*, *60*, 70–85. doi:10.1016/S0019-9958(84)80022-4

Manilla, H. (1985). Measures of presortedness and optimal sorting algorithms. *IEEE Transactions on Computers*, *34*(4), 318–325. doi:10.1109/TC.1985.5009382

Mitchell, M. (2006). Network thinking. *Artificial Intelligence*, *170*, 1194–1212. doi:10.1016/j.artint.2006.10.002

Mitchell, M., Hraber, P. T., & Crutchfield, J. P. (1993). Revisiting the edge of chaos: Evolving cellular automata to perform computations. *Complex Systems*, *7*, 89–130.

Mustafa, N.H., & Pekeč. (2001). Majority consensus and the local majority rule. In *Proceedings of International Colloquium on Automata, Languages and Programming* (pp. 530–542). Crete, Greece: Springer.

Prasath, R. (2010). Algorithms for Distributed Sorting and Prefix Computation in Static Ad Hoc Mobile Networks. In *Proceedings of International Conference on Electronics and Information Engineering* (Vol. 2, pp. 144-148). Kyoto, Japan: Academic Press.

Ross, S. (2002). The Spreadsort High-performance General-case Sorting Algorithm. In *Proceedings of the International Conference on Parallel and Distributed Processing Techniques and Applications* (Vol. 3, pp. 1100-1106). Las Vegas, NV: CSREA Press.

Roughgarden, T. (2003). The Price of Anarchy is Independent of the Network Topology. *Journal of Computer and System Sciences*, *67*(2), 341–364. doi:10.1016/S0022-0000(03)00044-8

Sasaki, A. (2002). A time-optimal distributed sorting algorithm on a line network. *Information Processing Letters*, *83*(1), 21–26. doi:10.1016/S0020-0190(01)00307-6

Sauerwald, T. (2008). *Randomized Protocols for Information Dissemination*. (PhD Thesis). University of Paderborn.

Scharnow, J., Tinnenfeld, & Wegener. (2004). The Analysis of Evolutionary Algorithms on Sorting and Shortest Paths Problems. *Journal of Mathematical Modelling and Algorithms*, *3*, 349–366. doi:10.1023/B:JMMA.0000049379.14872.f5

Van Doorn, E. A., & Pollett. (2009). Quasi-Stationary Distributions for Reducible Absorbing Markov Chains in Discrete Time. *Markov Processes and Related Fields*, *15*, 191–204.

Wilson, S. W. (1986). *Classifier system learning of a boolean function*. Cambridge, MA: Rowland Institute for Science.

KEY TERMS AND DEFINITIONS

Adaptive Sorting: A sorting algorithm that exploits regularities or unusual distributions in the sequence to be sorted.

Genetic Algorithm: A randomized search technique whereby candidate solutions are competitively evaluated against each other, with the best ones proceeding to a next round of competitive evaluation, allowing for candidate solutions to exchange parts among themselves and to mutate themselves in order to avoid local maxima/minima, until a best solution is pronounced after a number of rounds (generations).

Grid Computing: The infrastructure and services associated with the operation of heterogeneous, distributed computing systems that are primarily targeted at CPU intensive applications which admit parallelism.

Markov Process: A process described by a collection of random variables, whereby the current state suffices for one to predict possible future states, without having to revert to earlier history.

Swarm Intelligence: The collective behavior of individuals, which may act in a distributed, decentralized fashion, with limited knowledge of their peers, and which still manage to demonstrate some progress towards a grander goal that the individuals themselves may be unaware of.

ENDNOTES

[1]   http://wiki.hellasgrid.gr/wiki/bin/view/HellasGrid/GOC/WS-PGRADEUserGuide

APPENDIX: 3-LONG NEIGHBORHOODS AND ALTERNATING RUNS

Let a triple contains numbers a, b, c with $a < b < c$ and let its neighboring numbers be x and z, with $x < z$. Assuming a global sorting direction bias of A, we present in Table 10 all possible enumerations of the possible orderings of $\{x, z, a, b, c\}$, before and after local ordering, alongside with the corresponding measure of alternating runs. To facilitate reading we use actual numbers as follows: $a = 10$, $b = 15$, $c = 20$. We also select specific values for x, z to lie in all possible places outside and within the $[a..c]$ range. It turns out that half of the enumerated alternatives result in the number of alternating runs of the triple's extended neighborhood decreasing by 1 or 2. The rest result in that number staying the same. Since this local sorting does not affect what happens to the left or to the right of the triple's extended neighborhood, it also follows that the overall sequence's number of alternating runs also decreases by at least 1, or it stays the same; each with a probability of ½. These alternatives do not depend on the particular values we use in the example but on the relevant order of any such numbers; as all possible orders have been enumerated, the ½ probability on the modification of the number of alternating runs is a direct consequence of all possible orders being equiprobable (this is not too strong an assumption).

Table 10. Sequence snapshots before and after local sorting (alternating runs shown in parentheses)

Relative Order	BEFORE Sorting	AFTER Sorting
$x < a, z > c$	30 **10 20 15** 5 (3)	30 **10 15 20** 5 (3)
	5 **10 20 15** 30 (3)	5 **10 15 20** 30 (1)
$z < a$	1 **10 20 15** 2 (2)	1 **10 15 20** 2 (2)
	2 **10 20 15** 1 (2)	2 **10 15 20** 1 (2)
$x > c$	40 **10 20 15** 50 (4)	40 **10 15 20** 50 (2)
	50 **10 20 15** 40 (4)	50 **10 15 20** 40 (2)
$x < a, a < z < b$	5 **10 20 15** 12 (2)	5 **10 15 20** 12 (2)
	12 **10 20 15** 5 (3)	12 **10 15 20** 5 (3)
$x < a, b < z < c$	5 **10 20 15** 17 (3)	5 **10 15 20** 17 (2)
	17 **10 20 15** 5 (3)	17 **10 15 20** 5 (3)
$a < x < b, z > c$	12 **10 20 15** 30 (4)	12 **10 15 20** 30 (2)
	30 **10 20 15** 12 (3)	30 **10 15 20** 12 (3)
$b < x < c, z > c$	17 **10 20 15** 30 (4)	17 **10 15 20** 30 (2)
	30 **10 20 15** 17 (4)	30 **10 15 20** 17 (3)
$a < x < b, b < z < c$	12 **10 20 15** 17 (4)	12 **10 15 20** 17 (3)
	17 **10 20 15** 12 (3)	17 **10 15 20** 12 (3)

Chapter 13
Application of Biologically Inspired Techniques for Industrial and Environmental Research via Air Quality Monitoring Network

Tianxing Cai
Lamar University, USA

ABSTRACT

Industrial and environmental research will always involve the study of the cause-effect relationship between the emissions and the surrounding environment. Qualitative and mixed methods researchers have employed a variety of Information and Communication Technology (ICT) tools, simulated or virtual environments, information systems, information devices, and data analysis tools in this field. Machine-enhanced analytics has enabled the identification of aspects of interest such as correlations and anomalies from large datasets. Chemical facilities have high risks to originate air emission events. Based on an available air-quality monitoring network, the data integration technologies are applied to identify the scenarios of the possible emission source and the dynamic pollutant monitor result, so as to timely and effectively support diagnostic and prognostic decisions. In this chapter, the application of artificial neural networks for such applications have been developed according to the real application purpose. It includes two stages of modeling and optimization work: 1) the determination of background normal emission rates from multiple emission sources and 2) single-objective or multi-objective optimization for impact scenario identification and quantification. They have the capability to identify the potential emission profile and spatial-temporal characterization of pollutant dispersion for a specific region, including reverse estimation of the air quality issues. The methodology provides valuable information for accidental investigations and root cause analysis for an emission event; meanwhile, it helps evaluate the regional air quality impact caused by such an emission event as well. Case studies are employed to demonstrate the efficacy of the developed methodology.

DOI: 10.4018/978-1-4666-6078-6.ch013

INTRODUCTION

Biologically inspired techniques or biologically inspired algorithms is a category of algorithms that imitate the way nature performs. This category has been quite popular, since numerous problems can be solved without rigorous mathematical approaches. They have included the methodologies of artificial neural networks (ANN), genetic algorithms (GA), evolutionary algorithms (EA), particle swarm optimization (PSO), ant colony optimization (ACO), fuzzy logic (FL) and the other methods. This chapter aims to provide their potential application in the industrial and environmental research. Actually we will always involve the study of the cause-effect relationship between the emission and the surrounding environment. With the collection and representation of information in a range of ways, software tools have been created to manage and store this data. This data management enables more efficient searching ability of various types of electronic and digitized information. Various technologies have made the work of research more efficient. Biological inspired data mining techniques have been intensively used in different data mining applications such as data clustering, classification, association rules mining, sequential pattern mining, outlier detection, feature selection, and information extraction in healthcare and bioinformatics. The results of the qualitative or mixed methods research may be integrated to reach the research target. Right now, a lot of software tools are available for the analysis to identify patterns and represent new meanings. The programs extend the capabilities of the researcher in terms of information coding and meaning-making. Machine-enhanced analytics has enabled the identification of aspects of interest such as correlations and anomalies from large datasets. Industrial operations always need large amounts of chemicals and fuels in the processing of manufacturing. It have high risks to originate air emission events. Based on an available air-quality monitoring network,

the data integration technologies will be applied to identify the scenarios of the possible emission source and their impact to the environment, so as to timely and effectively support diagnostic and prognostic decisions. In this chapter, the application of biologically inspired techniques for such applications have been developed according to the real application purpose. They will have the capability to identify the potential emission profile and spatial-temporal characterization of pollutant dispersion for a specific region, including reversely estimation of the air quality issues. It provides valuable information for accidental investigations and root cause analysis for an emission event; meanwhile, it helps evaluate the regional air quality impact caused by such an emission event as well. Case studies are employed to demonstrate the efficacy of the developed methodology.

BACKGROUND

Biological inspired data mining techniques have been intensively used in different data mining applications such as data clustering, classification, association rules mining, sequential pattern mining, outlier detection, feature selection, and information extraction in healthcare and bioinformatics. The techniques include neural networks, fuzzy logic system, genetic algorithms, ant colony optimization, particle swarm optimization, artificial immune system, culture algorithm, social evolution, and artificial bee colony optimization. A huge increase in the number of papers and citations in the area has been observed in the previous decade, which is clear evidence of the popularity of these techniques. These have included the adoption of such kind of methodologies in the research field of polarization-difference imaging for observation through scattering media (Rowe, Pugh, Tyo, & Engheta, 1995), biologically inspired self-adaptive multi-path routing in overlay networks (Leibnitz, Wakamiya, & Murata, 2006), a biologically inspired system for action recognition

(Jhuang, Serre, Wolf, & Poggio, 2007), programmable self-assembly using biologically-inspired multiagent control (Nagpal, 2007), biologically inspired growth of hydroxyapatite nanocrystals inside self-assembled collagen fibers (Roveri, Falini, Sidoti, Tampieri, Landi, Sandri, & Parma, 2003), biologically inspired cognitive radio engine model utilizing distributed genetic algorithms for secure and robust wireless communications and networking (Rieser, 2004), biomimetics of biologically inspired technologies (Bar-Cohen, 2005), biologically inspired computing (DeCastro & von Zuben, 2005), and biologically inspired algorithms for financial modeling (Brabazon & O'Neill, 2006). Before we start to give the introduction of these techniques in the research field of industrial operation and environment sustainability, the brief introduction will be given for these techniques.

1. Artificial Neural Networks

In computer science and related fields, artificial neural networks are models are derived from animal central nervous systems (Wang & Fu, 2008). The biologically neural networks are capable of machine learning and pattern recognition. They can be regarded as systems of internally connected neurons. They can compute values from inputs by feeding information through the network (Stevens & Casillas, 2006). For example, in a neural network for image recognition, a set of input neurons may be activated by the pixels of an input image representing a shape or color. The activations of these neurons are then passed on, weighted and transformed by some function determined by the network's designer, to other neurons, etc., until finally an output neuron is activated that determines which image was recognized. Similar with other methods of machine learning, neural networks have been applied to solve a wide range of jobs which are difficult to solve using ordinary rule-based programming (Yang & Zhang, 2009). Generally, artificial neural network handles a problem with the combination of simple processing

elements which have complex global behavior. A class of statistical models will be called "neural" if they have sets of adaptive weights (numerical parameters that are tuned by a learning algorithm, and are capable of approximating non-linear functions of their inputs) (Patterson, 1998).

The adaptive weights are conceptually connection strengths between neurons. They will be activated during the period of model training and prediction. Neural networks can also perform functions collectively and in parallel by the units, which are also similar to biological neural networks. The terminology of neural network usually means the model with the integration of statistics, cognitive psychology and artificial intelligence (Sarle, 1994). They are part of theoretical neuroscience and computational neuroscience. In modern software implementations of artificial neural networks, the approach inspired by biology has been largely abandoned according to statistics and signal processing (Holler, Tam, Castro, & Benson, 1989). In some of these systems, neural networks or parts of neural networks can form components in larger systems that combine both adaptive and non-adaptive elements (Cochocki & Unbehauen, 1993). The general approach of such systems is feasible for real-world problem solving while it has been different from the traditional artificial intelligence connectionist models, which adopt the principles of non-linear, distributed, parallel and local processing and adaptation.

2. Fuzzy Logic System

Fuzzy logic is a logic form of multiple values. It helps to handle the problems which are not fixed and exact. Compared to traditional binary variables, fuzzy logic variables may have a truth value that ranges in degree between 0 and 1. It can be regarded as the concept of partial truth, where the truth value may range between completely true and completely false (Perfilieva & Mockor, 1999). The term "fuzzy logic" was introduced with the proposal of fuzzy set theory by Lotfi

A. Zadeh (2003; 1965). It has been applied in many fields of control theory and artificial intelligence. A basic application might characterize subranges of a continuous variable. For instance, a temperature measurement for anti-lock brakes might have several separate membership functions defining particular temperature ranges needed to control the brakes properly. Each function maps the same temperature value to a truth value in the 0 to 1 range. These truth values can then be used to determine how the brakes should be controlled.

3. Genetic Algorithms

In the field of artificial intelligence, a genetic algorithm (GA) is a search heuristic with the process of natural selection. This heuristic is normally used to generate useful solutions to optimization and search problems. Genetic algorithms is one of the algorithm of evolutionary algorithms (EA) (Whitley, 1994). The evolutionary algorithm applies the evolution techniques of inheritance, mutation, selection, and crossover to generate solutions to optimization problems. It can be used in bioinformatics, computational science, engineering, economics, manufacturing, mathematics, physics, chemistry, and other fields (Goldberg & Holland, 1988). In a genetic algorithm, a population of candidate solutions to an optimization problem is evolved to better generations of solutions. Each candidate solution has a set of properties of chromosomes which can be mutated and altered. The procedures usually start from a population of randomly generated individuals. Then the iterative process will provide a new generation of population in each iteration (Vose, 1999). The fitness of every individual in the population is evaluated in each generation. It is usually the value of the objective function in the optimization problem being minimized or maximized. The more fit individuals are selected from the current population, and each individual's genome is changed through recombination and possibly randomly mutation to form a new generation. The new generation of

candidate solutions is then used in the next iteration of the algorithm. Commonly, the algorithm terminates when either a maximum number of generations has been produced, or a satisfactory fitness level has been reached for the population. A typical genetic algorithm requires: a genetic representation of the solution domain, a fitness function to evaluate the solution domain. A standard representation of each candidate solution is as an array of bits. The main property that makes these genetic representations convenient is that their parts are easily aligned due to their fixed size, which facilitates simple crossover operations. Variable length representations may also be used, but crossover implementation is more complex in this case. Tree-like representations are explored in genetic programming and graph-form representations are explored in evolutionary programming; a mix of both linear chromosomes and trees is explored in gene expression programming. When the genetic representation and the fitness function are defined, a GA proceeds to initialize a population of solutions and then to improve it through repetitive application of the mutation, crossover, inversion and selection operators. Initially many individual solutions are randomly generated to form an initial population. The population size is based on the nature of the problem, but typically contains thousands of possible solutions. Normally, the population is generated randomly in order to cover the entire range of possible solutions in the searching space. During each successive generation, a proportion of the existing population is selected to breed a new generation. Individual solutions are selected through a fitness-based process, where fitter solutions are typically more likely to be selected. The selection methods help to rate the fitness of each solution and select the best solutions. The next step is to generate a second generation population of solutions from those selected through genetic operators: crossover and/or mutation. For each new solution to be produced, a pair of parent solutions is selected for breeding from the previously selected pool. By producing a "child" solution using the above methods of crossover and mutation, a new solution is created which typically shares many of the characteristics of its "parents". New parents are selected for each new child, and the process continues until a new population of solutions of appropriate size is generated. These processes ultimately result in the next generation population of chromosomes that is different from the initial generation. Generally the average fitness will have increased by this procedure for the population, since only the best organisms from the first generation are selected for breeding, along with a small proportion of less fit solutions. These less fit solutions ensure genetic diversity within the genetic pool of the parents and therefore ensure the genetic diversity of the subsequent generation of children. The attention should be paid to the tuning parameters such as the mutation probability, crossover probability and population size to find reasonable settings for the problem solving. There are theoretical but not yet practical upper and lower bounds for these parameters that can help guide selection through experiments. This above introduced processes are repeated until a termination condition has been reached. Common terminating conditions are the achievement of the identification of solution to satisfy criteria, fixed number of generations, allocated budget of computation time and the highest ranking solution's fitness (Deb, 2001).

4. Ant Colony Optimization

The ant colony optimization algorithm (ACO) is a probabilistic technique for solving computational problems which can be reduced to finding good paths through graphs (Dorigo & Birattari, 2010). This algorithm is one of the ant colony algorithms family of swarm intelligence methods and some meta-heuristic optimizations (Dorigo, 2007). Ant colony optimization algorithms have been applied to many combinatorial optimization problems, ranging from quadratic assignment to

protein folding or routing vehicles and a lot of derived methods have been adapted to dynamic problems in real variables, stochastic problems, multi-targets and parallel implementations. It has also been used to produce near-optimal solutions to the travelling salesman problem (Dorigo, 2006). They have an advantage over simulated annealing and genetic algorithm approaches of similar problems when the graph may change dynamically; the ant colony algorithm can be run continuously and adapt to changes in real time. This is of interest in network routing and urban transportation systems (Dorigo, 2006).

5. Particle Swarm Optimization

Particle swarm optimization (PSO) helps to optimize a problem by iteratively trying to improve a candidate solution with regard to a given measure of quality (Kennedy, 2010). PSO optimizes a problem by having a population of candidate solutions of dubbed particles and moving these particles around in the search-space according to simple mathematical formulae over the particle's position and velocity (Kennedy, 2010; Poli, Kennedy, & Blackwell, 2007). Each particle's movement is determined by its local best known position and guided toward the best known positions in the search-space. They are updated as better positions found by other particles. PSO is a meta-heuristic due to its characterization with few or no assumptions about the problem being optimized and can search very large spaces of candidate solutions. However, meta-heuristics such as PSO do not guarantee an optimal solution is ever found. More specifically, PSO does not use the gradient of the problem being optimized, which means PSO does not require that the optimization problem be differentiable as is required by classic optimization methods such as gradient descent and quasi-Newton methods (Vent & Sobieszczanski-Sobieski, 2003). A basic variant of the PSO algorithm works by having a population (called a swarm) of candidate solutions (called particles). These particles are moved around in the search-space according to a few simple formulae (Clerc, 2006). The movements of the particles are guided by their own best known position in the search-space as well as the entire swarm's best known position. When improved positions are being discovered these will then come to guide the movements of the swarm. The process is repeated and by doing so it is hoped, but not guaranteed, that a satisfactory solution will eventually be discovered. PSO has also been applied to multi-objective problems, in which the objective function comparison takes Pareto dominance into account when moving the PSO particles and non-dominated solutions are stored so as to approximate the Pareto front (Lazinica, 2009).

6. Artificial Immune System

Artificial immune systems (AIS) are a class of computationally intelligent systems inspired by the principles and processes of the vertebrate immune system. The algorithms typically exploit the immune system's characteristics of learning and memory to solve a problem. The field of Artificial Immune Systems (AIS) is concerned with abstracting the structure and function of the immune system to computational systems, and investigating the application of these systems towards solving computational problems from mathematics, engineering, and information technology. AIS is a sub-field of Biologically-inspired computing, and Natural computation, with interests in Machine Learning and belonging to the broader field of Artificial Intelligence. Artificial Immune Systems (AIS) are adaptive systems, inspired by theoretical immunology and observed immune functions, principles and models, which are applied to problem solving. AIS is distinct from computational immunology and theoretical biology that are concerned with simulating immunology using computational and mathematical models towards better understanding the immune system, although such models initiated the field

of AIS and continue to provide a fertile ground for inspiration. Finally, the field of AIS is not concerned with the investigation of the immune system as a substrate computation, such as DNA computing. The common techniques are inspired by specific immunological theories that explain the function and behavior of the mammalian adaptive immune system (Hofmeyr & Forrest, 2000; Timmis, Neal, & Hunt, 2000; Timmis & Neal, 2001; DasGupta, 1999; Coello & Coetes, 2005; Lei, 2002; Coello & Cortes, 2002).

Clonal Selection Algorithm: A class of algorithms inspired by the clonal selection theory of acquired immunity that explains how B and T lymphocytes improve their response to antigens over time called affinity maturation. These algorithms focus on the Darwinian attributes of the theory where selection is inspired by the affinity of antigen-antibody interactions, reproduction is inspired by cell division, and variation is inspired by somatic hypermutation. Clonal selection algorithms are most commonly applied to optimization and pattern recognition domains, some of which resemble parallel hill climbing and the genetic algorithm without the recombination operator.

Negative Selection Algorithm: Inspired by the positive and negative selection processes that occur during the maturation of T cells in the thymus called T cell tolerance. Negative selection refers to the identification and deletion (apoptosis) of self-reacting cells, that is T cells that may select for and attack self tissues. This class of algorithms are typically used for classification and pattern recognition problem domains where the problem space is modeled in the complement of available knowledge. For example in the case of an anomaly detection domain the algorithm prepares a set of exemplar pattern detectors trained on normal (non-anomalous) patterns that model and detect unseen or anomalous patterns.

Immune Network Algorithms: Algorithms inspired by the idiotypic network theory proposed by Niels Kaj Jerne that describes the regulation of the immune system by anti-idiotypic antibodies (antibodies that select for other antibodies). This class of algorithms focus on the network graph structures involved where antibodies (or antibody producing cells) represent the nodes and the training algorithm involves growing or pruning edges between the nodes based on affinity (similarity in the problems representation space). Immune network algorithms have been used in clustering, data visualization, control, and optimization domains, and share properties with artificial neural networks.

Dendritic Cell Algorithms: The Dendritic Cell Algorithm (DCA) is an example of an immune inspired algorithm developed using a multi-scale approach. This algorithm is based on an abstract model of dendritic cells (DCs). The DCA is abstracted and implemented through a process of examining and modeling various aspects of DC function, from the molecular networks present within the cell to the behaviour exhibited by a population of cells as a whole. Within the DCA information is granulated at different layers, achieved through multi-scale processing (Hofmeyr & Forrest, 2000; Timmis, Neal, & Hunt, 2000; Timmis & Neal, 2001; DasGupta, 1999; Coello & Coetes, 2005; Lei, 2002; Coello & Cortes, 2002).

7. Culture Algorithm

Cultural algorithms (CA) are a branch of evolutionary computation where there is a knowledge component that is called the belief space in addition to the population component (Reynolds & Sverdlik, 1994; Reynolds, 1994). In this sense, cultural algorithms can be seen as an extension to a conventional genetic algorithm (Coello & Becerra, 2004). The belief space of a cultural algorithm is divided into distinct categories. These categories represent different domains of knowledge that the population has of the search space. The belief space is updated after each iteration by the best individuals of the population. The best individuals can be selected using a fitness function that assesses the performance of each individual in population

much like in genetic algorithms. The population component of the cultural algorithm is approximately the same as that of the genetic algorithm. Cultural algorithms require an interface between the population and belief space (Jin & Reynolds, 1999). The best individuals of the population can update the belief space via the update function. Also, the knowledge categories of the belief space can affect the population component via the influence function. The influence function can affect population by altering the genome or the actions of the individuals (Chung & Reynolds, 1996).

MOTIVATION

The operation of chemical facilities will always handle large amounts of chemicals and fuels. The manufacturing will have the risk to cause potential air emission events. The normal emissions originate from plant normal operations. They will have a large impact on the pollution concentration profile in the surrounding region. The air emission events may also be caused by severe process upsets due to planned operations such as plant scheduled start-ups or shut downs. Therefore, it is very necessary to conduct industrial and environmental research to investigate the cause-effect relationship between the emission and the surrounding environment. Chemical plant emission events can also be caused by uncontrollable and unpredictable uncertainties such as emergency shutdown, nature disaster, or terrorist attack. For example, an oil refinery at eastern Japan exploded with huge amounts of toxic emissions due to Japan's tsunami and earthquake occurred on March 11th of 2011 (NDTV, 2011). In another emission event on March 22nd of 2011, the blast of a carbide plant in Louisville, Kentucky, fired calcium carbide and produced a large amounts of inhalation hazardous gases (United States Chemical Safety Board, 2013).

The air-quality impacts from chemical plant emission events can be serious to both local communities and their surrounding environments. One of the major concerns is the exposure of acute or short-term toxicity. Release of acutely toxic contaminants, such as SO2 and chlorine, would likely be transported to a populated area and pose an immediate threat to the public health and environment quality. Generally, the plant personnel should document and report emission details in response to an emission event, so that valuable information of hazardous releasing rate, possible transportation speed and directions, and potential harmful impacts on exposed populations and ecosystems can be estimated to support responsible decision makings. Since such responsible decisions are very critical, independent supporting information such as real-time measurements from a local air-quality monitoring network is vitally needed, especially in industrial zones populated heavily by various chemical facilities.

A local air-quality monitoring network can measure and record multiple pollutant concentrations simultaneously and alarm dangerous events in a real-time fashion. Meanwhile, based on measurement data from each monitoring station, plus regional meteorological conditions during the event time period, a monitoring network could help estimate possible emission source locations or even their emission rates. This inverse characterization of abnormal emission sources is very valuable to all stake holders, including government environmental agencies, chemical plants, and residential communities.

In the bulk of previous research, inverse modeling ideas were originated by the adoption of atmospheric dispersion models, which was normally used in the forward modeling problem to determine downwind contamination concentrations with given meteorological conditions and emission rates. "Gaussian Plume Model" is an approximate analytical method for point-source emissions for calculation of air pollutant concentration in the downwind area (Bowman, 1996; Turner, Bender, Pierce, & Petersen, 1989; Griffths, 1994; Halitsky, 1989; Slade, 1986; Seinfeld, 1986; Hanna, Briggs,

& Kosker, 1982; Turner, 1979; 1994; Pasquill, 1961; 1974; Church, 1949; Goldsmith & Friberg, 1976). Even though inverse modeling methods based on Gaussian plume models have been reported (Hogan, Cooper, Wagner, & Wallstorm, 2005; Jeong, Kim, Suh, Hwang, Han, & Lee, 2005; MacKay, McKee, & Mulholland; 2006), they are generally used to estimate emission rates of point sources in an average long-time period based on measurements from multiple monitoring stations. It means their emissions are assumed under steady-state conditions and their values are treated as constants. Therefore, there is still a lack of studies on the reverse modeling for abnormal emission identifications with the consideration of dynamic emission rates of point emission sources.

Based on an available air-quality monitoring network, the data integration technologies will be applied to identify the scenarios of the possible emission source and the dynamic pollutant monitor result, so as to timely and effectively support diagnostic and prognostic decisions. Qualitative and mixed methods researchers have employed a variety of information and communication technology (ICT) tools, simulated or virtual environments, information systems, information devices and data analysis tools in this field. With the collection and representation of information in a range of ways, software tools have been created to manage and store these data. This data management enables more efficient searching ability of various types of digitized information. Various technologies have made the work of research more efficient. The results of the qualitative or mixed methods research may be integrated to reach the research target. Right now, a lot of software tools are available for the analysis to identify knowledge patterns and represent new meanings. The programs extend the capabilities of the researcher in terms of information coding and meaning-making. Machine-enhanced analytics has enabled the identification of aspects of interest such as correlations and anomalies from large datasets.

In this chapter, the application of artificial neural networks for such applications have been developed according to the real application purpose. It includes two stages of modeling and optimization work:

- The determination of background normal emission rates from multiple emission sources and
- Single-objective or multi-objective optimization for impact scenario identification and quantification.

They will have the capability to identify the potential emission profile and spatial-temporal characterization of pollutant dispersion for a specific region, including reversely estimation of the air quality issues. It provides valuable information for accidental investigations and root cause analysis for an emission event; meanwhile, it helps evaluate the regional air quality impact caused by such an emission event as well. Case studies are employed to demonstrate the efficacy of the developed methodology.

DATA SOURCE

The basic mission of the industrial and environment research with web service is to preserve and improve the air quality of our living environment. To accomplish this, we must be able to evaluate the status of the atmosphere as compared to clean air standards and historical information. The following are some of the topics associated with monitoring air pollution (United States Environment Protection Agency, 2013).

In USA, the Clean Air Act requires every state to establish a network of air monitoring stations for criteria pollutants, using criteria set by OAQPS for their location and operation. The monitoring stations in this network are called the State and Local Air Monitoring Stations (SLAMS). The states must provide OAQPS with an annual summary of monitoring results at each SLAMS monitor, and detailed results must be available to OAQPS upon request. To obtain more timely and detailed information about air quality in strategic locations across the nation, OAQPS established an additional network of monitors: the National Air Monitoring Stations (NAMS). NAMS sites, which are part of the SLAMS network, must meet more stringent monitor siting, equipment type, and quality assurance criteria. NAMS monitors also must submit detailed quarterly and annual monitoring results to OAQPS.

Between the years 1900 and 1970, the emission of six principal pollutants increased significantly. These six pollutants, also called criteria pollutants, are: particulate matter, sulfur dioxide, carbon monoxide, nitrogen dioxide, ozone, and lead. In 1970, the Clean Air Act (CAA) was signed into law. The CAA and its amendments provides the framework for all pertinent organizations to protect air quality. EPA's principal responsibilities under the CAA, as amended in 1990 include:

- Setting National Air Quality Standards (NAAQS) for pollutants considered harmful to the public health and environment;
- Ensuring the air quality standards are met or attained (in cooperation with the States) through national standards and strategies to control air emission standards from sources;
- Ensuring the sources of toxic air pollutants are well controlled;
- Monitoring the effectiveness of the program.

One way to protect and assess air quality was through the development of an Ambient Air Monitoring Program. Air quality samples are generally collected for one or more of the following purposes:

- To judge compliance with and/or progress made towards meeting ambient air quality standards.

- To activate emergency control procedures that prevent or alleviate air pollution episodes.
- To observe pollution trends throughout the region, including non-urban areas.
- To provide a data base for research evaluation of effects: urban, land-use, and transportation planning; development and evaluation of abatement strategies; and development and validation of diffusion models.

With the end use of the air quality samples as a prime consideration, the network should be designed to meet one of four basic monitoring objectives listed as follows:

- To determine highest concentrations expected to occur in the area covered by the network;
- To determine representative concentrations in areas of high population density;
- To determine the impact on ambient pollution levels of significant sources or source categories;
- To determine general background concentration levels.

These four objectives indicate the nature of the samples that the monitoring network will collect which must be representative of the spatial area being studied.

The EPA's ambient air quality monitoring program is carried out by State and local agencies and consists of three major categories of monitoring stations, State and Local Air Monitoring Stations (SLAMS), National Air Monitoring Stations (NAMS), and Special Purpose Monitoring Stations (SPMS), that measure the criteria pollutants. Additionally, a fourth category of a monitoring station, the Photochemical Assessment Monitoring Stations (PAMS), which measures ozone precursors (approximately 60 volatile hydrocarbons and carbonyl) has been required by the 1990 Amendments to the Clean Air Act.

State and Local Air Monitoring Stations (SLAMS)

The SLAMS consist of a network of ~ 4,000 monitoring stations whose size and distribution is largely determined by the needs of State and local air pollution control agencies to meet their respective State implementation plan (SIP) requirements (Figure 1).

National Air Monitoring Stations (NAMS)

The NAMS (1,080 stations) are a subset of the SLAMS network with emphasis being given to urban and multi-source areas. In effect, they are key sites under SLAMS, with emphasis on areas of maximum concentrations and high population density (Figure 2).

Special Purpose Monitoring Stations (SPMS)

Special Purpose Monitoring Stations provide for special studies needed by the State and local agencies to support State implementation plans and other air program activities. The SPMS are not permanently established and, can be adjusted easily to accommodate changing needs and priorities. The SPMS are used to supplement the fixed monitoring network as circumstances require and resources permit. If the data from SPMS are used for SIP purposes, they must meet all QA and methodology requirements for SLAMS monitoring.

Photochemical Assessment Monitoring Stations (PAMS)

A PAMS network is required in each ozone nonattainment area that is designated serious, severe,

Figure 1. State and local monitoring (SLAMS) network

Figure 2. National air monitoring (NAMS) network

or extreme. The required networks will have from two to five sites, depending on the population of the area. There will be a phase-in period of one site per year starting in 1994. The ultimate PAMS network could exceed 90 sites at the end of the 5-year phase-in period (Figure 3).

The AirData website gives you access to air quality data collected at outdoor monitors across the United States, Puerto Rico, and the U.S. Virgin Islands. The data comes primarily from the AQS (Air Quality System) database. You can choose from several ways of looking at the data:

- Download data into a file (or view it on the screen).
- Output the data into one of AirData's standard reports.
- Create graphical displays using one of the visualization tools.

Figure 3. Photochemical assessment monitoring network

- Investigate monitor locations using an interactive map.

AirData assists a wide range of people, from the concerned citizen who wants to know how many unhealthy air quality days there were in his county last year to air quality analysts in the regulatory, academic, and health research communities who need raw data.

AirData lets you display and download monitored hourly, daily, and annual concentration data, AQI data, and speciated particle pollution data. If you need data that AirData does not have (such as emissions data) please see Other Sources of Data.

There are four main parts of the AirData website: Download Data, Reports, Visualize Data, and the Interactive Map.

Download Data

This part of the website has two query tools. The first tool provides daily summary concentrations and Air Quality Index values for the criteria pollutants for each monitoring site in the location you select. The second tool provides raw data for a specific location and time for any pollutant.

Reports

This part of the website provides a way to generate customized reports based on criteria you select (pollutant, location, etc.). The About Reports page explains exactly what is in each report, including individual column descriptions.

- **Air Quality Index (AQI) Report:** This report displays a yearly summary of AQI values in a county or city (specifically a CBSA - Core Based Statistical Area) . The summary values include maximum, 90th percentile and median AQI, the count of days in each AQI category, and the count of days when the AQI could be attributed to each criteria pollutant.
- **Air Quality Statistics Report:** This report shows yearly summaries of air pollution values for a city or county. The report shows the highest values reported during

the year by all monitors in the CBSA or county. The report uses highlighted text to show values that exceed the level of an air quality standard.

- **Monitor Values Report:** This report shows a yearly summary (first through fourth maximum values, number of samples, etc.) of the measurements at individual monitors and provides descriptive information about the sites.

- **Air Quality Index Daily Values Report:** This report provides daily Air Quality Index values for the specified year and location.

Visualize Data

Sometimes "seeing" the data is the best way to understand it. AirData's visualization tools display data in unique and helpful ways.

- **AQI Plot:** Compare AQI values for multiple pollutants for a specific location and time period. This tool displays an entire year of AQI values – two pollutants at a time - and is useful for seeing how the number of unhealthy days can vary throughout the year for each pollutant.

- **Tile Plot:** Plot daily AQI values for a specific location and time period. Each square or "tile" represents one day of the year and is color-coded based on the AQI level for that day. The legend tallies the number of days in each AQI category.

- **Concentration Plot:** Generate a time series plot for a specific location and time period. This tool displays daily air quality summary statistics for the criteria pollutants by monitor. You can choose to plot all monitors in a county or CBSA, or you can select specific monitors.

- **Concentration Map:** Generate an animated series of daily concentration maps for

a specific time period. Daily air quality is displayed in terms of the Air Quality Index (AQI) for the criteria pollutants, or in concentration ranges for certain PM species like organic carbon, nitrates, and sulfates. This tool may be useful for tracking an air pollution episode like a wildfire event.

- **Ozone Exceedances:** Compare 8-hour ozone "exceedances" from this year with previous years. Comparisons are presented in three ways. The first plot shows the comparisons by MONTH. The second plot shows the comparisons by DAY (for cumulative counts). The third plot shows the comparisons by YEAR.

The Interactive Map

Use the interactive map to see where air quality monitors are located, get information about the monitor, and download data from the monitor. You can select which monitoring networks to display on the map.

There are also other sources of air data about the monitoring network files and air quality data (Table 1).

From the web service, the following information is available

Types of Data

Monitoring Data: Ambient (outdoor) concentrations of pollutants are measured at more than 4000 monitoring stations owned and operated mainly by state environmental agencies. The agencies send hourly or daily measurements of pollutant concentrations to EPA's database called AQS (Air Quality System). AirData retrieves data from AQS.

Emissions Data: EPA keeps track of the amount of pollution that comes from a variety of sources such as vehicles, power plants, and industries. The emissions data reported to EPA by state environmental agencies can be an actual reading taken at a source or an estimate made us-

Table 1. Summary table of data source website

Name	Type of Data
AirNow	Air quality forecasts and real-time data in a visual format for public health protection
AirCompare	AQI summaries for comparison of counties
AirTrends	Trends of air quality and emissions
Air Emission Sources	Emissions - national, state, and county-level summaries for criteria pollutant emissions
The National Emissions Inventory	Emissions - a comprehensive and detailed estimate of air emissions of both Criteria and Hazardous air pollutants from all air emissions sources
AQS Data Mart	Monitored ambient air quality data from AQS; for those who need large volumes of data
AQS Data Page	The most requested data from the Air Quality System (AQS) are posted on this web page
CASTNET	The Clean Air Status and Trends Network (CASTNET) is the nation's primary source for data on dry acidic deposition and rural, ground-level ozone
Remote Sensing Information Gateway (RSIG)	Air quality monitoring, modeling, and satellite data
Radiation Monitoring Data	Air quality and emissions; Links to databases and maps
EPA Data Finder	Air, Water, other EPA data
Visibility Information Exchange Web System (VIEWS)	Air quality monitoring, modeling, emissions, and satellite data
DataFed	Air quality monitoring, modeling, emissions, and satellite data
Data.Gov	Air, Water, other U.S. Federal Executive Branch datasets

ing a mathematical calculation. AirData does not contain emissions data at this time. Emissions data can be obtained from the Air Emissions Sources website (for general summaries) and the NEI browser (for detailed reports).

Types of Air Pollutants

Criteria Air Pollutants: EPA sets national air quality standards for six common pollutants, also called criteria pollutants, to protect public health. Monitoring sites report data to EPA for these six criteria air pollutants:

- Ozone (O3)
- Particulate matter (PM10 and PM2.5)
- Carbon monoxide (CO)
- Nitrogen dioxide (NO2)
- Sulfur dioxide (SO2)
- Lead (Pb)

(PM10 includes particles less than or equal to 10 micrometers in diameter. PM2.5 includes particles less than or equal to 2.5 micrometers and is also called fine particle pollution.)

Hazardous Air Pollutants (HAPs) / Toxic Air Pollutants: Hazardous air pollutants (HAPs) (also called toxic air pollutants or air toxics) are pollutants that are known or suspected to cause serious health problems such as cancer. There are 188 hazardous air pollutants. Examples of toxic air pollutants include benzene, which is found in gasoline; perchlorethlyene, which is emitted from some dry cleaning facilities; and methylene chloride, which is used as a solvent and paint stripper. Examples of other listed air toxics include dioxin, asbestos, toluene, and metals such as cadmium, mercury, chromium, and lead compounds. The National-Scale Air Toxics Assessment (NATA) is EPA's ongoing comprehensive evaluation of air toxics in the U.S.

The AQI (Air Quality Index)

AirData uses the Air Quality Index (AQI) in some of its reports and tables and to display data using the visualization tools. The AQI is an index for reporting daily air quality. It tells how clean or polluted the air is, and what associated health effects might be a concern, especially for ground-level ozone and particle pollution.

Think of the AQI as a yardstick that runs from 0 to 500. The higher the AQI value, the greater the level of air pollution and the greater the health concern. For example, an AQI value of 50 represents good air quality with little potential to affect public health, while an AQI value over 300 represents hazardous air quality.

An AQI value of 100 generally corresponds to the national air quality standard for the pollutant, which is the level EPA has set to protect public health. AQI values below 100 are generally thought of as satisfactory. When AQI values are above 100, air quality is considered to be unhealthy-at first for certain sensitive groups of people, then for everyone as AQI values get higher. The AQI is divided into six categories(Good, Moderate, Unhealthy for Sensitive Groups, Unhealthy, Very Unhealthy, Hazardous). Each category corresponds to a different level of health concern. The six levels of health concern and what they mean are:

- "Good" AQI is 0 - 50. Air quality is considered satisfactory, and air pollution poses little or no risk.
- "Moderate" AQI is 51 - 100. Air quality is acceptable; however, for some pollutants there may be a moderate health concern for a very small number of people. For example, people who are unusually sensitive to ozone may experience respiratory symptoms.
- "Unhealthy for Sensitive Groups" AQI is 101 - 150. Although general public is not likely to be affected at this AQI range, people with lung disease, older adults and children are at a greater risk from exposure to ozone, whereas persons with heart and lung disease, older adults and children are at greater risk from the presence of particles in the air.
- "Unhealthy" AQI is 151 - 200. Everyone may begin to experience some adverse health effects, and members of the sensitive groups may experience more serious effects.
- "Very Unhealthy" AQI is 201 - 300. This would trigger a health alert signifying that everyone may experience more serious health effects.
- "Hazardous" AQI greater than 300. This would trigger health warnings of emergency conditions. The entire population is more likely to be affected.

PROBLEM STATEMENT

Based on the aforementioned, the studied problem is to develop a systematic methodology to reversely detect the emission conditions from a list of candidates (local chemical plants) according to the abnormal air-quality measurements from an available monitoring network, so as to support diagnostic and prognostic decisions timely and effectively. The outcome of the developed methodology should provide information of emission source location, starting time, time duration, total emission amount, and dynamic emission rate and pattern from the abnormal emission sources. The methodology will firstly determine the background normal emission rates for a given list of candidate emission sources in the region. Next, an optimization model will be employed for reverse emission source detection based on abnormal air-quality measurements. For clarity, the problem statements are summarized in the following.

Assumptions:

1. An air-quality event in a region is caused by abnormal emissions from one and only one emission source based on a given list of candidate emission sources, whose abnormal emission pattern belongs to one of those shown in Table 2;

2. Each candidate emission source has a constant emission rate during its normal operational conditions;

3. Emission transportation follows Gaussian dispersion model and there is no secondary consumption or generation of the pollutant during its air transportation;

4. When the emitted pollutant reached ground through dispersion, it will be absorbed, i.e., there is no pollutant reflection from the ground during its air transportation;

5. Meteorological conditions (e.g., local wind direction and wind speed) during the considered scheduling time horizon are constant (or near constant) in the region.

Given Information:

1. Spatial locations of each emission sources and monitoring stations;

2. Emission source stack parameters, such as stack height and outlet temperature;

3. Dynamic monitoring results at each monitoring station;

4. Meteorological conditions in the studied region during the event time period.

Information to be Determined:

1. Which emission source caused the investigated pollutant concentration pattern;

2. What are the emission pattern and dynamic emission rate for the identified emission source.

GENERAL METHODOLOGY

The input parameters at the modeling stage include geographical information (locations of every possible emission source and monitoring station), meteorological condition (e.g., wind direction, speed, and atmospheric stability), measurements at each monitoring station, and emission source data (e.g., stack height, exit diameter and outlet temperature). The next step is to map locations of candidate emission sources and monitoring stations into a rectangular coordinator system (see Appendix). Then, the firs- stage modeling aims at the determination of normal emission rates from every emission source. The task is accomplished through a regression model based on Gaussian-dispersion model to minimize the sum of squared error (SSE) between the model calculated results and monitoring results from multiple monitoring stations. Since the normal emission rate of each emission source is the background emission during plant steady-state operational conditions, it is also called steady-state emission rate.

This regression model is to identify the normal emission rate for each candidate emission source by minimizing SSE between the model predicting results and the monitoring results from multiple monitoring stations at normal emission status (without emission events).

1. Objective Function

$$\varphi_1 = \min_{m_i^S} \sum_{t \in T^0} \sum_{j \in J} \left(\bar{C}_j - C_{j,t}^S \right)^2 \qquad (2)$$

where j represents the index of monitoring stations grouped by set J; T^s represents a selected steady-state time set when each emission source has a normal emission rate. T^s contains multiple time instants indexed by t. $\bar{C}_j$ and $C_{j,t}^S$ respectively represents model calculated and measured pollutant concentrations at the j-th monitoring station at time t. Equation (2) suggests the objective function is to minimize SSE between $\bar{C}_j$ and $C_{j,t}^S$.

The model calculated pollutant concentration at the j-th monitoring station $\left(\bar{C}_j\right)$ should be the cumulative of $\bar{C}_{i,j}$ from all the emission sources, which can be formulated by Equation (3).

$$\bar{C}_j = \sum_{i \in I} \bar{C}_{i,j}, \forall j \in J \qquad (3)$$

2. Dispersion Transportation Principle

Note that $\bar{C}_{i,j}$ should be calculated by the following Equation (4). It represents pollutant dispersion from emission sources to monitoring stations under the impact of meteorological conditions. The associated details of Equation (4) can be referenced in the Appendix.

$$\bar{C}_{i,j} = \frac{m_i^S\, f\left(Z_{i,j}, H_i\right)}{2U_i\, \pi\, \sigma_{Y_{i,j}}\, \sigma_{Z_{i,j}}} \exp\left[-\frac{1}{2}\left(\frac{Y_{i,j}}{\sigma_{Y_{i,j}}}\right)^2\right], \forall\ i \in I,$$
$$j \in J \qquad (4)$$

where $\bar{C}_{i,j}$ is the pollutant concentration at the j-th monitoring station caused by the emission from the i-th emission source; $Y_{i,j}$ is the projection of $d_{i,j}$ along Y direction (Here, X direction is the same as the wind direction; Y direction is horizontally perpendicular to X direction); $Z_{i,j}$ is the ground height difference between the i-th emission source to the j-th monitoring station; H_i is the

plume height above the ground for source i; $\sigma_{Y_{i,j}}$ and $\sigma_{Z_{i,j}}$ are the standard deviations of the emission plume's probability distribution function along Y and Z directions, respectively; $f(Z_{i,j}, H_i)$ is a function with respect to $Z_{i,j}$ and H_i; m_i^S represents the constant emission rate at the i-th emission source in the normal condition.

The related equations and procedures to calculate the parameters shown in Equation (4) has been included in the Gaussian dispersion model area (Pasquill, 1961 and 1974; Turner, 1979 and 1994; Hanna et al., 1982; Seinfeld, 1986; Slade, 1986; Halitsky, 1989; Griffiths, 1994; Turner et al., 1989; Bowman, 1996, pp. 47-59).

3. Artificial Neural Network Model

Among all the above mentioned techniques, one of the commonly used methodologies is artificial neural network. In computer science and related fields, artificial neural networks are models inspired by animal central nervous systems that are capable of machine learning and pattern recognition. They are usually presented as systems of interconnected "neurons" that can compute values from inputs by feeding information through the network. Like other machine learning methods, neural networks have been used to solve a wide variety of tasks that are hard to solve using ordinary rule-based programming, including computer vision and speech recognition.

Generally, it involves a network of simple processing elements exhibiting complex global behavior determined by the connections between the processing elements and element parameters. Commonly, though, a class of statistical models will be called "neural" if they

1. They consist of sets of adaptive weights, i.e. numerical parameters that are tuned by a learning algorithm, and

2.   They are capable of approximating non-
linear functions of their inputs.

The adaptive weights are conceptually connection strengths between neurons, which are
activated during training and prediction.

Neural network models in artificial intelligence
are usually referred to as artificial neural networks
(ANNs); these are essentially simple mathematical models defining a function of $f: X \rightarrow Y$ or a
distribution over X or both X and Y, but sometimes models are also intimately associated with
a particular learning algorithm or learning rule.
A common use of the phrase ANN model really
means the definition of a class of such functions
where members of the class are obtained by varying parameters, connection weights, or specifics
of the architecture such as the number of neurons
or their connectivity.

The word network in the term 'artificial neural
network' refers to the inter-connections between
the neurons in the different layers of each system.
An example system has three layers. The first layer
has input neurons, which send data via synapses
to the second layer of neurons, and then via more
synapses to the third layer of output neurons.
More complex systems will have more layers of
neurons with some having increased layers of input
neurons and output neurons. The synapses store
parameters called "weights" that manipulate the
data in the calculations.

An ANN is typically defined by three types
of parameters:

- The interconnection pattern between different layers of neurons
- The learning process for updating the
weights of the interconnections
- The activation function that converts
a neuron's weighted input to its output
activation.

To train the artificial neural network we obtain
a generalized transfer function of the values of
emission rate and the pollutant concentrations
which are normalized in the procedure of model
preparation. The normalized features were used
to give the training on the neural network with
the Lavenberg - Marquardt back propagation
algorithm. Different numbers of hidden neurons
were used and we found a good approximation
and generalization with 1000 neurons. Riva-Rocci
based measurement is used as the target values. The
measurement of the dynamic emission rate changes
is not easy because the systolic and diastolic values
are measured at different time instances. There are
total 7000 samples have participated the modeling of the artificial neural network. 70% of the
samples are training samples, which are presented
to the network during training, and the network is
adjusted according to its error. 15% of the samples
are validation samples, which are used to measure
network generalization, and to halt training when
generalization stops improving. The rest 15% of
the samples are testing samples. These have no
effect on training and so provide an independent
measure of network performance during and after
training (Figures 4, 5, and 6).

15% of the samples are validation samples,
which are used to measure network generalization, and to halt training when generalization
stops improving. The rest 15% of the samples are
testing samples. These have no effect on training
and so provide an independent measure of network
performance during and after training.

CASE STUDY

To demonstrate the efficacy of the developed
systematic methodology, two case studies including the detection of a real SO_2 emission event are
conducted.

As shown in Figure 7, the studied involves five
chemical emission sources (E1, E2, E3, E4, and
E5 represented by red dots) and four monitoring
stations (S1, S2, S3, and S4 represented by green
dots) distributed in a squared region (30 km×30

Figure 4. Percentage selection of the samples for validation and test data

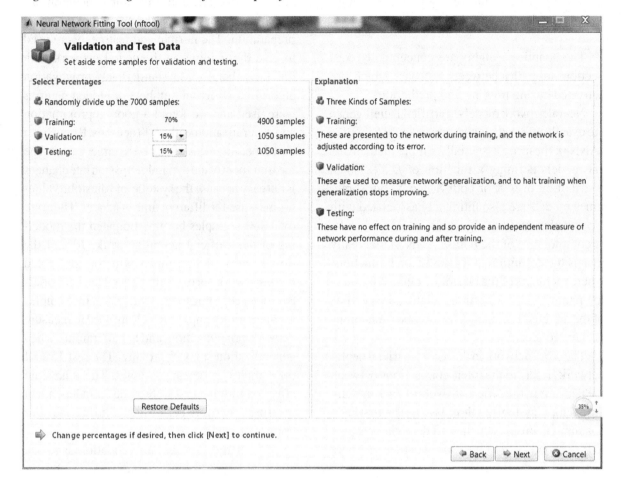

km). The entire region is gridded and the edge length of each gridded cell is 1 km. The surface wind blows from the southwest to northeast as shown in Figure 7. A common pollutant emitted from these five emission sources is monitored by the monitoring stations through hourly measurements.

The plume and stack parameters of the five emission sources are given in Table 2. During the event time period, the lapse rate was 4 K/km, the wind speed was 1.6m/s at 10-meter height, and the ambient temperature was 20 °C. For the investigation, the entire time period has been separated into two parts: steady-state time period and dynamic time period. The data in the steady-state has been applied to determine the normal emission rates for each emission source.

The modeling result for the developed artificial neural network has been plot in the Figure 8. It can be seen that the training has the R square value of 0.41802 while the validation and test has the R-square of 0.15516 and 0.13702 respectively. It can be seen that the R square value among the periods of training, validation and test are quite similar and the overall R square value has been 0.16433. This has shown that the artificial

Figure 5. Setting for the hidden neurons

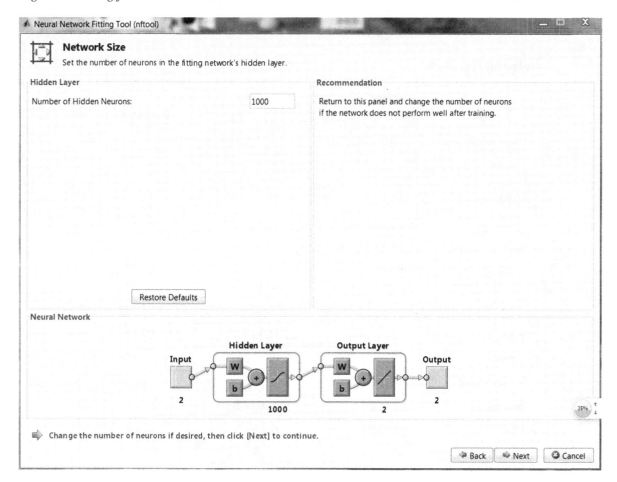

neural network model can give the quantitative identification of the normal emission rate. The results of m_1^S through m_5^S are identified as 10.8, 10.5, 10.1, 9.2, and 9.8 kg/h, respectively.

CONCLUSION

A local air-quality monitoring network has potentials to proactively identify abnormal emission events. In this chapter, a systematic methodology for simultaneous identification of a emission source and its emission rate has been developed to conduct regression for background emission rate determination and emission source identification and quantification. The case study is employed to demonstrate the efficacy of the developed methodology. This study lays out a solid foundation for multiple stake holders on diagnostic and prognostic decisions in face of an industrial air-pollution event, including government environmental agencies, regional chemical plants, and local communities. Based on an available air-quality monitoring network, the data integration technologies will be applied to identify the scenarios of the possible emission source and the dynamic pollutant monitor result, so as to timely and effectively support diagnostic and prognostic

Figure 6. Training neural network

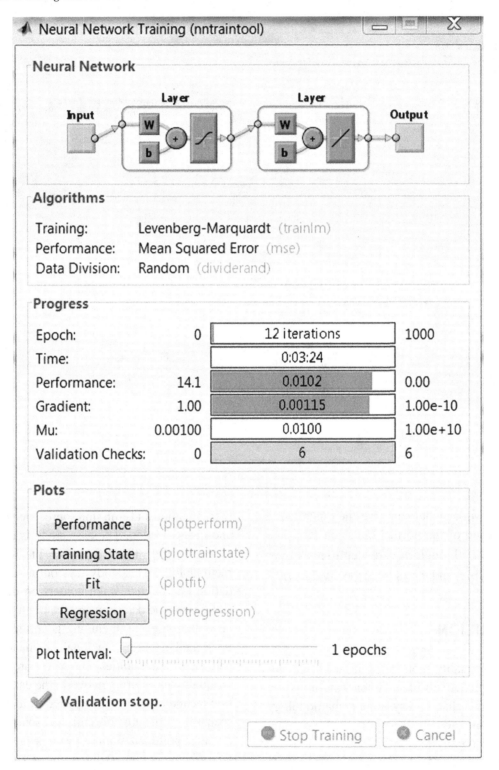

Figure 7. Spatial scope of case study

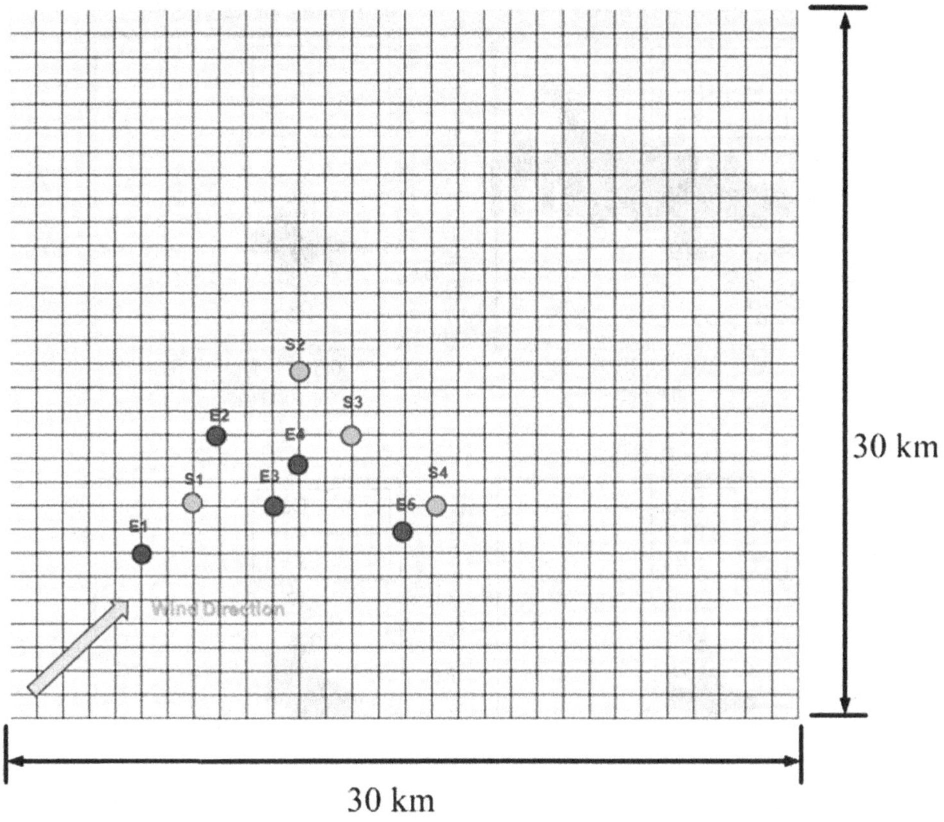

30 km

30 km

Table 2. Plume and stack parameters for each emission source

Chemical Emission Sources	E1	E2	E3	E4	E5
Stack Height H_i (m)	80	110	95	100	105
Stack Exit Temperature $T_{s,i}$ (K)	480	400	460	440	430
Stack Exit Velocity $V_{s,i}$ (m/s)	17.5	13.0	15.6	14.2	16.1
Stack Exit Diameter $D_{s,i}$ (m)	1.6	1.9	1.5	1.7	1.8

decisions. The application of artificial neural networks for such applications have been developed according to the real application purpose.

FUTURE RESEARCH DIRECTIONS

This study can not only determine emission source location, starting time, and time duration responsible for an observed emission event, but also reversely estimate the dynamic emission rate and the total emission amount from the accidental emission source. It provides valuable information for accidental investigations and root cause analysis for an emission event; meanwhile, it helps evaluate the regional air-quality impact caused by such an emission event as well. It lays out a solid foundation for multiple stake holders

Figure 8. Regression result for training, validation, and test

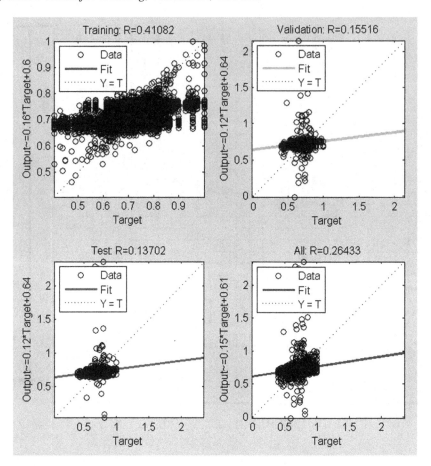

on diagnostic and prognostic decisions in face of an industrial air-pollution event, including government environmental agencies, regional chemical plants, and local communities.

It is necessary to further extend the current research to be integrated into the website service of environmental protection agency. Similar case studies and applications in using technologies and fundamental theory can be applied and demonstrated in the representative service domains with the combination of e-business services, mobile services, social networking services, cloud services, legal services, healthcare services, logistics services and educational services taking into account demands from government, organization, enterprise, community, individual, customer, and citizen.

REFERENCES

Bar-Cohen, Y. (2005). *Biomimetics: biologically inspired technologies*. Boca Raton, FL: CRC Press.

Bowman, W. A. (1996). Maximum ground level concentrations with downwash: the urban stability mode. *Journal of the Air & Waste Management Association*, *46*, 615–620. doi:10.1080/1047328 9.1996.10467495

Brabazon, A., & O'Neill, M. (2006). *Biologically inspired algorithms for financial modelling*. Berlin: Springer.

Chung, C. J., & Reynolds, R. G. (1996). A Testbed for Solving Optimization Problems Using Cultural Algorithms. In *Evolutionary Programming* (pp. 225–236). Academic Press.

Church, P. E. (1949). Dilution of Waste stack gases in the atmosphere. *Industrial & Engineering Chemistry, 41,* 2753–2756. doi:10.1021/ie50480a022

Clerc, M. (2006). *Particle swarm optimization* (Vol. 243). London: ISTE. doi:10.1002/9780470612163

Cochocki, A., & Unbehauen, R. (1993). *Neural networks for optimization and signal processing.* Hoboken, NJ: John Wiley & Sons, Inc.

Coello, C. A., & Becerra, R. L. (2004). Efficient evolutionary optimization through the use of a cultural algorithm. *Engineering Optimization, 36*(2), 219–236. doi:10.1080/03052150410001647966

Coello, C. A. C., & Cortés, N. C. (2002). An approach to solve multiobjective optimization problems based on an artificial immune system. In *Proceedings of 1st International Conference on Artificial Immune Systems (ICARIS).* ICARIS.

Coello, C. A. C., & Cortés, N. C. (2005). Solving multiobjective optimization problems using an artificial immune system. *Genetic Programming and Evolvable Machines, 6*(2), 163–190. doi:10.1007/s10710-005-6164-x

DasGupta, D. (1999). *An overview of artificial immune systems and their applications.* Berlin: Springer. doi:10.1007/978-3-642-59901-9

Deb, K. (2001). Multi-objective optimization. In *Multi-objective optimization using evolutionary algorithms* (pp. 13–46). Academic Press.

DeCastro, L. N., & von Zuben, F. J. (Eds.). (2005). *Recent developments in biologically inspired computing.* Hershey, PA: IGI Global.

Dorigo, M. (Ed.). (2006). *Ant Colony Optimization and Swarm Intelligence: 5th International Workshop, ANTS 2006,* (Vol. 4150). Springer-Verlag New York Incorporated.

Dorigo, M. (2007). Ant colony optimization. *Scholarpedia, 2*(3), 1461. doi:10.4249/scholarpedia.1461

Dorigo, M., & Birattari, M. (2010). Ant colony optimization. In Encyclopedia of Machine Learning (pp. 36-39). Springer US.

Dorigo, M., & Di Caro, G. (1999). Ant colony optimization: a new meta-heuristic. In *Proceedings of Evolutionary Computation* (Vol. 2). IEEE.

Goldberg, D. E., & Holland, J. H. (1988). Genetic algorithms and machine learning. *Machine Learning, 3*(2), 95–99. doi:10.1023/A:1022602019183

Goldsmith, J. R., & Friberg, L. T. (1976). Effects of air pollution on human health, Air Pollution. In *The Effects of Air Pollution* (Vol. 2, pp. 457–610). Academic Press.

Griffiths, R. F. (1994). Errors in the use of the Briggs parameterization for atmospheric dispersion coefficients. *Atmospheric Environment, 28*(17), 2861–2865. doi:10.1016/1352-2310(94)90086-8

Halitsky, J. (1989). A jet plume model for short stacks. *Journal of the Air Pollution Control Association, 39*(6), 856–858.

Hanna, S. R., Briggs, G. A., & Kosker, R. P. (1982). *Hand book on Atmospheric Diffusion.* NTIS. doi:10.2172/5591108

Hofmeyr, S. A., & Forrest, S. (2000). Architecture for an artificial immune system. *Evolutionary Computation, 8*(4), 443–473. doi:10.1162/106365600568257 PMID:11130924

Hogan, W. R., Cooper, G. F., Wagner, M. M., & Wallstrom, G. L. (2005). *An inverted Gaussian Plume Model for estimating the location and amount of Release of airborne agents from downwind atmospheric concentrations (RODS Technical Report)*. Pittsburgh, PA: University of Pittsburgh.

Holler, M., Tam, S., Castro, H., & Benson, R. (1989). An electrically trainable artificial neural network (etann) with 10240'floating gate'synapses. In *Proceedings of Neural Networks* (pp. 191–196). IEEE. doi:10.1109/IJCNN.1989.118698

Jeong, H. J., Kim, E. H., Suh, K. S., Hwang, W. T., Han, M. H., & Lee, H. K. (2005). Determination of the source rate released into the environment from a nuclear power plant. *Radiation Protection Dosimetry*, *113*(3), 308–313. doi:10.1093/rpd/nch460 PMID:15687109

Jhuang, H., Serre, T., Wolf, L., & Poggio, T. (2007). A biologically inspired system for action recognition. In *Proceedings of Computer Vision* (pp. 1–8). IEEE. doi:10.1109/ICCV.2007.4408988

Jin, X., & Reynolds, R. G. (1999). Using knowledge-based evolutionary computation to solve nonlinear constraint optimization problems: a cultural algorithm approach. In *Proceedings of Evolutionary Computation, 1999*. Academic Press.

Kennedy, J. (2010). Particle swarm optimization. In Encyclopedia of Machine Learning (pp. 760-766). Springer US.

Lazinica, A. (Ed.). (2009). *Particle swarm optimization*. Rijeka, Croatia: InTech. doi:10.5772/109

Lei, X. R. B. W. (2002). Artificial Immune System: Principle, Models, Analysis and Perspectives. *Chinese Journal of Computers, 12.*

Leibnitz, K., Wakamiya, N., & Murata, M. (2006). Biologically inspired self-adaptive multi-path routing in overlay networks. *Communications of the ACM*, *49*(3), 62–67. doi:10.1145/1118178.1118203

MacKay, C., McKee, S., & Mulholland, A. J. (2006). Diffusion and convection of gaseous and fine particulate from a chimney. *IMA Journal of Applied Mathematics*, *71*, 670–691. doi:10.1093/imamat/hxl016

Nagpal, R. (2002). Programmable self-assembly using biologically-inspired multiagent control. In *Proceedings of the first international joint conference on Autonomous agents and multiagent systems: part 1* (pp. 418-425). ACM.

NDTV. (2011). *Japan: Earthquake triggers oil refinery fire*. Retrieved from http://www.ndtv.com

Pasquill, F. (1961). The Estimation of the Dispersion of Windborne Material. *The Meteorological Magazine*, *90*(1063), 33–49.

Pasquill, F. (1974). *Atmospheric Diffusion* (2nd ed.). Halsted Press, John Wiley & Sons.

Patterson, D. W. (1998). *Artificial neural networks: Theory and applications*. Upper Saddle River, NJ: Prentice Hall PTR.

Perfilieva, I., & Močkoř, J. (1999). *Mathematical principles of fuzzy logic*. Berlin: Springer.

Poli, R., Kennedy, J., & Blackwell, T. (2007). Particle swarm optimization. *Swarm Intelligence*, *1*(1), 33–57. doi:10.1007/s11721-007-0002-0

Reynolds, R. G. (1994). An introduction to cultural algorithms. In *Proceedings of the third annual conference on evolutionary programming* (pp. 131-139). World Scientific.

Reynolds, R. G., & Sverdlik, W. (1994). Problem solving using cultural algorithms. In *Proceedings of Evolutionary Computation* (pp. 645–650). IEEE.

Rieser, C. J. (2004). *Biologically inspired cognitive radio engine model utilizing distributed genetic algorithms for secure and robust wireless communications and networking.* (Doctoral dissertation). Virginia Polytechnic Institute and State University, Blacksburg, VA.

Roveri, N., Falini, G., Sidoti, M. C., Tampieri, A., Landi, E., Sandri, M., & Parma, B. (2003). Biologically inspired growth of hydroxyapatite nanocrystals inside self-assembled collagen fibers. *Materials Science and Engineering C, 23*(3), 441–446. doi:10.1016/S0928-4931(02)00318-1

Rowe, M. P., Pugh, E. N. Jr, Tyo, J. S., & Engheta, N. (1995). Polarization-difference imaging: A biologically inspired technique for observation through scattering media. *Optics Letters, 20*(6), 608–610. doi:10.1364/OL.20.000608 PMID:19859271

Sarle, W. S. (1994). Neural networks and statistical models. In *Proceedings of the Nineteenth Annual SAS Users Group International Conference.* Cary, NC: SAS Institute.

Seinfeld, J. H. (1986). *Atmospheric Chemistry and Physics of Air Pollution. J.* Wiley.

Slade, D. H. (Ed.). (1986). *Meteorology and Atomic Energy. U.S.* Atomic Energy Commission, Air Resources Laboratories, Research Laboratories, Environmental Science Services Administration, U.S Department of Commerce.

Stevens, R., & Casillas, A. (2006). Artificial neural networks. In *Automated Scoring of Complex Tasks in Computer Based Testing: An Introduction.* Lawrence Erlbaum.

Timmis, J., & Neal, M. (2001). A resource limited artificial immune system for data analysis. *Knowledge-Based Systems, 14*(3), 121–130. doi:10.1016/S0950-7051(01)00088-0

Timmis, J., Neal, M., & Hunt, J. (2000). An artificial immune system for data analysis. *Bio Systems, 55*(1), 143–150. doi:10.1016/S0303-2647(99)00092-1 PMID:10745118

Turner, D. B. (1979). Atmospheric Dispersion Modeling. *Journal of the Air Pollution Control Association, 29*(5), 502–519. doi:10.1080/00022470.1979.10470821

Turner, D. B. (1994). *Workbook of Atmospheric Dispersion Estimates: An Introduction to Dispersion Modeling* (2nd ed.). Lewis Publishers.

Turner, D. B., Bender, L. W., Pierce, T. E., & Petersen, W. B. (1989). Air Quality Simulation Models from EPA. *Environmental Software, 4*(2), 52–61. doi:10.1016/0266-9838(89)90031-2

United States Chemical Safety Board. (2013). Retrieved from http://www.csb.gov

Venter, G., & Sobieszczanski-Sobieski, J. (2003). Particle swarm optimization. *AIAA Journal, 41*(8), 1583–1589. doi:10.2514/2.2111

Vose, M. D. (1999). *The simple genetic algorithm: Foundations and theory* (Vol. 12). Cambridge, MA: The MIT Press.

Wang, L., & Fu, K. (2008). *Artificial neural networks.* Hoboken, NJ: John Wiley & Sons, Inc.

Whitley, D. (1994). A genetic algorithm tutorial. *Statistics and Computing, 4*(2), 65–85. doi:10.1007/BF00175354

Yang, X., & Zheng, J. (2009). Artificial neural networks. In *Handbook of Research on Geoinformatics.* Academic Press. doi:10.4018/978-1-59140-995-3.ch016

Zadeh, L. A. (1965). Fuzzy sets. *Information and Control*, 8(3), 338–353. doi:10.1016/S0019-9958(65)90241-X

Zalta, E. N. (Ed.). (2003). *Stanford encyclopedia of philosophy*. Retrieved from http://plato.stanford.edu/

KEY TERMS AND DEFINITIONS

Ant Colony Optimization (ACO): In computer science and operations research, the ant colony optimization algorithm (ACO) is a probabilistic technique for solving computational problems which can be reduced to finding good paths through graphs.

Artificial Neural Networks (ANN): They are computational models inspired by animals' central nervous systems that are capable of machine learning and pattern recognition.

Environmental Protection: It is a practice of protecting the natural environment on individual, organizational or governmental levels, for the benefit of both the natural environment and humans.

Evolutionary Algorithm: It is a subset of evolutionary computation, a generic population-based metaheuristic optimization algorithm. It uses mechanisms inspired by biological evolution, such as reproduction, mutation, recombination, and selection.

Fuzzy Logic: It is a form of many-valued logic; it deals with reasoning that is approximate rather than fixed and exact.

Genetic Algorithm: In the computer science field of artificial intelligence, genetic algorithm (GA) is a search heuristic that mimics the process of natural selection.

Industrial Operation: It is concerned with the development, improvement, implementation and evaluation of integrated systems of people, money, knowledge, information, equipment, energy, materials, analysis and synthesis, as well as the mathematical, physical and social sciences together with the principles and methods of engineering design to specify, predict, and evaluate the results to be obtained from such systems or processes.

Particle Swarm Optimization (PSO): It is a computational method that optimizes a problem by iteratively trying to improve a candidate solution with regard to a given measure of quality.

Chapter 14
Online Prediction of Blood Glucose Levels using Genetic Algorithm

Khaled Eskaf
Arab Academy for Science, Technology and Maritime Transport, Egypt

Tim Ritchings
University of Salford, UK

Osama Bedawy
Arab Academy for Science, Technology and Maritime Transport, Egypt

ABSTRACT

Diabetes mellitus is one of the most common chronic diseases. The number of cases of diabetes in the world is likely to increase more than two fold in the next 30 years: from 115 million in 2000 to 284 million in 2030. This chapter is concerned with helping diabetic patients to manage themselves by developing a computer system that predicts their Blood Glucose Level (BGL) after 30 minutes on the basis of their current levels, so that they can administer insulin. This will enable the diabetic patient to continue living a normal daily life, as much as is possible. The prediction of BGLs based on the current levels BGLs become feasible through the advent of Continuous Glucose Monitoring (CGM) systems, which are able to sample patients' BGLs, typically 5 minutes, and computer systems that can process and analyse these samples. The approach taken in this chapter uses machine-learning techniques, specifically Genetic Algorithms (GA), to learn BGL patterns over an hour and the resulting value 30 minutes later, without questioning the patients about their food intake and activities. The GAs were invested using the raw BGLs as input and metadata derived from a Diabetic Dynamic Model of BGLs supplemented by the changes in patients' BGLs over the previous hour. The results obtained in a preliminary study including 4 virtual patients taken from the AIDA diabetes simulation software and 3 volunteers using the DexCom SEVEN system, show that the metadata approach gives more accurate predictions. Online learning, whereby new BGL patterns were incorporated into the prediction system as they were encountered, improved the results further.

DOI: 10.4018/978-1-4666-6078-6.ch014

INTRODUCTION

One of the most common medical chronic diseases is diabetes mellitus, and in 2000, the World Health Organization, stated that there were at least 171 million people worldwide suffering from diabetes, and that the number was increasing rapidly, and expected to almost double by 2030 (World Health Organization, n.d.). Diabetes is a chronic disease that occurs either when the pancreas does not provide enough insulin or leads to an uncontrolled increase in blood glucose (Type I), or the body cannot effectively use the insulin it produces, typically because of excess body weight or physical inactivity (Type II).

Diabetic patients are predisposed to many complications associated with their disease and these may results in hospitalisation, permanent disabilities, and death. These complications may be classified as acute (quick manifestation and correctable) or chronic (taking years or decades to develop). Acute complications include hypoglycemia, hyperglycemia, and diabetic ketoacidosis (DKA), while macrovascular (atherosclerosis) and microvascular (nephropathy, neuropathy, and retinopathy) diseases are the most common chronic complications.

People with diabetes have an important role in their own medical care, and self-glucose monitoring is an opportunity for people with diabetes to take control of their health and wellbeing. At present, most diabetics monitor their BGLs by sampling a drop of capillary blood, typically from the fingertip, and measuring its BGL with a blood glucose meter (Rossetti, 2008). The stages are shown in Figure 1. First, a lancet is used to prick a finger (2), drawing forth a small droplet of blood (3). The blood is then added to a strip which is either separate or built in to the glucose monitor (4), and finally the glucose monitor then gives a reading of the concentration of glucose in the blood (5).

Recently, several sensors have been developed which allow continuous glucose monitoring (CGM) for several days. These systems are noninvasive or minimally invasive, and in many cases are portable and so can allow their use in patient daily life. Although the clinical validation of some of the CGM devices is still under way, there is a general agreement that in the near future these devices will enable the tuning of appropriate changes in the daily management of diabetes in order to achieve better metabolic control (Medtronic diabetes and health care providers company, 2012) (Dexcom medical device company, 2012) (Abbott Diabetes Care Company, n.d.). A summary of the features of the four CGM systems that are FDA approved is given in Table 1. The BGL is usually shown on a display, and in one case (Dexcom SEVEN System) the BGL data can be downloaded to a PC for computer analysis.

Figure 1. Self BGL monitoring system

Table 1. Comparison of the four FDA approved continuous BGL monitoring systems (Children with Diabetes, 2006)

Companies	Guardian REAL-Time Continuous Glucose Monitoring System	Dexcom SEVEN	MiniMed Paradigm® REAL-Time System	Abbott FreeStyle Navigator®
Availability	FDA approved in June 2006 (monitor) and February 2007 (MiniLink Transmitter)	FDA approved in March, 2006	FDA approved in March of 2006	FDA approved in March of 2008
Price	$1339 for monitor, transmitter, charger, and 4 sensors $35 per sensor	$800 for receiver, case, charger, transmitter $60 per 7 day sensors	$999 in addition to initial pump cost, $35 per 3 day sensor	
Sensor Life	3 days	7 days	3 days	5 days
Insertion Device	Sens-serter, manual insertion possible	DexCom SEVEN Applicator	Sens-serter, manual insertion possible	Automatic, comes with sensor
Start-Up Initialization Time	2 hours	2 hours	2 hours	10 hours
Calibration	2 hours after insertion, within next 6 hours after first, then every 12 hours. Will alarm if calibration value not entered.	every 12 hours	2 hours after insertion, within next 6 hours after first, then every 12 hours. Will alarm if calibration value not entered.	Calibrate at 10, 12, 24 and 72 hours after insertion, no calibration for the final 2 days of the 5 day wear
Displays Glucose Numbers	Every 5 minutes	Every 5 minutes	Every 5 minutes	Every 1-2 minutes
Displays Directional Trends	Yes, 3, 6, 12, and 24 hour graphs	Yes, displays a 1, 3, or 9 hour glucose graph	Yes, 3 and 24 hour graphs	5 TRU™ Directional Glucose Arrows indicating rate and direction of change
Waterproof Transmitter	Yes, hot water not suggested	Yes, up to 3 ft for 30 min	Yes, hot water not suggested	Yes, up to 3 ft for 30 min

BACKGROUND

Earlier computer-based approaches to predict BGLs have typically applied linear (Ståhl, 2009; Mathews, 2009; Schauer, 2007) and non-linear algorithms, including Artificial Intelligent Algorithms (Kok, 2004; Tresp, 1999; Bellazzi, 2001; Andrianasy, 1997; Hackzell, 1999; Zitar, 2005; Pender, 1997; Sandham, 1998; Nikoletou, 1997; Haque, 1999; Zecchin, 2012) to patient data. These approaches tended to use mainly qualitative information provided by the diabetic, such as food intake, but some quantitative measures including BGLs and the amount of insulin intake (Tresp, 1999; Liszka, 1999; Pender, 1997;

Sandham, 1998; Nikoletou, 1998; Haque, 1999; Zecchin, 2012). These algorithms were developed predominantly using virtual patient derived from the AIDA diabetic software simulator (Diabetic Software Simulator, 2006), although a few studies used data from a single patient (Kok, 2004; Tresp, 1999). A comparative summary of projects predicting BGLs is given in Table 2.

The accuracy of each approach is usually given in term of the Root-Mean-Square-Error (RMSE) in the predicted BLGs, although some authors quote errors. Table 3, taken primarily from Kok (2004), gives the reported prediction accuracies obtained by many researchers using Artificial Neural Networks.

Table 2. Comparative summary of projects predicting BGLs

Project	Source of Data	Methodology	Processing Steps	Prediction Time	Learning Time	Type of Error Measured
Kok (Kok, 2004)	Real (one only) patient	Model based approach (ANN)	Split day time for 3 intervals	Separate prediction	77 days	RMSE (1.8 – 2.4 mmoml/l)
Tresp (Tresp,1999)	Real (one only) patient	ANN	Depends on question (patient answers)	Prediction after 15 minutes		RMSE (2.5 mmol/l)
Bellazzi (Bellazzi,2001)	Virtual patient	ANN	Dependent on patient answer (BGL-Carbohydrate intake-insulin)			Not evaluated
Andrianasy&Milgram (Andrianasy, 1997)	Virtual patient	ANN	Dependent on BG values and amount on insulin taken	Separate day to 10 interval at fixed time (not include any patient activity).		0.06-0.15 mean relative error
Liszka-Hackzell (Liszka, 1999)	Virtual patient	ANN	Dependent on patient answer (insulin dose, body mass, level of activity, level of stress)	The system is designed for specific patient	15 days	Correlative coefficient 0.76-0.33 mmol/l
Zitar(Zitar, 2005)	Real patient	ANN	Split day four interval			
Pender (Pender, 1997)	Virtual patient	ANN	Depend on patient answer	Predict the BGL after 2 hour		Average error IAIDA-ANNI (I0.25-1.18I) mmol/l
Sandham et al (Sandham, 1998)	Virtual patient	ANN	Trained NN on sets of BGL patterns	After 2 hour		Error 1.5 mmol/l
Sandham et al (Nikoletou, 1998)	Virtual patient	ANN	Depend on patient answer	After k+1 time		Average error 0.7 mmol/l
Haque (Haque, 1999)	Virtual patient	ANN	Depend on patient answer	After t+1 time	Training time 2 days	Error 12% - 24%
Chung (CJ, 2006)	Real Patient	NIR	Near infrared sensor scan patient finger			
Schauer (Schauer, 2007)	Real Patient	Linear model	Linear discrete time transfer function			
Mathews Mathews, **2008)**	Real Patients	Linear function	Depend on patient answer			
Sparacino (Sparacino, 2007)	Real Patients	AR model		After 30 minutes		
Reifman (Reifman, 2007)	Real Patient	Autoregressive model		After 30 minutes		RMSE = 22.2 mg/dl
Cinar (Cinar, 2006)	Virtual Patient	ARMA		After 30 minutes		
Stahl (Stahl, 2003)	Real Patient	Linear model		After 2 hours		1 mmol/l
Andriansy (Andrianasy, 1997)	Real patients	ANN				I real – predictedI = 27 mg/dl
Oruklu (Oruklu, 2007)	Real Patient + virtual Patient	Linear recursive algorithm				SSPE=3.792

Table 3. Reported accuracies obtained for predicting BGLs using ANNs

Project	ERROR or RMSE
Kok (Kok, 2004)	1.8 -2.4 RMSE (mmol/l)
Lehmann and Deutsch(Lehmann, 1998)	2.8-3.5 RMSE (mmol/l)
Pender (Pender, 1997)	1.18-0.25 average Error(mmol/l)
Sandham et al (Sandham, 1998)	1.5 average Error (mmol/l)
Sandham et al (Nikoletou, 1998)	0.77 mmol/l
Haque (Haque, 1999)	12% - 24% Error
Zecchin et al (Zecchin, 2012)	0.7 mmol/l
McNulty and Mauze (McNulty, 1998)	4.77-4.96 RMSEP

This study is concerned with investigating the ability of Machine Learning techniques, specifically Genetic Algorithms (GA), to predict a specific patient's blood glucose levels in the near future directly from patterns related to the BGLs over the previous hour, with no information taken from the diabetic about food intake. While the techniques that have been investigated could predict the BGLs at various times in the near future, 30minutes ahead was arbitrarily chosen since this amount of warning would permit the diabetic to take action before the BGL reached a potentially dangerous level.

The GAs were invested using the raw BGL time-series as input, and metadata derived from a Diabetic Dynamic Model of the variations in the BGLs (WU, 2005), which reflects the oscillatory nature in the BGL due to external food intake or any human daily activities, supplemented by the changes in patient's BGLs over the previous hour. The BGL data was derived for virtual patients taken from the AIDA diabetes simulation software, and three volunteers using the DexCom SEVEN CGM system.

METHODOLOGY

The general approach involved the supervised training of several GA using two different sets of input patterns related to the BGLs over an hour, with the actual BGLs 30mins later being the target output. The raw BGLs formed one pattern, while the second pattern included metadata derived from a Diabetic Dynamic Model of BGLs, supplemented by the changes in patient's BGLs over the previous hour.

The same input patterns and training/testing regimes were used for the GAs technique in order to ensure a fair comparison of the performance of GAs in this application.

The potential improvement in performance using of on-line learning, whereby patterns that gave a predicted BGL that was not within $\pm10\%$ of the actual BGL, were considered as new patterns and were incorporated into the system as they were encountered, was also investigated.

Finally, the best results achieved by the GA, with and without the on-line learning technique, are compared, with published results for BGL prediction techniques that involved knowledge of a patient's food intake.

Data Collection

Patient data was derived from two sources; virtual diabetic patients generated from the AIDA system, and volunteers using a CGM device.

AIDA is an educational simulation program of glucose-insulin interaction and insulin dosage & dietary adjustment in diabetes mellitus (Diabetic Software Simulator, n.d.). BGL data can be derived at regular intervals for a specified period of time for virtual patients. In this study data was generated for 4 virtual patients at intervals chosen to match the capabilities of the CGM device.

The CGM device that was used in this study was the DexCom SEVEN CGM system (Dexcom medical device company, 2012), which is intended for use by patients at home and in health care facilities, and is waterproof so the patient can shower or swim wearing it. The DexCom SEVEN system comprises of 3 components: a tiny, flexible, platinum wire-based Sensor that goes just under the skin to read glucose levels, and is attached to the skin by a small, adhesive patch; a small and lightweight water-resistant Transmitter that snaps into the Sensor to form a small and discreet unit; and a wireless Receiver that has a large display for easy viewing, and shows the wearer's glucose level and trend. The Receiver provides easy viewing of current glucose readings and 1-, 3- and 9-hour glucose trends. The Transmitter sends information related to the current glucose levels to the Receiver every 5 minutes, and the Receiver can store up to 30 days of data. A total of 3 volunteers, 2 of whom were diabetics, used this system and led a normal life during the recordings, and were not subjected to any prescribed regimen such as restricted exercise or fixed meal times or sizes.

Diabetic Dynamic Model

The model used to derive metadata for the prediction algorithms was based on the Dynamic Damping Model proposed by Wu [21]; the rational being that the post-prandial blood glucose excursion could be considered as a hormone regulated resilient system, with the food intake being treated as a bolus injection of glucose. This model is depicted in Figure 2, where the impulse Force, F(t), represents the bolus injection of glucose, and the Damping Factor, β, reflects the combined effects of exercises and hypoglycemic medication.

Using this model, the BGLs over the baseline at time t, x(t), can be described by the standard the differential equation of a damped oscillatory system:

$$F\left(t\right) = \frac{d^2x}{dt^2} + \beta\frac{dx}{dt} + \omega_0^2 x \tag{1}$$

where ω_0 is the system's natural frequency [20]. If F(t) takes the form of the Dirac delta function at t=0, the solution of Equation 1 is

$$x\left(t\right) = \frac{F}{\omega}e^{-\beta t/2}\sin\omega t \tag{2}$$

Figure 2. Diabetic dynamic model

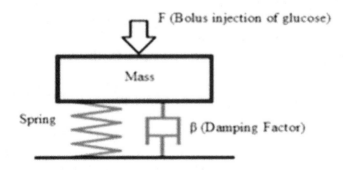

where

$$\omega = \sqrt{\omega_0^2 - \left(\frac{\beta}{2}\right)^2} \qquad (3)$$

is the frequency of the system at time t.

As, ω and ω_0 can be derived directly from the short-term and long-term variations in the diabetic's BGLs, the Damping Factor can be calculated from Equation 3 as

$$\beta = 2 * \sqrt{{\omega_0}^2 + \omega^2} \qquad (4)$$

(ω_0 is always greater than ω when F(t) takes the form of the Dirac delta function), and then the bolus injection of glucose from Equation 2

$$F(t) = \frac{X(t) * \omega}{e^{-\beta t/2} * \sin \omega t} \qquad (5)$$

It should be noted that while the metadata, F and β, are of interest because of their tangible nature, and depend to some extent on the diabetic's activities, they do not require direct input from the diabetic, such as the amount of carbohydrates eaten.

Data Preprocessing

In this study, blood glucose measurements were generated from the AIDA system or using the DexCom system every 5 minutes for 24 hours over 7 days. The Discrete Fourier Transform (DFT) was applied to the whole dataset to derive ω_0. This was found to correspond to the 3.27 hours that the Diabetic doctors observe the BGLs respond to food intake. The DFT was also applied to a 1-hour sliding window (12 samples) to obtain ω for that 1-hour period.

The average values of F and β for that period were then calculated. The actual 12 BGLs, x(t-55), ... x(t-5), x(t), and the value 30mins after that period, x(t+30) were also recorded. This 1-hour dataset is shown diagrammatically in Figure 3.

The full dataset comprised of 168 1-hour datasets (24*7), amounting to 2016 BGL samples.

Data Analysis

The GA used the following patterns from these 1-hour BGL datasets to train and then evaluate the prediction system:

1. The 12 BGL data over a hour, x(t-55),... x(t) as input and the predicted BGL after 30mins, $x_p(t+30)$ as the output.

Figure 3. The BGL 1-hour dataset at time t

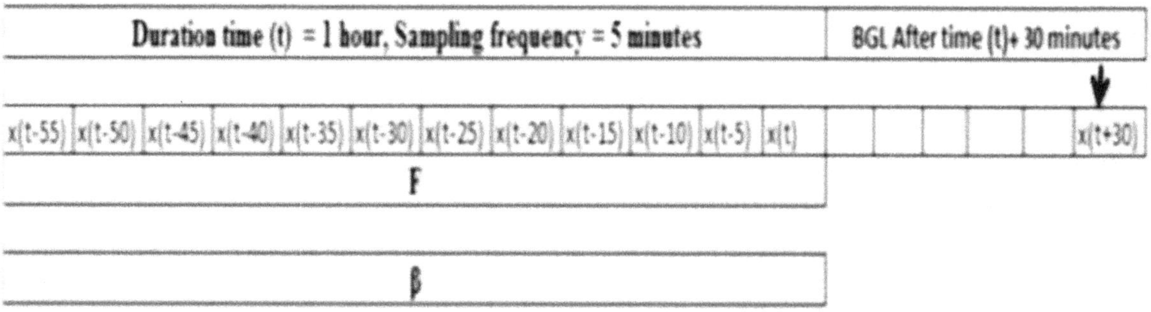

Duration time (t) = 1 hour, Sampling frequency = 5 minutes												BGL After time (t)+ 30 minutes					
x(t-55)	x(t-50)	x(t-45)	x(t-40)	x(t-35)	x(t-30)	x(t-25)	x(t-20)	x(t-15)	x(t-10)	x(t-5)	x(t)						x(t+30)
F																	
β																	

2. The metadata, F and β, and the 11 changes in the values of the BGLs x(t-55)-x(t-50) ... x(t-5)-x(t) as input and the predicted percentage change in BGL over the following 30mins, Δx(t+30), as the output; the predicted BGL x_p, being calculated from: $x_p(t+30) = x(t)+ x(t)*Δx(t+30)$

In all cases, the techniques minimized the Root Mean Square Error (RMSE) between the predicted BGL, $x_p(t+30)$, and the actual BGL, x(t+30)

$$RMSE = \sqrt{\frac{1}{N}\sum_{i=1}^{N}\left(x_p\left(t+30\right)_i - x\left(t+30\right)_i\right)^2}$$

where $x_p(t+30)$ is the output of the GA, x(t+30) the target output (the measured value) and N the number of samples.

The RMSE was chosen because large errors are weighed proportionally heavier than small errors (Kok, 2004), while taking the square root expresses the error in the same units as the BGLs (mmol/l) and thus gives some insight into the accuracy of the techniques with the different datasets, and also permits comparisons with the results of other researchers.

The leave-one-out cross-validation technique was adopted throughout. In view of the large number of samples, the number of folds was chosen to be 10 (Mitchell, 1997; Berthold, 2007) leading to a total of 200 successive samples which were systematically left out (just under 24hours of samples), leaving 1816 samples each time for training. The accuracy of each techniques quoted in the results was the average of the 10 RMSE results for each technique.

The GA was implemented using the Matlab version 2010 Genetic Algorithm toolbox with specific architectures described below. Each 1-hour dataset represented a chromosome, and the population was the remainder of the whole dataset (after removing the 1-hour dataset for the cross-validation technique). For testing and prediction, the GA applied genetic-like operators representing selection, crossover and mutation to each of the chromosomes to find the best match to the input dataset. The predicted BGL for the input dataset was calculated from the percentage change associated with the best match dataset. An extension to these basic approaches to BGL prediction data analysis involved on-line learning, whereby new data patterns were incorporated into the prediction system as they were encountered. A pattern was considered new if $x_p(t+30)$ was not within ±10% of x(t+30). In this event, the pattern was added to the GA chromosome dataset as appropriate.

RESULTS AND DISCUSSION

The typical variation in BGLs in the dataset is shown in Figure 4 for one of the real patients.

Figure 4. Difference between the actual value and predicted value of BGL for a real diabetic using GA

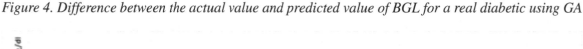
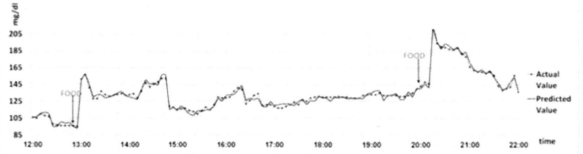

A variety of parameters, including chromosome representation, reproduction, crossover and mutation were investigated and the lowest RMSE values obtained for the raw BGL data (pattern 1) different combinations of the meta-data and BGL changes (pattern 2) are shown in Table 4.

In the case of the on-line learning approach, results were obtained for the 2nd and 3rd week using the architecture derived from the 1st week's training datasets, and then using the on-line training approach are shown in Table 5. In this case the number of 'new' patterns that were found and used to update the chromosome population are shown in the Table. Two of the volunteers chose not to participate for the 2nd and 3rd week, and so there are only results for 1 (diabetic) volunteer.

The results that are shown in these Tables may be summarized as follows:

1. The RMSE values for the virtual patients generated by the AIDA system and the volunteers are close, confirming the suitability of using the AIDA data in this type of study

2. The RMSE values obtained using the metadata and BGL changes patterns are much lower that for raw BGL patterns, the combination of metadata supplemented with the BGL changes giving the best results.

3. The RMSE values obtained using the on-line learning approach were lower than those obtain with for the basic approach with both types of algorithm, as would be expected when the algorithms were leaning and incorporating new patterns

4. The RMSE values are lower than those cited in Table 1 for previous research in BGL prediction

In addition to appearing to produce better results than previous researchers, this approach does not have the disadvantage of Haque (1999), Sandham (1998) and Pender (1997), where their data was dependent on patient answers, or the work of Kok (2004), which needed a long time period (77 days) in the learning phase. Furthermore and some projects such as Zitar (2004) and Kok (2004) used coarse time interval for prediction (morning, afternoon, and evening) while this approach appears to provide a faster, as well as a more accurate response to a potentially dangerous situation.

Finally, it should be noted that the GAs approach outperformed the predicted BGLs using ANNs (Eskaf, 2011), as found in other comparative studies involving biomedical data (Ritchings, 2002; 2008, pp. 27, 28).

Table 4. RMSE values (mmol/l) for different GA input parameters

Data Source	BGL	F, β	BGL Changes	F, β, BGL Changes
4 virtual diabetics	>10	0.68±0.10	1.12±0.32	0.54±0.07
3 volunteers	>9	0.7±0.11	1.5±0.1	0.4±0.01

Table 5. RMSE values (mmol/l) for different GA input parameters

Data Source	2nd Week	3rd Week	2nd Week (25 Updates)	3rd Week (16 Updates)
4 virtual diabetics	0.42±0.05	0.36±0.07	0.32±0.05	0.22±0.05
1 volunteer	0.46	0.43	0.3	0.2

CONCLUSION

The work considered prediction of BLGs without the need for patient input, using a Machine Learning technique, namely Genetic Algorithms,. The meta-data approach using the Dynamic Data Model gave much better results that simply applying the algorithms to the raw BGL data. The results are comparable with those reported from other approaches to BGL prediction, which required patient input.

This study has been based on a virtual patient simulator, and a very small number of volunteers. For the future work, the prediction algorithms (GA) must be evaluated with a larger numbers of diabetic patients (Type I and Type II) in order to confirm these conclusions.

REFERENCES

Abbott Diabetes Care Company. (n.d.). Retrieved from http://www.abbottdiabetescare.com

Andrianasy, A., & Milgram. (1997). Applying Artificial Neural Networks to adjust insulin pump doses. In *Proceedings of Artificial Neural Networks for Signal Processing VII Proceedings of the IEEE Signal Processing Society Workshop*, (pp. 182 – 188). IEEE.

Andrianasy, F., & Milgram, M. (1997). Applying Artificial Neural Networks to adjust insulin pump doses. In *Proceedings of Artificial Neural Networks for Signal Processing VII Proceedings of the IEEE Signal Processing Society Workshop*. The Institute of Electrical and Electronic Engineers, Inc.

Bellazzi, R., Nucci, G., & Cobelli, C. (2001). The subcutaneous route to insulin dependent diabetes therapy. *IEEE Engineering in Medicine and Biology Magazine*. Retrieved from https://ieeexplore.ieee.org

Berthold, M. R., & Hand, D. J. (2007). *Intelligent Data Analysis*. Springer.

Children with Diabetes. (n.d.). Retrieved from http://www.childrenwithdiabetes.com/continuous.htm

Cinar, A. Quinn, & Smith. (2006). Low-Order Linear Dynamic Models for Prediction of Blood Glucose Concentration. In *Proceedings of AIChE Annual Meeting*. San Francisco, CA: AIChE.

Dexcom medical device company. (n.d.). Retrieved from http://www.dexcom.com

Diabetic Software Simulator. (n.d.). Retrieved from http://www.2aida.net

Eskaf, K. (2011). *Blood Glucose Level prediction for diabetic patients using Intelligent Techniques.* (Ph.D. thesis). Salford University, Salford, UK.

Haque, A. (1999). *Modelling human metabolism using Artificial Neural Network*. London: Brunel University.

Kok, P. (2004). *Predicting blood glucose levels of diabetics using Artificial Neural Networks*. Delft University of Technology.

Lehmann, E. D., & Deutsch, T. (1998). Compartmental model for glycaemic prediction and decision support in clinical diabetes care: promise and reality. *Computer Methods and Programs in Biomedicine, 56*(2), 193–204. doi:10.1016/S0169-2607(98)00025-X PMID:9700433

Liszka Hackzell, J. (1999). Prediction of blood glucose levels in diabetic patients using a hybrid AI technique. In *Proceedings of Computers and Biomedical Research*. Linköping, Sweden: Academic Press. doi:10.1006/cbmr.1998.1506

Mathews, A. Eduard. (n.d.). *A dietary system: Blood sugar predicting system*. Retrieved from http://www.wipo.int/pctdb/en/wo.jsp?wo=2002100266

Mathews, A., & Eduard, J. H. (2009). *A Dietary system: blood sugar predicting system*. World Intellectual Property Organization. Retrieved from http://www.wipo.int

McNulty & Mauze. (1998). Wavelet analysis for determining glucose concentrations of aqueous solutions using NIR spectroscopy. In *Proc. Biomedical Optics'98*. Academic Press.

Medtronic diabetes and health care providers company. (n.d.). Retrieved from http:// www.medtronicdiabetes.com

Mitchell, T. (1997). *Machine Learning*. McGraw Hill.

Nikoletou, D., Sandham, W. A., Hamilton, D. J., Patterson, K., Japp, A., & MacGregor, C. (1998). Blood glucose prediction for diabetes therapy using a recurrent artificial neural network. In *Proceedings, EUSIPCO-98, IX European Signal Processing Conference*, (Vol. 11, pp. 673-676). EUSIPCO.

Oruklu, M. Cinar, Quinnand, & Smith. (2007). Adaptive control strategy for glucose regulation using recursive linear models. In *Proceedings of 10th International IFAC Symposium on Computer Applications in Biotechnology*, (pp. 153-158). IFAC.

Pender, J. E. (1997). *Modelling of blood glucose levels using Artificial Neural Networks*. (PhD Thesis). University of Strathclyde.

Reifman, J, Rajaraman, Gribok, & Ward. (2007). Predictive Monitoring for Improved Management of Glucose Levels. *Journal of Diabetes Science and Technology*, *1*(4), 468–478. doi:10.1177/193229680700100405 PMID:19885110

Ritchings, R. T., Berry, C., & Sheta, W. (2008). Comparing ANNs and Genetic Programming for voice quality assessment post-treatment. *Applied Artificial Intelligence Journal*, *22*(3), 198–207. doi:10.1080/08839510701734343

Ritchings, R. T., & McGillion, M. C. J. (2002). Pathological voice quality assessment using artificial neural networks. *Medical Engineering and Physics Journal*, *24*, 561–564. doi:10.1016/S1350-4533(02)00064-4 PMID:12237054

Rossetti, P., Porcellati, F., Bolli, B., & Fanelli, G. (2008). Prevention of Hypoglycemia While Achieving Good Glycemic Control in Type 1 Diabetes: The role of insulin analogs. *Diabetes Care*, *31*(Supp 2), S113–S120. doi:10.2337/dc08-s227 PMID:18227470

Sandham, W. A., Hamilton, D. J., Japp, A., & Patterson, K. (1998). Artificial Neural Network and neuro-fuzzy systems for improving diabetes therapy. In *Proceedings, 20th International Conference of the IEEE Engineering in Medicine and Biology Society*, (vol. 20, pp. 673–676). IEEE.

Schauer, T., & Raisch. (2007). Model-based predictive control of blood-sugar level in intensive care. In *Proc. 15th IEEE Mediterranean Conference on Control and Automation* (MED '07). IEEE.

Schauer, T., & Raisch, J. (2007). Model-based predictive control of blood-sugar level in intensive care, control & automation. In *Proc. 15th IEEE Mediterranean Conference on Control and Automation* (MED '07). Athens, Greece: MED.

Sparacino, G., Zanderigo, Corazza, Maran, Facchinetti, & Cobelli. (2007). Glucose Concentration can be Predicted Ahead in Time From Continuous Glucose Monitoring Sensor Time-Series. *IEEE Transactions on Bio-Medical Engineering*, *54*(5), 931–938. doi:10.1109/TBME.2006.889774 PMID:17518291

Stahl, F. (2003). *Diabetes Mellitus Modelling Based on Blood Glucose Measurements*. Department of Automatic Control Lund Institute of Technology.

Ståhl, F., Cescon, M., Johansson, R., & Landin-Olsson, M. (2009). Subspace-based model identification of diabetic blood glucose dynamics. In *Proc. 15th Symposium on System Identification* (SYSID2009), (pp. 233-238). Saint-Malo, France: SYSID.

Tresp, V., Briegel, T., & Moody, J. (1999). Neural-network models for the blood glucose metabolism of a diabetic. *IEEE Transactions on Neural Networks*, *10*, 1204. doi:10.1109/72.788659 PMID:18252621

WaiYee, Lun Wong, Shing, ChakHing, Ching, Chung Man, & Yin Ki. (2006). *Method for predicting a blood glucose level of a person*. Academic Press.

World Health Organization. (n.d.). Retrieved from http://www.who.int

Wu, H.-I. (2005). A case study of type 2 diabetes self-management. *Biomedical Engineering Online*, *4*(4). doi: doi:10.1186/1475-925X-4-4 PMID:15644138

Zecchin, C., Facchinetti, A., Sparacino, G., De Nicolao, G., & Cobelli, C. (2012). Neural network incorporating meal information improves accuracy of short-time prediction of glucose concentration. *IEEE Transactions on Bio-Medical Engineering*, *59*, 1550–1560. doi:10.1109/TBME.2012.2188893 PMID:22374344

Zitar, A. (2005). Towards Artificial Neural Networks Model for Insulin/Glucose in Diabetics. *Journal Informatica*, *29*(2), 227–232.

KEY TERMS AND DEFINITIONS

Blood Glucose: The main sugar can be found in the blood and is the main source of energy for the human body.

Blood Glucose Monitoring: Checking blood glucose level on a regular time in order to manage diabetes. A blood glucose meter will be used for frequent blood glucose monitoring.

Continuous Glucose Monitoring Systems: Continuous glucose monitoring systems typically consist of a sensor that is applied on the diabetic body to measure glucose concentrations, and transmitter that is attached to the sensor will send data to a receiver unit that communicates wirelessly with the transmitter and on which glucose data are displayed.

Diabetes Dynamic Model: Diabetes dynamic model is mathematical model that simulate the behavior of the real physiological blood glucose regulatory system of human.

Diabetes Mellitus: Diabetes mellitus is a condition in which the pancreas will not be able to produces enough insulin or cells stop responding to the insulin that is produced.

Genetic Algorithm: Genetic algorithm is heuristic search that mimics the process of natural selection. The mechanics of natural selection and genetics are emulated artificially in order to search for a global optimum solution to a given problem.

Machine Learning: Machine learning is a branch of artificial intelligence. Machine learning allows computerized system to handle new situations via analysis and self re-training.

Online Learning: Online learning is the method that adds the new cases to the system in order to improve its performance based on previous results.

Predicting Blood Glucose Level: Predict the blood glucose level of a diabetic patient after 30 or 60 minutes from the current blood glucose level.

Chapter 15
Security of Wireless Devices using Biological–Inspired RF Fingerprinting Technique

Saeed ur Rehman
Unitec Institute of Technology, New Zealand

Shafiq Alam
University of Auckland, New Zealand

Iman T. Ardekani
Unitec Institute of Technology, New Zealand

ABSTRACT

Radio Frequency (RF) fingerprinting is a security mechanism inspired by biological fingerprint identification systems. RF fingerprinting is proposed as a means of providing an additional layer of security for wireless devices. RF fingerprinting classification is performed by selecting an "unknown" signal from the pool, generating its RF fingerprint, and using a classifier to correlate the received RF fingerprint with each profile RF fingerprint stored in the database. Unlike a human biological fingerprint, RF fingerprint of a wireless device changes with the received Signal to Noise Ratio (SNR) and varies due to mobility of the transmitter/receiver and environment. The variations in the features of RF fingerprints affect the classification results of the RF fingerprinting. This chapter evaluates the performance of the KNN and neural network classification for varying SNR. Performance analysis is performed for three scenarios that correspond to the situation, when either transmitter or receiver is mobile, and SNR changes from low to high or vice versa.

INTRODUCTION

The inventor of wireless communication, Guglielmo Marconi demonstrated the communication of telegraphic messages in the late nineteen-century. Since then, the world has seen an explosive growth in the field of wireless communication. Particularly in the last ten years, several new wireless technologies have been invented to expand the growing application of wireless communications. In the coming days, wireless modules will be embedded in various objects, such as home

DOI: 10.4018/978-1-4666-6078-6.ch015

appliances, transport, clothes, gadgets, toys, food carts, roads, bridge, farms, buildings, animals and people.

The continued proliferation of inexpensive wireless Radio Frequency (RF) devices provides worldwide communication connectivity to virtually every individual. These wireless devices broadcast information to intended recipients in the form of an electromagnetic emission. However, the electromagnetic emission may be remotely monitored, recorded, intercepted or analyzed by unintended recipients owing to the broadcasting nature of the wireless medium. Generally, the communicators are unaware of this activity, and moreover, the intentions of unintended recipients vary. The unintended recipient may simply listen to the communication activity and remain passive – an activity that is difficult to detect– or may become active and compromise the identity of the wireless device by launching "spoofing" or "man in the middle" type attacks (Meyer & Wetzel, 2004). For example, the software within a wireless device allows the Medium Access Control (MAC) address of a network interface card to be modified and thus it is vulnerable to a spoofing attack (Faria & Cheriton, 2006). Similarly, the Erasable Programmable Read Only Memory (EPROM) of a cellular phone carries the phone's Electronic Serial Number (ESN) and Mobile Identification Number (MIN), which can be changed by replacing the EPROM, hence allowing the identity of the phone to be changed (Nguyen, et al., 2011). Compromising the identity of wireless devices makes them vulnerable to a variety of attacks, which can take the form of impersonation, intrusion, theft of bandwidth and denial of service.

To increase network security and mitigate identity theft attacks, much of the research is focused on traditional bit-level algorithmic. In conventional wireless networks, security issues are primarily considered above the physical layer and are usually based on cryptographic methods, where the cryptographic algorithms are mainly used for establishing the identity of a legitimate wireless device. A two-way communication is required to establish a session key in the cryptography. However, the security algorithm would be compromised upon access to the key, thus making it difficult to distinguish a legitimate key/device and cloned key/device (Mathur, et al., 2010). Additionally, higher-layer security key distribution and management may be difficult to implement and may be vulnerable to attacks in some environments, such as ad-hoc or relay networks, in which transceivers may join or leave randomly (Debbah, 2008; Kauffmann, et al., 2007). Furthermore, some recent wireless technologies do not allow an interactive communication for establishing a cryptography key due to its unique architecture. One such example is Cognitive Radio Network (CRN), which is invented in order to increase the efficient utilization of the spectrum. However, if a Primary User Emulation (PUE) attack is launched then the whole operation of CRN is jeopardize by effectively limiting the access of legitimate users to idle spectrum (Chen, et al., 2008).

More recently consideration has been given to detecting and mitigating spoofing near or at the bottom of the Open Systems Interconnection (OSI) network stack. One such work includes the addition of a "lightweight security layer" hosted within the Medium Access Control (MAC) layer to detect spoofing and anomalous traffic (Li & Trappe, 2007). Other recent efforts have focused on Physical (PHY) layer implementations with a goal of exploiting RF characteristics (radio and environmental) that are difficult to mimic, thus minimizing the opportunity for spoofing. Hence, identity theft can be effectively tackled using physical layer security. Physical layer security based on the extraction of unique feature from the analog signal is called RF fingerprinting.

The classification process of RF fingerprinting can be divided into training phase (for generating the profile RF fingerprint of a specific transmitter) and the testing phase (for identifying the wireless device). Majority of the existing RF fingerprinting techniques have either used high SNR signals or no information is provided regarding the signals used in training phase (Bonne & Capkun, 2007; Danev, et al., 2010; Edman & Yener, 2009; Hall, et al., 2004; Kennedy, et al., 2008; Polak, et al., 2011; Woelfle, et al., 2009; Rehman, et al., 2012). However, the SNR of the signals changes in a typical wireless environment due to mobility of transmitter/ receivers, interference and environment.

Therefore, high receiver SNR signals are not always available in a typical wireless environment. This study provides the initial results on the effect of the varying receiver SNR on the classification performance of RF fingerprinting. KNN and Neural network is used as classifiers and their performance is compared for varying SNR. The analysis is performed for three low-end (low cost) receivers and one high-end receiver setup.

The rest of the chapter is organized as follows. First, a background on physical layer security and its different categories are provided. Second, the experiment setup and RF fingerprinting technique used in this chapter are explained. Then the classifiers used in this research work are explained. Performance evaluation and conclusion are discussed at the end of the chapter.

PHY LAYER SECURITY

Physical layer security is a new concept for securing the identity of wireless devices by extracting the unique features embedded in the electromagnetic waves emitted from the transmitters. These unique features are due to inherent randomness in the manufacturing process. Physical layer security that is based on recognizing wireless devices through these unique features is known as Radio Frequency (RF) fingerprinting (Danev, et al., 2010). Transmitter imperfections that can produce RF fingerprints are originated from analogous components. The analog components (digital-to-analog converters, band-pass filters,

frequency mixers and power amplifiers) present in the radio transmit chain are mainly responsible for the unique features (Gard, et al., 2005).

As with almost every technology, RF fingerprinting also stems from the military. The first RF fingerprinting system was utilized in the Vietnam War to differentiate between a friendly and foe radar (Nansai Hu, 2012). In the past few years, researchers explored many RF fingerprinting techniques for identification of transmitters in commercial spheres (Marcus, 1992; Hippenstiel & Payal, 1996; Xu, et al., 2008; Toonstra & Kinsner, 2002; Zamora, et al., 2010). One such example is in cellular industry, where RF fingerprinting is used to prevent cell phone cloning (Kaplan & Stanhope, 1999; Hoogerwerf, et al., 2000). RF fingerprinting has been evaluated for a number of wireless devices operating on different standards, which include Cognitive Radio Networks (CRN) (Kim, et al.; Nansai Hu, 2012), Universal Mobile Telecommunications System (UMTS) (Scanlon, et al., 2010), Wi-Fi (Kim, et al.; Suski II, et al., 2008), push-to-talk transmitters (Toonstra & Kinsner, 2002), Bluetooth (Woelfle, et al., 2009; Ur Rehman, et al., 2012) and Radio-Frequency Identification (RFID) (Zanetti, et al., 2010; Bertoncini, et al., 2012). It has been found that every transmitter has a unique RF fingerprint due to imperfection in the analog components present in the RF front end (Danev, et al., 2010).

A generic rudimentary block diagram of a digital radio communications system is shown in Figure 1, which shows the transformation of an information (baseband) signal from origination at the transmitter to its reception at the receiver. Figure 1 shows the components (in grey) of a typical digital transmitter, which are the sources of RF fingerprints. The imperfections include modulation errors at the modulator, Phase Noise (PN) at oscillators, spurious tones from mixers and Power Amplifiers (PA), non- linearity distortion at PA, power ramp distortions (due to transients), and distortions of the various filters including IF

Figure 1. Radiometric block diagram showing different sources of impairments in overall digital communication system

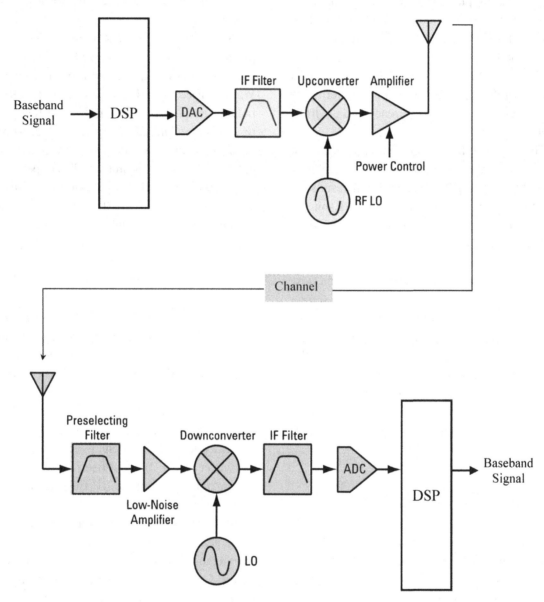

and RF filters. All these hardware imperfections contribute in the creation of a unique RF fingerprint of a specific transmitter. Though, it may be possible to eliminate these hardware imperfections through more precise manufacturing and quality control. However, this will greatly increase device cost. In fact, most common technology standards including 802.11, 802.15.4, 802.22 explicitly require different wireless devices to tolerate rather wide ranges of RF variations in received signals for seamless operation. Therefore, these transmitter specific RF imperfections can be utilized to establish the identity of the transmitter.

Classification of RF Fingerprinting

RF fingerprinting is used to identify wireless nodes using the unique structure of the electromagnetic waves emitted from the transmitters. It has been shown that every transmitter has a unique RF fingerprint owing to imperfections in its analog components (Danev, et al., 2009). The main goal of RF fingerprinting is to extract the unique features of a transmitted signal that enable identification of the signal's transmitter. RF fingerprinting is further divided into transient and steady-state (modulation) based techniques. Figure 2 shows the transient and steady-state parts of an actual signal captured from a Bluetooth device

Transient-Based RF Fingerprinting

In transient-based RF fingerprinting, the transition of a transmitter from the Off state to the On state generates unique features that appear before the transmission of the actual packet. These features are transmitter specific, they vary across different transmitters, and they can be used to identify the transmitter (Toonstra & Kinsner, 2002; Shiu, et al., 2011). In (Kim et al., 2008) six different WLAN cards were identified using the transients of the 802.11a/g OFDM signals. In the experimental setup, the signature interceptor was placed 40 cm away from the WLAN card, so a high Signal-to-Noise Ratio (SNR) and line-of-sight propagation

Figure 2. Bluetooth transmitter signal captured from a Bluetooth transmitter embedded in a cellular phone

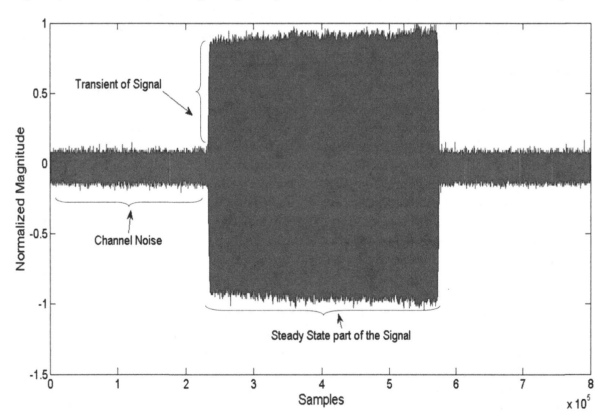

were assumed. Hall et al. used frequency and amplitude information to create RF fingerprints from ten different transient features for identifying WLAN and Bluetooth transmitters (Hall, et al., 2006; 2004; 2003; 2005). VHF radios were identified using RF fingerprints created from amplitude and phase information (Ellis & Serinken, 2001). Ellis and Serinken found that some transmitters were virtually indistinguishable using their amplitude, phase and frequency profiles. They concluded that the feature set is highly dependent on the transmitters; a feature that is dominant in one transmitter may be insignificant in other transmitters. A similar analysis was performed for OFDM 802.11a/g signals using amplitude and phase based transient detection, in which spectral correlation was used to classify the RF fingerprint. The experimental set-up consisted of three WLAN cards in an office environment with line-of-sight propagation and a high SNR (Suski II, et al., 2008). In these experiments high-end equipment were used to capture and extract the transient.

Transient-based identification of Wireless Sensor Node (WSN) was demonstrated in (Bonne & Capkun, 2007), in which an RF fingerprint was formed visually by looking at the physical shape of the signals transient. The RF fingerprint consisted of the transient duration, the number of peaks and the difference between the normalized mean and normalized maximum value of the peaks. This work was extended using an RF fingerprint formed by extracting spectral Fisher-features from the captured signals, and using a linear transformation derived from Linear Discriminant Analysis (LDA) (Danev & Čapkun, 2009). The Fisher LDA is a well-established technique used for discriminating between different human biometrics (Martínez & Kak, 2001; Zhao, et al., 1998). Furthermore, the RF fingerprinting performance was investigated with respect to distance; antenna polarization and variable power supply voltage. It was found that there is little variation in the RF fingerprint due to large fixed distances and variable volt-

ages. However, antenna polarization and varying distance distort the RF fingerprint. In (Afolabi, et al., 2009), a secure electromagnetic signature based detection scheme was proposed for CRNs. In this scheme simulated pre-processed transient signals were generated in MATLAB. Amplitude, frequency and phase were extracted from the transient signals for three different transceivers and classification was performed to identify a PUE attacker.

Steady-State-Based RF Fingerprinting

Steady-state based RF fingerprinting uses the unique features introduced by the transmitter during the modulation phase. In (Brik, et al., 2008), a Passive RAdiometric Device Identification System (PARADIS) is proposed to identify the transmitters in 802.11 networks. PARADIS uses modulation imperfection (caused by analog transmitter hardware) to identify specific devices. Mainly, the offset in Inphase/Quadrature (I/Q) components, frequency error, phase and magnitude errors of the frames were used as an RF fingerprint of the transmitter. A similar approach was adopted in (Shi & Jensen, 2011), where Multiple Input Multiple Output (MIMO) devices were identified using the radiometric features in the modulation domain. In (Kennedy, et al., 2008b), frequency domain characteristics were used to identify transmitters. In the experimental setup, Universal Software Radio Peripherals (USRPs) were used to produce the Random Access CHannel (RACH) preamble of the Universal Mobile Telecommunication System (UMTS). The transmission sources were connected directly to a spectrum analyzer via a coaxial cable in order to minimize the interference. This work has been further extended to real UMTS devices and experiments have been performed in an anechoic chamber (Kennedy, et al., 2008; Zamora, et al. 2010). Suski et al. identified wireless transmitter using the Power Spectral Density (PSD) coefficients of the IEEE

802.11a/g preamble signal (Suski II, et al., 2008). They extracted features from the IEEE 802.11a/g preamble signal to form the RF fingerprint of a transmitter. In (Danev, et al., 2009a), the unique features extracted from the modulation shape, and the spectral features emitted from an RFID transponders, were used for identification. The experiments were performed in a controlled environment, in which a well-formed RFID reader signals was passed through RFID transponders and measured using high-end equipment in close proximity.

Initially, the research community gave more attention to transient-based RF fingerprinting, owing to the unavailability of a steady-state signal common to all transmitters. The attraction of transient based RF fingerprinting is because it will always occur in a transmission. The rationale was given that a steady-state signal cannot be used reliably for RF fingerprinting because a steady-state signal will vary from one transmission to another. However, a higher sampling rate is required for the transient detection and extraction owing to its relatively short period compared to a steady state signal (Kennedy, et al., 2008b). Therefore, real-time implementation of transient-based fingerprinting presents serious technical challenges. On the other hand, the need for a common steady-state signal for steady-state based RF fingerprinting is no longer an issue in the modern digital communication era. Nowadays, almost all digital communication systems (CRN, WSN, RFID, Wireless Local Area Network (WLAN), UMTS etc.) introduce a preamble at the start of packet transmission in order to simplify the receiver design (Scanlon, et al., 2010). The preamble provides the common signal necessary for successful fingerprinting. Therefore, a typical modulation based RF fingerprinting technique is analyzed in this chapter.

Overview of the Experimental Setup

Suski et al. have identified wireless transmitter using the Power Spectral Density (PSD) of the IEEE 802.11a preamble signal (Suski II, et al., 2008). They have extracted features from the IEEE 802.11a preamble signal to form the RF fingerprint of a transmitter. His work is evaluated in this chapter for different training set. For this purpose, a reference IEEE 802.11a preamble signal is generated in MATLAB and transmitted with three different USRP transmitters. The preamble signal is then captured with the measurement setup, explained in next Section. The classification is implemented by extracting the preamble from the signals and computing the PSD coefficients. The PSD coefficients are then used to develop the RF fingerprint for different transmitters and classification are performed using the K Nearest Neighbor (KNN) classifier and neural network. In classification, training is performed with low SNR and high SNR signals. Then testing is performed for varying SNR signals in order to analyze the effect of received SNR on the classification performance of RF fingerprinting.

UNIVERSAL SOFTWARE RADIO PERIPHERAL

The Ettus Universal Software Radio Peripheral (USRP) is the most widely used Software Defined Radio (SDR) platform, owing to its low cost and open source software architecture (Ettus, 2012). Developed by Ettus Research LLC, the USRP platform is a RF software-programmable radio transceiver designed for wireless communications research. A block diagram of USRP is shown in Figure 3. A USRP consists of three main blocks. In the first block, the RF front end is implemented

Figure 3. USRP N210 functional block diagram showing different components involved in processing (Ettus, 2012)

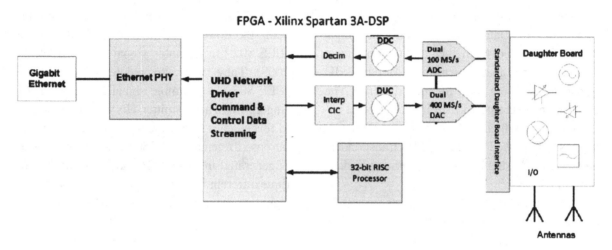

on daughterboards and serves as an interface to the analog RF domain. Each USRP daughterboard provides an independent transmit and receive path capable of full duplex operation in some hardware configurations. A second block is implemented on the motherboard and acts as an interface between the digital and analog domains. The main components of motherboard are the FPGA, ADCs and DACs. Some part of DSP is implemented in FPGA, but it is completely reconfigurable. In the third block, the digital signal processing is performed in a host computer via a USB or GB ETHERNET port. Connecting the USRP hardware to a host PC allows the PC to act as a software-defined radio with host-based digital signal processing. Several versions of the USRP are available that are categorized based on their motherboard and the interface with the host computer. The three categories are; USRP bus series, USRP network series and the USRP embedded series (USRP, 2013).

The USRP bus series is the derivative of the original USRP1, which was the first USRP to be built. The USRP1 has a USB 2.0 host interface that can stream up to 8 Mega samples per second (MS/s) of data to the host computer. The USRP1 motherboard has four slots for daughterboards. The USRP embedded series consists of the E100 and

E110 versions. This series contains a TI OMPA3 embedded processor with 4 GB of flash space and 512 MB of RAM. High processing speed allows significant processing to be performed on the board itself. The USRP networked series consists of N200 and N210 models. This series enables high rate data streaming to the host computer using its Gigabit Ethernet interface and has been designed for SDR systems with more demanding performance requirements.

In this research work, the USRP N210 was chosen as the SDR platform. The Gigabit Ethernet interface supports high data rate communication with the host computer. The high speed ADC/DAC enables sampling of signals with large bandwidths, which is required for IEEE 802.11a/g signals. RF front ends are implemented on daughterboards. Therefore, the effect of different front ends on RF fingerprinting can be analyzed by replacing only the daughterboards in USRPs. Another important factor in favor of the USRP was the modular nature of the hardware, together with the low price of the daughterboards that enabled us to purchase a more extensive system. Furthermore, the availability of daughterboards schematic gives us details of the analog components used in different versions of daughterboards.

Measurement Setup

The measurement setup used for capturing the wireless signals from three different USRP transmitters is shown in Figure 4. Four receivers are used to capture the preamble signal transmitted by each transmitter. Three of the receivers are USRP devices, representing low-end receivers, while a spectrum analyzer/oscilloscope setup represents a high-end receiver. Three USRP N210 devices equipped with SBX transceiver daughter boards and vert2450 antennas are used. The SBX daughter boards act as a front end and have a frequency range from 0.4 GHz to 4.4 GHz, which allows transmitting and receiving in the 2.4 GHz ISM band. The USRP N210 is equipped with a dual 14-bit Analog to Digital Converter (ADC) operating at 100 MHz and dual 16-bit Digital to Analog Converter (DAC) operating at 400 MHz. The USRP N210 transmits complex base band samples at 25 MSample/s to the host computer via a direct gigabit Ethernet link (Ettus, 2012).

The complex In-phase (I) and Quadrature (Q) components are stored in the computer for further processing.

The preamble signal is captured through an antenna connected to an Agilent spectrum analyzer in the high-end receiver setup. The spectrum analyzer acts as an Intermediate Frequency (IF) converter. The IF signal is then fed to a 4 GSample/s oscilloscope. The oscilloscope is used as an analog to digital converter in order to get the time domain signal. The captured signal is then transferred to computer via GPIB Bus and stored in digital format for further processing.

Data Collection

All the measurements were carried out in an office environment, representing a typical reception scenario. Each 802.11a/g signal includes the preamble information at the start of each RF burst to aid in diversity selection, timing/frequency acquisition and channel estimation (Suski, et al., 2008). The

Figure 4. Measurement setup for RF fingerprinting of IEEE 802.11a/g preamble. Only one transmitter is shown while three transmitters are used for experiments. Measurements are performed in an office environment. RX1, RX2, RX3 are low-end receivers while RX4 is a high-end receiver.

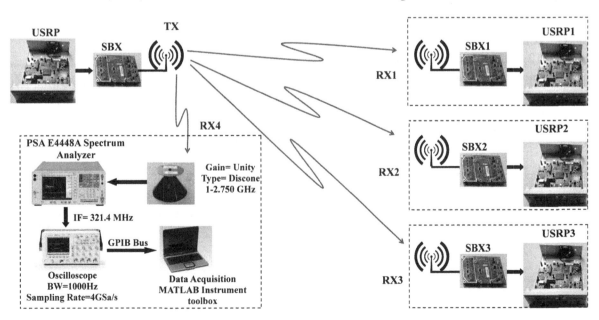

IEEE 802.11a/g preamble is generated as per the standard, which consists of 10 short and 2 long fixed symbols standards (IEEE, et al., 2003). The wireless signal transmissions from the three different transmitters were captured using the measurement setup shown in Figure 4. A total of 4000 signals from each transmitter were captured and stored at each of the receivers, giving a total data set of 48000 received signals.

Preamble and Feature Extraction

In order to extract the preamble from each acquired signal, the signal is first normalized and then the preamble is extracted from each acquired signal using the amplitude-based variance detection technique described given in (Bonne & Capkun, 2007; Ur Rehman, et al., 2012; Suski II, et al., 2008).

$$V_i = K \frac{1}{w-1} \sum_{n=1}^{w} (X_{m-n} - \bar{X}_w)^2 \tag{1}$$

The goal of the feature extraction is to form a unique RF fingerprint, which distinctly characterizes a transmitter from the rest of the transmitters. In previous work, the coefficients of Power Spectral Density (PSD) are used to create the RF fingerprint of transmitters (Suski, et al., 2008; Suski II, et al., 2008; Scanlon, et al., 2010; Rehman, et al., 2012). Therefore in this evaluation, the RF fingerprint of a specific transmitter consists of normalized Power Spectral Density (PSD) coefficient values and is given by (Suski, et al., 2008).

$$\psi_x(k) = \frac{|X(k)|^2}{\sum_{k=1}^{K} |X(k)|^2} \tag{2}$$

where $X(k)$ are the coefficients of discrete Fourier transform for the input signal $x(m)$ given by

$$X(k) = \frac{1}{N_F} \sum_{m=1}^{N_F} x(m) e^{\left[\frac{-2\pi j}{N_F}(m-1)(k-1)\right]} \tag{3}$$

CLASSIFICATION METHODOLOGY

The classification process of RF fingerprinting can be divided into training phase (for generating the profile RF fingerprint of a specific transmitter) and the testing phase (for identifying the wireless device) as shown in Figure 5. In the training phase, signals of a specific transmitter are used to create the profile RF fingerprint of the transmitter. Whereas in the testing phase, an RF fingerprint is created from an input test signal. Then a classifier is used to classify this test RF fingerprint against the existing profiles of the transmitter. Training and testing is equivalent to initialization and network operation phase in RF fingerprinting. Two classifiers are used for evaluation purpose. One of the classifier is based on K Nearest neighbor algorithms, while other utilizes Artificial Neural Networks (ANN) for classification. Details are given below

K Nearest Neighbor

The K Nearest Neighbor (KNN) is the simplest supervised machine learning algorithm and used as a benchmark for other classifier. KNN is used in various applications such as image processing, bioinformatics, data compression, computer vision, document retrieval, market data analysis and multimedia databases. The KNN classifier is used to classify an input feature vector into one of

Figure 5. RF Fingerprinting classification process

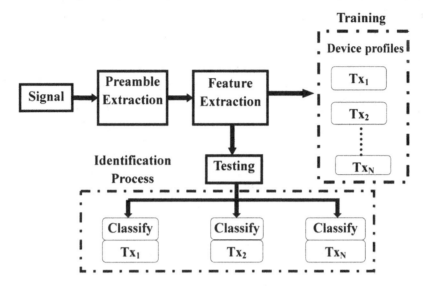

the class based on the closest training examples available in the feature space (Danev, et al., 2010). In training phase, the KNN stores all the training examples along with its label. In testing phase, following steps are carried out to make a class prediction of an unknown test example

1. The KNN classifier first computes the distance of test example to every training example available in the feature space. In this research work, Euclidean function is chosen for computing the distance and is given as.

$$d\left(X,Y\right) = x - y = \sqrt{\sum_{i=1}^{k}\left(x_i - y_i\right)^2}$$

2. KNN keeps the closest K training examples based on the computed distance, where $K \geq 1$ and is defined as the number of nearest neighbors. K is normally kept odd fixed integer in order to avoid ties among the closest training examples.

3. The predicted class of the unknown example is the class that appears most often in the closest examples of step 2.

In this work K-Nearest Neighbor (KNN) with three nearest neighbors is used as a classifier.

ARTIFICIAL NEURAL NETWORK

Artificial Neural Network (ANN) is a biological inspired computational model, which replicate human brain's functionality (Jain, et al., 1996). It is composed of a large number of interconnected processing units called artificial neuron (like a neuron in human brain) in order to solve complex problems. A mathematical function computes the output of an artificial neuron, which consists of inputs (synapses), multiplied by weights (strength of the signals). The weight controls the activation of an artificial neuron. An input with higher weight has strong impact on activation of neuron while a negative weight has less impact.

A commonly used multi-layer perceptron (MLP) neural network is used for identification in this research work (Widrow & Lehr, 1990; Jain, et al., 1996). The MLP network is shown in Figure 6. The MLP is a supervised neural network, where it is first trained by computing the parameters from the known examples. Later, the trained network is used to predict the class of an unknown input. The inputs to the MLP network are the RF features of transmitters, while outputs are the prediction about the identity of transmitters. In the training phase, a pair of input training data $\left(x_k(m),\ t_{id} \right)$ is applied to the network. $x_k\left(m \right)$

is the kth training instance of the m dimensional input feature vector and t_{id} is the transmitter identity. In Figure 6, $x_k\left(M \right)$ is the kth training instance of the m dimensional input vector and $Y_k\left(N \right)$ is the output vector from the trained mlp network for kth instance.

The inputs $x_k\left(M \right)$ to the hidden neuron unit are multiplied by the weights W_{Hi} and summed up with the constant bias term Θ_i^1. The input to ith hidden neuron is given as

Figure 6. Multilayer perceptron artificial neural network with one hidden layer

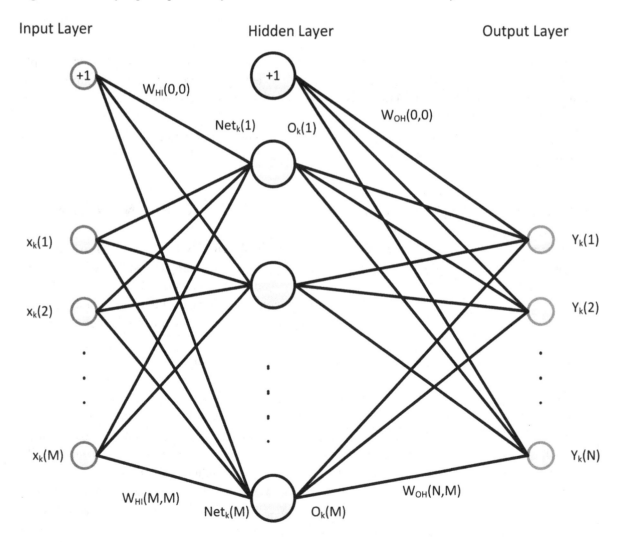

$$Net_k\left(i\right) = \sum_{m=1}^{M} W_{HI}\left(i,m\right) x_k\left(m\right) + \Theta_i^1; 1 \le i \le M$$

(4)

Equation 4 is the input to the activation function g. Activation means the value computed and output by the neuron based on a mathematical function. The output activation for the kth input is given as

$$O_k\left(i\right) = g(Net_k\left(i\right)) = g\left(\sum_{m=1}^{M} W_{HI}\left(i,m\right) x_k\left(m\right) + \Theta_i^1\right)$$

(5)

A commonly used sigmoid function is chosen as nonlinear activation function given below

$$g(Net_k\left(i\right)) = \frac{1}{1 + e^{-Net_k(i)}}$$

(6)

In Equation (5) and Equation (6), index m is the input features and $W_{HI}\left(i,m\right)$ denotes the weights connecting mth input feature to the ith hidden neuron unit.

In the output layer, the final output for the kth training example is expressed as

$$Y_k\left(j\right) = \sum_{i=1}^{N} W_{OH}\left(j,i\right) O_k\left(i\right) + \Theta_j^2$$

(7)

$$Y_k\left(j\right) = \sum_{i=1}^{N} W_{OH}\left(j,i\right) g\left(\left(\sum_{m=1}^{M} W_{HI}\left(i,m\right) x_k\left(m\right) + \Theta_i^1\right)\right) + \Theta_j^2$$

(8)

where $W_{HI}\left(i,m\right)$ are the weights from the input to the hidden neurons, $W_{OH}\left(j,i\right)$ represents the weight from the hidden nodes to the output nodes, Θ_i^1 is the constant input bias for the input layer 1 and Θ_j^2 is the constant input bias for the hidden layer 2.

In this chapter, three layer MLP neural network is used. The RF fingerprint has 512 features. Therefore, input to MLP is 512 and hidden layer consists of 25 neurons.

PERFORMANCE EVALUATION

In the evaluation, K Nearest Neighbor (KNN) with 3 nearest neighbors is used. The ANN is trained with the back-propagation. MATLAB and its associated toolboxes are used for processing and evaluation. The RF fingerprinting performance evaluation is carried out for a more realistic environment, where receiver SNR changes with time either due to mobility of transmitter/ receiver or due to environment. To the best knowledge of the author, the effect of SNR during the training and testing phase is not evaluated for different classifiers. Three scenarios are considered for the evaluation.

1. The first scenario considers the situation when the mobile receiver is nearby the transmitter during the training phase and later on, the receiver SNR either decreases or increases due to the mobility of transmitter or receiver. In this scenario, both classifiers are trained with high SNR signals and testing is performed with varying SNR. Hence, the profile RF fingerprint is created with high SNR signals.

2. In second scenario, the mobile receiver is considered at a location where SNR is low during the training phase and later on, the receiver SNR decreases or increases due to mobility of transmitter. This scenario is evaluated by training the classifiers with low receiver SNR signal and then testing is performed with varying SNR.

3. Third scenario considers the case, where the receiver SNR changes from low to high or vice versa during the training phase.

In all three scenarios, the profile RF fingerprints of the three transmitters are created with 40% preamble signals from each transmitter. The rest of the signals from each transmitter are used for testing purposes. This process is repeated for each of the four receivers; i.e. training and testing is performed with signals captured by one specific receiver and the same process is repeated for signals captured with three other receivers. Simulated Additive White Gaussian Noise (AWGN) is added to the collected signals in order to simulate the three scenarios and assess the effect of Signal-to-Noise Ratio (SNR). The process is repeated for each of the four receivers (three low-end and one high-end).

Figure 7, 8 and 9 shows the classification accuracy for both the classifiers under varying SNR. Rx1, Rx2 and Rx3 are the low-end receivers while Rx4 is the high-end receiver in the figures. As expected, the high-end receiver shows good classification results irrespective of the training SNR/classifiers and confirms the accurate results reported in the literature, which are based on the high-end receivers (Suski II, et al., 2008; Scanlon, et al., 2010). However, all low-end receivers perform differently for the same set of transmitters.

The accurate classification results of scenario one is shown in Figure 7. High SNR signals allow to precisely extract unique features of a specific transmitter, which is unique to different transmit-

Figure 7. Scenario one, where classifier is trained with 40% signals from 15 to 30 SNR signals

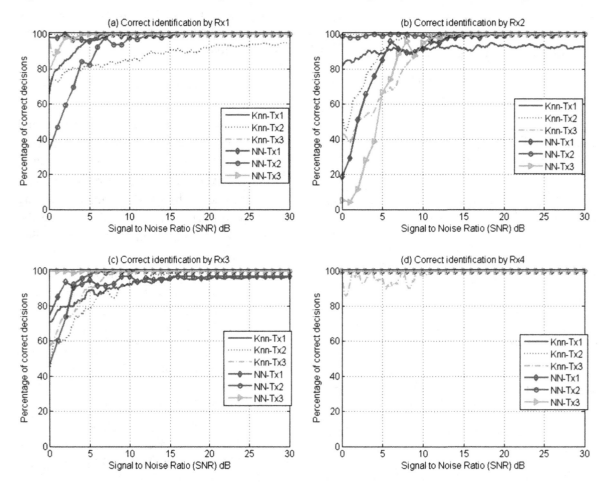

Figure 8. Scenario two, where classifier is trained with 40% signals from 0 to 15 SNR signals

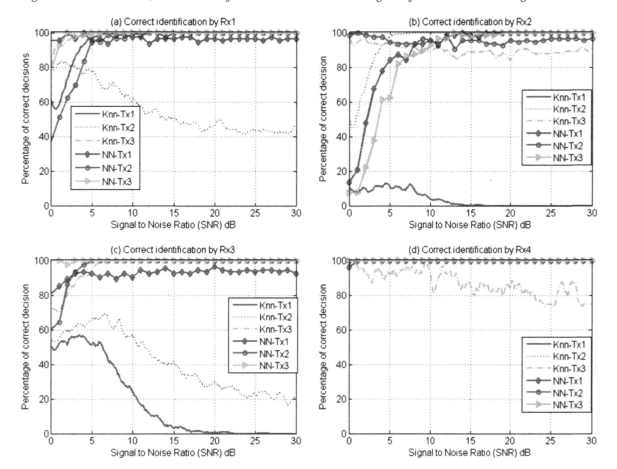

ters. This is evident from the results of the Figure 7, which has used high SNR signals for training. RF fingerprints are distinct in features space. Therefore, classification results of both classifiers are comparable for scenario one. However, high SNR scenario is rare in a typical wireless environment and collecting the high SNR signals is a tedious and time consuming task.

In a typical wireless environment, the receiver SNR is from 5 to 15dB. Scenario two corresponds to the typical real time wireless environment. In scenario two, the classifiers is trained with 0 to 15 dB receiver SNR signals and then testing is performed with varying SNR signals. The classification results are shown in Figure 8. The overall trend of scenario two result shows that training with low SNR signals deteriorates the classification

accuracy for KNN classifier while neural network provide the same accuracy as of scenario one and it is not affected by the training SNR.

Figure 9 shows the classification results, when classifier is trained with both low and high SNR signals. The hypothesis was that this scenario would provide the accurate classification results for KNN classifier because it has the training samples from both low and high SNR but when testing was performed with high SNR signals then Rx2 and Rx3 results deteriorated.

KNN is the simplest classifier and it is unable to provide good classification as compared to neural network, which provides accurate result even if it has low SNR signals for the training. The overall accuracy of KNN classifier is poor for scenario one and three as KNN uses Euclidean distance for

Figure 9. Scenario three, where classifier is trained with 40% signals from 0 to 15 SNR signals

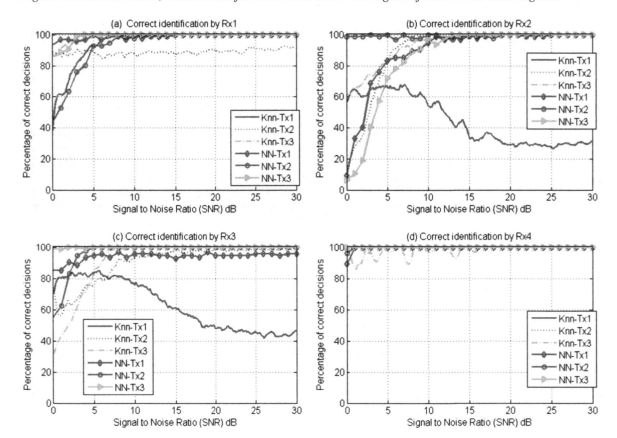

correlation while neural network provides accurate classification irrespective of the training SNR. However, neural network is more complex and resource hungry as compared to KNN.

CONCLUSION

This chapter has experimentally analyzed the effect of receiver SNR in terms of the training data in order to analyze the effect on the performance of overall RF fingerprinting process. Three low-end and one high-end receiver are used for the analysis. Two classifiers; KNN and neural network performance are compared and it was found that neural network provide accurate classification and it is not dependent on receiver SNR whereas KNN classifier provide accurate results, when it is trained with high SNR signals.

Our results suggest that the real-time implementation of RF fingerprinting using today's typical low-end receivers is considerably more challenging than might be suggested by experiments carried out with high-end receivers in controlled environments and sophisticated classifiers. Our results suggest that the accuracy of classification results varies with receiver SNR if a simple classifier like KNN is used. However, a more complex classifier like neural network would provide good classification results but then it is complex to implement in the low resources mobile transceivers.

REFERENCES

Afolabi, O., Kim, K., & Ahmad, A. (2009). On Secure Spectrum Sensing in Cognitive Radio Networks Using Emitters Electromagnetic Signature. In *Proceedings of IEEE 18th International Conference on Computer Communications and Networks*. IEEE.

Bertoncini, C., Rudd, K., Nousain, B., & Hinders, M. (2012). Wavelet fingerprinting of radio frequency identification (RFID) tags. *IEEE Transactions on Industrial Electronics*, *59*(12), 4843–4850. doi:10.1109/TIE.2011.2179276

Bonne Rasmussen, K., & Capkun, S. (2007). Implications of radio fingerprinting on the security of sensor networks. In *Proceedings of Security and Privacy in Communications Networks and the Workshops* (pp. 331–340). Nice, France: IEEE. doi:10.1109/SECCOM.2007.4550352

Brik, V., Banerjee, S., Gruteser, M., & Oh, S. (2008). Wireless device identification with radiometric signatures. In *Proceedings of the 14th ACM international conference on Mobile computing and networking*, (pp. 116-127). New York, NY: ACM.

Chen, R., Park, J., & Reed, J. (2008). Defense against primary user emulation attacks in cognitive radio networks. *IEEE Journal on Selected Areas in Communications*, *26*(1), 25–37. doi:10.1109/JSAC.2008.080104

Danev, B., & Čapkun, S. (2009). Transient-based identification of wireless sensor nodes. In *Proceedings of the 8th IEEE/ACM Information Processing in Sensor Networks*, (pp. 25-36). Washington, DC: IEEE/ACM.

Danev, B., Heydt-Benjamin, T. S., & Čapkun, S. (2009). Physical-layer identification of RFID devices. In *Proceedings of the 18th USENIX Security Symposium*, (pp. 125-136). Montreal, Canada: USENIX.

Danev, B., Luecken, H., Capkun, S., & El Defrawy, K. (2010). Attacks on physical-layer identification. In *Proc. ACM Conf on Wireless network security*, (pp. 89-98). ACM.

Debbah, M. (2008). Mobile flexible networks: The challenges ahead. In *Proceedings of International Conference on Advanced Technologies for Communications*. ATC.

Edman, M., & Yener, B. (2009). *Active attacks against modulation-based radiometric identification*. Rensselaer Institute of Technology, Technical report, pages 09-02. Retrieved on 10 January, 2014 from http://www.cs.rpi.edu/research/pdf/09-02.pdf

Ellis, K., & Serinken, N. (2001). Characteristics of radio transmitter fingerprints. *Radio Science*, *36*(4), 585–597. doi:10.1029/2000RS002345

Ettus, M. (2012). *Universal software radio peripheral*. Ettus Research. Retrieved on 10 Jan, 2014 from www.ettus.com

Faria, D., & Cheriton, D. (2006). Detecting identity-based attacks in wireless networks using signalprints. In *Proceedings of the 5th ACM workshop on Wireless security*, (pp. 43-52). ACM.

Gard, K., Larson, L., & Steer, M. (2005). The impact of rf front-end characteristics on the spectral regrowth of communications signals. *IEEE Transactions on Microwave Theory and Techniques*, *53*(6), 2179–2186. doi:10.1109/TMTT.2005.848801

Hall, J., Barbeau, M., & Kranakis, E. (2003). Detection of transient in radio frequency fingerprinting using signal phase. In *Proceedings of Wireless and Optical Communications* (pp. 13–18). Academic Press.

Hall, J., Barbeau, M., & Kranakis, E. (2004). Enhancing intrusion detection in wireless networks using radio frequency fingerprinting. In *Proceedings of the 3rd IASTED International Conference on Communications, Internet and Information Technology* (CIIT), (pp. 201-206). IASTED.

Hall, J., Barbeau, M., & Kranakis, E. (2005). *Radio frequency fingerprinting for intrusion detection in wireless networks*. IEEE Transactions on Defendable and Secure Computing.

Hall, J., Barbeau, M., & Kranakis, E. (2006). Detecting rogue devices in bluetooth networks using radio frequency fingerprinting. In *Proceedings of IASTED International Conference on Communications and Computer Networks*. IASTED.

Hippenstiel, R., & Payal, Y. (1996). Wavelet based transmitter identification. [). IEEE.]. *Proceedings of Signal Processing and Its Applications*, *2*, 740–742.

Hoogerwerf, D., Green, E., Stanhope, D., & McKernan, R. (2000). *Active waveform collection for use in transmitter identification* (US Patent 6,035,188). Washington, DC: US Patent Office.

Jain, A., Mao, J., & Mohiuddin, K. M. (1996). Artificial neural networks: a tutorial. *Computer*, *29*(3), 31–44. doi:10.1109/2.485891

Kaplan, D., & Stanhope, D. (1999). *Waveform collection for use in wireless telephone identification* (US Patent 5,999,806). Washington, DC: US Patent Office.

Kauffmann, B., Baccelli, F., Chaintreau, A., Mhatre, V., Papagiannaki, K., & Diot, C. (2007). Measurement-based self-organization of interfering 802.11 wireless access networks. In *Proceedings of 26th IEEE international Conference on Computer Communications*. IEEE.

Kennedy, I., Scanlon, P., & Buddhikot, M. (2008a). Passive steady state rf fingerprinting: a cognitive technique for scalable deployment of co-channel femto cell underlays. In *Proceedings of 3rd IEEE Symposium on New Frontiers in Dynamic Spectrum Access Networks*. IEEE.

Kennedy, I., Scanlon, P., Mullany, F., Buddhikot, M., Nolan, K., & Rondeau, T. (2008b). Radio transmitter fingerprinting: A steady state frequency domain approach. In *Proceedings of IEEE 68th Vehicular Technology Conference*. IEEE.

Kim, K., Spooner, C., Akbar, I., & Reed, J. (2008). Specific emitter identification for cognitive radio with application to IEEE 802.11. In *Proceedings of Global Telecommunications Conference*. IEEE.

Li, Q., & Trappe, W. (2007). Detecting spoofing and anomalous traffic in wireless networks via forge-resistant relationships. *IEEE Transactions on Information Forensics and Security*, *2*(4), 793–808. doi:10.1109/TIFS.2007.910236

Marcus, M. (1992). *Progress in vhf/nhf mobile transmitter identification*. University of Manitoba.

Martínez, A. M., & Kak, A. C. (2001). PCA versus LDA. *IEEE Transactions on Pattern Analysis and Machine Intelligence*, *23*(2), 228–233. doi:10.1109/34.908974

Mathur, S., Reznik, A., Ye, C., Mukherjee, R., Rahman, A., & Shah, Y. et al. (2010). Exploiting the physical layer for enhanced security. *IEEE Wireless Communications*, *17*(5), 63–70. doi:10.1109/MWC.2010.5601960

Meyer, U., & Wetzel, S. (2004). A man-in-the-middle attack on umts. In *Proceedings of the 3rd ACM workshop on Wireless security*, (pp. 90-97). Philadelphia, PA: ACM.

Nansai Hu, Y.-D. Y. (2012). Identification of legacy radios in a cognitive radio network using a radio frequency fingerprinting based method. In *Proceedings of IEEE International Conference on Communications* (pp. 1597—1602). Ottawa, Canada: IEEE.

Nguyen, N., Zheng, G., Han, Z., & Zheng, R. (2011).Device fingerprinting to enhance wireless security using nonparametric bayesian method. In *Proceedings of INFOCOM*, (pp. 1404-1412). Shanghai, China: IEEE.

Polak, A., Dolatshahi, S., & Goeckel, D. (2011). Identifying wireless users via transmitter imperfections. *IEEE Journal on Selected Areas in Communications*, 29(7), 1469–1479. doi:10.1109/JSAC.2011.110812

Rehman, S., Sowerby, K., & Coghill, C. (2012). RF fingerprint extraction from the energy envelope of an instantaneous transient signal. In *Proceedings of Communications Theory Workshop* (AusCTW), (pp. 90-95). Wellington, New Zealand: AusCTW.

Scanlon, P., Kennedy, I., & Liu, Y. (2010). Feature extraction approaches to rf fingerprinting for device identification in femtocells. *Bell Labs Technical Journal*, 15(3), 141–151. doi:10.1002/bltj.20462

Shi, Y., & Jensen, M. (2011). Improved radiometric identification of wireless devices using mimo transmission. *IEEE Transactions on Information Forensics and Security*, 6(4), 1346–1354. doi:10.1109/TIFS.2011.2162949

Shiu, Y., Chang, S., Wu, H., Huang, S., & Chen, H. (2011). Physical layer security in wireless networks: A tutorial. *IEEE Wireless Communications*, 18(2), 66–74. doi:10.1109/MWC.2011.5751298

Standards Committee. L., et al. (2003). Part 11: Wireless LAN medium access control (MAC) and physical layer (PHY) specifications. IEEE-SA Standards Board.

Suski, W., Temple, M., Mendenhall, M., & Mills, R. (2008). Using spectral fingerprints to improve wireless network security. In *Proceedings of Global Telecommunications Conference*. IEEE.

Suski, W. II, Temple, M., Mendenhall, M., & Mills, R. (2008). Radio frequency fingerprinting commercial communication devices to enhance electronic security. *International Journal of Electronic Security and Digital Forensics*, 1(3), 301–322. doi:10.1504/IJESDF.2008.020946

Toonstra, J., & Kinsner, W. (2002). A radio transmitter fingerprinting system ODO-1. In *Proceedings of Canadian Conference on Electrical and Computer Engineering*, (vol. 1, pp. 60-63). IEEE.

USRP. (2013). *USRP products*. Retrieved January 10, 2014 from https://www.ettus.com/product

Widrow, B., & Lehr, M. (1990). 30 years of adaptive neural networks: perceptron, madaline, and backpropagation. *Proceedings of the IEEE*, 78(9), 1415–1442. doi:10.1109/5.58323

Woelfle, M., Temple, M., Mullins, M., & Mendenhall, M. (2009). Detecting, identifying and locating bluetooth devices using RF fingerprints. In *Proceedings of 2009 Military Communications Conference* (MILCOM 2009). Boston, MA: MILCOM.

Xu, S., Xu, L., Xu, Z., & Huang, B. (2008). Individual radio transmitter identification based on spurious modulation characteristics of signal envelop. In *Proceedings of IEEE Military Communications Conference*. IEEE.

Zamora, G., Bergin, S., & Kennedy, I. (2010). Using Support Vector Machines for Passive Steady State RF Fingerprinting. In *Novel Algorithms and Techniques in Telecommunications and Networking* (pp. 183–188). Academic Press. doi:10.1007/978-90-481-3662-9_31

Zanetti, D., Danev, B., & Čapkun, S. (2010). Physical-layer identification of UHF RFID tags. In *Proceedings of the 16th ACM Conference on Mobile Computing and Networking* (pp. 353-364). Chicago: ACM.

Zhao, W., Krishnaswamy, A., Chellappa, R., Swets, D. L., & Weng, J. (1998). Discriminant analysis of principal components for face recognition. In *Face Recognition* (pp. 73–85). Springer. doi:10.1007/978-3-642-72201-1_4

KEY TERMS AND DEFINITIONS

GNU Radio: GNU Radio is a free open-source software platform that is natively supported by Linux (Blossom, 2004). GNU radio provides libraries of signal processing blocks to implement a software-defined radio that can be coupled with an appropriate hardware platform such as USRP.

RF Fingerprinting: The process of identifying wireless nodes using the unique features extracted from the electromagnetic waves emitted from the transmitters.

Universal Software Radio Peripheral (USRP): A software radio platform used to generate the waveforms in GNU radio and transmitted through USRP hardware.

Compilation of References

Abbott Diabetes Care Company. (n.d.). Retrieved from http://www.abbottdiabetescare.com

Abolpour, B., Javan, M., & Karamouz, M. (2007). Water allocation improvement in river basin using adaptive neural fuzzy reinforcement learning approach. *Applied Soft Computing, 7*(1), 265–285. doi:10.1016/j.asoc.2005.02.007

Abonyi, J., Feil, B., & Abraham, A. (2005). Computational Intelligence in Data Mining. *Informatica, 29*, 3–12.

Abraham, A., Guo, H., & Liu, H. (2006). Swarm intelligence: foundations, perspectives and applications. In *Swarm Intelligent Systems* (pp. 3–25). Springer. doi:10.1007/978-3-540-33869-7_1

Afolabi, O., Kim, K., & Ahmad, A. (2009). On Secure Spectrum Sensing in Cognitive Radio Networks Using Emitters Electromagnetic Signature. In *Proceedings of IEEE 18th International Conference on Computer Communications and Networks.* IEEE.

Afshin, M., Sadeghian, A., & Raahemifar, K. (2007). On Efficient Tuning of LS-SVM Hyper-Parameters in Short-Term Load Forecasting: A Comparative Study. In *Procedings of the IEEE Power Engineering Society General Meeting.* Tampa, FL: IEEE.

Agarwal, M., Goyal, M., & Deo, M. C. (2010). Locally weighted projection regression for predicting hydraulic parameters. *Civil Engineering and Environmental Systems, 27*(1), 71–80. doi:10.1080/10286600802517491

Ahmed Farid, J., & Salahudin, F. (2010). *Risk Frameworks and Applications* (2nd ed.). Karachi: Alchemy Technologies Pvt. Ltd.

Akbani, R., Kwek, S., & Japkowicz, N. (2004). Applying support vector machines to imbalanced datasets. In *Proceedings of the 2004 European conference on machine learning* (pp. 39-50). Pisa, Italy: Academic Press.

Akdag, U., Komur, M. A., & Ozguc, A. F. (2009). Estimation of heat transfer in oscillating annular flow using artifical neural networks. *Advances in Engineering Software, 40*(9), 864–870. doi:10.1016/j.advengsoft.2009.01.010

Alam, M. S., Ul Kabir, M. W., & Islam, M. M. (2010). Self-adaptation of mutation step size in Artificial Bee Colony algorithm for continuous function optimization. In *Proceedings of the 13th International Conference on Computer and Information Technology* (ICCIT). Dhaka, Bangladesh: ICCIT.

Alam, S. (2012). *Clustering, swarms and recommender systems.* (Doctoral dissertation). ResearchSpace@ Auckland.

Alam, S., Dobbie, G., & Riddle, P. (2008). An evolutionary particle swarm optimization algorithm for data clustering. In *Proceedings of IEEE Swarm Intelligence Symposium,* (pp. 1-6). IEEE.

Alam, S., Dobbie, G., Koh, Y. S., & Riddle, P. (2014). Web Bots Detection Using Particle Swarm Optimization Based Clustering. In *Proceedings of IEEE Congress on Evolutionary Computation* (CEC). Beijing, China. IEEE.

Alam, S., Dobbie, G., Riddle, P., & Naeem, M. A. (2010). A swarm intelligence based clustering approach for outlier detection. In *Proceedings of IEEE Congress on Evolutionary Computation* (CEC), (pp. 1-7). IEEE.

Alam, S., Dobbie, G., Riddle, P., & Naeem, M. A. (2010). Particle swarm optimization based hierarchical agglomerative clustering. In *Proceedings of IEEE/WIC/ACM International Conference on Web Intelligence and Intelligent Agent Technology* (WI-IAT), (Vol. 2, pp. 64-68). Toronto, Canada: IEEE.

Alam, S., Dobbie, G., Sing Koh, Y., Riddle, P., & Ur Rehman, S. (2014). Research on Particle Swarm Optimization Based Clustering: A systematic review of literature and techniques. In *Swarm and Evolutionary Computation*. Elsevier. doi:10.1016/j.swevo.2014.02.001

Allen, S.M., Colombo, & Whitaker. (2010). Cooperation through self-similar social networks. *ACM Transactions on Autonomous and Adaptive Systems, 5*(1), Article 4.

Allen, L. (2010). *An introduction to stochastic processes with applications to biology* (2nd ed.). Chapman and Hall/CRC.

Al-Shalabi, L., Shaaban, Z., & Kasasbeh, B. (2006). Data Mining: A Preprocessing Engine. *Journal of Computer Science, 2*(9), 735–739. doi:10.3844/jcssp.2006.735.739

Altrock, C. V. (1995). *Fuzzy logic and neurofuzzy applications explained*. Prentice-Hall.

Amaefule, J. O., Altunbay, M., Tiab, D., Kersey, D. G., & Keelan, D. K. (1993). Enhanced reservoir description: using core and log data to identify hydraulic (flow) units and predict permeability in uncored intervals/wells. In *Proceedings of the SPE 68th Annual Technical Conference and Exhibition*. Houston, TX: SPE/Onepetro Database.

Amyx, J. W., Bass, D. M. Jr, & Whiting, R. L. (1960). *Petroleum Reservoir Engineering, Physical Properties*. New York: McGraw-Hill.

Andre, D., Bennett, F. H., III, & Koza, J. R. (1996). Discovery by genetic programming of a cellular automata rule that is better than any known rule for the majority classification problem. In *Proceedings of First Annual Conference on Genetic Programming* (pp. 3-11). Stanford, CA: Academic Press.

Andrianasy, F., & Milgram, M. (1997). Applying Artificial Neural Networks to adjust insulin pump doses. In *Proceedings of Artificial Neural Networks for Signal Processing VII Proceedings of the IEEE Signal Processing Society Workshop*. The Institute of Electrical and Electronic Engineers, Inc.

Angiulli, F., & Pizzuti, C. (2005). Outlier mining in large high-dimensional data sets. *IEEE Transactions on Knowledge and Data Engineering, 17*(2), 203–215. doi:10.1109/TKDE.2005.31

Anifowose, F., Labadin, J., & Abdulraheem, A. (2013b). Ensemble learning model for petroleum reservoir characterization: A case of feed-forward back-propagation neural networks. In J. Li, et al. (Eds.), *International Workshop on Data Mining Applications in Industry and Government under the 17th Pacific-Asia Conference on Knowledge Discovery and Data Mining, Gold Trends and Applications in Knowledge Discovery and Data Mining* (LNCS), (vol. 7867, pp. 71-82). Berlin: Springer.

Anifowose, F., Labadin, J., & Abdulraheem, A. (2013c). Ensemble Model of artificial neural networks with randomized number of hidden neurons. In *Proceedings of the 8th International Conference on Information Technology in Asia* (pp. 1-5). Kuching, Malaysia: IEEEXplore.

Anifowose, F., Labadin, J., & Abdulraheem, A. (2013a). A least square-driven functional networks type-2 fuzzy logic hybrid model for efficient petroleum reservoir properties prediction. *Neural Computing & Applications*. doi:10.1007/s00521-012-1298-2

Ansari, A. Q., Biswas, R., & Aggarwal, S. (2012). Neutrosophic classifier: An extension of fuzzy classifer. *Applied Soft Computing, 13*, 563–573. doi:10.1016/j.asoc.2012.08.002

Armstrong, J. S. (2001). *A Handbook for Researchers and Practitioners*. New York: Springer.

Arora, S., & Barak, B. (2009). *Computational complexity: a modern approach*. New York: Cambridge University Press. doi:10.1017/CBO9780511804090

ASCE Task Committee on Application of Artificial Neural Networks in Hydrology. (2000). Artificial neural networks in hydrology. *Journal of Hydrologic Engineering*, *5*(2), 115–137. doi:10.1061/(ASCE)1084-0699(2000)5:2(115)

Aysal, T. C. Coates, & Rabbat. (2007). Distributed average consensus using probabilistic quantization. In *Proceedings of IEEE 14th Workshop on Statistical Signal Processing* (pp. 640-644). Madison, WI: IEEE.

Azamathulla, H. M., & Zahiri, A. (2012). Flow discharge prediction in compound channels using linear genetic programming. *Journal of Hydrology (Amsterdam)*, *454-455*, 203–207. doi:10.1016/j.jhydrol.2012.05.065

Babaoglu, O., Canright, Deutsch, di Caro, Ducatelle, Gambardella, Ganguly, …. Urnes, T. (2006). Design patterns from biology to distributed computing. *ACM Transactions on Autonomous and Adaptive Systems*, *1*(1), 26-66.

Babayigit, B., & Ozdemir, R. (2012). A modified artificial bee colony algorithm for numerical function optimization. In *Proceedings of the IEEE Symposium on Computers and Communications* (ISCC). Cappadocia, Turkey: IEEE.

Bache, K., & Lichman, M. (2013). *UCI Machine Learning Repository*. Irvine, CA: University of California, School of Information and Computer Science.

Bao, Y., Zhang, X., Yu, L., Lai, K. K., & Wang, S. (2011). An Integrated Model Using Wavelet Decomposition and Least Squares Support Vector Machines for Monthly Crude Oil Prices Forecasting. *New Mathematics and Natural Computation*, *7*(2), 299–311. doi:10.1142/S1793005711001949

Barchart. (2012). Retrieved November, 2011, from http://www.barchart.com/historicalquote.php?view=quote&sym=CLY00&txtDate=12%2F31%2F09&submit=Get+Data

Bar-Cohen, Y. (2005). *Biomimetics: biologically inspired technologies*. Boca Raton, FL: CRC Press.

Baruah, S. K., & Goossens, J. (2003). Rate-Monotonic scheduling on uniform multiprocessors. *IEEE Transactions on Computers*, *52*(7), 966–970. doi:10.1109/TC.2003.1214344

Barua, S., Monirul Islam, M., Yao, X., & Murase, K. (2013). MWMOTE: Majority weighted minority oversampling technique for imbalanced data set learning. *IEEE Transactions on Knowledge and Data Engineering*.

Baruque, B., & Corchado, E. (2010). The committee of experts approach: ensemble learning. In *Fusion Method for Unsupervised Learning Ensembles* (pp. 31–47). Springer-Verlag. doi:10.1007/978-3-642-16205-3_3

Bastos, J. A. (2013). Ensemble predictions of recovery rates. *Journal of Financial Services Research*, 1–17.

Batyrshin, I. (2004). On linguistic representation of quantitative dependencies. *Expert Systems with Applications*, *26*, 95–104. doi:10.1016/S0957-4174(03)00111-8

Batyrshin, I., Kaynak, O., & Rudas, I. (2002). Fuzzy modeling based on generalized conjunction operations. *IEEE Transactions on Fuzzy Systems*, *10*(5), 678–683. doi:10.1109/TFUZZ.2002.803500

Bavdaž, M. (2010). Sources of Measurement Errors in Business Surveys. *Journal of Official Statistics*, *26*, 25–42.

Bay, S. D., & Schwabacher, M. (2003). Mining distance-based outliers in near linear time with randomization and a simple pruning rule. In *Proceedings of the ninth ACM SIGKDD international conference on Knowledge discovery and data mining* (pp. 29-38). Washington, DC: ACM.

Baylar, A. (2002). *Study on the effect of type selection of weir aerators on oxygen transfer*. (Ph.D. thesis). Firat University, Elazig, Turkey.

Baylar, A. (2003). An investigation on the use of venturi weirs as an aerator. *Water Quality Research Journal of Canada*, *38*(4), 753–767.

Baylar, A., & Bagatur, T. (2000). Aeration performance of weirs. *Water S.A.*, *26*(4), 521–526.

Baylar, A., & Bagatur, T. (2001a). Aeration performance of weirs. *Water Engineering & Management*, *148*(3), 33–36.

Baylar, A., & Bagatur, T. (2006). Experimental studies on air entrainment and oxygen content downstream of sharp-crested weirs. *Water and Environment Journal*, *20*(4), 210–216. doi:10.1111/j.1747-6593.2005.00002.x

Baylar, A., Bagatur, T., & Tuna, A. (2001a). Aeration performance of triangular notch weirs at recirculating system. *Water Quality Research Journal of Canada*, *36*(1), 121–132.

Baylar, A., Bagatur, T., & Tuna, A. (2001b). Aeration performance of triangular-notch weirs. *Journal of the Chartered Institution of Water and Environmental Management*, *15*(3), 203–206. doi:10.1111/j.1747-6593.2001.tb00334.x

Baylar, A., & Emiroglu, M. E. (2007). The role of weir types in entrainment of air bubbles. *International Journal of Science and Technology*, *2*(2), 143–154.

Baylar, A., Hanbay, D., & Ozpolat, E. (2007). Modeling aeration efficiency of stepped cascades by using ANFIS. *Clean – Soil, Air. Water*, *35*(2), 186–192.

Baylar, A., Hanbay, D., & Ozpolat, E. (2008). An expert system for predicting aeration performance of weirs by using ANFIS. *Expert Systems with Applications*, *35*, 1214–1222. doi:10.1016/j.eswa.2007.08.019

Bellazzi, R., Nucci, G., & Cobelli, C. (2001). The subcutaneous route to insulin dependent diabetes therapy. *IEEE Engineering in Medicine and Biology Magazine*. Retrieved from https://ieeexplore.ieee.org

Bell, D. A., & Wang, H. (2000). A formalism for relevance and its application in feature subset selection. *Machine Learning*, *41*(2), 175–195. doi:10.1023/A:1007612503587

Bénézit, F. Thiran, & Vetterli. (2009). Interval Consensus: From Quantized Gossip to Voting. In *Proceedings of IEEE International Conference on Acoustics, Speech, and Signal Processing* (pp. 3661-3664). Taipei, Taiwan: IEEE.

Bénézit, F., Dimakis, Thiran, & Vetterli. (2010). Order-Optimal Consensus Through Randomized Path Averaging. *IEEE Transactions on Information Theory*, *56*(10), 5150–5167. doi:10.1109/TIT.2010.2060050

Bénézit, F., Thiran, P., & Vetterli, M. (2011). The Distributed Multiple Voting Problem. *IEEE Journal of Selected Topics in Signal Processing*, *5*(4), 791–804. doi:10.1109/JSTSP.2011.2114326

Ben-Gal, I. (2004). An upper bound for the weight-balanced testing procedure with multiple searchers. *IIE Transactions*, *36*(5), 481–493. doi:10.1080/07408170490426206

Ben-Gal, I., & Caramanis, M. (2002). Sequential DOE via dynamic programming. *IIE Transactions*, *34*(12), 1087–1100. doi:10.1080/07408170208928937

Ben-Gal, I., Herer, Y., & Raz, T. (2002). Self-correcting inspection procedure under inspection errors. *IIE Transactions*, *34*(6), 529–540. doi:10.1080/07408170208928889

Ben-Gal, I., Morag, G., & Smilovichi, A. (2003). A monitoring procedure for state dependent processes. *Technometrics*, *45*(4), 293–311. doi:10.1198/004017003000000122

Ben-Gal, I., & Singer, G. (2004). Statistical process control via context modeling of finite states processes. *IIE Transactions*, *36*(5), 401–415. doi:10.1080/07408170490426125

Benichou, O., Loverdo, C., Moreau, M., & Voituriez, R. (2011). *Intermittent search strategies*. Retrieved February 13, 2013, from arXiv.org:1104.0639

Benichou, O., Coppey, M., Moreau, M., Suet, P.-H., & Voituriez, R. (2005). Optimal search strategies for hidden targets. *Physical Review Letters*, *94*, 1–4. doi:10.1103/PhysRevLett.94.198101 PMID:16090215

Benioff, P. (1998). Quantum robots and environments. *Physical Review A.*, *58*, 893–904. doi:10.1103/PhysRevA.58.893

Bergstrom, C. T., & Lachmann, M. (1997). Signaling among relatives: Is signaling too costly? *Philosophical Transactions of London Royal Society B*, *352*, 609–617. doi:10.1098/rstb.1997.0041

Bergstrom, C. T., & Lachmann, M. (1998a). Signaling among relatives: Beyond the tower of Babel. *Theoretical Population Biology*, *54*, 146–160. doi:10.1006/tpbi.1997.1372 PMID:9733656

Bergstrom, C. T., & Lachmann, M. (1998b). Signaling among relatives: Talk is cheap. *Proceedings of the National Academy of Sciences of the United States of America*, *95*, 5100–5105. doi:10.1073/pnas.95.9.5100 PMID:9560235

Berlanga, F., Rivera, A., Del Jesus, M., & Herrera, F. (2010). GP-COACH: Genetic Programming-based learning of COmpact and ACcurate fuzzy rule-based classification systems for High-dimensional problems. *Information Sciences*, *180*, 1183–1200. doi:10.1016/j.ins.2009.12.020

Berthold, M. R., & Hand, D. J. (2007). *Intelligent Data Analysis*. Springer.

Bertoncini, C., Rudd, K., Nousain, B., & Hinders, M. (2012). Wavelet fingerprinting of radio frequency identification (RFID) tags. *IEEE Transactions on Industrial Electronics*, *59*(12), 4843–4850. doi:10.1109/TIE.2011.2179276

Bhatt, A. (2002). *Reservoir properties from well logs using neural networks*. (Unpublished doctoral dissertation). Norwegian University of Science and Technology.

Biedl, T., Chan, T., Demaine, E. D., Fleischer, R., Golin, M., King, J. A., & Munro, J.-I. (2004). Fun-Sort – or the Chaos of Unordered Binary Search. *Discrete Applied Mathematics*, *144*, 231–236. doi:10.1016/j.dam.2004.01.003

Bies, R. R., Muldoon, M. F., Pollock, B. G., Manuck, S., Smith, G., & Sale, M. E. (2006). A genetic algorithm-based, hybrid machine learning approach to model selection. *Journal of Pharmacokinetics and Pharmacodynamics*, *33*(2), 195–221. doi:10.1007/s10928-006-9004-6 PMID:16565924

Bishop, C. H., & Svens'en, M. (2003). Bayesian hierarchical mixtures of experts. In *Uncertainty in Artificial Intelligence: Proceedings of the Nineteenth Conference* (pp. 57-64). Morgan Kaufmann.

Black, P. E. (2010). Gnome sort. In *Dictionary of Algorithms and Data Structures*. Retrieved from http://www.nist.gov/dads/HTML/gnomeSort.html

Blagus, R. (2013). Improved shrunken centroid classifiers for high-dimensional class-imbalanced data. *BMC Bioinformatics*, *14*(1), 64–76. doi:10.1186/1471-2105-14-64 PMID:23433084

Bogdan, M. W. (2009). Neural network architecture and learning algorithms: how not to be frustrated with neural networks. *IEEE Industrial Electronics Magazine*, *3*(4), 56–63. doi:10.1109/MIE.2009.934790

Bojarczuk, C., Lopes, H., Freitas, A., & Michalkiewicz, E. (2004). A constrained-syntax genetic programming system for discovering classification rules: Application to medical data sets. *Artificial Intelligence in Medicine*, *30*, 27–48. doi:10.1016/j.artmed.2003.06.001 PMID:14684263

Bolaji, A. L. A., Khader, A. T., Al-Betar, M. A., & Awadallah, M. A. (2013). Artificial Bee Colony Algorithm, its Variants and Applications: A Survey. *Journal of Theoritical and Applied Information Technology*, *47*(2), 434–459.

Bonabeau, E. Dorigo, & Theraulaz. (1999). Swarm Intelligence: From Natural to Artificial Systems. Oxford University Press.

Bonabeau, E. (1997). From classical models of morphogenesis to agent-based models of pattern formation. *Artificial Life*, *3*(3), 191–209. doi:10.1162/artl.1997.3.3.191 PMID:9385734

Bonabeau, E., Theraulaz, & Deneubourg. (1998). Fixed Response Thresholds and the Regulation of Division of Labour in Insect Societies. *Bulletin of Mathematical Biology*, *60*, 753–807. doi:10.1006/bulm.1998.0041

Bonabeau, E., & Meyer, C. (2001). Swarm intelligence: A whole new way to think about business. *Harvard Business Review*, *79*(5), 106–114. PMID:11345907

Bonne Rasmussen, K., & Capkun, S. (2007). Implications of radio fingerprinting on the security of sensor networks. In *Proceedings of Security and Privacy in Communications Networks and the Workshops* (pp. 331–340). Nice, France: IEEE. doi:10.1109/SECCOM.2007.4550352

Booker, L.B., Goldberg, & Holland. (1989). Classifier Systems and Genetic Algorithms. *Artificial Intelligence*, *40*(2), 235–282. doi:10.1016/0004-3702(89)90050-7

Bosc, P., Kraft, D., & Petry, F. (2005). Fuzzy sets in database and information systems, status and opportunities. *Fuzzy Sets and Systems*, *156*, 418–426. doi:10.1016/j.fss.2005.05.039

Bosc, P., & Pivert, O. (2000). SQLf query functionality on top of a regular relational database management system. In M. Pons, M. A. Vila, & J. Kacprzyk (Eds.), *Knowledge Management in Fuzzy Databases* (pp. 171–190). Heidelberg, Germany: Physica-Verlag. doi:10.1007/978-3-7908-1865-9_11

Bovet, D. P., & Crescenzi, P. (2006). *Introduction to the theory of complexity*. San Francisco, CA: Prentice Hall.

Bovet, P., & Benhamou, S. (1988). Spatial analysis of animals' movements using a correlated random walk model. *Journal of Theoretical Biology, 131*, 419–433. doi:10.1016/S0022-5193(88)80038-9

Bowman, W. A. (1996). Maximum ground level concentrations with downwash: the urban stability mode. *Journal of the Air & Waste Management Association, 46*, 615–620. doi:10.1080/10473289.1996.10467495

Boyd, S., Ghosh, A., Prabhakar, B., & Shah, D. (2005). Gossip algorithms: Design, analysis and applications. In *Proceedings of 24th Annual Joint Conference of the IEEE and Communication Societies* (Vol. 3, pp. 1653-1664). Miami, FL: IEEE.

Brabazon, A., & O'Neill, M. (2006). *Biologically inspired algorithms for financial modelling*. Berlin: Springer.

Braitenberg, V. (1986). *Vehicles: Experiments in synthetic psychology*. Cambridge, MA: MIT Press.

Breiman, L. (1996). Bagging predictors. *Machine Learning, 24*(2), 123–140. doi:10.1007/BF00058655

Breiman, L. (2001). Random forests. *Machine Learning, 45*(1), 5–32. doi:10.1023/A:1010933404324

Breukelaar, R., & Bäck, T. (2005). Using a Genetic Algorithm to Evolve Behaviour in Multi Dimensional Cellular Automata. In *Proceedings of Conference on Genetic and Evolutionary Computation* (pp. 107-114). Washington, DC: Academic Press.

Breunig, M. M., Kriegel, H. P., Ng, R. T., & Sander, J. (2000). LOF: Identifying density-based local outliers. *SIGMOD Record, 29*(2), 93–104. doi:10.1145/335191.335388

Brik, V., Banerjee, S., Gruteser, M., & Oh, S. (2008). Wireless device identification with radiometric signatures. In *Proceedings of the 14th ACM international conference on Mobile computing and networking*, (pp. 116-127). New York, NY: ACM.

Brock, W. A., Scheinkman, J. A., Dechert, W. D., & LeBaron, B. (1996). A Test for Independence on the Correlation Dimension. *Econometrics Reviews, 15*(3), 197–235. doi:10.1080/07474939608800353

Brown, G., Wyatt, J., Harris, R., & Yao, X. (2005). Diversity creation methods: a survey and categorization. *Information Fusion, 6*(1), 5–20. doi:10.1016/j.inffus.2004.04.004

Brown, M., & Harris, C. (1994). *Neurofuzzy adaptive modeling and control*. Prentice-Hall.

Burke, E. K., Hyde, M., Kendall, G., Ochoa, G., Özcan, E., & Woodward, J. R. (2010). A classification of hyper-heuristic approaches. In Handbook of Metaheuristics (pp. 449-468). Springer US.

Burke, E., Kendall, G., Newall, J., Hart, E., Ross, P., & Schulenburg, S. (2003). Hyper-heuristics: An emerging direction in modern search technology. In International series in operations research and management science, (pp. 457-474). Springer.

Buttazzo, G., Spuri, M., & Sensini, F. (1995). Value vs. Deadline scheduling in overload conditions. In *Proceeding of Real-Time System Symposium,* (pp. 90-99). Academic Press.

Calenge, C., Dray, S., & Royer-Carenzi, M. (2009). The concept of animal's trajectories from a data analysis perspective. *Ecological Informatics, 4*, 34–41. doi:10.1016/j.ecoinf.2008.10.002

Campbell, A., & Wu, A. S. (2011). Multi-agent role allocation: Issues, approaches, and multiple perspectives. *Autonomous Agents and Multi-Agent Systems, 22*(2), 317–355. doi:10.1007/s10458-010-9127-4

Cano, A., Zafra, A., & Ventura, S. (2011). An EP algorithm for learning highly interpretable classifiers. In *Proceedings of Intelligent Systems Design and Applications (ISDA)* (pp. 325–330). Cordoba, Spain: IEEE. doi:10.1109/ISDA.2011.6121676

Cao, Z., & Kandel, A. (1989). Applicability of some fuzzy implication operators. *Fuzzy Sets and Systems, 31*, 151–186. doi:10.1016/0165-0114(89)90002-X

Capcarrere, M.S., & Sipper. (2001). Necessary conditions for density classification by cellular automata. *Physical Review E: Statistical, Nonlinear, and Soft Matter Physics, 64*(3), 036113. doi:10.1103/PhysRevE.64.036113 PMID:11580400

Carlisle, A., & Dozier, G. (2001). an off-the-shelf PSO. In *Proceedings of Particle Swarm Optimization Workshop* (pp. 1-6). Academic Press.

Carman, P. C. (1937). Fluid flow through a granular bed. *Transactions of the Institution of Chemical Engineers, 15*, 150–156.

Carnap, R. (1967). *Logical foundations of probability.* University of Chicago Press.

Carvalho, M., & Ludermir, T. B. (2007). Particle swarm optimization of neural network architectures and weights. In *Proceedings of the 7th international conference on hybrid intelligent systems* (pp. 336-339). Kaiserlautern, Australia: Academic Press.

Casadei, M., Gardelli, L., & Viroli, M. (2006). Collective Sorting Tuple Spaces. In *Proceedings of 11ᵗʰ International Workshop on Cooperative Information Agents* (pp. 255-269). Delft, The Netherlands: Academic Press.

Casadei, M., Menezes, R., Viroli, M., & Tolksdorf, R. (2007). Using Ant's Brood Sorting to Increase Fault Tolerance in Linda's Tuple Distribution Mechanism. In *Proceedings of 7ᵗʰ Workshop from Objects to Agents* (pp. 173-180). Catania, Italy: Academic Press.

Castillo-Ortega, R., Marín, N., Sánchez, D., & Tettamanzi, A. (2012). Quality Assessment in Linguistic Summaries of Data. In S. Greco, B. Bouchon-Meunier, G. Coletti, M. Fedrizzi, B. Matarazzo, & R. Yager (Eds.), *14ᵗʰ International Conference on Information Processing and Management of Uncertainty in Knowledge-Based Systems IPMU 2012* (pp. 285-294). Berlin: Springer-Verlag.

Cervantes, A., Galván, O. M., & Isasi, P. (2009). AMPSO: A new particle swarm method for nearest neighborhood classification. *IEEE Transactions on Systems, Man, and Cybernetics. Part B, Cybernetics, 39*(5), 1082–1091. doi:10.1109/TSMCB.2008.2011816 PMID:19336325

Chandrasekaran, B., & Chen, D. W. (1969). Stochastic automata games. *IEEE Transaction on Systems Science and Cybernetics, 5*(2), 145–149. doi:10.1109/TSSC.1969.300206

Chang, P. C., Wu, I. W., Shann, J.-J., & Chung, C. P. (2008). *ETAHM: An energy-aware task allocation algorithm for heterogeneous multiprocessor.* DAC. doi:10.1145/1391469.1391667

Chávez, M. C., Casas, G., Falcón, R., Moreira, J. E., & Grau, R. (2007). Building fine bayesian networks aided by PSO-based feature selection. In *Proceedings of Advances in Artificial Intelligence* (pp. 441–451). Academic Press. doi:10.1007/978-3-540-76631-5_42

Chawla, N. V., & Sylvester, J. (2007). Exploiting diversity in ensembles: Improving the performance on unbalanced datasets. In *Proceedings of the 7th International Workshop on Multiple Classifier Systems* (pp. 397-406). Prague, Czech Republic: Academic Press.

Chawla, N. V., Lazarevic, A., Hall, L. O., & Bowyer, K. W. (2003). SMOTEBoost: Improving prediction of the minority class in boosting. In *Proceedings of the Seventh European conference Principles and Practice of Knowledge Discovery in Databases* (pp. 107-119). Cavtat-Dubrovnik, Croatia: Academic Press.

Chawla, N. V., Bowyer, K. W., Hall, L. O., & Kegelmeyer, W. P. (2002). SMOTE: Synthetic minority over-sampling technique. *Journal of Artificial Intelligence Research, 16*, 321–357.

Chawla, N. V., Cieslak, D. A., Hall, L. O., & Joshi, A. (2008). Automatically countering imbalance and its empirical relationship to cost. *Data Mining and Knowledge Discovery, 17*(2), 225–252. doi:10.1007/s10618-008-0087-0

Chawla, N. V., Japkowicz, N., & Kolcz, A. (2004). Editorial: special issue on learning from imbalanced data sets. *SIGKDD Explorations, 6*(1), 1–6. doi:10.1145/1007730.1007733

Chen, C. Y., & Ye, F. (2004). Particle swarm optimization algorithm and its application to clustering analysis. In *Proceedings of IEEE International Conference on Networking, Sensing and Control, 2004* (Vol. 2, pp. 789-794). Taipei, Taiwan: IEEE.

Chen, D., Quirein, J., Hamid, S., Smith, H., & Grable, J. (2004). Neural network ensemble selection using multiobjective genetic algorithm in processing pulsed neutron data. In *Proceedings of the 45th Annual Logging Symposium.* Noordwijk, The Netherlands: SPE/Onepetro database.

Chen, J., & Zhang, H. (2007). Research on application of clustering algorithm based on PSO for the web usage pattern. In *Proceedings of International Conference on Wireless Communications, Networking and Mobile Computing WiCom 2007* (pp. 3705-3708). Shanghai, China: IEEE.

Chen, Q., Wu, Y., & Chen, X. (2008). Research on Customers Demand Forecasting for E-business Web Site Based on LS-SVM. In *Proceedings of the International Symposium on Electronic Commerce and Security.* Nachang City, China: Academic Press.

Chen, X., Wang, J., Sun, D., & Liang, J. (2008). Time Series Forecasting Based on Novel Support Vector Machine Using Artificial Fish Swarm Algorithm. In *Proceedings of the Fourth International Conference on Natural Computation* (ICNC). Jinan, China: ICNC.

Chen, C. H., & Lin, Z. S. (2006). A committee machine with empirical formulas for permeability prediction. *Computers & Geosciences, 32*(4), 485–496. doi:10.1016/j.cageo.2005.08.003

Chen, G., Kerre, E. E., & Vandenbulcke, J. (1996). Normalization based on fuzzy functional dependency in a fuzzy relational data model. *Information Systems, 21,* 299–310. doi:10.1016/0306-4379(96)00016-6

Cheng, Q., Varshney, P. K., & Arora, M. K. (2006). Logistic regression for feature selection and soft classification of remote sensing data. *IEEE Geoscience and Remote Sensing Letters, 3*(4), 491–494. doi:10.1109/LGRS.2006.877949

Chen, R., Park, J., & Reed, J. (2008). Defense against primary user emulation attacks in cognitive radio networks. *IEEE Journal on Selected Areas in Communications, 26*(1), 25–37. doi:10.1109/JSAC.2008.080104

Chen, W., & Du, Y. (2009). Using neural networks and data mining techniques for the financial distress prediction model. *Expert Systems with Applications, 36,* 4075–4086. doi:10.1016/j.eswa.2008.03.020

Chen, Y., & Zhao, Y. (2008). A novel ensemble of classifiers for microarray data classification. *Applied Soft Computing, 8,* 1664–1669. doi:10.1016/j.asoc.2008.01.006

Chenyang, L., Stankovic, J. A., Gang, T., & Sang, H. S. (1999). Design and evaluation of a feedback control EDF scheduling algorithm. In *Proceedings of IEEE Real-Time System Symposium,* (pp. 56-67). IEEE.

Chernikhovsky, G., Kagan, E., Goren, G., & Ben-Gal, I. (2012). Path planning for sea vessel search using wideband sonar. In *Proceedings of 27th IEEE Convention of Electrical and Electronics Engineers in Israel.* IEEE. doi:10.1109/EEEI.2012.6377122

Children with Diabetes. (n.d.). Retrieved from http://www.childrenwithdiabetes.com/continuous.htm

Cho, Y. H., Kim, J. K., & Kim, S. H. (2002). A personalized recommender system based on web usage mining and decision tree induction. *Expert Systems with Applications, 23*(3), 329–342. doi:10.1016/S0957-4174(02)00052-0

Chris, S., Taghi, M. K., Jason, V. H., & Amri, N. (2008). A comparative study of data sampling and cost sensitive learning. In *Proceedings of IEEE International Conference on Data Mining Workshops.* Pisa, Italy: IEEE.

Chung, C. J., & Reynolds, R. G. (1996). A Testbed for Solving Optimization Problems Using Cultural Algorithms. In *Evolutionary Programming* (pp. 225–236). Academic Press.

Chung, T. H., Hollinger, G. A., & Isler, V. (2011). Search and pursuit-evasion in mobile robotics: A survey. *Autonomous Robots, 31*(4), 299–316. doi:10.1007/s10514-011-9241-4

Church, P. E. (1949). Dilution of Waste stack gases in the atmosphere. *Industrial & Engineering Chemistry, 41,* 2753–2756. doi:10.1021/ie50480a022

Cigizoğlu, H. K. (2005). Application of generalized regression neural networks to intermittent flow forecasting and estimation. *J. Hydrol. Engng ASCE, 10*(4), 336–341. doi:10.1061/(ASCE)1084-0699(2005)10:4(336)

Cinar, A. Quinn, & Smith. (2006). Low-Order Linear Dynamic Models for Prediction of Blood Glucose Concentration. In *Proceedings of AIChE Annual Meeting*. San Francisco, CA: AIChE.

Clark, A. (1997). *Being there: Putting brain, body and world together again*. Cambridge, MA: MIT Press.

Clerc, M. (2006). *Particle swarm optimization* (Vol. 243). London: ISTE. doi:10.1002/9780470612163

Cleveland, W. S. (1979). Robust locally weighted regression and smoothing scatterplots. *Journal of the American Statistical Association*, 74, 829–836. doi:10.1080/01621 459.1979.10481038

Coates, G. R., Menger, S., Prammer, M., & Miller, D. (1997). Applying NMR Total and Effective Porosity to Formation Evaluation. In *Proceedings of the 1997 SPE Annual Technical Conference and Exhibition*. San Antonio, TX: SPE/Onepetro database.

Coates, G., & Denoo, S. (1981). The producibility answer product. *Technology Review*, 29(2), 55–63.

Cochocki, A., & Unbehauen, R. (1993). *Neural networks for optimization and signal processing*. Hoboken, NJ: John Wiley & Sons, Inc.

Coello, C. A. C., & Cortés, N. C. (2002). An approach to solve multiobjective optimization problems based on an artificial immune system. In *Proceedings of 1st International Conference on Artificial Immune Systems (ICARIS)*. ICARIS.

Coello, C. A. C., & Cortés, N. C. (2005). Solving multiobjective optimization problems using an artificial immune system. *Genetic Programming and Evolvable Machines*, 6(2), 163–190. doi:10.1007/s10710-005-6164-x

Coello, C. A., & Becerra, R. L. (2004). Efficient evolutionary optimization through the use of a cultural algorithm. *Engineering Optimization*, 36(2), 219–236. doi:10.1080 /03052150410001647966

Cohen, S. C., & de Castro, L. N. (2006). Data clustering with particle swarms. In *Proceedings of IEEE Congress on Evolutionary Computation*, (pp. 1792-1798). Vancouver, Canada: IEEE.

Cohen, W. (1995). Fast effective rule induction. In *Proceedings of International Conference on Machine Learning (ICML)*, (pp. 115-123). Tahoe City, CA: ICML.

Cole, B. J., & Cheshire, D. (1996). Mobile cellular automat models of ant behavior: Movement activity of leptothorax allardycei. *American Naturalist*, 148(1), 1–15. doi:10.1086/285908

Condamin, S., Benichou, O., Tejedor, V., Voituriez, R., & Klafter, J. (2007). First-passage times in complex scale-invariant media. *Nature*, 450, 77–80. doi:10.1038/ nature06201 PMID:17972880

Cormen, T. H., Leicerson, C. E., Rivest, R. L., & Stein, C. (2009). *Introduction to Algorithms* (3rd ed.). MIT Press.

Couzin, I. D., Krause, J., Franks, N. R., & Levin, S. A. (2005). Effective leadership and decision making in animal groups on move. *Nature*, 433, 513–516. doi:10.1038/ nature03236 PMID:15690039

Cubero, J. C., Medina, J. M., Pons, O., & Vila, M. A. (1999). Data summarization in relational databases through fuzzy dependencies. *Information Sciences*, 121, 233–270. doi:10.1016/S0020-0255(99)00104-8

Cunningham, P., & Zenobi, G. (2001). Case representation issues for case-based reasoning from ensemble research. In Case-Based Reasoning Research and Development (LNCS), (vol. 2080, pp. 146-157). Springer.

Cutler, A., Cutler, D. R., & Stevens, J. R. (2012). Random forests. In C. Zhang, & Y. Ma (Eds.), *Ensemble Machine Learning* (pp. 157–175). Springer. doi:10.1007/978-1-4419-9326-7_5

Danev, B., & Čapkun, S. (2009). Transient-based identification of wireless sensor nodes. In *Proceedings of the 8th IEEE/ACM Information Processing in Sensor Networks*, (pp. 25-36). Washington, DC: IEEE/ACM.

Danev, B., Heydt-Benjamin, T. S., & Čapkun, S. (2009). Physical-layer identification of RFID devices. In *Proceedings of the 18th USENIX Security Symposium*, (pp. 125-136). Montreal, Canada: USENIX.

Danev, B., Luecken, H., Capkun, S., & El Defrawy, K. (2010). Attacks on physical-layer identification. In *Proc. ACM Conf on Wireless network security*, (pp. 89-98). ACM.

Das, S., Chowdhury, A., & Abraham, A. (2009). A bacterial evolutionary algorithm for automatic data clustering. In *Proceedings of IEEE Congress on Evolutionary Computation*, (pp. 2403-2410). Trondheim, Norway. IEEE.

DasGupta, D. (1999). *An overview of artificial immune systems and their applications*. Berlin: Springer. doi:10.1007/978-3-642-59901-9

de Leeuw, E., Hox, J., & Huisman, M. (2003). Prevention and Treatment of Item Nonresponse. *Journal of Official Statistics*, *19*(2), 153–176.

Debbah, M. (2008). Mobile flexible networks: The challenges ahead. In *Proceedings of International Conference on Advanced Technologies for Communications*. ATC.

Deb, K. (2001). Multi-objective optimization. In *Multi-objective optimization using evolutionary algorithms* (pp. 13–46). Academic Press.

DeCastro, L. N., & von Zuben, F. J. (Eds.). (2005). *Recent developments in biologically inspired computing*. Hershey, PA: IGI Global.

Dehuri, S., Patnaik, S., Ghosh, A., & Mall, R. (2008). Application of elitist multi-objective genetic algorithm for classification rule generation. *Applied Soft Computing*, *8*, 477–487. doi:10.1016/j.asoc.2007.02.009

Demsar, J. (2006). Statistical comparisons of classifiers over multiple data sets. *Journal of Machine Learning Research*, *7*, 1–30.

Demuth, H. B., & Beale, M. (1999). *Neural Network Toolbox, users guide*. Natick, MA: The Mathworks, Inc.

Demuth, H., Beale, M., & Hagan, M. (2009). *Neural Network Toolbox™ 6 User's Guide*. New York: The MathWorks Inc.

Dertouzos, M., & Ogata, K. (1974). Control Robotics: The procedural control of physical process. In *Proceeding of IFIP Congress*, (pp. 807-813). IFIP.

Dexcom medical device company. (n.d.). Retrieved from http://www.dexcom.com

Diabetic Software Simulator. (n.d.). Retrieved from http://www.2aida.net

Dietterich, T. G. (2000). Ensemble methods in machine learning. In *International Workshop on Multiple Classifier Systems* (LNCS), (vol. 1857, pp. 1-15). Springer-Verlag. DOI: 10.1007/s10693-013-0165-3

Dijkstra, E. W. (1974). Self-stabilizing systems in spite of distributed control. *Communications of the ACM*, *17*(11), 643–644. doi:10.1145/361179.361202

Dimakis, A.D.G., Sarwate, & Wainright. (2008). Geographic gossip: Efficient averaging for sensor networks. *IEEE Transactions on Signal Processing*, *56*(3), 1205–1216. doi:10.1109/TSP.2007.908946

Doerr, B. (2011). Analyzing randomized search heuristics: Tools from probability theory. In *Theory of Randomized Search Heuristics: Foundations and Recent Developments*. World Scientific. doi:10.1142/9789814282673_0001

Dolev, D., Klawe, & Rodeh. (1982). An $O(n\log n)$ unidirectional distributed algorithm for extrema finding in a circle. *Journal of Algorithms*, *3*(3), 245–260. doi:10.1016/0196-6774(82)90023-2

Dombi, J. (1982). A general class of fuzzy operators, the DeMorgan class of fuzzy operators and fuzziness measures induced by fuzzy operators. *Fuzzy Sets and Systems*, *8*(2), 149–163. doi:10.1016/0165-0114(82)90005-7

Domingos, P. (2000). Bayesian averaging of classifiers and the overfitting problem. In *Proceedings of the 17th International Conference on Machine Learning (ICML)* (pp. 223—230). San Francisco, CA: Morgan Kaufmann.

Dorigo, M. (Ed.). (2006). *Ant Colony Optimization and Swarm Intelligence: 5th International Workshop, ANTS 2006*, (Vol. 4150). Springer-Verlag New York Incorporated.

Dorigo, M., & Birattari, M. (2010). Ant colony optimization. In Encyclopedia of Machine Learning (pp. 36-39). Springer US.

Dorigo, M. (2007). Ant colony optimization. *Scholarpedia*, *2*(3), 1461. doi:10.4249/scholarpedia.1461

Dorigo, M., & Caro, G. D. (1999). The Ant Colony Optimization metaheuristic. In *New Ideas in Optimization*. McGraw-Hill.

Dorigo, M., & Di Caro, G. (1999). Ant colony optimization: a new meta-heuristic. In *Proceedings of Evolutionary Computation* (Vol. 2). IEEE.

Dorigo, M., & Gambardella, L. M. (1997). Ant colony system: A cooperative learning approach to the traveling salesman problem. *IEEE Transactions on Evolutionary Computation, 1*(1), 53–66. doi:10.1109/4235.585892

Dorigo, M., Maniezzo, V., & Colorni, A. (1996). The ant system: Optimization by a colony of cooperating agents. *IEEE Transaction on Systems. Man and Cybernetics- Part B, 26*, 29–41. doi:10.1109/3477.484436

Dorigo, M., & Stutzle, T. (Eds.). (2004). *Ant colony optimization*. Cambridge, MA: MIT Press/Bradford Book. doi:10.1007/b99492

Dos Santos, G. S., Luvizotto, L. G. J., Mariani, V. C., & Dos Santos Coelho, L. (2012). Least Squares Support Vector Machines with tuning based on Differential Evolution Approach Applied to the Identification of a Thermal Process. *Expert Systems with Applications, 39*, 4805–4812. doi:10.1016/j.eswa.2011.09.137

Draief, M., & Vojnović. (2012). Convergence speed of binary interval consensus. *SIAM Journal on Control and Optimization, 50*(3), 1087–1109. doi:10.1137/110823018

Droste, S., Jansen, & Wegener. (2002). On the analysis of the (1 + 1) evolutionary algorithm. *Theoretical Computer Science, 276*, 51–81. doi:10.1016/S0304-3975(01)00182-7

Dunsby, A., Eckstein, J., Gaspar, J., & Mulholland, S. (2008). *Commodity Investing: Maximizing Returns Through Fundamental Analysis*. John Wiley & Sons.

Dutta, H. (2009). Measuring diversity in regression ensembles. In B. Prasad, P. Lingras, & A. Ram (Eds.), *Proceedings of the 4th Indian International Conference on Artificial Intelligence* (pp. 2220-2236). New York: IICAI.

Džeroski, S., & Zenko, Z. (2004). Is Combining classifiers better than selecting the best one? *Machine Learning, 54*(3), 255–273. doi:10.1023/B:MACH.0000015881.36452.6e

Eberhart, R. C., Shi, Y., & Kennedy, J. (2001). *Swarm intelligence*. Elsevier.

Edman, M., & Yener, B. (2009). *Active attacks against modulation-based radiometric identification*. Rensselaer Institute of Technology, Technical report, pages 09-02. Retrieved on 10 January, 2014 from http://www.cs.rpi.edu/research/pdf/09-02.pdf

Ellis, K., & Serinken, N. (2001). Characteristics of radio transmitter fingerprints. *Radio Science, 36*(4), 585–597. doi:10.1029/2000RS002345

El-Sebakhy, E. A., Asparouhov, O., Abdulraheem, A., Al-Majed, A., Wu, D., Latinski, K., & Raharja, I. (2012). Functional networks as a new data mining predictive paradigm to predict permeability in a carbonate reservoir. *Expert Systems with Applications, 39*(12), 10359–10375. doi:10.1016/j.eswa.2012.01.157

Emiroglu, M. E., & Baylar, A. (2003a). Experimental study of the influence of different weir types on the rate of air entrainment. *Water Quality Research Journal of Canada, 38*(4), 769–783.

Emiroglu, M. E., & Baylar, A. (2003b). The effect of broad-crested weir shape on air entrainment. *Journal of Hydraulic Research, 41*(6), 649–655. doi:10.1080/00221680309506897

Emiroglu, M. E., & Baylar, A. (2005). The influence of included angle and sill slope on air entrainment of triangular planform labyrinth weirs. *Journal of Hydraulic Engineering, 131*(3), 184–189. doi:10.1061/(ASCE)0733-9429(2005)131:3(184)

Engelbrecht, A. P. (2006). *Fundamentals of computational swarm intelligence*. John Wiley & Sons.

Ervine, D. A. (1998). Air entrainment in hydraulic structures: A review. *Proceedings of the Institution of Civil Engineers Water Maritime and Energy, 130*(3), 142–153. doi:10.1680/iwtme.1998.30973

Eskaf, K. (2011). *Blood Glucose Level prediction for diabetic patients using Intelligent Techniques*. (Ph.D. thesis). Salford University, Salford, UK.

Eskandari, H., Rezaee, M.R., & Mohammadnia, M. (2004). Application of multiple regression and artificial neural network techniques to predict shear wave velocity from wireline log data for a carbonate reservoir, South-West Iran. *CSEG Recorder,* 42 - 48.

Espejo, P., Ventura, S., & Herrera, F. (2010). Article. *IEEE Transactions on Systems, Man and Cybernetics. Part C, Applications and Reviews, 40*(2), 121–144. doi:10.1109/TSMCC.2009.2033566

Estivill–Castro, V., & Wood. (1992). A Survey of Adaptive Sorting Algorithms. *ACM Computing Surveys, 24*(4), 441–476. doi:10.1145/146370.146381

Ettus, M. (2012). *Universal software radio peripheral.* Ettus Research. Retrieved on 10 Jan, 2014 from www.ettus.com

Fan, B., Ji, P., & Zhou, K. (2012). The implementation of pipe climbing robot's real-time speech control based on the generalized regression neural network in embedded system. *Applied Mechanics and Materials, 220-223,* 1986–1989. doi:10.4028/www.scientific.net/AMM.220-223.1986

Faria, D., & Cheriton, D. (2006). Detecting identity-based attacks in wireless networks using signalprints. In *Proceedings of the 5th ACM workshop on Wireless security,* (pp. 43-52). ACM.

Fawcett, T. (2006). An introduction to ROC analysis. *Pattern Recognition Letters, 27,* 861–874. doi:10.1016/j.patrec.2005.10.010

Fayyad, U., & Irani, K. (1993). Multi-interval discretization of continuous-valued attributes for classification learning. In *Proceedings of International Joint Conference on Uncertainly in Artificial Intelligence (IJCAI),* (pp. 1022-1029). Chambéry, France: IJCAI.

Fayyad, U. M., Piatestku-Shapiro, G., & Smyth, P. (1996). Knowledge discovery and data mining: Towards a unifying framework. In E. Simoudis, J. Han, & U. M. Fayyad (Eds.), *Advances in Knowledge Discovery and Data Mining* (pp. 82–88). Palo Alto, CA: AAAI/MIT Press.

Feil, B., & Abonyi, J. (2008). Introduction to fuzzy data mining methods. In J. Galindo (Ed.), *Handbook of Research on Fuzzy Information Processing in Databases* (pp. 55–96). London: IGI Global. doi:10.4018/978-1-59904-853-6.ch003

Fernández, A., García, S., & Herrera, F. (2011). Addressing the classification with imbalanced data: Open problems and new challenges on class distribution. In *Proceedings of International Conference on Hybrid Artificial Intelligent Systems (HAIS)* (pp. 1-10). Wroclaw, Poland: Springer.

Fernández, A., García, S., & Herrera, F. (2011). *International Conference on Hybrid Artificial Intelligence Systems (HAIS),* (LNAI), (vol. 6678, pp. 1-10). Berlin: Springer.

Ferreira, A. J., & Figueiredo, M. A. T. (2012). Boosting algorithms: a review of methods, theory, and applications. In C. Zhang, & Y. Ma (Eds.), Ensemble Machine Learning (pp. 35-85). Springer Science+Business Media.

Flocchini, P., Kranakis, E., Krizanc, D., Luccio, F. L., & Santoro, N. (2004). Sorting and election in anonymous asynchronous rings. *Journal of Parallel and Distributed Computing, 64,* 254–265. doi:10.1016/j.jpdc.2003.11.007

Fodor, J., Rudas, I. J., & Bede, B. (2004). Uninorms and absorbing norms with applications to image processing. In *Proceedings of the 4th Serbian-Hungarian Joint Symposium on Intelligent Systems* (pp. 59-72). Academic Press.

Fodor, J. C. (1991). On fuzzy implication operators. *Fuzzy Sets and Systems, 42,* 293–300. doi:10.1016/0165-0114(91)90108-3

Fodor, J., Yager, R., & Rybalov, A. (1997). Structure of uninorms. *International Journal on Uncertainty. Fuzziness and Knowledge-Based Systems, 5,* 411–427. doi:10.1142/S0218488597000312

Fong, H. (2013). Opportunities and Challenges of Integrating Bio-Inspired Optimization and Data Mining Algorithms. In X. S. Yang, Z. Cui, R. Xiao, A. H. Gandomi, & M. Karamanoglu (Eds.), *Swarm Intelligence and Bio-inspired Computation: Theory and Applications* (pp. 385–402). London: Elsevier. doi:10.1016/B978-0-12-405163-8.00018-1

Frank, E., & Witten, I. (1998). Generating accurate rule sets without global optimization. In *Proceedings of International Conference on Machine Learning*, (pp. 144-151). Madison, WI: Academic Press.

Franks, N.R., & Ssendova-Franks. (1992). Brood sorting by ants: distributing the workload over the work-surface. *Behavioral Ecology and Sociobiology, 30*(2), 109–123. doi:10.1007/BF00173947

From Animals to Animats. (2012). *Proceedings of international conference on simulation and adaptive behavior.* Bradford books/MIT Press/Springer.

Fu, H., Liu, S., & Sun, F. (2010). Ship Motion Prediction Based on AGA-LSSVM. In *Proceedings of the International Conference on Mechatronics and Automation (ICMA)*. Xi'an, China: ICMA.

Fu, K. S. (1967). Stochastic automata as models of learning systems. In J. T. Lou (Ed.), *Computer and information sciences II* (pp. 177–191). New York: Academic Press.

Fu, K. S., & Li, T. J. (1969). Formulation of learning automata and automata games. *Information Sciences, 1*(3), 237–256. doi:10.1016/S0020-0255(69)80010-1

Fukś, H. (1997). Solution of the density classification problem with two cellular automata rules. *Physical Review E: Statistical Physics, Plasmas, Fluids, and Related Interdisciplinary Topics, 55*(3), 2081–2084. doi:10.1103/PhysRevE.55.R2081

Galar, M., Fernández, A., Barrenechea, E., Bustince, H., & Herrera, F. (2011). An overview of ensemble methods for binary classifiers in multi-class problems: Experimental study on one-vs-one and one-vs-all schemes. *Pattern Recognition, 44*(8), 1761–1776. doi:10.1016/j.patcog.2011.01.017

Galar, M., Fernández, A., Barrenechea, E., & Herrera, F. (2013). Eusboost: Enhancing Ensembles for Highly Imbalanced Data-sets by Evolutionary Undersampling. *Pattern Recognition.* doi:10.1016/j.patcog.2013.05.006

Galindo, J. (2008). Introduction and Trends to Fuzzy Logic and Fuzzy Databases. In J. Galindo (Ed.), *Handbook of Research on Fuzzy Information Processing in Databases* (pp. 1–33). London: IGI Global. doi:10.4018/978-1-59904-853-6.ch001

Gao, M., Hong, X., Chen, S., & Harris, C. J. (2011). A combined SMOTE and PSO based RBF classifier for two-class imbalanced problems. *Neurocomputing, 74,* 3456–3466. doi:10.1016/j.neucom.2011.06.010

Gao, W. (2012). Study on new improved hybrid genetic algorithm. In D. Zeng (Ed.), *Advances in Information Technology and Industry Applications (LNEE)* (Vol. 136, pp. 505–512). SpringerLink. doi:10.1007/978-3-642-26001-8_66

Gao, W., & Liu, S. (2012). A Modified Artificial Bee Colony. *Computers & Operations Research, 39,* 687–697. doi:10.1016/j.cor.2011.06.007

Gärdenfors, P. (1978). On the logic of relevance. *Synthese, 37*(3), 351–367. doi:10.1007/BF00873245

Gard, K., Larson, L., & Steer, M. (2005). The impact of rf front-end characteristics on the spectral regrowth of communications signals. *IEEE Transactions on Microwave Theory and Techniques, 53*(6), 2179–2186. doi:10.1109/TMTT.2005.848801

Garg, V., & Jothiprakash, V. (2013). Evaluation of reservoir sedimentation using data driven techniques. *Applied Soft Computing Journal, 13*(8), 3567–3581. doi:10.1016/j.asoc.2013.04.019

Garnier, S., Combe, M., Jost, C., & Theraulaz, G. (2013). Do ants need to estimate the geometrical properties of trail bifurcations to find an efficient route? A swarm robotics test bed. *PLoS Computational Biology, 9*(3), e1002903. doi:10.1371/journal.pcbi.1002903 PMID:23555202

Gazi, V., & Passino, K. M. (2011). *Swarm stability and optimization.* Berlin: Springer. doi:10.1007/978-3-642-18041-5

Gerstel, O., & Zaks. (1997). The bit complexity of distributed sorting. *Algorithmica, 18,* 405–416. doi:10.1007/PL00009163

Geyer-Schulz, A. (1995). *Fuzzy rule-based expert systems and genetic machine learning.* Physica-Verlag.

Ge, Z., & Song, Z. (2013). *Multivariate statistical process control: Process monitoring methods and applications.* London, UK: Springer. doi:10.1007/978-1-4471-4513-4

Giesen, D. (Ed.). (2011). *Response Burden in Official Business Surveys: Measurement and Reduction Practices of National Statistical Institutes*. BLUE-ETS Project Report. Retrieved May 10, 2012, from http://www.blue-ets.istat.it/index.php?id=7

Glöckner, I. (2006). Quantifier Selection for Linguistic Data Summarization. In *Proceedings of IEEE International Conference on Fuzzy Systems* (pp. 720 – 727). Institute of Electrical and Electronics Engineers (IEEE).

Goldberg, D. (1989). *Genetic Algorithms in Search, Optimization & Machine Learning*. Reading, MA: Addison-Wesley.

Goldberg, D. E., & Holland, J. H. (1988). Genetic algorithms and machine learning. *Machine Learning*, *3*(2), 95–99. doi:10.1023/A:1022602019183

Goldsmith, J. R., & Friberg, L. T. (1976). Effects of air pollution on human health, Air Pollution. In *The Effects of Air Pollution* (Vol. 2, pp. 457–610). Academic Press.

Gonzaga de Sa, P., & Maes, C. (1992). The Gacs-Kurdyumov-Levin automaton revisited. *Journal of Statistical Physics*, *67*(3-4), 507–522. doi:10.1007/BF01049718

Gordillo, J. L., & Luna, J. V. (1994). Parallel sort on a linear array of cellular automata. In *Proceedings of International Conference on Systems, Man and Cybernetics* (Vol. 2, pp. 1903-1907). San Antonio, TX: Academic Press.

Gordon, D. M. (2010). *Ant encounters: Interaction networks and colony behavior*. Princeton, NJ: Princeton University Press.

Griffiths, R. F. (1994). Errors in the use of the Briggs parameterization for atmospheric dispersion coefficients. *Atmospheric Environment*, *28*(17), 2861–2865. doi:10.1016/1352-2310(94)90086-8

Gruber, H., Holzer, M., & Ruepp, O. (2007). Sorting the slow way: an analysis of perversely awful randomized sorting algorithms. In *Proceedings of 4th International Conference on Fun with Algorithms* (pp. 183-197). Castiglioncello, Italy: Springer.

Gupta, M. M., & Qi, J. (1991). Theory of t-norms and fuzzy inference methods. *Fuzzy Sets and Systems*, *40*, 431–450. doi:10.1016/0165-0114(91)90171-L

Guven, A., Md. Azamathulla, H., & Zakaria, N. A. (2009). Linear genetic programming for prediction of circular pile scour. *Ocean Engineering*, *36*(12-13), 985–991. doi:10.1016/j.oceaneng.2009.05.010

Gu, Y., Wu, C. Q., Liu, X., & Yu, D. (2013). Distributed Throughput Optimization for Large-Scale Scientific Workflows Under Fault-Tolerance Constraint. *Journal of Grid Computing*, *11*, 361–379. doi:10.1007/s10723-013-9266-3

Hagan, M. T., & Menhaj, M. B. (1994). Training Feedforward Networks with the Marquardt Algorithm. *IEEE Transactions on Neural Networks*, 5. PMID:18267874

Haidar, I., & Wolff, R. C. (2011). Forecasting of Crude Oil Price (Revisited). In *Proceedings of the 30th USAEE Conference*. Washington, DC: USAEE.

Halitsky, J. (1989). A jet plume model for short stacks. *Journal of the Air Pollution Control Association*, *39*(6), 856–858.

Hall, J., Barbeau, M., & Kranakis, E. (2004). Enhancing intrusion detection in wireless networks using radio frequency fingerprinting. In *Proceedings of the 3rd IASTED International Conference on Communications, Internet and Information Technology* (CIIT), (pp. 201-206). IASTED.

Hall, J., Barbeau, M., & Kranakis, E. (2006). Detecting rogue devices in bluetooth networks using radio frequency fingerprinting. In *Proceedings of IASTED International Conference on Communications and Computer Networks*. IASTED.

Hall, J., Barbeau, M., & Kranakis, E. (2003). Detection of transient in radio frequency fingerprinting using signal phase. In *Proceedings of Wireless and Optical Communications* (pp. 13–18). Academic Press.

Hall, J., Barbeau, M., & Kranakis, E. (2005). *Radio frequency fingerprinting for intrusion detection in wireless networks*. IEEE Transactions on Defendable and Secure Computing.

Hamann, H. (2010). *Space-time continuous models of swarm robotic systems: Supporting global-to-local programming*. Berlin: Springer. doi:10.1007/978-3-642-13377-0

Hanbay, D., Turkoglu, I., & Demir, Y. (2006a). Complex systems modeling by using ANFIS. In *Proceedings of International Fifteenth Turkish Symposium on Artificial Intelligence and Neural Networks* (pp. 83–90). Academic Press.

Hanbay, D., Turkoglu, I., & Demir, Y. (2006b). A wavelet neural network for intelligent modeling. In *Proceedings of International fifteenth Turkish symposium on artificial intelligence and neural networks* (pp. 175–182). Academic Press.

Hanbay, D., Turkoglu, I., & Demir, Y. (2007). Predicting chemical oxygen demand (COD) based on wavelet decomposition and neural networks. *Clean – Soil, Air. Water, 35*(3), 250–254.

Handl, J., & Meyer. (2008). Ant-based and swarm-based clustering. *Swarm Intelligence, 1*(2), 95–113. doi:10.1007/s11721-007-0008-7

Hanna, S. R., Briggs, G. A., & Kosker, R. P. (1982). *Hand book on Atmospheric Diffusion*. NTIS. doi:10.2172/5591108

Haque, A. (1999). *Modelling human metabolism using Artificial Neural Network*. London: Brunel University.

Hassan, R., Cohanim, B., De Weck, O., & Venter, G. (2005). A comparison of particle swarm optimization and the genetic algorithm. In *Proceedings of 46th AIAA/ASME/ASCE/AHS/ASC Structures, Structural Dynamics, and Materials Conference* (pp. 1-13). Austin, TX: AIAA.

Hassan, S.A., & Ingram. (2010). Modeling of a Co-operative One-Dimensional Multi-Hop Network using Quasi-Stationary Markov Chains. In *Proceedings of IEEE Global Telecommunication Conference* (pp. 1-5). Miami, FL: IEEE.

Hassin, Y., & Peleg. (2001). Distributed Probabilistic Polling and Applications to Proportionate Agreement. *Information and Computation, 171*, 248–268. doi:10.1006/inco.2001.3088

Hastie, T., Tibshirani, R., & Friedman, J. (2009). *The elements of statistical learning: data mining, inference, and prediction* (2nd ed.). Springer-Verlag. doi:10.1007/978-0-387-84858-7

Haupt, R. L., & Haupt, S. E. (1998). *Practical genetic algorithms*. New York: Wiley Pub.

Haussler, D., Kearns, M., & Schapire, R. E. (1994). Bounds on the sample complexity of Bayesian learning using information theory and the VC dimension. *Machine Learning, 14*, 83–113. doi:10.1007/BF00993163

Hawkins, D. M. (1980). *Identification of outliers* (Vol. 11). London: Chapman and Hall. doi:10.1007/978-94-015-3994-4

Hayashi, Y., Yuki, M., Sugawara, K., Kikuchi, T., & Tsuji, K. (2008). Analysis and modeling of ant's behavior from single to multi-body. *Artificial Life and Robotics, 13*, 120–123. doi:10.1007/s10015-008-0571-z

He, H., & Ma, Y. (2013). *Imbalanced Learning: Foundations, Algorithms, and Applications*. Wiley-IEEE.

Heating Oil Explained. (2012). Retrieved October 22, 2013, from http://www.eia.gov/energyexplained/index.cfm?page=heating_oil_home

Hebb, D. O. (1949). *The organization of behaviour*. Wiley. McCulloch, W.S., & Pitts, W. (1943). A logical calculus in the ideas immanent in nervous activity. *The Bulletin of Mathematical Biophysics, 5*, 115–133.

He, H., & Garcia, E. A. (2009). Learning from imbalanced data. *IEEE Transactions on Knowledge and Data Engineering, 21*(9), 1263–1284. doi:10.1109/TKDE.2008.239

He, J., & Yao. (2001). Drift analysis and average time complexity of evolutionary algorithms. *Artificial Intelligence, 127*, 57–85. doi:10.1016/S0004-3702(01)00058-3

Helmy, T., Al-Harthi, M. A., & Faheem, M. T. (2012). Adaptive ensemble and hybrid models for classification of bioinformatics datasets. *Transaction on Fuzzy. Neural Network and Bioinformatics: Global Journal of Technology and Optimization, 3*(1), 20–29.

Helmy, T., Anifowose, F., & Faisal, K. (2010). Hybrid computational models for the characterization of oil and gas reservoirs. *International Journal of Expert Systems with Application, 37*, 5353–5363. doi:10.1016/j.eswa.2010.01.021

Helmy, T., Rahman, S. M., Hossain, M. I., & Abdulraheem, A. (2013). Non-linear heterogeneous ensemble model for permeability prediction of oil reservoirs. *Arab Journal of Science and Engineering*, *38*, 1379–1395. doi:10.1007/s13369-013-0588-z

Hippenstiel, R., & Payal, Y. (1996). Wavelet based transmitter identification.[). IEEE.]. *Proceedings of Signal Processing and Its Applications*, *2*, 740–742.

Hoeting, J. A., Madigan, D., Raftery, A. E., & Volinsky, C. T. (1999). Bayesian model averaging: a tutorial. *Statistical Science*, *14*(4), 382–401.

Hofmeyr, S. A., & Forrest, S. (2000). Architecture for an artificial immune system. *Evolutionary Computation*, *8*(4), 443–473. doi:10.1162/106365600568257 PMID:11130924

Hofstee, H.P., Martin, & van de Snepscheut. (1990). Distributed sorting. *Science of Computer Programming*, *15*(2-3), 119–133. doi:10.1016/0167-6423(90)90081-N

Hogan, W. R., Cooper, G. F., Wagner, M. M., & Wallstrom, G. L. (2005). *An inverted Gaussian Plume Model for estimating the location and amount of Release of airborne agents from downwind atmospheric concentrations (RODS Technical Report)*. Pittsburgh, PA: University of Pittsburgh.

Holden, N., & Freitas, A. (2008). A hybrid PSO/ACO algorithm for discovering classification rules in data mining. *Journal of Artificial Evolution and Applications*, *2*, 1–11. doi:10.1155/2008/316145

Holler, M., Tam, S., Castro, H., & Benson, R. (1989). An electrically trainable artificial neural network (etann) with 10240' floating gate' synapses. In *Proceedings of Neural Networks* (pp. 191–196). IEEE. doi:10.1109/IJCNN.1989.118698

Hong, P. T., Lee, Y. C., & Wu, M. T. (2014). An effective parallel approach for genetic-fuzzy data mining. *Expert Systems with Applications*, *41*, 655–662. doi:10.1016/j.eswa.2013.07.090

Hoogerwerf, D., Green, E., Stanhope, D., & McKernan, R. (2000). *Active waveform collection for use in transmitter identification* (US Patent 6,035,188). Washington, DC: US Patent Office.

Hsu, C.W., Chang, C.C., & Lin, C.J. (2003). *A Practical Guide to Support vector Classification*. National Taiwan University Technical Report.

Huang, G. B., & Babri, H. A. (1998). Upper bounds on the number of hidden neurons in feedforward networks with arbitrary bounded nonlinear activation functions. *IEEE Transactions on Neural Networks*, *9*(1), 224–229. doi:10.1109/72.655045 PMID:18252445

Hudec, M. (2013a). Applicability of Linguistic summaries. In N. Mladenović, G. Savić, M. Kuzmanović, D. Makajić-Nikolić, & M. Stanojević (Eds.), *11th Balkan conference on operational research* (pp. 133-140). Belgrade, Serbia: Faculty of Organizational Sciences.

Hudec, M. (2013c). Fuzzy database queries in official statistics: Perspective of using linguistic terms in query conditions. *Statistical journal of the IAOS, 4*, 315-323.

Hudec, M., & Juriová, J. (2013). *Evaluation and checking non-response data by soft computing approaches - Case of business and trade statistics*. Paper presented at the New Techniques and Technologies in Statistics, (NTTS 2013). Brussels, Belgium.

Hudec, M., & Sudzina, F. (2012). Construction of fuzzy sets and applying aggregation operators for fuzzy queries. In J. Cordeiro, A. Cuzzocrea, & L. Maciaszek (Eds.), *14th International Conference on Enterprise Information Systems* (ICEIS 2012) (pp. 253-257). Setubal: SciTe Press.

Hudec, M., Balbi, S., Juriová, J., Kľúčik, M., Marino, M., & Scepi, G. … Triunfo, N. (2012). *Report on principles of fuzzy methodology and tools developed for use in data collection (Soft computing and text mining tools for Official Statistics)*. BLUE-ETS Project Report. Retrieved May 15, 2013, from http://www.blue-ets.istat.it/index.php?id=7

Hudec, M. (2003). Urban and Municipal Statistics Project and Information System of the Slovak Republic. *INFOM, 5*, 20–22.

Hudec, M. (2009). An Approach to Fuzzy Database Querying, Analysis and Realisation. *Computer Science and Information Systems*, *6*(2), 127–140. doi:10.2298/CSIS0902127H

Hudec, M. (2011). Fuzzy improvement of the SQL. *Yugoslav Journal of Operations Research, 21*, 239–251. doi:10.2298/YJOR1102239H

Hudec, M. (2013b). Issues in construction of linguistic summaries. In R. Mesiar, & T. Bacigál (Eds.), *Proceedings of Uncertainty Modelling 2013* (pp. 35–44). Bratislava: STU.

Hutteger, S. M., & Zollman, K. J. S. (2010). Dynamics stability and basins of attraction in the Sir Philip Sidney game. *Proceedings. Biological Sciences*. doi:10.1098/rspb.2009.2105

Hyndman, R. J., & Koehler, A. B. (2006). Another Look at Measures of Forecast Accuracy. *International Journal of Forecasting, 22*, 679–688. doi:10.1016/j.ijforecast.2006.03.001

Irie, B., & Miyanki, S. (1988). Capabilities of three layer perceptrons. *In Proceedings of IEEE second Int. Conf. on Neural networks* (pp. 641-648). IEEE.

Israel, M., Khmelnitsky, E., & Kagan, E. (2012). Search for a mobile target by ground vehicle on a topographic terrain. In *Proceedings of 27th IEEE Convention of Electrical and Electronics Engineers in Israel*. IEEE. doi:10.1109/EEEI.2012.6377123

Israeli, A., & Jalfon, M. (1993). Uniform Self-Stabilizing Ring Orientation. *Information and Computation, 104*(2-3), 175–196. doi:10.1006/inco.1993.1029

Jain, A., Mao, J., & Mohiuddin, K. M. (1996). Artificial neural networks: a tutorial. *Computer, 29*(3), 31–44. doi:10.1109/2.485891

Jammazi, R., & Aloui, C. (2012). Crude oil price forecasting: Experimental evidence from wavelet decomposition and neural network modeling. *Energy Economics, 34*, 828–841. doi:10.1016/j.eneco.2011.07.018

Jeong, H. J., Kim, E. H., Suh, K. S., Hwang, W. T., Han, M. H., & Lee, H. K. (2005). Determination of the source rate released into the environment from a nuclear power plant. *Radiation Protection Dosimetry, 113*(3), 308–313. doi:10.1093/rpd/nch460 PMID:15687109

Jhuang, H., Serre, T., Wolf, L., & Poggio, T. (2007). A biologically inspired system for action recognition. In *Proceedings of Computer Vision* (pp. 1–8). IEEE. doi:10.1109/ICCV.2007.4408988

Jiang, B. T., & Zhao, F. Y. (2013). Particle Swarm Optimization-based Least Squares Support Vector Regression for Critical Heat Flux Prediction. *Annals of Nuclear Energy, 53*, 69–81. doi:10.1016/j.anucene.2012.09.020

Jiménez, A., Aroba, J., de la Torre, M. L., Andujar, J. M., & Grande, J. A. (2009). Model of behaviour of conductivity versus pH in acid mine drainage water, based on fuzzy logic and data mining techniques. *Journal of Hydroinformatics, 11*(2), 147–153. doi:10.2166/hydro.2009.015

Jin, X., & Reynolds, R. G. (1999). Using knowledge-based evolutionary computation to solve nonlinear constraint optimization problems: a cultural algorithm approach. In *Proceedings of Evolutionary Computation, 1999*. Academic Press.

Johansson, U., Löfström, T., & Norinder, U. (2009). Evaluating ensembles on QSAR classification. In *Proceeding of Skövde Workshop on Information Fusion Topics* (pp. 49-54). Skövde, Sweden: Univeristy of Skövde.

Jones, W. P., & Hoskins, J. (1987, October). Back–propagation a generalized delta learning rule. *BYTE,* 155-162.

Jong-Se, L. (2005). Reservoir properties determination using fuzzy logic and neural networks from well data in offshore Korea. *Petroleum Science and Engineering, 49*, 182–192. doi:10.1016/j.petrol.2005.05.005

Juriová, J. (2012). *Neural Network Approach Applied for Classification in Business and Trade Statistics*. Paper presented at the 46th Scientific Meeting of the Italian Statistical Society. Rome, Italy.

Kacprzyk, J., & Yager, R. (2001). Linguistic summaries of data using fuzzy logic. *International Journal of General Systems, 30*, 33–154. doi:10.1080/03081070108960702

Kacprzyk, J., & Zadrożny, S. (1995). FQUERY for Access: Fuzzy querying for windows-based DBMS. In P. Bosc, & J. Kacprzyk (Eds.), *Fuzziness in Database Management Systems* (pp. 415–433). Berlin: Physica-Verlag. doi:10.1007/978-3-7908-1897-0_18

Kacprzyk, J., & Zadrożny, S. (2009). Protoforms of Linguistic Database Summaries as a Human Consistent Tool for Using Natural Language in Data Mining. *International Journal of Software Science and Computational Intelligence*, *1*, 1–11. doi:10.4018/jssci.2009010107

Kagan, E., Goren, G., & Ben-Gal, I. (2010). Probabilistic double-distance algorithm of search after static or moving target by autonomous mobile agent. In *Proceedings of 26th IEEE Convention of Electrical and Electronics Engineers in Israel* (pp. 160-164). IEEE.

Kagan, E., Goren, G., & Ben-Gal, I. (2012). Algorithm of search for static or moving target by autonomous mobile agent with erroneous sensor. In *Proceedings of 27th IEEE Convention of Electrical and Electronics Engineers in Israel*. IEEE. doi:10.1109/EEEI.2012.6377124

Kagan, E., & Ben-Gal, I. (2011). Navigation of quantum-controlled mobile robots. In A. V. Topalov (Ed.), *Recent advances in mobile robotics* (pp. 311–326). Rijeka, Croatia: InTech. doi:10.5772/25944

Kagan, E., & Ben-Gal, I. (2013a). *Probabilistic search for tracking targets: Theory and modern applications*. Chichester, UK: John Wiley & Sons. doi:10.1002/9781118596593

Kagan, E., & Ben-Gal, I. (2013b). Moving target search algorithm with informational distance measures. *Open Applied Informatics Journal*, *6*, 1–10. doi:10.2174/1874136320130604001

Kagan, E., & Ben-Gal, I. (2014). A group-testing algorithm with online informational learning. *IIE Transactions*, *46*(2), 164–184. doi:10.1080/0740817X.2013.803639

Kagan, E., Rybalov, A., Siegelmann, H., & Yager, R. (2013). Probability-generated aggregators. *International Journal of Intelligent Systems*, *28*(7), 709–727. doi:10.1002/int.21598

Kalles, D., & Papagelis. (2001). Breeding decision trees using evolutionary techniques. In *Proceedings of the International Conference on Machine Learning* (pp. 393-400). Williamstown, MA: Academic Press.

Kalles, D., Mperoukli, V., & Papanderadis, A.-C. (2012). Emerge-Sort: Swarm Intelligence Sorting. In *Proceedings of Panhellenic Conference on Artificial Intelligence* (pp. 98-105). Lamia, Greece: Springer.

Kaplan, D., & Stanhope, D. (1999). *Waveform collection for use in wireless telephone identification* (US Patent 5,999,806). Washington, DC: US Patent Office.

Karaboga, D. (2005). *An Idea Based on Honey Bee Swarm for Numerical Optimization (Technical Report)*. Erciyes University.

Karaboga, D., & Akay, B. (2009). A comparative study of Artificial Bee Colony. *Applied Mathematics and Computation*, *214*, 108–132. doi:10.1016/j.amc.2009.03.090

Kauffmann, B., Baccelli, F., Chaintreau, A., Mhatre, V., Papagiannaki, K., & Diot, C. (2007). Measurement-based self-organization of interfering 802.11 wireless access networks. In *Proceedings of 26th IEEE international Conference on Computer Communications*. IEEE.

Kempe, D., Dobra, A., & Gehrke, J. (2003). Gossip-based computation of aggregate information. In *Proceedings of IEEE Conference on Foundations of Computer Science* (pp. 482-491). Cambridge, MA: IEEE.

Kennedy, I., Scanlon, P., & Buddhikot, M. (2008a). Passive steady state rf fingerprinting: a cognitive technique for scalable deployment of co-channel femto cell underlays. In *Proceedings of 3rd IEEE Symposium on New Frontiers in Dynamic Spectrum Access Networks*. IEEE.

Kennedy, I., Scanlon, P., Mullany, F., Buddhikot, M., Nolan, K., & Rondeau, T. (2008b). Radio transmitter fingerprinting: A steady state frequency domain approach. In *Proceedings of IEEE 68th Vehicular Technology Conference*. IEEE.

Kennedy, J. (2010). Particle swarm optimization. In *Encyclopedia of Machine Learning* (pp. 760-766). Springer US.

Kennedy, J., & Eberhart, R. (1995). Particle swarm optimization. In *Proceedings of IEEE International Conference on Neural Networks* (Vol. 4, No. 2, pp. 1942-1948). Perth, Australia. IEEE.

Keynes, J. M. (1909). A treatise on probability. *Diamond (Philadelphia, Pa.), 3*(2), 12.

Khanesar, M. A., Teshnehlab, M., & Shoorehdeli, M. A. (2007). A novel binary particle swarm optimization. In *Proceedings of Mediterranean Conference on Control & Automation* (pp. 1–6). Athens, Greece: Academic Press.

Khashman, A., & Nwulu, N. I. (2011). Intelligent Prediction of Crudei Oil Price Using Support Vector Machines. In *Proceedings of the 9th IEEE International Symposium on Applied Machine Intelligenc abd Informatics*. Smolenice, Slovakia: IEEE.

Khosravi, A., Nahavandi, S., & Creighton, D. (2013). Quantifying uncertainties of neural network-based electricity price forecasts. *Applied Energy, 112*, 120–129. doi:10.1016/j.apenergy.2013.05.075

Kim, K., Spooner, C., Akbar, I., & Reed, J. (2008). Specific emitter identification for cognitive radio with application to IEEE 802.11. In *Proceedings of Global Telecommunications Conference*. IEEE.

Kisi, O. (2004a). River flow modeling using artificial neural networks. *Journal of Hydrologic Engineering, 9*(1), 60–63. doi:10.1061/(ASCE)1084-0699(2004)9:1(60)

Kisi, O. (2004b). Multi-layer perceptions with Levenberg–Marquardt optimization algorithm for suspended sediment concentration prediction and estimation. *Hydrological Sciences Journal, 49*(6), 1025–1040.

Klement, W., Wilk, S., Michaowski, W., & Matwin, S. (2009). Dealing with Severely Imbalanced Data. In *Proceedings of Workshop on Data Mining When Classes are Imbalanced and Errors Have Costs, PAKDD*. Bangkok, Thailand: PAKDD.

Klement, E. P., Mesiar, R., & Pap, E. (2000). *Triangular Norms*. Dordrecht, The Netherlands: Kluwer Academic Publishers. doi:10.1007/978-94-015-9540-7

Klir, G., & Yuan, B. (1995). *Fuzzy sets and fuzzy logic, theory and applications*. Prentice Hall.

Kľúčik, M. (2011). *Introducing New Tool for Official Statistics: Genetic Programming*. Paper presented at the New Techniques and Technologies in Statistics (NTTS 2011). Brussels, Belgium.

Kľúčik, M. (2012). *Estimates of Foreign Trade Using Genetic Programming*. Paper presented at the 46th Scientific Meeting of the Italian Statistical Society. Rome, Italy.

Knox, E. M., & Ng, R. T. (1998). Algorithms for mining distancebased outliers in large datasets. In *Proceedings of the International Conference on Very Large Data Bases* (pp. 392-403). Berlin: Morgan Kaufmann Publishers.

Knuth, D. E. (1973). The Art of Computer Programming: Vol. 3. *Sorting and Searching*. Reading, MA: Addison-Wesley.

Kohavi, R., & John, G. H. (1997). Wrappers for feature subset selection. *Artificial Intelligence, 97*(1), 273–324. doi:10.1016/S0004-3702(97)00043-X

Kok, P. (2004). *Predicting blood glucose levels of diabetics using Artificial Neural Networks*. Delft University of Technology.

Koren, G., & Shasha, D. (1995). D^{Over}: An optimal on-line scheduling algorithm for overloaded real-time systems. *SIAM Journal on Computing, 24*(2), 318–339. doi:10.1137/S0097539792236882

Kostrykin, V., & Oleynik, A. (2013). On the existence of unstable bumps in neural networks. *Integral Equations and Operator Theory, 75*(4), 445–458. doi:10.1007/s00020-013-2045-5

Kotsiantis, S., Kanellopoulos, D., & Pintelas, P. (2006). Handling imbalanced datasets: A review. *GESTS International Transactions on Computer Science and Engineering, 30*(1), 25–36.

Koza, J. R. (1991). Concept formation and decision tree induction using the genetic programming paradigm. In *Parallel problem solving from nature*. Springer Verlag. doi:10.1007/BFb0029742

Koza, J. R. (1992). *Genetic Programming: On the programming of computers by means of natural selection* (Vol. 1). Cambridge, MA: MIT Press.

Kozeny, J. (1927). Uber Kapillare Leitung des Wassers im Boden: Sitzungsber. *Akad. Wiss. Wien, 136,* 271–306.

Kubat, M., & Matwin, S. (1997). Addressing the Curse of Imbalanced Training Sets: One-Sided Selection. In *Proceedings of the 14th International Conference on Machine Learning* (vol. 97, pp. 179-186). Academic Press.

Kukar, M., & Kononenko, I. (1998). Cost-sensitive learning with neural networks. In *Proceedings of European Conference on Artificial Intelligence* (pp.445–449). Brighton, UK: Academic Press.

Kulkarni, S., & Haidar, I. (2009). Forecasting Model for Crude Oil Price Using Artificial Neural Networks and Commodity Futures Prices. *International Journal of Computer Science and Information Security, 2*(1).

Kuncheva, L., & Whitaker, C. (2003). Measures of diversity in classifier ensembles. *Machine Learning, 51,* 181–207. doi:10.1023/A:1022859003006

Kuntz, P. Layzell, & Snyers. (1997). A colony of ant-like agents for partitioning in VLSI technology. In *Proceedings of the 4ᵗʰ European Conference on Artificial Life* (pp. 417-424). Brighton, UK: MIT Press.

Kuo, R. J., Wang, M. J., & Huang, T. W. (2011). An application of particle swarm optimization algorithm to clustering analysis. *Soft Computing, 15*(3), 533–542. doi:10.1007/s00500-009-0539-5

Landgrebe, T., Paclik, P., Duin, R., & Bradley, A. (2006). Precision-recall operating characteristic (P-ROC) curves in imprecise environments. In *Proceedings of International Conference on Pattern Recognition (ICPR),* (pp. 123-127). Hong Kong, China: ICPR.

Land, M., & Belew. (1995). No Perfect Two-State Cellular Automata for Density Classification Exists. *Physical Review Letters, 74*(25), 5148–5150. doi:10.1103/PhysRevLett.74.5148 PMID:10058695

Last, M., Kandel, A., & Maimon, O. (2001). Information-theoretic algorithm for feature selection. *Pattern Recognition Letters, 22*(6), 799–811. doi:10.1016/S0167-8655(01)00019-8

Lee, C.-Y., & Yao, X. (2004). Evolutionary programming using mutations based on the Levy probability distribution. *IEEE Transactions on Evolutionary Computation, 8*(1), 1–13. doi:10.1109/TEVC.2003.816583

Lehmann, E. D., & Deutsch, T. (1998). Compartmental model for glycaemic prediction and decision support in clinical diabetes care: promise and reality. *Computer Methods and Programs in Biomedicine, 56*(2), 193–204. doi:10.1016/S0169-2607(98)00025-X PMID:9700433

Lei, X. R. B. W. (2002). Artificial Immune System: Principle, Models, Analysis and Perspectives. *Chinese Journal of Computers, 12.*

Leibnitz, K., Wakamiya, N., & Murata, M. (2006). Biologically inspired self-adaptive multi-path routing in overlay networks. *Communications of the ACM, 49*(3), 62–67. doi:10.1145/1118178.1118203

Lendasse, A., Ji, Y., Reyhani, N., & Verleysen, M. (2005). LS-SVM Hyperparameter Selection with a Nonparametric Noise Estimator. In *Proceedings of the 15th International Conference on Artificial Neural Networks: Formal Models and Their Applications* (ICANN). Warsaw, Poland: ICANN.

Lerman, K., Martinoli, A., & Galstyan, A. (2005). A review of probabilistic macroscopic models for swarm robotic systems. In E. Sahin, & W. M. Spears (Eds.), *Swarm robotics (LNCS)* (Vol. 3342, pp. 143–152). Heidelberg, Germany: Springer. doi:10.1007/978-3-540-30552-1_12

Lessman, S., Caserta, M., & Arango, I. M. (2011). Tuning metaheuristics: A data mining based approach for particle swarm optimization. *Expert Systems with Applications, 38,* 12826–12838. doi:10.1016/j.eswa.2011.04.075

Levy, P. (1937). *Theorie de l'Addition des Veriables Aleatoires.* Paris, France: Gauthier-Villars.

Liao, R., Zheng, H., Grzybowski, S., & Yang, L. (2011). Particle Swarm Optimization-Least Squares Support Vector Regression based Forecasting model on Dissolved Gases in Oil-Filled Power Transformers. *Electric Power Systems Research, 81,* 2074–2080. doi:10.1016/j.epsr.2011.07.020

Liao, S.-H., Chu, P.-H., & Hsiao, P.-Y. (2012). Data mining techniques and applications – A decade review from 2000 to 2011. *Expert Systems with Applications, 39*, 11303–11311. doi:10.1016/j.eswa.2012.02.063

Liao, W., & Balzen, Z. (2013). LSSVM Network Flow Prediction Based on the Self-adaptive Genetic Algorithm Optimization. *Journal of Networks, 8*(2), 507–512.

Lin, Y., & Jeon, Y. (2002). *Random forests and adaptive nearest neighbors* (Technical Report No. 1055). University of Wisconsin.

Li, N., Tsang, I., & Zhou, Z. (2013). Efficient Optimization of Performance Measures by Classifier Adaptation. *IEEE Transactions on Pattern Analysis and Machine Intelligence, 35*(6), 1370–1382. doi:10.1109/TPAMI.2012.172 PMID:22868653

Ling, C. X., Huang, J., & Zhang, H. (2003). AUC: A Statistical Consistent and More Discriminating Measure than Accuracy. In *Proceedings of the 18th International Conference on Artificial Intelligence* (pp. 329-341). Acapulco, Mexico: Academic Press.

Ling, C. X., & Sheng, V. S. (2008). Cost-sensitive learning and the class imbalance problem. In *Encyclopedia of Machine Learning* (pp. 231–235). Academic Press.

Lippert, R. (2013). *The wisdom of crowds: using ensembles for machine learning*. Retrieved from http://blog.factual.com/the-wisdom-of-crowds

Li, Q. (2007). Recent progress in computer-aided diagnosis of lung nodules on thin-section CT. *Computerized Medical Imaging and Graphics, 31*, 248–257. doi:10.1016/j.compmedimag.2007.02.005 PMID:17369020

Li, Q., & Trappe, W. (2007). Detecting spoofing and anomalous traffic in wireless networks via forge-resistant relationships. *IEEE Transactions on Information Forensics and Security, 2*(4), 793–808. doi:10.1109/TIFS.2007.910236

Liszka Hackzell, J. (1999). Prediction of blood glucose levels in diabetic patients using a hybrid AI technique. In *Proceedings of Computers and Biomedical Research*. Linköping, Sweden: Academic Press. doi:10.1006/cbmr.1998.1506

Liu, H., & Setiono, R. (1995). Chi2: Feature selection and discretization of numeric attributes. In *Proceedings of the Seventh International Conference on Tools with Artificial Intelligence* (pp. 388-391). IEEE.

Liu, W., Chawla, S., Cieslak, D., & Chawla, N. (2010). A robust decision tree algorithm for imbalanced data sets. In *Proceedings of SIAM International Conference on Data Mining (SDM)*, (pp. 766-777). Columbus, OH: SIAM.

Liu, B. (2011). Uncertain Logic for Modeling Human Language. *Journal of Uncertain Systems, 5*, 3–20.

Liu, C. L., & Layland, J. W. (1973). Scheduling algorithms for multiprogramming in a hard real-time environment. *Journal of the ACM, 20*(1), 46–61. doi:10.1145/321738.321743

Liu, J. W. S. (2001). *Real-Time Systems*. Pearson Education.

Li, X. H., Fan, Y. S., Cai, Y. X., Zhao, W. D., & Yin, H. Y. (2013). Optimization of biomass vacuum pyrolysis process based on GRNN. *Applied Mechanics and Materials, 411-414*, 3016–3022. doi:10.4028/www.scientific.net/AMM.411-414.3016

Locke, C. D. (1986). *Best Effort Decision Making for Real-Time Scheduling*. (Doctoral thesis). Computer Science Department, Carnegie-Mellon University, Pittsburgh, PA.

Lomax, R. G. (2007). *An Introduction to Statistical Concepts*. Lawrence Erlbaum Associates, Inc.

Loui, M. C. (1984). The complexity of sorting on distributed systems. *Information and Control, 60*, 70–85. doi:10.1016/S0019-9958(84)80022-4

Luu, T. P., Low, K. H., Qu, X., Lim, H. B., & Hoon, K. H. (2014). An individual-specific gait pattern prediction model based on generalized regression neural networks. *Gait & Posture, 39*(1), 443–448. doi:10.1016/j.gaitpost.2013.08.028 PMID:24071020

MacKay, C., McKee, S., & Mulholland, A. J. (2006). Diffusion and convection of gaseous and fine particulate from a chimney. *IMA Journal of Applied Mathematics, 71*, 670–691. doi:10.1093/imamat/hxl016

Maertens, K., Baerdemaeker, J. D., & Babuska, R. (2006). Genetic polynomial regression as input selection algorithm for non-linear identification. *Journal of Soft Computing*, *10*, 785–795. doi:10.1007/s00500-005-0008-8

Malliaris, M. E., & Malliaris, S. G. (2008). Forecasting Inter-Related Energy Product Prices. *European Journal of Finance*, *14*(6), 453–468. doi:10.1080/13518470701705793

Maloof, M. A. (2003). Learning when data sets are imbalanced and when costs are unequal and unknown. In *Proceedings of International Conference on Machine Learning Workshop on Learning from Imbalanced Data Sets*. Melbourne, FL: Academic Press.

Manilla, H. (1985). Measures of presortedness and optimal sorting algorithms. *IEEE Transactions on Computers*, *34*(4), 318–325. doi:10.1109/TC.1985.5009382

Marcus, M. (1992). *Progress in vhf/nhf mobile transmitter identification*. University of Manitoba.

Mardi, M., Nurozi, H., & Edalatkhah, S. (2011). A water saturation prediction using artificial neural networks and an investigation on cementation factors and saturation exponent variations in an Iranian oil well. *Petroleum Science and Technology*, *30*(4), 425–434. doi:10.1080/10916460903452033

Marsland, S. (2009). Machine Learning An Algorithm Perspective. Boca Raton, FL: A Chapman & Hall Book.

Martens, D., Baesens, B., & Fawcett, T. (2011). Editorial Survey: Swarm Intelligence for Data Mining. *Machine Learning*, *82*(1), 1–42. doi:10.1007/s10994-010-5216-5

Martens, D., De Backer, M., Vanthienen, J., Snoeck, M., & Baesens, B. (2007). Classification with ant colony optimization. *IEEE Transactions on Evolutionary Computation*, *11*, 651–665. doi:10.1109/TEVC.2006.890229

Martínez, A. M., & Kak, A. C. (2001). PCA versus LDA. *IEEE Transactions on Pattern Analysis and Machine Intelligence*, *23*(2), 228–233. doi:10.1109/34.908974

Marzio, M. D., & Taylor, C. C. (2012). Boosting kernel estimators. In C. Zhang, & Y. Ma (Eds.), *Ensemble Machine Learning* (pp. 87–115). New York, NY: Springer. doi:10.1007/978-1-4419-9326-7_3

Masoudnia, S., & Ebrahimpour, R. (2012). Mixture of experts: a literature survey. *Artificial Intelligence Review*. doi:10.1007/s10462-012-9338-y

Mathews, A., & Eduard, J. H. (2009). *A Dietary system: blood sugar predicting system*. World Intellectual Property Organization. Retrieved from http://www.wipo.int

Mathur, S., Reznik, A., Ye, C., Mukherjee, R., Rahman, A., & Shah, Y. et al. (2010). Exploiting the physical layer for enhanced security. *IEEE Wireless Communications*, *17*(5), 63–70. doi:10.1109/MWC.2010.5601960

Ma, Z. (2006). *Fuzzy database modeling of imprecise and uncertain engineering information*. Berlin: Springer.

Mazurowski, M. A., Habas, P. A., Zurada, J. M., Lo, J. Y., Baker, J. A., & Tourassi, G. D. (2008). Training neural network classifiers for medical decision making: The effects of imbalanced datasets on classification performance. *Neural Networks*, *21*, 427–436. doi:10.1016/j.neunet.2007.12.031 PMID:18272329

McCulloch, J. H. (1996). *J. Huston McCulloch*. Retrieved March 15, 2012, 2012, from http://economics.sbs.ohio-state.edu/jhm/programs/STABRND.M

McFarland, D., & Bösser, T. (1993). *Intelligent behavior in animals and robots*. Cambridge, MA: MIT Press/Bradford books.

McNulty & Mauze. (1998). Wavelet analysis for determining glucose concentrations of aqueous solutions using NIR spectroscopy. In *Proc. Biomedical Optics'98*. Academic Press.

Md. Azamathulla, H., Wu, F. C., Ghani, A. A., Narulkar, S. M., Zakaria, N. A., & Chang, C. K. (2008). Comparison between genetic algorithm and linear programming approach for real time operation. *Journal of Hydro-environment Research*, *2*(3), 172–181. doi:10.1016/j.jher.2008.10.001

Medtronic diabetes and health care providers company. (n.d.). Retrieved from http://www.medtronicdiabetes.com

Mellit, A., Massi Pavan, A., & Benghanem, M. (2013). Least Squares Support Vector Machine for Short-Term Prediction of Meteorological Time Series. *Theoretical and Applied Climatology*, (111): 297–307. doi:10.1007/s00704-012-0661-7

Metzler, R., & Klafter, J. (2000). The random walk's guide to anomalous diffusion: A fractional dynamics approach. *Physics Reports*, *339*, 1–77. doi:10.1016/S0370-1573(00)00070-3

Meyer, U., & Wetzel, S. (2004). A man-in-the-middle attack on umts. In *Proceedings of the 3rd ACM workshop on Wireless security*, (pp. 90-97). Philadelphia, PA: ACM.

Minku, L. L., White, A. P., & Yao, X. (2010). The impact of diversity on online ensemble learning in the presence of concept drift. *IEEE Transactions on Knowledge and Data Engineering*, *22*(5), 730–742. doi:10.1109/TKDE.2009.156

Mitchell, M. (2006). Network thinking. *Artificial Intelligence*, *170*, 1194–1212. doi:10.1016/j.artint.2006.10.002

Mitchell, M., Hraber, P. T., & Crutchfield, J. P. (1993). Revisiting the edge of chaos: Evolving cellular automata to perform computations. *Complex Systems*, *7*, 89–130.

Mitchell, T. (1997). *Machine learning*. Boston, MA: WCB/McGraw-Hill.

Mobasher, B., Cooley, R., & Srivastava, J. (2000). Automatic personalization based on Web usage mining. *Communications of the ACM*, *43*(8), 142–151. doi:10.1145/345124.345169

Mobasher, B., Dai, H., Luo, T., Sun, Y., & Zhu, J. (2000). Integrating web usage and content mining for more effective personalization. In *Electronic commerce and web technologies* (pp. 165–176). Springer. doi:10.1007/3-540-44463-7_15

Mohemmed, A. W., Zhang, M., & Browne, W. N. (2010). Particle swarm optimisation for outlier detection. In *Proceedings of the 12th annual conference on Genetic and evolutionary computation* (pp. 83-84). Portland, OR: ACM.

Mok, A. (1983). *Fundamental design problems of distributed systems for the hard-real time environment*. (Doctoral thesis). MIT, Cambridge, MA.

More, J. J. (1977). The Levenberg-Marquardt algorithm: Implementation and theory. In G. A. Watson (Ed.), *Numerical Analysis* (pp. 105–116). Springer.

Moreno-Torres, J. G., Raeder, T., Alaiz-Rodríguez, R., Chawla, N. V., & Herrera, F. (2012). A unifying view on dataset shift in classification. *Pattern Recognition*, *45*(1), 521–530. doi:10.1016/j.patcog.2011.06.019

Mustafa, N.H., & Pekeč. (2001). Majority consensus and the local majority rule. In *Proceedings of International Colloquium on Automata, Languages and Programming* (pp. 530–542). Crete, Greece: Springer.

Mustafa, M. W., Sulaiman, M. H., Shareef, H., & Khalid, S. N. A. (2012). Reactive power tracing in pool-based power system utilising the hybrid genetic algorithm and least squares support vector machine. *IET, Generation. Transmission & Distribution*, *6*(2), 133–141. doi:10.1049/iet-gtd.2011.0166

Mustaffa, Z., & Yusof, Y. (2011). Optimizing LSSVM using ABC for Non-Volatile Financial Prediction. *Australian Journal of Basic and Applied Sciences*, *5*(11), 549–556.

Nabavi-Kerizi, S. H., Abadi, M., & Kabir, E. (2010). A PSO-based weighting method for linear combination of neural networks. *Computers & Electrical Engineering*, *36*(5), 886–894. doi:10.1016/j.compeleceng.2008.04.006

Nagpal, R. (2002). Programmable self-assembly using biologically-inspired multiagent control. In *Proceedings of the first international joint conference on Autonomous agents and multiagent systems: part 1* (pp. 418-425). ACM.

Nansai Hu, Y.-D. Y. (2012). Identification of legacy radios in a cognitive radio network using a radio frequency fingerprinting based method. In *Proceedings of IEEE International Conference on Communications* (pp. 1597—1602). Ottawa, Canada: IEEE.

Nawi, N. M., Hamid, N. A., & Zainun, N. Y. (2012). A new modified back-propagation algorithm for forecasting Malaysian housing demand. *Applied Mechanics and Materials*, *232*, 908–912. doi:10.4028/www.scientific.net/AMM.232.908

NDTV. (2011). *Japan: Earthquake triggers oil refinery fire*. Retrieved from http://www.ndtv.com

Nguyen, N., Zheng, G., Han, Z., & Zheng, R. (2011). Device fingerprinting to enhance wireless security using nonparametric bayesian method. In *Proceedings of INFOCOM*, (pp. 1404-1412). Shanghai, China: IEEE.

Nikoletou, D., Sandham, W. A., Hamilton, D. J., Patterson, K., Japp, A., & MacGregor, C. (1998). Blood glucose prediction for diabetes therapy using a recurrent artificial neural network. In *Proceedings, EUSIPCO-98, IX European Signal Processing Conference*, (Vol. 11, pp. 673-676). EUSIPCO.

Nouvellet, P., Bacon, J. P., & Waxman, D. (2009). Fundamental insights into the random movement of animals from a single distance-related statistic. *American Naturalist, 174*(4), 506–514. doi:10.1086/605404 PMID:19737110

O'zcan, E., Bilgin, B., & Korkmaz, E. (2008). A comprehensive analysis of hyper-heuristics. *Intelligent Data Analysis, 12*(1), 3–23.

Oakland, J. S. (2003). *Statistical process control* (5th ed.). Oxford, UK: Butteworth/Heinemann.

Oh, K. W., & Bandler, W. (1987). Properties of fuzzy implication operators. *International Journal of Approximate Reasoning, 3*, 273–285. doi:10.1016/S0888-613X(87)80002-6

Oh, Y., & Son, S. H. (1995). Allocating fixed-priority periodic tasks on multiprocessor systems. *J. of Real-Time Systems, 9*(3), 207–239. doi:10.1007/BF01088806

Olmo, J., Luna, J., Romero, J., & Ventura, S. (2013). Mining association rules with single and multi-objective grammar guided ant programming. *Integrated Computer-Aided Engineering, 20*(3), 217–234.

Olmo, J., Romero, J., & Ventura, S. (2011). Article. *IEEE Transactions on Systems, Man, and Cybernetics. Part B, Cybernetics, 41*(6), 1585–1599. doi:10.1109/TSMCB.2011.2157681

Olmo, J. L., Cano, A., Romero, J. R., & Ventura, S. (2012). Binary and multiclass imbalanced classification using multi-objective ant programming. In *Proceedings of International Conference on Intelligent Systems Design and Applications (ISDA)*, 70-76. doi: 10.1109/ISDA.2012.6416515

Omran, M., Salman, A., & Engelbrecht, A. P. (2005). Dynamic clustering using particle swarm optimization with application in unsupervised image classification. In *Proceedings of Fifth World Enformatika Conference (ICCI 2005)* (pp. 199-204). Springer.

Oruklu, M. Cinar, Quinnand, & Smith. (2007). Adaptive control strategy for glucose regulation using recursive linear models. In *Proceedings of 10th International IFAC Symposium on Computer Applications in Biotechnology*, (pp. 153-158). IFAC.

Paoli, D. D., Goscinski, A., Hobbs, M., & Joyce, P. (1996). Performance comparison of process migration with remote process creation mechanism in RHODOS. In *Proc. of 16th ICDCS*, (pp. 554-561). Hong Kong: ICDCS.

Park, J.-B., Jeong, Y.-W., Shin, J.-R., & Lee, K. Y. (2010). An Improved Particle Swarm Optimization for Nonconvex Economic Dispatch Problems. *IEEE Transactions on Power Systems, 25*(1), 156–165. doi:10.1109/TPWRS.2009.2030293

Parpinelli, R., Freitas, A., & Lopes, H. (2002). Data mining with an ant colony optimization algorithm. *IEEE Transactions on Evolutionary Computation, 6*, 321–332. doi:10.1109/TEVC.2002.802452

Pasquill, F. (1961). The Estimation of the Dispersion of Windborne Material. *The Meteorological Magazine, 90*(1063), 33–49.

Pasquill, F. (1974). *Atmospheric Diffusion* (2nd ed.). Halsted Press, John Wiley & Sons.

Passino, K. M. (2004). *Biomimicry for optimization, control, and automation*. London: Springer.

Patterson, D. W. (1998). *Artificial neural networks: Theory and applications*. Upper Saddle River, NJ: Prentice Hall PTR.

Pavlus, J. (2012). Machines of the infinitive – searching for easy answers to hard. *Scientific American, 307*, 52–57.

Payton, D., Daily, M., Estowski, R., Howard, M., & Lee, C. (2001). Pheromone robotics. *Autonomous Robots, 11*, 319–324. doi:10.1023/A:1012411712038

Pelkmans, K., Suykens, J. A. K., Gestel, T. V., Brabanter, J. D., Lukas, L., Hamer, B., et al. (2002). *LS-SVMlab: A Matlab/C Toolbox for Least Squares Support Vector Machines.* Retrieved from www.esat.kuleuven.be/sista/lssvmlab/

Pender, J. E. (1997). *Modelling of blood glucose levels using Artificial Neural Networks.* (PhD Thesis). University of Strathclyde.

Peng, H., Long, F., & Ding, C. (2005). Feature selection based on mutual information criteria of max-dependency, max-relevance, and min-redundancy. *IEEE Transactions on Pattern Analysis and Machine Intelligence*, 27(8), 1226–1238. doi:10.1109/TPAMI.2005.159 PMID:16119262

Peng, Y. (2006). A novel ensemble machine learning for robust microarray data classification. *Computers in Biology and Medicine*, 36, 553–573. doi:10.1016/j.compbiomed.2005.04.001 PMID:15978569

Perfilieva, I., & Močkoř, J. (1999). *Mathematical principles of fuzzy logic.* Berlin: Springer.

Petrus, J. B., Thuijsman, F., & Weijters, A. J. (1995). *Artificial Neural Networks: An Introduction to ANN Theory and Practice.* Springer.

Polak, A., Dolatshahi, S., & Goeckel, D. (2011). Identifying wireless users via transmitter imperfections. *IEEE Journal on Selected Areas in Communications*, 29(7), 1469–1479. doi:10.1109/JSAC.2011.110812

Poli, R., & Graff, M. (2009). There Is a Free Lunch for Hyper-Heuristics, Genetic Programming and Computer Scientists. In *Proceedings of the 12th European Conference on Genetic Programming* (pp. 195-207). Berlin: Springer-Verlag.

Polikar, R. (2006). Ensemble based systems in decision making. *IEEE Circuits and Systems Magazine*, 21-45.

Polikar, R. (2009). Ensemble learning. *Scholarpedia*, 4(1), 2776. doi:10.4249/scholarpedia.2776

Poli, R., Kennedy, J., & Blackwell, T. (2007). Particle swarm optimization. *Swarm Intelligence*, 1(1), 33–57. doi:10.1007/s11721-007-0002-0

Prasath, R. (2010). Algorithms for Distributed Sorting and Prefix Computation in Static Ad Hoc Mobile Networks. In *Proceedings of International Conference on Electronics and Information Engineering* (Vol. 2, pp. 144-148). Kyoto, Japan: Academic Press.

Pyke, G. H. (1984). Optimal foraging theory: A critical review. *Annual Review of Ecology and Systematics*, 15, 523–575. doi:10.1146/annurev.es.15.110184.002515

Qiao, C., Sun, S., & Hou, Y. (2013). Design of strong classifier based on adaboost M2 and back propagation network. *Journal of Computational and Theoretical Nanoscience*, 10(12), 2836–2840. doi:10.1166/jctn.2013.3287

Radojević, D. (2008a). Interpolative Realization of Boolean Algebra as a Consistent Frame for Gradation and/or Fuzziness. In M. Nikravesh, & L. Zadeh (Eds.), *Forging New Frontiers: Fuzzy Pioneers II Studies in Fuzziness and Soft Computing* (pp. 295–318). Berlin: Springer-Verlag. doi:10.1007/978-3-540-73185-6_13

Radojević, D. (2008b). Real sets as consistent boolean generalisation of classical sets. In L. Zadeh, D. Tufis, F. Filip, & F. G. Diztac (Eds.), *From natural language to soft computing: New paradigms in artificial intelligence* (pp. 150–171). Bucharest: Editing House of Romanian Academy.

Raghuvanshi, A., Fan, Y., Woyke, M., & Perkowski, M. (2007). Quantum robots for teenagers. In *Proceedings of 37-th International Symposium on Multi-Valued Logic.* Oslo, Norway: Academic Press.

Rajasekhar, A., Abraham, A., & Pant, M. (2011). Levy Mutated Artificial Bee Colony Algorithm for Global Optimization. In *Proceedings of the IEEE International Conference on Systems, Man, and Cybernetics* (SMC). Anchorage, AK: IEEE.

Ramamritham, K., & Stankovic, J. A. (1994). Scheduling algorithms and operating support for real-time systems. *Proceedings of the IEEE*, 82(1), 55–67. doi:10.1109/5.259426

Ramamritham, K., Stankovic, J. A., & Shiah, P. F. (1990). Efficient scheduling algorithms for real-time multiprocessor systems. *IEEE Transactions on Parallel and Distributed Systems*, 1(2), 184–194. doi:10.1109/71.80146

Ramos, V., Muge, F., & Pina, P. (2002). Self-organized data and image retrieval as a consequence of inter-dynamic synergistic relationships in artificial ant colonies. In *Proceedings of Second International Conference on Hybrid Intelligent System*, (pp. 500-512). Academic Press.

Rao, R. B., Fung, G., Krishnapuram, B., Bi, J., Dundar, M., & Raykar, V. … Stoeckel, J. (2009). Mining medical images. In *Proceedings of the Third Workshop on Data Mining Case Studies and Practice Prize, Fifteenth Annual SIGKDD International Conference on Knowledge Discovery and Data Mining (KDD 2009)*. Paris, France: ACM.

Rasmussen, D., & Yager, R. (1997). Summary SQL - A Fuzzy Tool for Data Mining. *Intelligent Data Analysis*, *1*, 49–58. doi:10.1016/S1088-467X(98)00009-2

Razin, N., Eckmann, J. P., & Feinerman, O. (2013). Desert ants achieve reliable recruitment across noisy interactions. *Journal of the Royal Society, Interface*, *10*(82), 20130079. doi:10.1098/rsif.2013.0079 PMID:23486172

Rehman, S., Sowerby, K., & Coghill, C. (2012). RF fingerprint extraction from the energy envelope of an instantaneous transient signal. In *Proceedings of Communications Theory Workshop* (AusCTW), (pp. 90 -95). Wellington, New Zealand: AusCTW.

Reifman, J, Rajaraman, Gribok, & Ward. (2007). Predictive Monitoring for Improved Management of Glucose Levels. *Journal of Diabetes Science and Technology*, *1*(4), 468–478. doi:10.1177/193229680700100405 PMID:19885110

Re, M., & Valentini, G. (2010). Simple ensemble methods are competitive with state-of-the-art data integration methods for gene function prediction.[). DLBP.]. *Proceedings of the Machine Learning in System Biology*, *8*, 98–111.

Resnick, P., & Varian, H. R. (1997). Recommender systems. *Communications of the ACM*, *40*(3), 56–58. doi:10.1145/245108.245121

Reynolds, R. G. (1994). An introduction to cultural algorithms. In *Proceedings of the third annual conference on evolutionary programming* (pp. 131-139). World Scientific.

Reynolds, R. G., & Sverdlik, W. (1994). Problem solving using cultural algorithms. In *Proceedings of Evolutionary Computation* (pp. 645–650). IEEE.

Richardson, T. O., Christensen, K., Franks, N. R., Jensen, H. J., & Sendova-Franks, A. B. (2011). Ants in a labyrinth: A statistical mechanics approach to the division labor. *PLoS ONE*, *6*(4), e18416. doi:10.1371/journal.pone.0018416 PMID:21541019

Rieser, C. J. (2004). *Biologically inspired cognitive radio engine model utilizing distributed genetic algorithms for secure and robust wireless communications and networking*. (Doctoral dissertation). Virginia Polytechnic Institute and State University, Blacksburg, VA.

Ritchings, R. T., Berry, C., & Sheta, W. (2008). Comparing ANNs and Genetic Programming for voice quality assessment post-treatment. *Applied Artificial Intelligence Journal*, *22*(3), 198–207. doi:10.1080/08839510701734343

Ritchings, R. T., & McGillion, M. C. J. (2002). Pathological voice quality assessment using artificial neural networks. *Medical Engineering and Physics Journal*, *24*, 561–564. doi:10.1016/S1350-4533(02)00064-4 PMID:12237054

Rokach, L. (2010). Ensemble-based classifiers. *Artificial Intelligence Review*, *33*(1-2), 1–39. doi:10.1007/s10462-009-9124-7

Rosenblatt, F. (1958). The perceptron: a probabilistic model for information storage and organization in the brain. *Psychological Review*, *68*, 386–408. doi:10.1037/h0042519 PMID:13602029

Ross, S. (2002). The Spreadsort High-performance General-case Sorting Algorithm. In *Proceedings of the International Conference on Parallel and Distributed Processing Techniques and Applications* (Vol. 3, pp. 1100-1106). Las Vegas, NV: CSREA Press.

Rossetti, P., Porcellati, F., Bolli, B., & Fanelli, G. (2008). Prevention of Hypoglycemia While Achieving Good Glycemic Control in Type 1 Diabetes: The role of insulin analogs. *Diabetes Care*, *31*(Supp 2), S113–S120. doi:10.2337/dc08-s227 PMID:18227470

Roughgarden, T. (2003). The Price of Anarchy is Independent of the Network Topology. *Journal of Computer and System Sciences, 67*(2), 341–364. doi:10.1016/S0022-0000(03)00044-8

Roux, O., & Fonlupt, C. (2000). Ant programming: or how to use ants for automatic programming. In *Proceedings of International Conference on Swarm Intelligence (ANTS)*, (pp. 121-129). Brussels, Belgium: ANTS.

Roveri, N., Falini, G., Sidoti, M. C., Tampieri, A., Landi, E., Sandri, M., & Parma, B. (2003). Biologically inspired growth of hydroxyapatite nanocrystals inside self-assembled collagen fibers. *Materials Science and Engineering C, 23*(3), 441–446. doi:10.1016/S0928-4931(02)00318-1

Rowe, M. P., Pugh, E. N. Jr, Tyo, J. S., & Engheta, N. (1995). Polarization-difference imaging: A biologically inspired technique for observation through scattering media. *Optics Letters, 20*(6), 608–610. doi:10.1364/OL.20.000608 PMID:19859271

Rybalov, A., Kagan, E., & Yager, R. (2012). Parameterized uninorm and absorbing norm and their application for logic design. In *Proceedings of 27th IEEE Convention of Electrical and Electronics Engineers in Israel*. IEEE. doi:10.1109/EEEI.2012.6377125

Rybalov, A., Kagan, E., Manor, Y., & Ben-Gal, I. (2010). Fuzzy model of control for quantum-controlled mobile robots. In *Proceedings of 26th IEEE Convention of Electrical and Electronics Engineers in Israel* (pp. 19-23). IEEE.

Saad, E. M., Adawy, M. E., & Habashy, S. M. (2006). Reconfigurable parallel processing system based on a modified ant colony system. In *Proc. of NRSC*, (pp. 1-11). NRSC.

Sadeghi, R., Kadkhodaie, A., Rafiei, B., Yosefpour, M., & Khodabakhsh, S. (2011). A committee machine approach for predicting permeability from well log data: A case study from a heterogeneous carbonate reservoir, Balal oil Field, Persian Gulf. *Journal of Geopercia, 1*(2), 1–10.

Saini, G. (2005). Application of fuzzy-logic to real-time scheduling. In *Proceedings of 14th IEEE-NPSS Real-Time Conference*, (pp. 60-63). IEEE.

Sandham, W. A., Hamilton, D. J., Japp, A., & Patterson, K. (1998). Artificial Neural Network and neuro-fuzzy systems for improving diabetes therapy. In *Proceedings, 20th International Conference of the IEEE Engineering in Medicine and Biology Society*, (vol. 20, pp. 673–676). IEEE.

Saraswathi, R., Saseetharan, M. K., & Suja, S. (2012). ANN-based predictive model for performance evaluation of paper and pulp effluent treatment plant. *International Journal of Computer Applications in Technology, 45*(4), 280–289. doi:10.1504/IJCAT.2012.051128

Sarle, W. S. (1994). Neural networks and statistical models. In *Proceedings of the Nineteenth Annual SAS Users Group International Conference*. Cary, NC: SAS Institute.

Sasaki, A. (2002). A time-optimal distributed sorting algorithm on a line network. *Information Processing Letters, 83*(1), 21–26. doi:10.1016/S0020-0190(01)00307-6

Sauerwald, T. (2008). *Randomized Protocols for Information Dissemination*. (PhD Thesis). University of Paderborn.

Scanlon, P., Kennedy, I., & Liu, Y. (2010). Feature extraction approaches to rf fingerprinting for device identification in femtocells. *Bell Labs Technical Journal, 15*(3), 141–151. doi:10.1002/bltj.20462

Schapire, R. E. (2003). The boosting approach to machine learning: an overview. In *Nonlinear Estimation and Classification* (pp. 143–171). New York, NY: Springer. doi:10.1007/978-0-387-21579-2_9

Scharnow, J., Tinnenfeld, & Wegener. (2004). The Analysis of Evolutionary Algorithms on Sorting and Shortest Paths Problems. *Journal of Mathematical Modelling and Algorithms, 3*, 349–366. doi:10.1023/B:JMMA.0000049379.14872.f5

Schauer, T., & Raisch, J. (2007). Model-based predictive control of blood-sugar level in intensive care, control & automation. In *Proc. 15th IEEE Mediterranean Conference on Control and Automation* (MED '07). Athens, Greece: MED.

Schlumberger Oilfield Glossary, Reservoir Characterization. (n.d.). Retrieved August 19, 2013, from http://www.glossary.oilfield.slb.com/en/

Schweitzer, F. (2003). *Brownian agents and active particles. Collective dynamics in the natural and social sciences.* Berlin: Springer.

Searle, J. R. (2001). *Rationality in action.* Cambridge, MA: MIT Press/Bradford books.

Seinfeld, J. H. (1986). *Atmospheric Chemistry and Physics of Air Pollution. J.* Wiley.

Shah, A., Kotecha, K., & Shah, D. (2010). Dynamic scheduling for real-time distributed systems using ACO. *International Journal of Intelligent Computing and Cybernetics, 3*(2), 279–292. doi:10.1108/17563781011049205

Shang, B. Z., Hamman, J. G., Chen, H., & Caldwell, D. H. (2003). A model to correlate permeability with efficient porosity and irreducible water saturation. In *Proceedings of the SPE Annual Technical Conference and Exhibition.* SPE/Onepetro database.

Shapiro, L. (2011). *Embodied cognition.* London: Routledge/Taylor & Francis.

Sharma, T. K., Pant, M., & Bhardwaj, T. (2011). PSO Ingrained Artificial Bee Colony Algorithms for Solving Continuous Optimization Problems. In *Proceedings of the International Conference on Computer Applications and Industrial Electronics* (ICCAIE). Penang, Malaysia: ICCAIE.

Sharma, M., & Ponselva, A. (2010). Delayed coker heater analysis using an artifical neural network: The model was used to study the effects of the many variables that affect coke formation. *Hydrocarbon Processing, 89*(2), 75–79.

Shen, W., Zhang, Y., & Ma, X. (2009). Stock Return Forecast with LS-SVM and Particle Swarm Optimization. In *Proceedings of the International Conference on Business Intelligence and Financial Engineering* (BIFE). Beijing, China: BIFE.

Shi, X., Li, Y., Li, H., Guan, R., Wang, L., & Liang, Y. (2010). An integrated algorithm based on artificial bee colony and particle swarm optimization. In *Proceedings of the Sixth International Conference on Natural Computation* (ICNC). Yantai, China: ICNC.

Shiu, Y., Chang, S., Wu, H., Huang, S., & Chen, H. (2011). Physical layer security in wireless networks: A tutorial. *IEEE Wireless Communications, 18*(2), 66–74. doi:10.1109/MWC.2011.5751298

Shi, Y., & Jensen, M. (2011). Improved radiometric identification of wireless devices using mimo transmission. *IEEE Transactions on Information Forensics and Security, 6*(4), 1346–1354. doi:10.1109/TIFS.2011.2162949

Siegelmann, H. (1998). *Neural networks and analog computation: beyond the Turing limit.* Boston: Birkhüuser.

Siegwart, R., & Nourbakhsh, I. R. (2004). *Introduction to autonomous mobile robots.* Cambridge, MA: MIT Press/Bradford books.

Singh, B., & Arya, S. R. (2014). Back-propagation control algorithm for power quality improvement using DSTATCOM. *IEEE Transactions on Industrial Electronics, 61*(3), 1204–1212. doi:10.1109/TIE.2013.2258303

Slade, D. H. (Ed.). (1986). *Meteorology and Atomic Energy. U.S.* Atomic Energy Commission, Air Resources Laboratories, Research Laboratories, Environmental Science Services Administration, U.S Department of Commerce.

Sousa, T., Silva, A., & Neves, A. (2004). Particle swarm based data mining algorithms for classification tasks. *Parallel Computing, 30*(5-6), 767–783. doi:10.1016/j.parco.2003.12.015

Sözat, M. I., & Yazici, A. (2001). A complete axiomatization for fuzzy functional and multivalued dependencies in fuzzy database relations. *Fuzzy Sets and Systems, 117,* 161–181. doi:10.1016/S0165-0114(98)00152-3

Sparacino, G., Zanderigo, Corazza, Maran, Facchinetti, & Cobelli. (2007). Glucose Concentration can be Predicted Ahead in Time From Continuous Glucose Monitoring Sensor Time-Series. *IEEE Transactions on Bio-Medical Engineering, 54*(5), 931–938. doi:10.1109/TBME.2006.889774 PMID:17518291

Specht, D. F. (1991). A general regression neural network. *IEEE Transactions on Neural Networks, 2,* 568–576. doi:10.1109/72.97934 PMID:18282872

Ståhl, F., Cescon, M., Johansson, R., & Landin-Olsson, M. (2009). Subspace-based model identification of diabetic blood glucose dynamics. In *Proc. 15th Symposium on System Identification* (SYSID2009), (pp. 233-238). Saint-Malo, France: SYSID.

Stahl, F. (2003). *Diabetes Mellitus Modelling Based on Blood Glucose Measurements*. Department of Automatic Control Lund Institute of Technology.

Standards Committee. L., et al. (2003). Part 11: Wireless LAN medium access control (MAC) and physical layer (PHY) specifications. IEEE-SA Standards Board.

Stergiou, C. (2013). *What is a neural network?* Retrieved August 25, 2013, from http://www.doc.ic.ac.uk/~nd/surprise_96/journal/vol1/cs11/article1.html

Steshenko, J., Kagan, E., & Ben-Gal, I. (2011). A simple protocol for a society of NXT robots communicating via Bluetooth. In *Proceedings of IEEE Conference ELMAR'11* (pp. 381-384). IEEE.

Stevens, R., & Casillas, A. (2006). Artificial neural networks. In *Automated Scoring of Complex Tasks in Computer Based Testing: An Introduction*. Lawrence Erlbaum.

Stone, L. D. (1983). The process of search planning: current approaches and continuing problems. *Operations Research*, *31*(2), 207–233. doi:10.1287/opre.31.2.207

Stutzle, T. (1998). An ant approach for the flow shop problem. In *Proceeding of EUFIT-98*, (pp. 1560-1564). EUFIT.

Subotic, M. (2011). Artificial Bee Colony Algorithm with Multiple Onlookers for Constrained Optimization Problems. In *Procedings of the European Computing Conference* (ECC). Paris: ECC.

Sumpter, D. J. T. (2010). *Collective animal behavior*. Princeton, NJ: Princeton University Press.

Sun, Y., Kamel, M. S., Wong, A. K., & Wang, Y. (2007). Cost-sensitive boosting for classification of imbalanced data. *Pattern Recognition*, *40*, 3358–3378. doi:10.1016/j.patcog.2007.04.009

Suski, W., Temple, M., Mendenhall, M., & Mills, R. (2008). Using spectral fingerprints to improve wireless network security. In *Proceedings of Global Telecommunications Conference*. IEEE.

Suski, W. II, Temple, M., Mendenhall, M., & Mills, R. (2008). Radio frequency fingerprinting commercial communication devices to enhance electronic security. *International Journal of Electronic Security and Digital Forensics*, *1*(3), 301–322. doi:10.1504/IJESDF.2008.020946

Suykens, J. A. K., Van Gestel, T., De Brabanter, J., De Moor, B., & Vandewalle, J. (2002). *Least Squares Support Vector Machines*. Leuven, Belgium: World Scientific Publishing Co. Pte. Ltd.

Tan, K., Tay, A., Lee, T., & Heng, C. (2002). Mining multiple comprehensible classification rules using genetic programming. In *Proceedings of IEEE Congress on Evolutionary Computation (IEEE CEC)* (pp. 1302-1307). Honolulu, HI: IEEE.

Tang, K., Wang, R., & Chen, T. (2011). Towards maximizing the area under the ROC Curve for multi-class classification problems. In *Proceedings of the 25th AAAI Conference on Artificial Intelligence* (pp. 483-488). San Francisco, CA: AAAI.

Tan, G., Yan, J., Gao, C., & Yang, S. (2012). Prediction of water quality time series data based on least squares support vector machines. *Procedia Engineering*, *31*, 1194–1199. doi:10.1016/j.proeng.2012.01.1162

Tang, Y., Zhang, Y., Chawla, N., & Krasser, S. (2009). SVMs modeling for highly imbalanced classification. *IEEE Transactions on Systems, Man, and Cybernetics. Part B, Cybernetics*, *39*(1), 281–288. doi:10.1109/TSMCB.2008.2002909 PMID:19068445

Tan, S. T. (2010). *Applied Mathematics for the Managerial, Life, and Social Sciences* (6th ed.). Richard Stratton.

Tehrani, R., & Khodayar, F. (2011). A hybrid optimized Artificial Intelligent Model to Forecast Crude Oil using Genetic Algorithm. *African Journal of Bussiness Management*, *5*(34), 13130–13135.

Thai, N. D. (2002). Real-time scheduling in distributed systems. In *Proc of PARELEC'02*, (pp. 165-170). PARELEC.

Timmis, J., & Neal, M. (2001). A resource limited artificial immune system for data analysis. *Knowledge-Based Systems*, *14*(3), 121–130. doi:10.1016/S0950-7051(01)00088-0

Timmis, J., Neal, M., & Hunt, J. (2000). An artificial immune system for data analysis. *Bio Systems*, *55*(1), 143–150. doi:10.1016/S0303-2647(99)00092-1 PMID:10745118

Timur, A. (1968, July-August). An investigation of permeability, porosity, and residual water saturation relationship for sandstone reservoirs. *The Log Analyst*.

Ting, K. M. (2002). An instance-weighting method to induce cost-sensitive trees. *IEEE Transactions on Knowledge and Data Engineering*, *14*, 659–665. doi:10.1109/TKDE.2002.1000348

Tomek, I. (1976). Two modifications of CNN. *IEEE Transactions on Systems, Man, and Cybernetics*, *6*, 769–772. doi:10.1109/TSMC.1976.4309452

Toonstra, J., & Kinsner, W. (2002). A radio transmitter fingerprinting system ODO-1. In *Proceedings of Canadian Conference on Electrical and Computer Engineering*, (vol. 1, pp. 60-63). IEEE.

Tresp, V., Briegel, T., & Moody, J. (1999). Neural-network models for the blood glucose metabolism of a diabetic. *IEEE Transactions on Neural Networks*, *10*, 1204. doi:10.1109/72.788659 PMID:18252621

Trianni, V. (2008). *Evolutionary swarm robotics: Evolving self-organising behaviors in groups of autonomous robots*. Berlin: Springer. doi:10.1007/978-3-540-77612-3

Trillas, E., Cubillo, S., & del Campo, C. (2000). When QM-operators are implication functions and conditional fuzzy relations? *International Journal of Intelligent Systems*, *15*, 647–655. doi:10.1002/(SICI)1098-111X(200007)15:7<647::AID-INT5>3.0.CO;2-T

Tsetlin, M. L. (1963). Finite automata and models of simple forms of behavior. *Russian Mathematical Surveys*, *18*(1), 1–27. doi:10.1070/RM1963v018n04ABEH001139

Tsetlin, M. L. (1973). *Automaton theory and modeling of biological systems*. New York: Academic Press.

Tsymbal, A., Pechenizkiy, M., & Cunningham, P. (2005). Diversity in search strategies for ensemble feature selection. *Inference*, *6*(1), 83–98.

Tudorie, C. (2008). Qualifying objects in classical relational database querying. In J. Galindo (Ed.), *Handbook of Research on Fuzzy Information Processing in Databases* (pp. 218–245). London: IGI Global. doi:10.4018/978-1-59904-853-6.ch009

Tudorie, C. (2009). Intelligent interfaces for database fuzzy querying. *The Annals of Dunarea de Jos University of Galati. Fascicle III*, *32*(2), 33–37.

Turchin, P. (2003). *Complex population dynamics: A theoretical/empirical synthesis*. Princeton, NJ: Princeton University Press.

Turneo, A., Pilato, C., Frrandi, F., et al. (2008). Ant colony optimization for mapping and scheduling in heterogeneous multiprocessor systems. In *Proceedings of International Conference on Embedded Computer Systems: Architectures, Modeling and Simulation*, (pp. 142-149). Academic Press.

Turner, D. B. (1979). Atmospheric Dispersion Modeling. *Journal of the Air Pollution Control Association*, *29*(5), 502–519. doi:10.1080/00022470.1979.10470821

Turner, D. B. (1994). *Workbook of Atmospheric Dispersion Estimates: An Introduction to Dispersion Modeling* (2nd ed.). Lewis Publishers.

Turner, D. B., Bender, L. W., Pierce, T. E., & Petersen, W. B. (1989). Air Quality Simulation Models from EPA. *Environmental Software*, *4*(2), 52–61. doi:10.1016/0266-9838(89)90031-2

United States Chemical Safety Board. (2013). Retrieved from http://www.csb.gov

USRP. (2013). *USRP products*. Retrieved January 10, 2014 from https://www.ettus.com/product

van der Heide, A., & Trivino, G. (2009). Automatically generated linguistic summaries of energy consumption data. In A. Abraham, J. Sánchez, F. Herrera, V. Loia, F. Marcelloni, & S. Senatore (Eds.), *Intelligent Systems Design and Applications* (ISDA 2009) (pp. 553 – 559). Los Alamitos, CA: CPS.

Van der Merwe, D. W., & Engelbrecht, A. P. (2003). Data clustering using particle swarm optimization. In *Proceedings of IEEE Congress on Evolutionary Computation*, (Vol. 1, pp. 215-220). Canberra, Australia. IEEE.

Van Doorn, E.A., & Pollett. (2009). Quasi-Stationary Distributions for Reducible Absorbing Markov Chains in Discrete Time. *Markov Processes and Related Fields*, *15*, 191–204.

Van Hulse, J., Khoshgoftaar, T. M., Napolitano, A., & Wald, R. (2009). Feature selection with high dimensional imbalanced data. In *Proceedings of the 9th IEEE International Conference on Data Mining Workshops* (pp. 507–514). Miami, FL: IEEE.

Vapnik, V. N. (1995). *The Nature of Statistical Learning Theory* (2nd ed.). New York: Springer-Verlag. doi:10.1007/978-1-4757-2440-0

Venter, G., & Sobieszczanski-Sobieski, J. (2003). Particle swarm optimization. *AIAA Journal*, *41*(8), 1583–1589. doi:10.2514/2.2111

Verbeeck, K., & Nowé, A. (2002). Colonies of learning automata. *IEEE Transactions on Systems, Man, and Cybernetics B*, *32*(6), 772–780. doi:10.1109/TSMCB.2002.1049611 PMID:18244883

Veropoulos, K., Campbell, C., & Cristianini, N. (1999). Controlling the sensitivity of support vector machines. In *Proceedings of the international joint conference on artificial intelligence* (pp. 55–60). Stockholm, Sweden: Academic Press.

Viswanathan, G. M., Buldyrev, S. V., Havlin, S., Da Luz, M. G. E., Raposo, E. P., & Stanley, H. E. (1999). Optimizing the success of random searchers. *Nature*, *401*, 911–914. doi:10.1038/44831 PMID:10553906

Viswanathan, G. M., Da Luz, M. G. E., Raposo, E. P., & Stanley, H. E. (2011). *The physics of foraging: an introduction to random searchers and biological encounters*. New York: Cambridge University Press. doi:10.1017/CBO9780511902680

Vlad, S. (2010). Investigation of Chaotic Behavior in Euro-Leu Exchange Rate. *Journal of Applied Computer Science and Mathematics*, *8*(4), 67–71.

Vose, M. D. (1999). *The simple genetic algorithm: Foundations and theory* (Vol. 12). Cambridge, MA: The MIT Press.

Vucetic, M., Hudec, M., & Vujošević, M. (2013). A new method for computing fuzzy functional dependencies in relational database systems. *Expert Systems with Applications*, *40*(7), 2738–2745. doi:10.1016/j.eswa.2012.11.019

WaiYee, Lun Wong, Shing, ChakHing, Ching, Chung Man, & Yin Ki. (2006). *Method for predicting a blood glucose level of a person*. Academic Press.

Wang, T. C., Lee, H. D., & Chen, C. M. (2007). Intelligent queries based on fuzzy set theory and SQL. In P. Wang (Ed.), *Joint Conference on Information Science* (pp. 1426–1432). Washington, DC: Word Scientific.

Wang, L., & Fu, K. (2008). *Artificial neural networks*. Hoboken, NJ: John Wiley & Sons, Inc.

Wang, S., & Yao, X. (2013). Relationships between diversity of classification ensembles and single-class performance measures. *IEEE Transactions on Knowledge and Data Engineering*, *25*(1), 206–219. doi:10.1109/TKDE.2011.207

Weiss, G., McCarthy, K., & Zabar, B. (2007). Cost-sensitive learning vs. sampling: Which is best for handling unbalanced classes with unequal error costs? In *Proceedings of the 2007 International Conference on Data Mining* (pp. 35-41). CSREA Press.

Weiss, G. (Ed.). (1999). *Multiagent systems: a modern approach to distributed artificial intelligence*. Cambridge, MA: MIT Press.

Whigham, P. A., & Crapper, P. F. (2001). Modelling rainfall-runoff using genetic programming. *Mathematical and Computer Modelling*, *33*, 707–721. doi:10.1016/S0895-7177(00)00274-0

Whitley, D. (1994). A genetic algorithm tutorial. *Statistics and Computing*, *4*(2), 65–85. doi:10.1007/BF00175354

Widrow, B., & Lehr, M. (1990). 30 years of adaptive neural networks: perceptron, madaline, and backpropagation. *Proceedings of the IEEE*, *78*(9), 1415–1442. doi:10.1109/5.58323

Wilson, D., & Martinez, T. (2000). Reduction techniques for instance-based learning algorithms. *Machine Learning*, *38*, 257–286. doi:10.1023/A:1007626913721

Wilson, S. W. (1986). *Classifier system learning of a boolean function*. Cambridge, MA: Rowland Institute for Science.

Wittlinger, M., Wehner, R., & Wolf, H. (2006). The ant odometer: Stepping on stilts and stumps. *Science*, *312*, 1965–1967. doi:10.1126/science.1126912 PMID:16809544

Wittlinger, M., Wehner, R., & Wolf, H. (2007). The desert ant odometer: A stride integrator that accounts for stride length and walking speed. *The Journal of Experimental Biology*, *210*, 198–207. doi:10.1242/jeb.02657 PMID:17210957

Woelfle, M., Temple, M., Mullins, M., & Mendenhall, M. (2009). Detecting, identifying and locating bluetooth devices using RF fingerprints. In *Proceedings of 2009 Military Communications Conference* (MILCOM 2009). Boston, MA: MILCOM.

Wolpert, D., & Macready, W. (1997). No free lunch theorems for optimization. *IEEE Transactions on Evolutionary Computation*, *1*(1), 67–82. doi:10.1109/4235.585893

Woolley, A. W., Chabris, C. F., Pentland, A., Hashmi, N., & Malone, T. W. (2010). Evidence for a collective intelligence factor in the performance of human groups. *Science*, *330*, 686–688. doi:10.1126/science.1193147 PMID:20929725

World Health Organization. (n.d.). Retrieved from http://www.who.int

Wu, J., & Niu, D. (2009). Short-Term Power Load Forecasting Using Least Squares Support Vector Machines (LS-SVM). In *Proceedings of the Second International Workshop on Computer Science and Engineering* (WCSE). Qingdao, China: WCSE.

Wu, D., Feng, S., & He, Y. (2007). Infrared Spectroscopy Technique for the Nondestructive measurement of Fat Content in Milk Powder. *Journal of Dairy Science*, *90*, 3613–3619. doi:10.3168/jds.2007-0164 PMID:17638971

Wu, H.-I. (2005). A case study of type 2 diabetes self-management. *Biomedical Engineering Online*, *4*(4). doi: doi:10.1186/1475-925X-4-4 PMID:15644138

Wyllie, M.R.J., & Rose, W.D. (1950). Some theoretical considerations related to the quantitative evaluation of the physical characteristics of reservoir rock from electrical log data. *Transactions of the American Institute of Mechanical Engineers*, 105–118.

Wyllie, M. R. J., Gregory, A. R., & Gardner, G. H. F. (1956). Elastic wave velocity in heterogeneous and porous media. *Geophysics*, 41–70. doi:10.1190/1.1438217

Xiang, Y., & Jiang, L. (2009). Water Quality Prediction Using LS-SVM and Particle Swarm Optimization. In *Proceedings of the Second International Workshop on Knowledge Discovery and Data Mining* (WKDD). Moscow, Russia: WKDD.

Xiao, X., Dow, E. R., Eberhart, R., Ben Miled, Z., & Oppelt, R. J. (2004). A hybrid self-organizing maps and particle swarm optimization approach. *Concurrency and Computation*, *16*(9), 895–915. doi:10.1002/cpe.812

Xie, H.-L., Li, N., Lu, F.-C., & Xie, Q. (2009). Application of LS-SVM by GA for Dissolved Gas Concentration Forecasting in Power Transformer Oil. In *Proceedings of the Asia-Pacific Power and Energy Engineering Conference* (APPEEC). Wuhan, China: APPEEC.

Xu, S., Xu, L., Xu, Z., & Huang, B. (2008). Individual radio transmitter identification based on spurious modulation characteristics of signal envelop. In *Proceedings of IEEE Military Communications Conference*. IEEE.

Xu, L., & Amari, S. (2009). Combining Classifiers and Learning Mixture-of-Experts. In J. Rabuñal Dopico, J. Dorado, & A. Pazos (Eds.), *Encyclopedia of Artificial Intelligence* (pp. 318–326). Hershey, PA: Information Science Reference.

Yager, R. R. (1989). On linguistic summaries of data. In G. Piatetsky-Shapiro & W. Frawley (Eds.), *IJCAI Workshop on Knowledge Discovery in Databases* (pp. 378–389). Waltham, MA: GTE Laboratories Incorporated.

Yager, R. (1982). A new approach to the summarization of data. *Information Sciences*, *28*, 69–86. doi:10.1016/0020-0255(82)90033-0

Yager, R. (1988). On ordered weighted avaraging operators in multicriteria decision making. *IEEE Transactions on Systems, Man, and Cybernetics*, *18*, 183–190. doi:10.1109/21.87068

Yager, R., & Kacprzyk, J. (Eds.). (1997). *The Ordered Weighted Averaging Operators: Theory and Applications*. Boston: Kluwer. doi:10.1007/978-1-4615-6123-1

Yager, R., & Rybalov, A. (1996). Uninorm aggregation operators. *Fuzzy Sets and Systems*, *80*, 111–120. doi:10.1016/0165-0114(95)00133-6

Yang, X., Zheng, Y., Siddique, M., & Beddoe, G. (2008). Learning from imbalanced data: a comparative study for colon CAD. In *Proceedings of the Medical Imaging* (Vol. 6915). Academic Press.

Yang, F., Sun, T., & Zhang, C. (2009). An efficient hybrid data clustering method based on K-harmonic means and Particle Swarm Optimization. *Expert Systems with Applications*, *36*(6), 9847–9852. doi:10.1016/j.eswa.2009.02.003

Yang, Q., & Wu, X. (2006). 10 challenging problems in data mining research. *International Journal of Information Technology & Decision Making*, *5*(4), 597–604. doi:10.1142/S0219622006002258

Yang, X., & Zheng, J. (2009). Artificial neural networks. In *Handbook of Research on Geoinformatics*. Academic Press. doi:10.4018/978-1-59140-995-3.ch016

Yen, S., & Lee, Y. (2006). Cluster-Based Sampling Approaches to Imbalanced Data Distributions. In *Data Warehousing and Knowledge Discovery* (pp. 427–436). Springer. doi:10.1007/11823728_41

Yi, L., & Kang, W. (2011). A new genetic programming algorithm for building decision tree. *Procedia Engineering*, *15*, 3658–3662. doi:10.1016/j.proeng.2011.08.685

Ying, M. (2002). Implication operators in fuzzy logic. *IEEE Transactions on Fuzzy Systems*, *10*(1), 88–91. doi:10.1109/91.983282

Yongcheng, L., & Roy, C. (1995). A dynamic priority based scheduling method in distributed systems. In *Proceedings of the International Conference on Parallel and Distributed Processing Techniques and Applications*, (pp. 177-186). Academic Press.

Yorucu, V. (2003). The Analysis of Forecasting Performance by Using Time Series Data for Two Mediterranean Islands. *Review of Social. Economic & Business Studies*, *2*, 175–196.

Yuan, B., & Liu, W. H. (2011). A Measure Oriented Training Scheme for Imbalanced Classification Problems. In *Proceedings of the Pacific-Asia Conference on Knowledge Discovery and Data Mining Workshop on Biologically Inspired Techniques for Data Mining* (pp. 293–303). Shenzhen, China: Academic Press.

Yuan, B., & Ma, X. (2012). Sampling + Reweighting: Boosting the Performance of AdaBoost on Imbalanced Datasets. In *Proceedings of the 2012 International Joint Conference on Neural Networks* (pp. 2680–2685). Brisbane, Australia: Academic Press.

Yu, H., Ni, J., & Zhao, J. (2013). ACOSampling: An ant colony optimization-based undersampling method for classifying imbalanced DNA microarray data. *Neurocomputing*, *101*, 309–318. doi:10.1016/j.neucom.2012.08.018

Yuksel, S. E., Wilson, J. N., & Gader, P. D. (2012). Twenty years of mixture of experts. *IEEE Transactions on Neural Networks and Learning Systems*, *23*(8), 1177–1193. doi:10.1109/TNNLS.2012.2200299 PMID:24807516

Yu, L., Chen, H., Wang, S., & Lai, K. K. (2009). Evolving Least Squares Support Vector Machines for Stock Market Trend Mining. *IEEE Transactions on Evolutionary Computation*, *13*(1), 87–102. doi:10.1109/TEVC.2008.928176

Yusof, N., & Rashid, A. R., & Mohamed, Z. (2010). Malaysia Crude Oil Production Estimation: An Application of ARIMA Model. In *Proceedings of the International Conference on Science and Social Research* (CSSR). Kuala Lumpur, Malaysia: CSSR.

Zadeh, L. A. (1965). Fuzzy sets. *Information and Control*, *8*(3), 338–353. doi:10.1016/S0019-9958(65)90241-X

Zadeh, L. A. (1983). A computational approach to fuzzy quantifiers in natural languages. *Computers & Mathematics with Applications (Oxford, England)*, *9*, 149–184. doi:10.1016/0898-1221(83)90013-5

Zadeh, L. A. (2002). From computing with numbers to computing with words – From manipulation of measurements to manipulation of perceptions. *International Journal of Applied Mathematics and Computer Science*, *12*(3), 307–324.

Zadrożny, S., & Kacprzyk, J. (2009). Issues in the practical use of the OWA operators in fuzzy querying. *Journal of Intelligent Information Systems*, *33*, 307–325. doi:10.1007/s10844-008-0068-1

Zahara, E., & Kao, Y. T. (2009). Hybrid Nelder–Mead simplex search and particle swarm optimization for constrained engineering design problems. *Expert Systems with Applications*, *36*(2), 3880–3886. doi:10.1016/j.eswa.2008.02.039

Zalta, E. N. (Ed.). (2003). *Stanford encyclopedia of philosophy*. Retrieved from http://plato.stanford.edu/

Zamora, G., Bergin, S., & Kennedy, I. (2010). Using Support Vector Machines for Passive Steady State RF Fingerprinting. In *Novel Algorithms and Techniques in Telecommunications and Networking* (pp. 183–188). Academic Press. doi:10.1007/978-90-481-3662-9_31

Zanetti, D., Danev, B., & Čapkun, S. (2010). Physical-layer identification of UHF RFID tags. In *Proceedings of the 16th ACM Conference on Mobile Computing and Networking* (pp. 353-364). Chicago: ACM.

Zecchin, C., Facchinetti, A., Sparacino, G., De Nicolao, G., & Cobelli, C. (2012). Neural network incorporating meal information improves accuracy of short-time prediction of glucose concentration. *IEEE Transactions on Bio-Medical Engineering*, *59*, 1550–1560. doi:10.1109/TBME.2012.2188893 PMID:22374344

Zhai, J., & Huang, L. (2013). Marketing Prediction Based on Time Series Prediction Algorithm of Least Squares Support Vector Machines.[JCIT]. *Journal of Convergence Information Technology*, *8*(3), 245–250. doi:10.4156/jcit.vol8.issue3.29

Zhang, G., Jiang, W., & Su, X. (2008). Discussion on the optimization of BP neural network in GPS height conversion. *Journal of Geomatics*, *33*(4), 18–20.

Zhang, G., Patuwo, B. E., & Hu, M. Y. (1998). Forecasting with Artificial Neural Network: The State of Art. *International Journal of Forecasting*, *14*, 35–62. doi:10.1016/S0169-2070(97)00044-7

Zhang, W., Niu, P., Li, G., & Li, P. (2013). Forecasting of Turbine Heat Rate with Online Least Squares Support Vector Machine based on Gravitational Search Algorithm. *Knowledge-Based Systems*, *39*, 34–44. doi:10.1016/j.knosys.2012.10.004

Zhao, W., Krishnaswamy, A., Chellappa, R., Swets, D. L., & Weng, J. (1998). Discriminant analysis of principal components for face recognition. In *Face Recognition* (pp. 73–85). Springer. doi:10.1007/978-3-642-72201-1_4

Zheng, Z., Wu, X., & Srihari, R. (2004). Feature selection for text categorization on imbalanced data. *ACM SIGKDD Explorations*, *6*(1), 80–89. doi:10.1145/1007730.1007741

Zhou, Z. H., & Liu, X. Y. (2006). Training Cost-Sensitive Neural Networks with Methods Addressing the Class Imbalance Problem. *IEEE Transactions on Knowledge and Data Engineering*, *18*(1), 63–77. doi:10.1109/TKDE.2006.17

Zhou, Z.-H. (2009). Ensemble learning. In S. Z. Li (Ed.), *Encyclopedia of Biometrics* (pp. 270–273). Berlin: Springer.

Zitar, A. (2005). Towards Artificial Neural Networks Model for Insulin/Glucose in Diabetics. *Journal Informatica*, *29*(2), 227–232.

About the Contributors

Shafiq Alam received his Ph.D. degree from the University of Auckland and is currently working as a research fellow in the Department of Computer Science, University of Auckland. His research interests include optimization-based data mining, Web usage mining, and computational intelligence. He has two Master's, one in Information Technology and another in Computer Science. He has a B.Sc. in Computer Science. Shafiq Alam has held the positions of Lecturer, Assistant Professor, and Academic Coordinator at university level. He has been on the Program Committees of A-ranked data mining conferences and computational intelligence conferences.

Gillian Dobbie worked in industry for a couple of years before lecturing and doing research at the University of Melbourne, Victoria University of Wellington and the National University of Singapore. Her main areas of interest pertain to databases and the Web. She has worked in the foundations of database systems, defining logical models for various kinds of database systems, and reasoning about the correctness of algorithms in that setting. With colleagues at the National University of Singapore, she has defined a data model for semistructured data (called ORA-SS), providing a language independent description of the data. The group she was working with has used the ORA-SS data model to define a normal form for ORA-SS schema, defined valid views for semistructured databases, and described a storage structure for semistructured databases using object relational databases. Gill has a wide range of research interests, including databases, the Web, and software engineering. She is interested both in structured and semistructured data. More specifically, she is interested in how data can best be organized and managed, how the semantics of the data can be retained and expressed, and how querying can be carried out efficiently.

Yun Sing Koh is currently a senior lecturer at the Department of Computer Science, University of Auckland. After completing a Bachelor's degree in Computer Science and Masters in Software Engineering at University Malaya, she went on to do her PhD in Computer Science at University of Otago, New Zealand. Her current research interests include data mining, machine learning, and information retrieval. Most of her current research revolves around finding rare patterns/rules within datasets and data stream mining. She has also developed a keen interest in several other areas including particle swarm optimization, social network mining, and online auction fraud detection.

Saeed ur Rehman has submitted PhD thesis for examination at the University of Auckland, New Zealand. He has received his ME in Electrical and Electronic Engineering with first class honors from the University of Auckland, New Zealand and the B.Sc Electrical Engineering from NWFP University of Engineering and Technology, Pakistan in 2009 and 2004, respectively. He is currently working as a lecturer in Unitec Institute of Technology, Auckland, New Zealand. His doctoral research is focused on physical layer security of wireless networks. His ME thesis was on the Analytical and simulation analysis of MAC for Wireless Sensor Network. Following graduation, he has worked in cellular companies for three years as a Telecom Engineer (2005-08) and as a research assistant in CISTER/IPP-HURRAY Research unit, Portugal (2009). His current interests include cyber security, physical layer security of wireless networks and, in particular, analysis and design of radio fingerprinting for low cost transceivers.

* * *

Abdulazeez Abdulraheem is an Associate Professor in the department of Petroleum Engineering, King Fahd University of Petroleum and Minerals, Saudi Arabia. He earned a Ph.D. degree in Civil Engineering with specialization in Rock Mechanics from the University of Oklahoma, Norman, USA in 1994, a Master degree in Civil Engineering from the Indian Institute of Science, Bangalore, India, in 1985, and a Bachelor degree in Civil Engineering from the Osmania University, Hyderabad, India, in 1983. His areas of research interests include application of Artificial Intelligence, theoretical and experimental rock mechanics, constitutive (material behavior) modeling, and numerical simulation using finite element and finite difference, soil mechanics, and structural dynamics.

Fatai Anifowose is a PhD student in the Faculty of Computer Science and Information Technology, Universiti Malaysia Sarawak. Presently, he works as a Research Engineer in the Center for Petroleum and Minerals, Research Institute, King Fahd University of Petroleum and Minerals (KFUPM), Saudi Arabia. He obtained his Bachelor of Technology (B. Tech.) degree in Computer Science from Federal University of Technology, Akure, Nigeria in 1999 and a Master degree in Information and Computer Science from KFUPM in 2009. His research interests include Hybrid Intelligent Systems, Ensemble Machine Learning, and Big Data Analysis, especially in petroleum reservoir characterization. He is a member of professional societies such as Society of Petroleum Engineers, type2fuzzylogic.org, UK, International Association of Computer Science and Information Technology and Nigeria Computer Society.

Iman T. Ardekani has received his PhD degree from the University of Auckland. After a post-doctoral research fellowship experience, he has joined Unitec Institute of Technology as a lecturer in the department of Computing and Information Technology. He is known internationally for his novel approach to active noise control. He has accumulated academic and industrial experience in active noise control. He has had substantial experience in signal processing and mathematical modeling: essential ingredients for this proposal. His thesis on active noise control was nominated for the University of Auckland's Top Doctoral Thesis Award. He also won a FRDF grant for his 2-year postdoctoral research on active noise control in the University of Auckland. Currently, he is the Director of Unitec Smart Rooms labs, where various research projects on acoustic and image signal processing are conducted.

Tianxing Cai is a reseracher in the Dan. F Smith Department of Chemical Engineering, Lamar University. Tianxing specialized in the research fields of modeling, simulation and optimization for the industrial operation, process safety, and environment protection. His major research is the development of optimization models (Linear Programming, Quadratic Constraint Programming, Nonlinear Programming, Mixed Integer Programming, Relaxed Mixed Integer Programming, Mixed Integer Quadratic Constraint Programming, Mixed Integer Nonlinear Programming, Relaxed Mixed Integer Quadratic Constraint Programming) to realize the synthesis of energy and water systems, manufacturing planning and scheduling, and plant-wide optimization. Besides that, he also involves the software application of Aspen, HYSYS, ProII, MATLAB, and gPROMS to conduct simulation and optimization for the process design, environment impact reduction, and safety assessment.

Peng Cao is a PhD student enrolled in the Northeastern University, China. Peng has been working with the Alberta Innovates Center for Machine Learning (AICML)-Computing Science at the University of Alberta, since 2011. Peng received an MSc in Computer Science from Northeastern University, China, in 2005. His research interests are imbalanced data learning, medical image mining.

Anthony Chatzinouskas was born March 18, 1970 in Athens. He is married and has a daughter 6 years old. He is a graduate of Hellenic Open University from 2013 (in computer science). He has attended many seminars and conferences. He is working in German polytechnic company Henkel Hellas since 1992 as IT Business Consultant reporting to Local IT Manager. His key job responsibilities are: Support Global Applications (User support of SAP processes and local variant, Local customer reference for problem management and incident first level of escalation), Support change Application (Coordination and execution of local project rollout in the office), Run Local Applications and Infrastructures (Manage interfaces of Global applications/infrastructures, Contribution in inventory and cost allocation management of cell phones, blackberries, UNTS cards, telephone devices, ADSL line connections and PCs), and Contribution in systematic backup procedures in Data Center located in the HQ.

Dhruvan Choubisa is an undergraduate student in School of Mechanical and Building Science at VIT University. His research interests cover a wide range of subjects in civil engineering, including geotechnical engineering, environmental, slope stability, pile foundation, structural designs, and super-structure designs.

Khaled Eskaf is an assistance Professor of intelligent systems in College of computing and Information Technology at The Arab Academy for Science, Technology and Maritime Transport – Alexandria branch, Egypt. He received his BSc (Hons) in Computer Engineering, College of Engineering and Technology, The Arab Academy for Science, Technology and Maritime Transport, Egypt (1995). In addition, he received his MSc in Computer Engineering, College of Engineering and Technology, The Arab Academy for Science, Technology and Maritime Transport, Egypt (2000). Furthermore, he received the PhD in Computer Science, School of Computing, Science and Engineering, College of Science and Technology, The University of Salford, UK, in 2011. His research is related to the development and evaluation of novel intelligent and visualization systems that involve the digital signals and images using artificial intelligent techniques and pattern recognition in order to help in their interpretation and understanding of the data and extract knowledge. Of particular interest at present are applications focusing on effective and reliable systems that can solve real life problems especially with biomedical applications and other application such as pattern recognition, computer vision, robotics, intelligent system, cloud computing, and mobile computing.

Miroslav Hudec is a researcher and assistant professor at the University of Economics in Bratislava, department of Applied Informatics, recently moved from the Institute of Informatics and Statistics (Infostat), Bratislava. He received the Master and PhD degrees from the University of Belgrade, under the supervision of Professor Mirko Vujosevic. His work is focused on data mining, fuzzy logic, and information systems mainly in fields of official statistics. He is the author of approximately 40 scientific papers and member of program committee of several international conferences. He was research leader of two working packages of recently finished Blue-ETS project (FP7) focused on the modernization of data collection in official statistics. He was the representative of Slovakia on UNECE/Eurostat/OECD Meeting on the Management of Statistical Information Systems in years 2005-2009 and 2013.

Osama Mohamed Badawy Abd El Kader was born on 1949 in Al Minya, Egypt, became a Maintenance Engineer for electronic equipment in the Egyptian Marine Forces on 1971, then a Tutorial Instructor and Assistant Lecturer in the Faculty of Military Technical Engineering on 1975, then a Trainer and Educational developer for Computers and Electronics under contract of maintenance and training between the Saudi Arabian and the American government in Saudi Arabia on 1982, then a Second Lecturer in Arab Academy for Science and Technology and Maritime Transport (AAST), in the Computer Engineering department on October 1993, then a First Lecturer in Arab Academy for Science and Technology and Maritime Transport (AAST), in the Computer Engineering department October 1994, then a Professor, Computer Engineering department in the AAST January 2003. After that, he became a Professor and Head of Departments, College of Computing and Information Technology in the AAST September 2003, then a Professor and Assistant Dean for students and education fairs, College of Computing and Information Technology in the AAST July 2008. Finally, he became a Professor and Vice Dean for Community Service and Environment Development Affairs, College of Computing and Information Technology in the AAST September 2010.

Eugene Kagan earned his MSc in Computer Engineering (1991) from Taganrog Radio-Engineering University (Russia), and PhD (2010) in Industrial Engineering from Tel-Aviv University (Israel). He has more than 20 years' research experience in applied mathematics and engineering and more than 10 years of practical experience in industrial applications of mathematical methods and software engineering. E. Kagan has published more than 20 scientific papers; he is a co-author of a recently published book and has contributed to many collective monographs in the field of robotics and application of probabilistic algorithms.

Dimitris Kalles actively researches artificial intelligence, machine learning, and e-learning technologies. While with Hellenic Open University, he has been involved in the design and implementation of study programs and of infrastructures and services for e-learning. He has taught several subjects in Informatics at undergraduate and postgraduate levels and has supervised over 40 dissertations and theses. He has worked as a project evaluator for the European Commission, for the Corallia Clusters Initiative, and for the University of Porto, and as a proposal evaluator for the European Commission, for the General Secretariat for Research and Technology (Greece), and for other organisations (Ministry of Education, Greece, University of Patras, Greece, Region of Piemonte, Italy). He was a member of the Organising Committee of the 18th European Conference on Artificial Intelligence (2008) and of the 24th IEEE International Conference on Tools with Artificial Intelligence (2012). He is Co-Chair of the 8th Panhellenic Conference on Artificial Intelligence. He serves as Chair of the Board of the Hellenic Society for Artificial Intelligence. He has published over 50 papers in scientific journals and conference proceedings. He is a skilled programmer (C, Java, Prolog, Maple, Unix shell).

Siti Sakira Kamaruddin is currently a senior lecturer in the School of Computing, Universiti Utara Malaysia (UUM), Sintok, Kedah, Malaysia. Before joining UUM in 2001, she was a faculty member in Universiti Teknologi Malaysia (UTM), Skudai, Johor, Malaysia for 5 years. She obtained a B.Sc. and M.Sc. in Computer Science from UTM in 1995 and 1998, respectively, and a PhD in Science and System Management from Universiti Kebangsaan Malaysia, Bangi, Selangor, Malaysia in 2011. Her research interests include text mining, knowledge discovery, information extraction, information retrieval, and anomaly detection. She has published various articles in scientific journals and international conferences in the area of computational intelligence and data mining. She is a member of the Computational and Intelligence Group and The Science and Information Organization.

Alexis Kaporis got his first academic degree from the Department of Mathematics, University of Patras, Greece. He got his PhD Department from the Department of Computer Engineering and Informatics, University of Patras, Greece. He served as post doctoral researcher at the same Department. He has been supported in his research by Computer Technology Institute and Press "Diophantus." He serves as Assistant Professor at the Department of Information and Communication Systems, University of the Aegean, Greece.

Jane Labadin is currently an Associate Professor at the Faculty of Computer Science and Information Technology, Universiti Malaysia Sarawak (UNIMAS). She received her PhD in Computational Mathematics specializing in Fluid Dynamics from the Imperial College of Science, Technology, and Medicine, London, UK in 2002. Her Bachelor degree in Applied Mathematics was from the same university in 1995. She obtained her Master in Computation in 1997 from the University of Manchester, Institute of Science and Technology, UK. Her research interest is in computational modeling of dynamical systems.

Vassiliki Mperoukli received a Bachelor in Computer Science from the Hellenic Open University in 2010. Since 2000, she has been working for SingularLogic and LogicDIS (DIS Group of Companies) as Project Manager, as Senior Applications Developer, and as Systems Analyst. She has been involved in the design, development, testing, and support of two ERP Systems, in the supervision and coordination of a small team of developers and in the cooperation with business consultants for user requirements analysis.

Zuriani Mustaffa received her Bachelor of Science (Computer) majoring in Software Engineering from Universiti Teknologi Malaysia, Johor, Malaysia in 2004 and Master of Science in Information Technology from Universiti Utara Malaysia, Kedah, Malaysia in 2011. She is currently pursuing her PhD degree in Computer Science at School of Computing, Universiti Utara Malaysia. Her research interest include Computational Intelligence algorithm, specifically in machine learning and Swarm Intelligence techniques, which is inspired from biological systems. Her research area focuses on hybrid algorithms, which involves optimization and machine learning techniques with particular attention for financial predictive analysis. She has authored and co-authored various scientific articles in the field of interest.

Juan Luis Olmo was born in Cordoba, Spain, in 1984. He received the M.Sc. degree from the University Oberta of Catalonia, Barcelona, in 2007, and the Ph.D. degree from the University of Córdoba in 2013, both in Computer Science. Since 2009, he has been with the Department of Computer Science and Numerical Analysis, the University of Córdoba, where he holds a postdoc position, as well as developing teaching and research tasks. His research interests include the application of evolutionary computation and swarm intelligence to data mining. He is a member of the IEEE Computer Society and the IEEE Systems, Man, and Cybernetics Society.

R. T. Ritchings is the Professor of Intelligent Systems in the Computer Science and Software Engineering Department in the School of Computing, Science, and Engineering at the University of Salford. He was Head of School for 5 years, after being Head of Computer Science for 3 years. Prior to joining Salford in 2001 as a Reader in Computer Science, he was a Senior Lecturer in Computation at UMIST. He was educated and the University of Manchester, receiving 1st Class BSc (Hons) in Physics in 1972, followed by a PhD in Radio-astronomy in 1976. His research interests are related to the development and evaluation of novel Intelligent Systems that involve the digital signals and images, using Pattern Recognition and AI techniques to help in their interpretation and understanding of the data. His focus has been on effective and reliable systems that address significant real-world issues, and has been principally concerned with biomedical applications. Recent key projects include: objective computer-based techniques to monitor and assess the quality of a patient's voice following treatment for cancer of the larynx, the automated registration of time-separated retinopathy images for monitoring the progression of glaucoma and diabetes, and the real-time prediction of Blood Glucose Levels in diabetics. Other interests involve visualisation, interactive, context-aware multimedia applications involving Augmented and Mixed Reality and Mobile/Wearable computing. His work has been published in over 30 journals articles and chapters in books and more than 60 international refereed conferences. He is a Chartered Engineer and a Chartered IT Professional and a Fellow of both the Royal Astronomical Society and the British Computer Society and a Member of the Institute of Engineering and Technology.

José Raúl Romero received his PhD in Computer Science from the University of Málaga, Spain, in 2007. He has worked as an IT consultant for important business consulting and technology companies for several years. He is currently an Associate Professor at the Department of Computer Science of the University of Córdoba, Spain. His current research interests include the use of bio-inspired algorithms for data mining, the development of intelligent systems for industrial use, and model-based software development and its applications. Dr. Romero is a member of IEEE, the ACM, and the Spanish Technical Normalization Committee AEN/CTN 71/SC7 of AENOR. He can also be reached at http://www.jrromero.net.

Alexander Rybalov earned his PhD from the City University of New York (1996). He is an investigator of fundamental concept of uninorm, which was presented in one of the most cited papers in the field of fuzzy logic. In addition, Alexander contributed to many papers and books in artificial intelligence and computer science and to several projects in mobile robots systems and their applications. His research interests include applications of the data-mining techniques, mobile robotics and artificial intelligence methods.

Pijush Samui is a professor at Centre for Disaster Mitigation and Management in VIT University, Vellore, India. He obtained his B.E. at Bengal Engineering and Science University, M.Sc. at Indian Institute of Science, Ph.D. at Indian Institute of Science. He worked as a postdoctoral fellow at University of Pittsburgh (USA) and Tampere University of Technology (Finland). He is the recipient of CIMO fellowship from Finland. Dr. Samui worked as a guest editor in *Disaster Advances* journal. He also serves as an editorial board member in several international journals. Dr. Samui is editor of *International Journal of Geomatics and Geosciences*. He is the reviewer of several journal papers. Dr. Samui is a Fellow of the International Congress of Disaster Management and Earth Science India. He is the recipient of Shamsher Prakash Research Award for the year of 2011.

Alon Sela earned his B.Sc. in Industrial Engineering (1998) as well as an Honored MBA (2003) from Beer-Sheva University. He has more than ten years of experience as an industrial engineer in diverse fields and industries including supply chain, healthcare, and consulting firms. Alon is currently in his PhD studies in the field of collective information sharing and crowd wisdom. He is happily married to Sharon and a proud father to three young children: Eden, Mika, and Eitan.

Apurva Shah has done his PhD in Computer Engineering from Sardar Patel University and currently working as Associate Professor, Dept of Computer Science and Engineering, Faculty of Technology and Engineering, The M S University of Baroda, India. He is also working as Hon. Director, Computer Center, The M S University of Baroda, India. He has more than 15 years of teaching experience at under graduate and postgraduate level. He has published 8 international journal papers, 9 international conference papers, and a book chapter. He has visited USA, Hong Kong, Canada, and Singapore for research and academic purposes. His research interest includes real-time systems, distributed computing, and artificial intelligence.

Akash Sharda is an undergraduate student in School of Mechanical and Building Science at VIT University. His research interests cover a wide range of subjects in water resource engineering, including modeling of rainfall, ground water, slope stability, pile foundation, structural designs, and superstructure designs.

Hava Siegelmann earned her MSc (cum laude) from Hebrew University of Jerusalem and PhD (fellow of excellence) from Rutgers University both in Computer Science, and currently, she is a full professor of Computer Science at the University of Massachusetts, Amherst. Her research focuses on the understanding of biologically inspired computational systems. In particular, she studies the computational and dynamical complexity of neural systems as well as genetic-networks. Hava published a fundamental book on Super-Turing computation and numerous papers in the field.

Jennie Steshenko graduated from the Tel-Aviv University (2011) and currently is a fellow of the MSc/PhD program in Computer Science at the University of Massachusetts, Amherst. Jennie has more than five years' experience in systems' design in leading companies (including Intel Corp.), and contributed to several research projects in robotics and system analysis. Jennie's research interests are in the field of system analysis and mobile networks.

Sebastián Ventura is currently an Associate Professor in the Department of Computer Science and Numerical Analysis at the University of Córdoba, where he heads the Knowledge Discovery and Intelligent Systems Research Laboratory. He received his BSc and Ph.D. degrees in sciences from the University of Córdoba, Spain, in 1989 and 1996, respectively. He has published more than 150 papers in journals and scientific conferences, and he has edited 3 books and several special issues in international journals. He has also been engaged in 11 research projects (being the coordinator of 3 of them) supported by the Spanish and Andalusian governments and the European Union. His main research interests are in the fields of soft-computing, machine learning, data mining, and their applications. Dr. Ventura is a senior member of the IEEE Computer, the IEEE Computational Intelligence, and the IEEE Systems, Man, and Cybernetics Societies, as well as senior member of the Association of Computing Machinery(ACM).

Miljan Vučetić was born on March 28th 1984 in Sarajevo, Bosnia and Hercegovina. He graduated from the Faculty of Transport and Traffic Engineering, telecommunication department with excellent mark as well as the best student from its founding. He received PhD at the Faculty of Organizational Science, Information Technology department, under the mentorship of Professor Mirko Vujosevic. He has published more than 20 papers in national and internatioanal conferences as well as national and SCI journals. He is recognized as IT enthusiast, Microsoft Technology Specialist and Solution Expert for Private Cloud. Areas of interest include fuzzy logic, artiffical inteligence, data mining, knowledge discovery, information technology, and ERP.

Mirko Vujošević was born in Podgorica, Montenegro, 1951, and graduated in electrical engineering at Belgrade University, where he finished his postgraduated studies and earned his doctorate. From 1976 to 1995, he was with Mihailo Pupin Institute, Belgrade, and now he is full professor at the Faculty for Organizational Sciences, Belgrade University, teaching various courses from the field of Operational Research and Management Science, and leading the chair for Operations Research and Statistics. He is author or co-author of about 180 professional articles and 10 books. He is one of the founders of Yugoslav Operations Research Society and its president from 1994 until 2003. He is regular member of Academy of Engineering Sciences of Serbia.

Kesheng Wang holds a Ph.D. in production engineering from the Norwegian University of Science and Technology (NTNU), Norway. Since 1993, he has been appointed Professor at the Department of Production and Quality Engineering, NTNU. He is a director of the Knowledge Discovery Laboratory (KDL) at NTNU at present. He is also an active researcher and serves as a technical adviser in SINTEF. He was elected member of the Norwegian Academy of Technological Sciences in 2006. He has published 18 books, 10 book chapters, and over 220 technical peer-reviewed papers in international journals and conferences. Prof. Wang's current areas of interest are intelligent manufacturing systems, applied computational intelligence, data mining and knowledge discovery, swarm intelligence, condition-based maintenance, and structured light systems for 3D measurements and RFID.

Yi Wang is a Lecturer, Ph. D, at the University of Manchester, UK. He has published 2 books, 7 book chapters, and over 31 technical peer-reviews papers in international journals and conferences. His current areas of research interest are operations management, computational intelligence, intelligent maintenance, strategy selection, marketing/manufacturing integration, and data mining and causality analysis.

Yuhanis Yusof is a senior lecturer in School of Computing, Universiti Utara Malaysia (UUM), Malaysia. She obtained her PhD in 2007 in the area of Computer Science from Cardiff University, UK. She also holds aMSc degree in Computer Science from Universiti Sains Malaysia and Bachelor of Information Technology from Universiti Utara Malaysia. Her research interest is broadly in data analysis and management for large scale computing. This includes the area of computational intelligence, particularly focusing on designing algorithms that discovers useful patterns and trends (big data analytics) that is important to future business decisions. Special attention is given to meta-heuristics algorithms that come from nature-inspired computing. To complement such interest, she is also involved in grid computing where managing dynamic resource allocation becomes an interesting challenge. Her research works have been published in international journals as well as in proceedings of national and international conferences.

Osmar Zaiane received his PhD in Computing Science from Simon Fraser University, Canada, in 1999, specializing in data mining. He is a professor at the University of Alberta, Canada, with research interest in novel data mining techniques and currently focuses on Social Network Analysis as well as Health Informatics applications. He is the Scientific Director of AICML (Alberta Innovates Centre for Machine Learning). He regularly serves on the program committees of international conferences in the field of knowledge discovery and data mining and was the program co-chair for the IEEE international conference on data mining ICDM'2007, and the general chair for ICDM'2011. He is the Associate Editor of *Knowledge and Information Systems* and *Data Mining and Knowledge Discovery*.

Zhenyou Zhang is a senior engineer in wind turbine condition monitoring at the Department of Wind Park Management of Kongsberg Maritime AS. He graduated in Mechanical Engineering at Shanghai University as Master Student in 2009 and then started his PhD work of Condition-based Maintenance (CBM) in Norwegian University of Science and Technology (NTNU). He is currently responsible for data analysis and algorithm development of fault diagnosis and prognosis for wind turbine condition monitoring system.

Dazhe Zhao received her PhD in Computer science from Berlin Institute of Technology, Germany, in 1996. Dazhe is a professor in the College of Information Science and Engineering, Northeastern University, and the director in Key Laboratory of Medical Image Computing of the Chinese Ministry of Education. She is also the president of the research institute of Neusoft corporation.

Index

A

B

C

D

E

F

G

Genetic Algorithm 57, 75, 84, 150, 204-205, 246, 259-260, 270, 275-278, 298-299, 306, 310

Genetic Programming 108, 128, 204-205, 220, 224, 227, 229, 232, 235, 259, 275

Grid Computing 270

H

Hidden Neurons 76-77, 81, 84, 87, 95, 97-99, 106, 210, 212, 289, 291, 323

Hyper-Heuristics 227, 235

I

Imbalanced Data 48-51, 53, 55-57, 59, 61, 65-66, 69, 71-72, 75, 117, 121, 125

Industrial and Environmental Research 272-273, 278

Industrial Operation 274, 298

K

k-Fold Cross Validation 128

L

Least Squares Support Vector Machines 149-150, 173

Levy Probability Distribution 151, 157, 173

Linear Search 76, 84, 87, 99, 106

Linguistic Summary 186, 203

M

Markov Process 255, 270

Misclassification Cost 48-49, 52-53, 56, 58-59, 63-66, 69, 71, 75, 224

Mobile Agent 13, 16-19, 23-28, 32, 40, 47

Mutation 66, 149, 151, 157-159, 165, 173, 210, 261-262, 275-276, 298, 306-307

N

Niching Method 128

O

Online Learning 299, 310

Outlier Detection 1-2, 5, 7, 10, 273

P

parallel processing 239

Pareto Dominance 115, 128, 277

Particle Swarm Intelligence 55, 75

Particle Swarm Optimization (PSO) 10

Permeability 77-80, 84, 95, 97-99, 106

Petroleum Reservoir Characterization 76-80, 106

Porosity 77-80, 84, 95, 97-99, 106

Predicting Blood Glucose Level 310

Predictive Analysis 149-153, 160, 162-163, 168, 173

Proximity Relation 180-181, 203

R

Randomized Algorithm 78-79, 87, 98-99, 106

Real-Time system 236, 240, 248

Redundancy 221, 223-224, 235

Relational Database 174-175, 181, 183, 194, 202-203

Relevance Measure 221, 224, 226-227, 229, 232-233, 235

Rule-Based Classifier 128

S

Scheduling 2, 129, 236-237, 239-244, 246, 248, 250

Self-Organizing Map (SOM) 129-132, 143, 148

Static Scheduling 243, 248

Swarm Intelligence 1-3, 7, 10, 54-57, 59, 71, 75, 127, 237, 248-250, 263, 270, 276

T

Time Series 153, 160, 162, 173

Triangular Sharp-Crested Weir 204-207, 216, 220

Tsetlin Automaton 11, 18-20, 22-24, 41, 47

U

Universal Software Radio Peripheral (USRP) 317, 330

W

Web Bot Detection 6, 10

Web Usage Mining 10